Coaching Psychology: Meta-theoretical perspectives and applications in multicultural contexts

Llewellyn E. van Zyl • Marius W. Stander
Aletta Odendaal
Editors

Coaching Psychology: Meta-theoretical perspectives and applications in multicultural contexts

Springer

Editors
Llewellyn E. van Zyl
Optentia Research Focus Area,
Department of Industrial Psychology,
School for Behavioural Sciences
North-West University
Vanderbijlpark, South Africa

Marius W. Stander
Optentia Research Focus Area,
Department of Industrial Psychology,
School for Behavioural Sciences
North-West University
Vanderbijlpark, South Africa

Aletta Odendaal
Department of Industrial
Psychology & People Management
University of Johannesburg
Johannesburg, Gauteng, South Africa

ISBN 978-3-319-31010-7 ISBN 978-3-319-31012-1 (eBook)
DOI 10.1007/978-3-319-31012-1

Library of Congress Control Number: 2016943055

Printed on acid-free paper

This Springer imprint is published by Springer Nature
The registered company is Springer International Publishing AG Switzerland

Foreword

It is almost a cliché these days to describe coaching as being a dynamic cross-disciplinary approach to creating purposeful positive change. But that's the fact. Coaching has become a widely used and highly valued change methodology; one that is increasingly evidence-based and theoretically grounded – and one that is more and more being used on a worldwide basis. Despite the global interest in using coaching methodologies, there has been relatively little discussion about the use of coaching psychology in cross-cultural environments. It is this context that makes this book an important and useful contribution to the coaching literature.

The core of any emerging discipline is its theoretical foundation. Coaching psychology is informed by a broad range of theoretical approaches. These range from the ones more frequently associated with coaching, such as positive psychology, strengths-based approaches and appreciative enquiry, to more psychodynamic approaches such as Jungian psychology and systemic approaches to leadership and organizational development. This book explores these issues and makes an important contribution in doing so.

In addition to theoretical frameworks, we also need to know that what we do in coaching is indeed effective. This is the domain of research. The research base for coaching has grown significantly. Whilst still small compared to helping traditions such as counselling that have been established for considerable periods of time, we now have an emerging empirical evidence base. The coaching research covers a broad and fascinating range of issues, from the impact of coaching on goal attainment to the dynamics of the coaching relationship, to systemic issues in organizational contexts. This is truly a dynamic area of psychology. Because of the growing complexity of the coaching research it is not easy to grasp the major research trends and key studies – and this book addresses these issues in a clear and accessible manner.

One consistent finding in the coaching outcome literature is that good coaching almost invariably helps people develop a broader range of perspectives, expands their sense of self and helps enhance personal resilience.

These are vital aspects in these complex and uncertain times. Individuals, teams and organizations are grappling to work with increasing social diversity and uncertain economic and political landscapes. By helping our coaching clients to develop their perspective-taking capacity and personal resilience, coaching, as a theoretically grounded discipline, is ideally placed to be of significant benefit to individuals, organizations and the broader social enterprise.

Our discipline of coaching psychology is indeed an exciting and vibrant place. We have the opportunity to make significant contributions to the well-being of society. This book presents a new benchmark in multicultural aspects of coaching – an inclusive approach that is solely needed globally. I encourage you to enjoy and unitize these insights. Onwards!

The University of Sydney, Australia Anthony M. Grant

Preface

Coaching in psychology has emerged as a growing field in both the discipline and profession of broader psychological practice. Within the last decade, research within this discipline has increased exponentially, ranging from theoretical contributions to validated coaching psychological interventions. Similarly, within the profession, various professional psychological societies (e.g. the Australian Psychology Society Interest Group for Coaching Psychology, the British Psychological Society, the Society for Industrial and Organizational Psychology of South Africa) have formed professional interest groups to further the practice of coaching psychology within industry. Further, alternative professional societies specifically focused on coaching psychology have also been formed (e.g. International Society for Coaching Psychology), which aids in the professionalization of the profession. As such, various tertiary educational institutions have started to either incorporate coaching psychology as part of modules within the professional training of psychologists or develop dedicated courses to aid in the development of professional coaching psychologists. This provides evidence for not only the interest in the field but also emphasizes the need for further exploration, professionalization and application within alternative contexts.

With this increased interest, a need was identified to investigate coaching psychological processes, practices and contributions within multi-cultural contexts. Limited research within popular psychological media, scientific journals and specialist books exists relating to the use of coaching psychological practices within multi-cultural, trans-cultural or cross-cultural contexts. Although a limited amount of coaching models, methodologies and approaches which have been validated could be found within multi-cultural or cross-cultural scientific literature, none of which are consumed by the mass-market as a result of the restrictions regarding consumption/distribution imposed by scientific journals. In further support, increased technological developments and an enhanced focus on globalization emphasize the need for research and practice guidelines on the (a) fundamentals of coaching psychology, (b) psychological approaches towards coaching psychology and (c) meta-theoretical perspectives and professional applications of coaching psychology within multi-cultural contexts. Moreover, multi-cultural specific psychological approaches, alternative coaching frameworks, models, strategies, practice guidelines as well as the competencies required for multi-cultural coaching need to be developed.

In order to address these needs, this book attempts to facilitate and stimulate further interest in the field of multi-cultural coaching psychology through providing not only context to theoretical advances in the field but to provide practice guidelines and approaches. The aim of this book is therefore to synthesize empirical-research-based and theoretical perspectives on coaching psychology in order to provide a comprehensible perspective on contemporary research and practice which is accessible to researchers and practicing psychology professionals globally.

Those aspects discussed in the various chapters provides not only context and practice guidelines to professional coaching from a psychological perspective but will elaborate upon its complexity within multi-cultural contexts. This book therefore provides researchers and practitioners with guidelines to effective coaching within multi-cultural environments. This is done through three sections.

Part I: *Fundamentals of coaching psychology within multi-cultural contexts*. The purpose of this section is to contextualize the fundamental processes, principles and practice guidelines of coaching psychology within multi-cultural contexts. The aim is to provide an interpretive framework through which Part 2 and 3 can be understood and approached. This section is divided into five chapters. Chapter 1 aimed to contextualize coaching, coaching psychology and multi-cultural coaching. Chapter 2 provides a meta-synthesis of the literature relating to research within the field of coaching psychology applied within multi-cultural contexts. Chapter 3 attempted to provide context to the relationship between the coach and coachee through introducing the coach as a fellow human companion. Chapter 4 introduces a coaching supervision framework to aid in the professional development of coaching psychologists within multi-cultural contexts. Finally, Chap. 5 presents a philosophical and normative analysis on ethical issues, challenges and approaches within coaching psychology applied to the multi-cultural contest. These five chapters provides context to the alternative psychological approaches towards multi-cultural coaching psychology which is presented in Part 2.

Part II: *Psychological approaches towards coaching within multi-cultural contexts*. This section proposed to introduce, develop and contrast psychological models, approaches and paradigms which are applicable to multi-cultural coaching contexts. Similar to Part I, this section also comprises five chapters. First, Chap. 6 explores the theory underlying the role that psychological ownership can play when applied to the GROW model of coaching within a multi-cultural context. Second, Chap. 7 presents an evidence-based, theoretical multi-cultural coaching framework for authentic leadership development. Third, Chap. 8 presents a narrative on the use of appreciative inquiry as a coaching methodology through elaborating on the underlying principles of the paradigm through two case studies. Fourth, Chap. 9 presents a Jungian approach towards coaching psychology through elaborating on the use of archetypes within multi-cultural contexts. Finally, Chap. 10 introduces systems thinking and trans-cultural perspectives to coaching psychology through presenting an alternative multi-cultural systems coaching framework.

Part III: *Meta-theoretical perspectives and applications within multi-cultural contexts*. The final section of this book is focused on presenting theoretical perspectives and professional applications of coaching psychology within multi-cultural contexts. The aim of this section is to provide an outlet for theoretical research within the field of multi-cultural psychological coaching psychology as well as provide an orientation to the professional applications of coaching psychology. Chapter 11 introduces an elective depth psychological approach towards conceptualizing the coaching psychologist as a container within team coaching approaches. Chapter 12 focuses on establishing the relationship between emotional intelligences, the SOAR and team-based collaboration within a coaching psychological process. In Chap. 13, the author discusses strengths-based coaching as an enabler of positive psychological outcomes of athletes in multi-cultural sporting environments. Chapter 14 highlights the use of symbolism, art, myths and dreams as projective tools within the coaching relationship. Within Chapter Chap. 15, the authors aim to contrast two prominent paradigms in psychology (positive psychology and the person-centred approach) against a strengths-based multi-cultural coaching model. Chapter 16 aims to evaluate the experiences of emerging psychologists relating to an evidence-based training methodology in order to provide structured guidelines for the development of a multi-cultural coaching training programme. Chapter 17 aims to develop a coaching relationship competency framework through evidence-based coaching practices. Finally, Chap. 18 of this book focuses on determining the future direction of multi-cultural coaching psychology for both the discipline (research) and the profession (practice) presented against the backdrop of the preceding chapters.

Through the systematic integration of the aforementioned chapters, a comprehensive overview of multi-cultural coaching psychology is presented. It acts as a conduit to link the dynamic world of coaching psychology, to the unique approaches, challenges and opportunities within multi-cultural contexts. As the editors of this text, we hope that this provides both researchers and practitioners with insight, guidelines and practical 'tools' for practicing coaching psychology within multi-cultural contexts. We believe that this volume will act as a roadmap and guideline for multi-cultural coaching psychologists in the years to come.

Vanderbijlpark, South Africa — Llewellyn E. van Zyl
Vanderbijlpark, South Africa — Marius W. Stander
Johannesburg, Gauteng, South Africa — Aletta Odendaal
November 2015

Acknowledgements

As the editors of this manuscript we would like to acknowledge the extent towards which each author and reviewer have contributed to the advancement of the meta-theoretical perspectives and applications of coaching psychology within multi-cultural contexts through their respective works. Each chapter makes a unique contribution to the discipline of coaching psychology through professional, scientific and theoretical research. We are truly grateful to all those whom have shared both the direction of this book as well as contributed to future understanding relating to coaching psychology within multi-cultural contexts.

The editors of this book would like to extend our appreciation to Springer, the authors and the peer-reviewers who contributed to the quality of this book. Each of the 18 chapters was subjected to an independent, double-blind peer-reviewed process. Each chapter was initially examined by the editorial staff, and two independent expert reviewers were assigned to evaluate each manuscript based on the focus and scope of the chapter. This book and the quality of its contents would not have been possible without the selfless investment of both the time and expertise of the reviewers. We would like to thank all 36 reviewers for their contribution to the quality of this manuscript.

Finally, the editors would like to extend a special work of thanks to Janlé Horn, a dedicated master student of the North-West University (Potchefstroom, South Africa) and emerging psychologist, for her valuable contributions to the technical editing of this manuscript. Her dedication, diligence and professionalism are qualities which were welcomed in the finalization of this project.

Contents

Contributors

Steven Breger DynamicDIALOGUE®, Johannesburg, South Africa

Matthew L. Cole College of Management, Lawrence Technological University, Southfield, MI, USA

Freddie Crous University of Johannesburg, Johannesburg, South Africa

Chantelle Christine Blandin de Chalain Optentia Research Focus Area, North-West University, Vanderbijlpark, South Africa

Jeremias J. De Klerk University of Stellenbosch, Stellenbosch, South Africa

Daniel Hercules du Toit Optentia Research Focus Area, North-West University, Vanderbijlpark, South Africa

Lené Ilyna Jorgensen Department of Industrial Psychology, School of Human Resource Sciences, Work-Well Research Unit, North-West University, Potchefstroom, South Africa

Pieter Koortzen Investec, Johannesburg, South Africa

Yi-Ling Michelle Lai Organisation Studies and HRM, University of Portsmouth, Portsmouth, UK

Department of Organizational Psychology, Birkbeck, University of London, London, UK

Anna-Rosa le Roux Woolworths Financial Services, Cape Town, South Africa

Claude-Hélène Mayer Department of Indsutrial and Organisational Psychology, University of South Africa, South Africa

Almuth McDowell Organisation Studies & HRM, University of Portsmouth, Portsmouth, UK

Renate Motschnig-Pitrik University of Vienna, Vienna, Austria

Aletta Odendaal Department of Industrial Psychology & People Management, University of Johannesburg, Johannesburg, Gauteng, South Africa

Chantal Olckers University of Pretoria, Pretoria, South Africa

Jonathan Passmore Department of Psychology, University of Evora, Evora, Portugal

Frederick Wilhelm Stander Department of Industrial Psychology, Optentia Research Focus Area, North-West University, Vanderbijlpark, South Africa

Marius W. Stander Optentia Research Focus Area, Department of Industrial Psychology, School for Behavioural Sciences, North-West University, Vanderbijlpark, South Africa

Jacqueline M. Stavros College of Management, Lawrence Technological University, Southfield, MI, USA

Reinhard Stelter Coaching Psychology Unit, NEXS, University of Copenhagen, Copenhagen, Denmark

Tim Theeboom Department of Work and Organizational Psychology, University of Amsterdam, Amsterdam, The Netherlands

Llewellyn E. van Zyl Optentia Research Focus Area, Department of Industrial Psychology, School for Behavioural Sciences, North-West University, Vanderbijlpark, South Africa

Rian Viviers University of South Africa, Pretoria, South Africa

Gail Wrogemann Industrial Psychologist, Team and Systems Coach, Systems Consultant, Johannesburg, South Africa

About the Authors

Steven Breger is a registered industrial and organizational psychologist and qualified coach. He founded Dynamic DIALOGUE® in 2006 and provides organizational consulting, customized leadership coaching, transformational interventions and communication training programmes. He applies his work experience in consulting psychology, organizational development and facilitation to his passion for the behavioural dynamics of authentic team and individual leadership. He has presented papers at various local and international events and conferences since 2011. These include the 1st International Congress of Coaching Psychology, 2011 (Pretoria); the 2011 SIOPSA Conference (Pretoria); the 2012 International Congress of Psychology (Cape Town); and the 4th European Coaching Psychology Conference, 2013 (Edinburgh). This model is used to diagnose and address intra-, inter-personal and team dynamics – the aim being to develop authentic leaders and to enhance interpersonal interaction and team cohesion. He incorporates an evidence-based and cognitive-behavioural coaching approach with narrative, neuroscience and emotional intelligence theory, continually drawing on his experience in corporate role-play and professional theatre and television. He has worked with various industry sectors (across Southern Africa), including banking, insurance, academic institutions, mining, finance, manufacturing, energy, public service departments and para-statals. He serves on the Executive of the Society for Industrial and Organizational Society (SIOPSA) in his role of Chairperson of the IGCCP SA (Interest Group in Coaching and Consulting Psychology South Africa) and is a past chairperson of the SIOPSA Johannesburg Branch.

Matthew L. Cole is Assistant Professor of Management, Chair of the Institutional Review Board and Chair of the Research Support Services Committee at Lawrence Technological University. He teaches biostatistics, business statistics, research design-quantitative methods, entrepreneurship, industrial/organizational psychology and principles of management. He received his doctoral degree from Wayne State University (Detroit, MI) in Cognitive and Social Psychology across the Lifespan (CaSPaL). His research interests focus on the science of teams, cognitive styles in problem solving, strategic thinking capacity, positive organizational scholarship, entrepreneurship and research methodology. He has facilitated national and international workshops, seminars and strategic planning sessions on SOAR and Appreciative Inquiry with his research collaborator.

Freddie Crous is Professor of Industrial Psychology at the University of Johannesburg. He does his best to approach life in general and his work in particular from an appreciative stance. In 1990, Freddie joined the programme in Industrial Psychology at the erstwhile Rand Afrikaans University, now the University of Johannesburg. From 1998 to 2002, he served as its programme leader. He has 22 years' lecturing and research experience in a wide range of domains, such as consumer psychology, social psychology, career development, industrial psychological design, performance management, strategic management, organizational wellness, positive industrial psychology, facilitation of change and coaching psychology. He obtained an M.Com. with distinction, with a dissertation in the domain of consumer decision-making. His doctoral thesis contributed to the contextualization of entrepreneurship. He has published a variety of scientific articles, contributed to several books and read papers at conferences both nationally and internationally. Freddie is a registered psychologist and a member of the Society for Industrial and Organisational Psychology of South Africa. He served on the editorial board of the *SA Journal of Industrial Psychology* for 12 years and is a consultant to various organizations and individuals.

Chantelle Christine Blandin de Chalain is an Organizational Solutions Coaching Specialist at the Independent Counselling and Advisory Services (ICAS), an Employee Wellbeing provider in South Africa. Her coaching philosophy is that of strength-based coaching, focusing on the integration of positive psychology and appreciative techniques in the coaching methodology offered. She is a student psychologist in the process of completing a master's degree in Industrial Psychology with the North-West University. She has a passion for people, organizations and understanding organizational dynamics and is driven to re-humanize organizations through the element of appreciation and strength-based techniques.

Mias de Klerk was the Chief Ethics Officer of a major South African organization, which operates in 30 countries with more than 34,000 employees. He worked extensively as an organizational development consultant and coach, specializing in personal and organizational transformation, workplace spirituality, motivation and business ethics. He facilitated transformation workshops on most continents, including countries such as India, Qatar, China, Uzbekistan, South Africa, Germany, UAE, UK, Canada and the USA. Mias has extensive management experience, gained from several senior management appointments during his career. Apart from his permanent employment as Chief Ethics Officer, he is an associate professor in Organizational Behaviour and Business Ethics at the University of Pretoria and visiting professor in Business Management and Leadership at the University of the Free State. He believes in teaching his students the value and necessity of critical thinking. His qualifications include a Ph.D. in Organizational Behaviour, a Master's

Degree in Business leadership and Bachelor's degree in Engineering (Mech). He has published widely in international scholarly journals and conferences on topics relating to business ethics and organizational psychology. He is a member of the American Academy of Management, Psychological Association, Business Ethics Network of Africa (BEN-Africa), Viktor Frankl Institute of Logotherapy and the Society of Industrial and Organizational Psychology of South Africa. He is currently a professor at the Stellenbosch Business School.

Daniel Hercules du Toit (B.A., M.Com.; D.Com.) is a registered Industrial Psychologist, senior lecturer at the North-West University teaching mainly post-graduate students and giving study guidance for magister and doctoral research. He is a co-author of peer-reviewed articles, a chapter in a text book and presenter at numerous national and international conferences. He divides his time between academic work, consulting to organizations and individual growth interventions. He spent 20 years in business organizations in various human resource management and development positions before joining the academic world. His main areas of interest are applying Jungian concepts in organizations and research; focusing on personal growth and leadership development using art therapy; stress, gender inequality in the workplace, conflict management and relationship adaptation; and dealing with fear and anger.

Lené Ilyna Jorgensen is an associate professor at the School of Human Resource Science on the North-West University's Potchefstroom Campus. Her career started in the South African Police Service (SAPS) where she was responsible for managing the well-being of police personnel in the North West Province. After 10 years in the police service, she joined the university where her subsequent teaching experience of 7 years include teaching applied counselling and trauma management, psychometric assessment and practical work for intern-psychometrists. Her research mainly is focussed on the development of psychometrists, HR personnel and industrial psychologists in the skills they need to address the human capital needs in South Africa. She consults in her private practice on a regular basis including assessments, team development and counselling.

Pieter Koortzen (D.Com. – Doctor of Commerce) is a counselling and industrial/organizational psychologist. He obtained a doctorate in I/O Psychology from the University of South Africa in 1998. As practitioner, he specializes in training and development, leadership development, executive coaching, facilitation, group relations from a systems psychodynamic stance, trauma debriefing and post-trauma counselling. In his private practice, he has been rendering consulting and development services to various South African organizations for the last 18 years. Until May 2007, he was employed as a professor in Industrial/Organizational Psychology at the University of South Africa where he worked for 13 years. His teaching responsibilities included courses from the undergraduate to doctoral level. During 2001, he also taught industrial/organizational and consulting psychology as a visiting faculty member at Alliant International University in San Diego, United States of America. Apart from his teaching responsibilities, he conducts research and supervises masters' dissertations and doctoral theses. Pieter has presented numerous research papers at national and international conferences and publishes continuously. From 2005 to May 2007, he served as the coordinator of a doctoral programme in Consulting Psychology at UNISA. From October 2007 to 2012, Pieter was involved at Resolve Encounter Consulting where he managed the assessment centre, coordinated large-scale assessment projects, acted as an executive coach for a number of organizations, conducted leadership and team development interventions and presented training programmes. Currently, he has a part-time faculty position in the Department of Industrial/Organizational Psychology and People Management at the University of Johannesburg and consults privately.

Claude-Hélène Mayer holds a Master's in Cultural Anthropology and a Doctorate in Political Sciences from the Georg-August-University, Göttingen, Germany. She also holds a Ph.D. in Management from Rhodes University and has been a Post-doc fellow from March 2007 to December 2008. Since 2009, she is Professor of Intercultural Business Communication at the University of Applied Studies in Hamburg, Germany, and Senior Research Associate at the Department of Management at Rhodes University. Her research areas are transcultural conflict management in organizations, transcultural mediation, managerial identity and values, health and salutogenesis in transcultural management and (health) counselling in transcultural organizations.

Renate Motschnig-Pitrik is Professor at the Faculty of Computer Science at the University of Vienna and head of the Computer Science Didactics and Learning Research Center. Until 1996, she has repeatedly been a Visiting Professor at the Computer Science Department of the University of Toronto, Canada. In 1995/1996, she was on the faculty of the Computer Science Department of the RWTH-Aachen, Germany. Currently, she also teaches courses on communication for computer scientists at the Masaryk University in Brno/CZ. Renate received her Dipl.-Ing. degree in Computer Science (Informatik) in 1982 and her Dr. techn. in Computer Science in 1988, both from the Vienna University of Technology, Austria. In 1996, she got the "venia docendi" in Practical and Applied Computer Science from the University of Vienna. In 2004 and 2005, she participated in the La Jolla Program of the Center for the Studies of the Person.

Aletta Odendaal is a practicing industrial psychologist and academic and is currently the qualification leader for the new Masters in Leadership Coaching at the University of Johannesburg. She has more than 20 years' experience in strategic executive leadership development, coaching and assessment interventions across all levels in different organizations in South Africa that include mining, retail, engineering, academic institutions, Government, NGO's, media and communications. Her research interests are primarily in the field of psychological assessment, leadership development and coaching psychology. As a scholar, she has presented a number of papers at national and international conferences and published research results in academic journals. Aletta is a co-author and editor of the Southern African edition of Stephen Robbins and Timothy Judge's *Organizational Behaviour* book. Her passion and commitment to the development of coaching psychology and service to industrial psychology is reflected in her national and international leadership and involvement. She participated in the Global Convention of Coaching in 2007 in New York and represented SIOPSA in 2008 in Dublin. She was President of SIOPSA for the period June 2002 to June 2006, Chair of People Assessment in Industry (2008–2011) and was awarded honorary membership of SIOPSA in 2006. She is currently serving her term as elected council member of the International Test Commission (ITC). Aletta is a founder member of the Interest Group in Coaching and Consulting Psychology and also co-represented South Africa in the First International Congress of Coaching Psychology in London (2010), Pretoria (2011) and Barcelona (2011). She is a member of the International Steering Committee and Honorary Vice President of the International Society of Coaching Psychology. She holds an M.Phil. (cum laude) and D.Phil. in Industrial Psychology from the University of Johannesburg.

Chantal Olckers holds a Ph.D. in Human Resource Management from the University of Pretoria, South Africa. She is currently employed as a Senior Lecturer in the Department of Human Resource Management at the University of Pretoria. She has delivered numerous papers at national and international conferences and published several refereed articles in subject-related journals. She is registered as an Industrial Psychologist with the Health Professions Council of South Africa, registered as a Master Human Resource Practitioner (Generalist) with the South African Board for People Practice as well as a certified Assessor of the ETQA of the South African Board of People practice. Her research focuses on Psychological Ownership in organizations and the validation of measuring instruments.

Jonathan Passmore is Professor of Psychology at the University of Evora, Portugal, and managing director of Embrion, a psychology consulting company working across EMEA. He is a chartered psychologist, holds five degrees and has an international reputation for his work in coaching and leadership. He has published 14 books on the themes of leadership, personal development and change, including editing the Association for Coaching series of coaching titles and the Wiley Blackwell Series on Industrial and Organizational Psychology. He speaks widely at conferences across the world from the USA to Europe and Asia and has published over 100 journal papers and book chapters. He was awarded the Association for Coaching' Global Coaching Award for his contribution to practice and research in 2010 and the British Psychology Society Research Award for his research into safety coaching in 2012. He sits on the editorial board of several journals including Coaching: An International Journal and the International Coaching Psychology Review. Jonathan lives with his wife and two small children in the UK. In his spare time, he keeps bees and likes to swim, walk and run.

Frederick Wilhelm Stander is a registered psychologist (category: Industrial, PS 0123145) with the Health Professions Council of South Africa. He currently lectures Organisational Development at the North-West University, Vaal Triangle Campus, where he also heads up the Industrial Psychology department. In 2011, he started a niche sport psychological performance company called Performi Focus (Pty) Ltd and has since conducted various projects with some of the country's leading sport organizations, including SA Cricket, the South African Football Association, Kaizer Chiefs Football Club and the Leopards Rugby Union. He is a professional member of the Association for Applied Sport Psychology.

Marius W. Stander is a professor and management consultant specializing in the assessment and optimization of talented people and teams. He has been lecturing Industrial Psychology on post-graduate level at the Potchefstroom University, North-West University (Potchefstroom and Vaal Triangle campus) as well as UJ (previously RAU) and the University of Namibia. He studied at the University of Potchefstroom and North-West University and holds an M.Com. (cum laude) and Ph.D. in Industrial Psychology. Previously, he was GM of an outsourcing company for 2 years. He is currently the co-managing director of Psychai Management Consultants. He is a registered industrial psychologist (HPCSA), mentor and a master HR practitioner (SABPP). He has been consulting in South Africa and Namibia for various companies and local authorities over the past 28 years. His fields of expertise include talent management, assessment of potential, leadership development, team building and coaching psychology.

Jacqueline M. Stavros is Professor of Management and Director of the DBA Program at Lawrence Technological University. She teaches strategy, organization development and change, leading change, research design, qualitative research methods and business sustainability. She received her doctoral degree from Case Western Reserve University's Weatherhead School of Management (Cleveland, OH). Her research interests include positive organizational scholarship, organization development and change, appreciative inquiry, sustainability and strategy. She has written 4 books, 26 journal articles and 8 book chapters from her research agenda. She has travelled to over a dozen countries as an invited speaker and conference presenter on Appreciative Inquiry and SOAR.

Reinhard Stelter holds a Ph.D. in Psychology and is Professor of Sport and Coaching Psychology at the University of Copenhagen and visiting professor at the Copenhagen Business School (Master of Public Governance). He is the Head of Section Human and Social Sciences and Head of the Coaching Psychology Unit at the Department of Nutrition, Exercise and Sports, University of Copenhagen. He is Honorary Vice President of the International Society of Coaching Psychology and Scientific Advisory Council member of the Institute of Coaching associated with Harvard Medical School. In 2014, Springer launched his new book "Third Generation Coaching – A Guide to Narrative-Collaborative Theory and Practice". www.nexs.ku.dk/coaching and www.rstelter.dk.

Tim Theeboom is a lecturer at the University of Amsterdam and course director of the post-graduate programme at the university. He is completing his Ph.D. in coaching. His interests lie in exploring basic questions which still need to be answered. What is coaching exactly? How should we assess the effects of coaching? Do perceptions about effectiveness differ between coaches and coachees? He is also active in research into positive psychology, mindfulness and stress. In addition to his academic life, he works as a coach, trainer and consultant.

Llewellyn E. van Zyl, (Ph.D.) is an associate professor of industrial psychology with the North-West University (Vaal Triangle Campus) and a registered psychologist (Category: Industrial) with the Health Professions Council of South Africa. He has completed a Doctorate degree in the field of Industrial Psychology, specializing in positive psychological interventions. He also holds a Master of Commerce, an Honours and a Bachelor's degree in Industrial Psychology, which were obtained from the North-West University (cum laude) at the top of his class. Llewellyn is a respected researcher, with contributions to peer-reviewed journals and chapters in international peer-reviewed books, and has conducted presentations at both national and international conferences. Llewellyn was involved with the South African Journal of Industrial Psychology as a Section Editor and hosted a special edition on positive organizational behaviour. As of April 2012, he has taken over the role as co-editor for the South African Journal of Industrial Psychology and has been nominated to take over the role as editor in 2019. He also serves on the editorial board for the Journal of leadership and organizational studies. Furthermore, as of July 2014, he has served as the President (/Elect) of the Society for Industrial and Organisational Psychology of South Africa. He has extensive experience within the tertiary educational environment (as a lecturer and researcher) as well as within the private and public sectors (as a consultant). Llewellyn has a passion for human resource development initiatives. Specifically, online strengths-based people development, coaching psychology, happiness and flourishing at work.

Rian Viviers is Professor in the Department of Industrial and Organizational Psychology at UNISA. His interests lie mainly in the fields of assessment centre technology, positive psychology and employee wellness. He has been working for SHL as part-time consultant and has done numerous assessments for a wide range of organizations. In the field of assessment centre design, he developed expertise over many years in diverse settings. He started his career in Transnet within the assessment centre division and was extensively involved in the development and running of centres for senior and middle management. Thereafter, he joined UNIISA and in this capacity teaches assessment centre methodology to students on post-graduate level. He frequently assists in doing assessment centres for SHL for a variety of clients – from government institutions to private organizations. Assessment and development centres for Executive Management and CEOs down to middle management centres are being done regularly, both locally and in neighbouring countries. He also gained extensive experience in the UK where he worked at SHL's headquarters and gained experience in the development of simulation exercises. He has been involved in the ACSG as committee member for three consecutive terms.

Gail Wrogemann is an organizational development consultant, specializing in systems thinking, team and organizational integration and leadership in complex systems. She is a registered Industrial Psychologist, systems and relationship coach, executive and team coach and coach supervisor, with many years' experience in coaching, facilitating, training, organizational development and change management processes. She has worked across many industries, across different groupings of client and at many levels of interactions. Specific programs designed, led and delivered include 18 month to 2 year change management and organizational development processes, leadership development in the form of personal mastery facilitation and coaching, organizational strategy processes and business development and sales coaching. Specific focus has been on team coaching for development, integration and strategy and planning. Longer-term programs designed for training and mentoring of coaches and consultants specifically on the aspects of systems development have also been delivered. She has been a guest speaker on 702 and has presented at various conferences – at international, national and regional level. She is currently completing her Ph.D. on the topic of Systems Complexity.

Part I
Fundamentals of Coaching Psychology in Multi-cultural Contexts

Contextualising Coaching Psychology Within Multi-cultural Contexts

Aletta Odendaal and Anna-Rosa le Roux

Abstract The purpose of this chapter is to discuss the meta-context in which coaching psychology[1] has emerged. The aim is to contextualise coaching, coaching psychology and multi-cultural coaching. The emphasis is further on developments within these domains in both the discipline and profession of broader psychological practice. The chapter is based on inputs received from various stakeholders in the coaching industry and extends on current knowledge, practices and positioning statements both nationally and internationally. A South African definition as well as the value proposition of coaching psychology is presented, followed by a descriptive overview of a meta-framework for further research in the application of coaching psychology in multi-cultural contexts.

Keywords Coaching • Coaching psychology • Multi-cultural • Professionalization • Coaching context

1 Introduction

Since the seminal statement of Anthony Grant in 2000 that coaching psychology[1] has come of age, both the discipline and the profession has developed considerably. First, within the discipline more than 4733 academic articles and 311 specialist books have been published with coaching or coaching psychology as keywords within the last decade. This upsurge in research aided in the development of various coaching theories, methodologies, developmental models and intervention strategies (Van Zyl and Stander in press). These attempts to

[1] There is no provision in the regulations defining the scope of the profession of psychology in South Africa for registered practitioners that coach to register as a coaching psychologist.

A. Odendaal (✉)
Department of Industrial Psychology & People Management, University of Johannesburg, Johannesburg, Gauteng, South Africa
e-mail: aodendaal@uj.ac.za

A.-R. le Roux
Woolworths Financial Services, Cape Town, South Africa
e-mail: Anna-RosaLeRoux@wfs.co.za

L.E. van Zyl et al. (eds.), *Coaching Psychology: Meta-theoretical perspectives and applications in multicultural contexts*, DOI 10.1007/978-3-319-31012-1_1

further the academic understanding of coaching psychology has aided in the professionalisation of coaching and coaching psychology as active practice domains in order to provide evidence of its effectiveness as a strategy to optimise the potential of individuals and teams (Grant et al. 2010; Odendaal 2011; Palmer and Whybrow 2014). Second, within the profession, various interest groups within professional psychological societies and coaching domain specific professional associations have formed to further the professionalisation of coaching and coaching psychology (Grant 2011; Odendaal 2011; Van Zyl et al. in press) through aiding in the development of practice guidelines and formalising/organising professional coaching services (ISFCP 2015; Palmer and Whybrow 2014). In further support, given the high demand for professional coaching, the industry has grown exponentially; a global survey estimates that approximately 47,500 active coaches are practicing worldwide (ICF 2013). Coaching, especially leadership and executive coaching, has further emerged as a key strategy in leadership development and succession management programmes in various organisations (Elliott 2011; Stelter 2014; Sperry 2013) and as such have become an integral part to facilitate and sustain the fiscal development of organisations (Beattie et al. 2014). This increasing demand for coaching theory and services has manifested in various ways ranging from a significant increase in coaching conference papers delivered at global conferences, and the establishment of professional coaching psychological training programmes through to concerted efforts of professional coaching and coaching psychology bodies to enhance credibility and professional standards of practice on a global scale.

Although both coaching and coaching psychology has emerged as independent professional disciplines within the literature (Grant et al. 2010; Gray 2011; Van Zyl and Stander 2013), the diversification of coaching psychological practices, methodologies and approaches have caused endless debate, contrasting views and misalignment between conceptual coaching approaches (Cox et al. 2014; Palmer and Whybrow 2014). Therefore, discussions about the definition, teaching of coaching psychology, boundaries within the profession of psychology, relation to the broader coaching industry, as well as the enhancement of its roots in psychology remain critical and demand continuous reflection (Grant 2011; Lai and McDowall 2014). These are however not easy questions to address, especially in the context of an increasingly complex and fast changing business environment (Cavanagh and Palmer et al. 2011) influenced by globalisation and developments in technology and characterised by increased mobility, volatility and uncertainty (cf. Johansen 2012; Stacey 2007).

The identity of coaching psychology and its associated value proposition to business, and other stakeholders are however evolving and being defined, even as this chapter is written. Various professional bodies representing a diversity of coaches, application domains, methodological approaches, as well as training and continuous professional development activities are participating in the discourse expressing different recommendations regarding the professionalization of the broader coaching industry as well as the value of registration or chartered status as coaching psychologist (Grant et al. 2010; Lane et al. 2010; Palmer and Whybrow 2014). Furthermore, the ability to operate effectively in multi-cultural contexts and to apply coaching psychology within a diverse workforce as well as across national boundaries is an evolving and growing area of interest worldwide (Booysen 2015; Plaister-Ten 2013). This manuscript therefore comes at a critical point in the development of multi-cultural coaching psychology, as an emerging profession globally, providing a comprehensive overview of multi-cultural coaching psychology theory and practice.

Therefore, the aim of the chapter is to provide an overview of the meta-context impacting the development of coaching psychology, followed by a discussion of global trends and specific developments in the professionalisation of coaching psychology within the multi-cultural South African context. Coaching and coaching psychology are further defined and positioned within a multi-cultural context. To contextualise the development of coaching psychology in South Africa, positioning statements will be presented and discussed as strategic departure points.

2 The Meta-context Impacting the Development of Coaching Psychology

2.1 Global Trends and Developments

Broader contextual issues such as regulatory requirements, economic as well as the multi-cultural context are important considerations beyond the field of psychology that influences the required knowledge, skills and attributes required for effective coaching outcomes. In a recent McKinsey study amongst global Fortune 500 companies, it was evident that the nature of the global business landscape has shifted from a 5 % representation of these organisations in emerging regions in the 1990s, to a 17 % representation in 2010 and a forecasted representation of 45 % in 2025 (McKinsey 2013). The broader contextual issues further solicit the question of "What does it take to be a successful global coach?" The authors belief that effective coaching requires not only a coaching and consulting competence but also a multicultural competence positioning the coach to be effective in environments characterised by complexity. As such, complexity not only in quality of physical conditions, job security, safety, or labour market characteristics, but also where different perspectives, thinking patterns, behaviours and rules of social engagement are formed and driven by value drivers unique to the culture(s) that exist in the context of the coaching engagement.

2.2 Contextualising Coaching and Coaching Psychology in South Africa

Positioning Statement 1 **The contextual factors evident in each country will shape and influence the development of Coaching Psychology as a profession.** There is general agreement within the coaching and coaching psychology community on the importance of understanding the context in which the client operates. A review of the published literature conducted by Nieminen et al. (2013), however suggest a paucity of evidence related to the integration and understanding of the influence of contextual factors on the science and practice of coaching. This lack of rigor when assessing the contexts of coaching is furthermore in stark contrast to the abundance of assessments related to the individual differences that are often also accompanied by the use of multi-rater feedback instruments (Nowack and Mashihi 2012).

South Africa, in particular is a country that bears evidence of a rich multi-cultural setting. With 11 official languages and 53 million people of different backgrounds, cultures, languages and beliefs (41.1-million African, 4.5-million White, 4.6-million Coloured[2] and 1.2-million Indian/Asian), we are known to the world as the 'rainbow nation' (Statistics South Africa 2012). It should further be noted that although more than three-quarters of the population is Black African, this does not imply that the majority is similar in culture or language spoken (Odendaal 2013). Given the highly diverse and complex South African society it is increasingly important for coaches to understand both the country and global developments faced by clients (coachee and organisation) that are from a systems perspective interrelated. By understanding the embeddedness of the individual in a complex system of circumstances, relationships and processes the coaching intervention can be tailored to optimise development and obtain alignment with organisational outcomes (Cavanagh and Lane 2012; Clarke 2013). The main focus is therefore on the individual within the broader system, as the interaction between the system and its external context also give rise to unexpected and even unpredictable outcomes.

Although South Africa as developing country has recently been accepted within the BRICS states (Brazil, Russia, India, China and South Africa), it has been challenged with various socio-political and socio-economic dilemmas at a national level that coaching psychologist must be cognisant of. Unemployment remains a significant challenge and has reached 24.3 % at the end of 2014 with youth unemployment at 49 % (South African Economic Outlook 2015). This statistic represents an average of 24 % of unemployment in the last 15 years leading to high and growing levels in poverty and crime (South African Economic Outlook 2015). In addition, the healthcare systems are continuously under pressure with complex challenges around development and maintenance (Deloitte 2015). Similarly, the educational sector is constrained not only from a facilities perspective, but also by a lack of strong

[2]The term Coloured is used to refer to people of mixed racial descent and is used by the South African government as part of its official racial categorisation scheme.

leadership to steer towards the desired production of human capital for sustained economic development (Department of Education 2009).

At an organisational level, coaching and consulting psychologists are pressured to develop woman leaders, to provide accelerated career paths to create not only technical talent pools, but also talent pools that strengthen leadership succession benches (Bersin 2013). Coaching practitioners are further tasked to navigate the corporate landscape in an ethical way and build organisational cultures that are sustainable and fit for purpose to compete globally (de Klerk in press; Simon et al. 2014; Thompson and Dieffenbach 2015). Lastly, organisational leaders are asked to implement broad based black economic empowerment as a legislative frame created to distribute wealth across a broad a spectrum of previously disadvantaged (black) South Africans in an effective and sustainable manner (Broad Based Black Economic Empowerment 2013).

At an individual level, acknowledgement is needed that individuals differ in culturally important ways e.g. race, gender, religion, socioeconomic status, language, education, sexual orientation and ethnicity (Odendaal 2011). Coaching practitioners are therefore increasingly exposed to diverse work environments necessitating higher levels of intercultural competence to succeed (Geber and Keane 2013; Jorgensen, et al. in press; Plaister-Ten 2013; Milner et al. 2013). Work-life balance, employee wellbeing and engagement are increasingly discussed as some of the top issues on people agendas in organisations (Leonard et al. 2013). Only when coaching is approached systemically with a clear appreciation of the diversity of coaching needs at individual, group and organisational levels, together with the multi-cultural complexities that plays out when global business landscapes are considered, will clients experience value in a meaningful and sustainable way (Leonard et al. 2013; Lowman 2013).

In summary, the professionalisation of coaching psychology within South Africa is shaped by a set of contextual factors that are unique to its status as a developing country. These contextual factors impacts on the accelerated growth and professionalisation of coaching psychology as a sub-discipline of psychology in South Africa, where specific emphasis is on how: (i) employment equity legislation creates a need for accelerated leadership development, (ii) the multi-cultural and political landscape in South Africa drives ethical, value based developmental approaches, (iii) legislation provides a mandate to the Health Professions Council of South Africa (HPCSA) as a regulatory body for psychology, (iv) consumers of coaching psychological services are growing in sophistication, (v) accredited academic institutions offers coaching psychology modules and qualifications (Odendaal 2011; Odendaal and Le Roux 2011).

Similarly, the unique South African multi-cultural context provides interesting challenges/restraining forces for the professionalisation of the coaching industry. First, a lack of alignment between professional bodies, as well as regulators which is characterised by diverse views on professionalisation of coaching psychology. Second, an unregulated coaching industry with evidence of a ‘marketing’ driven industry in the form of proprietary models and credentialing which distracts from the credibility of both the discipline and the profession. Finally, a lack of minimum standards on education, training, continued competence development and practice guidelines exist to further the professionalisation of coaching psychology within the multi-cultural South African context.

2.3 The Role of Professional Bodies in the Development of Coaching Psychology

Positioning Statement 2 **Coaching Psychology is growing as an applied sub-discipline of Psychology**. Contextualising coaching and coaching psychology will not be complete without a short discussion of the development of coaching psychology within the South African context. The development of coaching psychology has been an international action process with key drivers the formation of different interest groups in coaching psychology that are associated with recognised national psychological societies, followed by the establishment of joint publications of peer-reviewed coaching psychology journals (Grant 2011). Central to the development of coaching psychology as theoretical and applied sub-discipline of psychology was the establishment of an Interest Group in Coaching Psychology within the Australian Psychological Society in 2002[3] and the Special Group in Coaching Psychology within the British Psychological Society in 2004 (Palmer and Whybrow 2006). Several other coaching psychology related bodies followed e.g. Society for Evidence-based Coaching as part of the Danish Psychological Association in 2007.

Similarly to global trends, the development of coaching psychology in South Africa gained momentum with the establishment of the Consulting Psychology Interest Group (CPIG) in June 2006 within the Society of Industrial and Organisational Psychology of South Africa (SIOPSA),[4] with coaching psychology positioned as consultation intervention, competency and role function of the consultant. In September 2010 the CPIG announced a name change to the Interest Group of Coaching and Consulting Psychology (IGCCP) to create a dedicated focus for Coaching Psychology in line with international developments (Odendaal 2011). Highlights within the development path were the participation of IGCCP representing SIOPSA in the Global Coaching Community (GCC)[5] with subsequent endorsement of the declaration of intent in 2008. In October 2009 the CPIG partnered with the International Organisation Development Association (IODA[6]) to host the 29th

[3] Retrieved from APS website 12 November 2015.

[4] Detailed information and timelines for the development of IGCCP see https://www.siopsa.org.za/pages/interest_groups#igccp.

[5] The GCC was a year-long collaborative framework of stakeholders in coaching, established with the aim of discussing the difficult issues facing the professionalising of coaching. Nine Working Groups were constituted to address a variety of topics and issues important to the future of coaching (GCC Declaration of Intent 2008).

[6] The IODA is dedicated to supporting and strengthening OD principles at international level through research, academic OD programs, peer mentoring and coaching, networking and sharing of knowledge, international OD projects and cultural exchange.

International OD conference. The CPIG leveraged its positioning within the Society to actively play a role in the international community. Subsequent developments were the signing of a Memorandum of Understanding (MoU) with the Society for Coaching Psychology in May 2010 (which later changed its name to the International Society for Coaching Psychology - ISCP), an international professional membership body established specifically to further the discipline and profession of coaching psychology. A series of International Congresses in Coaching Psychology (ICCP) under the ambit of ISCP provided opportunities for the development of the theory, practice and research of coaching psychology globally (Odendaal and Le Roux 2011). South Africa hosted the First International Congress of Coaching Psychology: Southern Hemisphere event in May 2011.

A further highlight was the formation of a strategic partnership in 2010 with the Australian Psychological Society's (APS) Interest Group in Coaching Psychology and the British Psychological Society (BPS) Special Group in Coaching Psychology (Odendaal and Le Roux 2010). In 2011 the IGCCP was invited to participate in an international discussion on the development of a teaching agenda for coaching psychology (Odendaal 2011). In addition, the IGCCP signed a MoU with the Section of the Psychology of Organisations and Work (SPOT) of the Col·legi Oficial de Psicòlegs de Catalunya (COPC) in October 2011 with the intent to collaborate and work together, in support of the development of the coaching psychology profession both in South Africa and in Spain (Odendaal and Le Roux 2011). At a local front, the IGCCP commissioned research in 2011 amongst all coaching professional bodies in South Africa to define the nature of coaching as an emerging discipline in South Africa (Odendaal et al 2011). Furthermore the IGCCP followed an inclusive stakeholder engagement model and were in regular conversation with Coaches and Mentors Association of South Africa (COMENSA) regarding the development and professionalisation of the coaching industry in general (Odendaal and Le Roux 2010).

2.4 Professional Status of Coaching and Coaching Psychology: Accreditation, Registration and Certification

Positioning Statement 3 **Psychology is a well-regulated profession, ideally positioned to facilitate the professionalisation of coaching psychology**. Coaching psychology is currently being defined within the legal frameworks and specific contextual landscapes of different countries where coaching psychology is emerging (Grant 2011; Odendaal 2011; Palmer and Whybrow 2006; Passmore 2011). As a professional area of practice, the core qualifying criteria around certification, accreditation and registration are being defined globally by various regulatory, professional coaching and coaching psychology bodies (Cavanagh and Palmer et al. 2011; Grant 2011). As such, registration or chartered status as a psychologists (e.g. UK, Australia and South Africa) require accredited undergraduate degree in psychology, then a post-graduate degree (in South Africa a Honours degree followed by a Masters' degree), followed by a supervised internship and in some countries also a National Board examination (Odendaal 2011; Passmore 2011). It should be noted that an undergraduate degree in psychology is however not an entry requirement into PsyD degrees and subsequent licensing as psychologist in the US (Grant 2011). Accreditation of the different training programmes/courses in psychology typically resides with recognised structures as mandated in the specific country, e.g. Health Professions Council of South Africa (HPCSA). Depending applied area of practice, post-registration supervision is also mandated in some countries (Odendaal and Kwiatkowski in press).

Psychology is a recognised profession globally and meets all accepted criteria for professional status (cf. Bennett 2006; Gray 2011) in that there are clear entry requirements based on qualifications, adherence to an enforceable Code of Ethics and standards of practice, compliance to applicable regulations (e.g. scope of practice and scope of the profession), continuous professional development and a common body of knowledge and skill. Psychology as profession is therefore ideally positioned to facilitate the professionalisation of coaching psychology, with Grant (2006) arguing that psychology

> …with its attendant rigorous educational programmes and professional ethos and qualifications has, I believe, noticeably raised the bar for the coaching industry in general (p. 15).

In this regard Cavanagh and Palmer et al. (2011) argue that how we define and distinguish the practices of coaching psychologists from coaches who are not psychologists and the relationship of coaching psychology relative to other applied areas of practice remain unanswered questions. It is evident that whether the status of coaching psychology should be that of independent registration category or applied sub-discipline of Psychology is a debate that is still unfolding.

In contrast, there is general agreement that the coaching industry is not meeting the criteria of a profession (Grant et al. 2010). The International Coach Federation (ICF) however designates coaching as a profession in support that it has developed its own certification process and code of ethics (ICF 2013). Critical gaps towards recognition as a profession however remains that there are still no barrier to entry, a lack of universal standards towards minimum and on-going training and qualifications, and no enforceable and binding ethical practice and standards. In addition, the general public and related professions do not recognise coaching as a profession. There is however an emerging knowledge base supported by the acknowledgement and increased efforts towards evidence-based theoretical and practical research (Gray 2011; Lane et al. 2010).

A typical pattern of an emerging profession is that developments and applications in practice tends to precede the development of a strong theoretical and empirical foundation. Change in the pattern is starting to emerge with the establishment of the International Coaching Research Forum (ICRF) that promotes the value of research and the development of a coaching knowledge base that informs evidence-based practice. Within the coaching industry there is furthermore a large body of skilled and experienced practitioners that is now starting to be visible in the peer reviewed publications (Grant et al. 2010). The recognised Journals in the field are the 'International Coaching Psychology Review', 'Coaching: An International Journal of Theory Research and Practice' and the 'International Journal of Evidence-based Coaching and Mentoring'. Current concern is that the Journals have not yet reached acceptable international distribution and citation levels as what were indeed hoped for within the coaching community (Zarris 2011). On the local front the 'SA Journal of Industrial Psychology' and 'SA Journal of Human Resource Management' are key journals where research on coaching and coaching psychology are published (Coetzee and Van Zyl 2014). Critical to continuous growth as a profession is a rigorous and coherent body of coaching and coaching psychology specific research (Passmore and Theeboom in press) and in this regard Lowman (2013) asserts that research is primarily the major source of professional differentiation between coaching and coaching psychology practice.

Apart from professional qualifications and research as core criteria towards professionalisation, is adherence to acceptable standards of practice, typically endorsed through certification and accreditation processes by coach training providers (Standards Australia 2010). The accreditation of coaches is however controversial globally as well as in South Africa with the true value of the certifications in many cases questionable (for a detailed discussion see Grant et al. (2010). There appears to be a high need for credibility that is perceived to be anchored in accreditation by practitioners wishing to work and be recognised as a coach (Grant and Cavanagh 2004). Uninformed practitioners and the general public is furthermore not in a position to determine the worth of the various psychological qualifications and accreditations. In this regard Grant (2006) asserts that there are a lucrative industry offering coach certification courses and programmes that appear to make more money than actually coaching by coaching practitioners. It is furthermore important to acknowledge that coaching organisations such as European Mentoring and Coaching Council (EMCC), World Association of Business Coaches (WABC) and the International Coach Federation (ICF) have put significant effort into establishing credentialing processes and developing coaching competencies (Grant et al. 2010) in a quest to set standards for coaching in an industry that is unregulated.

In setting standards, competence to practice is a core ethical principle that informs psychology as a profession and registered or licensed psychology practitioners are therefore required to practice exclusively within the boundaries of their competence (Ethical Rules of Conduct 2006). To ensure competence in the emerging sub-discipline of coaching psychology several professional coaching psychology bodies are introducing steps towards self-regulation that further solicits the question of 'What will be the minimum standards/quality assurance required for Coaching?' Self-regulation within voluntary professional bodies is typically supported by acceptable principles and values, voluntary codes of ethics, and recommended standards of competence – in some instances certification (Lane et al. 2010). Noteworthy are the Standards Australia Handbook for Coaching in Organisations (2010) that offers guidelines for the professional practice of coaching in organisations as well as the Graduate School Alliance for Executive Coaching (GSAEC 2012), setting standards for teaching executive and leadership coaching at university level.

In support of self-regulation within the coaching psychology domain the IGCCP in South Africa introduced the Code of Practice for Registered Psychology Practitioners in Coaching (2014) with the primary objective

> …to ensure that registered practitioners who practice as a coach conduct their services appropriately, professionally and ethically, with due regard to the needs and rights of those involved in the coaching process, the purpose for the coaching, and the broader context in which the coaching takes place. To achieve these outcomes, it is assumed that the registered practitioner has the necessary competence (including knowledge and understanding) of the coaching process, and the psychological frameworks and theories that inform and underpin this process (p. 9)

In addition to setting standards, the accreditation of coaching psychologists is of major concern globally. In order to provide recognition of coaching psychology expertise and enabling differentiation to a range of users of coaching and coaching psychology services the British Psychological Society (BPS no date) introduced a Register of Coaching Psychologists and the International Society for Coaching Psychology (ISFCP no date) a process of accreditation. Aligned to international developments, the IGCCP Code of Practice for Registered Psychology Practitioners in Coaching (2014) proposed a List of Registered Psychology Practitioners in Coaching. Table 1 provides a description of the proposed criteria for inclusion on the List of Coaching Psychology practitioners in South Africa benchmarked against the BPS Register of Coaching Psychologists and the ISCP process of accreditation to MISCP status. The positioning of compulsory supervision and number of continuous educational units in a continuous professional development (CPD) cycle in South Africa differs from the international benchmarks and is still under discussion.

In summary, research is primarily the major source of professional differentiation (Lowman 2013) and it is therefore pertinent that coaching psychology is positioned within a scientist- practitioner model vis-a-vis. a reflective practitioner model or an informed-practitioner model (Passmore and Theeboom in press). To enhance professional status coaching psychology should further develop within regulatory frameworks that determine boundaries of practice with a clear differentiation between coaching, counselling and therapy (Grant et al. 2010). Lastly, it is pertinent to identify and unpack issues pertinent to governance, ethics and continuing professional development to allow coaching psychology to develop within the boundaries of what constitutes a profession (Bennett 2006; Gray 2011).

2.5 *Coaching Psychology in a Multi-cultural Context*

Against the meta-context as previously described coaching psychologists are increasingly working within complex and multicultural environments at individual, team, organisational, national and international levels (Plaister-Ten 2013). It is

Table 1 Proposed criteria for inclusion in register of coaching psychologists

IGCCP proposed criteria	BPS register of coaching psychologists	ISCP process of accreditation MISCP status
Registered psychologists who practice coaching	Chartered psychologists	Chartership/registration/license
Member of IGCCP	Member of special group of coaching psychology	Member of recognised professional society
Satisfactory evidence of CPD related to coaching psychology (amount of CEU's in consultation)	Supervision from supervisor who is either a chartered psychologist or registered with the Health Professions Council (HPC)	CPD – 30 h of 40 related to coaching psychology in a 2 year cycle
Two supporting references and self-declaration	Self-declaration of competence plus two references (one must be current supervisor)	Evidence of supervision by qualified psychologist
Evidence of professional indemnity insurance		Evidence of professional indemnity insurance

essential that coaches understand the influence of culture in the execution of roles and responsibilities (Geber and Keane 2013; Griffiths 2010; Peterson 2007) and incorporating intercultural perspectives into coaching are therefore increasingly acknowledged (Gilbert and Rosinski 2008). There are however several descriptors that refer to coaching and culture when reviewing coaching and coaching psychology literature that in some instances are used interchangeably i.e. cross-cultural, multicultural and transcultural (for detailed discussion on differentiation based on view from anthropology and sociology (see Marotta 2014). There is still no consensus on defining the term *culture* (Booysen 2015). Typically, culture is defined as deeply entrenched values and beliefs (referred to as implied cultural occurrences) and displayed mainly by observed symbols and rituals (Triandis 2004) that manifest at the individual, group, organisational and national level (Hofstede et al. 2010).

The inclusion of culture into coaching practices gained momentum with the publication of Rosinski (2003) that refers specifically to coaching across culture or coaching from a cultural perspective. Several books and chapters within books followed that were more descriptive in nature and not based on empirical research. Cross-cultural coaching relates specifically to the coaching process where the coach and the coachee are from different cultural backgrounds (Milner et al. 2013; Plaister-Ten 2013; Rojon and McDowall 2010). Furthermore, a distinction is made between the topic under discussion within a coaching conversation e.g. how culture influence own beliefs and behaviours (Booysen 2015) and the broader cultural context. In this regard Lowman (2007, p. 297) argues that it is important that a coach understands the difference between culture as context and culture as a contributing factor towards behaviour. Within cross-cultural coaching the coach typically work from their own reference system to understand another person, whereas within multicultural and transcultural work the coach work across cultural differences and will thus be able to function within the worldview of another individual or group. It is further evident that there is a clear gap between coaching practices in multi-cultural environments and evidence-based and theoretically grounded research (Van Zyl and Stander in press).

Based on a body of empirical cross-cultural research, the main departure point within psychology is that 'all individuals exist in social, political, historical and economic contexts' and psychologists in different applied domains of psychology are therefore expected to understand the influence of these contexts on behaviour (American Psychological Association 2003, p. 377). To this end the 'Guidelines on Multicultural Education, Training, Research, Practice and Organizational Change for Psychologists' was developed in 2003, intended as a 'living document' providing guidelines towards the develop of deeper knowledge and awareness in addressing multiculturalism and diversity in education, research and practices of psychologists in the various areas of application in psychology (p. 395). The Guidelines further uses the term *culture-centered* to encourage the use of a cultural lens as central focus of professional behaviour. To this end, Triandis (2004) differentiates between cultural psychology, cross-cultural psychology and indigenous psychology. The main focus of cultural and indigenous psychology is to understand the individual within a traditional and socio-cultural context (also referred to as the emic position). Culture is seen as part of the individual and culture and behaviour are thus viewed as inseparable. In contrast, cross-cultural researchers are specifically interested in understanding cross-cultural similarities and differences towards an understanding of cultural universals, also referred to as the etic approach (Sullivan and Cottone 2010).

The abovementioned discussion is important and provides a meta-framework for further research on the application of coaching psychology in a multi-cultural context. Increased attention is therefore placed on the importance of multi-cultural interactions within work processes and is typically defined within three overarching factors: awareness and mindset, knowledge and skill (Handin and Steinwedel 2006; Inman and DeBoer Kreider 2013). To this end meta-cultural competence is viewed as critical to ethical coaching practices. The study of Plaister-Ten (2013) proposed that change occur over a lifespan due to multiple and continuous intercultural experiences and therefore the coach must work with 'unlearning' as key intercultural competency (p. 53). Furthermore, the complexity of coaching in multi-cultural context are confirmed with findings supporting the importance of cultural intelligence (Booysen 2015; Deng and Gibson 2008; Van Zyl et al. 2011), awareness and application of global mindedness (Wilson 2013) and focusing on the link between cultural and spiritual values (Griffiths 2010) with a general paucity of literature on coaching with African values (Geber and Keane 2013). Important questions regarding the influence of westernised worldviews in current coaching practices remains, especially how methods and approaches rooted in a western worldview can be applied to other cultures (Milner et al. 2013; Plaister-Ten 2013). A qualitative study utilising critical incidents with German coaches reported the main areas impacting coaching as communication patterns, the coach-client relationship, the coach setting and role understanding (Milner et al. 2013).

In support of an indigenous or emic approach to the study of the influence of culture in coaching, is the discussion paper of Geber and Keane (2013) that argued for the need to include indigenous knowledge as an important aspect of transformation and redress on individual and systems level within coaching research in South Africa. They proceed to refer specifically to the African paradigm of Ubuntu, a relationship-centred paradigm (for detailed discussion see Mbigi 2002 and Metz 2007) as different ontological perspective and well suited framework for coaching and coach training in Africa. Questions of universality versus culture-specificity remain a main area of research especially utilising cultural orientation frameworks (Dorfman et al. 2012; House et al. 2004; Peterson 2007) and endorsing universal leadership attributes as well as identifying universally undesirable leadership attributes. Furthermore, research caution against superficial use and knowledge of national culture that promotes stereotypical thinking (Friedman and Antal 2005) and could lead to cultural misunderstandings if differences observed are misinterpreted. In the application of cross-cultural research utilising cultural dimensions as presented in cultural orientation frameworks, researchers should be mindful that on individual level personality is a more reliable predictor of individual behaviour than culture (Booysen 2015; Hofstede et al. 2010).

Application of cross-cultural coaching models is popular in books and chapters with validity research starting to emerge. Research on the use of models and frameworks of cultural difference as guide on the levels of intercultural competence that map the stages individuals go through as they become more transculturally effective, are steadily growing (Bird et al. 2009; Dorfman et al. 2012). Within these models awareness or intercultural sensitivity and cultural experiences are precursors to the development of intercultural competence that requires further research. In addition, research should also focus on alternative models such as the dynamic constructivist approach (Friedman and Antal 2005) where reality is negotiated (based on action science) to the adaptation approaches that uses general models of cultural differences (such as cultural orientation frameworks and models of intercultural competence).

3 Coaching and Coaching Psychology

3.1 Contemporary Coaching Practice

Positioning Statement 4 **There is a high degree of interdependence between psychology and coaching and it is therefore important to globally define coaching psychology and the associated value proposition thereof**. From a global perspective there are no clear boundaries between coaching as emerging practice and coaching psychology as sub-discipline in psychology (Grant et al. 2010).

Reviewing different scholarly works on the development of coaching and the psychology of coaching, it is evident that different disciplines including psychology, sociology, and anthropology informs coaching practices (Grant et al. 2010; Palmer and Whybrow 2006). The development of coaching within the field of psychology can further be traced back to the humanistic approach and the emergence of positive psychology (Biswas-Diener and Dean 2007; Grant 2006; Motschnig-Pitrik et al. in press). Bachkirova et al. (2014, p. 3) proposed that typical attempts at defining coaching usually emphasise the "purpose (what it is for?), type of clients (who uses the service?) or process (how it is done?) or a combination of these".

Pavur (2013) revisited the main purposes of coaching by exploring client's perceived needs for coaching in organisations. He identified three main categories of purpose that help us to reflect on the drivers of the exponential growth of the coaching industry. The *first* category relates to training and development. The organisation engages the coach primarily to facilitate manager self-awareness, to build social skills, align motives and values to the culture of the organisation and to improve organisational outcomes and performance. The *second* category relates to health and self-actualisation. Here the organisation engages the coaching primarily to promote mental health, to support work-life balance and to improve the quality of life, work satisfaction and engagement. The *third* category relates to adaptation and resilience where the coach is contracted to interpret ethical challenges, work with complex problems by engaging stakeholders, improve functions in uncertain environments, modify organisational architecture, change culture, prepare for multiple possible futures and to improve functioning across cultures.

In a literature review it was evident that definitions of Coaching differ considerably but are generally anchored in relationship and outcome, i.e. coaching is "a collaborative relationship formed between coach and coachee for the purpose of attaining professional or personal development outcomes which are valued by the coachee" (Grant et al. 2010, p. 3). Definitions further differs according to the domain of application within which a coaching engagement takes place (i.e. executive and leadership coaching), theoretical approaches, perspectives and methodologies utilised in the coaching assignment as well as definitions that focus on the outcomes to achieve i.e. performance, skill and developmental coaching (Standards Australia 2010). The lack of clear boundaries between coaching and coaching psychology is further evident by the statement of Sperry (2013, p. 284) that 'executive coaching has come of age both inside and outside the field of consulting psychology'. Coaching Psychology as a specialised discipline in psychology has steadily grown since the landmark publication in 1996 of a special edition on executive coaching and consultation in the *Consulting Psychology Journal: Research and Practice* (CPJ). Reviewing articles published between 2008 and 2013 in CPJ, coaching theory and practice were referenced in 15.8 % of the articles published – an increase of 15.5 % for the period between 1998 and 2007 (Leonard et al. 2013).

3.2 Coaching Psychology: Towards a South African Definition

In a quest to set standards for professional coaching psychology in South Africa and to clarify boundaries within the profession of psychology it was important to benchmark and reflect on how other professional bodies defined coaching psychology. In line with the evolving nature of Coaching Psychology internationally, the following definitions of the British Psychological Society Special Group in Coaching Psychology (SGCP), as well as the Australian Psychological Society's Interest Group for Coaching Psychology (IGCP) served as initial working definitions within South Africa:

- *British Psychological Society (BPS) Special Group in Coaching Psychology (SGCP)*:
- Coaching psychology is for enhancing well-being and performance in personal life and work domains underpinned by models of coaching grounded in established adult learning or psychological approaches"(Palmer and Whybrow 2006).
- *Australian Psychological Society (APS), Interest group in Coaching Psychology (IGCP)*:
- Coaching psychology, as an applied positive psychology, draws on and develops established psychological approaches, and can be understood as being the systematic application of behavioural science to the enhancement of life experience, work performance and wellbeing for individuals, groups and organisations who do not have clinically significant mental health issues or abnormal levels of distress (IGCCP 2002).

Given the multi-cultural context of coaching in South Africa, informed by the rapid pace of globalisation and associated complexity of a multicultural society, the lack of reference to culture within the definitions of APS and BPS are viewed as a major omission. Subsequent debates in the international arena regarding what should be included in the definition of coaching psychology to inform the development of an agenda for the teaching of coaching psychology recognised the inclusion of: (1) the purpose of coaching psychology, (2) the contextual issues as important considerations beyond psychology, as well as (3) the exclusion of direct treatment of mental illness or abnormal levels of stress (Cavanagh and Palmer et al. 2011; Grant 2011). Important for the inclusion of contextual influences was the recognition that people may differ in a number of culturally important ways such as race, gender, education, socio-economic status, language, religion, sexual orientation and ethnicity (Odendaal 2011). Multicultural competence is therefore a critical competency for effective coaching and within the domain of leadership and executive coaching Booysen (2015) posits that intercultural sensitivity and the ability to operate in different cultural contexts can be regarded as a requirement for all leaders (Booysen 2015).

Against this background, the Society for Industrial and Organisational Psychology of South Africa's Interest Group in Coaching and Consulting Psychology (IGCCP) started an inclusive process to formulate a South African definition. Initially two focus groups were held in 2010/2011 at the SIOPSA, as well as the Psychological Society of South Africa (PsySSA) annual conferences. A total of 55 participants from SIOPSA and PsySSA participated in two phases of data gathering. In phase 1 the data obtained from the focus groups were interpreted utilising content analysis. The recurring themes were then incorporated into a South African definition and value proposition that was also subsequently included in the Code of Practice for Registered Psychology Practitioners in Coaching (2014). A draft definition was presented at the First International Congress of Coaching Psychology in Spain (Odendaal and Le Roux 2011). In phase two, a working definition was distributed to the participants and feedback solicited via the Delphi technique. A final definition was presented at the International Psychology Conference in Cape Town in 2012, as well as the SIOPSA Annual Conference in 2013 (Odendaal and Le Roux 2013):

> Coaching psychology, as practiced by a 'coaching' psychologist is a conversational process of facilitating positive development and change towards optimal functioning, well-being and increased performance within work and personal life domains, in the absence of clinically significant mental health issues, and through the application of a wide range of psychological theories and principles. The intervention is action orientated with measureable outcomes, but also reflective towards creating greater self-awareness and meaning and directed at individuals, groups, organisations and communities within a culturally specific context.

The definition included several important features as emphasised by practitioners, namely: (1) the differentiation between the *field/industry* of coaching and the *practice* of coaching psychology, in that only registered psychologists practice coaching psychology; (2) that coaching psychology can be applied to different domains (life coaching and coaching within organisational context); (3) registered practitioners utilise and should be competent in a wide range of psychological theories and principles, (4) an inclusion of a present-centred focus with reference to action and goal orientated interventions; (5) with measureable outcomes; (6) a reflective focus that referred to greater self-awareness, a sense of purpose and meaning. Similar to international definitions, South African registered practitioners also emphasised (7) growth and development, learning and positive change; and (8) the emphasis on mentally healthy clients. Highlighting the importance of contextual factors, South African practitioners have (9) included diversity into their definition with specific reference to work in a culturally specific context at (10) individual, group, organisation and community level.

Reviewing the definitions of coaching and coaching psychology, Grant and Palmer (2002) concluded that coaching psychology practice is different from coaching practice with the main differentiation the theoretical bases of coaching psychology practice. Passmore however argue that this may have been true in 2002 but in 2011 the coaching industry is strongly informed by coaching standards of professional bodies and evidence-based approaches. Passmore (2011, p. 107) position the differentiation between coaching psychology practice and coaching practice by focusing on the 'scientific study of behaviour, cognitive and emotion within coaching practice'. In addition, Passmore asserts that all coaches must have a good understanding of the specific domain they are working in, be educated in ethics and ethical decision making as well as mental health and psychological conditions to know when it is appropriate to refer.

Lowman (2013) also highlights research as the primarily source of professional differentiation. It is therefore pertinent that coaching psychology is positioned within a scientist-practitioner model vis-a-vis a reflective practitioner model or an informed-practitioner model. Training in coaching psychology further places an emphasis on the science behind the practice and not just on skills (i.e. competency approach) and the coaching process (i.e. proprietary models) (Grant et al. 2010).

3.3 Value Proposition for Coaching Psychology

In addition to the definition, South African psychologists practicing coaching have also collectively unpacked the value proposition of coaching psychology (Odendaal and Le Roux 2011) that are presented in Table 2 with supporting comments as obtained from the focus groups.

Firstly, psychologists positioned Coaching Psychology within the ambit of the profession of Psychology that is recognised and governed under the Health Professions Act (Act 56 of 1974 as amended by Act 29 of 2007). Practicing a profession requires training that is theoretically grounded and leads to a scientist-practitioner approach in practice. Furthermore, practicing as a psychologist requires demonstrating competence in the registered domain of practice (i.e. scope of practice) with clear referral to registration categories equipped, trained and registered to deliver work under each practice area. Secondly, psychologists recognised the importance of rapport and client interface and the fact that as professionals they are trained to navigate complex client relationships in different individual, team and organisational contexts allowing them a deep understanding of the subject. Thirdly, psychologists recognised that they are trained behavioural scientists competent to optimise the life experience, well-being and work performance of individuals, groups and organisations. Lastly, South African psychologists have identified strength in their ability to work with diversity as a result of the rich multi-cultural heritage of South Africa as a country.

4 In Conclusion

This chapter focused specifically on contextualising coaching, coaching psychology and multi-cultural coaching within a multi-cultural context. The chapter indicates that coaching psychology requires an active approach towards professionalisation, with professional bodies having a strategic role to play. It is evident from preceding discussions that there are strong alignment with a degree of interdependence between the broader discipline of psychology and coaching. Requirements for

Table 2 Value proposition for coaching psychologists in South Africa

Theme	Comment
Behaviour expert	Theoretical and practical background as a registered practitioner prepares the practitioner for his/her role as behavioural and relationship expert
Recognised profession	Registered Psychologists in South Africa are professionals and psychology is recognised as a profession
Evidence based tools grounded in psychology – (refer to scientist-practitioner model)	Formal training as a psychologist provides a foundation and meta-orientation in a variety of theoretical frameworks to understand the complexity of human behaviour
Scope of practice	Psychologists understand boundaries of work and will refer to registration categories equipped, trained and registered to deliver work under each practice area
Coaching relationship and client interface	Psychologists are trained to facilitate complex client relationships and interactions
Development focus	Psychologists have the knowledge and experience to systematically apply behavioural science to enhance the life experience, work performance and wellbeing of individuals, groups and organisations where clinical pathology and/or abnormal stress levels are absent
Levels of analysis	Psychologists are trained to analyse problems systemically and behaviours holistically on individual, group and organisational level which allow them a deep understanding of the subject
Organisational positioning	Psychologists in the workplace has access to managers and their broader organisation enhancing the objective to support personal and work performance of individuals and teams within the relevant organisational context
Practical coaching competencies	Training as psychologists provides an inherent competency in a wide range of coaching and counselling skills
Diversity	Psychologists in South Africa are trained and have experience in a broad spectrum of context that is prominent in the country's heritage

Society for Industrial and Organisational Psychology of South Africa's Interest Group in Coaching and Consulting Psychology's Code of Practice for Registered Psychology Practitioners in Coaching 2014

future development must therefore focus on establishing and maintaining a sound foundation of empirical knowledge within a shared framework of evidence-based practice, taking into account differentiation in training and education as well as professional standards. Global trends point towards increased participation and interdisciplinary cooperation amongst professional coaching bodies to address remaining challenges regarding (i) access to professional registration versus accreditation or certification, (ii) endorsement of a specific Code of Ethics with appropriate sanctions should transgressions occur, (iii) level of competence around the variety of approaches and professional applications of coaching psychology within multi-cultural contexts, (iv) endorsement of minimum standards of practice and

(v) recognition of boundaries of professional practice based on qualification, experience and level of competence in coaching psychology.

References

African Economic Outlook. (2015). *South Africa 2015*. Retrieved November 29, 2015, from africaneconomicoutlook.org

American Psychological Association. (2003). Guidelines on multicultural education, training, research, practice, and organizational change for psychologists. *American Psychologist, 58*(5), 377–402. doi:10.1037/0003-066X.58.5.377.

Bachkirova, T., Cox, E., & Clutterbuck, D. (2014). Introduction. In E. Cox, T. Bachkirova, & D. Clutterbuck (Eds.), *The complete handbook of coaching* (2nd ed., pp. 1–20). London: Sage.

Beattie, R. S., Kim, S., Hagen, M. S., Egan, T. M., Ellinger, A. D., & Hamlin, R. G. (2014). Managerial coaching: A review of the empirical literature and development of a model to guide future practice. *Advances in Developing Human Resources, 16*(2), 184–201. doi:10.1177/1523422313520476.

Bersin, J. (2013). *Building a strong talent pipeline for the global economic recovery – Time for innovative and integrated talent and HR strategies*. Bersin by Deloitte Consulting LLP, Retrieved from: http://www.bersin.com/library

Bennett, J. L. (2006). An agenda for coaching-related research: A challenge for researchers. *Consulting Psychology Journal: Practice and Research, 58*, 240–249.

Bird, A., Mendenhall, M., Stevens, M. J., & Oddou, G. (2009). Defining the content domain of intercultural competence for global leaders. *Journal of Managerial Psychology, 25*(8), 810–828. doi:10.1108/02683941011089107.

Biswas-Diener, R., & Dean, B. (2007). *Positive psychology coaching: Putting the science of happiness to work for your clients*. Hoboken: Wiley.

Booysen, L. A. E. (2015). Cross-cultural coaching. Chapter 10. In D. Riddle, E. Hoole, E. Gullette (Eds.), *Center for creative leadership handbook of coaching in organizations* (pp. 241–288). Wiley: Jossey-Bass. ISBN 978-1-118-84148-8.

British Psychological Society. (n.d.). *FAQ's – Register for coaching psychologists*. Retrieved from www.bps.org.uk

Broad Based Black Economic Empowerment Act. (2013). Amendment 46 of 2013. Government Gazette 2011.

Cavanagh, M., & Lane, D. (2012). Coaching psychology coming of age: The challenges we face in the messy world of complexity. *International Coaching Psychology Review, 7*(1), 75–90.

Cavanagh, M., Palmer, S., et al. (2011). Educating coaching psychologists: Responses from the field. *International Coaching Psychology Review, 6*(1), 100–127.

Clarke, N. (2013). Model of complexity leadership development. *Human Resource Development International, 16*(2), 135–150. doi:10.1080/13678868.2012.756155.

Coetzee, M., & Van Zyl, L. E. (2014). A review of a decade's scholarly publications. *South African Journal of Industrial Psychology/SA Tydskrif vir Bedryfsielkunde, 40*(1), 16. doi:10.4102/sajip.v40i1.1227.

Cox, E. E., Bachkirova, T., & Clutterbuck, D. (2014). Theoretical traditions and coaching genres: Mapping the territory. *Advances in Developing Human Resources, 16*(2), 139–160. doi:10.1177/1523422313520194.

De Klerk, M. (in press). Morality on the executive's couch: Ethical perspectives on coaching psychology, theory and praxis. In L. E. Van Zyl, M. W. Stander, & A. Odendaal (Eds.), *Coaching psychology: Meta-theoretical perspectives and applications in multi-cultural contexts.* New York: Springer.

Deloitte. (2015). *Health care outlook South Africa.* Retrieved from https://www2.deloitte.com/content/dam/Deloitte/global/Documents/Life-Sciences-Health-Care/gx-lshc-2015-health-care-outlook-south-africa.pdf

Deng, L., & Gibson, P. (2008). A qualitative evaluation on the role of cultural intelligence in cross-cultural leadership effectiveness. *International Journal of Leadership Studies, 3*(2), 181–197.

Department of Education. (2009). *Challenges facing education in South Africa.* An interview with Martin Prew, director of the Centre for Education Policy Development (CEPD) and former director and acting chief director for the National Department of Education Management and Governance.

Dorfman, P., Javidan, M., Hanges, P., Dastmalchian, A., & House, R. (2012). GLOBE: A twenty year journey into the intriguing world of culture and leadership. *Journal Of World Business October.* doi:10.1016/j.jwb.2012.01.004.

Elliott, R. (2011). Utilising evidence-based leadership theories in coaching for leadership development: Towards a comprehensive integrating conceptual framework. *International Coaching Psychology Review, 6*(1), 46–70.

Ethical rules of conduct for practitioners registered under the Health Professions Act, 1974. (2006). Government Gazette, 29079, Cape Town, 4 August.

Friedman, V. J., & Antal, A. B. (2005). Negotiating reality: A theory of action approach to intercultural competence. *Management Learning, 36*(1), 69–86. doi:0117713505076050198811

Geber, H., & Keane, M. (2013). Extending the worldview of coaching research and practice in Southern Africa: The concept of Ubuntu. *International Journal of Evidence Based Coaching and Mentoring, 11*(2), 8–17.

Gilbert, K., & Rosinski, P. (2008). Accessing cultural orientations: The online cultural orientations framework assessment as a tool for coaching. *Coaching: An International Journal of Theory, Research and Practice, 1*(1), 81–92.

Global Community of Coaches. (2008). The Dublin declaration on coaching, including appendices. Version 1.3. August 2008. Retrieved from http://www.pdf.net/Files/Dublin%20Declaration%20on%20Coaching.pdf

Graduate School Alliance for Executive Coaching. (2012, March 30). *Academic standards for graduate programes in executive and organisational coaching: Executive summary.* Version: 30 March 2012. Retrieved from www.gsaec.orgwww.gsaec.org

Grant, A. M. (2000). Coaching psychology comes of age. *Psychology News, 4*(4), 12–14.

Grant, A. (2006). A personal perspective on professional coaching and the development of coaching psychology. *International Coaching Psychology Review, 1*(1), 12–20.

Grant, A. M. (2011). Developing an agenda for teaching coaching psychology. *International Review of Industrial and Organizational Psychology, 6*(1), 84–99.

Grant, A. M., & Cavanagh, M. (2004). Towards a profession of coaching: Sixty five years of progress and challenges for the future. *International Journal of Evidence-based Coaching and Mentoring, 2*(1), 8–21.

Grant, A. M., & Palmer, S. (2002). *Coaching psychology workshop.* In Annual Conference of the Counselling Psychology Division of the British Psychological Society, Torquay, UK, 18 May.

Grant, A. M., Passmore, J., Cavanagh, M. J., & Parker, H. (2010). The state of play in coaching today: A comprehensive review of the field. *International Review of Industrial and Organizational Psychology, 25,* 125–167. doi:10.1002/9780470661628.

Gray, D. E. (2011). Journeys towards the professionalization of coaching: Dilemmas, dialogues and decisions along the global pathway. *Coaching: An International Journal of Theory, Practice and Research, 4*(1), 4–19.

Griffiths, A. (2010). Coaching and spiritual values in the workplace: Exploring the perspectives of coaches. *International Journal of Evidence Based Coaching and Mentoring, 4,* 65–82.

Handin, K., & Steinwedel, J. (2006). Developing global leaders: Executive coaching targets cross-cultural competencies. *Global Business and Organizational Excellence, 26*(1), 18–28.

Hofstede, G., Hofstede, G. J., & Minkov, M. (2010). *Cultures and organisations software of the mind, Intercultural cooperation and its importance to survival* (3rd ed.). New York: McGraw Hill.

House, R. J., Hanges, P. J., Javidan, M., Dorfman, P. W., & Gupta, V. (2004). *Culture, leadership and organisations: The GLOBE study of 62 societies*. Thousand Oaks: Sage Publications.

Inman, A. G., & DeBoer Kreider, E. (2013). Multicultural competence: Psychotherapy practice and supervision. *Psychotherapy, 50*, 346–350. doi:10.1037/a0032029.

Interest Group of Coaching Psychology. (2002). *Definition of coaching psychology.* Retrieved December 29, 2010, from www.groups.psychology.org.au/igcp/

Interest Group of Coaching and Consulting Psychology. (2013). *General information*. Retrieved https://www.siopsa.org.za/pages/interest_groups#igccp

Interest Group of Coaching and Consulting Psychology. (2014). *Code of practice for registered psychology practitioners in coaching*. Publication of the Society of Industrial and Organisational Psychology of South Africa. Retrieved from www.siopsa.org.za

International Coach Federation. (2013). *Individual credentialing*. Retrieved from http://coachfederation.org/credential/?navItemNumber_502

International Society for Coaching Psychology. (2015). *Objectives of the international society for coaching psychology: An international professional membership organisation*. Retrieved form http://www.isfcp.net/objectives.htm

International Society for Coaching Psychology. (n.d.). *Roots to accreditation/certification*. Retrieved from www.isfcp.net

Johansen, B. (2012). *Leaders make the future: Ten new leadership skills for an uncertain world*. San Francisco: Berrett-Koehler Publishers.

Jorgensen, L. I., Van Zyl, L. E., & Stander, M. W. (in press). Training emerging psychologists as multi-cultural contextual coaches. In L. E. Van Zyl, M. W. Stander, & A. Odendaal (Eds.), *Coaching psychology: Meta-theoretical perspectives and applications in multi-cultural contexts*. New York: Springer.

Lai, Y., & McDowall, A. (2014). A systematic review (SR) of coaching psychology: Focusing on the attributes of effective coaching psychologists. *International Coaching Psychology Review, 9*(2), 118–134.

Lane, D. A., Stelter, R., & Stout-Rostron, S. S. (2010). The future of coaching as a profession. In E. Cox, T. Bachkirova, & D. Clutterbuck (Eds.), *The complete handbook of coaching* (pp. 357–369). London: Sage.

Leonard, H. S., Freedman, A. M., & Kilburg, R. (2013). Tribal elders' view of consulting psychology's past, present and future. *Consulting Psychology Journal, Practice and Research, 65*(4), 266–277.

Lowman, R. L. (2007). Coaching and consulting in multicultural contexts integrating themes and issues. *Consulting Psychology Journal: Practice and Research, 59*(4), 296–303. doi:10.1037/1065-9293.59.4.296.

Lowman, R. L. (2013). What have we learned? Where are headed? *Consulting Psychology Journal, Practice and Research, 65*(4), 325–328.

Marotta, V. (2014). The multicultural, intercultural and the transcultural subject. In F. Mansouri & B. E. de B'béri (Eds.), *Global perspectives on the politics of multiculturalism in the 21st century: A case study analysis*. New York: Routledge. http://www.researchgate.net/publication/261216820

Mbigi, L. (2002). The spirit of African leadership: A comparative African perspective. *Journal for Convergence, 3*(4), 18–23.

McKinsey. (2013). *Urban world: The shifting global business landscape*. McKinsey Global Institute. Retrieved www.mckinsey.com/mgi

Metz, T. (2007). Ubuntu as a moral theory: Reply to four critics. *South African Journal of Philosophy, 26*, 369–387.

Milner, J., Ostmeier, E., & franke. (2013). Critical incidents in cross-cultural coaching: The view from German coaches. *International Journal of Evidence Based Coaching and Mentoring, 11*(2), 19–30.

Motschnig-Pitrik, R., Van Zyl, L. E., & Stander, M. W. (in press). Exploring positive psychology and person-centered psychology in coaching. In L. E. Van Zyl, M. W. Stander, & A. Odendaal (Eds.), *Coaching psychology: Meta-theoretical perspectives and applications in multi-cultural contexts*. New York: Springer.

Nieminen, L., Biermeier-Hanson, B., & Denison, D. (2013). Aligning leadership and organisational culture: The leader-culture fir framework for coaching organizational leaders. *Consulting Psychology Journal: Practice and Research, 65*(3), 177–198.

Norwack, K. M., & Mashini, S. (2012). Evidence-based answers to 15 questions about leveraging 360-degree feedback. *Consulting Psychology Journal: Practice and Research, 64*(3), 157–182.

Nowack, K., & Mashihi, S. (2012). Evidence-based answers to 15 questions about leveraging 360-degree feedback. *Consulting Psychology Journal: Practice and Research, 64*, 157–182. doi:10.1037/a0030011.

Odendaal, A. (2011). Response to: Developing an agenda for teaching coaching psychology. In M. Cavanagh, & S. Palmer, et al. (Eds.), *Educating coaching psychologists: Responses from the field*. International Coaching Psychology Review, *6*(1), 100–127.

Odendaal, A. (2013). *The measurement of social desirability: A cross-cultural perspective*. Unpublished doctoral thesis. University of Johannesburg, Johannesburg, South Africa.

Odendaal, A., & Kwiatkowski, R. (in press). Supervision in industrial, organisational, work and occupational psychology. In D. A. Lane, M. Watts, & S. Corrie (Eds.), *Psychological supervision – emergence and growth in practice*. London: Open University Press.

Odendaal, A., & Le Roux, A. (2010, December 14–15). *Towards the development of coaching psychology in South Africa: A stakeholder analysis*. Paper presented at the 1st international congress of coaching psychology, 14–15 Dec, City University, London.

Odendaal, A., & Le Roux, A. (2011, October 12). *Emerging trends and challenges in the professionalization of the coaching industry: A South African coaching psychology perspective*. Paper presented at the 1st international congress of coaching psychology, 12 October, Barcelona.

Odendaal, A., & Le Roux, A. (2013). *The professionalisation of coaching psychology: Introducing a draft code of practice and register/List for registered practitioners*. Paper presented at the 15th annual conference of the Society for Industrial and Organisational Psychology of South Africa, 29–31 July, CSIR Conference Centre, Pretoria, South Africa.

Odendaal, A., Le Roux, A., & Steenkamp, H. (2011) *Profiling the coaching industry in South Africa*. Paper presented at the 1st International Congress of Coaching Psychology, Southern Hemisphere, 11 May, CSIR Conference Centre, Pretoria, South Africa.

Palmer, S., & Whybrow, A. (2006). The coaching psychology movement and its development within the British Psychological Society. *International Coaching Psychology Review, 1*(1), 5–11.

Palmer, S., & Whybrow, A. (2014). *Handbook of coaching psychology: A guide for practitioners*. London: Routledge.

Passmore, J. (2011). Response to: Developing an agenda for teaching coaching psychology. In M. Cavanagh, & S. Palmer (Eds.), *Educating coaching psychologists: Responses from the field*. International Coaching Psychology Review, *6*(1), 100–127.

Plaister-Ten, J. (2013). Raising culturally-derived awareness and building culturally-appropriate responsibility: The development of the cross-cultural kaleidoscope. *International Journal of Evidence Based Coaching and Mentoring, 11*(2), 53–69.

Passmore, J., & Theeboom, T. (in press). Coaching psychology: A journey of development in research. In L. E. van Zyl, M. W. Stander, & A. Odendaal (Eds.), *Coaching psychology: Meta-theoretical perspectives and applications in multi-cultural contexts*.

Pavur, E. J. (2013). Why do organisations want their leaders to be coached? *Consulting Psychology Journal, Practice and Research, 65*(4), 289–293.

Peterson, D. (2007). Executive coaching in a cross-cultural context. *Consulting Psychology Journal: Practice and Research, 59*(4), 261–271.

Republic of South Africa. (1974). *Health professions act, no. 56 of 1974*. Retrieved from http://www.health.gov.za

Rojon, C., & McDowall, A. (2010). Cultural Orientation Framework (COF) assessment questionnaire in cross-cultural coaching: A cross-validation with wave focus styles. *International Journal of Evidence Based Coaching and Mentoring, 8*(2), 1–26.

Rosinski, P. (2003). *Coaching across cultures*. London: Nicholas Brealey Publishing.

Simon, C. E., Odendaal, A., & Goosen, X. (2014). Exploring the contemporary ethical challenges in coaching psychology in South Africa. *South African Journal of Industrial Psychology/SA Tydskrif vir Bedryfsielkunde, 40*(1). doi:10.4102/.

Sperry, L. (2013). Executive coaching and leadership assessment: Past, present and future. *Consulting Psychology Journal, Practice and Research, 65*(4), 284–288.

Stacey, R. (2007). The challenge of human interdependence: Consequences for thinking about the day to day practice of management in organizations. *European Business Review, 19*(4), 292–302.

Standards Australia Guidelines for Coaching in Organisations. (2010). Sydney: SAI Global Limited under licence from Standards Australia Limited.

Statistics South Africa. (2012). *Census 2011 methodology and highlights of key results*. Published by Statistics South Africa. Retrieved from www.statssa.gov.za

Stelter, R. (2014). Intervention theories in coaching and coaching psychology. In *A guide to third generation coaching* (pp. 45–109). Dordrecht: Springer.

Sullivan, C., & Cottone, R. R. (2010). Emergent characteristics of effective cross-cultural research: A review of the literature. *Journal of Counseling & Development, 88*, 357–362. doi:10.1002/j.1556-6678.2010.tb00033.x.

Thompson, M., & Dieffenbach, K. (2015). Measuring professional ethics in coaching: Development of the PISC-Q. *Ethics & Behavior, (in press)*, 1–17.

Triandis, H. C. (2004). The many dimensions of culture. *Academy of Management Executive, 18*(1), 88–93. doi:10.5465/AME.2004.12689599.

Van Zyl, L. E., & Stander, M. W. (2013). A strengths-based approach towards coaching in a multicultural environment. In J. H. D. Cornelius-White, R. Motschnig-Pitrik, & M. Lux (Eds.), *Interdisciplinary handbook of the person-centered approach* (pp. 245–257). New York: Springer.

Van Zyl, L. E., & Stander, M. W. (in press). The future of multi-cultural coaching psychology. In L. E Van Zyl, M. W. Stander, A. Odendaal (Eds.), *Coaching psychology: Meta-theoretical perspectives and applications in multi-cultural contexts*. New York: Springer.

Van Zyl, E. S., Kleynhans, R., & Du Plessis, M. (2011). Understanding and approaching the cultural gap between first world leaders and their third world workforce: An African focus. *African Journal of Business Management, 5*(17), 7171–7178.

Van Zyl, L. E., Stander, M. W., & Odendaal, A. (in press). Preface. In L. E. Van Zyl, M. W. Stander, & A. Odendaal (Eds.), *Coaching psychology: Meta-theoretical perspectives and applications in multi-cultural contexts*. New York: Springer.

Wilson, W. (2013). Coaching with a global mindset. *International Journal of Evidence Based Coaching and Mentoring, 11*(2), 33–52.

Zarris, P. (2011). Response to: Developing an agenda for teaching coaching psychology. In M. Cavanagh, & S. Palmer, et al. (Eds.), *Educating coaching psychologists: Responses from the field*. International Coaching Psychology Review, *6*(1), 100–127.

Coaching Psychology Research: A Journey of Development in Research

Jonathan Passmore and Tim Theeboom

Abstract The purpose of this chapter is to explore the developmental journey of coaching research. The paper suggests that coaching research, like other areas, has migrated through a number of phases. It started with case study papers (phase 1) which largely looked at individuals or individual organizations from the perspective of the coach (usually a consultant). The second and third phases (phase 2 and 3) were more qualitative in nature, and included surveys and more sophisticated approaches such as grounded theory. The next phase (phase 4) has been the growth in randomised control trails. These papers have offered stronger evidence about the efficacy of coaching as an intervention. More recently (phase 5) there have been a number of meta-analysis papers published. For each phase, the authors will illustrate their arguments by selecting one or two relevant papers and offering a critical review of the paper, as well as specific phase of the research journey. The paper will conclude with a projected overview of the future of coaching psychology research and practice.

Keywords Coaching psychology • Coaching research • Coaching context • Multi-cultural coaching

1 Introduction

In this chapter we aim to review the developing journey of coaching psychology research, which has emerged over the past two decades from ad hoc, grass roots research to dynamic, serious academic study.

The chapter explores the theme of coaching psychology research by considering its development through a series of research phases. Our selection of phases reflects

J. Passmore (✉)
Department of Psychology, University of Evora, Evora, Portugal
e-mail: jonathancpassmore@yahoo.co.uk

T. Theeboom
Department of Work and Organizational Psychology, University of Amsterdam, Amsterdam, The Netherlands
e-mail: timtheeboom@gmail.com

L.E. van Zyl et al. (eds.), *Coaching Psychology: Meta-theoretical perspectives and applications in multicultural contexts*, DOI 10.1007/978-3-319-31012-1_2

how we see this journey of development looking back from 2014. We recognize there are other ways the journey could be segmented, and that our view is just one perspective.

To illustrate these phases we have selected a sample paper from each period that we believe illustrates many of the points we are raising about the phase in question. By selecting these papers we are not suggesting they are the worst or the best examples, but rather the example is typical of the research that was being undertaken, referenced and quoted in coaching research papers at the time, including by ourselves. In fact just to balance up the critique of these papers, we have deliberately included one paper written by one of us, to show that our own work is not beyond criticism or improvement.

Our aspiration is that the chapter will provide future students and those studying coaching research with a summarized 'history' of the development of coaching psychology, which shows its emergence towards a respected strand of psychological research. Further, we will argue that such a journey of development is typical for most emerging areas of research.

2 A Brief Review of Coaching Psychology Research

As researchers we have both been challenged in the past by practitioners; 'So why is research important? I know it works and that is enough'. For many practitioners, that is enough. However, when decisions need to be made about the impact of coaching, we would argue as psychologists that companies and individuals need to ensure that they can demonstrate that coaching is both the right intervention to address the perceived problem and secondly that it actually works – i.e. that it will deliver the perceived benefits.

We would argue that research can provide valuable benefits for us as practitioners. Research aims to identify and define the knowledge base upon which practitioners work – what is coaching's combination of knowledge and skills which differentiate what coaches do from other helping and learning interventions? Such a differentiation is essential for any consideration of coaching.

With the idea of an evolving and developing knowledge base, supplied by appropriate research, there comes the potential of enhancing coaching performance of current coaches. Training and development therefore becomes a process of continuous professional development for coaching practitioners.

Further, with increased demand for coaching, new coaches also need to be trained. Formal training too should be based on evidence from research about what works and how. Those involved in coach training need to understand what works, and why. This knowledge needs to be grounded in research, as well as theory. For example do open questions make a difference in coaching? If so how? Are listening and empathy enough to help provide a space for reflection, learning and change? Or do support and empathy need to be matched by challenge? Does it matter if the coach moves from one approach to another within a coaching session, or is consistency in approach important in producing effective outcomes? What approaches work best with different presenting issues, for example is Transpersonal coaching the most effective model for career coaching and Cognitive behavioural coaching most effective for coaching on skill development? When should we coach and when should other interventions be used from instruction, or mentoring? These are important questions and we still do not know adequate answers to all of these questions, although the past two decades have given us a much better insight to the process and the experience of coaching.

The past 25 years have seen an explosion of coaching psychology research. This research has gone through a number of phases, as our understanding of coaching continues to grow and the expertise of researchers developed to push the boundaries towards as yet unanswered questions.

Each phase has required different methodologies and instruments. In the first phase the approach was experiential and theoretical. In this phase the focus was on individuals sharing their examples of practice and debating the boundaries of an emerging domain. In the second phase the case study and survey became popular tools for helping to explore the phenomena. Later in phase three and four qualitative studies sought to build our theoretical knowledge, while small scale quantitative studies, often Randomised Controlled Trials (RCT's) provided interesting insights to specific populations. Most recently we believe we have embarked upon a fifth phase where meta studies are providing insights into collections of studies, to provide a more definitive answer to the question, does coaching work?

In the following sections we aim to look at each of these phases with a particular focus on a single paper which illustrates the phase. We will start by considering the first phase, which was dominate during 1990–2005, but has now almost slipped from the literature. Of course prior to this there were a number of early studies of coaching, staring with (Gorby's 1937) paper (Gorby 1937) looking at the impact of coaching in a manufacturing setting. This was quickly followed by a second study in 1938 (Bigelow 1938).

In the 62 years following 1937, to the end of the century, there were a total of 93 articles, PhDs and empirical studies published. The 1937 and 1938 papers were followed by a slow trickle of papers. One research paper was published in the 1940s (Lewis 1947) and this was followed by nine studies in the 1950s, the majority concentred in the latter half of the decade. This was followed by three studies in the 1960s and three in the 1970s. It was not until the 1980s that the first signs of growth were seen. Several of these early papers hinted at the potential that coaching may be a separate organisational intervention, or as a complimentary intervention to help in skills transfer after training. An example is Holoviak's study (Holoviak 1982) that examined training programmes in relationship to variations in company productivity levels in the coal industry. The study used a semi-structured interview method and identified that companies which provided greater amounts of management and supervisory training, including coaching, achieved higher productivity. It was not until the 1990s that coaching research papers became a common occurrence in the literature with 41 papers cited by the search engines PsycINFO and Dissertation Abstracts International for this period.

2.1 Phase 1: Boundaries and Theories

There has been considerable debate about coaching and coaching psychology. Are they the same thing or different things. Some writers have implied that coaching psychology is a different discipline. That is not our view. We hold the view that coaching and coaching psychology are parallel disciplines. The evidence appears to support this view. In a UK based study of non-psychologically trained coaches and coaching psychologists the results indicated that both groups reported employing similar behaviours (Jenkins et al. 2012).

Early in the journey of coaching psychology Grant and Palmer (2002) defined coaching psychology as:

> Coaching psychology is for enhancing performance in work and personal life domains with normal, non-clinical populations, underpinned by models of coaching grounded in established therapeutic approaches.

The implication of the definition was that coaching psychology was distinctive from coaching. Further the definition of coaching makes clear that the intervention is one targeted at 'normal' and non-clinical populations. However, more recently coaching is being extended into new areas including smoking cessation and other health related areas. This trend is likely to continue as coaching skills continue to be adopted by clinically trained staff for use in medical settings. Secondly, Grant and Palmer's original definition suggests that coaching psychology must draw on models grounded in therapeutic approaches. This potentially limits coaching and restricts the development of approaches which are grounded in organisational practice or are specifically developed for coaching. In response to these and other points Palmer and Grant updated their definition:

> Coaching Psychology is for enhancing well-being and performance in personal life and work domains, underpinned by models of coaching grounded in established adult learning or psychological approaches, (adapted Grant and Palmer 2002).

Rather than focusing on process, one of us (Passmore 2010) have previous offered an alternative definition for coaching psychology:

> Coaching psychology is the scientific study of behaviour, cognitive and emotion within coaching practice to deepen our understanding and enhance our practice within coaching.

While there remains some discussion about these issues, the trend in coaching psychology research has moved away from definitions towards areas of practice and impact, specifically the use of case studies and surveys. This shift in the primary focus is itself a reflection of a growing confidence in what the focus of study is. This is the theme for the next section.

2.2 *Phase 2: Case Studies and Surveys*

In phase two the focus was on case studies and survey based research. These studies can be found in the two journals that were actively publishing coaching psychology research during the mid 1990s to around 2009. These were *Consulting Psychology Journal*: *Practice & Research* and *International Coaching Psychology Review* (from 2006).

During this phase papers were focused on the experience of coaching, either from the perspective of the coach in the form of a case study, or drawing on the experiences of coaches through surveys. One example of the survey-based approach that looked at both the views of coaches and coaches was Hall et al. (1999). This paper sought to identify the key behaviours which participants perceived to make a material difference in the process. What is most interesting about this paper is that looking back the study identified most of the key behaviours subsequently referred to in research papers focusing on coach behaviours over the coming two decades. While the method may be challenged as being basic, the outcome provided a useful platform for future multiple studies on coach behaviour that followed. Tables 1 and 2 below provide a summary of the Hall et al. (1999) study.

The second popular methodology used during this phase was the case study. This type of paper offered the coach (mostly psychologists) perspective on their work and on the coaching process. In this sense the approach is limited by the impact of attribution bias in reporting our own work.

A commonly cited example is Winum's paper (Winum 2005). The paper offers a case study of coaching a black American coachee. The first three quarters of the paper is presented in a story format, rather than as a classic academic paper or even as a business case study. There is little critical reflection, and little insights as to the coaches personal learning from the process. In some senses this style of paper can

Table 1 What works best in coaching (Adapted from Hall et al. 1999)

Coaches	Coachees
Honest, realistic, challenging feedback (positive and negative)	Connecting personally, recognizing where client is
Good listening, sounding board	Good listening, being a sounding board
Good action ideas, pointers	Reflecting
Clear objective	Caring
No personal agenda	Learning, demonstrating trial and error attitude
Accessibility, availability	Checking back, following up
Straight feedback	Committing to client success and good organizational outcome
Competence, sophistication	
Seeing a good model of effectiveness	Demonstrating integrity, honesty
Coach has seen other career paths	Openness, initiative of client coaching
	Having good coach/client fit
	Knowing the "unwritten rules"
	"Pushing" the client when necessary

Table 2 What works least well in coaching

Coaches	Coachees
Nothing	Being judgmental
When recommendations are self-serving for the coach	Poor timing or impatience regarding executive's readiness
When feedback is all negative	Finding the right degree of bluntness and honesty for the individual
Feedback only, no action ideas	
When feedback deals with others' feelings, not results	
Invasion of privacy	
When recommended actions seem naive or unrealistic	

be viewed as soft marketing, presenting a rosy perspective of the work undertaken by the individual or by the consulting company concerned. Too frequently the unspoken implication is '*see what we did, we can do this for you*', as opposed to '*see what we did, if you learned from our mistakes you could do this even better yourself*'.

In the Winum paper, the final quarter of the paper, the paper partly redeems itself by offering a hand full of insights into the coaching process. These include the importance of challenge and candid feedback for the coachee and organizational clients, the role of contracting with all of the stakeholders, including coachee, organizational client and peers who have a view about the outcome, and the role of organizational culture in supporting the coaching process.

This is not to say that case study papers cannot make a significant contribution to the literature, examples such as Freedman and Perry's (2010), case study from one to one coaching with a client from the nuclear industry offers fresh insights into both the coaching process and the coach. Although this paper, suffers the same core limitation of not being able to move from the specific to the general – for the reader to generalise, with any reliability, to their own work.

2.3 *Phase 3: Qualitative*

The third phase which we have described as qualitative, emerges around 2005 and continues to be a feature within the literature. In this phase researchers drew on qualitative research methodologies, such as Grounded Theory (Bryant and Charmaz 2007; Glaser and Strauss 1967), Interpretative Phenomenological Analysis, Thematic Analysis (Smith and Osborn 2003; Smith et al. 2009). This would also include Discourse Analysis, an as yet unused coaching research methodology, but in our view one which offers a rich vein to explore, particularly with respect to the role of power within the coach-coachee and the coach-organizational client dyads.

Table 3 Ethical principles in decision making (Adapted from Duff and Passmore 2010)

Personal ethics
Moral values
Duty to society
Standards of practice
Relevant laws for the region in which they worked
Conversations with others such as supervisors
Experience, respected others "views"
Implicit and explicit contract with clients along with boundaries
Implications involved with a situation

Such methodologies are useful in building theory and also diving deeper to understand the personal and less tangible aspects of coaching as a phenomenon of human relationships and interpersonal processes. One example of a paper in this area is Duff and Passmore (2010).

In this paper Duff and Passmore, apply the Grounded Theory approach to understand coaching decision making with a view to building an ethical decision making model. The study used a semi-structured interview design, complemented by a focus group of experienced coaches. The study identified key elements used by coaching psychologists in making decisions which include ethical principles such as those presented in professional codes and relevant literature (see Table 3).

These elements were used to build firstly descriptive and later conceptual codes and from these a decision-making framework was developed and tested on coaching psychologists.

The outcome of the research was an ethical decision making model which the authors claimed offered a sequential but non-linear model to guide the subsequent decision making of practitioners.

Such models offer the opportunity for further testing, for example by assessing their value to practice through the use of RCT's, comparing the model with a placebo approach to decision making or practitioners who don't use a model in their decision making.

Thus, qualitative research methods can provide valuable insights into the potential benefits of coaching, as well as the processes underlying effective coaching (Grant 2012). Indeed, it has been argued that qualitative research methods are especially suited for studying individualized interventions such as coaching. First, coaching is a client-directed intervention (Grant 2003): each coachee has his or her own unique problems and/or goals. Thus, the standardization in both the coaching intervention and the targeted outcomes needed for quantitative studies is often problematic. Second, (most) coaching is based on socratic dialogue and is therefore non-linear and unpredictable in nature. In this sense, qualitative research methods are possibly most suited for capturing the organic nature and the richness of individuals' lived experience (Grant 2012).

However, while qualitative approaches may be insightful about the participants in such studies, they lack the ability to generalize the results from one sample to the wider population or to offer definitive answers to questions, such as 'does coaching work' or what behaviours used by coaches create the biggest outcomes. In this sense we argue that qualitative studies need to go hand in hand with quantitative studies in mixed methods research. Specifically, the numerical data provided by quantitative studies allows for comparisons with related developmental interactions such as mentoring and training (D'Abate et al. 2003) and could thus provide a reference point for the human resource development decisions and strategies for both organizations and individual clients. To conclude, both qualitative and quantitative methodologies have answers to give, but only by bringing different methodologies together can maximum insight be gained by the process in question.

2.4 Phase 4: Quantitative – RCT Studies

The area of quantitative research too has grown over a similar period, from early 2000s and remains a popular topic of coaching psychology research. In this category we consider RCT's to be the gold standard of research methodology, although quasi-experimental design and similar methodologies have also been used. RCT's provide a unique opportunity to control for confounding influences that cannot be addressed by other research designs (Cook and Campbell 1979). Especially relevant for coaching, RCT designs allow us to control for selection effects (e.g. coachees that participate in a study are strongly motivated for change), placebo effects and natural maturation (change that cannot be ascribed to the intervention). Research on related interventions such as psychotherapy consistently shows that these factors play a significant role in determining the effectiveness of interventions, and even are stronger predictors of effectiveness than the specific type of intervention used in the study (McKenna and Davis 2009; Messer and Wampold 2002).

The exact number of RCT's in coaching is hard to measure because it depends how the literature search categories are defined (see Theeboom et al. 2014). Anthony Grant, who actively maintains a bibliography of coaching research, has suggested, there are less than 50 such papers. However, a larger net, collecting papers from health and education, as well, business and psychology, is likely to see the number of RCT's rise beyond 100. This reflects the spread of coaching into health and education and the popularity of RCT as a method for use in such domains. These numbers are still relatively low when compared to studies in related areas such as therapy and mentoring. As Grant notes "*For some observers the small number of randomised controlled outcome studies may be considered to be the major shortcoming in the literature on coaching efficacy*" (Grant 2012). Table 4 below (adapted from Grant 2012) provides an overview of the current RCT studies to the knowledge of the current authors.

In the light of the relatively small number of studies, it is encouraging to observe that the amount of RCT studies has increased substantially in the period 2001–2011 (Grant 2012; Grant et al. 2010). Anthony Grant has been one of the most active contributors to the research in this area and has published a number of the RCT studies. One exemplary study that combines a RCT design with qualitative research

Table 4 Randomized control trail and experimental design coaching research

Study	Intervention overview	Type of study	Key findings
Gyllensten and Palmer (2005)	31 participants from UK finance organization	Quasi-experimental field study (a) coaching group; (b) control group	Anxiety and stress decreased more in the coaching group compared to control group
Evers et al. (2006)	60 managers of the federal government	Quasi-experimental field study (a) coaching group; (b) control group	Coaching increased outcome expectancies' and self-efficacy
Green et al. (2006)	56 adults (community sample) took part in SF-CB life coaching program	Randomised controlled study (a) group-based life coaching; (b) waitlist control	Coaching increased goal attainment, well-being, and hope. 30-week follow-up found gains were maintained
Green et al. (2007)	56 female high school students took part in SF-CB life coaching program for 10 individual coaching sessions over 2 school terms	Randomised controlled study (a) coaching group; (b) waitlist control group	Coaching increased cognitive hardiness, mental health and hope
Spence and Grant (2007)	63 adults (community sample) took part in SF-CB life coaching program	Randomised controlled study (a) professional coaching group; (b) peer coaching group; (c) waitlist control group	Professional coaching more effective in increasing goal commitment, goal attainment and environmental mastery
Duijts et al. (2008)	Dutch employees assessed for the effectiveness of a preventive coaching program on sickness absence due to psychosocial health complaints and on wellbeing outcomes	Randomised controlled study (a) 6 month course of preventive coaching; (b) control group	Significant improvements in health, life satisfaction, burnout, psychological wellbeing but no improvement in self-reported sickness absence
Spence et al. (2008)	45 adults (community sample) took part in mindfulness-based health coaching over 8 weeks	(a) Randomised controlled study: SF-CB coaching followed by mindfulness training (MT); (b) mindfulness training followed by SF-CB coaching; (c) health education only control group	Goal attainment greater in coaching than in the educative/directive format. No significant differences were found for goal attainment between the two MT/ CB-SF conditions

(continued)

Table 4 (continued)

Study	Intervention overview	Type of study	Key findings
Fielden et al. (2009)	Nurses from six UK Health Care Trusts were allocated to a coaching group ($n = 15$) or a mentoring group ($n = 15$)	Quasi-experimental field study (a) coaching group; (b) mentoring group in 6-month coaching/mentoring programme. Qualitative and quantitative data at (T1 = baseline, T2 = 4 months and T3 = 9 months)	Mentoring was perceived to be 'support' and coaching was 'action', both reported significant development in career development, leadership skills and capabilities, mentees reported the highest level of development with significantly higher scores in eight areas of leadership and management and in three areas of career impact
Franklin and Doran (2009)	First-year students: co-coaching with preparation, action, adaptive learning coaching or self-regulation coaching PAAL ($N = 27$) or self-regulation ($N = 25$)	A double-blind random control trial in which participants were randomly allocated to either a preparation, action, adaptive learning (PAAL), or a self-regulation co-coaching	Both co-coaching conditions produced significant increases in self-efficacy and resilience, however, only those in the PAAL condition performed significantly better on decisional balance, hope, self-compassion, the incremental theory of change, and independently assessed academic performance
Grant et al. (2009)	41 executives in a public health agency received 360-degree feedback and four SF-CB coaching sessions over 10 week period	Randomised controlled study (a) coaching group; (b) waitlist control group	Coaching enhanced goal attainment, resilience and workplace well-being and reduced depression and stress and helped participants deal with organisational change

(continued)

Table 4 (continued)

Study	Intervention overview	Type of study	Key findings
Aust et al. (2010)	Seven intervention units ($n = 128$) and seven non-randomized reference units ($n = 103$) of a large hospital in Denmark participated in an intervention project with the goal of improving the psychosocial working conditions	Quasi-experimental field study (a) coaching group; (b) control group	In the intervention units there was a statistically significant worsening in six out of 13 work environment scales. The decrease was most pronounced for aspects of interpersonal relations and leadership. In comparison, the reference group showed statistically significant changes in only two scales. Process evaluation revealed that a large part of the implementation failed and that different implicit theories were at play
Cerni et al. (2010)	14 secondary school principals: all school staff in the 14 schools were invited to rate their school principal using the MLQ (5X) questionnaire	Pre-test, post-test control-group research design (a) coaching group; (b) control group	This study provides initial evidence that by creating changes to rational and constructive thinking, it is possible to increase coachee's use of transformational leadership techniques
Grant et al. (2010)	44 high school teachers were randomly assigned to either SF-CB coaching or a waitlist control group	This study was both an experimental (randomly assigned) and a WS (pre-post) study	Participation in coaching was associated with increased goal attainment, reduced stress, and enhanced workplace well-being and resilience. Pre-post analyses for the coaching group indicated that coaching enhanced self-reported achievement and humanistic-encouraging components of constructive leadership styles

(continued)

Table 4 (continued)

Study	Intervention overview	Type of study	Key findings
Kauffeld and Lehmann-Willenbrock (2010)	Spaced and massed training are compared using behavioural and outcome criteria. 64 bank employees (n=32 in each training group)	Quasi-experimental follow-up research design with a sample of 64 bank employees (n=32 in each training group) is used	Spaced rather than massed training practice resulted in greater transfer quality, higher self-reports of sales competence, and improved key figures. Spaced training did not surpass massed training in terms of transfer quantity
Kines et al. (2010)	Foremen in two intervention groups are coached and given bi-weekly feedback about their daily verbal safety communications with their workers	A pre-post intervention-control design with five construction work gangs: Foremen-worker verbal safety exchanges (experience sampling method, n=1693 interviews), construction site safety level (correct vs. incorrect, n=22,077 single observations), and safety climate (seven dimensions, n=105 questionnaires) a measured over 42 weeks	Coaching construction site foremen to include safety in their daily verbal exchanges with workers has a significantly positive and lasting effect on the level of safety, which is a proximal estimate for work-related accidents
Kochanowski et al. (2010)	Experimental group of managers received individual coaching several weeks after attending a feedback workshop. The control group of managers also attended a feedback workshop but did not receive the follow-up coaching	Quasi-experimental field study (a) feedback plus coaching group; (b) feedback only control group	Coaching significantly increased the use of collaboration with subordinates, but results for the other three "core" tactics were mixed
Leonard-Cross (2010)	Investigated the impact and process of developmental coaching evaluating coaching which took place over a 2-year period	The study used action research (Lewin 1946) and a quasi-experimental method. Coachees and the comparative group of non-coached staff completed questionnaires	Participants that had received developmental coaching (N=61) had higher levels of self-efficacy than the control group of participants (N=57) who had not received coaching

(continued)

Table 4 (continued)

Study	Intervention overview	Type of study	Key findings
Passmore and Rehman (2012)	The study investigated the efficacy of learning methodologies, comparing a blended coaching and instruction approach with an instruction approach	Randomized control trial, involving 208 participants drawn for the armed services	Participants in instruction and coaching group (104 participants) had reduced learning period and higher level of pass rate than the instruction group (104 participants)
Passmore and Velez (2012)	The study investigated driver behaviour in HGV drivers, comparing blended coaching and instruction with an instruction method for a 1 h refresher course for 327 HGV drivers	Randomized control trial involving 327 participants and 12 coaches and 12 instructors	Participants in the two groups reported similar speed convictions and similar occurrence of accidents Results may be due to limited 1 h of coaching or instruction, neither of which led to a behavioural change in long-term driver behaviour over the forthcoming 12 month period

methods is a study by Grant et al. (2009). In their study, 41 executives in an Australian public health agency were randomly allocated to either a coaching condition (half-day workshop plus four individual solution-focused coaching sessions over 10 weeks) or a wait-list control condition (half-day workshop only). The quantitative data showed that coaching enhanced goal-attainment, resilience and well-being and decreased stress and depression as compared to the control condition. The qualitative data indicated that coaching also fostered self-confidence, personal insight and helped the managers to develop their managerial skills. In our view, studies such as these reflect the ongoing development of coaching as a field over the past decades and contribute substantially to the evidence-base of coaching.

All in all, the amount of rigorous and methodologically sophisticated quantitative studies seems to be on the rise. This is good news for scholars and practitioners alike. In order to establish coaching as evidence-based practice and respected academic field, we need to recognize and embrace the diversity of research methodologies (as well as practice-based insights) that can capture the equally diverse ways in which coaching is applied as a change methodology. At the same time, this rise of RCT studies also poses new challenges. In this sense, the use of RCT's in coaching reflects the common challenges of applying interventions in non-health based and specifically in organizational settings.

Firstly, most of the coaching papers published draw on small sample sizes, often 30, but usually less than 50 in each condition. Secondly, the most common samples consist of students based in educational settings. These two aspects reflect that accessing students and working with small, contained groups, is substantially easier than working with samples of 100 or more in organizational settings. Thirdly, given the samples, the focus of the RCT studies has often been towards exploring psychological dimensions such as goal setting, hope or resilience, in contrast with leadership dimensions or personal work based performance. Once again such dimensions are more challenging to collect and to maintain a group where meaningful comparison over time can be achieved.

Last but not least, we hope that future research will be theoretically enriched. Coaching is frequently defined as a change methodology ultimately aimed at enhanced well-being and functioning (Grant 2003). By incorporating seminal psychological theories on for example individual change (e.g. self-regulation and adult learning) and its' ultimate aims of well-being and functioning (e.g. Self-Determination Theory; Deci and Ryan 1985) we can gain insight into the question how coaching works rather than if coaching works (Latham 2007; Spence and Oaedes 2011). These insights could be used to develop both existing and new coaching interventions as well as the development of the cumulative knowledge framework needed to advance coaching psychology as a field of practice and an academic discipline.

2.5 Phase 5: Meta Research

As mentioned above, the literature on coaching has grown substantially over the past two decades. This growth has mainly been driven by (scientist-) practitioner. Most of this research focuses either on a specific type of intervention (e.g. cognitive-behavioural solution-focused coaching) or outcome (e.g. burn-out) that is of interest to the researcher and/or sponsors of the research such as the companies hiring scientist-practitioners. As a result, the current literature is somewhat fragmented and this has resulted in a mixture of scepticism and confusion with regard to coaching psychology as a domain of practice and research (Theeboom et al. 2014).

In response to this increasing scepticism and confusion, several excellent qualitative literature reviews have been published over the years (e.g. Brock 2008; Grant et al. 2010; Feldman and Lankau 2005; Kampa-Kokesch and Anderson 2001). In addition to these qualitative reviews, recent meta-analytic reviews form a welcome addition to the literature for two interrelated reasons. First, meta-analyses use statistical methods rather than narrative reviews in order to synthesize data from multiple individual studies. In this sense, meta-analyses can provide a more objective review of the literature (Wilkinson 1999). Second, meta-analytic reviews can provide insight into the between study variability and the generalizability of results (Borenstein et al. 2009). In this way, meta-analyses can shed light on potential theoretical (e.g. number of sessions) and methodological (e.g. study design) moderators of coaching effectiveness. Identifying these moderating factors can have strong implications for future research on coaching. At the time of writing, four meta analytic studies have been published and will be discussed below (De Meuse et al. 2009; Theeboom et al. 2014; Jones et al. 2015; Sonesh et al. 2015).

In the first meta-analysis in the field of coaching, De Meuse et al. (2009) used meta-analytic techniques to estimate the effects of executive coaching interventions. They identified six studies that met their four criteria for inclusion: (1) coaching was targeted at executives (2) coaching was provided by external coaches (3) the methodological design included pre and post coaching ratings and (4) the statistical information provided was sufficient for estimating effect sizes. As an outcome variable, they took an average of all outcome variables included in the studies under analysis. Furthermore, they distinguished between self-ratings by the coachee, and ratings by others (managers and/or peers).

According to the standards of Cohen (1988), effect sizes less than 0.30 can be considered to be small, an effect size between 0.31 and 0.50 would be moderate and effect sizes above 0.50 would be considered large. The results of their analysis showed that coaching can have moderate to large positive effects depending on who was responsible for the ratings. The estimated population effect sizes were much larger when the outcome was rated by the coachee (1.27) rather than by others (0.50). This was in line with the results of a study by Peterson (1993) that showed that relative to the estimates of others (e.g. supervisors), coachees tend to overestimate the effectiveness of coaching interventions. Furthermore, the results showed that the effectiveness of coaching was highly inconsistent. In other words, there were major between-study differences in effect sizes. In addition to the small number of studies, the authors identified several factors that might have contributed to this inconsistency: differences in outcome criteria, characteristics of the coaching intervention (e.g. type of coaching) and methodological rigor of the studies.

These factors were explicitly addressed in a recently published meta-analysis by the second author of this chapter and his colleagues (Theeboom et al. 2014). The team used similar inclusion-criteria for our meta-analysis as De Meuse et al. (2009) with two notable differences. First, the team focused on all studies investigating the effects of coaching interventions in organizational settings (thus not only coaching targeted at executives). Second, the team only included studies in which the influence of other interventions (e.g. when coaching was part of a broader leadership development program) could be ruled out. This resulted in a total of 18 studies included in the final analysis.

Regarding the differences in outcome criteria encountered by De Meuse et al. (2009), the team used both a bottom-up (looking at available data) and top-down (looking at well-known outcomes in the broader psychological literature) approach to categorize the various outcomes into five clusters: performance and skills (e.g. transformational leadership behaviour), well-being (e.g. mental health), coping (e.g. problem vs. emotion focused coping), work attitudes (e.g. job satisfaction) and goal-directed self-regulation (e.g. goal attainment). The results showed that coaching had positive effects on all of these categories (see Table 5). In line with the

Table 5 Summary of effect sizes

Outcome category	Effect size
Performance/skills	0.60
Wellbeing	0.46
Coping	0.43
Self-regulation	0.74
Work attitudes	0.54

results of De Meuse et al. (2009) however, the team also found that effect sizes differed considerably between studies – even when comparable outcome measures were clustered into the five categories mentioned above.

In order to check whether the between study variance could be attributed to factors related to either characteristics of the coaching intervention and/or the methodological design of the studies included in the analyses, we performed two different meta-regressions. Regarding the characteristics of the coaching intervention, the team tested whether the number of coaching sessions had an influence on coaching effectiveness. Somewhat surprisingly, the team did not find an effect. In other words, the number of coaching sessions seemed to be unrelated to the effects of coaching interventions on the coachees. Two possible explanations were proposed by the authors. First, it could be that in the studies included in the analyses, the number of sessions was related to the severity of the problems that the coachees were coached for. If this were the case, more severe problems would require more sessions to attain a similar effect (rather than having a larger effect). A second possibility is that the lack of differences between studies with more or less coaching sessions was due to the nature of the type of intervention in the majority of studies. Most of the coaching interventions were solution-focused in nature and solution-focused coaching (derived from solution focused brief therapy) is well known for its quick results and its ability to 'jump to the heart of things' (Kim 2008). From this perspective, the fact that there was no difference in effectiveness between studies using more or less sessions may simply reflect a psychological equivalent to economics law of diminishing returns (Theeboom et al. 2014).

The team performed a meta-regression in order to check whether the methodological design of studies impacted the effectiveness of in the studies included in the analysis. Specifically, the team checked whether there were differences in effect sizes for studies incorporating a control group (mixed within between subject designs) and thus controlled for additional sources of bias (see above) as opposed to studies lacking a control group (within-subject designs). The Theeboom team found that effect sizes in the latter were significantly larger, hinting at the idea that confounding factors such as natural maturation of coachees and placebo effects should be a concern in future studies addressing the effectiveness of coaching interventions.

The Jones et al. (2015) study has provided a number of interesting insights, both supporting and challenging the findings from the other two studies. Jones and her team found that coaching had a positive effect on affective, skill-based and individual level outcomes. Secondly, contrary to their prediction, Jones et al. (2015) did not find significant discrepancies in effect sizes between the different types of research design analysed. This result conflicts with the result from Theeboom et al. (2014), and raises the question why is there a difference, and more importantly, which is correct? Thirdly, the study found that the period of coaching had no influence on coaching effectiveness. This appears to be counter-intuitive, as one would expect to find a gradual increase in the impact of coaching over several sessions, before the effect plateaued.

In sum, the three meta-analytic studies reviewed in this chapter show that coaching can be an effective change-methodology, but that additional (methodologically rigorous) research is needed to build an evidence-base for coaching and to explore some of the new questions raised by these studies. Furthermore, the meta-analysis by Theeboom et al. (2014) indicated that the coaching literature and (meta-analytic) estimates of overall effectiveness might be susceptible to publication bias: an over representation of studies displaying significant positive results in the literature. Although the problem of publication bias is by no means limited to the field of coaching research, it is worth mentioning explicitly since the estimated $2 billion yearly global revenue on coaching (International Coach Federation 2012) seems a potent precursor for wishful thinking regarding its effectiveness. To conclude, the meta-analytic research up to date seems provide a fruitful starting point for future research.

3 Conclusion

This chapter has briefly reviewed the journey of coaching psychology research. We have argued that coaching psychology research has transitioned from small scale and highly personal to larger studies and meta-analysis. This journey echoes coaching psychologies own journey from a emergent discipline within psychology to a discipline which is growing in maturity and an evidence basis.

References

Aust, B., Rugulies, R., Finken, A., & Jensen, C. (2010). When workplace interventions lead to negative effects: Learning from failures. *Scandinavian Journal of Public Health, 38*(3), 106–119.

Bigelow, B. (1938). Building an effective training program for field salesmen. *Personnel, 14*, 142–150.

Borenstein, M., Hedges, L. V., Higgins, J. P. T., & Rothstein, H. R. (2009). *Introduction to meta-analysis*. Cornwall: Wiley.

Brock, V. G. (2008). *Grounded theory of the roots and emergence of coaching*. Doctoral dissertation, International University of Professional Studies, 2008. Retrieved from http://libraryofprofessionalcoaching.com/wp-content/uploads/2011/10/dissertation.pdf

Bryant, A., & Charmaz, K. (2007). *The Sage handbook of grounded theory*. Los Angeles: Sage.

Cerni, T., Curtis, G. J., & Colmar, S. H. (2010). Executive coaching can enhance transformational leadership. *International Coaching Psychology Review, 5*(1), 81–85.

Cohen, J. (1988). *Statistical power analysis for the behavioral sciences* (2nd ed.). Hillsdale: Eribaum.

Cook, T., & Campbell, D. (1979). *Quasi-experimentation: Design and analysis for field settings*. New York: Rand-McNally.

D'Abate, C., Eddy, E., & Tannenbaum, S. T. (2003). What's in a name? A literature-based approach to understanding mentoring, coaching, and other constructs that describe developmental interactions. *Human Resource Development Review, 2*, 360–384.

De Meuse, K. P., Dai, G., & Lee, R. J. (2009). Evaluating the effectiveness of executive coaching: Beyond ROI? *Coaching: An International Journal of Theory, Research and Practice, 2*, 117–134.

Deci, E. L., & Ryan, R. M. (1985). *Intrinsic motivation and self-determination in human behavior*. New York: Plenum.

Duff, M., & Passmore, J. (2010). Coaching ethics: A decision making model. *International Coaching Psychology Review., 5*(2), 140–151.

Duijts, S. F. A. P., Kant, I. P., van den Brandt, P. A. P., & Swaen, G. M. H. P. (2008). Effectiveness of a preventive coaching intervention for employees at risk for sickness absence due to psychosocial health complaints: Results of a randomized controlled trial. *Journal of Occupational & Environmental Medicine, 50*(7), 765–776.

Evers, W. J., Brouwers, A., & Tomic, W. (2006). A quasi-experimental study on management coaching effectiveness. *Consulting Psychology Journal: Practice & Research, 58*, 174–182.

Feldman, D. C., & Lankau, M. J. (2005). Executive coaching: A review and agenda for future research. *Journal of Management, 31*, 829–848.

Fielden, S. L., Davidson, M. J., & Sutherland, V. J. (2009). Innovations in coaching and mentoring: Implications for nurse leadership development. *Health Services Management Research, 22*(2), 92–99.

Franklin, J., & Doran, J. (2009). Does all coaching enhance objective performance independently evaluated by blind assessors? The importance of the coaching model and content. *International Coaching Psychology Review, 4*(2), 128–144.

Freedman, A. M., & Perry, J. A. (2010). Executive consulting under pressure: A case study. *Consulting Psychology Journal: Practice & Research, 62*(3), 189–202.

Glaser, B. G., & Strauss, A. (1967). *The discovery of grounded theory: Strategies for qualitative research*. Chicago: Aldine Publishing Co.

Gorby, C. (1937). Everyone gets a share of the profits. *Factory Management & Maintenance, 95*, 82–83.

Grant, A. M. (2003). The impact of life coaching on goal-attainment, metacognition and mental health. *Social Behavior and Personality, 31*, 253–264.

Grant, A. M. (2012). The efficacy of coaching. In J. Passmore, D. Peterson, & T. Freire (Eds.), *Wiley Blackwell handbook of the psychology of coaching & mentoring*. Chichester: Wiley.

Grant, A. M. & Palmer, S. (2002, May 18). *Coaching psychology workshop*. Annual conference of the Counselling Psychology Division of the BPS. Torquay.

Grant, A. M., Curtayne, L., & Burton, G. (2009). Executive coaching enhances goal attainment, resilience and workplace well-being: A randomized controlled study. *The Journal of Positive Psychology, 4*, 396–407.

Grant, A. M., Passmore, J., Cavanagh, M. J., & Parker, H. M. (2010). 4 The state of play in coaching today: A comprehensive review of the field. *International Review of Industrial and Organizational Psychology, 25*(1), 125–167.

Green, L. S., Oades, L. G., & Grant, A. M. (2006). Cognitive-behavioral, solution-focused life coaching: Enhancing goal striving, well-being, and hope. *The Journal of Positive Psychology, 1*(3), 142–149.

Green, L. S., Grant, A. M., & Rynsaardt, J. (2007). Evidence-based life coaching for senior high school students: Building hardiness and hope. *International Coaching Psychology Review, 2*(1), 24–32.

Gyllensten, K., & Palmer, S. (2005). Can coaching reduce workplace stress: A quasi-experimental study. *International Journal of Evidence Based Coaching and Mentoring, 3*(2), 75–85.

Hall, D. T., Otazo, K. L., & Hollenbeck, G. P. (1999). Behind closed doors: What really happens in executive coaching. *Organizational Dynamics, 27*(3), 39–53.

Holoviak, S. J. (1982). The impact of training on company productivity levels. *Performance & Instruction, 21*(5), 6–8.

International Coach Federation. (2012). Retrieved May 16, 2012, from http://www.coachfederation.org/about-icf/overview/

Jenkins, L., Passmore, J., Palmer, S., & Short, E. (2012). The nature and focus of coaching in the UK today: A UK survey report. *Coaching: An International Journal of Theory, Practice & Research, 5*(2), 132–150.

Jones, R. J., Woods, S. A., & Guillaume, Y. R. F. (2015). The effectiveness of workplace coaching: A meta-analysis of learning and performance outcomes from coaching. *Journal of Occupational and Organizational Psychology*. doi:10.1111/joop.12119.

Kampa-Kokesch, S., & Anderson, M. Z. (2001). Executive coaching: A comprehensive review of the literature. *Consulting Psychology Journal: Practice and Research, 53*, 205–228.

Kauffeld, S., & Lehmann-Willenbrock, N. (2010). Sales training: Effects of spaced practice on training transfer. *Journal of European Industrial Training, 34*(1), 23–37.

Kim, J. S. (2008). Examining the effectiveness of solution-focused brief therapy: A meta-analysis. *Research on Social Work Practice, 18*, 107–116.

Kines, P., Andersen, L. P., Spangenberg, S., Mikkelsen, K. L., Dyreborg, J., & Zohar, D. (2010). Improving construction site safety through leader-based verbal safety communication. *Journal of Safety Research, 41*(5), 399–406.

Kochanowski, S., Seifert, C. F., & Yukl, G. (2010). Using coaching to enhance the effects of behavioral feedback to managers. *Journal of Leadership & Organizational Studies, 17*(4), 363–369.

Latham, G. P. (2007). Theory and research on coaching practices. *Australian Psychologist, 42*, 268–270.

Leonard-Cross, E. (2010). Developmental coaching: Business benefit – fact or fad? An evaluative study to explore the impact of coaching in the workplace. *International Coaching Psychology Review, 5*, 36–47.

Lewis, P. B. (1947). Supervisory training methods. *Personnel Journal, 25*, 316–322.

McKenna, D. D., & Davis, S. L. (2009). Hidden in plain sight: The active ingredients of executive coaching. *Industrial and Organizational Psychology, 2*(3), 244–260.

Messer, S. B., & Wampold, B. E. (2002). Let's face facts: Common factors are more potent than specific therapy ingredients. *Clinical Psychology: Science and Practice, 9*(1), 21–25.

Passmore, J. (2010, December 15). *1st international coaching psychology congress*. Keynote: Leadership coaching. City University, London.

Passmore, J., & Rehman, H. (2012). Coaching as a learning methodology – A mixed methods study in driver development – A randomised controlled trial and thematic analysis. *International Coaching Psychology Review, 7*(2), 166–184.

Passmore, J., & Velez, M. J. (2012). Coaching fleet drivers – A randomized controlled trial (RCT) of 'short coaching' interventions to improve driver safety in fleet drivers. *The Coaching Psychologist, 8*(1), 20–26.

Peterson, D. B. (1993). *Measuring change: A psychometric approach to evaluating individual training outcomes*. In Symposium conducted at the eighth annual conference of the society for industrial and organizational psychologists, San Francisco.

Smith, J. A., & Osborn, M. (2003). Interpretative phenomenological analysis. In J. A. Smith (Ed.), *Qualitative psychology: A practical guide to methods*. London: Sage.

Smith, J. A., Flowers, P., & Larkin, M. (2009). *Interpretative phenomenological analysis: Theory method and research*. London: Sage.

Sonesh, S., Coultas, C. W., Lacerenza, C. N., Marlow, S. L., Benishek, L. E., & Salas, E. (2015). The power of coaching: A meta-analytic investigation. *Coaching: An International Journal of Theory, Practice & Research, 8*(2), 73–95.

Spence, G. B., & Grant, A. (2007). Professional and peer life coaching and the enhancement of goal striving and well-being: An exploratory study. *The Journal of Positive Psychology, 2*, 185–194.

Spence, G. B., & Oaedes, L. G. (2011). Coaching with self-determination in mind: Using theory to advance evidence-based coaching practice. *International Journal of Evidence Based Coaching and Mentoring, 9*, 37–55.

Spence, G. B., Cavanagh, M. J., & Grant, A. M. (2008). The integration of mindfulness training and health coaching: An exploratory study. *Coaching: An International Journal of Theory, Research and practice, 1*(2), 145–163.

Theeboom, T., Beersma, B., & van Vianen, A. E. (2014). Does coaching work? A meta-analysis on the effects of coaching on individual level outcomes in an organizational context. *The Journal of Positive Psychology, 9*(1), 1–18.

Wilkinson, L. (1999). Statistical methods in psychology journals: Guidelines and explanations. *American Psychologist, 54*, 594–604.

Winum, P. (2005). Effectiveness of a high potential African American Executive: The anatomy of a coaching engagement. *Consulting Psychology Journal: Practice & Research, 57*(1), 71–89.

The Coach as a Fellow Human Companion

Reinhard Stelter

Abstract The relationship between coach and coaching partner is presented as a main condition for successful coaching. The role of this relationship seems to be even more important when current societal changes are taken into account, changes which are often the pivotal point for the understanding and necessity of coaching in our society: We live in a hypercomplex society in which both individuals and organizations struggle with increasing diversity and organizational challenges, and where it has become impossible to reach unequivocal and long-lasting solutions to these challenges. The agenda for the coaching conversation is to provide a space for new reflections by initiating a process that leads to transformation, a new self-understanding and enhanced agency. This transformational process may be inspired by third-generation coaching, where the coach and coachee are collaborative partners, and where the dialogical focus is on value reflection and the striving for meaning-making. Based on research into 'common factors', the main intention of the chapter is to unfold and illustrate key dimensions that lead towards the coach as a fellow human companion of the coaching partner: (1) The dialogical dimension, (2) The narrative-collaborative dimension, (3) The protreptic dimension; (4) Mentalization and (5) Feedback as collaborative and outcome-oriented practice. The intention of this chapter is to show the importance of relationship with a 'human face' as the most important influencing factor in coaching, a factor that is also recognized with growing interest and evidence in both psychotherapy and coaching research.

Keywords Dialogue • Hypercomplexity • Collaboration • Meaning-making • Narrative approach • Self and identity • Third-generation coaching • Transformational learning • Value-orientation

---

R. Stelter (✉)
Coaching Psychology Unit, NEXS, University of Copenhagen, Copenhagen, Denmark
e-mail: rstelter@nexs.ku.dk

L.E. van Zyl et al. (eds.), *Coaching Psychology: Meta-theoretical perspectives and applications in multicultural contexts*, DOI 10.1007/978-3-319-31012-1_3

1 Introduction

We live in a hypercomplex society (Qvortrup 2003) in which both individuals and organizations struggle with the increasing diversity and growing organizational challenges, and where it has become impossible to reach unequivocal and long-lasting solutions to these challenges.

These social changes and specific challenges are often the pivotal point for the understanding and necessity of coaching in our society, a form of dialogue that has to be further developed and refined when society and its organizations and institutions change. The agenda of coaching conversations and coaching-inspired dialogues has to provide a space for new reflections by initiating a process that leads to a transformation, a new self-understanding and enhanced agency. A coaching agenda that focuses exclusively on goals and quick solutions will fail to meet the needs of postmodern, late modern and hypercomplex societies, where the challenges and demands on the individual are changing very rapidly.

With this societal context in mind, it is fundamental to develop a coaching format that puts *sustainability* on the agenda. In this context, sustainability means that clients or coachees can reach a state of renewed independence and self-assurance. Coaching and coaching-inspired dialogues lead to a new stage in the coaching partner's mindset and self-understanding. This transformational process may be inspired by third-generation coaching (Stelter 2014a), where the coach and coachee are understood as collaborative partners, and where the dialogical focus is on value reflection and on striving for meaning-making. A coach, consultant, leader or psychologist inspired by third-generation coaching will aim to develop a dialogical format that matches some of the following key dimensions:

- The coaching process is focused less on goals and quick fixes, because the coachee needs *room for self-reflection* in order to be able to take an action-oriented approach in his or her practice as a manager, employee, job-seeker, person struggling with stress, career-maker etc. The basic idea is that the in-depth meaning-making and value-oriented dialogue between coach and coachee should ultimately enable the coachee to link his or her personal and professional identities with specific action perspectives.
- Coaching is a *reflective process* that considers both an existential-experiential and a relational perspective. The reflexive aspect is also expressed in the special position of the coach. The coach is not merely a facilitator but, in certain stages of the dialogue, an equal self-reflective fellow human being and a generous listener, who is able to reflect on the challenges that the coachee is facing, and which the coach relates to in the coachee's life perspective with the intention of supporting the coachee in his or her reflective process. In a coaching dialogue that involves both sides in a reflective process, often based on value reflection and meaning-making, the relationship between coach and coachee will at times be *symmetrical*.
- The coaching conversation is based on a close link between person (i.e. coachee) and context. This inclusion of the context and the specific situation promotes

meaning-making in the dialogue. The coachee thus becomes more aware of the impact of certain actions on his or her identity and self-concept, and how these actions are involved in representing certain life values and convictions.
- The coaching conversation facilitates a new narrative in relation to the challenge that currently concerns the coachee. This *narrative is a product of the collaborative dialogue practice* as it unfolds between the coach and coachee and also reflects the developmental process of the dialogue. The art of coaching is about changing the person's past history collaboratively by incorporating new events and persons and by creating and challenging the story's plot. Earlier – often troubling – narratives are always treated with respect and may form the basis of new narratives that emerge in the dialogue between coach and coachee.

This chapter does not, however, set out to present a new coaching model. The author's intention is mainly to enhance the understanding of the coaching partnership. In the following, therefore, the term *coaching partner* will be used to replace the terms *client* or *coachee*, as these terms might not fully describe the intention of coaching as a fellow human companionship. The essence of coaching from a third-generation perspective – as described above – will be illustrated through the following relationship dimensions:

1. The dialogical dimension
2. The narrative-collaborative dimension
3. The protreptic or value dimension
4. Mentalization
5. Feedback as collaborative and outcome-oriented practice

The unfolding of these dimensions should help the coach or coaching psychologist to develop an intensive and collaborative attitude to his or her coaching partner.

2 Dimensions Towards Fellow Human Companionship

In the following, these five dimensions will be unfolded. The author will argue for the central importance of these dimensions for a good coaching practice. Whatever their preferred coaching model, all coaches can adapt and include some or all of these dimensions in their work. The intention is to present these dimensions on the basis of a literature study and by including results from both research and professional practice.

2.1 The Dialogical Dimension

In the present context, coaching is understood as a dialogue form that appreciates the coaching partner as a fellow human companion. From this dialogical stance, the term intervention should be avoided. Intervention means 'to come between, to interrupt' (Online Etymology Dictionary) and thus implies an understanding associated with a medical model, where the focus is on dysfunctions within the patient, and where the physician is responsible for providing a problem-solving treatment (see also Farlex Partner Medical Dictionary 2012). Intervention can therefore be interpreted as an act where something is done to the patient by an external provider. This intervention-oriented understanding is quite far removed from the understanding of the collaborative partnership in coaching that is promoted in this chapter.

From an etymological perspective, the term dialogue is quite broad. Here, dialogue is understood in its original Greek connotation: dia-logue = through (διά/dia) speech, meaning or discourse (λόγος/logos). The participants in a dialogue develop a mutual relationship through speech and discourse. The dialogue becomes the art of conversation, where one simultaneously engages with the other and with oneself. When the emphasis is on shaping something new in the coaching dialogue, the focus has to be on how something new can unfold in the dialogue between coach and coaching partner, and what these new developments can be. The English communication theorist Shotter (2006) suggested the term *withness-thinking* to describe the profound character of the dialogue. In his writing, Shotter generally tried to link a social constructionist and a phenomenological position. In dialogue, we co-create reality by listening and sharing ideas with each other on the basis of our own understanding and sense-making. The term withness-talk or withness-thinking seeks to grasp this intense meeting with the other:

> Withness (dialogic)-talk/thinking occurs in those reflective interactions that involve our coming into living, interactive contact with an other's living being, with their utterance, with their bodily expressions, with their words, their 'works'. It is a meeting of outsides, of surfaces, of two kinds of 'flesh' (Merleau-Ponty 1968), such that they come into 'touch' or 'contact' with each other… In the interplay of living moments intertwining with each other, new possibilities of relation are engendered, new interconnections are made, new 'shapes' of experience can emerge (p. 600).

The most significant point in this quote is probably the emphasis on *coming into touch with* the other. In times of accelerating hyper information, where we mostly only receive messages and possibly 'Likes' via online social media, it is important to *linger* on one's own and the other's thoughts. Sharing one another's thoughts or reflections in a trustful and empathic way is fundamental to the quality of the dialogue and the ultimate basis of a successful relationship between coach and coaching partner(s). Being *in touch* can be compared to *being empathic*, which I would describe as being passionate on behalf of the other and sensing with the other. Carl Rogers (1975), still one of the greatest figures in counselling and psychotherapy, recognized being empathic as a central element of counselling and offered the following definition:

> Being empathic means entering the private perceptual world of the other and becoming thoroughly at home in it. It involves being sensitive, moment to moment, to the changing felt meaning which flow in the other person … It means temporarily living in his/her life, moving about in it delicately without making judgments … It includes communicating your sensing of his/her world … (p. 4)

Here, Rogers' phenomenological understanding is evident. He applied the term 'felt meaning' to describe a meeting place for the counsellor and client. The notion of felt meaning or felt sense goes back to Gendlin (1997), who nowadays is known for his focusing approach (Gendlin 1978, 1996). Felt meaning or felt sense can be regarded as a possible starting point for the coaching partner's own in-depth understanding of his/her life. When the coaching partner grasps his or her felt meaning and shares this understanding with the coach, both parties achieve a sense of mutual closeness where withness-thinking and withness-talk unfold, and where the coach is deeply involved in meeting and understanding the coaching partner's lifeworld.

This intensive meeting can be further described as the basis for a *relational attunement* that can be established between dialogical companions. As mentioned earlier (Stelter 2014a), as the foundation for this companionship, both coaching partners 'have to demonstrate a willingness to be involved in each other and to show sympathy' (p. 94). The aim of the dialogue is to develop a presence and an attunement where the participants are constantly trying to tune in to each other's thoughts, feelings and reflections. But something more develops in this process: When listening to the other's story, one can pay attention to oneself and the sensations, feelings and thoughts that the story might produce in one's own mind. Ultimately, relational attunement also means to reflect back on what one has heard, and how it might have an impact on oneself. We *wonder* about what we hear, share our questions with each other and try to make sense in collaboration – through dialogue. From this perspective, relational attunement can be defined as 'a shared or co-created articulation, where a sensation, a sensory impression or a theme is addressed collectively, and where the participants achieve a meeting' (Stelter 2014a, p. 94). This leads to the following conclusion: 'People become each other's sounding boards … in a relationship characterized by mutual responsiveness' (Stelter 2014a, p. 94).

Dialogue philosophers like Søren Kierkegaard and Martin Buber might help us gain a better understanding of the importance of the other for self-development. Kierkegaard (2010) spoke about the double reflection of the message, which may grasp these important moments of symmetry, as the first person becomes the 'midwife' of the other's thought and reflection, and where the other ultimately finds him/herself in the co-reflective process with the first person. Similarly, Buber (1983) stated: Through the *Thou*, a person becomes *I*. In this perspective, dialogue is grounded in the mutuality between partners where both sides are provided with the opportunity to understand, develop and grow in a process of giving, receiving and sharing.

2.2 The Narrative-Collaborative Dimension

In the post-modern world, the meta-narratives or grand narratives have lost their value and explanatory power. These narratives used to help people find a broadly accepted understanding of historical changes and placed big events into a widely culturally accepted frame of reference. However, the 'small stories', the narratives of everyday life, where people talk about uplifting events or hard times, are still the foundation for all humans wishing to understand and share their world with each other. Telling stories is the basis of social interaction, building culture and – ultimately – being a human being. Sharing stories can have a healing effect and can provide support for tackling challenging life situations (Charon 2011; Frank 1995). Narratives help us develop our identity. They tell us something about who we are, what we stand for, and what we dream of, and hopefully they anchor us in an appreciative context with the listener. At best, we feel understood, relieved and uplifted. And as the philosopher David Carr (1986) put it: 'Lives are told in being lived and lived in being told' (p. 61).

In a coaching dialogue inspired by a narrative-collaborative practice, the coach will use narratives actively to build a collaborative partnership where the coaching partners feel safe and open to sharing, and where they are open to modify their understanding, view or perspective with the aim of developing and further discovering who they are. In stories we always highlight (a series of) specific events with the intention of relating something specific; thus, every story has a plot that enables the story-teller to make a specific point. At the same time, stories do not tell 'the whole story'; we leave out events that do not fit the plot of the story. Acting as a dialogical partner, the coach is a co-creator of new and hopefully more uplifting stories that are shaped in collaboration with the coaching partner. The narrative-collaborative coach works from the basic assumption that narratives can be transformed and developed – a position that clearly lies in the extension of social constructionist epistemology.

There are a number of strategies and dialogical approaches available in narrative and collaborative practices aimed at inviting the coaching partner to embrace new perspectives of stories to be told (see Drake and Stelter 2014; Stelter 2014a, b; Stelter and Law 2010). In the following, the readers' attention is drawn to the most collaborative activity in the coaching partnership, where the coach appears as a fellow human companion of the coaching partner, and where coach and coaching partner take up a relative position that contains *moments of symmetry* in their mutual relationship – a totally new and innovative feature of coaching that can place the coach into an actively collaborative position in relation to the coaching partner(s) with the intention of optimally promoting their reflective process. In group or team coaching, this role of a collaborative partner can be easily adopted by all participants of a coaching group. Moments of symmetry may occur when the coach or a coaching group participant shares his or her reflections on specific descriptions, statements, feeling or thoughts of the coaching partner in focus. It is a form of *resonating* to what is said by the coaching partner in focus. To resonate means to be a sounding board for the words, phrases or storylines presented. Hearing another's words is an encounter, an interchange of experiences, feelings, thoughts, where we not only respond to the other but also reflect on our own experiences, feelings and thoughts. As co-reflecting partners, the coach or coaching group members tend to hear the other's stories through the perspective of their own experiences and sense-making. And these experiences, thoughts and reflections might prove beneficial to the coaching partner in focus. A space of collaborative reflections and mutual understanding emerges where all coaching participants feel enriched and enlightened: All the participants reflect on each other's sense-making and stories in the light of their own sense-making and stories. It is important to remember that the contribution of the coach or coaching group participants should encourage and contribute to new reflections and new understanding for the coaching partner in focus. It would be unfortunate if the contribution of the other derailed the topical focus of the conversation.

Chené Swart (2013), a narrative coach and consultant from South Africa, described the act of 'being moved or touched by the stories being listened to' (p. 168) as a *gift*. Sharing the reflections of the coaching partner in focus by offering one's own reflections means *receiving* or *handing out a gift*: (1) By appreciating the words of the coaching partner in focus we receive a gift by becoming clearer about our own feelings, thoughts or challenges, and (2) By reflecting back what has been said, we deal out gifts to the coaching partner in focus, who might construe the words of the other as valuable in regard to the challenge at hand. Receiving and dealing out gifts appears a nice metaphor that elucidates the value of the collaborative nature of coaching. Narrative-collaborative coaching can infuse new life into a dialogical format that seems more important and necessary than ever in our hypercomplex world, where people need inspiration and mutual reflection, both in their private and working life, to help them to handle their challenges. Receiving and dealing out gifts means also to share one's cultural background with the other. Hypercomplexity means always to appreciate multi-cultural perspectives and by that to understand the many ways to make sense of the world. Figure 1 illustrates how a coach or a coaching group participant can be an *outsider-withness* who either receives or deals out a gift. Narrative coaching is embodied in the coaching partner's descriptions, statements or reflections, which are either related to specific actions/activities (the landscape of action, e.g. 'Recently, when I started up a new project, which was quite complex, I managed to organize my people in a way that helps us all work with focus and energy …') or based on specific personal convictions, attitudes, values, dreams, intentions, expectations etc. (landscapes of identity, e.g. 'I believe it's crucial to have a good working climate in the team.'). Figure 1 illustrates the different perspectives of possible outsider-withnessing.

In the therapeutic literature, outsider withnessing would often be defined as *self-disclosure*, although the two terms are not completely identical in meaning. In psychotherapy, the benefits of self-disclosure are appreciated, and the potential risks are highlighted (Sturges 2012). In a collaborative practice which is the approach promoted here, this sharing of gifts, as this form of interaction could also be framed, is promoted as a valuable feature that strengthens the working alliance between coach and coaching partners. As Norcross (2010) mentioned in regard to psychotherapy, self-disclosure can be perceived as helpful for enhancing empathy and immediate outcomes; however, he also underlined the importance of avoiding self-disclosures that merely serve the counsellor's need, as they only remove focus from the client. This warning cannot be taken seriously enough. However, outsider withnessing goes beyond the intention of self-disclosure. Sharing gifts means more than creating a good atmosphere in the dialogue. It means developing our understanding

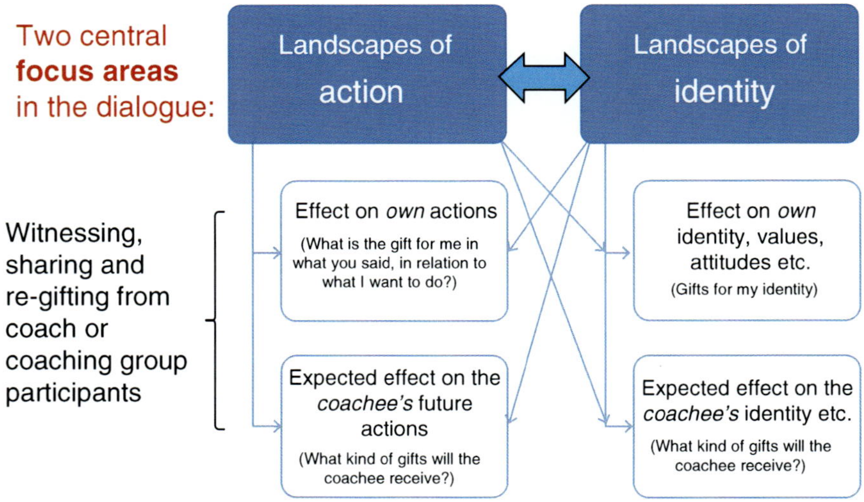

Fig. 1 Outsider withness procedure as a process of receiving and dealing out 'gifts'

and inviting different perspectives into the conversation, new perspectives that help the coaching partners develop and shape new meaning and new narratives about themselves, about specific events and, ultimately, their lives.

2.3 The Protreptic or Value Dimension

Values, convictions, ambitions or dreams are central aspects of what is described as *landscapes of identity* in narrative practice. In a broader sense, values can be seen as the guiding star for an individual to act in a specific way. Values are the key to people's sense of agency and their capacity to be in charge of themselves and their life. Kirkeby (2009), a professor of management philosophy at Copenhagen Business School, has revived the ancient Greek concept of *protreptic*, a form of dialogue that would nowadays be understood as executive coaching. This form of dialogue was founded in the Greek academies around 400 B.C. and developed by Plato with the goal of achieving the Socratic concept of 'eupratein', the ethically mastered life, and turning another person into the most essential entity in his or her own life. The root of the term *protreptic* is 'trépo'/'trópos' meaning *turn*. To elucidate the principles of protreptic processes, Kirkeby (2009) stated the following:

> On the basis of the magnum opus of Aristotle we can define protreptic as *dialectic applied with the aim of prompting a person to liberate himself by reflecting on her/his basic values.* Thus protreptic is bound to social dialogue, and to the possibility of becoming the master of one's own inner dialogue (p. 13).

A protreptic process is aimed at a central goal that is 'desirable for its own sake' (see Aristotle's 'The Art of Rhetoric I', quoted by Kirkeby 2009, p.14) and should ultimately lead to *eudaimonia* – translated as happiness, welfare or human flourishing. From this perspective, there might be a parallel to positive psychology in a very broad sense. A protreptic process is not, however, a psychological tool but a path for getting in touch with the guiding values, principles and convictions that drive individuals' actions in the world. Coaching, especially earlier generations[1] was very much focused on helping a person to meet a specific goal, moving a person from A to B. Protreptic, value-based coaching principles, on the other hand, are applied to give coaching a broad and generally human approach to promote the coaching partner's self-understanding. Thus, they are not aimed directly at promoting actions, events or situations but have a more abstract focus on specific values that are somehow essential for the coaching partner (and ultimately also for the coach). The focus is on what lies behind one's action and what can define the meaningfulness of an action, an event or a situation for the individual or a group. This broad focus on the central values of the individual, group or team guarantees that coaching is *sustainable*, meaning that the knowledge and the reflection in the dialogue have a long-lasting and general impact on the life and actions of the coaching partner(s). Protreptic or value-oriented coaching unfolds the implicit drivers that cause the individual to act in a specific way.

These values are not necessarily eternal and universal – some might be, but often, they are rooted in local practices and events. Surely, freedom, love or justice can be described as eternal values, but in our everyday life, interactions and cooperation with others will be additional values that are highly contextualized. The ultimate goal of coaching is to facilitate and improve leadership, communication and cooperation by reflecting on key values as a fundamental condition and quality in human endeavours and activities that will continue to provide a sense of direction in relation to specific goals. In this value-oriented process, a coach acting as a collaborative partner can be a helpful reflective companion in the coaching partnership. From this perspective, values are also a product of a co-active process unfolding between coach and coaching partners. Listening to each other's voices and all the dialogue, participants can become rooted within themselves and what they stand for. They will find commonalities, differences and possibly a path where they can co-create meaning in a reflective community of practice.

The following presents some theoretical reflections on the way in which values and meaning-making are founded as the driving force or guiding star of an individual or a working team. Values are a central part of our identity. In narrative practice, we speak about *landscapes of consciousness* (White 2007) or *landscapes of identity* (Stelter 2014a). Narratives presented by the coaching partner will touch on key issues with regard to what is important in life for him or her – in more or less explicit terms. Here, it is the task of the coach or other group participants to act as outsider withnesses, focusing on what they heard in regard to identity issues or spe-

[1] See a description of the three generations of coaching in Stelter (2014a, b). First-generation coaching is very goal-driven, e.g. applying the GROW model, while second-generation coaching is more solution, future or strength-oriented.

cific commitments, values or dreams. Focusing and reflecting on values marks an attempt to highlight the most central aspects in the coaching partner's life.

Referring back to my reflection on the *sustainability* of coaching, values are an anchor or a guiding star for the individual. Kirkeby (2009) underlined that values represent 'a possible mode of certainty' (p. 155). And he continued: 'A value is an "I can" based on knowledge, and knowledge of what we have done, and will be able to do, and guided by ethical imagination by both deliberate and intuitive judgment' (p. 156).

Values are the entrance to our lived knowledge and our practical wisdom, in Greek *phronesis*. The critical social scientist Flyvbjerg (2001) regarded *phronesis* as important, because instrumental rationality needs to be balanced by value rationality, a balance that 'is crucial to the sustained happiness of the citizens in any society, according to Aristotle' (p. 4). Through *phronesis*, people implicitly base their actions on specific values – through lived knowledge that is often immediately unfolded while acting. Individuals, groups or teams are always situated and anchored in the context in which they live, and which they shape through their doing. Values help to prepare the individual to be implicitly ready in the moment. Values help to establish our way of acting based on gut feelings or intuition.

An example to complete this section on protreptic and value-oriented coaching: The conversation can take its starting point in the reflection of a specific term – for example *trust* or *responsibility*. In this version, the *coach* presents a term and asks the coaching partner to reflect on the term. Another option is if the coaching partner is familiar with this dialogue form, he or she may suggest a term that is important to him or her. In a further version that seems to be easier to include in any kind of coaching, the procedure is the following: Coach and coaching partner talk about a specific challenge and event facing the coaching partner. At some point, the coach invites the coaching partner to step back from the specific issue and move towards a reflection on values, commitments, convictions or dreams. The landscapes of identity, initially connected to the specific issue, are generalized and elevated to a protreptic reflection on a specific important value that becomes apparent in the coaching dialogue; this value could, for example, be trust or responsibility.

2.4 Mentalization

With this topic we return to a more psychological position, a perspective that stresses what happens *inside* the individual, but also how a sensitive insight might be the first step towards understanding the other or form the basis for an intensified relationship between the dialogue partners. The concept of mentalization, which is presented in the following, was developed by, among others, Peter Fonagy, a psychodynamic psychotherapist and researcher, and Eia Asen, a systemically oriented family therapist (see Asen and Fonagy 2011). Mentalization-based work is not considered a specific intervention or therapy form but rather an approach that can be integrated into a wide range of conversation approaches and methods. In general, mentalization-based approaches are aimed at the following goals for the client: (1) better behavioural control, (2) improved affect regulation, (3) more intimate and gratifying relationships and (4) the ability to pursue life goals (Fonagy and Bateman 2006).

The concept of mentalization is included here as a source of inspiration to highlight the relation between coach and coaching partner and as a way to strengthen the individual awareness and attentiveness of both coach and coaching partner in regard to their sensing and perceptual processes. The capacity for mentalization can be considered one of the most essential factors in any form of conversation-based intervention and a basic requirement for understanding oneself and others. Asen and Fonagy (2011) describe mentalization as 'seeing ourselves from the outside and seeing others from the inside' (p. 347).

To strengthen their mutual relationship and companionship, coach and coaching partner(s) will benefit from improving their ability to mentalize, i.e., to get in touch with one's own senses, feelings and thoughts about what happens inside oneself, and on the other hand, to get in touch with what happens inside the other. Earlier, the term *withness-thinking* was introduced, which seems to be closely related to what is expressed here. If this process of mutual mentalization is developed in the coaching relationship, the term *relational attunement* – presented earlier in this chapter – is a fairly apt description of the intensity of the relationship between coach and coaching partner.

With reference to Asen and Fonagy (2011), various possibilities for strengthening mentalization – especially with a focus on developing the coaching partnership – may be suggested:

Through *openness and a wondering stance*, the coach shows genuine interest in the coaching partner's perspective. By exploring the coaching partner's life, the coach challenges the coaching partner to examine his or her own emotions and thoughts. The coach's wondering position, which includes encouraging the coaching partner to reassess certain assumptions in his or her perception of the outside world, the coach supports the coaching partner in taking a fresh look at him/herself and his or her interactions with others.

This helps the coaching partner achieve better *impact awareness*: Open, curious and wondering questions can strengthen the coaching partner's capability for developing mentalization skills and thus the awareness and understanding of how one's own emotions, thoughts and actions might affect others, and how they contribute to creating a reality for others. The ability to see the other from the inside in regard to this impact can generate vital changes in the coaching partner. Systemic coaching circular questions (Tomaschek 2006; Tomm 1988) may further help to develop the coaching partner's awareness of the position of others and thus help to paint a broader picture of the world.

The final stage in the coaching partnership may lead to a form of mutual *reflective contemplation*, which can be viewed as a mentalizing stance. There is a situationally adapted and relaxed attitude in the coach and coaching partner as they each relate to the other's specific descriptions, feelings, thoughts or reflections. Involving the other in how these descriptions, feelings, thoughts or reflections resonate in one's own system, i.e., what happens inside when one listens to the other, can form the basis for further development of the coaching partner's perception and understanding of his or her reality. In turn, it may thus change some of the coaching partner's specific stories about him/herself or specific events. The ability to mentalize by seeing others from the inside can help create these new realities and serve as the starting point for deeper understanding for the coaching partner. It is especially important for the coach to act with *humility*, as this is a condition for understanding the coaching partner. This requires a willingness to be surprised and to learn from the other. Importantly, this perspective must apply to both parties in the coaching dialogue. With this attitude, both coach and coaching partner(s) will have a real sense of companionship on their shared journey.

2.5 Feedback as a Collaborative and Outcome-Oriented Practice

Despite the intention to view coaching as a *collaborative activity* where the coach or the coaching psychologist functions as a fellow human companion, which goes beyond the role of neutral facilitator, the bottom line remains the same: The coaching partner or client should reach a state of change and development. And, coaching is a fee-based service delivered by a professional that should serve the client's interests as efficiently as possible. From this perspective, it is important to keep in mind that coaches have to do their best to meet their clients' needs, and therefore, they can only be the fellow human companion that is promoted in this chapter if they strive towards outcomes that are in line with the interests and progress of their clients. The concept of being a collaborative partner is (only) highlighted here with the intention of *intensifying the coaching relationship* and thus to improve the effectiveness of the coaching process. Another purpose of intensifying the relationship is to give professional dialogues a 'human face'. Only when the clients accept the coach as both a competent professional and a fellow human companion, with all the qualities described above, can the dialogue unfold in an efficient and human manner.

On this basis, the coaching relationship can be improved by focusing directly on outcomes. Systematic work and research – albeit based on psychotherapy – is presented by Scott Miller and his colleagues (2007, 2013), Miller and Hubble (2011), and Duncan and colleagues (2007). Some of these ideas should now be transferred to coaching, especially with a focus on the *real-time feedback* during the session. In the present context, I do not want to go so far as to promote written outcome assessments of the sessions, as Miller and his colleagues (2003) suggested. That would also go beyond the scope of this chapter. My objective here is to encourage coaches both to include the coaching partner/client more actively in the process and to engage actively in the dialogue as reflective partners. By providing mutual feedback, the coaching partnership can be elevated to a new and intensified collaborative level. Duncan and Miller's (2000) praise for the *heroic client* can also be a useful stance in coaching. These authors moved beyond the medical model by recasting the client as a central protagonist in the dialogue: 'The client's view of the relationship is the "trump card" in therapy outcomes, second only to the winning hand of the client's strength' (p. 72). From this position, the collaborative aspects of the relationship and the usefulness of mutual feedback will be at the centre of the rest of the chapter. As mentioned earlier, the movement advocated here is a move *away from intervention* and towards seeing coaching as an *interaction*; a position that highlights the collaborative nature of the dialogue (see also De Haan 2008). Based on the work of Miller and his colleagues (2006, 2007, 2011) and the author's own theoretical work presented earlier in this chapter, several aspects can help to unfold the collaborative and feedback-informed nature of the coaching relationship:

Create a Culture of Collaboration and Feedback

From the very beginning, it is important to make clear how the relationship should unfold. Therefore it is crucial, as part of the psychological contract, to describe central features of the collaboration. Coaching partners need to see themselves as active partners in the working alliance. Progress and development have to be visible from the beginning, and it is helpful in building a sound working alliance if the coaching partner/client provides feedback about the development, progress and possible setbacks. For the coach it is important to develop some of the feedback qualities described above, for example, withness-thinking and outsider withness procedures.

Integrate Alliance and Outcome Feedback

To establish a good working alliance, it is helpful to look at how the coach and the coaching partner interact, how they establish and work on their relationship, and what degree of progress they are making in regard to the path they have agreed on. This may, for example, include small comments such as, 'I am really happy that you're sharing this with me,' questions or suggestions about how to proceed after having reflected on progresses made or sharing reflections on something the other said. The coach may also offer feedback when coupling some aspects of the coaching partner's story with events or reflections that were mentioned earlier by the coaching partner. This latter example is not only a way to offer feedback; it is also a way to develop new stories or a new understanding that may serve as the basis for change. Sometimes it may also be necessary to ask the coaching partner(s) for feedback about:

- How the coaching partner(s) experience(s) the relationship,
- What seems to work,
- How things make sense, and
- Any wishes and ideas that stand out.

Use Your Intuition and Be on Perceptive Tiptoes

Make sure not to overload the client with demands for feedback. It is important for the coach to sharpen his or her awareness of changes and to be attentive to what happens with the coaching partner and in the relationship. A few questions from the coach about these observations may be enough to develop a clear enough picture. Sometimes, it is enough just to notice nonverbal feedback in order to readjust the alliance. *Empathy* plays a decisive role here and can be linked to positive outcomes (see Elliott et al. 2011; Norcross 2010). To ensure the progress of the session and the working relationship between coach and coaching partner(s), it is important not to take things for granted and to be willing to step out of one's own comfort zone (Duncan et al. 2007).

Be Non-judgemental

Being mindful of one's own perceptions as a coach also means being non-judgemental, being accepting and clearly expressing this stance. This gives the coaching partner the feeling of being okay, and it helps to ease the conversation. The coach needs to be curious and investigate possible differences in perceptions and understandings of the world; appreciate the coaching partner's perspective and be curious about understanding this perspective even better. Judgements would only disturb the working alliance between coach and coaching partner(s), but a question that invites the coaching partner to unfold his or lifeworld helps to bring both parties closer to one another. A non-judgemental stance is also import for the coaching partner to develop. Being critical of oneself and being judgemental about the way one thinks, feels and acts can undermine open reflections and, ultimately, self-acceptance. The coach should help the coaching partner move towards being open-minded to whatever comes up in the coaching process.

Learn to 'fail successfully'

Any coach can make mistakes, fail on the basis of the specific assumptions they make about the relationship, about the coaching partner's position or about the way the situation is perceived. It is important to remain open-minded in regard to the coaching partner's possible self-understanding and understanding of the world. The flow of mutual understanding and the process of meaning-making between coach and coaching partner are essential. If the coach gets the sense that 'something' went wrong, it is important to pause, involve the coaching partner in sorting out the possible misunderstanding and then re-build the case and re-structure the process of the dialogue.

The idea of presenting these guidelines on feedback is to help the coach and all other dialogue partners to be open to a collaborative process where they engage as professional partners and as fellow human companions and to an interaction that has the ultimate goal of helping the coaching partner change and develop.

3 Research Evidence for Relationship Issues in Coaching

Since the beginning of this century there has been a growing interest in the impact of relationship issues in regard to the efficacy of psychotherapy and lately also of coaching. The interest has recently moved away from focusing on approaches, methods and techniques towards a strong acknowledgement of the importance of *common factors* and especially the *working alliance* as the key ingredient in all forms of psychotherapy, coaching or counselling. There is a growing awareness that psychotherapy and other dialogue forms do not always work in the same way, as medicine does, i.e. that specific psychological treatments should work for specific disorders (Duncan et al. 2010). There appear to be relational and other common factors that have a decisive impact on change and development, but which are hard to pin down, and which may be even very complex and difficult for a practitioner to acquire. From this perspective, it is difficult to predict when a psychotherapist, coach or counsellor is going to do a good job (see Miller et al. 2007 about their attempt to offer guidelines to psychotherapists).

A growing number of studies and publications have shed light on relationship and common factors issues (see De Haan and Duckworth 2013, for coaching and Horvath 2011, for psychotherapy). Many of these research findings are presented with a special focus on psychotherapy, simply because this area has a longer research tradition than coaching. It will be made clear to the reader what these studies are based on – psychotherapy or coaching – but on the other hand, when speaking about relational and common factors, it can be assumed that many results from therapy research may also be applicable and valuable in coaching and coaching psychology. Let us now take a look at what research has brought to light:

Lambert and Barley (2002) made the following summary of results in regard to what accounts for change and development of clients in psychotherapy: The *relationship* between therapist and client accounts for 30 % of the variance in outcomes, with 40 % of the variance attributed to external or contextual factors, 15 % to hope or expectancy effects and only 15 % to specific theory or techniques. This study makes clear that the relationship is the one single factor that has the highest significance in regard to therapeutic success. With reference to a psychotherapy studies of Wampold (2001) the following results appear even more shocking in that sense that client and extra-therapeutic factors account for 87 % of the variance of change, leaving only 13 % accounted for by treatment (see Fig. 2).

The small circle (treatment effects) inside the big circle (client and extra-therapeutic factors) in the upper left corner of the figure is enlarged into the biggest circle on the right in Fig. 2. If we take a closer look at the big circle, we see that only 1 % of the variance can be accounted for by the therapeutic model or technique. The heroes are our clients. Their readiness and willingness to change is the cornerstone

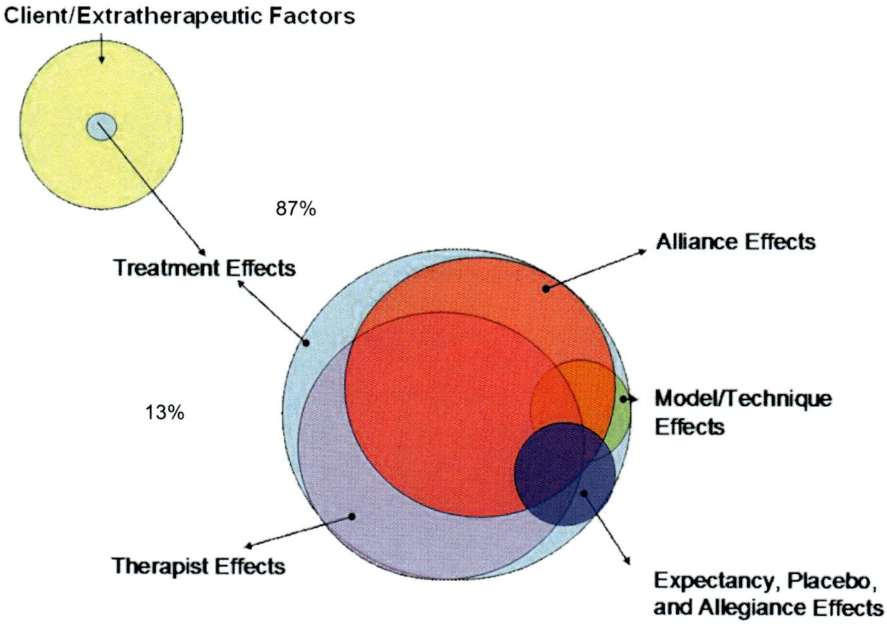

Fig. 2 Common factors with a proposed feedback factor (Duncan et al. 2010, p. 366)

of their capacity for development and progress. But this readiness and willingness also needs to be kept alive during the session, and here, the client's positive perception of the working alliance is of central importance.

In the following, some results that focus on relationship issues shall be highlighted. Let us have a look at one of the most recent studies in the area of coaching:

De Haan and colleagues (2013) found in their outcome study that the clients' perception of the relationship is the key factor in determining how clients perceive the outcome of coaching, and that outcomes are significantly related to the working alliance, client self-efficacy and the perceptions of the coaching interventions ('generalised techniques'). They found that the working alliance scores by clients predict 25 % of the variance in coaching outcome. However, they also cautioned coaches not simply to assume that their perception of the relationship necessarily matches the perception of their clients:

> We think it is fascinating that despite the high predictive value of the client estimate of the coaching relationship, the coach estimate of that same relationship neither correlates with the coaching outcomes nor with the strength of the relationship as measured by the client (p. 54).

This is a warning to all coaches, on the one hand, to work seriously towards improving the alliance with their coaching partner(s), and, on the other hand, to work towards including real-time feedback strategies and collaborative practices in their coaching and thus improve the effectiveness and impact of the dialogue on the change and development achieved by their coaching partner(s).

Boyce and colleagues (2010) carried out a study based on 74 coach-client relationships in the US military, including senior military leaders as coaches and cadets as clients, and reported that the relationship affected outcomes significantly, as assessed both by the client, with an explained proportion of variance around 50 %, and by the coach, with an explained proportion of variance around 25 %. Similar results were presented by Baron and Morin (2009, 2012). They documented that the coaching outcomes correlated with the coaching clients' rating of the *working alliance*, which they used as a measure for the strength of the coaching.

On the basis of a large number of research studies, Horvath and colleagues (2015) presented a number of recommendations for psychotherapists, which are probably equally valuable for coaches and coaching psychologists (see further recommendations in Norcross 2010):

- The development of a good alliance is essential for the success of psychotherapy, regardless of the type of treatment.
- The ability of the therapist to bridge the client's needs, expectations, and abilities into a therapeutic plan is important in building the alliance.
- Because the therapist and client often judge the quality of the alliance differently, active monitoring of the alliance throughout therapy is recommended.
- Responding non-defensively to a client's hostility or negativity is critical to establishing and maintaining a strong alliance.
- Clients' evaluation of the quality of the alliance is the best predictor of outcome; however, the therapist's input has a strong influence on the client and is therefore critical.

4 Implications for Future Research

On the basis of this short presentation of research that is relevant for the topic of this chapter, the following can be highlighted as focus areas for future research: Clearly, the chapter has included many references from psychotherapy research. The central statements of this chapter would even be more valuable if they could be supported by evidence from coaching research. The suggestions for future research are twofold: (1) Bearing the topic of this chapter in mind, it is essential to strengthen the practitioners' understanding of relationship issues and to help them to gain insight into what happens in the working alliance with their coaching partner. Therefore, it would be a big step forward to conduct studies that are based on video observation and interviews with both the coach and the coaching partner. That would offer insights into what happens in the relationship, and how things work when the coaching partner appreciates the coach's specific approach. (2) It is worthwhile to promote research that focuses on the impact of specific relational topics on the coaching outcomes.

5 Conclusion

The objective of this chapter was to unfold the importance of the relationship between coach and coaching partner(s). The aim was *not* to present the tools that novice coaches often call for, but rather to encourage coaching professionals to develop a fundamental *attitude* to improve their working alliance with their coaching partner(s). It would be unfortunate to approach coaching as a form of treatment. It is essentially a meeting of two (or more) people, where one – the coach – seeks to support the other(s) – the coaching partner(s) – on their path. The aim of this chapter was to improve the awareness of coaches of the impact of elements that seem difficult to grasp and to operationalize; concepts such as *withness-thinking, relational attunement* or the whole matter of *receiving and dealing out gifts*, just to mention some of the central concepts presented in this chapter.

I encourage the reader to focus less on specific goals and instead invite their coaching partner to *linger on* thoughts and feelings and to make time for reflection. In our time, we have lost the idea of simply having time. Coaching has to be a dialogue form where we reinvent the concept of just lingering, of having time to be on a journey with another person. It is a journey into the unknown, where neither the coach nor the coaching partner clearly knows the destination or the route. It is a journey of discovery into relatively unknown territory, where both parties are travel companions, and neither knows anything for sure about the road ahead.

References

Asen, E., & Fonagy, P. (2011). Mentalization-based therapeutic intervention for families. *Journal of Family Therapy, 34*(4), 347–370. doi:10.1111/j.1467-6427.2011.00552.x.

Baron, L., & Morin, L. (2009). The coach-coachee relationship in executive coaching: A field study. *Human Resource Development Quarterly, 20*(1), 85–106.

Baron, L., & Morin, L. (2012). The working alliance in executive coaching: Its impact on outcomes and how coaches can influence it. In E. De Haan & C. Sills (Eds.), *Coaching relationships* (pp. 213–226). Faringdon: Libri.

Boyce, L. A., Jackson, R. J., & Neal, L. J. (2010). Building successful leadership coaching relationships: Examining impact of matching criteria in a leadership coaching programme. *Journal of Management Development [Special Issue on Coaching and the Relationship], 29*(10), 914–931.

Buber, M. (1983). *Ich und Du*. Heidelberg: Verlag Lambert Schneider.

Carr, D. (1986). *Time, narrative and history*. Bloomington: Indiana University Press.

Charon, R. (2011). The novelization of the body, or how medicine and stories need one another. *Narrative, 19*, 33–50.

De Haan, E. (2008). *Relational coaching – journey towards mastering one-to-one learning*. Chichester: Wiley.

De Haan, E., & Duckworth, A. (2013). Signalling a new trend in executive coaching outcome research. *International Coaching Psycholog Review, 8*(1), 6–19.

De Haan, E., Duckworth, A., Birch, D., & Jones, C. (2013). Executive coaching outcome research: The contribution of common factors such as relationship, personality match, and self-efficacy. *Consulting Psychology Journal: Practice and Research, 65*(1), 40–57.

Drake, D., & Stelter, R. (2014). Narrative coaching. In J. Passmore (Ed.), *Mastery in coaching – A complete psychological toolkit for advanced coaching* (pp. 65–94). London: KoganPage.
Duncan, B. L., & Miller, S. D. (2000). *The heroic client. Doing client-directed, outcome-informed therapy*. San Francisco: Jossey-Bass.
Duncan, B., Miller, S. D., & Hubble, M. (2007). How being bad can make you better. *Psychotherapy Networker, 31*(5), 36–46.
Duncan, B. L., Miller, S. D., Wampold, B. E., & Hubble, M. A. (2010). *The heart & soul of change* (2nd ed.). Washington, DC: American Psychological Association.
Elliott, R., Bohart, A. C., Watson, J. C., & Greenberg, L. S. (2011). Empathy. *Psychotherapy: Theory, Research, Practice & Training, 48*, 43–49. doi:10.1037/a0022187.
Farlex Partner Medical Dictionary. (2012). *Medical model*. Retrieved February 2015, from http://medical-dictionary.thefreedictionary.com/medical+model
Flyvbjerg, B. (2001). *Making social science matter*. Cambridge: Cambridge University Press.
Fonagy, P., & Bateman, A. (2006). Mechanism of change in mentalization based treatment of borderline personality disorder. *Journal of Clinical Psychology, 62*, 411–430.
Frank, A. (1995). *The wounded storyteller*. Chicago: The University of Chicago Press.
Gendlin, E. T. (1978). *Focusing*. New York: Everest House.
Gendlin, E. T. (1996). *Focusing-oriented psychotherapy*. New York: The Guildford Press.
Gendlin, E. T. (1997). *Experiencing and the creation of meaning*. Evanston: North-Western University Press. (original from 1962)
Horvath, A. O. (2011). Alliance in common factor land: A view through the research lens. *Research in Psychotherapy: Psychopathology, Process and Outcome, 14*(1), 121–135.
Horvath, A.O., Del Re, A.C., Flückiger, C., Symonds, D. (2015). *Alliance in individual psychotherapy*. Retrieved February 14, 2015, from http://www.nrepp.samhsa.gov/Norcross.aspx#chapter2)
Kierkegaard, S. A. (2010). *Kierkegaards skrifter, SKS**. Copenhagen: Søren Kierkegaard Forskningscenter. (online edition: www.sks.dk)
Kirkeby, O. F. (2009). *The new protreptic – the concept and the art*. Copenhagen: Copenhagen Business School Press.
Lambert, M. J., & Barley, D. E. (2002). Research summary on therapeutic relationship and psychotherapy outcome. In J. Norcross (Ed.), *Psychotherapy relationship that works* (pp. 17–32). Oxford: Oxford University Press.
Merleau-Ponty, M. (1968). *Sense and non-sense*. Evanston: Northwestern University Press.
Miller, S. D., & Hubble, M. (2011). The road to mastery. *Psychotherapy Networker, 35*(2), 22–60.
Miller, S. D., Duncan, B. L., Brown, J., Sparks, J. A., & Claud, D. A. (2003). The outcome rating scale: A preliminary study of the reliability, validity, and feasibility of a brief visual analog measure. *Journal of Brief Therapy, 2*(2), 91–100.
Miller, S. D., Duncan, B. L., Sorrell, R., Brown, G. S., & Chalk, M. B. (2006). Using outcome to inform therapy practice. *Journal of Brief Therapy, 5*(1), 5–22.
Miller, S. D., Hubble, M. A., & Duncan, B. L. (2007). Supershrinks. *Psychotherapy Networker, 31*(56), 26–35.
Miller, S. D., Hubble, M. A., Chow, D. L., & Seidel, J. A. (2013). The outcome of psychotherapy: Yesterday, today, and tomorrow. *Psychotherapy, 50*(1), 88–97.
Norcross, J. C. (2010). The therapeutic relationship. In B. L. Duncan, S. D. Miller, B. B. E. Wampold, & M. A. Hubble (Eds.), *The heart & soul of change* (2nd ed., pp. 113–141). Washington, DC: American Psychological Association.
Qvortrup, L. (2003). *The hypercomplex society*. New York: Peter Lang Publishers.
Rogers, C. (1975). Empathic – An unappreciated way of being. *The Counseling Psychologist, 5*(2), 2–10.
Shotter, J. (2006). Understanding process from within: An argument for 'withness'-thinking. *Organization Studies, 27*, 585–604.
Stelter, R. (2014a). *A guide to third generation coaching. Narrative-collaborative theory and practice*. Dordrecht: Springer Science+Business Media.

Stelter, R. (2014b). Third-generation coaching– striving towards value-oriented and collaborative dialogues. *International Coaching Psychology Review, 9*(1), 33–48.
Stelter, R., & Law, H. (2010). Coaching – Narrative-collaborative practice. *International Coaching Psychology Review, 5*(2), 152–164.
Sturges, J. W. (2012). Use of therapist self-disclosure and self-involving statements. *The Behavior Therapist, 35*(5), 90–93.
Swart, C. (2013). *Re-authoring the world: The narrative lens and practices for organisations, communities and individuals*. Bryanston: Knowledge Resources.
Tomaschek, N. (2006). *Systemic coaching. A target-oriented approach to consulting*. Heidelberg: Carl Auer International.
Tomm, K. (1988). Interventive interviewing: Part III. Intending to ask lineal, circular, strategic, or reflexive questions? *Family Process, 27*(1), 1–15.
Wampold, B. E. (2001). *The great psychotherapy debate: Models, methods and findings*. Mahwah: Lawrence Erlbaum.
White, M. (2007). *Maps of narrative practice*. New York: Norton.

Coaching Supervision: Towards a Systemic Coaching Supervision Framework

Pieter Koortzen and Aletta Odendaal

Abstract Coaching supervision is an emerging and at the same time a contentious development intervention to improve coaching practices (Grant AM, Int J Evid Based Coach Mentor 10(2):17–33, 2012). While professional supervision is strongly recommended by coaching bodies and coaching organizations (Standards Australia, SAI Global Limited under licence from Standards Australia Limited, Sydney, 2010), its rate of development and uptake varies considerably across the world with potentially more coaching supervisors trained in UK and Germany than the rest of the world combined (Hawkins P, Smith N, Coaching, mentoring, and organisational consultancy: Supervision, skills and development. McGraw-Hill Education, Maidenhead, 2013). Given an increasing awareness regarding the role of supervision in professional development and in enhancing standards of practice (Lawrence P, White A, Coach Int J Theory Res Pract 7(1):39–55. doi:10.1080/17521882.2013.878370, 2014; Passmore J, Supervision in coaching: Supervision, ethics, and continuous professional development. Kogan Page, London, 2011), very little attention has been paid in the published literature to the need for specific training, anchored in theoretically-grounded and evidence-based programmes (Grant Am, Int J Evid Based Coach Mentor, 10(2):17–33, 2012). As scientist/practitioners it is therefore imperative to firstly understand the broader landscape in which coaching supervision training will take place. From a systems perspective the landscape includes all the different components which need to be considered in designing a coaching supervision training programme. In the light of this, the aim of this chapter is to present a coaching supervision framework based on a systemic approach to supervision, according to which the training and development of potential supervisors can be structured. A systemic perspective highlights the multitude of components that shape the supervision process. The chapter further aims to stimulate discussion regarding the critical building blocks included in the framework from a multicultural perspective and a number of design questions are therefore posed at the end of each section.

P. Koortzen (✉)
Investec, Johannesburg, South Africa
e-mail: Pieter.Koortzen@investec.co.za

A. Odendaal
Department of Industrial Psychology & People Management, University of Johannesburg, Johannesburg, Gauteng, South Africa
e-mail: aodendaal@uj.ac.za

L.E. van Zyl et al. (eds.), *Coaching Psychology: Meta-theoretical perspectives and applications in multicultural contexts*, DOI 10.1007/978-3-319-31012-1_4

These questions also represent areas for future research in coaching supervision. The framework emerged from a conceptual analysis of current practices, scholarly research and the collective experience of the authors as leadership and executive coaches who also provide supervision.

Keywords Coaching • Supervision • Coaching supervision • Supervision training • Multicultural competence

1 Introduction

Supervision for practitioners-in-training as well as for professional practitioners after completion of formal training is universally seen as a crucial ingredient to enhance standards of practice of a wide range of professional groups, including psychologists, social workers and medical professionals (Carroll 2006; Grant 2012; Hawkins and Shohet 2012). Initial developments regarding the theory and practice of coaching supervision therefore have its roots strongly anchored in the therapeutic disciplines (Moyes 2009; O'Donovan et al. 2011). The existing literature on supervision from the helping professions can certainly contribute to an understanding of different models of supervision, the purpose and primary functions of supervision as well as the processes followed in supervision as there are likely to be theories and practices that can be applied to all types of supervision. This remains a key debate within the coaching community with Butwell (2006) and Hawkins and Smith (2006) questioning the 'borrowing' of ideas from therapy. Within the helping professions the main emphasis is however strongly focused, with some exceptions, on supervision at an individual level – the coach, also referred to as 'coaching the coach' (Blanton 2014; Moyes 2009) without addressing group and organizational levels or understanding the client system – coach-client and client-organization system (Hawkins and Smith 2013; Lawrence and White 2014). Carroll (2006) particularly emphasized the importance of acknowledging the interrelatedness of subsystems within a supervision process, even though some of the interactions may not be visible to all participants – referred to by Oshry as 'system blindness' (1994).

The authors have noticed limited reference within the current literature to the broader organization system, more specifically the organization-society interface where the emphasis is on the influence of the broader context (including a multicultural, country and industry perspective). Hawkins and Shohet included descriptions of the wider context into the developmental model of supervision in 2012, remaining however mostly descriptive rather than empirical. Given the rapid rate of change in the world of work, Cavanagh and Lane (2012) assert that coaches must be able to deal with the complexities faced by their clients and Stacey (cf. Stacey 2007) also introduced certain features of the dynamic nature of the organizational contexts and its impact on the supervision process. This raises the question of which components should be considered when developing a coaching supervision training programme in order to deliver supervisors who can work and provide supervision in complex, multicultural systems. Our position is aligned to that of Cavanagh and Lane (2012) in that we need to move beyond the traditional linear models which have informed coaching supervision towards the development of systemic practitioners that are multiculturally competent. In this regard, there is a call in the coaching community for the development of models, theories and supervision training programmes that are fit for purpose (Hawkins and Schwenk 2006; Moyes 2009). We have also noticed an emergence of new models and theories on the supervision process itself but less research on the development of coaching supervision training programmes.

There has further been a call from both coaching clients and professional bodies for professional supervision on a regular basis to maintain professional standards of coaching around the world (Standards Australia 2010). This is in line with the general ethos in the helping professions that professional development does not end with certification – or registration and licensing, but that working with a supervisor can be seen as an additional intervention towards continuous professional growth and personal career development (Annan and Ryba 2013; Blanton 2014; Passmore 2011). While coaching supervision may be acceptable practice in Europe, reviewing the current discussions and applications with the South African context, the authors support the statement made by Passmore and McGoldrick in 2009 that there are indeed huge variations in patterns of use from country to country suggesting that even in 2015 in some countries it may still be spoken about more often than it is practiced. It is further evident that coaches and purchasing organizations have different needs for supervision (Hawkins and Smith 2006), contributing towards the debate regarding the benefits of supervision compared to other professional development activities (Passmore and McGoldrick 2009) especially at different stages of professional development (Passmore 2011).

Drawing on our collective experience we have further observed that many organizations in South Africa, that have large panels of internal and external coaches, regard *supervision* as an important standard of coaching practice. Several organizations have therefore developed organizational policies and guidelines for the implementation of supervision, clearly stipulating the requirement that all coaches within the organisation must engage in supervision. Given an increase in awareness regarding the role of supervision in professional coaching practice and the need for specific training anchored in theoretically-grounded and evidence-based programmes (Grant 2012), we present in this chapter a coaching supervision framework based on a systemic approach to supervision, according to which the training and development of potential supervisors can be structured. The framework emerged from a conceptual analysis of current practices, scholarly research and our collective experience as leadership and executive coaches, of providing and receiving supervision, of assisting organizations in implementing coaching strategies as well as in teaching coaching psychology on postgraduate level. The first part of the chapter provides a brief overview of definitions and functions of coaching supervision, followed by an introduction of the Systemic Coaching Supervision Framework. We propose to examine and stimulate discussion regarding the critical building blocks included in the framework from a multicultural and systemic perspective and then move towards explaining the importance of carefully considering each of the components in the framework when designing a teaching programme. We conclude with a summary of the most important considerations according to the framework.

2 A Brief Overview of Supervision and Supervision in Coaching

In the following section we introduce the concepts supervision and coaching supervision as well as the purpose of coaching supervision.

2.1 What Is Supervision and Coaching Supervision?

Supervision in the broadest sense means to 'oversee' and in the context of work typically refers to a managerial function or role that implies a hierarchical relationship with certain power differentiation inherent to the role. In the helping professions supervision started out quite similar to apprenticeships in other fields, where a master or expert guides and directs a novice or trainee towards independent work (Drake 2014; Mead et al. 1999). In professional psychology, the term supervision is typically used when discussing the overseeing of work while in training and in internship settings and is a requirement for registration (licensure) to practice psychology (Blanton 2014; Hawkins and Shohet 2012). The practice of post-registration supervision however differs significantly across the applied areas of practice with limited application in industrial psychology (cf. Odendaal and Kwiatkowski In Press). Within the applied areas of clinical, counselling and education psychology, post-registration supervision is utilized predominantly for reflective practice and development (O'Donovan et al. 2011; Passmore and McGoldrick 2009).

Reviewing the coaching literature there is no agreed definition of coaching supervision. Grant (2012, p. 17) integrated the main themes and adapted the definition of Hawkins and Schwenk (2006) to refer to supervision in coaching

> …as a structured process for coaches designed to help coaches attend to improving the quality of the coaching, to grow their coaching capabilities and support themselves and their practice with the help of a coaching supervisor.

The Standards Australia Handbook for Coaching in Organisations (2010) also emphasizes that coaching supervision should be a mutually agreed arrangement and that the supervisor should be a competent and experienced coaching practitioner (p. 11). Hawkins and Schwenk (2006) point towards the interpersonal nature of coaching supervision that can be applied on individual level in the format of a one-on-one relationship, in groups or even in peer groups. They further emphasise the importance of reflection on client work within the supervision relationship. In this regard Lawrence and White (2014) refer to the 'facilitation of reflective practice', such that coaches can provide supervision to each other (p. 41). Hawkins and Shohet (2012) made certain additions to their initial definition of coaching supervision to also include a description of the wider systemic context, which they believe not only set out to serve key stakeholders, but also to improve the quality of their work.

Reviewing the literature a further differentiation is made between coaching supervision and coaching psychology supervision. In this regard Moyes (2009) argue that coaching psychology supervision addresses 'the psychological nature of the coaching process, as well as the application of psychological theory and methods within the coaching process' (p. 163). Given the Systemic Coaching Supervision Framework introduced in this chapter we further highlight the importance of multicultural interactions within the supervisory process. Strongly informed by the research of Inman and DeBoer Kreider (2013) and Soheilian et al. (2014), we emphasize the importance of creating sensitivity and awareness regarding the influence of culture when working with differences and developing multicultural competence within the supervision process. This includes both a multicultural awareness to coaches with different backgrounds, as well as sensitivity towards different organizational cultures in which the coaching services are provided.

2.2 *The Purpose of Supervision*

Supervision is undertaken to address different needs and while the models of supervision may vary considerably across professions, there are rather consistencies in what is perceived as the purpose of professional supervision. It should however be noted that different researchers provide different labels to the core purposes even though the content and meaning may be similar. According to Hawkins and Smith (2006) coaching supervision has developmental [also referred to as formative (Proctor 1987) or educative (Kadushin 1992)]; resourcing [referred to as restorative (Proctor 1987) or supportive (Kadushin 1992)] and qualitative purposes [referred to as normative (Proctor 1987) or managerial/administrative function of supervision (Kadushin 1992)]. The developmental purpose focuses on providing opportunities to coaches to develop competence, the resourcing purpose focus on the development of internal psychological resources to cope with the role of a coach while the qualitative purpose focus on an acute awareness of the quality of one's coaching. These purposes are however not independent and more than one purpose may be achieved at the same time during supervision. Standards Australia (2010) further emphasizes that the qualitative (normative) function refers specifically to the advancement as well as continuous maintenance of generally acceptable standards of practice. Table 1 provides the main categories of focus in coaching supervision with a classification of the three functional categories as described by Hawkins (2010). The authors subscribe to these broad functions/purposes of coaching supervision, which address self-awareness, competence and a willingness to learn and develop. More specifically we support the core applications of supervision for coaching as proposed by Hawkins (2010) because it aligns with the most pressing developing needs of coaches as observed in our supervision practices.

Table 1 Primary foci of supervision (Source: Hawkins in Passmore 2010, p. 217)

Main categories of focus	Function category
To provide a regular space for the supervisees to reflect upon the *content and process* of their work	Developmental
To develop understanding and skills within the work	Developmental
To receive information and another perspective concerning one's work	Developmental/resourcing
To receive both content and process feedback	Developmental/resourcing
To be validated and supported both as a person and as a worker	Resourcing
To ensure that as a person and as a worker one is not left to carry, unnecessary, difficulties, problems and projections alone	Resourcing
To have space to explore and express personal distress, re-stimulation, transference or counter transference that may be brought up by the work	Qualitative/resourcing
To plan and utilize their *personal and professional* resources better	Qualitative/resourcing
To be proactive rather than reactive	Qualitative/resourcing
To ensure quality of work	Qualitative

It is further of interest to note the difference in view of purpose of supervision from the perspective of coaches and purchasing organizations. The research of Hawkins and Smith (2006) showed that coaches emphasized the developmental and quality assurance function, whereas purchasing organizations highlighted the managerial aspect of supervision in minimising the organizational risk of unethical or unprofessional practice. This is especially important if the organization has a pool of internal and/or external coaches that coach from different perspectives and approaches. Hawkins and Smith (2006) suggest the appointment of a Lead Coach that aims to facilitate joint meetings between the external and internal coaches and the organization to provide high level feedback on emerging systemic and cultural patterns, as well as general progress on contracted outcomes achieved during the coaching intervention. In our opinion this lead coach should ideally be a senior internal coach in the organization but the role can also be fulfilled by an external coach with a sound knowledge of the organization. The Lead Coach further acts as knowledge broker to ensure that the coaches are fully informed on emerging strategic challenges and other developments or interventions within the organization that may have a direct impact on the coaching outcomes to be achieved. In addition, the Lead Coach seeks to balance the expectations of both the client and the organization within the boundaries of confidentiality. We also believe that this lead coach would be an ideal candidate to fulfil the role of supervisor.

Regarding the role of the supervisor, it is important to be mindful that the coaches that participated in the research of Hawkins and Smith (2006) also indicated that supervisors must have business knowledge, must appreciate organizational dynamics and be able to think in a systemic way. There is however limited research, if any, on what happens in coaching supervision and whether any of the identified purposes are indeed achieved through coaching supervision. Next, we introduce a systemic coaching supervision framework according to which the training and development of potential supervisors can be structured.

3 A Systemic Coaching Supervision Framework

In this section we firstly provide a brief introduction to the framework and then a detailed discussion of the components in the framework.

3.1 *Brief Introduction*

In recent years we have seen an exponential increase in published literature on the changes in the operating context of business, from relative stable, orderly and predictive to operating arenas characterized by contextual volatility, uncertainty, complexity and ambiguity (cf. Johansen 2012; Stacey 2007; Veldsman 2013). In this regard the recent global economic and socio-political turmoil serve as examples. In our experience, the majority of leaders and executives we coached introduced topics that manifested across different sub-systems that required work on multiple levels at the same time. There is an old Shona saying in South Africa that 'the fish is as strong as the water it swims in' which implies that a leader should have both relationships and relatedness with other leaders in the system, and must also take into account the influence of the immediate and broader context in order to function effectively. This has a direct influence on the way that coaches, coach in the organization and on the way in which supervisors support coaches in working in a systemic way. This principle guided our initial exploration on what should be included in a coaching supervision framework and provided the impetus for including general systems theory and systems thinking as broad conceptual approach. Fuqua and Newman (2002) introduced different principles of systems theory that informed the supervision framework: (1) a system comprises of multiple subsystems that are interdependent and interacts with the environment; (2) any change in one part of the system has the potential to create unintended (residual) effects on other parts; and (3) within the context of human systems and their complex and interactive nature different paths can lead to the same results. We found some support in the more recent adaptations Hawkins and Smith (2013, p. 170) made to the developmental model of coaching supervision where they define systemic supervision to be based on four pillars:

> Informed by a systemic perspective; in service of all parts of the system; attends to the client in relation to their systemic context(s); and includes and reflects upon the supervisee and supervisor as part of the systemic field.

The Systemic Coaching Supervision Framework is presented in Fig. 1. The aim with this framework is firstly, to present and describe the different components which should be considered when providing coaching supervision from a systemic perspective and secondly to highlight some of the design questions, which should be asked in developing a systemic coaching supervision training programme. In the next section the different building blocks are subsequently discussed in more detail. The first building block focuses on the broader and immediate business contexts

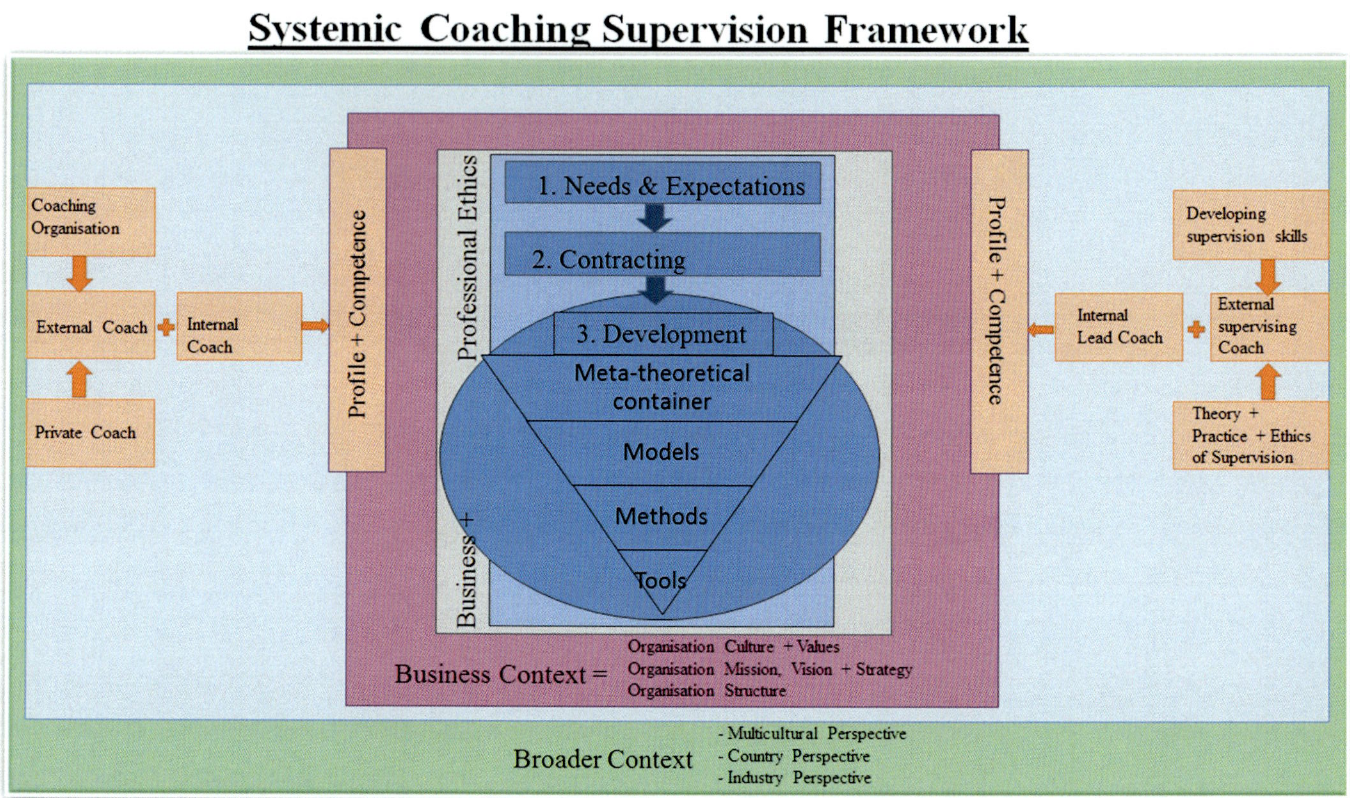

Fig. 1 Systemic coaching supervision framework

within which the supervision is provided as well as the reflective space created by coaching supervisors. This is followed by a discussion on the profiles and competencies of coaches and supervisors with special reference to the differences between these roles with regards to the theoretical, ethical and practical foundations. The authors then highlight the coaching supervision development process. The last two sections of the chapter focus on specific meta-theoretical container to coaching supervision and a number of different models, which can be used in the development process.

3.2 Broader Context

Working from the outside to the inside of the Systemic Coaching Supervision Framework, the broader context is discussed first. This broader context requires an awareness and impact of multicultural, country and industry perspectives on the supervisory process. The supervisor has to take into account the national and regional political, economic, social, technological, legal and environmental issues (PESTLE analysis - popular strategic tool to identify external factors that may impact the organization) that are operating in the background but could create challenges for the coach and client organization. With regards to the trends and critical events in the broader social context in South Africa, the following can be seen as challenges faced by leaders: socioeconomic status and poverty, education, health, crime and sexual orientation (e.g. homophobia).

Given the highly diverse and complex South African society it is increasingly important to deal with both the country and industry challenges faced by coaches as well as the cultural differences, which may exist between coaches and supervisors in the supervision process. Christiansen et al (2011) further acknowledge that people differ in a number of culturally important ways, such as race, gender, religion, socioeconomic status, language, education, sexual orientation and ethnicity. Our search on multicultural supervision guided us to research in the therapeutic context where multicultural competence is considered a core competency in the provision of ethical clinical practice (Falender and Shafranske 2007; Soheilian et al. 2014). It is further recognized that to be multicultural competent, the emphasis must be on both cultural awareness (cognitive process where culturally relevant information is processed intellectually) and cultural sensitivity (that refers to the emotional reaction that result in an intercultural significant experience) when working with differences (Christiansen et al. 2011).

There are different models applied within the coaching domain (e.g. Rosinski 2003) utilizing cultural orientation frameworks as language to talk about culture. Bennett (2004) introduced a useful empirical model mapping the stages people go through towards intercultural sensitivity: from denial, defence, minimisation, and acceptance to cognitive and behavioural adaptations. The first three stages are termed 'ethnocentric' where people view their own culture as central to their experiences and the last three 'ethnorelative' where people view their own culture as only one worldview from many possibilities. Bennett (2004) thus refer to intercultural sensitivity as the ability to discriminate between and experience cultural differences, in contrast intercultural competence is referred to as the ability to think and act in intercultural appropriate ways (p. 62). Inman and DeBoer Kreider (2013) are of the opinion that in order to enhance multicultural competence the focus must be on awareness, knowledge and skill. In this regard Soheilian et al. (2014, p. 380) emphasize the importance of working on cultural identity for both the supervisor and supervisee and refer to multicultural supervision as

> the supervisor's ability to address and facilitate cultural discussions in supervision, incorporate culturally sensitive interventions, assessments, client conceptualisations; and evaluate the multicultural competence of her or his supervisee.

Hawkins and Smith (2013) make a further differention between cross-cultural work (where the individual approach and try to understand another person from his/her own culture – ethnocentric in nature) and work that is transcultural (where the individual moves beyond cultural differences and is able to function within the context of other cultures – ethnorelative in nature). Reviewing the different definitions there appears to be strong alignment between transcultural and multicultural work. In conducting multicultural supervision Christiansen et al. (2011) further describes two perspectives to enhance cultural sensitivity, the cultural differences and the cultural affiliation perspective. If supervision is approach from a cultural difference perspective the style and approach of supervision will be strongly anchored in understanding cultural differences based on certain customs, language, traditions, beliefs and values. The argument is that multicultural supervision in this perspective requires a systemic approach with additional interventions for both the supervisor and supervisee to expand their world view and engage in continuous multicultural education. The cultural affiliation perspective, on the other hand, explores the degree to which individuals identify with their cultural group, the dominant culture or both. Christiansen et al. (2011) argue that multicultural supervision within this perspective focuses on racial identity stages of the supervisor and coach and it is then important to match a coach and supervisor from different cultural backgrounds. Working in the multicultural domain raises serious ethical concerns if the supervisor lacked sensitivity to cultural issues that could ultimately result in a negative supervision experience. In this regard Wong et al. (2013) argue that it is the responsibility of supervisors to ensure that supervisees develop multicultural competence.

There appears to be general support that little is known about what transpires within a supervision relationship where the emphasis is on the development of multicultural competence. Within a clinical supervision context where the emphasis was on multicultural events, race was identified as a frequent topic followed by gender-related discussions and potential gender role conflict (Christiansen et al. 2011; Inman and Ladany 2014; Soheilian et al. 2014; Wong et al. 2013). Gender and gender-related differences that have received some attention in the coaching literature but with limited focus in research within coaching supervision literature. In our collective experience and with acknowledgement to Soheilian et al. (2014) we support the view that race and gender are believed to be noticeable topics in supervision, especially given historical and socio-political climate in South Africa. Gender-related critical events in coaching supervision warrants further research.

3.3 *Business Context*

As alluded to previously, all the different components of the Systemic Coaching Supervision Framework are interconnected and can unintentionally impact the supervisee-client as well as the supervisor-supervisee system. Using an onion as metaphor, it is all about reviewing the influence of each subsequent level on the next. Within the immediate business context the emphasis is on organizational culture, climate and ethics; organizational mission, vision and strategy as well as organizational structure. Hawkins and Smith (2013) refer specifically to the influence and expectations of 'the client organization and its stakeholders, the coach's organization and its stakeholders as well as the supervisor and its organizational and professional context' (p. 200). As the contextual complexity of an organization changes, the organizational and leadership requirements will also change. For example, a shift in strategy from a local market to a global market impacts the leadership competency requirements towards that of a global mindset and intercultural sensitivity (Veldsman 2013).

Working effectively within and across the different levels therefore require associated knowledge, skill and abilities from both coach and the supervisor. We also believe that coaching involves coaching the individual in role, in their team and in a specific organizational context. Given this perspective, the challenges faced by the coaches, the dynamics of the team in which they operate and the organizational values and culture will be important points of discussion and exploration during the supervision process. This implies that the supervising coach also needs a thorough understanding of the business context if he or she is to assist the coach in delivering a successful coaching intervention. In the following section the reflective space followed by the supervision process are discussed.

3.4 *Reflective Space*

Core to the Systems Coaching Supervision Framework is the development of reflective practices, where coaches can reflect on their work. In this regard Schwenk and Jack (2013) indicated that supervision should be viewed as facilitated reflective practice, and Falender and Shafranske (2007) argue that a prerequisite to this meta-competence is the ability for introspection. Within the coaching supervision process this is achieved by encouraging and reinforcing the supervisee's skills in self-assessment and reflection. The work of Schön (1983), which refers specifically to reflection-on-action (looking back on the experience to gain further understanding) and reflection-in-action, (considering actions while in action) has received considerable attention within coaching and supervision. To be able to get to critical reflection, Thompson and Pascal (2012) included reflection-for-action (planning or thinking ahead). Effective reflection therefore requires a high level of introspection, open-minded analysis and self-regulation. In this regard Campone (2011, p. 15)

Table 2 Design questions to be asked in developing a systemic coaching supervision teaching programme

Systems component	Design questions
Broader context	Do the supervisors in training understand the way in which the multicultural, country and industry contexts influence the supervision process?
	Do the supervisors have an acceptable level of knowledge about the national and regional political nuances, the economic and social challenges; and the legal and environmental issues faced by the coaches?
	How can the multicultural competence (cultural awareness and sensitivity) of the supervisors be improved?
	In what way can the supervisors' competence in working across race and gender be developed?
Business context	How can the supervisors be educated on the organizational culture, climate and ethics; organizational mission, vision and strategy as well as organizational structure?
	How will they use this knowledge in guiding the coach to operate within this context?
Reflective space	What are the abilities required in providing a reflective space and how can the supervisor's ability to provide this space for coachees be developed?
	What is the current level of the supervisor's reflective ability and how can this be developed?

states that reflective practice within supervision is characterised by *intention* (the motivation to approach supervision as learning opportunity), with a *purpose* (to enable learning from experience) and *structure* (systematic process to capture personal experiences and specific strategies for meaning making). The creating of such a reflection space and practice is achieved through the supervision process (Table 2).

3.5 Coach and Supervisor Profiles and Competences

A core assumption of the Systemic Coaching Supervision Framework is that within a supervisory context all the sub-systems are connected, multileveled and open. Apart from the broader context, the framework also depicts the coaches and coaching supervisors who enter the system. We conceptualized the framework by thus secondly concentrating on the two most important role players namely the coach and the coaching supervisor. Both these individuals enter the system with a specific profiles and competencies as indicated in the far left and right parts of the framework.

Competence is a core ethical principle that informs psychology as profession. As both authors are registered psychologists and coaches we are mandated to practice exclusively within our boundaries of competence (Ethical Code of Conduct 2006,

p. 16) and this therefore strongly inform our approach to both coaching and supervision. Especially meta-competence as organizing principle (knowing what you know and do not know) is of importance in the training and development of psychologists (Falender and Shafranske 2007; Grus 2013) and, we propose, also in the transition from coach towards becoming a supervisor. Competencies are measureable human capabilities that involve knowledge, skill and attitudes (Soheilian et al. 2014). The principle of competence is also strongly anchored in competency frameworks of different coaching professional bodies. We therefore believe that coaches entering the organization to provide coaching and receive supervision should already have the basic competencies of coaching as well as an understanding of the importance of supervision. Similarly we require coaching supervisors to be well equipped to deliver on the different supervision needs, which are described in this chapter.

There are indeed a shared knowledge base or core knowledge, skills and abilities applicable to almost all coaching activities. In this chapter we have indicated, where applicable, the evidence based theories and models required on both micro and macro levels. The Standard Australia Handbook for Coaching in Organisations (2010) provides a valuable summary of coaching competency frameworks from different professional societies around the world. It also lists the major evidence bases upon which these competencies rest and refers specifically to four skills sets (cf. Standards Australia 2010, p. 34–35 for a comprehensive discussion of the following generic coaching competencies and supporting knowledge bases) to which we added a fifth namely, multicultural skills:

- foundational or micro skills
- conceptual and technical skills
- self-management and development skills
- boundary management skills
- multicultural skills

Providers of coaching can further be divided into internal and external coaches. Top executives and leaders are typically coached by external coaches and employees by internal coaches, which can be their direct managers or other managers in the organization (Spaten and Flensborg 2013). The goal or outcome to be achieved may be similar but the major difference is in the coaching relationship where the executive will select a coach whereas the employee usually has no influence on who will coach them. Coaches can be employed by a coaching organization or consultancy that may utilize specific proprietary models or frameworks in the coaching intervention. It is not the purpose of this chapter to go into a detailed discussion regarding the type (one-on-one, peer or group/team coaching and supervision), role and responsibility as well as supporting knowledge, skill and attributes required in each. It is however important to emphasize that depending the specific role profile and type of coaching and supervision applied, supporting competencies may be different. Empirical evidence in this area is emerging with power relations and boundary management identified as key areas for further research. There are furthermore differentiation in the role of the supervisor as determined by the purpose of supervision (refer to the discussion Sect. 2.2 on the responsibilities of the lead coach).

In determining the competence of coaching supervisors we were further informed by the work of Drake (2014) that provided an underlying architecture for the development of supervisors. He positioned three windows (a frame through which the supervisor can view the changing internal and external landscape) through which choices are made in supervision: (1) the artistry window focuses on the use of energy and own somatic experiences in supervision – anchored in the neuroscience of self-regulation; (2) the identity window represents the roles and functions attended to in supervision; and (3) the mastery window represents the domains of knowledge and evidence needed by supervisors. His conceptualization, not empirically tested, highlighted specifically two domains of knowledge often neglected in formal education – personal and contextual knowledge. Of further value is that each window is based on two axes, the vertical representing interpersonal competence (levels of consciousness) and the horizontal representing levels of technical competence (levels of expertise and ability to manage complexity) (cf. Drake 2014, p. 40.)

Evidence in support of the essential components of different coaching competency frameworks is starting to emerge, however peer-reviewed research on the competence of coaching supervision still lags, including identifying effective education and teaching practices to promote supervisor competence development. Reviewing theories of supervision, contemporary supervision practice as well as recent research, key mediators of effective supervision in the clinical domain were cited as supervisory working alliance, supervisor style, supervisor competence in supervision as well as supervisor multicultural competence (Inman and DeBoer Kreider 2013; Ladany et al. 2013; Soheilian et al. 2014). These areas require further exploration within the field of coaching supervision. Aligned with a systemic approach, a holistic aim is to develop supervisors that can operate at increased levels of competence with the ability to manage increased levels of complexity. Next, the coaching supervision development process is briefly introduced (Table 3).

Table 3 Design questions to be asked in developing a systemic coaching supervision teaching programme

Systems component	Design questions
Coach competencies	Do coaches with different levels of competence (for example, junior, senior and master) require different forms of supervision and how should this be considered in matching the coach with a supervisor?
	How will the supervisors enhance the foundational micro, conceptual and technical, self-management and development, boundary management and multicultural skills during the supervision process?
Supervisor competencies	On what basis will trainee coaching supervisors be selected?
	How can the supervisor's current level of interpersonal competence (levels of consciousness) and technical competence (levels of expertise and ability to manage complexity) be determined at the onset of training?
	How can the supervisors' skills in developing an effective working alliance, their supervision styles, and multicultural competence be developed?

3.6 Coaching Supervision Development Process

The Systemic Coaching Supervision Framework presented in this chapter, includes a description of the coaching supervision process in three stages. This process consists of needs and expectations, contracting and development stages. These stages are described next.

The Needs and Expectations Stage

Similar to the well-known coaching life cycles, which are used by coaches to structure a coaching process with their clients, supervising coaches use a similar process to plan, structure and deliver coaching supervision interventions. The first stage is called the needs and expectation stage. In this stage the organization, supervisor and coach or group coaches, clarify their needs and expectations of each other before entering into a formal supervision contract. The individual coach often approached a lead coach or supervisor with one or more objectives in order to develop their individual coaching competencies, while a group of coaches may express the need to develop both individual and team coaching competencies. When coaching in the same system, a group of coaches may also express the need to develop their individual coaching skills as well as, for example, their competence in analysing the system psychodynamics operating in the organization. Either way, for the majority of coaches, the supervising process is mostly designed as a co-learning or collective learning process in which both supervisors and coaches take part in the learning (Carroll 2010).

Apart from developing coaching competencies, novice coaches also request coaching supervision in order to develop their "business or coaching practice skills" in an attempt to improve their marketing, business strategies, networking and report writing skills. The Association for Coaching (2012) states that the third objective revolves around regular monitoring and reviewing of the coache's work which is essential in maintaining the standards of practice, providing ethical services and staying within the boundaries of the work of a coach. The Association also believes that supervision provides a space to develop emotional intelligence, to gain support, bring theory and practice together, gain new insights in order to develop into a successful coach. The Association also believes that coaches should opt for supervision because it is a place to develop their emotional intelligence, gain support, relate theory to practice, gain new insights and develop into an excellent coach. The Association for Coaching (2012) suggests finding a qualified and experienced supervising coach who has also trained as a coaching supervisor. The Association also points out that not all qualified supervisors come from a purely coaching background. It is however more important that they have practised as a coach. They may for example be psychologists or psychotherapists who are also coaches. Most importantly they should have the knowledge and skills to enhance the coachee's learning and development and be familiar with the supervision process (Standards Australia 2010). It is also not uncommon to find a coach in two relationships with two different supervisors who address different development needs (Passmore 2011).

Murdoch and Arnold (2013) believes that selecting a supervisor with high emotional intelligence will also meet the psychological development needs of coaches. In addition, Christiansen et al. (2011) emphasize the need for supervisors to be culturally sensitive when working with a client that is culturally different from themselves. The best way to develop multicultural sensitivity is a topic that requires further research. We propose that emotional intelligence will be instrumental in developing multicultural competence which will assist greatly in staying positive in difficult situations. The authors also believe that part of supervision involves the development of stress tolerance, impulse control, positive self-regard, social responsibility, optimism and happiness and that these characteristics can significantly improve the success of any coaching assignment, especially within a multicultural context.

Contracting Stage

The Association for Coaching (2012) suggests different forms of coaching supervision. These include: One-to-one coaching supervisor, one-to-one peer coaching supervision, group coaching supervision, peer group supervision, telephone or video-conference supervision and e-mail supervision.

Creating a supervision contract, however, entails significantly more than just deciding on the form of supervision. It is about establishing and managing professional boundaries based on a clear understanding of the roles and responsibilities of each party, including the sponsoring organization (Gray 2007). In agreeing and formulating a supervision contract, most supervisors will expect each coach to be fully responsible for his or her own learning process. This is especially true with regards to the frequency, content and intensity of the supervision sessions. Most coaches also expect coaches to take responsibility for the personal reflections, insights and conclusions, which they may have during and after the supervision sessions. The clarity with which the contact is designed will contribute significantly to meaningful and productive relationship. In developing the contract the authors suggest focusing on the following:

- Address the practical aspects of the contract as well as the psychological components e.g. conflicts, transference, premature termination
- Agree that each coach is responsible to regularly expressing new needs, which may arise
- Agree that every coach should participate actively in presenting content, facilitating learning and reflecting e.g. action learning methodology
- Discuss clear boundaries and stress that these are learning and not therapy sessions and that coaches should create an alternative support structure for support of a more personal nature
- Agree on the broad development objectives and manage the process accordingly but with the necessary flexibility to introduce new and related objectives e.g. individual, team and system psychodynamic competencies

- Decide on the different methodologies to be included in the supervision process. This can include journaling, reflecting, action learning and other forms of development
- Co-create or design the sessions creatively and allow the coach to take more responsibility in this as the process progresses
- Decide on the time frame of the cycle and the dates, duration and venue of each session
- Agree on the confidential nature of the content and clients being discussed during the sessions
- Address the way in which group supervision sessions will be structured and the way that differences and diversity will be dealt with
- Detail the process for dealing with any differences or disputes and clearly discuss termination procedure especially in the role as supervising coach
- Usually a contract will also attend to the investment linked to the supervision e.g. associated cost and what it includes

Development Stage

Although the literature on models for supervision is expanding very few fit for purpose models have been developed for coaching supervision within a highly diverse, multicultural and complex system. As with the well-known Seven-eyed model of Hawkins (2007) the majority of models were initially developed in the social work, nursing or counselling psychology disciplines. This implies that a great need exists for the development of unique coach supervision models and it is encouraging to notice attempts by different authors to conceptualise such models (Table 4).

In the next section the authors present a number of models, which are used in the coaching supervision context. As indicated in the Systemic Coaching Supervision Framework the development stage can be based on an array of different approaches and theories, which also include, to varying degrees, different methods and tools on coaching supervision. It is safe to say that the solution to new, unique coaching supervision models may not be found in one specific model, but in a combination of models. At the start of this section we however want to present a meta-theoretical container which describes the important components of the coaching supervision process and sessions.

3.7 A Meta-theoretical Container

At the time of publication, the authors reviewed a number of different conceptualizations and approaches to coaching supervision, which included the work of Alderfer (1977), Holton and Swanson (2011), and Alison Hodge (2014). The last mentioned author combines different theories into an integrative development framework. This container is presented with a number of expansions based on the

Table 4 Design questions to be asked in developing a systemic coaching supervision teaching programme

Systems component	Design questions
Supervision needs and expectations	In what way will the supervisors ensure that they enter into the relationship with the necessary emotional intelligence and cultural sensitivity?
	How will the supervisors identify the different supervision needs which individuals and groups may have?
	How will the supervisors address the needs to develop process and system psychodynamic (below the surface) coaching skills?
	In what way will the supervisor ensure that ample time is provided for the development of business and coaching practice skills?
Contracting	Which factors play a role in the form of supervision which can include one-to-one, one-to-one peer, group, peer group and telephone or video-conferencing supervision?
	In what way will the supervisor negotiate the practical and psychological aspects and the boundaries of the contract?
	In what way can the supervisor ensure that the roles and responsibilities of both parties are clear and that the coach takes responsibility for his or her own learning?
	How will the two parties settle disputes during the supervision process?
Development	How will the supervisor ensure that models of supervision are used in highly diverse, multicultural and complex system?

authors' experiences. We believe that this meta-theoretical container aligns well with our thinking in that it focuses on three non-negotiable aspects of coaching supervision. By including this container in a coaching supervision training programme, trainees are provided with three ingredients, which will contribute significantly to a successful supervision process.

Based on her doctoral research into supervision Hodge (2014), developed a framework, which she believes act as a container for coaching supervision and which rests on three pillars (Fig. 2). These Pillars she calls (1) The supervision relationship, (2) Creating the core conditions of adult learning, and (3) Promoting the value of reflective practice. She also views these pillars as the core ingredients that support coaches in their ongoing wellbeing and development.

With regards to the supervision relationship pillar Hodge (2014) focuses on the purpose or functions of coaching supervision and stresses how the process and relationship between the supervisor and coach provide important evidence on the dynamics operating in the relationship and organisational system. This is in line with our thinking with regards to clear purposes and a sound understanding of the system dynamics in the organization. She mentions that parallel processes can emerge in the supervision space, which can raise awareness in the coach and provide insights into what is happening in the client system. The 'here and now' processes in the supervision may also be indicative of what is happening in the coach/client relationship or in the coachee's system and this may give the coach new direction in terms of how to proceed in the coaching.

Some researchers, including Alderfer (1977) have found that dynamics in one part of an organization (supervision context) can be reflected in another part of the organization (coaching context). Alderfer developed the concept of parallel processes, which refers to any apparent resonance or similarities between two engaged social systems. This implies that dynamics that developed collectively in organizations can manifest in different parts of the system simultaneously. Coaches, therefore, need to be cognisant of the fact that manifested behaviour in the coaching relationship might be the result of what is happening elsewhere in the system. The coaching process therefore often resembles some of the dynamics of the broader system and the role of the supervisor is to assist the coach in studying these dynamics. Of great importance in a multicultural context, is an awareness of the cultural dynamics, which may surface in both the coaching and supervision processes.

Hodge (2014) also explains that becoming aware of parallel processes occurs through a process of observation, modelling and feedback on the relational dynamics that exist in the supervision relationship. This can especially be helpful in raining the self-awareness and insights which coaches can use with great effect in their coaching relationships (Critchley 2010; Drake 2011). The trust and safety created in this way, facilitates the sharing of concerns and vulnerabilities by the coach. Hodge (2014) furthermore explains that the supervision relationship pillar relates directly to the purpose of the supervision, which she describes as formative, restorative and normative according to the work of Proctor (1987). In this regard we prefer the Hawkins' set of purposes as described in Sect. 2.2 of this chapter. Nevertheless, we agree on the importance of having clear purposes in coaching supervision.

The second pillar of supervision refers to the creation of the core conditions of adult learning. Hodge (2014) believes that supervision should mainly be positioned as an adult learning process, which provides a reflective learning space and a positive rather than punitive experience. Hodge (2014) also believes that when coaches understand how they learn, they are also better able to identify the most appropriate forms of reflection for themselves which in turn will make them more effective learners. In a multicultural context the supervising coach need to pay special attention to this aspect to ensure that individuals with different cultural backgrounds and learning styles benefit equally from the supervision. As Whybrow and Palmer (2006) suggest, that supervision models which developed in the counselling psychology field may also have some relevance in industry and in evidence-based coaching because these models focus primarily on vulnerable adult clients. This lead us to believe that adult learning principles, by which each coach takes responsibility for their own learning, as self-directed, autonomous adults are a fundamental container in coaching supervision. More specifically, adult learning is defined by Knowles et al. (2011) as "the extension and clarification of the meaning of one's experience" (p. 11). These authors argue that adult learning is an implicit part of every coaching session and with adult learning come change. Significant changes in behaviours or attitudes can suggest that learning has taken place (Bachkirova et al. 2014).

In his theory on 'Andragogy', Knowles (1990) for example identified six main characteristics of adult learners that influences how the way they learn. In the coaching supervision context, these principles can be explained as follows:

- Adults need and want to know what the learning is about and what the benefits are. This emphasises their independence as adult learners and keeps the responsibility for the learning in their hands. The agenda should thus belong to the coach (Bachkirova et al. 2014).
- As self-directed individuals, adult learners generally become more autonomous as they mature. (Knowles et al., 2011). In this regard the supervising coach should treat them as adults and respect the knowledge they already have. This will include providing coaches with very specific feedback that is free of evaluation and judgment (Cox 2012).
- Adults also have a significant wealth of prior experience. Coaches who attend supervision sessions will draw on their past experiences and these experiences can become a vital catalyst in learning and unlearning (Cox 2012).
- It should also be recognised that adults will learn when they have a need to learn and the same should apply to coaches. Coaches generally seek supervision when their coaching engagements or practice create a need to know or understand or when they relies that their existing knowledge, skills and competencies are not effective in the situations they need to deal with.
- Adults also learn best when the learning is relevant they can apply it immediately.
- As internally motivated learners, adults are motivated by learning that helps them to solve problems and learning that can help them to feel more confidant and self-actualised (Knowles et al. 2011).

The third pillar of supervision is reflection on practice (Hodge 2014). The author's research showed that coaches should prepare for supervision by writing reflections after their coaching sessions and bringing these to the supervision sessions. Coaches can use various ways of capturing their reflections and these include notes, journaling, drawings and e-mails, which allow them to record behavioural themes, patterns, and insights gained during their daily activities. In this way coaches are developing their own form of 'internal supervisor' as Casement (1985) calls it (Table 5).

In the last section in this chapter, two different models of coaching supervision are presented. Each of these models suggest different processes, methods and tools which form part of our Systemic Coaching Supervision Framework. In selecting the models to be included in this chapter we specifically focused on a model which represents the skills and supervision process (7-Eyed Model) and the required theoretical knowledge bases, methods and tools (Full Spectrum Model) which all align to our Systemic Coaching Supervision Framework.

Table 5 Design questions to be asked in developing a systemic coaching supervision teaching programme

Systems component	Design questions
Meta-theoretical container	What competencies do supervisors need in establishing and maintaining effective supervision relationships?
	What competencies and process skills are needed in creating the core conditions of adult learning?
	Which skills and methods will the supervisor need to optimise the value of the reflective process?

3.8 *Models of Coaching Supervision*

Various models of supervision can be found in the literature and these include the 7-eyed process model (Hawkins and Smith 2013), the Full Spectrum Model (Murdoch et al. 2010) and the Systemic Model (cf. Gray and Jackson 2011). Passmore (cf. 2011) also refers to the Reflective coaching practitioner model, the Action learning supervision model, and the Gestalt supervision model. An overview of the first two models is provided in this section because these align closely to the components in our framework.

The 7-Eyed Process Model The original model can be traced back to 1985 when Hawkins and Shohet (Hawkins and Shohet 1989) developed a model to assist supervisees and supervisors with the purpose of exploring the various different influences on supervisory activities. This model, however, had a wide range of applications and has been used by many different professionals in many countries. It eventually also found its way into the coaching supervision context (Hawkins and Smith 2013). Since 2006 it has become one of the most used models of supervision.

The 7-eyed process model is described by Hawkins as a model, which provides a systemic understanding of the supervision process. It also allows for the integration of insights, some psychological aspects and the internal life of the individuals involved in this process. The model can be used by both supervisors and coaches to analyse their supervision process and practices by focusing on a number of prominent areas. The model can be presented graphically in the following way.

As indicated in Fig. 2, the model focuses on the interplay between the supervisory and coaching systems and the seven spaces or modes of communication or relationship (Hawkins 2010). The supervising coach uses different skills in the seven modes to assist the coach in reflecting and learning. The discussion in each of the modes may differ in content, process and dynamics, and if done effectively, contributes to the coach's understanding of the way he or she operates in the coaching role and some of the practices that may affect his or her performance. Hawkins and Smith (2013) provide the following explanation of the supervision process using the 7- eyed model.

The Coachee When focusing on the coachee the focus is on what is happening for the coachee in his or her role and the content and experiences they bring to the

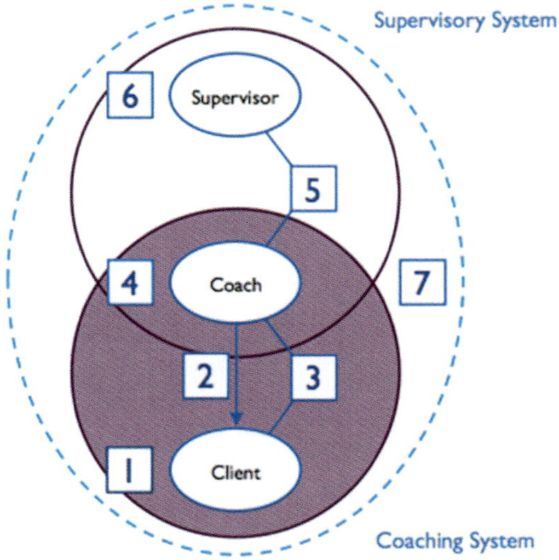

Fig. 2 The 7-eyed process model (Hawkins 2010)

coaching sessions. This includes the problems the coachee needs help with and how these may be representative of some of the problems manifesting in the coachee sessions. By reflecting on this, mode one is described as ta process whereby the supervisor is helping the coach to review what actually happened with the coachee. This includes the problems the coachee seeks help with and how they are presenting the issues in the coachee sechees and the resulting sensations and emotions. What the coach saw, heard and felt during the sessions, and at the same time separating the factual content from the coach's preconceptions, assumptions and interpretations (Hawkins 2010). As part of this reflection the coach is also assisted in reflecting on what happened when the coachee crossed the boundaries at the beginning and end of the sessions. The way in which coaches cross the supervision boundaries and what they start to speak about first, often holds evidence of richest unconscious content that needs to be explored in the supervising session (Hawkins and Smith 2013).

The Coach's Interventions When exploring the coach's interventions the supervisor and coach focus on the different interpretations and interventions the coach made during the coaching session and the alternative interventions, which could have been made. This may often lead to a discussion on the interventions, which coaches feel unsure or concerned about. This type of discussion involves exploring the different options and the possible impact of each. The mode two skill often involves assisting coaches with working through a deadlock situation which they have reached in the coaching process (Hawkins 2010). The coach may, for example, ask if he or she should collude with a situation or confront the issue? A skilful supervisor will avoid these 'either-or' discussions and rather make the coach aware of the way in which they limit their choice to two polarised possibilities without brainstorming alternatives. In this mode the advantages and possible consequences of these alternatives can be explored and even role-played in preparation of the next coaching session (Hawkins and Smith 2013). Many conflicting filled situations can develop when coaching in multicultural contexts and the coach needs to be aware of the cultural sensitive topics he or she tends to shy away from. The exploration of these topics and the underlying dynamics of the coach will need special attention when this appears.

The Relationship Between the Coach and the Coachee The mode three skill focuses on the relationship, which the coach and coachee have created and this requires that the coach figuratively lifts themselves out of the relationship in order to view the relationship from a new angle and perhaps gain new insights on it (Hawkins and Smith 2013). This allows the coach to explore both the conscious and unconscious dynamics, which may be operating in the coaching relationship. Many authors agree that a good working relationship forms the basis for the success of an executive coaching intervention (Kampa and White 2002; Kampa-Kokesch and Anderson 2001; Kilburg 2001; Lowman 2005). For this reason the coach should constantly be aware of the relationship dynamics, which may affect the success of the coaching process. In providing coaching supervision to coaches from different cultural backgrounds, supervisors need to be acutely aware of the way in which for example, value differences can impact their relationship.

The Coach According to Hawkins and Smith (2013) the coach should reflect on themselves with regards to what is being triggered in them by what the coachee shares with them, and also the way in which they use the 'self as instrument' in detecting, exploring and gaining insight in unconscious material. The mode four skill therefore represents the way in which the supervisor assists the coach in processing the feelings which were triggered during the work with the coachee. The focus, however, is not only on exploring the coach's feelings, but also on understanding how these feelings may be very useful in understanding what the coachee is experiencing but unable to verbalise. In this process the coach also explores how his or her personal 'blocks', including diversity and cultural dynamics, may prevent them from providing the necessary opportunities for the coachee and their system to change (Hawkins 2010).

The Parallel Process In this mode the focus is on what the coach has unconsciously absorbed or internalised from the coachee system and how this at times is played out in the supervision session. The assumption therefore is that the coach can unconsciously replicate the behaviour of the coachee and threat the supervisor in the way they were treated in the coaching session. The Mode five skill requires from the supervisor not only to attend to what they are being told about the coaching system, but also how it plays out in the 'here and now' of the supervision session (Hawkins 2010). When becoming aware of these dynamics the supervisor then offers tentative reflections or working hypotheses on the impact of these dynamics on the coaching relationship. When done effectively this process can assist the coach in becoming aware of how their conscious understanding of the coaching situation may however also have emotional, irrational and unconscious impacts on them (Hawkins and Smith 2013). This may even include assisting a coach with a valence for multicultural dynamics and the strong emotions, which may have been projected onto them.

The Supervisor Self-Reflection According to Hawkins and Smith (2013), the focus for mode six is the supervisor's 'here and now' experience while with the coach and what can be learnt about the coach/coachee relationship from their own response to the coach and what the coach presents. The Mode six skill therefore involves the supervisor attending to both the presented material and its impact on the 'here and now' relationship and their own internal process (Hawkins and Smith 2006). In this process the supervisor is bound to discover unconscious material related to the coaching relationship, by attending to his or her own feelings, thoughts and fantasies (Hawkins 2010).

(7) The Wider Context Hawkins (2010) describes mode seven as the mode in which the focus is on the organisational, social, cultural, ethical and contractual context in which the coaching is taking place. This requires an awareness of a wide array of stakeholders, which may impact the coaching process. Some of these stakeholders, which may impact the process include the client organisation, the coach's organisation as well as the professional network of which the supervisor may be part of (Hawkins, 2010). The Mode seven skill thus requires that the supervisor and coach consider how these different contexts or parts of the larger system can impact their cognitions, emotions and behaviours (Hawkins and Smith 2006). This involves for example the exploration and understanding how the culture of different system may create misconceptions, delusions and even unconscious collusions in both the coach and supervisor. To attend to mode seven the supervisor will need a high level of transcultural competence in order to assist the coachee in exploring and understanding the unique dynamics and processes operating in different organisational cultures (Hawkins and Shohet 2000).

Full Spectrum Model According to Murdoch and Arnold (2013) the Full Spectrum Model provides an in-depth description of the practice of supervision. In this model the authors address the meta-theories, supervision models, skills and tools. In essence, this inclusive model illustrates how supervision draws on adult learning theory, systems theory, reflection, mindfulness, interpersonal psychology, neuroscience and dialoguing. In combination these theories and practices provide the basis of supervision as a reflective practice.

When studying the model in detail it is clear that the authors attempted to focus on the relationship nature of supervision. According to Murdoch and Arnold (2013), the work takes place in the relationship and through the conversation. When the supervisor and coach create an open and equal learning partnership where both are learning and where they push each other's learning, new ideas and insights can emerge. Even though both may be learning, the focus is always on the coachee and his or her practice and the actions, processes and dynamics that impact this practice. Murdoch and Arnold (2013) and Passmore (2011) believe that working in this way the coach can over time improve his or her work. In this way it is possible to attend to the core tasks of coaching supervision, which are in line with the systemic and multicultural approached presented in this chapter:

- Assuring professionalism, integrity and ethical practice of the coach.
- Ensuring the continuous personal and professional learning and development of the coach.
- Learning to be present, mindful and transpersonal when working with coaches in order to facilitate the development of these skills in them. These authors thus go beyond the multicultural perspective presented in this chapter with a transpersonal perspective, which implies experiences in which the self extends beyond (trans) the individual or personal and includes the wider aspects of humankind, life and intra psychic experiences.
- Using clear explanations and interpretations of the psychodynamics, which are operating in the different relationships and assisting the coach with exploring these.
- Practical modelling of reflective learning skills.
- Assisting the coach to focus on rest, refuelling and restoration.
- Celebrating and honouring the work and successes of the coach.

In order to do this Murdoch and Arnold (2013) suggest that amongst other things a number of theoretical knowledge bases and tools are required, which they grouped into four categories. These categories are presented in Table 6.

This model is therefore by no means a step-by-step tool of supervision but rather a representation of the multi-layered nature of supervision. The Full Spectrum

Table 6 The coaching supervision academy's full spectrum model (From: Murdock and Arnold, 2013, p xxiv)

Theoretical knowledge bases	**Meta skills, self-support, reflection**
Quantum physics Systems Psychologies of:	Energy management
Development	Presence/mindfulness
Change	Internal supervisor
Groups	Parallel process
Organizations	Who you are is how you supervise
Sociology of:	Books and articles
Organizations	Reviews
Relationship building and sustaining tasks	**Methods, tools and actions**
Create working alliance	Psychometrics
Support and challenge	Multi-party contracting
Teach and develop	Arts based approaches
Ensure ethical and professional standards	7-eyed model (Hawkins)
	Developing reflective practice
	Coaching psychology

Table 7 Design questions to be asked in developing a systemic coaching supervision teaching programme

Systems component	Design questions
Models, methods and tools of coaching supervision	What supervision modes are available to supervisors and in what way can they work with their own psychological process and that of the coach and coachee and organization in the supervision process?
	What are the different theoretical knowledge bases that supervisors should have given the fact that they will supervise coaches with an array of clients in different organizational systems who are going through different developmental stages and career and organizational changes?
	What methods and tools should supervisors have available to assist them in the supervision process?

Model can be seen as a collection of methods, approaches and ways of being for the supervisor to support new insights, awareness and transformation (Murdoch and Arnold 2013) (Table 7).

4 Summary

The Systemic Coaching Supervision Framework is a first attempt towards identifying and integrating a multitude of principles and practices of coaching supervision with the goal of identifying those components which should be considered in designing a coaching supervision training programme. The framework can be seen as a systemic, process framework, which highlights both the contexts, tasks, competencies required and the developmental process. In order to provide effective coaching supervision, supervisors firstly, need to understand the broader context within which the coaching supervision is provided. This includes developing a clear perspective on the unique nature of the country and industry as well as the multicultural dynamics in which the service is provided. Given the highly diverse and complex South African society it is increasingly important to deal with both the country and industry challenges faced by coaches as well as the cultural differences, which may affect the coaching and coaching supervision process.

Secondly, we emphasize the principle that coaching supervisors should understand the business context in which the coach is delivering services. This includes the culture and values of the organization; the mission, vision and strategy and the structure of the organization. This contextual understanding will assist the supervising coach in exploring organizational (systems), team and leadership dynamics, which impact the coaching. This will allow the coaching supervisor to focus on the coach, client, organization and the business and broader country context, and the interactions between the different sub-systems.

Thirdly, the supervisor needs to understand the relationship nature of coaching supervision and that the success of the intervention depends on the relationship, which is created in this reflective space. The creation of a safe and non-judgemental reflection space as well as an effective development process requires specific competencies from the supervising coach. Both coaches and coaching supervisors enter the relationship with specific profiles and competencies, which may affect the way in which they perform their tasks and learn collaboratively in the supervision space. A certain level of self-awareness, an understanding of one's competencies and a learning attitude is required to get optimal value from the supervision relationship. This will also assist in making an initial evaluation of the competency gaps, which may exist and in defining the needs and expectations of the coach. Essential components, specifically to multicultural supervision, are further positioned as supervisor-supervisee relationship (and the interrelationship with all the sub-systems), supervisor competence in supervision as well as supervisor multicultural competence. Research within the clinical domain has further pointed towards specific outcomes such as supervisee multicultural competence or supervisor and supervisee meta-competence that may be linked to effective and ineffective supervision.

Fourthly, the Systemic Coaching Supervision Framework highlights the scientific and ethical practice of supervision by emphasizing knowledge, skills and attributes (and their integration) required to meet professional standards of supervision practice. Competence is not optional and is positioned as a critical outcome of training as a supervisor. An important aspect of competence is meta-competence – knowing your limitations and having the ability to evaluate your own performance. Build into the framework is therefore the continuous focus on reflection and introspection with the aid of different structured methods and tools.

Fifthly, the framework focuses on the three stages in the development process, which includes the clarification of needs and expectations, contracting and development. Clarifying the needs and expectations of the coach or coaches assists in identifying the purpose of the supervision while the contract solidifies the boundaries of the engagement.

Finally, the framework focuses on a meta-theoretical container which provides three pillars on which supervision is based as well as two coaching supervision models which focus on the supervision process and modes of supervision, and theoretical knowledge bases, methods and tools required to deliver effective supervision sessions. The focus can then shift to determining content to be learned and the range of options available to facilitate the learning. This chapter therefore also provides a number of design questions for consideration when designing a coaching supervision training programme.

References

Alderfer, C. P. (1977). Improving organisational communication through long-term intergroup intervention. *Journal of Applied Behavioral Science, 13*, 193–210.

Annan, J., & Ryba, K. (2013). Networks of professional supervision. *School Psychology Quarterly, 28*(2), 170–182.

Association for Coaching. (2012). *Supervision report*. Downloaded from www.associationforcoaching.com

Bachkirova, T., Cox, E., & Clutterbuck, D. (2014). Introduction. In E. Cox, T. Bachkirova, & D. Clutterbuck (Eds.), *The complete handbook of coaching* (2nd ed., pp. 1–20). London: Sage.

Bennett, M. J. (2004). Becoming interculturally competent. In J. Wurzel (Ed.), *Toward multiculturalism: A reader in multicultural education* (2nd ed., pp. 62–77). Newton: Intercultural Resource Corporation.

Blanton, J. S. (2014). Supervision practices in consulting and industrial-organisational psychology doctoral programs and consulting firms. *Consulting Psychology Journal: Practice and Research, 66*(1), 53–76. doi:10.1037/a0035681.

Butwell, J. (2006). Group supervision for coaches: Is it worthwhile? A study of the process in a major professional organisation. *International Journal of Evidence Based Coaching and Mentoring, 4*(2), 43–53.

Campone, F. (2011). The reflective coaching practitioner model. In J. Passmore (Ed.), *Supervision in coaching: Supervision, ethics and continuous professional development* (pp. 11–29). London: Kogan Page.

Carroll, M. (2006). Key issues in coaching psychology supervision. *The Coaching Psychologist, 2*(1), 4–8.

Carroll, M. (2010). Supervision: Critical reflection for transformational learning (Part 2). *The Clinical Supervisor, 29*(1), 1–19. doi:10.1080/07325221003730301.

Casement, P. (1985). *On learning from the patient*. East Sussex: Routledge.

Cavanagh, M., & Lane, D. (2012). Coaching psychology coming of age: The challenges we face in the messy world of complexity. *International Coaching Psychology Review, 7*(1), 75–90.

Christiansen, A. T., Thomas, V., Kafescioglu, N., Karakurt, G., Lowe, W., Smith, W., & Wittenborn, A. (2011). Multicultural supervision: Lessons learned about an ongoing struggle. *Journal of Marital and Family Therapy, 37*, 109–119. doi:10.1111/j.1752-0606.2009.00138.x.

Cox, E. (2012). Individual and organisational trust in a reciprocal peer coaching context. *Mentoring & Tutoring, 20*, 427–443.

Critchley, B. (2010). Relational coaching: Taking the coaching high road. *Journal of Management Development, 29*(10), 851–863.

Drake, D. B. (2011). What do coaches need to know? Using the mastery window to assess and develop expertise. *Coaching an International Journal of Theory, Research and Practice, 4*, 138–155.

Drake, D. B. (2014). Three windows of development: A postprofessional perspective on supervision. *International Coaching Psychology Review, 9*, 38–48.

Ethical Rules of Conduct for Practitioners Registered Under the Health Professions Act, 1974 (2006, August 4). *Government Gazette*, 29079, Cape Town.

Falender, C. A., & Shafranske, E. P. (2007). Competence in competency-based supervision practice: Construct and application. *Professional Psychology: Research and Practice, 38*(3), 232–240.

Fuqua, D. R., & Newman, J. L. (2002). The role of systems theory in consulting psychology. In R. L. Lowman (Ed.), *The California School of Organisational Studies. A comprehensive guide to theory, skills, and techniques: Handbook of organisational consulting psychology* (pp. 76–105). San Francisco: Jossey-Bass.

Grant, A. M. (2012). Australian Coaches' views on coaching supervision: A study with implications for Australian coach education, training and practice. *International Journal of Evidence Based Coaching and Mentoring, 10*(2), 17–33.

Gray, D. (2007). Towards a systemic model of coaching supervision: Some lessons from psychotherapeutic and counselling models. *Australian Psychologist, 42*(4), 300–309.

Gray, D. E., & Jackson, P. (2011). Coaching supervision in the historical context of psychotherapeutic and counselling models: A meta-model. In J. Bachkirova, P. Jackson, & D. Clutterbuck (Eds.), *Coaching and mentoring supervision: Theory and practice*. Berkshire: Mcqraw-Hill.

Grus, C. L. (2013). The supervision competency: Advancing competency-based education and training in professional psychology. *The Counseling Psychologist, 41*(1), 131–139.

Hawkins, P. (2010). Coaching supervision. In J. Passmore (Ed.), *Excellence in coaching: The industry guide* (pp. 215–225). London: Kogan Page.

Hawkins, P., & Schwenk, G. (2006, September). *Coaching supervision*. Paper presented at the CIPD coaching conference. London, UK. Retrieved from http://www.cipd.co.uk/NR/rdonlyres/C76BD1C9-317C-4A2C-B0D3708F3ED2EC81/0/coac hsupevrp.pdf

Hawkins, P., & Shohet, R. (1989). *Supervision in the helping professions*. Buckingham: Open University Press.

Hawkins, P., & Shohet, R. (2000). *Supervision in the helping professions*. Buckingham: Open University Press.

Hawkins, P., & Shohet, R. (2012). *Supervision in helping professions* (4th ed.). Maidenhead: Open University Press.

Hawkins, P., & Smith, N. (2006). *Coaching, mentoring and organisational consultancy: Supervision and development*. Maidenhead: Open University Press.

Hawkins, P., & Smith, N. (2013). *Coaching, mentoring, and organisational consultancy: Supervision, skills and development*. Maidenhead: McGraw-Hill Education.

Hodge, A. (2014). Pillars of support. *Coaching at Work, 9*(4), 35–38.

Holton, E. F., & Swanson, R. A. (2011). *Foundations of human resource management*. Retrieved from http://www.readhowyouwant.com

Inman, A. G., & DeBoer Kreider, E. (2013). Multicultural competence: Psychotherapy practice and supervision. *Psychotherapy, 50*, 346–350. doi:10.1037/a0032029.

Inman, A. G., & Ladany, N. (2014). Multicultural competence in psychotherapy supervision. In F. L. Leong, L. Comas-Díaz, G. C. Nagayama Hall, V. C. McLoyd, & J. E. Trimble (Eds.), *APA handbook of multicultural training* (pp. 643–658). Washington, DC: APA. doi:10.1037/14187-036.

Johansen, B. (2012). *Leaders make the future: Ten new leadership skills for an uncertain world*. San Francisco: Berrett-Koehler Publishers.

Kadushin, A. (1992). What's wrong, what's right with social work supervision. *The Clinical Supervisor, 10*(1), 3–19.

Kampa, S., & White, R. P. (2002). The effectiveness of executive coaching: What we know and what we still need to know. In R. L. Lowman (Ed.), *The California School of Organisational Studies. A comprehensive guide to theory, skills, and techniques: Handbook of organisational consulting psychology* (pp. 139–158). San Francisco: Jossey-Bass.

Kampa-Kokesch, S., & Anderson, M. Z. (2001). Executive coaching: A comprehensive review of the literature. *Consulting Psychology Journal: Practice and Research, 53*(4), 205–228.

Kilburg, R. R. (2001). Facilitating intervention adherence in executive coaching: A model and methods. *Consulting Psychology Journal: Practice & Research, 53*(4), 251–267.

Knowles, M. S. (1990). *The adult learner: A neglected species* (4th ed.). Houston: Gulf.

Knowles, M., Holton, E. F., & Swanson, R. A. (2011). *The adult learner*. Burlington: Elsevier.

Ladany, N., Mori, Y., & Mehr, K. E. (2013). Effective and ineffective supervision. *The Counseling Psychologist, 41*, 26–45.

Lawrence, P., & White, A. (2014). What is coaching supervision and is it important? *Coaching: An International Journal of Theory, Research and Practice, 7*(1), 39–55. doi:10.1080/17521882.2013.878370.

Lowman, R. L. (2005). Executive coaching: The road to Dodoville needs paving with more than good assumptions. *Consulting Psychology Journal: Practice and Research, 57*(1), 90–96.

Mead, G., Campbell, J., & Milan, M. (1999). Mentor and Athene: Supervising professional coaches and mentors. *Career Development International, 4*(5), 283–290.

Moyes, B. (2009). Literature review of coaching supervision. *International Coaching Psychology Review, 4*, 162–173.

Murdoch, E., & Arnold, J. (2013). *Full spectrum supervision: "Who we are is how you supervise"*. St Albans: Panoma Press.

O'Donovan, A., Halford, W. K., & Walters, B. (2011). Towards best practice supervision of clinical psychology trainees. *Australian Psychologist, 46*, 101–112.

Odendaal, A., & Kwiatkowski, R. (in press). Supervision in industrial, organisational, work and occupational psychology. In D. A. Lane, M. Watts, & S. Corrie (Eds.), *Psychological supervision – emergence and growth in practice*. London: Open University Press.

Oshry, B. (1994). *Seeing systems: Unlocking the mysteries of organisational life*. San Francisco: Berrett-Koehler.

Passmore, J. (2010). *Excellence in coaching: The industry guide*. London: Kogan Page.

Passmore, J. (2011). *Supervision in coaching: Supervision, ethics, and continuous professional development*. London: Kogan Page.

Passmore, J., & McGoldrick, S. (2009). Super-vision, extra-vision or blind faith? A grounded theory study of the efficacy of coaching supervision. *International Coaching Psychology Review, 4*(2), 145–161.

Proctor, B. (1987). Supervision: A co-operative exercise in accountability. In M. Marken & M. Payne (Eds.), *Enabling and ensuring supervision in practice*. Leicester: National Youth Bureau.

Rosinski, P. (2003). *Coaching across cultures: New tools for leveraging national, corporate and professional differences*. London: Nicholas Brealey Publishing.

Schön, D. A. (1983). *The reflective practitioner*. San Francisco: Jossey-Bass.

Schwenk, G., & Jack, R. (2013). Leading the way. *Coaching at Work, 8*(5), 32–36.

Soheilian, S. S., Inman, A. G., Klinger, R. S., Isenberg, D. S., & Kulp, L. E. (2014). Multicultural supervision: Supervisees' reflections on culturally competent supervision. *Counselling Psychology Quarterly, 27*(4), 379–392. doi:10.1080/09515070.2014.961408.

Spaten, O. M., & Flensborg, W. (2013). When middle managers are doing employee coaching. *International Coaching Psychology Review, 8*(2), 18–39.

Stacey, R. D. (2007). *Strategic management and organisational dynamics: The challenge of complexity* (5th ed.). London: Financial Times.

Standards Australia Guidelines for Coaching in Organisations. (2010). Sydney: SAI Global Limited under licence from Standards Australia Limited.

Thompson, N., & Pascal, J. (2012). Developing critically reflective practice. *Reflective Practice: International and Multi-disciplinary Perspectives, 13*(2), 311–325. doi:10.1080/14623943.2012.657795.

Veldsman, T. H. (2013). People professionals fit for emerging economies. In S. Bluen (Ed.), *Talent management in emerging markets* (pp. 179–202). Johannesburg: Knowres.

Whybrow, A., & Palmer, S. (2006). Taking stock: A survey of coaching psychologists' practices and perspectives'. *International Coaching Psychology Review, 1*(1), 56–75.

Wong, L. C. J., Wong, P. T. P., & Ishiyama, I. F. (2013). What helps and what hinders in cross-cultural clinical supervision: A critical incident study. *The Counseling Psychologist, 41*(1), 66–85. doi:10.1177/0011000012442652.

Morality on the Executive's Couch: Ethical Perspectives on Coaching Psychology, Theory and Praxis

Jeremias J. De Klerk

Abstract Coaching is one of the fastest growing industries. However, ethical insights on coaching are not developing at the same rate. Even highly qualified coaches can find themselves involved in serious ethical issues, especially in a multicultural context. This chapter is a philosophical and normative analysis from a meta-theoretical literature review. Ethical issues are identified, questionable approaches in coaching psychology is critiqued and a model for ethical coaching in a multi-cultural context is developed under eight themes: coaching regulation, scientific foundation, normative issues, diagnostic assessments, confidentiality and conflicting interests, dependency, keeping coaching boundaries and coaching proficiency. Coaching ethically is complex and fraught with ethical issues that can easily be missed. Identification of the ethical issues in coaching psychology creates better understanding of potential ethical pitfalls and how to avoid them. This can lead to a more ethical, and thus sustainable coaching industry.

Keywords Ethics • Cross-cultural • Morality • Coaching

1 Introduction

Coaching psychology and theory is operationalized through the practices of coaching practitioners coming from a diverse range of backgrounds. Coaching is also being done with people from every conceivable ethnic and cultural background. Coaching is an eclectic field of study in psychology, with every coaching event providing ample opportunity for both ethical and unethical behaviour to manifest. In order to ensure morally responsible coaching, ethical matters in coaching psychology, theory and praxis should be proactively identified, acknowledged and dealt with appropriately. This is especially true when coaching across cultural differences.

J.J. De Klerk (✉)
University of Stellenbosch, Stellenbosch, South Africa
e-mail: Mias.deKlerk@usb.ac.za

L.E. van Zyl et al. (eds.), *Coaching Psychology: Meta-theoretical perspectives and applications in multicultural contexts*, DOI 10.1007/978-3-319-31012-1_5

Executive coaching is one of the fastest growing industries worldwide (Yi-Ling and McDowall 2014). Executive coaching is considered to be one of the most effective talent management activities, but also the most significant developments within the field of consulting psychology over the past decade (Sperry 2013; Yi-Ling and McDowall 2014). The implication of coaching across cultures is a relatively new consideration in coaching psychology and interest on its impacts is also rapidly expanding (Plaister-Ten 2013).

There are several drivers behind the dramatic growth in the coaching industry. In global surveys, coaches consistently attest to coaching's very positive impact on executive effectiveness and organizational performance (Corbett and Kennedy 2014). The fast growing coaching industry presents lucrative careers to potential coaches – the earnings of executive coaches average around USD 335/h globally (Corbett and Kennedy 2014). Coaches come from almost every conceivable professional background, often with very little coaching training (Hannafey and Vitulano 2013; Yi-Ling and McDowall 2014). In an industry with almost no entry barriers – who would not like to join in the fun?

The fast growing, yet weakly regulated field of coaching is open to many ethical risks and hidden pitfalls, even the most highly qualified coaches can find themselves in situations that are ethically problematic. Some of the ethical risks of coaching are obvious. Any person can sell his or her service as executive coach and there is confusion about professional and ethical standards in coaching (Hannafey and Vitulano 2013). Generally the executive coach is hired by an organization, normally by HR or the line manager on behalf of the manager who will be the focus of the coaching. As result, ethical risks related to confidentiality and conflict of interests naturally originate from this arrangement. Coaching across cultures presents coaches with several difficulties and ethical risks due to cultural differences, which include different nuances in preferences and taboos. These issues represent only the proverbial tip of the iceberg of ethical risks in coaching psychology and praxis. Yet, the importance of ethics in coaching is often being neglected (Rostron 2014). Few research studies can be found that specifically investigated ethical issues in coaching (Hannafey and Vitulano 2013). Although large surveys are regularly conducted on the coaching industry and practices, little or no attention is given to ethical aspects of coaching in these surveys, especially when it comes to cross-cultural coaching ethical issues. Some examples of comprehensive international coaching surveys that refrained from including a specific focus on ethical issues, include the surveys by Corbett and Kennedy (2014), International Coaching Federation (2013), Larcker et al. (2013), and Underhill et al. (2013).

As the number of coaches and coaching events in culturally diverse environments expands, it becomes increasingly important that the ethical integrity in the coaching industry is assured. However, the development of an ethical compass does not appear to be growing at the same rate as the industry praxis. Not enough substantive consideration is being given to some of the complex ethical issues that arise from the complex coaching relationships (Hannafey and Vitulano 2013). The ethical issues in coaching psychology, theory and praxis need to be clearly identified, recognised and addressed on a broader basis or the ethical integrity of coaching psychology will remain questionable.

The purpose of investigating and promoting ethics in coaching psychology, theory and practice is to present a sound knowledge base of ethical issues and how to deal with the unique challenges in order to protect clients, the public, and the coach (Cavanagh and Lane 2012; Duffy and Passmore 2010). The aim of this chapter is to identify some of the most crucial ethical issues and complexities in coaching psychology and coaching praxis, and will provide some guidance on how to deal with these challenges. Cross cultural coaching is a specific focus under the overarching coaching psychology. Discussions on general ethical issues thus form the basis for the analyses and discussions in this chapter, which is then elaborated on to include specific focus on cross-culture coaching ethical issues.

2 Background

Coaching has its roots in the area of sport and dates back as far as ancient Greece where coaches were paid to train athletes for competing in the Olympic Games (American Management Association 2008). Coaching in the workplace is a much more recent development. The initial focus of coaching managers was directed at remedial actions to address destructive behaviours of talented executives (Corbett and Kennedy 2014; Kauffmann and Coutu 2009). Although the residual stigma still remains that coaching is remedial, coaching has developed into a popular proactive approach to leadership development, rather than being remedial (Corbett and Kennedy 2014; Gavett 2013).

Coaching of managers in the workplace (generally called executive coaching), is defined as "partnering with clients in a thought-provoking and creative process that inspires them to maximize their personal and professional potential" (ICF 2014). In this partnership, the coach is "an expert facilitator who provides structure, guidance, support and accountability, designed to create positive change in business behaviour" (Corbett and Kennedy 2014, p. 26). Coaching praxis is inextricably connected to coaching psychology, which should ideally provide the scientific foundation of all coaching practices.

The definition of coaching psychology contains four essential elements: coaching psychology is (1) the systematic application of behavioural science and psychological theories and principles, (2) to facilitate positive development and enhancement of wellbeing and work performance, (3) within a specific cultural context, (4) in the absence of clinically significant mental health issues or abnormal levels of distress (Grant 2006; SIOPSA 2014). These elements of the definition have specific significance as moral problems are likely to arise if they are not honoured.

Ethics is the science of morality and focus on what is considered to be good, right and appropriate, as opposed to those behaviours or actions that are considered to be bad, wrong, improper or unacceptable (Duffy and Passmore 2010). Ethical issues in coaching psychology and coaching praxis are often not obvious, but hidden within the subtleties of situations, which are not easily identifiable (Trevino and Brown 2004). Ethical coaching is about understanding and proactively attending to all the nuances of potential ethical issues relating to the coaching context (Allan and Law 2009). Ethical principles represent the most basic filters to assess whether something is ethical or not (Velasquez 2012). Although many ethical principles have been developed over the years, Passmore (2009) argues that ethical issues in coaching mainly relate to the principles of legality, consequentialism and deontology. In addition to these principles, the ethical principle of rights is also considered in this study to reflect on ethics in coaching psychology, theory and praxis. Although the ethical principles provide a good foundation from which to assess ethical issues, the guidance they provide can be vague and even in conflict. These principles and some of their limitations are briefly explained in the following sections.

2.1 Legality

Legality is about compliance to standards such as legislation, codes of conduct, policies and procedures as a minimum standard of behaviour (Velasques 2012). The legality position for coaching would be that ethical praxis must comply with legitimate legislation or prescribed professional codes of conduct in order to be ethical (Rossouw and Van Vuuren 2010). The principle of legality can be problematic in the absence of legislation, codes or standards – what do you measure or compare against? Legality can also be problematic to the extent that people could assume that what is not explicitly prohibited is deemed to be allowed.

2.2 Consequentialism

Consequentialism is the view that actions derive their moral value and worth solely from their outcomes or consequences; in layman's terms, it is often referred to as 'the end justifies the means'. In terms of consequentialism, coaching would be assumed to be ethical as long as the outcomes of the coaching practices is advantageous to the coachee and his or her organization, notwithstanding how it is achieved (Rossouw and Van Vuuren 2010). There are inherent ethical risks in consequentialism. History has shown that actions based on consequential motivations often resulted in devastating impacts on those who are affected by the process, rather the outcome. Another problem with consequentialism is that even with the best intentions, one very rarely has control over the final outcomes of a decision and even with the best intentions, unforeseen negative outcomes may realise.

2.3 Deontology

Deontology, or the science of moral duty, stands opposite to consequentialism. According to deontology, it is not only good consequences or outcomes of actions that make them ethical, but the nature of the actions themselves (Velasquez 2012). Immanuel Kant (1724–1804), the father of deontology, argued that behaviour is not simply a means to an end, but also an end in itself and one cannot achieve a moral consequence through immoral actions (Rossouw and Van Vuuren 2010). A person has a moral duty to always act morally, no matter what the outcome. Applied to coaching, deontology broadly means that all coaching practices must be appropriate and acceptable, notwithstanding whether outcomes are positive. Most ethical issues in coaching arise under the principle of deontology (Passmore 2009). Deontology is notoriously vague in its prescriptions and open for interpretation as to what is the right thing to do in different situations.

2.4 Rights

The principle of rights is based on the widely accepted view that all people have certain fundamental and equitable rights, with which no person or institution may interfere (Velasquez 2012). There is no hierarchy of rights, all rights are viewed as equal and should be respected unless there are good moral reasons for violating them. The Universal Declaration of Human Rights (UDHR), which has the status of international law, stipulates 30 pertinent rights ('articles') that form the most authoritative reference in the discourse on human rights (United Nations 2012). Behaviour, actions and decisions may not infringe on these rights in order to be regarded as morally good and ethical (United Nations 2012). Not all of the human rights stipulated in the UDHR relate specifically to coaching psychology or praxis (e.g. the right to a fair trial, the right to own property, the right to rest and leisure, etc.). Five human rights specifically relate to the realm of coaching; these are:

1. Basic human rights apply to every person, irrespective of origin, race, colour, sex and sexual orientation, language, religion and political opinion, without distinction of any kind (article 2);
2. The right not to be subjected to arbitrary interference with one's privacy, nor to attacks upon one's honour or reputation (article 12);
3. The right to freedom of thought, conscience and religion (article 18);
4. The right to freedom of opinion and expression without interference (article 19); and
5. The right to participate freely in the cultural life of one's community (article 27).

Applying the principle of human rights to assess ethical issues can become problematic when one specific right stands in contradiction with another right. One person's right to freedom of expression may conflict with another person's right to honour and reputation.

3 Design and Methodology

In this study, a philosophical analysis (Stanford University 2014) was conducted through a meta-theoretical literature review in order to identify a structure from which to analyse and describe potential ethical risks in coaching psychology, theory and praxis. The analyses include aspects of normative analysis, offering the researcher the opportunity to include personal views and judgements. Data was interpreted from the subjective perspective of the researcher who wrote from a place of tension; understanding the complexities of coaching from personal experience, but also the need for a stronger focus on ethical coaching.

The integration of ethics with coaching psychology sits at the intersection of foundational sciences, such as philosophy, sociology and psychology, with applied sciences (e.g. sports science, organizational behaviour and management) (Bachkirova 2012; Grant 2006). In developing a scientific theoretical contribution to the discourse on ethics in coaching, I considered contributions from all these fields and applied different lenses to develop synergy and integration (Okhuysen and Bonardi 2011). Data was gathered through an extensive literature search on the internet (e.g. coaching surveys and coaching associations and their codes of ethics) as well as a comprehensive set of scholarly databases.[1] Through various search words and phrases, relevant data was obtained and analysed. As the field of coaching is developing and growing rapidly, specific effort was made to attain the most recent information, data and views from the coaching industry and coaching psychology.

In the discussion of the results, the data was firstly analysed based on the characteristics of coaching psychology and the coaching industry. From this analysis, a structure of ethical themes was identified that seem to best represent the data, followed by a discussion on the possible ethical issues related to every theme. The idea behind the analysis was to extract themes whose relevance is driven by probability rather than absolute accuracy. This implies that the researcher asks the question 'what is hypothetically likely to happen?' rather than 'what is always happening?' No study can provide an exhaustive explanation of all ethical issues in coaching and so the aim was to explicate some of the more probable issues that contribute to, or distract from ethical coaching and coaching psychology. Practical application suggestions as well as suggestions for future research are presented in the final section of this chapter.

4 Findings

4.1 Characteristics of Coaching Psychology, Theory and Praxis

Coaching happens within a specific context that defines the characteristics of coaching praxis and the coaching relationship. One such characteristic is the relationship between a person leading the coaching event (the coach), and the person onto whom

[1] ABI/INFORM, APA, databases, EBSCOhost, Emerald, JSTOR, ProQuest, SAGE and Science Direct.

the coaching endeavour is focused (the coachee). In order to assess and abstract ethical themes in coaching psychology and praxis, the first step was to analyse relevant characteristics of coaching psychology and the coaching industry through assessment of available coaching surveys, research studies and other available information. This analysis is presented in the following paragraphs.

The value of research contributing scientifically to coaching psychology is the subject of much criticism. De Haan and Duckworth (2013), Passmore (2010), Passmore and Fillery-Travis (2011), and Yi-Ling and McDowall (2014) argue that executive coaching research generally is theoretical, anecdotal, mainly based on case studies and focused on outcomes of coaching praxis. Scientific research on cross-cultural coaching is somewhat limited. However, there are some attempts to rectify this situation, such as the 'International Journal of Evidence Based Coaching and Mentoring' that published a special issue on culture in coaching in 2013. Nevertheless, available coaching research was predominantly done with sample populations from Western cultures, with resulting coaching knowledge and practices mainly developed in the Western world (Geber and Keane 2013). The question therefore remains as to how much of these methodologies can be applied in the context of other cultures (Milner et al. 2013). No study could be found that specifically examine ethical issues in cross-cultural coaching.

In global surveys, coaches consistently attest to the fantastic positive impact of coaching on executive effectiveness and organizational performance (Corbett and Kennedy 2014). However, scientific methodologies to support these claims have been criticised as lacking. Most studies that assess coaching outcomes are based on subjective self-rating survey reports of coachees' personal satisfactions, rather than tracking actual behavioural changes or performance improvement and assessment of outcome effectiveness against control groups (De Haan and Duckworth 2013; Passmore and Fillery-Travis 2011; Tooth et al. 2013; Yi-Ling and McDowall 2014). Some researchers attempt to measure return of investment (ROI) from coaching, with one study infamously reporting a 570% ROI (Lawrence and Whyte 2014). Few individuals or organizations find these results credible as the causal link between coaching and financial outcomes remains at best hypothetical (Grant 2012; Lawrence and Whyte 2014). As coaching progressively became more developmental rather than remedial, the ambiguity is increasing about what is thought to constitute good coaching outcomes (De Haan and Duckworth 2013).

Executive coaching is a cross-disciplinary practice, which is not owned by one particular professional group (Yi-Ling and McDowall 2014). Coaches come from diverse backgrounds, often without any coaching training, accreditation or membership to any coaching association (Hannafey and Vitulano 2013). As far as could be established, no country has legislative regulations that define and regulate the profession or accreditation of coaches (ICF 2015; SIOPSA 2014). Some coaches are certified by self-appointed bodies, but most are not (ICF 2013; Kauffmann and Coutu 2009). Although some of these bodies provide decent training and guidance, there is no regulation over the large number of organisations that do training or certification of coaches (Underhill et al. 2013). There clearly is confusion around the training, certification and accreditation of coaches.

Almost every coaching organisation publishes a code of ethics for its members (Hannafey and Vitulano 2013; SIOPSA 2014; Standards Australia 2011). Most codes are well written and cover some important ethical issues relevant to coaching praxis (Standards Australia 2011). However, although some codes give fair attention to cultural issues (SIOPSA 2014) others give little or no attention to cross cultural issues. The only reference to cultural issues in the International Coach Federation's code of ethics is about setting culturally sensitive boundaries for physical contact (ICF 2014). The requirement to identify and comply with ethical principles as set out in a code of ethics is a fundamental component of any professional practice (Standards Australia 2011). The purpose of a code of ethics is to define and regulate acceptable behaviours relating to that profession and to establish a framework for professional behaviour and responsibilities (Rostron 2014). However, without accreditation obligations for coaches, codes are mostly informal and informational, rather than enforceable (ICF 2015; Standards Australia 2011).

Coaches tend to be well educated. Global surveys show that almost all coaches have a university degree, with a majority having masters degrees and some having doctoral degrees (Standards Australia 2011; Underhill et al. 2013). However, less than 10 % of the higher degrees relate to coaching; the vast majority of coaches only have some form of certificate as coaching qualification. Coaches mainly come from consulting and management backgrounds, with only around 15 % coming from careers in the behavioural sciences (Kauffmann and Coutu 2009; Newnham-Kanas et al. 2012; Pennington 2009). Practicing coaches tend not to rank a background in behavioural sciences such as psychology as an important coaching requirement, whereas criteria such as coaching experience, clear methodology and ability to measure outcomes are ranked much higher (Kauffmann and Coutu 2009; Marsden et al. 2010; Newnham-Kanas et al. 2012). The real situation is probably even more extreme as many coaching practitioners do not belong to coaching associations and were thus not included in these surveys' sample populations. As far as could be established, cross-cultural sensitivity and knowledge or cross-cultural coaching competencies were not once mentioned as requirements in the surveys. Cross-cultural competency does not appear to be on the radar of coaching practitioners.

It is not surprising that there is an on-going debate between psychologists and non-psychologists about whether coaching belongs to the field of psychology. Some argue that the diverse backgrounds of coaches represent a strength as it draws on a wide range of experience and methodological approaches (Lowman 2005; Spence et al. 2006). Others contend that a lack of training in mental health issues pose a risk as coaches are likely to encounter clients with various degrees of psychological conditions (Passmore 2009). There is the risk that a coach takes on a client to work on a simple performance issue, but clinical anxiety or depression may be at the root of this symptom. This risk seems to be a reality as between 25 % and 50 % of executives engaging in coaching interventions are estimated to suffer from clinically significant levels of anxiety, stress or depression (Green et al. 2005; Kauffmann and Coutu 2009; Spence et al. 2006). Some executives may also enter coaching as a more socially acceptable form of therapy (Spence and Grant 2005). Coaching cannot be anything else than psychology as its focus is behaviour alternating, developmental and guiding coachees towards personal insights. Specifically, the ability to identify and work with unconscious patterns of thinking and behaviour has been highlighted as a specific important coaching ability, especially with regards to coaching in a diverse and multi-cultural context (Cilliers and Terblanche 2010; Kilburg 2004; Motsoaledi and Cilliers 2012). Yet, Liston-Smith (2009) found that most coaches felt inadequately prepared to identify and work with unconscious processes.

Coaching psychology is positioned in the overlap between counselling psychology, clinical psychology, organisational psychology and business consulting (Fontaine and Schmidt 2009; Grant 2006). Several conceptual boundaries originate from this complex junction. One of the most important boundaries is that between coaching with counselling (Fontaine and Schmidt 2009; McKenna and Davis 2009). Whereas clinical and counselling psychologists work with a client who has mental or emotional problems, coaching psychologists per definition assume to work with mentally healthy clients (Grant 2006). Codes of ethics generally call on coaches to respect the boundary between coaching and counselling, but this boundary is somewhat conceptual and vague, with much fluidity in traversing this border (Campone 2014; ICF 2014).

There are also different types of coaching, each with different goals and each requiring a different approach and skillset (American Management Association 2008; Passmore 2010; Sperry 2008; Standards Australia 2011; Stern 2004). Cross cultural coaching is however generally not seen as a specific type of coaching endeavour. There is also a difference in cross-cultural coaching and intercultural coaching (Milner et al. 2013). While intercultural coaching focuses on assisting people to develop intercultural skills and capabilities (e.g. for an international assignment), cross-culture coaching is a situational complexity where there are cultural differences between the coach and coachee. At the advent of the coaching endeavour, coaches are supposed to contract for a specific type of coaching as well as the time boundary. Notwithstanding, Kauffmann and Coutu (2009) found that 94 % of coaches acknowledged that coaching goals and timelines generally shift over the course of engagements. Also, as the coach becomes trusted, it is not uncommon for the coach to become also an adviser on other aspects of the business than what was contracted for (Kaufmann and Coutu 2009).

Untrained individuals who call themselves coaches were viewed in a global survey as a primary risk to coaching (ICF 2013). Most coach training programmes tend to be short commercial courses, presented by self-appointed training organisations, based on in-house models of coaching, with little theoretical grounding in coaching psychology (ICF 2013). Nevertheless, a number of credible professional bodies are looking at substantive training and certification of coaches, with several universities already offering high quality postgraduate programmes in coaching (ICF 2015; SIOPSA 2014; University of Stellenbosch 2015; Wits Business School 2015). As far as could be established, cross-cultural aspects of coaching appear not to receive much attention, if any at all, in many of the coach training programmes on offer.

Increasing cultural diversification of countries and in the workplace is a worldwide phenomenon. As the workforce becomes more diverse, coaches face more challenges in dealing with diversity issues, including cross-cultural differences (Milner et al. 2013; Wilson 2013). It is becoming increasingly important for coaches to understand the effect of, and be able to work with cultural differences (Coultas et al. 2011; Wilson 2013). Coaches need for instance to appreciate that individuals from all cultures do not respond similarly to the same kind of feedback. Cultures high on individualism tend to prefer individual feedback, while those higher on collectivism are more comfortable with group feedback (Coultas et al. 2011). Concerns about keeping face, uncertainty avoidance, and collectivism often manifest as aversion to negative feedback. Participative goals are more effective in low power distance cultures; whereas high levels of power distance may require more directive goals from coaches (Coultas et al. 2011). Knowledge about cultural and indigenous specifics and differences, as well as sensitivity and tolerance towards these differences are becoming essential coaching competencies (Geber and Keane 2013).

Executive coaches are generally not contracted directly by the coachees, but by their employing organisations; either HR (most common) or the manager of the coachee (Corbett and Kennedy 2014; Gavett 2013). As result, coaching psychologists must deal not only with the coachee, but also work with complex dynamics of multiple dyadic relationships within the paying organisation (Hannafey and Vitulano 2013; Kuhn 2012; Pomerantz 2011). The main issues from the multiple dyadic relationships relate to confidentiality and conflicts of interest (Hannafey and Vitulano 2013). Given that the organization is paying, providing opportunities for the organization to set the agenda and get feedback on the outcome is a natural and necessary requirement (Passmore 2009). Although maintaining confidentiality is not simple, it is encouraging that surveys found that most coaches take confidentiality seriously (ICF 2013).

Coaches generally know that they should facilitate coachees to become self-reliant, but coachees routinely become dependent on their coaches. Kauffmann and Coutu (2009) found that 40 % of coaches had clients who became dependent upon them. They argue that the 60 % who think their clients do not become dependent is unrealistic as coaches have an economic incentive to exploit dependency of coachees on coaches. Coaches can also become dependent on their coachees. Apart from economic dependence, the desire of a coach to help can be driven from personal emotional needs to fulfil some sort of rescuer fantasy (Kets de Vries 2014).

From this analysis of the characteristics of coaching praxis and coaching psychology, the following eight themes have been identified:

1. The scientific foundation for coaching psychology and coaching praxis;
2. Confusion in the regulatory environment of coaching;
3. The requirement for coaching proficiency;
4. Normative issues relating to coaching across-cultures and other diversities;
5. Staying within respective coaching boundaries;
6. Making appropriate diagnoses;
7. Maintaining confidentiality and abstaining from conflicts of interests; and
8. Avoidance of dependency.

In the next sections, these themes are further analysed and discussed with respect to potential ethical pitfalls.

Coaching Psychology as a Scientific Foundation for Coaching Praxis

Coaching psychology is per definition an applied science that focuses on the application of behavioural science and psychological methods to develop managers (SIOPSA 2014; Whybrow 2008). It thus needs to adhere to scientific rigour, based on facts proven through rigorous scientific research, which provide validated theories and inform the coaching community of what principles and practices to consider as valid and acceptable.

As an applied science, coaching psychology requires strong support from scientific research to provide a theoretical foundation for coaching praxis to be considered ethical from a deontological perspective (Duffy and Passmore 2010; Passmore and Fillery-Travis 2011). If coaching practices are not based on scientific foundations, practitioners can apply any hocus-pocus and hope for a good outcome. From a deontological perspective, we need assurance that the practices in coaching interventions adhere to scientific validated practices and not just focus on the outcomes of coaching. After all, it was demonstrated that the claims of good outcomes from all coaching events could be scientifically questioned. Although there are some exciting research on cross-cultural issues in coaching (Coultas et al. 2011; Geber and Keane 2013; Milner et al. 2013; Plaister-Ten 2013; Wilson 2013), this focus of coaching research is still in its infancy and include little or no focus on ethical issues in cross-cultural coaching.

Coaching psychologists have an ethical duty to establish and strengthen the scientific foundation of coaching theory and praxis to ensure that ethically and scientifically defendable practices are consistently applied by coaches, rather than hanging on to a fantasy that any coaching always yields outcomes. There is a specific need to build the scientific foundation of cross-cultural coaching theory and praxis. The strong consumerist trend in the coaching industry presents the risk that scientific coaching psychology will be consumed by coaching praxis, masquerading as a psychological science and profitably selling this falsity to uninformed clients. This probability presents a deontological risk to both coaching psychology and coaching praxis.

Confusion in the Regulatory Environment of Coaching

With no entry barriers and accreditation regulation, it is virtually impossible to hold coaching practitioners accountable to the codes of ethics (Allan and Law 2009). There are a myriad of coaching organizations that publish codes of ethics. But because many coaches are not members of coaching bodies, it is up to each individual practitioner to uphold their own individual ethical standards (Rostron 2014). The absence of governing bodies presents deontological concerns as aggrieved clients have no remedial mechanisms from independent bodies to which they can refer complaints (Duffy and Passmore 2010). While contractual termination may resolve the issue of a specific unethical coaching incident, it is retrospective, reactive and fails to protect the wider public from misconduct, and the coaching profession from reputational damage (Passmore 2009).

With this confusion and situation in the regulatory environment of coaching, it is virtually impossible to comment on the legality in coaching praxis because there is none. It is apparent that ethical risks are significant in coaching psychology from both deontological and legality perspectives.

The Requirement for Coaching Proficiency

The absence of sufficient psychological knowledge of many coaching practitioners represents an ethical liability to coaching psychology. Coaching is inextricably tied to psychological approaches such as system psychodynamics, person-centeredness and cognitive interventions (Harakas 2013). Coaching is tailored to every individual and is therefore more psychological in nature than conventional training and development (De Haan and Duckworth 2013). From a deontological perspective, it appears to be essential that a coach has sufficient psychological knowledge in order to provide assurance that what happens in the coaching session is psychologically sound.

Per definition, coaching psychology is not about curing mental health problems (Grant 2011; SIOPSA 2014). However, a number of studies demonstrate that the senior managers being coached are not necessarily mentally robust (Green et al. 2005; Kauffmann and Coutu 2009; Spence et al. 2006). Coaches without psychological knowledge may not be able to recognise the coachees' mental health needs and may cause harm to them (Yi-Ling and McDowall 2014). For instance, a coach may cause harm by encouraging a clinically depressed client to set goals which are beyond his or her emotional capacity at the time (Campone 2014; Kilburg and Levinson 2008). From a deontological perspective is it concerning that so many practitioners do not have deeper psychological knowledge – even if just an understanding of when to refer clients to professional therapists for help (Campone 2014; Newnham-Kanas et al. 2012).

Coaching in the increasingly culturally diverse environments present new and unique proficiency challenges with several deontological implications (Coultas et al. 2011; Milner et al. 2013). Cross cultural coaching demands new competencies from coaches such as cultural sensitivity, appreciation for different cultural values, ability to adapt the coaching process to be relevant to the particular context, and proficiency to work on an equitable basis with a coachee from another culture. A specific difficulty facing coaching proficiency is the number of different cultures that may present for coaching. Doing coaching in only one organization, I've had to work in coaching relationships with individuals from South Africa (with our own rainbow of cultures), rest of Africa, Europe, the Far East, Middle East, and the Americas. Although many coaches with international experience may have the necessary vocabulary to discuss cross-cultural issues, this doesn't necessarily mean they are cross-culturally competent (Wilson 2013). It still may be difficult for them to ethically coach individuals from vastly different cultures.

The complexity of coaching and the number of permutations of what can happen during coaching events put significant proficiency demands on any coach and as a result create deontological risks. Coaches with a psychological background have a wealth of knowledge and insight into human behaviour and behavioural dynamics that cannot simply be gathered from business experience, an MBA or a short coaching course (McKenna and Davis 2009; Passmore 2009; Whybrow 2008). The coaching event and relationship is per definition a behavioural intervention and it is therefore essential that anyone who provides coaching must have substantive psychological training in order to have sufficient background and insight in psychological theories and applications. It is an ethical imperative that anyone serious to pursue an ethical career in coaching should obtain substantive behavioural or psychological training from an academic institution or coaching association that is widely recognised as credible and accountable (ICF 2015; USB 2015). It is equally important that these training programmes sufficiently address cross-cultural coaching issues and its ethical risks.

Normative Issues Relating to Coaching Across-Cultures and Other Diversities

Coaching across cultures and other diversities presents normative issues. These normative aspects present ethical risks, relating to deontological and human rights risks. Some of these risks include imposing value judgments onto others and not dealing objectively with them. It is a basic human right of every individual to be treated non-judgementally and without discrimination on their basic human differences and diversities such as ethnicity, religion, culture and sexual orientation (United Nations 2012). It is nearly impossible to be an effective coach in the modern cross-cultural environment without awareness of, and tolerance and appreciation for cultural differences and other diversities. However, it is unrealistic to expect from coaches to have a comprehensive knowledge of what is regarded as being right and appropriate in every culture and to be sensitive to every cultural nuance.

Coaches need a deep appreciation of cultural differences and how it might impact on the coaching process (Geber and Keane 2013; Wilson 2013). Coaching in culturally diverse environments requires sensitivity to recognise and acknowledge differences in cultural values and flexibility to adapt coaching techniques to be appropriate to such cultural values (Coultas et al. 2011; Milner et al. 2013). A general knowledge of cultural theories and typologies can provide valuable insights to the coach, but can also lead to a tendency to evaluate cultural values and dimensions too simplistically (Geber and Keane 2013; Plaister-Ten 2013). Culture sensitivity entails not succumbing to the ecological fallacy that individuals from a given country or culture will behave in a particular way (Coultas et al. 2011). Although cultural knowledge is useful, it would be inappropriate to project cultural knowledge into the coaching mix (Plaister-Ten 2013). Both deontology and human rights require that clients should always be seen and treated as individuals with their own personalities and differences, not as subjects from a specific culture (Milner et al. 2013).

Research has found that coaches are not necessarily ready for coaching across cultures (Wilson 2013). Too often Western bias is transported onto coaching praxis through coaching methods, practices and expectations (Geber and Keane 2013; Milner et al. 2013; Plaister-Ten 2013). It is for example not always appreciated that clients from religious dominant cultures may not have the same level of individual autonomy as individuals where state religion is side-lined (Plaister-Ten 2013). Different cultural values inform the meaning of constructs such as responsibility or accountability differently, and not all cultures appreciate the same level of choice by their members. To coach ethically across cultures, a coach must discard preconceived ways of thinking so as not to project their own beliefs and values onto the coachee.

As human beings, coaches often have great difficulty in separating their personal experiences, morals and values from what they are recommending to their clients (Kilburg and Levinson 2008). Coaches are often confronted by situations in client organizations or the behaviours of individual leaders that can severely challenge their own values or beliefs. There are plenty of examples, ranging from value judgments about sexual orientation, to religious extremism, racial or ethnic prejudice, to traditional views on gender roles, etc. It is tempting to rush to harsh judgment when executive or organizational actions or behaviours conflict with the values or convictions of the coach. But trust and confidentiality in the coaching relationship demand that coaches keep their personal agenda and value judgements to the minimum level that is humanly possible (Kaufmann and Coutu 2009). Coaches must be aware of their own prejudices and work to become acutely sensitive to the inherent moral complexities that presents itself unconsciously when working with their clients (Kilburg and Levinson 2008). Sensitivity to how one is influenced by such differences and tolerance to accept others' different perspective and put your own aside during the coaching event are indications of the professional maturity required from ethical coaches. Whilst being honest and authentic, coaches should be objective and non-judgemental, with real enthusiasm, commitment and motivation to help, notwithstanding the cultural background and values of the client (Yi-Lang and McDowall 2014).

Not only should cultural sensitivity improve coaching outcomes, but it is an ethical requirement from both the deontological and rights perspectives. Cultural sensitivity demonstrates respect for individuals and their cultures and thus also respect for their basic human rights (Coultas et al. 2011). Coachee's basic rights must always be respected, without interference or attacks on their honour or reputation, irrespective of cultural background and origin, race, colour, sex and sexual orientation, language or religion, without distinction of any kind (United Nations 2012). Individuals have the right to freedom of thought, conscience and religion, freedom of opinion and expression, the right to their own cultural life and their right to personal privacy (United Nations 2012). It is imperative from both deontology and human rights, that every coach show respect towards all individuals and organizations and their inherent diversity characteristics and cultures, establish and maintain fair, reasonable and equitable standards of engagement and avoid any conduct that could amount to harassment, discrimination or inappropriate relationships (SIOPSA 2014).

Deontological sound coaching is about unconditionally accepting different or opposing value systems, treating coachees equally, with dignity and respect notwithstanding what they do or whatever might be uncovered. To coach with integrity, means a coach will rather decline a coaching assignment where he or she cannot respect the diversities within the coachee, or to cease the relationship as soon as this irreconcilability becomes apparent (Rostron 2014).

Staying Within Respective Coaching Boundaries

As the field of executive coaching develops, the lines between what coaches should or shouldn't do become increasingly blurred (Pomerantz 2011). A qualified psychologist may find it necessary to deal with psychological or behavioural issues during a coaching session in order to progress with the coaching. On the other hand, central to the definition of coaching is the assumption of an absence of serious mental health problems in the client (Grant 2006; SIOPSA 2014). The majority of coachees seek developmental support and interventions based on a clinical psychological model will thus not be inappropriate (Grant 2006). This raises the question whether a coaching psychologist can ethically cross the boundary to counsel mental illness, whilst being contracted to providing coaching services to that person (Grant 2011)? Then again, many of the techniques that coaches use inside the coaching session closely relate to counselling activities (Pomerantz 2011). The boundary between coaching and counselling is ambiguous and its navigation fluid. From a psychologist as coach perspective, the ethical issue is much clearer and less of an ethical risk – the psychologist-coach will probably continue practising ethically as a psychologist is expected to do. However, the coach without psychological training who is expected to do coaching and to apply psychological principles ethically presents an ethical challenge and risk. It is therefore not a question whether or not a coach must have psychological training; proficiency in psychology and behaviour sciences is de facto a requirement in coaching. The dire need for a strong basis in psychology and behavioural sciences to underpin coaching praxis cannot be overemphasized.

It goes without saying that physical, economical and business boundaries should always be respected, for example not becoming sexually, financially or emotionally involved with coachees (Standards Australia 2011; Worldwide Association of Business Coaches 2007). In cross-cultural coaching, physical contact can be seen to be inappropriate even from simple actions that are generally accepted as normal and acceptable, even required. For instance, according to Western social protocol it would be generally considered to be normal for a male coach to greet a female coachee with a handshake. However, some Middle Eastern cultures do not even allow this kind of physical contact and would regard it as deontologically unethical.

Deontology demands that coaches agree upfront the type of coaching and goals that he or she contracts to do, understand the limits of this type coaching, stay within its conceptual boundaries, stay within the boundaries of their capabilities, have the knowledge to recognize when any type of referral is necessary, and have the courage to do so (ICF 2014; Pomerantz 2011; Underhill et al. 2013).

Making Appropriate Diagnoses

The ability to accurately diagnose the root cause of personal, interpersonal and organisational problems is not only essential for effective coaching, but a moral obligation (Rees and Porter 2013). An incorrect diagnosis is likely to derail a coaching intervention and send it in a wrong direction, significantly reducing the effectiveness and neglecting important aspects. Incorrect or improper diagnosis of personal issues, e.g. personality characteristics or strengths and weaknesses of coachees, is likely to result in improper coaching interventions, confusion and even psychological harm to the individual.

Executives are likely to be unaware of the root causes related to some of the complex problems they experience. It is the role of the coach to see beyond obvious problems and help the executive to see the root cause and work with it. This requires the ability to work more deeply than using basic diagnostic tools such as 360° feedback. It also demands the ability to look into the seemingly irrational world of what is happening in the collective unconscious of the organizational system and identify and interpret unconscious patterns of behaviour in individuals, groups, and organizations (Cilliers and Terblanche 2010; Kilburg 2004; Motsoaledi and Cilliers 2012; Turner and Goodrich 2010).

Diagnostic ability presents specific challenges in cross-cultural coaching interventions (Geber and Keane 2013; Wilson 2013). Diagnostic abilities may be impaired by untested assumptions that all individuals from certain cultures will behave in particular ways (ecological fallacy) (Coultas et al. 2011; Plaister-Ten 2013). For instance, a coachee may be shy or timid due to personality characteristics, not necessarily because of being from a more feminine or high power distance culture (Milner et al. 2013; Plaister-Ten 2013).

Deontological risks originate from making inaccurate or inappropriate diagnoses and pursuing undue or misplaced assessments. Coaches must understand the practical impacts of making incorrect or inappropriate diagnoses and the deontological risks that this present, not only for the coaching event, but also to the client. Coaching psychology has an ethical responsibility towards coachees from all cultures to ensure that the ability to make accurate diagnostic assessments is high on the radar in the coaching industry and in the training of coaches.

Maintaining Confidentiality and Abstaining from Conflicts of Interests

Coaches normally proclaim that sessions are confidential. This implies that all information shared is confidential. However, in several circumstances a coach may not only have an ethical right to break confidentiality, but also legal obligation to do so; for instance, when there is serious risk of harm to either the client or others, or serious illegality (Grant 2011; Pomerantz 2011). However, the decision to breach confidentiality is extremely subjective. For instance, how much evidence does the coach need to believe serious harm is likely to result? And when does something become serious? Should alcoholism be disclosed if the organization is not aware of it? Legally, the coach may be obliged to breach confidentiality and report the illegal activities, such as fraud (Pomerantz 2011). But what about 'petty fraud', e.g. does taking a pen home represent fraud that should be reported? If not, what is the cut-off point?

Pragmatic guidance to deal ethically with confidentiality, is that coaching psychologists generally do not disclose confidential information unless with explicit consent from the coachee. In cases where there is a legal obligation to divulge confidential information, or where the coachee is involved in illegal action, the coachee should be given the first opportunity to appropriately disclose the information (SIOPSA 2014). The principle is that information shared in coaching is owned by the coachee, and unless superseded by a higher ethical principle, the coachee should be empowered to manage that information (Standards Australia 2011).

The multiple dyadic relationships are at the basis of many deontological problems. Potential conflicts of interests originate automatically from dealing with multiple clients within the organizational hierarchy. One of the main conflict of interest issues is the question of who to honour as the real client? From psychological perspective and related ethical code one can argue that the true client is the person in front of the coach. However, from a non-psychological and pure business perspective, the client is the person who pays for the service and therefore the ethical risk and challenge. Although the primary obligation of the coach must always be to the coachee, the coach has an obligation to also serve the interest of the paying client (Hannafey and Vitulano 2013). The organization paying for the coaching has some right to know about progress. Ethical problems arise when tension exists between the executive and the organization as the coaching may then serve either the needs of the individual or the organization, but are unlikely to serve the needs of both. Coaching an executive towards leaving the organization may be in a coachee's best interest, but not necessarily for the organization (Standards Australia 2011). There is still much work to be done to provide ethical guidance as to who is the real client of executive coaching, the organisation or the client (Grant 2011).

Risks relating to confidentiality are de facto part of multiple dyadic relationships. Intimate knowledge of business issues will be a challenge to the coach to keep information appropriately confidential across hierarchical levels. Coaching across hierarchical levels is likely to result in conflict of interest issues between the coach's relationships with the different coachees. Although confidentiality and conflicts of interest issues and expectations on how to deal with it are to be clarified and agreed upfront (ICF 2014), a coach cannot foresee all the intricate issues and nuances. The proverbial devil lies in the detail (Kaufmann and Coutu 2009).

Maintaining confidentiality is a deontological and human rights requirement (the right to privacy). Coaches are to make specific effort to ensure individual clients and client organizations understand the problematic issues of confidentiality and its ethical implications (Pomerantz 2011).

Avoidance of Dependency

Effective coaching relationships require some level of co-dependency. A good indication of dependency is when the coachee is having conversations with the coach that he or she ought to be having with other colleagues within the organization (Kauffmann and Coutu 2009). When this happens, the coaching event is not serving the coachee and is even likely not to yield a good outcome and should thus be terminated. However, it was demonstrated that a large portion of coachees become overly dependent on their coaches, but that most coaches find it difficult to adhere to the agreed duration of the coaching endeavour, or to terminate coaching when needed. Moreover, selfish needs can influence coaches to create excessive dependencies in coachees (Kets de Vries 2014). Coaches should be sensitive to their own rescuer needs and have the courage to terminate the coaching endeavour if it becomes apparent.

Termination of a coaching endeavour is not without tension, for many coaches this is a challenging step to take when faced with the financial loss of terminating an assignment (Standards Australia 2011). However, it is the right thing to do from both a deontological and a consequentialist perspective. A coach has a moral responsibility to terminate the contract when there is evidence that the coachee is becoming overly dependent on him or her, or the other way around (ICF 2014).

5 Discussion and Practical Application

Coaching ethically is much more complex than it might appear at first glance. Coaching psychology, theory and praxis can be fraught with ethical risks relating to diagnostics, proficiency, dependency, confidentiality, normative and boundary issues that can easily be missed. If these are overlooked, the coaching endeavour may not result in much good at best; or at worst, harm the individual or the organization.

A lack of entry barriers and more formal regulation leaves coaching praxis ethically vulnerable (Cavanagh and Lane 2012; De Haan and Duckworth 2013; Yi-Ling and McDowall 2014). This does not have to stall the coaching praxis from making ethical progress in the delivering of coaching services. All coaching psychologists and other coaching practitioners have an ethical duty to ensure that they have sufficient psychological understanding and cross-cultural sensitivity and awareness required by their practices. The science-practitioner model applies to coaches, e.g. specific division between the rigors of science and the application of scientific results (Nielsen 2008). The coach as practitioner need to achieve results through application of psychological science based rules and methods. As coaching psychology grows from an industry to a scientific discipline and profession, it is essential that coaching psychologists rely on rigorous scientific research to inform their own coaching practices, especially as it relates to cross-cultural coaching. As the body of knowledge of coaching psychology grows, coaching psychologists must take effort to become clearer about the ethical boundaries in cross-cultural coaching and how to honour them.

Relevant academic training is an ethical necessity for the development of proficient coaching psychologists and other practitioners and needs to be expanded to develop coaching psychology beyond coaching praxis. And then, coaching psychologists and practitioners have a moral obligation to ensure that they expose themselves sufficiently to such training so as to build their cross-cultural coaching competencies and abilities. It is crucial to increase coaches' capacity to identify and respond to the diverse ethical challenges in coaching practice. Consequently, we need to expand the scientific foundation of coaching psychology and develop more universally applicable methods that are free from a Western bias. Improved awareness and understanding of the ethical pitfalls and how to avoid them, especially as it relates to cross-cultural coaching, can lead to improved ethical approaches and eventually to a more ethical and thus sustainable coaching industry.

6 Implications for Future Research

Coaching psychology research needs to move beyond researching the goodness of coaching outcomes through self-reporting questionnaires. More research evidence is required to identify and prescribe practices that are scientifically valid to inform the practices applied by coaches during coaching sessions. Although some research is available on cross-cultural issues in coaching, much more research is called for to fully comprehend all aspects of cross-cultural coaching (Coultas et al. 2011). Future research should specifically examine ethical issues relating to cross-cultural coaching, a research focus that has received little attention so far.

Coaching psychology is now in need of rigorous debate, vigorous empirical tests, and the revision of theory and practice based on these findings (De Haan and Duckworth 2013; Yi-Ling and McDowall 2014). Research must be used to create and ensure a sufficient scientific database for coaching to in order to counter deontological ethical risks and address consequentialist doubts. Such research needs to be expanded to develop coaching psychology as a professional scientific field beyond current questionable coaching praxis.

References

Allan, J., & Law, H. (2009). Ethical navigation in coaching psychology – a socratic workshop. *The Coaching Psychologist, 5*(2), 110–114.

American Management Association. (2008). *Coaching: A global study of successful practices.* Retrieved from www.amanet.org

Bachkirova, T. (2012). Let us not throw out the individual baby with the non-systemic bath water. *International Coaching Psychology Review, 7*(1), 98–100.

Campone, F. (2014). At the border: Coaching a client with dissociative identity disorder. *International Journal of Evidence Based Coaching and Mentoring, 12*(1), 1–13.

Cavanagh, M., & Lane, D. (2012). Coaching psychology coming of age: The challenges we face in the messy world of complexity. *International Coaching Psychology Review, 7*(1), 75–90.

Cilliers, F., & Terblanche, L. (2010). The systems psychodynamic leadership coaching experiences of nursing managers. *Health SA Gesondheid, 15*(1), 1–9.

Corbett, K., & Kennedy, J. (2014). *Executive coaching survey '14: Evidence and interaction.* Retrieved from http://www.sherpacoaching.com/pdf%20files/2014%20Executive%20Coaching%20Survey%20-%20Public%20report.pdf

Coultas, C. W., Bedwell, W. L., Burke, C. S., & Salas, E. (2011). Values sensitive coaching: The DELTA approach to coaching culturally diverse executives. *Consulting Psychology Journal: Practice and Research, 63*(3), 149–161.

De Haan, E., & Duckworth, A. (2013). Signalling a new trend in executive coaching outcome research. *International Coaching Psychology Review, 8*(1), 6–19.

Duffy, M., & Passmore, J. (2010). Ethics in coaching: An ethical decision making framework for coaching psychologists. *International Coaching Psychology Review, 5*(2), 140–151.

Fontaine, D., & Schmidt, G. F. (2009). The practice of executive coaching requires practice: A clarification and challenge to our field. *Industrial and Organizational Psychology: Perspectives on Science and Practice, 2*(3), 277–279.

Gavett, G. (2013). What CEOs really want from coaching. Retrieved from https://hbr.org/2013/08/research-ceos-and-the-coaching/

Geber, H., & Keane, M. (2013). Extending the worldview of coaching research and practice in southern Africa: The concept of Ubuntu. *International Journal of Evidence Based Coaching and Mentoring, 11*(2), 8–18.

Grant, A. M. (2006). A personal perspective on professional coaching and the development of coaching psychology. *International Coaching Psychology Review, 1*(1), 12–22.

Grant, A. M. (2011). Developing an agenda for teaching coaching psychology. *International Coaching Psychology Review, 6*(1), 84–99.

Grant, A. M. (2012). ROI is a poor measure of coaching success: Towards a more holistic approach using a well-being and engagement framework. *Coaching: An International Journal of Theory, Research and Practice, 5*(2), 1–12.

Green, S., Oades, L. G., & Grant, A. M. (2005). Theory, research and practice from the behavioural sciences. An evaluation of a life-coaching group programme: Initial findings from a waitlisted control study. In M. Cavanagh, A. M. Grant, & T. Kemp (Eds.), *Evidence-based coaching* (Vol. 1, pp. 127–142). Queensland: Australian Academic Press.

Hannafey, F. T., & Vitulano, L. A. (2013). Ethics and executive coaching: An agency theory approach. *Journal of Business Ethics, 115*(3), 599–603.

Harakas, P. (2013). Resistance, motivational interviewing, and executive coaching. *Consulting Psychology Journal: Practice and Research, 65*(2), 108–127.

International Coaching Federation. (2013). 2013 organizational coaching study. Retrieved from http://coachfederation.org/orgstudy

International Coaching Federation. (2014). Code of ethics. Retrieved from http://www.coachfederation.org/ethics/

International Coaching Federation. (2015). International coach federation. Retrieved from http://www.coachfederation.org

Kauffmann, C., & Coutu, D. (2009). The realities of executive coaching. *Harvard Business Review*, (Research Report), 1–32.
Kets de Vries, M. (2014). Mentor or martyr? Beware the rescuer trap. *Human Capital Review, 7*(3). Retrieved from Human Capital Review:http://www.humancapitalreview.org/content/default/asp?Article_ID=1348/
Kilburg, R. R. (2004). When shadows fall: Using psychodynamic approaches in executive coaching. *Consulting Psychology Journal: Practice and Research, 56*(4), 246.
Kilburg, R. R., & Levinson, H. (2008). Executive dilemmas: Coaching and the professional perspectives of Harry Levinson. *Consulting Psychology Journal: Practice and Research, 60*(1), 7–32.
Kuhn, L. (2012). Epistemological reflections on the complexity sciences and how they may inform coaching psychology. *International Coaching Psychology Review, 7*(1), 114–118.
Larcker, D. F., Miles, F., Tayan, B., & Gutman, M. E. (2013). *2013 executive coaching survey.* Retrieved from http://www.gsb.stanford.edu/sites/gsb/files/publication-pdf/cgri-survey-2013-executive-coaching.pdf
Lawrence, P., & Whyte, A. (2014). Return on investment in executive coaching: A practical model. *Coaching: An International Journal of Theory, Research and Practice, 7*(1), 4–17.
Liston-Smith, J. (2009). Highlighting the psychology in coaching. *The Coaching Psychologist, 5*(1), 45–52.
Lowman, R. L. (2005). Executive coaching: The road to Dodoville needs paving with more than good assumptions. *Consulting Psychology Journal: Practice and Research, 57*(1), 90–96.
Marsden, H., Humphrey, S., Stopford, J., & Houlder, D. (2010). Balancing business empathy and psychology in coaching practice. *The Coaching Psychologist, 6*(1), 16–23.
McKenna, D. D., & Davis, S. L. (2009). Hidden in plain sight: The active ingredients of executive coaching. *Industrial and Organizational Psychology: Perspectives on Science and Practice, 2*(3), 244–260.
Milner, J., Ostmeier, E. O., & Franke, R. (2013). Critical incidents in cross-cultural coaching: The view from German coaches. *International Journal of Evidence Based Coaching and Mentoring, 11*(2), 19–32.
Motsoaledi, L., & Cilliers, F. (2012). Executive coaching in diversity from the systems psychodynamic perspective. *South African Journal of Industrial Psychology, 38*(2), 1–11.
Newnham-Kanas, C., Morrow, D., & Irwin, J. D. (2012). Certified professional co-active coaches: Why they enjoy coaching. *International Journal of Evidence Based Coaching and Mentoring, 10*(1), 48–56.
Nielsen, K. (2008). On learning psychotherapy from clients. *Nordic Psychology, 60*(3), 163–182.
Okhuysen, G., & Bonardi, J. P. (2011). The challenges of building theory by combining lenses. *Academy of Management Review, 36*(1), 6–11.
Passmore, J. (2009). Coaching ethics: Making ethical decisions – Novices and experts. *The Coaching Psychologist, 5*(1), 6–10.
Passmore, J. (2010). A grounded theory study of the coachee experience: The implications for training and practice in coaching psychology. *International Coaching Psychology Review, 5*(1), 48–62.
Passmore, J., & Fillery-Travis, A. (2011). A critical review of executive coaching research: A decade of progress and what's to come. *Coaching: An International Journal of Theory, Research and Practice, 4*(2), 70–88.
Pennington, W. (2009). *Executive coaching world: A global perspective.* Retrieved from http://executivecoachingworld.com/home.htm
Plaister-Ten, J. (2013). Raising culturally-derived awareness and building culturally-appropriate responsibility: The development of the cross-cultural kaleidoscope. *International Journal of Evidence Based Coaching and Mentoring, 11*(2), 53–69.
Pomerantz, S. (2011). *Ethics in coaching, contracting and confidentiality: Drawing lines in the sand.* Retrieved from http://libraryofprofessionalcoaching.com/concepts/ethics/ethics-in-coaching-contracting-and-confidentiality-drawing-lines-in-the-sand/
Rees, W. D., & Porter, C. (2013). The development of diagnostic skills by management coaching. *International Coaching Psychology Review, 8*(2), 80–88.
Rossouw, G., & Van Vuuren, L. (2010). *Business ethics* (4th ed.). Johannesburg: Oxford University Press.

Rostron, S. S. (2014). *Ethics, values and integrity in coaching*. Retrieved from http://humancapitalreview.org/content/default.asp?Article_ID=965

SIOPSA. (2014). IGCCP – The code of practice for registered psychology practitioners in coaching. Retrieved from https://www.siopsa.org.za/news_articles

Spence, G. B., & Grant, A. M. (2005). Individual and group life-coaching: Initial findings from a randomised, controlled trial. In M. Cavanagh, A. M. Grant, & T. S. Kemp (Eds.), *Evidence-based coaching theory, research and practice from the behavioural sciences* (Vol. 1, pp. 143–158). Queensland: Australian Academic Press.

Spence, G., Cavanagh, M., & Grant, A. M. (2006). Duty of care in an unregulated industry: Initial findings on the diversity and practices of Australian coaches. *International Coaching Psychological Review, 1*(1), 71–85.

Sperry, L. (2008). Executive coaching: An intervention, role function, or profession? *Consulting Psychology Journal: Practice and Research, 60*(1), 33–37.

Sperry, L. (2013). Executive coaching and leadership assessment: Past, present, and future. *Consulting Psychology Journal: Practice and Research, 65*(4), 284–288.

Standards Australia. (2011). *Handbook: Coaching in organisations*. Retrieved from http://infostore.saiglobal.com/EMEA/default.aspx

Stanford University. (2014). *Analysis*. Retrieved from http://plato.stanford.edu/entries/analysis/

Stern, L. R. (2004). Executive coaching: A working definition. *Consulting Psychology Journal: Practice and Research, 56*(3), 154–162.

Tooth, J., Nielsen, S., & Armstrong, H. (2013). Coaching effectiveness survey instruments: Taking stock of measuring the immeasurable. *Coaching: An International Journal of Theory, Research and Practice, 6*(2), 137–151.

Trevino, L. K., & Brown, M. E. (2004). Managing to be ethical: Debunking five ethical myths. *Academy of Management Executive, 18*(2), 69–81.

Turner, R. A., & Goodrich, J. (2010). The case for eclecticism in executive coaching: Application to challenging assignments. *Consulting Psychology Journal: Practice and Research, 62*(1), 39–55.

Underhill, B. O., McAnally, K., Bastian, C., Desrosiers, E., Golay, L., & Tuller, M. (2013). *Executive coaching industry research: 2013 final report*. Retrieved from http://www.coachingsurveys.com/pdf-files/Executive_Coaching_Industry_Research_2013_Report.pdf

United Nations. (2012). *The universal declaration of human rights*. Retrieved from http://www.un.org/en/documents/udhr/index.shtml

University of Stellenbosch. (2015). *MPhil in management coaching*. Retrieved from http://www.usb.ac.za/MPhil-in-Management-Coaching/

USB. (2015). *MPhil in management coaching*. Retrieved from University of Stellenbosch Business School: http://www.usb.ac.za/MPhil-in-Management-Coaching/

Velasquez, M. G. (2012). *Business ethics: Concepts and cases* (7th ed.). New Jersey: Pearson Education.

Whybrow, A. (2008). Coaching psychology: Coming of age? *International Coaching Psychology Review, 3*(3), 227–240.

Wilson, W. (2013). Coaching with a global mindset. *International Journal of Evidence Based Coaching and Mentoring, 11*(2), 33–52.

Wits Business School. (2015). *MM in the field of business executive coaching*. Retrieved from http://www.wbs.ac.za/programmes/degrees/master_of_management_in_business_executive_coaching

Worldwide Association of Business Coaches. (2007). *Code of business coaching ethics and integrity*. Retrieved from http://www.wabccoaches.com/about/philosophies.htm

Yi-Ling, L., & McDowall, A. (2014). A systematic review (SR) of coaching psychology: Focusing on the attributes of effective coaching psychologists. *International Coaching Psychology Review, 9*(2), 118–134.

Part II
Psychological Approaches Towards Coaching Psychology in Multi-cultural Contexts

Exploring the Role of Psychological Ownership in the Coaching Process

Chantal Olckers

Abstract Psychological ownership is a cognitive-affective construct that is used to measure individuals' feelings of possessiveness towards material and immaterial objects. The existence of psychological ownership strengthens an individual's feelings of responsibility towards and influence over a target and has behavioural effects on both the individual and the organization for which the individual works. The aim of this chapter is to explore the theory underlying the role that psychological ownership can play when applied to the GROW model of coaching within a multicultural context. It is posited that psychological ownership can enhance a coach-client relationship and can help a client to solve problems, make better decisions, learn new skills, and even progress in a role or career. Furthermore, psychological ownership may enhance an individual's perception of meaningfulness and self-determination during the coaching process, which may have positive outcomes for both the individual and the individual's organization in a multicultural context such as South Africa.

Keywords Psychological ownership • GROW coaching model • Self-efficacy • Self-identity • Belongingness

1 Introduction

Traditionally, applied psychology focused on ameliorating distress and repairing dysfunctionality rather than on enhancing the well-being and goal attainment of normal, well-functioning individuals. According to Kauffman (2006, p. 220) the attention should be shifted away from what causes and drives pain to what "energises and pulls people forward." Positive psychology was defined by Seligman (2007) as the scientific study of positive emotion, engagement, and of meaning that lead to happiness, fulfilment, and flourishing. The purpose of positive psychology is

C. Olckers (✉)
University of Pretoria, Pretoria, South Africa
e-mail: Chantal.Olckers@up.ac.za

L.E. van Zyl et al. (eds.), *Coaching Psychology: Meta-theoretical perspectives and applications in multicultural contexts*, DOI 10.1007/978-3-319-31012-1_6

therefore to encourage people to look at what is good and going well in their lives to reinforce a positive disposition (Yves 2008). If a person experiences positive emotions, it widens their focus of attention and broadens access to their intellectual and psychological resources, resulting in improved performance (Kauffman 2006).

In exploring the implications of positive psychology for organizational behaviour, Luthans (2002, p. 59) incorporated the basic principles of positive psychology into his definition of the construct of positive organizational behaviour (POB) as "the study and application of positively orientated human resource strengths and psychological capacities that can be measured, developed, and effectively managed for performance improvement in today's workplace".

Psychological ownership has emerged as a positive psychological resource and it has been found to meet the recognised POB criteria because it is based on theory and research, can be measured, is open to change and development, and affects the performance of organizations (Avey et al. 2009a). Psychological ownership is defined by Pierce et al. (2003, p. 86) as "the state in which individuals feel as though the target of ownership or a piece of that target is theirs" and as a reflection of "an individual's awareness, thoughts, and beliefs regarding the target of ownership".

Coaching, which is rooted in some of the factors underpinning positive psychology, has become not only a very popular tool in the workplace, but also a powerful strategy in the twenty-first century workplace (Salavert 2015). According to Miles Downey, founder of the School of Coaching (see Hosking 2015), the need for coaching will be increasing in the new world of work. First due to several organizations that move away from more traditional hierarchical structures to work environments that are more flexible and accommodating to the needs of their employees and clients. Second as a result of increased job transition and self-employment caused in part by the restructuring and downsizing of organizations (particularly in the case of a multicultural context such as South Africa), employees have become more stressed and less focused and effective. Furthermore the younger generation that have a stronger sense of their own autonomy and independence and that want to work for themselves or in smaller groups, will need the assistance of a coach. Due to these changes coaching can play a small but not insignificant part in making this new world of work effective (Hosking 2015) by promoting the well-being (engendering hope and happiness) and enhancing the performance of individuals, thereby benefiting an organization and society as a whole (Yves 2008).

According to Myles Downey in Hosking (2015), in its purest form, coaching is about helping people to discover their own autonomy, their own authority, their own voice. Is it possible that psychological ownership could play a role in the coaching process, and, not only enhance the life experience of employees by helping them to find their own voice, but also strengthen their commitment to remain in the organization and to perform to the best of their ability?

2 Purpose of This Chapter

Psychological ownership plays a role in helping people define who they are and in shaping their emotions and subsequently much of their behaviours (Pierce et al. 2003). The purpose of coaching is to build on the client's strengths and to enhance positive emotions (Kauffman 2006) and to change behaviour. During the coaching process the coach can thus assist the client in helping them define who they are, helping them to identify with for example specific goals which might lead them to experience positive emotions such as meaningfulness and connectedness with the goal. If people feel that they can identify and control the object, the goal, the more possessive they will feel about that object, and the more that object will become part of the self (Pierce et al. 2003). This might enhance the self-efficacy of the person and they most probably will implement action (show certain behaviour) to complete the task successfully, or achieving the goal. It thus seems that if the coach could assist the client in creating a sense of psychological ownership, the client might achieve their goals ensuring a successful coaching process. To date, no research has been conducted on how psychological ownership can play a role during the coaching process and in this chapter the author would like to explore this relationship as a contribution to not only to the coaching literature but as well as to the development of psychological ownership theory. The purpose of this chapter is therefore to theoretically explore the role that psychological ownership can play in enhancing the coaching process within a multicultural context such as South Africa. The construct of psychological ownership will be discussed followed by a discussion on coaching indicating the role that psychological ownership could play during the coaching process.

3 Psychological Ownership

3.1 Psychological Ownership Defined

Pierce et al. (2001, 2003) defined psychological ownership in terms of possessive feelings that attach an individual to objects (either material or immaterial in nature), and these feelings are manifested in expressions such as 'my' and 'mine'. Thus, when a state of psychological ownership exists, the individual will feel psychologically tied to the object. Therefore, psychological ownership could provide an answer to the question 'What do I feel is mine?' The conceptual core of psychological ownership is possessiveness as well as a sense of control over psychologically owned objects (Van Dyne and Pierce 2004). Psychological ownership is at the core of a human being's individual and organizational existence; it is 'real' and it is also a 'state of mind'. Therefore, psychological ownership may exist in the absence of any legal connection with an object. According to Brown (1989, p. 15), "psychological ownership is people working as if they owned the place".

3.2 The 'Roots' of Psychological Ownership

Before the role that psychological ownership can possibly play during the coaching process can be explored, it is important to understand what the building blocks or so called 'roots' of psychological ownership are. We therefore ask ourselves the question: 'Why would people develop psychological ownership?' The reasons or motives for the existence of psychological ownership could be found, in part, in the need to experience efficacy, control and competence in one's environmental interactions, and in the need for self-identity and for 'having a place' or 'home' in which to dwell (Pierce et al. 2001, 2003). Only one motive, and not necessarily all three motives mentioned below, is needed for the emergence of psychological ownership.

The Effectance Motive

According to Van Dyne and Pierce (2004), the motive for possession lies in wanting to be in control because it will satisfy people's need to identify their needs as theirs. The need to explore and control the environment is part of the human condition. Feelings of possession and the psychological experience of ownership begin to develop within an individual as a result of wanting to exercise control over objects (Pierce et al. 2001, 2003). Exploring and controlling objects or the environment lead to experiences of self-efficacy and satisfaction. Therefore, people's belief that they can control objects or the environment is a psychological component of resultant feelings of self-efficacy. Self-efficacy is defined as the belief of people that they can take on and put in the necessary effort to implement action and complete a specific task successfully (Avey et al. 2009b).

The Need for Self-Identity

There is a close connection between people's possessions and their self-identity and individuality (Pierce et al. 2003). Through ownership of and interactions with objects (possessions), which could be tangible or intangible (such as an organization, a goal or a purpose), people are able to establish, maintain, reproduce and transform their self-identity (Rousseau 1998). Therefore, targets of ownership could be seen as descriptors of people's identity. According to Avey et al. 2009b, p. 178), "Feelings of psychological ownership over these objects may provide a foundation from which individuals can identify themselves as being unique, thus contributing to their personal identity."

O'Driscoll et al. (2006) stated that people had a strong drive to identify with the setting in which they worked and, therefore, they might identify with an organization, goal or purpose. Because people 'do' things because of what they 'are', they establish and affirm an identity for themselves (Shamir et al. 1993).

People experience meaningfulness and connectedness if they internalize an organizational identity or a goal, for example as a definition of the self. If they feel they have control over the target or even the environment, that target or object becomes part of the extended self since there is an interconnection between control and the self-identity functions of possession (Pierce et al. 2009). If targets appeal to people and are aligned with their values and self-identity, they may develop feelings of psychological ownership towards those targets (Avey et al. 2009a). According to Myles Downey in Hosking (2015, p. 12) "when people operate from a sense of their own identity or authority they achieve more, grow and experience more joy".

The Need for Having a Home

According to Pierce et al. (2003), having a 'home' or having a place in which to dwell translates into 'being in this world'. Being 'at home' addresses people's placement and understanding of themselves in time and space. Interaction with the environment, as well as personalisation, promotes familiarity and a discovery of the self within, and a sense of being one with a target creates a 'home' for an individual. A work environment in which an individual feels 'at home' will give that individual a purpose in life and help the individual to find the self (Pierce et al. 2009). Feeling 'at home' requires an investment of the self into the context, an intimate knowing of that context, and/or the discovery of personal identity in that context in such a manner that the context is seen as a reflection of the self. If an individual makes a considerable emotional investment in a particular possession, this possession will become 'home' to that individual and it will have a special meaning for that individual.

It is important for every human being 'to be' and to 'have roots'. Feelings of ownership are linked to an individual's need to have a place and to be at 'home' (Olckers and Du Plessis 2015; Pierce et al. 2003, 2009). People will defend this 'home' because it provides them with security and they have made an effort to invest in it. Having a 'home' satisfies the individual's psychological need to belong. A place or object becomes 'home' to a person through the attachment to or strong sense of identification with that place or object. The existence of psychological ownership reflects our need to be 'at home' and to create a place for ourselves (Pierce et al. 2009).

3.3 The 'Routes' to Psychological Ownership

When considering the emergence of psychological ownership the following questions arise: 'What drives psychological ownership?', and 'How do people come to feel psychological ownership?' Pierce et al. (2001, 2003) pointed out that there were three basic ways in which people came to experience an object or a target which lay outside the self as part of the self: They need to (1) be able to control the object; (2) to know the object; and (3) to invest in the object. The more they invest in and spend time with the object, the more the self will become attached to that object.

Controlling the Object or Target

The ability of a person to control or manipulate an object or target causes that person to develop feelings of ownership towards that object or target (Olckers and Du Plessis 2015). Control is a critical determinant of feelings of ownership, and the more people believe they can control and influence an object, the more possessive they will feel about that object, and the more that object will become part of the self. Therefore, the feeling of ownership is related to the ability to use and control the use of objects. Objects over which people exercise the most control are objects experienced as 'mine', in other words objects towards which they experience ownership (Pierce et al. 2009). Only those objects that people can control will become part of the self and objects they cannot control will not become part of the self. Environmental conditions, for example in the case of an organization that provides employees with the opportunity to exercise control and to experience personal control, will satisfy not only people's need for control, but also their need for effectance, competence, and feelings of efficacy (Avey et al. 2009a).

Knowing the Target or Object

People will develop feelings of ownership for objects which they have a living relationship with, in other words, objects (people, places or things) that are with them for a period of time and eventually become psychologically 'theirs'. Objects become part of the self through knowing them passionately (intimately) (Pierce et al. 2001, 2003). It is through active participation or association with objects that knowledge about these objects or targets develops. The more knowledge or information a person gathers about an object, the more intimate the connection will become between the person and the object and the more attached the person will become to the object. The person will increasingly become one with the object. Through the attachment to an object the individual will discover themselves within and experiences a sense of being 'one with' the object and being 'at home' (Olckers and Du Plessis 2015).

Investing the Self in the Target

A sense of ownership will only develop if an investment of the self into a target takes place and the investment will only take place if a person spends energy, time and effort on a target so that the self becomes one with the target or object. Therefore, the object emerges from the self (Pierce et al. 2003). People can develop a sense of ownership towards machines, their work, the products they produce, and other people. Individuals' need for self-identity and for having a 'home' is satisfied if a personal investment of the self is made in the target, and if they become familiar with the target. In addition, by investing the self in the target, people exercise control over the target, giving rise to feelings of self-efficacy (Pierce et al. 2009).

Thus, people will come to feel they are one with the target because they have developed psychological ownership through controlling the target, knowing the target through close association with it, and immersing the self into creating and shaping the target of ownership.

3.4 The Benefits of Psychological Ownership

There are several benefits of psychological ownership, not only for an individual, but also for an organization.

Positive attitudes toward the target, enhanced self-concept, and a sense of responsibility are the three fundamental outcomes associated with feelings of possession. Van Dyne and Pierce (2004) suggested that this sense of possession (which allows individuals to satisfy their basic needs for efficacy and effectance, self-identity, and place) is the key to shaping work-related attitudes, self-concept, and behaviours. In this sense, psychological ownership is associated with positive motivational, attitudinal and behavioural consequences.

Psychological ownership has been associated with: (1) *greater commitment* to an organization – because employees experience a sense of attachment and belonging to the organization through a sense of possession (Avey et al. 2009a; Olckers 2013; Van Dyne and Pierce 2004); (2) *greater accountability* – because, through psychological ownership, employees' sense of the self will be closely linked to the organization and their desire to maintain, protect, or enhance the self, and this will result in an enhanced sense of accountability (Olckers 2013); (3) *greater job satisfaction* – because if employees feel possessive toward their organization as a result of having influence and control at work, if they have intimate knowledge of the organization, and if they feel they have invested themselves in their organizational roles, they should experience high levels of satisfaction which, in turn, would influence their job satisfaction (Avey et al. 2009a; Mayhew et al. 2007; Van Dyne and Pierce 2004); (4) *better organizational performance* – because if an organization provides employees with a valued sense of belonging, sense of efficacy and/or sense of self-identity the employees will develop feelings of responsibility, which will lead to their investing time and energy to the benefit of the organization (Van Dyne and Pierce 2004; Wagner et al. 2003); (5) *better organization-based self-esteem* – because employees who regard their organization as their personal psychological property will assess themselves positively as members of the organization since they recognize the value and importance of the relationship (Avey et al. 2009a; Van Dyne and Pierce 2004); (6) *more effort on the part of the individual to engage in organizational citizenship behaviours* – because individuals who experience psychological ownership will display behaviour that is intended to benefit others and not themselves (for example, employees will speak on behalf of their organization, they will assist others in the performance of their roles, and they will volunteer for tasks) (Avey et al. 2009a; Van Dyne and Pierce 2004); (7) *increase in extra-role behaviour* (Mayhew et al. 2007) – because individuals with higher levels of psychological ownership are more likely to engage in extra-role behaviour (constructive work efforts that benefit the organization and go beyond required work activities); (8) *intention to stay* in the organization – because employees feel the organization satisfies their need to have a 'home' and to belong (Avey et al. 2009a; Jeswani and Dave 2011, Olckers 2013); and (9) *happiness* – because employees who have control of their environment will experience feelings of pleasure, and employees who feel their organization is like a 'home' will experience a sense of comfort and security, and these feelings will have positive effects (George 2015).

The coaching construct will now be discussed, followed by a discussion indicating the role that psychological ownership could play during each phase of the coaching process.

4 Coaching

4.1 Coaching Defined

There has been an explosion of interest in coaching in recent years (Theeboom et al. 2015), and this has produced many definitions of coaching. According to Passmore (2010), coaching is a process that is solution-focused, results-orientated and systematically planned, and one in which a coach by way of a one-to-one supportive relationship helps a client to achieve fulfilling results in their personal and professional lives. By implication, the coach accepts responsibility for ensuring that clients improve their performances and enhance the quality of their lives (Wright 2005) through the building of trust, two-way communication, facilitation and a transparent process (Lai and McDowall 2014). According to Salavert (2015), it is the responsibility of a coach to ask the right questions and to elicit solutions and strategies from a client that will enable the client to focus on and achieve their goals by using their own resources. Coaches should believe in the significant untapped inner potential of their clients, and coaches should provide the necessary support to enhance the skills, resources and creativity that clients already have, regardless of culture (Linder-Pelz and Hall 2008).

The aim of coaching is to enhance the performance or life experiences of clients by assisting them in discovering what they are capable of doing, as stated by Whitmore (2003, p. 97) "optimising people's potential and performance". The coach is, therefore, a facilitator of learning who must help the client not by being directive but by applying their own knowledge, skills and techniques to assist the client in taking ownership and control of the self and processes in order to enhance performance (Lai and McDowall 2014).

4.2 Coaching Models

Brown (2010) defined a coaching model as a theoretical framework comprising different coaching elements that enable coaches to coach and develop their clients effectively. Several theoretical approaches to coaching have been developed and summarised by Ives (2008) as behaviourist, humanist, cognitive, goal-focused, adult development and learning, positive psychology, adventure-based and system-oriented. Each of the approaches to coaching is rooted in a different psychological school of thought, such as behaviourism (GROW coaching model), cognitive psychology (cognitive behavioural coaching), constructive-developmental psychology (developmental coaching), theories of human behaviour and behavioural change (solution-focused coaching), and integrated cognitive and behavioural psychology (integrated coaching). Not any one approach is better or right, but each approach would be more appropriate in a particular situation (Ives 2008). For the purpose of this chapter the focus will be on the GROW (Goal, Reality, Options, Wrap-up) model of coaching, which is grounded in the behaviourism school of thought.

An important contributor to classical behaviourism was Watson, who paved the way for Skinner's radical or operant behaviourism. According to behaviourism, behaviours can be measured, trained and changed. Therefore, behaviour can be studied in a systematic and observable manner without taking any internal mental states, such as emotions and cognitions, into consideration (Yves 2008). The GROW model will be discussed in more detail.

The GROW Model

The development of coaching has been strongly influenced by the GROW model which was devised by Sir John Whitmore and developed by Graham Alexander. This model is simple and effective to apply to individual coaching and coaching interaction, and captures a key aspect of coaching since, it enables people to grow, develop their skills, achieve performance, and gain fulfilment (Alexander 2010).

According to Hattingh (2008), the GROW model has been used in numerous coach training programmes as a framework to develop the coaching relationship and guide the coaching process. Coaching within this framework is natural, flowing and artistic with the purpose of strengthening the human bond and the relationship, and it is cyclical in nature. Throughout a coaching interaction the model will enable the coach to recap earlier phases of the GROW model and to allow the client to see the process clearly and move forward. The GROW model is visually depicted in Fig. 1.

The GROW model comprises five phases, which will be discussed briefly.

Fig. 1 The GROW model (Alexander 2010, p. 84)

Phase 1: Topic

Firstly the coach needs to start the discussion about the topic that will be covered. It is of critical importance to understand what the client wants to talk about, what space the client is in, the extent of the issue at hand, how important the topic is to the client, as well as what the long-term goal of the topic is (Koortzen and Oosthuizen 2010). During this phase the coach needs to build rapport with the client, ask relevant open-ended questions and listen actively in order to gain information (Lai and McDowall 2014). The purpose of open-ended questions is to help the client explore their current situation and develop different ways of thinking about it so as to empower the client to generate solutions by themselves (Dembkowski and Eldridge 2003). According to Alexander and Renshaw (2005), typical questions that could be asked in this phase are the following: 'What would you like to discuss in today's session?', 'What topic do you want to address?', and 'What will be the most valuable subject to focus on?' To allow the client to take ownership and control of the topic, it is of utmost importance that the coach allows the client to present their ideas and requirements. Therefore, the coach should refrain from imposing topics for discussion on the client. It is of critical importance especially in a multicultural context that the coach does not oppose his/her ideas onto the client but by asking relevant questions that promote self-reflection assist the client to develop their own topics and goals they want to achieve (Peterson 2007).

The Role of Psychological Ownership in Phase 1

Individuals want a purpose in life; they want to discover personal meaning; they want to understand not only themselves but also their placement in time and space (Pierce et al. 2003, 2009); and they want to feel that they belong. Some of the reasons why people approach a coach is to assist them in finding personal meaning in life and achieving their goals (Salavert 2015). Clients will respond positively to coaching only if they experience the coach as an expert partner and trusted advisor who will assist them in seeing the bigger picture and in accomplishing their goals (Salavert 2015). Only if the client invests the self into the context, in other words, explores their current situation and find meaning in what they want to achieve, will they feel at 'home' (Pierce et al. 2001, 2003). Therefore, the client needs to know the context, and to help the client discover the context as well as the client's personal identity within that context, the coach could play an important role by asking relevant questions (Yves 2008). Examples of such questions could be: 'What does it mean to you?', and 'How important is it to you?' The client will take control of a topic and it will become 'home' to them only if they regard the topic or goal as meaningful and worthy of investing a lot of their time and effort, because it will provide them with a purpose and with security. Regardless of culture, one of the key conditions according to Peterson (2007) for the client to develop themselves and to become more effective is the willingness to invest time and energy into what they want to accomplish.

The client will become psychologically attached to (come to feel at home with) a topic or goal that is theirs, that is familiar to them, that provides them with a sense of personal security, and that represents a place in which they feel safe to dwell (Pierce et al. 2001, 2003, 2009). If clients come up with their own topics and the goals they want to achieve (Yves 2008), these topics and goals are 'theirs', and because they own them, clients will be able to identify themselves with these topics and goals.

Phase 2: Goal

The coach should spend time with the client to establish the goal they wish to achieve through receiving coaching since this will have a big impact on the success of the coaching process. Goals should be clearly formulated conform to the principles of SMART (specific, measurable, achievable and attainable, relevant and realistic, time-bound and tangible) otherwise it will only lead to a frustrating and purposeless conversation (Alexander 2010).

Goals should not just be a restatement of organizational goals, but should have relevance for the client and be real to them, and, to achieve that, the coach needs to ask penetrating questions about goals (Yves 2008). By studying cultural dimensions and distinctions, a cross-cultural coach will be able to become familiar with the various ways that people differ and by asking the right questions, will spot the hidden meanings of their clients (Peterson 2007). According to Koortzen and

Oosthuizen (2010), typical questions that could be asked are the following: 'How will you know that you have achieved that goal?', and 'How will you know the problem has been solved?' Goals will be achieved only if they are meaningful to and have personal relevance for the client. As stated by Dembkowski and Eldridge (2003, p. 4): "The more it matters to the client the more it acts as a magnet; it will draw in the person rather than the person having to push for it". In addition, goals should be broken down into smaller, achievable goals.

It is also the coach's responsibility to provide the client with a real picture of how the goal will appear, and, to do this, the coach must approach a discussion of the goal with the end in mind. In this way, the goal will be made more achievable, the client will have a much clearer idea of what they are endeavouring to achieve, and they will also have a benchmark to measure their progress against, as they work towards the goal (Dembkowski and Eldridge 2003).

The Role of Psychological Ownership in Phase 2

In order for goals to be achieved, it is important that the client makes the goal their own: in other words, that they take possession of the goal. Possession of the goal will enable the client to feel safe because they will see this goal as theirs (Pierce et al. 2001, 2003, 2009). The ultimate meaning of ownership is the fusing of the target of ownership, in this case the goal the client wants to achieve, with the self: to have is to take into the self, and this is the ultimate form of control. The moment the client feels that they can control the goal, can control how they achieve the goal and use it, and use it as a mechanism to exert control over the environment, which, in this case could be either in their personal life or their work environment, they start to develop feelings of psychological ownership (Pierce et al. 2004). Furthermore, as a result of taking control of this goal, the client will experience feelings of competence and personal efficacy, autonomy and of psychological ownership (Pierce et al. 2004).

It is important to set goals for achievement that are relevant for the client and that the client can control. Only if clients feel they can control or manipulate the goal will they feel they possess it and will it become 'theirs'. It will become part of the self and they will experience feelings of ownership for that particular goal (Pierce et al. 2003, 2004, 2009). Therefore, this feeling of control over the goal will enhance the client's self-efficacy.

Phase 3: Reality

This phase is seen as a starting point to move towards the set goals. The coach should refrain from telling the client how to achieve their goals because it defeats the purpose of coaching and will prevent the client from learning and gaining insight into the goal (Stober and Grant 2006). During this phase the client is confronted with their perceived reality and truth. The environment should be non-threatening, especially in a multicultural context so that the client can become aware of their own achievements, capabilities and available resources whilst being challenged by limiting beliefs and feelings (Koortzen and Oosthuizen 2010; Peterson 2007).

To assist the client in seeing the situation they are in, and for them to face reality from an 'outside-in' perspective, the following open-ended questions, among others, could be asked: 'What is your understanding of the situation?', 'What resources will you need to face this situation?', 'What control do you have?', and 'What do you want to happen in this situation?' (Alexander and Renshaw 2005) To clarify the goal they want to achieve, broader types of questions are asked before focusing on more specific issues. This will enable the coach and client to explore a new reality.

The Role of Psychological Ownership in Phase 3

In order to achieve a goal, a client needs to believe that they can achieve the goal successfully and that they have the capacity and ability to achieve it; that is, that they have self-efficacy (Avey et al. 2009b). According to Peterson (2007), to be capable, to have the skills and knowledge to achieve a goal is a key condition for systematic learning and to help the client to develop themselves and to become more effective. Feelings of ownership emerge if the client feels they can control and manipulate the object, in this case the goal they want to achieve. The client's feeling of having control is a psychological component of the resultant feelings of self-efficacy (Avey et al. 2009b), which may promote a sense of psychological ownership concerning that particular goal. As stated by Avey et al. (2009a, p. 177), the client needs to be able to say "I need to do this task, I can do it, and therefore I own the responsibility for achieving success."

Phase 4: Options

Without being judgemental, especially in a multicultural context where individuals may vary in terms of what is meaningful to them (Peterson 2007), the coach, together with the client, must list all possible options of moving forward. Following on the Reality phase, the client should be able to identify goals and areas for development. Although some clients may have a high level of self-awareness and the ability to identify problems, others may need the coach to provide more support and encouragement to enable them to think 'outside the box' which is often more so within a multicultural context. It is important to keep in mind that the coaching process is non-directive (Stober and Grant 2006): the coach should not provide solutions to problems, but should draw out solutions from the client (Vickers and Bavister 2005). Long-term learning will only be achieved if the client has gained insight and has the confidence to come up with answers (Peterson 2007). During the Options phase the goal should be revisited to ensure that it is still relevant (Alexander and Renshaw 2005).

The coach can start off this phase by asking open-ended questions, such as: 'What options do you have?', What solutions are possible?', and 'What are the pros and cons of each option?' Thereafter, more probing questions can be asked, such as: 'If you were an expert in this area what would you do', and 'If you had all the resources in the world, what would you do?' (Alexander and Renshaw 2005).

In order to change the client's behaviour and beliefs, the client should be given the necessary support and time to think creatively and differently about how the goal could be achieved. In this phase, the client does not have to commit to a specific course of action or evaluate possible actions. Without being judged by the coach, the client needs to feel free to make statements about options in this phase. These options will only be evaluated in the Wrap-up phase.

The Role of Psychological Ownership in Phase 4

It is very important for clients to identify with their problems and with the goal they want to achieve. Clients will be able to establish, maintain and transform their self-identity only if they interact with their possessions (Van Dyne and Pierce 2004) in this case, the goals they want to achieve, and reflect upon their meaning (which is important during this phase of the coaching process). When one interacts with one's goals or possessions, one's identity is developed and cultivated because these goals or possessions, which are experienced as symbols of the self, provide space and pleasure (Pierce et al. 2003, 2009) and help the client to experience autonomy, which is one of the goals of coaching (Hosking 2015). The client will experience the goals as meaningful and will connect with them only if the client, with the support of the coach, is able to internalise them as a definition of the self (Pierce et al. 2009). The client may feel a sense of psychological ownership towards the goal to the extent that it appeals to and affirms their values and self-identity which will in a multicultural context differ from one another since according to Pierce et al. (2003) especially the expression of self-identity to others, will most probably be more significant in collectivistic cultures (because people care about how others perceive them).

In order for the coach to assist the client in generating different options and identifying advantages and disadvantages associated with all the options (Yves 2008), the client must have knowledge of the target or object, in this instance, the goal they would like to achieve. Once the client has attained the necessary knowledge of the goal to be achieved, the goal will become 'theirs'. Active participation with the target/object or goal is needed to gain knowledge of it (Pierce et al. 2003); therefore, it is important that the coach and the client spend some time on attaining this knowledge because only then will the client develop a sense of ownership towards the goal.

Phase 5: Wrap-Up

Most of the client's learning and awareness will take place during this phase because this is the time when dreams will be translated into reality (Koortzen and Oosthuizen 2010). The different options identified in the Options phase need to be weighed up in terms of short-term and long-term costs and benefits, and then be broken down into specific action steps. It is important to emphasise once again that the client should come up with their own decisions (Lai and McDowall 2014). Once the appropriate actions have been selected, the coach and the client must decide on a plan of action to bridge the gap between where the client is at the moment and where they want to be. In this phase the coach should obtain the client's commitment to take action and establish a time frame for achieving selected goals (Dembkowski and Eldridge 2003). The coach and the client also need to identify how they will go about overcoming obstacles and obtain clarity about the support the coach will provide. The coach must ensure that the client knows exactly what action steps will be taken, and these actions should be quite specific, measurable and time-bound (Alexander 2010).

Specific questions could be asked to ensure that the client will know when each action has been achieved, for instance, 'What are the implications of taking this action?, 'How realistic and practical is it?', and 'Is there anything that will stop you from doing it?'.

The Role of Psychological Ownership in Phase 5

By allowing the client to come up with their own decisions, they will be provided with the autonomy to achieve higher levels of control, which will increase the likelihood that feelings of ownership towards the goal will emerge (Pierce et al. 2003). As earlier stated, the purpose of coaching is to help people discovering their own autonomy, their own voice (Hosking 2015). This could however differ from different cultures since according to Peterson (2007) seeking independence and autonomy is more of an individualistic perspective. The client needs to be very clear about the action steps, because only if they have sufficient information about the goals they want to achieve and the steps they are going to take (Lai and McDowall 2014), and have considered the pros and cons of each step, will they develop psychological ownership of these goals. It is further important that the client invest some time and energy during this phase thinking about the practicality and implications of the actions to be taken as this will increase the possibility that the action steps will cause the self to become one with the actions and that feelings of ownership will develop (Peterson 2007). If the client experiences a sense of psychological ownership of the action steps to be followed to achieve the goals, they might experience responsibility directed not only towards themselves but also towards the organization (Pierce et al. 2009).

5 Psychological Ownership and Coaching in a Multicultural Context

The cultural aspects of a social context according to Pierce et al. (2003) will have a significant influence on the phenomenon of psychological ownership. Culture, which is reflected in customs, norms, traditions and beliefs in society (Hofstede 1980), shapes the individual's self-concept and values with regard to control, self-expression, self-identity, property, and ownership.

Pierce et al. (2003) propose that culture will have an influence on all the elements of the framework of psychological ownership: on the construct itself, the motives, the "routes", targets, individuals, and the process. Although possessive feelings are universal, it is possible that individuals from different cultural groups assign different meaning to possessions in terms of viewing them as part of their extended selves. Possessions may play a more significant role in the self-definition in some cultures than in others. Therefore, Pierce et al. (2003) suggest that feelings of ownership may be present in different cultures to a different extent.

There could be a difference in cultures with respect to the salience of the various ownership motives (roots). According to Hofstede (1980), the "efficacy and effectance" motive for example might be more prominent than the "having a place" motive in individualistic rather than in collectivistic cultures. The "identity" motive, especially the expression of self-identity to others, will most probably be more significant in collectivistic cultures (because people care about how others perceive them).

Pierce et al. (2003) also suggest cross-cultural differences with regard to the "routes" to psychological ownership. There will be a shift from the "control" and "investment of self" route to the "getting to intimately know" route if a person moves from a more deterministic and "doing" cultural orientation to a more fatalistic and "being" orientation.

According to Pierce et al. (2003), both the kind of target and the expression of feelings of ownership towards that target will vary greatly according to the culture and country in which the individual operates, and the locus of the self-concept in that society. Individualistic societies would place more emphasis on personal successes and achievements (Triandis 2004), and would focus ownership more on their material possessions and work that addresses these achievements. Other cultures are more collectivistic and place high value on the community, family and relationships (Triandis 2004); individuals from these cultures will probably develop feelings of ownership primarily towards social targets like the community and family.

According to Pierce et al. (2003), the level at which the feeling for psychological ownership resides, defined as individual versus collective, is a very important aspect of the construct. They theorise that in individualistic cultures (e.g. the US and Australia), the feeling of ownership will tend to be experienced at the individual level. In contrast, the more the self-concept is tied to the collective entity (as in collectivistic cultures like those of China and Japan), the more psychological ownership will be defined as a shared, collective feeling. There is very limited empirical evidence in support of such propositions. However, although Hartley (2015) did not find in her study conducted in the multicultural context of South Africa, that either an individualistic or collectivistic cultural approach has a significant influence on psychological ownership, small differences were found. For example, Hartley (2015) found that individualists are higher than collectivists on the effective motive as well as on their level accountability.

In a multi-cultural context such as in South Africa it is on the one hand of critical importance that a coaches' assumption about culture should never interfere with their coaching of an individual. This means that regardless of whether that individual was shaped by culture, education, family background, life experience or any other factors, it remains the coach's responsibility and challenge to know the person/client they are working with. On the other hand, if a coach broadens their understanding of culture, it will better assist them in identifying and understanding human behaviour and the meaning thereof (Peterson 2007). A good cultural-coach will realise that people look at the world through different lenses and therefore it is important that they familiarize themselves with the different cultural dimensions and distinctions.

Although understanding of a culture may help in understanding group behaviour, it doesn't necessary help in predicting individual behaviour since not all individuals fit the particular cultural style. Pierce et al. (2003) also emphasise the fact individuals differs regarding the strength of their motives of psychological ownership both across individuals and within individuals in time. Therefore this emphasises the fact that the coach should be aware of the different ways in which individuals may vary and what is meaningful to them. It is important that the coach always demonstrate a non-judgmental, accepting attitude in determining clients' primary values and motivations (Peterson 2007). A cross-cultural coach should never allow their own preferences to result in negative evaluations of what the client value. In order to coach across cultures it is of the utmost importance that a relationship of trust and understanding should be established between the coach and the client and that the coach will connect with the client regardless of culture (Renner 2007).

6 Chapter Summary

Most employees need a purpose in life, to discover personal meaning, to achieve goals, to understand not only themselves but also where in an organization they fit in, to feel that they belong in their organization and have a 'home' that provides them with comfort and security (Pierce et al. 2001, 2003, 2009). There could be several reasons why clients might approach a coach but in general they enter the coaching process because they want to learn and develop goals, increase their performance within their organization, or reflect upon their own behaviour (De Haan and Nieβ 2015). Clients would thus approach a coach to assist them to focus and to grow; to motivate and support them in achieving their goals in their personal and/or professional life (Linder-Pelz and Hall 2008; Yves 2008).

Psychological ownership can help employees define who they are and shape their emotions and subsequently much of their behaviours (Pierce et al. 2003). Because psychological ownership influences people's behaviour, it can play a major role during the coaching process, specifically if the GROW model of coaching is applied. The reason is because the focus of the GROW model is to establish if the client needs to change their behaviour or acquire new skills to be successful (Alexander 2010).

For the coach to assist the client in changing their behaviour so that they can achieve their goal, the coach needs to ensure that the client feels that they have control over their goal. The client will probably take control of a topic and it might become 'home' to them only if they experience achievement of their goal as meaningful, and if achieving the goal provides them with a purpose and feeling of security (Pierce et al. 2001, 2003). As a result of taking control of their goal, the client might experience feelings of competence and personal efficacy, and the psychological experience of ownership will most probably emerge. Clients can have control only if they have sufficient knowledge of and clarity about what they want to achieve (Peterson 2007). Furthermore, sufficient knowledge can only be attained if the client spends enough time, energy and effort to ensure understanding of the goal they want to achieve, as a result of which the self will become 'one' with their goal. Clients will most probably also become 'one' with the goal if they can identify with their goal (Hosking 2015). Only if the client, with the support of the coach, is able to internalise their goal as a definition of the self, might the client experience the goal as meaningful and might they connect with the goal. Being able to achieve their goal set might ensure the happiness and fulfilment of clients and will they most probably flourish (Yves 2008).

Although psychological ownership was predominantly discussed from the client's perspective, with indications of how the coach can help the client, the psychological ownership of the coach on his/her role in all of the aspects are of equal importance. The coach can also come to feel psychological ownership during the coaching process through the 'routes' of psychological ownership by controlling the object (client), knowing the object (client) and by investing in the object (client). By manipulating or rather guiding the client during the process by asking the right questions (Stober and Grant 2006) the coach can feel that they control the coaching process and therefore might develop feelings of psychological ownership towards the client. The effective management of the relationship between the coach and the client is vital during coaching (Yves 2008). To enhance this relationship it is therefore important that the coach and particularly a cross-cultural coach broader their understanding of culture since this will enable them to identify the different dimensions of human behaviour and to explore the meaning thereof (Peterson 2007). The more knowledge or information the coach gathers about the client, the more intimate the connection will become between the coach and the client (Pierce et al. 2003). Through this attachment with the client the coach might become to experience feelings of psychological ownership. By investing the self in the target (client) through spending time and energy with the client, making effort to understand the client and particularly learn about their culture the coach might develop feelings of psychological ownership towards the object which in this case is the client.

From this discussion it is clear that not only the client, but the coach as well can develop feelings of psychological ownership during the coaching process that might enhance their perceptions of meaningfulness and self-determination (for the client due to the achievement of their goals or learning that has taken place and for the coach due to the fact that they has achieve in assisting the client in finding meaning and achieving their goals).

7 Practical Implications of the Role of Psychological Ownership in the Coaching Process

In order to be successful and to survive in the twenty-first century world of work, it is ideal that all employees on all levels in an organization have a clear view of their personal goals, and these goals should be aligned with those of the organization. This alignment will only take place if the goals appeal to the employees and they feel they can identify with them.

The GROW model offers a useful structure for a coach to ensure the following: that a client comes to feel that they can identify with a goal; that the client develops psychological ownership as a result of controlling the way they will achieve the goal; that the client knows the goal through close association with it; and that it provides the client the opportunity to immerse themself and thereby shape and create their goal or target of ownership. Having control and influence over the goal might lead to the experience of feelings of competence, personal efficacy, and psychological ownership (Pierce et al. 2003, 2009). Psychological ownership may enhance the client's perception of meaningfulness and self-determination during the coaching process, which might ensure the improvement, development and growth of the client, leading to not only an enhancement of the quality of their lives, but also to a strengthening of their commitment to remain in the organization and to perform well.

During coaching the coach should always keep in mind that individuals have their own expectations and requirements of the coaching process and the relationship with their coach. Cultural differences will even increase the challenge. The coaching process will most probably be better anticipated and handled if a coach increases their knowledge of cultural differences. However, in the words by Peterson (2007, p. 270) "regardless of the amount of cultural knowledge a coach has, the best coaches will always be those who coach with an open attitude of curiosity and interest, who meet people where they are, who accept them for what they are, and who project a genuine desire to be helpful to each person on their own terms."

8 Concluding Remarks

This chapter contributes to the body of knowledge about the role that psychological ownership can play in the coaching process since this relationship has not yet been explored. Management, human resource practitioners and coaches can benefit from recognizing the importance that psychological ownership can play during the coaching process because employees who experience psychological ownership develop feelings of responsibility towards their targets of ownership, which, in this case, are their goals they want to achieve. They furthermore improve not only the quality of their own lives, but might also improve the performance of their organizations.

References

Alexander, G. (2010). Behavioural coaching – The GROW model. In J. Passmore (Ed.), *Excellence in coaching: The industry guide* (2nd ed.). London: Kogan Page Publishers.

Alexander, G., & Renshaw, B. (2005). *Super coaching*. London: Random House.

Avey, J. B., Avolio, B. J., Crossley, C. D., & Luthans, F. (2009a). Psychological ownership: Theoretical extensions, measurement and relation to work outcomes. *Journal of Organizational Behavior, 30*, 173–191.

Avey, J. B., Luthans, F., & Jensen, S. M. (2009b). Psychological capital: A positive resource for combating stress and turnover. *Human Resource Management, 48*(5), 677–693.

Brown, T. L. (1989, June 19). What will it take to win? *Industry Week*, p. 15.

Brown, G. (2010). *An exploratory study of the elements to develop a coaching model*. (Doctoral thesis). Retrieved from http://0-search.proquest.com.innopac.up.ac.za/docview/500018986?accountid=14717/

De Haan, E., & Nieβ, C. (2015). Differences between critical moments for clients, coaches, and sponsors of coaching. *International Coaching Psychology Review, 10*(1), 38–61.

Dembkowski, S., & Eldridge, F. (2003). Beyond grow: A new coaching model. *International Journal of Mentoring and Coaching, 1*(1), 1–6.

George, K. (2015). *The relation between happiness, work engagement and psychological ownership*. Unpublished master's thesis, University of Pretoria, Pretoria.

Hartley, M. (2015). *The relationship between the individualsm-collectivism factor and psychological ownership*. Unpublished master's thesis, University of Pretoria, Pretoria.

Hattingh, M. (2008). *An explorative comparison of the value and experiences of the coach and the coachee during executive coaching*. Unpublished master's thesis, University of Pretoria Pretoria, South Africa. Retrieved from: http://upetd.up.ac.za/thesis/available/etd-02162012-120517/

Hofstede, G. (1980). *Culture's consequences: International differences in work-related values*. Beverly Hills: Sage.

Hosking, A. (2015, May). Has coaching lost its edge – If it ever had one? *HRFuture*, p. 12–15.

Ives, Y. (2008). What is coaching? An exploration of conflicting paradigms. *International Journal of Evidence Based Coaching and Mentoring, 6*(2), 100–113.

Jeswani, S., & Dave, S. (2011). Conceptual framework on psychological ownership as predictor of turnover intentions. *KKIMRC International Journal of Research in Finance and Accounting, 1*(1), 52–70.

Kauffman, C. (2006). Positive psychology: The science at the heart of coaching. In F. Stober & A. M. Grant (Eds.), *Evidence-based coaching handbook*. New York: Wiley.

Koortzen, P., & Oosthuizen, R. (2010). A competence executive coaching model. *South African Journal of Industrial Psychology, 36*(1), 1–10. doi:10.4102/sajip.v36i1.837.

Lai, Y., & McDowall, A. (2014). A systematic review (SR) of coaching psychology: Focusing on the attributes of effective coaching psychologists. *International Coaching Psychology Review, 9*(2), 118–134.

Linder-Pelz, S., & Hall, M. (2008). Meta-coaching: A methodology grounded in psychological theory. *International Journal of Evidence-Based Coaching & Mentoring, 6*(1), 43–56.

Luthans, F. (2002). The need for and meaning of positive behavior. *Journal of Organizational Behavior, 23*(6), 695–706.

Mayhew, M. G., Ashkanasy, N. M., Bramble, T., & Gardner, J. (2007). A study of the antecedents and consequences of psychological ownership in organizational settings. *Journal of Social Psychology, 147*(5), 477–500.

O'Driscoll, M. P., Pierce, J. L., & Coglan, A. (2006). The psychology of ownership: Work environment structure, organizational commitment, and citizenship behaviour. *Group & Organization Management, 31*(3), 388–416.

Olckers, C. (2013). Psychological ownership: Development of an instrument. *SA Journal of Industrial Psychology/SA Tydskrif vir Bedryfsielkunde, 39*(2), 1–13. doi:10.4102/sajip.v39i2.1105.

Olckers, C., & Du Plessis, Y. (2015). Psychological ownership as a requisite for talent retention: The voice of highly skilled employees. *European Journal of International Management, 9*(1), 52–73.

Passmore, J. (2010). *Excellence in coaching: The industry guide* (2nd ed.). London: Kogan Page Publishers.

Peterson, D. B. (2007). Executive coaching in a cross-cultural context. *Consulting Psychology Journal: Practice and Research, 59*(4), 261–271. doi:10.1037/1065-9293.59.4.261.

Pierce, J. L., Kostova, T., & Dirks, K. T. (2001). Towards a theory of psychological ownership in organizations. *Academy of Management Review, 26*(2), 298–310.

Pierce, J. L., Kostova, T., & Dirks, K. T. (2003). The state of psychological ownership: Integrating and extending a century of research. *Review of General Psychology, 7*(1), 84–107.

Pierce, J. L., O'Driscoll, M. P., & Coghlan, A. M. (2004). Work environment structure and psychological ownership: The mediating effects of control. *Journal of Social Psychology, 144*(5), 507–534. doi:10.1002/job.550.

Pierce, J. L., Jussila, I., & Cummings, A. (2009). Psychological ownership within the job design context: Revision of the job characteristics model. *Journal of Organizational Behavior, 30*, 477–496.

Renner, J. C. (2007). Coaching abroad. *Consulting Psychology Journal: Practice and Research, 59*(4), 272–285. doi:10.1037/1065-9293.59.4.272.

Rousseau, D. M. (1998). Why workers still identify with organizations. *Journal of Organizational Behavior, 19*(3), 217–233.

Salavert, R. (2015). Coaching: An apprenticeship approach for the 21st century. *International Journal of Educational Leadership and Management, 3*(1), 4–24. doi:10.4471/ijelm.2015.02.

Seligman, M. E. P. (2007). Coaching and positive psychology. *Australian Psychologist, 24*, 266–267.

Shamir, B., House, R. J., & Arthur, M. B. (1993). The motivational effect of charismatic leadership: A self-concept based theory. *Organizational Science, 4*(4), 577–594.

Stober, D., & Grant, A. M. (2006). Toward a contextual approach to coaching models. In *Evidence-based coaching handbook*. New York: Wiley.

Theeboom, T., Beersma, B., & Van Vianen, A. E. M. (2015). Does coaching work? A meta-analysis on the effects of coaching on individual level outcomes in an organizational context. *The Journal of Positive Psychology: Dedicated to Furthering Research and Promoting Good Practice, 9*(1), 1–18. doi:10.1080/17439760.2013.83749999.

Triandis, H. C. (2004). Foreword. In D. Landis, J. M. Bennet, & M. J. Bennett (Eds.), *Handbook of intercultural training* (3rd ed.). Thousand Oaks: Sage.

Van Dyne, L., & Pierce, J. L. (2004). Psychological ownership and feelings of possession: Three field studies predicting employee attitudes and organizational citizenship behaviors. *Journal of Organizational Behavior, 25*(4), 439–459.

Vickers, A., & Bavister, S. (2005). *Coaching*. London: Hodder Arnold Publishers.

Wagner, S. H., Parker, C. P., & Christianson, N. D. (2003). Employees that think and act like owners: Effects of ownership beliefs and behaviors on organizational effectiveness. *Personnel Psychology, 56*, 847–871.

Whitmore, J. (2003). *Coaching for performance*. London: Nicholas Brealey Publishing.

Wright, J. (2005). Workplace coaching: What is that all about? *Work, 24*, 325–328.

Yves, Y. (2008). What is 'Coaching'? An exploration of conflicting paradigms. *International Journal of Evidence Based Coaching and Mentoring, 6*(2), 100–113.

Coaching and Consulting for Authentic Leadership: A Theoretical Foundation for an Evidence-Based Process Model

Steven Breger

Abstract This chapter explores how theory and evidence-based practice converge to establish a theoretically-grounded understanding of a model used for authentic-leadership coaching and consulting. The *Authentic-intention Model* (AiM) is a model that is used within the context of promoting, developing and managing values-based, authentic-leadership behaviour. It is used to facilitate a shift in relational dynamics for the coaching client (coachee): from displaying a nonconscious, unacknowledged and unarticulated reactive behaviour (possibly perceived as being an 'untrustworthy' *Agenda* by others), toward a consciously articulated and intentional *Dialogue* (potentially perceived as being 'trustworthy' by others). The overall evidence-based outcome of applying this model has culminated in coachees reducing their relational anxiety, and being empowered to adopt a neutral meta-position within the context of their leadership roles. The coachees are ultimately able to transform their reactive *Agenda* into a relational *Dialogue*. The theories discussed in this chapter provide evidence that the aforementioned is associated with authentic-leadership behaviour. Importantly, the AiM is used as the conceptual framework with which to articulate this exposition.

Keywords Intention • Authentic leadership • Coaching psychology • Values-based leadership • Mindfulness • Trustworthiness

> My life is a story of the self-realization of the unconscious. Everything in the unconscious seeks outward manifestation, and the personality too desires to evolve out of its unconscious conditions and to experience itself as a whole. I cannot employ the language of science to trace this process of growth in myself, for I cannot experience myself as a scientific problem. From C.G. Jung's (1961) *Memories, Dreams, Reflections*

The purpose of this chapter is to demonstrate that the relevant theories and the evidence-based practice of consulting and coaching psychology can converge to provide credence to the form, function and spirit of authentic, intentional leadership.

S. Breger (✉)
DynamicDIALOGUE®, Johannesburg, South Africa
e-mail: stevenb@dynamicdialogue.co.za

L.E. van Zyl et al. (eds.), *Coaching Psychology: Meta-theoretical perspectives and applications in multicultural contexts*, DOI 10.1007/978-3-319-31012-1_7

This chapter explores how the relevant theories, in combination with evidence-based practice, are used to articulate an *authentic-leadership* model. This model is used within the context of diagnosing, developing, managing and optimising intentional, conscious, and values-based authentic-leadership behaviour.

In order to explain and articulate the *Authentic-intention Model* (AiM), the following four theoretical domains, or domain groupings will be discussed: (1) Authentic-Leadership theory, (2) Self-Determination theory, (3) Approach-Avoidance Motivation and Trust theories, and (4) Mindfulness and Triple-Loop Learning theories. Each of these provides the combined theoretical and conceptual psychological foundation that represents the AiM model.

1 Overarching Assumptions of the AiM

The AiM has been founded and applied, based on the following assumptions:

(a) *Intentional leadership*, for the purpose of this chapter, means the same as *authentic leadership* (and vice versa).
(b) Being intentional is synonymous with being neutral, present and mindful—i.e., doing and saying something in full awareness and on purpose (for a reason).
(c) Intentional (authentic) leadership is essential to generating an inspiring organizational vision, and engaging individuals and teams to operationalise the intended outcome.
(d) Human beings cannot not have an intention: We *always* act on purpose, in order to fulfill our need(s). Consciously or nonconsciously, humans are inherently intentional beings.
(e) We are, prior to optimizing our awareness through coaching (and also through our life experiences), prone to being less aware, and therefore behaving less authentically. The authenticity of our behaviour may ideally be accelerated and optimised in accordance with the coachee acquiring the ability to recognise, acknowledge and name their underlying intentions. Coaching is therefore primarily a vehicle through which the coach facilitates a process whereby the coachee accumulates self awareness (intrapersonal), and awareness of self in relation to others (interpersonal). This ideally leads to a realisation and learning that results in the intended (coaching-focussed) behavioural shifts for the coachee. The coachee should, therefore, ideally transition from being in a reactive, nonconscious *avoid/away* inauthentic leader mode, to being able to consciously and intentionally create an *approach/toward* authentic-leadership mode.
(f) Humans are evolutionarily driven by the need to survive (which is essentially a protective/coping fight-flight-freeze 'threat-fear' mechanism), and thus we instinctively scrutinise for underlying (authentic/inauthentic) intentions in others. Relationships are therefore built when we are capable of trusting others

(to a greater or lesser degree). But, our survival instinct generates doubt or dissonance, before we can achieve optimal relational trust. Humans have the unique ability to say one thing but mean another—hence our need to discern, so that we may protect and defend ourselves from potential threats.

(g) When humans are in a reactive or *avoid/away* mode (i.e., when we fear, avoid or protect ourselves), we are probably less aware of our own underlying intentions than we are of and attuned to the underlying intentions of others. In other words, we seek potential ulterior motives in others.

(h) Our intentions reveal themselves, over time, through a consistent (cyclical) pattern of behavioural dynamics. These dynamics are initiated by deep-seated reactive triggers, which—if they remain unrecognized, unacknowledged, and unresolved—may result in blind-spot, nonconscious, reactive and inauthentic relational behaviour. It is important that these dynamics be addressed with the coachee, within their leader-manager coaching context.

(i) Change is threatening and humans resist it: We are creatures of habit; releasing 'old' and adopting 'new' habits induces fear, anxiety, stress, and doubt within us. When prolonged, this condition is likely to damage our personal and relational well-being.

(j) Our verbal content (our language and word choice), our physical movements, and our vocal tone are social cues of our intentions.

(k) An individual's intentions will be influenced by his or her values, attitudes, beliefs, assumptions, and generalizations.

(l) Recognizing, acknowledging and explicitly articulating our underlying intentions has the effect of neutralizing our *Agenda,* or the interpersonal effect of our outward expression or reaction, in the moment. This process of explicit articulation allows individuals the time and space to self-regulate and to curb their emotional reactivity, in a given situation.

(m) An explicitly articulated underlying intention (with accompanying neutral *Agenda*) is perceived by others as being more trustworthy, which is essential for being regarded as an 'authentic leader'. An example of this would be when a leader-manager (coachee) says: 'I believe you would feel more comfortable knowing the context, or where I am coming from, when I give you the following feedback....'

2 The Methodological Approach to Developing the AiM

During the various coaching projects and individual face-to-face coaching sessions, a primarily phenomenological, constructionist and *a posteriori* paradigm was applied, in order to conceptualize and develop the AiM. This process is ongoing, and articulating the theoretical underpinnings is but a single component of this model-building process.

The approaches used encompassed, predominantly, depth psychology, humanistic, person-centred, and solution-focused coaching.

There are multiple theories that were consulted throughout the process of developing this model—these include: authentic leadership; social-cognitive neuroscience; systems psychodynamics; self-determination and goal-focused theories; evolutionary brain; approach-avoidance motivation; social-role dynamics, narrative; mindfulness; emotional intelligence and action-learning theories.

The following models have also been consulted in the establishment of the AiM, and as part of the overall coaching process [discussed in some detail later]: the Authentic Leadership Questionnaire (ALQ; Gardner et al. 2006); the Self-Determination Theory model (Deci and Ryan 2000); Approach-Avoidance model, being an integral part of the AiM (Elliot 2006); the Ego-State [Parent-Adult-Child Transactional Analysis model] (Berne 1964); and the Triple-Loop Learning and Presencing (generative) models (Brown and Ryan 2003; Kabat-Zinn 2003; Scharmer 2000; Senge 1990)—particularly with regard to aiding the coachees in acquiring a mental model for the understanding and practice of mindfulness, self-regulation, and self-reflection.

3 Understanding Intention, Within Context

It is important to understand how the words *intention* and *Agenda* are applied in this chapter.

The intended meaning of the word *intention*, in this case, refers to a longer-term desired end-state, which is less accessible to immediate conscious, cognitive engagement, explanation, or articulation. The intended meaning of the word *Agenda* refers to one of the four behavioural-dynamic attitudes, as applied within the AiM, which is discussed later in this chapter.

The general dictionary definitions of *intention* refer to levels of conscious, executive (neocortex) functioning, such as 'determined', 'aimed', 'planned', 'purpose-' and 'goal-oriented' thoughts and actions. Perhaps a more all-encompassing label, for the purpose of this chapter, would be *underlying intention*.

Human beings cannot always articulate or explain the underlying reasons for our behaviours, particularly when we are in a reactive, fight-flight-freeze mental, emotional, and physiological state. It is therefore asserted that an individual's underlying intentions may be both conscious (accessible) and nonconscious (underlying, and therefore less accessible) to the individual; much of this would also depend on the specific contexts in which the individual's behaviours occur.

Underlying intentions, for the purpose of understanding the AiM, encompass an individual's belief system (i.e., their role-identities, values, beliefs, prejudices/biases, assumptions, and generalizations). This incorporates socio-cultural influences through which individuals perceive and make choices and decisions within their world. The assertion is that underlying intentions serve to energize and drive an individual's value-belief system in a particular direction, toward a particular desired outcome, and frame their intrapersonal and interpersonal (social) interactions within each of their given contexts.

The AiM is applied, in part, to assist coachees to bring their (nonconscious) underlying intentions to the level of conscious awareness, acknowledgement, and explicit (rather than implicit) articulation. By rendering underlying intentions explicit, through the act of cognition and verbal articulation (language), this ideally optimises an individual's abilities to self-regulate, to make choices and decisions, and to follow an optimized course of action.

It is asserted that human beings' underlying intentions are evolutionarily linked to, and contingent on, how trustworthy we perceive others to be, and how trustworthy others perceive us to be (Elliot 2006; Rousseau, et al. 1998). Our interpersonal relationships are powered by the deep-seated primal need to avoid potential threats and to survive (whether conscious or nonconscious). Therefore, assuming that we are continuously in survival mode, we could never *not* have an intention (theoretically speaking).

One of the overarching premises of this chapter, therefore, is that this underlying intention does not involve rational, neocortical decision-making, but rather emanates from the reactive paleomamallian emotional brain, as per MacLean's (1990) evolutionary Triune Brain theory. Contrary to the dictionary definitions mentioned previously, underlying intention is not (as discussed within the context of this chapter) a wholly conscious action, motive, decision, desire, or commitment toward any particular shorter-term end goal. Within this context, the intended meaning of underlying intention is closer to being a longer-term, unfocused, non-specific—and therefore an as-yet-to-be-cognitively-engaged-with (nonconscious)—desired outcome.

This chapter is built on the premise that all behaviour must be fuelled by either a conscious or an underlying (nonconscious) intention. In other words, being unaware or nonconscious does not infer that an individual's behaviour is, in any way, unintentional.

4 The Objectives and Context of the Coaching Interventions

4.1 The Objectives

The landscape for this authentic leadership-through-coaching-and-consulting chapter has been multi-contextual, in that the AiM has been applied, for each coachee, across their professional (work/organizational) and personal (home/life) contexts. Within the leadership-coaching environment, Grant (2012) asserts that our higher-order *meaning and purpose values* are often neglected in favour of our lower-order *deadline-driven goals*—as expounded by his goal-hierarchy-framework concept of values. Grant's position, in this regard, is supported by the coachees' objectives that they brought to the coaching process, which is elaborated on below.

The applied coaching philosophy and approach in this chapter therefore focuses on values-based, developmental coaching interventions. The individual coachee's higher-order values—i.e., their abstract meaning-oriented and purpose-oriented goals (e.g., "to be a more mindful and inclusive leader"), as well as the lower-order concrete or specific action-oriented goals (e.g., "to complete a project on time and below budget")—are factored into their reasons for being there, and their all-encompassing coaching objectives.

The assertion within this chapter is that authentic leadership can be optimized through the use of the following approach to leadership development: The overarching objective across the coaching process is for the coach to support each coachee to shift or transform the coachee's nonconscious and implicit underlying intention into a conscious and explicit intention—thereby, also shifting 'direction' from an *avoid/away* mode to an *approach/toward* mode.

From the coaching-intervention approach, as detailed below, it is asserted—from the coaching psychologist's subjective, evidence-based, and phenomenological experience—that personal change, paradigm shifts and transformations can occur for coachees only when they have achieved an intentional and conscious *approach/toward* emotional or psychological state. An *avoid/away* mode means that the coachee is more than likely still in a reactive and defensive/self-protective mode. While some coachees may be able to consciously recognize and articulate their underlying intention(s) while in this reactive state, they are usually not yet ready (or willing) to make the requisite shift from the *avoid/away* to the *approach/toward* mode. This shift appears to occur only once there is a conscious recognition, acknowledgement and cognitive reframing (self-regulation) of the particular habitual (reactive) mode of action. This serves to shift the coachee's emotional state from an *avoid/away* to an *approach/toward* mode. This particular terminology is expanded upon in the main *Authentic-intention Model* (*AiM*) section of this chapter.

4.2 Coaching-Intervention Process

The context of the coaching-project intervention included the following consultation and coaching phases:

(i) *Pre- and mid-coaching project stakeholder consultations* with the coach, coachee, and his or her direct report (senior manager):

   (a) The initial meeting occured prior to each project inception, in order to gather information with regard to facilitating the proposed coaching objectives (from both coachee's and manager's perspectives), and for overall system consultation and case conceptualization (Lane and Corrie 2009); to determine the mandate; to initiate the coaching contract and to delineate the confidentiality boundaries; to prime expectations; and, to engage both of the client stakeholders.

   (b) The second meeting occured mid-way through the overall coaching project, for the purpose of reflection: for re-engaging, re-focussing and the re-aligning of the initial coaching objectives.

(ii) *The coaching sessions* (coach and coachee), included elements of coaching-tool and mental-model explication and training—combined with ongoing reflection and feedback.
(iii) *Continual inter-coaching-session engagement*, between the coachee and senior manager—and feeding back of the salient issues to the coach during the coaching sessions.
(iv) *Post-coaching project communication and two-way feedback* with the coachee and senior manager—in order to confirm that the relevant changes occurred, on visible and tangible behavioural levels.

The AiM was applied longitudinally and iteratively over 12 h (±6 months) of bi-monthly coaching sessions—usually 1 or 1.5 h per session, per individual coachee, at middle, senior, and executive leader-manager levels.

The coach (via intra-session empathic attendance and post-session reflective presencing) applied thematic, intention, and narrative-analysis coding—thereby establishing each coachee's primary and secondary intention themes and patterns. While this process was coded in accordance with the AiM model, the question of the coach's subjectivity and resulting reliability of this process would require further research.

4.3 Diversity in Context

This chapter is based on the study of nine individual coachees (six females, three males), with a range of ages, ethnicities, qualifications, work experience, industry-sector and organizational levels. During their respective coaching interventions, all worked in corporate organizations as either executive managers, senior managers, middle managers, line managers, or specialists in their field. The definition and expectation of the label 'leader-manager' addresses the above factors.

The coachees represented multiple ethnicities that included black, white, Indian, and Chinese South Africans. All were proficient in English, although this was the second language for four of the nine coachees. All coaching sessions were conducted in English.

The coachees' objectives for coaching were similar, to some degree, in that they all wished to address relational boundaries, interpersonal authenticity and assertiveness, and difficult-conversation issues that overlapped with both their job and home roles. Certain coachees were transitioning between job levels and roles (i.e., being promoted and having to manage their former peers). For others, it was a career transition, to the next career and life stage. All, however, benefitted from their new-found intrapersonal awareness and insight. Their ability and skill in explicitly articulating their underlying intentions, and the congruence achieved between their own and others' expectations of their role(s) and role boundaries, were self-validating and self-empowering.

They each reported that the AiM, and, in particular, the knowledge of their roles in relation to the *avoid/away* and *approach/toward* dimension, proved to be extremely beneficial and significant—particularly with regard to their respective coaching objectives. According to their feedback, it provided them with an intuitive tool that helped them to focus and exercise their mindfulness, when exposed again to their usually-stressful work and home contexts. There was a consistency, in that all coachees felt empowered—rather than feeling trapped without options—and developed an assertiveness or a 'courageous authenticity', within each of their contextual roles.

5 The Authentic-intention Model (AiM)

5.1 The Purpose and Function of the AiM

Within the context of authentic leadership, the AiM serves as a coaching model that is used to optimize conscious, mindful behaviour, empathic awareness, and insightful observations. In both personal and work-related contexts, this model is also used to generate an emotional connection to a valued vision that has resonance and meaning for the respective coachees.

One of the purposes of this coaching model is to empower leader-manager coachees to enhance their facility for authentic interpersonal interactions through both generative and cognitive thinking, rather than being limited to using only cognitive (and often reactive) decision-making methods. Coachees would ideally transition from having, or being perceived as having, a nonconscious or 'untrustworthy' *Agenda*, to being empowered to demonstrate what would then be perceived as their having integrity and trustworthiness—i.e., through their conscious, intentional, and thereby authentic, leadership behaviour.

At its highest level, the AiM functions to guide coachees, both cognitively (through logic and reason) and viscerally (somatically, through the body), to be present to relational and behavioural dynamics; to recognize and to explicitly articulate their heretofore nonconscious intentions, role identities, beliefs, biases, assumptions and generalisations; and to understand social-role expectations—within their context of intra- and interpersonal relationships.

More specifically, this model could ideally be applied in various ways, as part of the overall (team or individual) coaching process: As a diagnostic tool (to determine the levels and intensities of the coachee's *approach* 'towardness' and *avoidance* 'awayness'); as a self-mastery and developmental tool; and, as an intra- and interpersonal-relationship management tool. The functionality of this approach is to elicit a tangible shift in relational dynamics—i.e., from the coachee's displaying of nonconscious, unacknowledged, and unarticulated reactive behaviour (possibly perceived by others as being an 'untrustworthy' intention), to the coachee's displaying of consciously articulated and intentional dialogue (possibly perceived by others as having a neutral *Agenda,* and therefore a 'trustworthy' intention).

As mentioned previously, the model has been designed using a grounded-theory-type (i.e., emergence of concepts from the data), *a posteriori* (from the latter), phenomenological, and constructionist research approach. A meta-theoretical literature review of behavioural dynamics and the psychology of intentions has also been used throughout. The model requires, from the consultant-coach and the coachees, continual and iterative reflecting and presencing (mindfulness, cognitive engagement), empathic awareness (somatic, visceral engagement), and insightful synthesis.

The AiM ideally serves as a dynamic coaching model for facilitating on-going conscious behaviour within specific behavioural contexts. The model combines a semi-linear coaching *process* model with a more *dynamic* coaching model. It is a *process* model in that it facilitates a structured process of recognition of personal meaning, motivation, and value for the coachee. This supports the coachee to become mindful of what they are moving *away* from—in order to become mindful of what they want to move *toward*—rather than remaining stuck in an habitually reactive, fear-based mode of *away* behaviour. The AiM is also a *dynamic* coaching model in that it acknowledges dispositional traits (e.g., mindfulness, and approach-avoidance tendencies), and developmental aspects (e.g., the ability to learn through an iterative action-reflection process of becoming increasingly mindful to the thinking, feeling, and behavioural components of the model).

In addition, the AiM provides a *mental* model for explaining (recognising and labelling) the 'intangible' behavioural dynamics, so that coachees are able to access and explicitly articulate their previously nonconscious underlying intentions—thereby assisting them to overcome their *awayness*, or avoidance of particular contextual situations.

The above requires that the coach be able to facilitate the coachee's shift (across the overall coaching intervention), from being nonconsciously 'incompetent' (unaware) to becoming consciously 'competent' (aware) of his or her ability to be mindful of specific personal, underlying intentions—encompassing values, attitudes, beliefs, assumptions, biases and generalisations.

To summarise, the functional outcomes of using the AiM are as follows:

1. To assist the coach and the coachee to access and to develop the coachee's ability to recognize and to acknowledge his or her underlying (nonconscious) intentions; and to transform previously unrecognized and unacknowledged intentions into those that are explicit, rather than remaining implicit; and
2. To raise the coach's and coachee's conscious-competence, through coaching, which culminates in explicitly articulated acknowledgements—which tend to result in lowered relational anxiety as well as optimised internalised self-regulation and personal empowerment (i.e., autonomy, relatedness, and competence) for the coachee (Ryan 2009).

5.2 The Structure and Process of the Authentic-intention Model

The AiM is based on the premise that our intentions are evolutionarily linked to how we protect and defend ourselves, and how we perceive our safety in relation to others. In other words, we perceive others as being potential threats, and as being untrustworthy (Elliot 2006; Rousseau et al. 1998). At its core, the model is used to elicit an individual coachee's own language descriptions for their context-specific

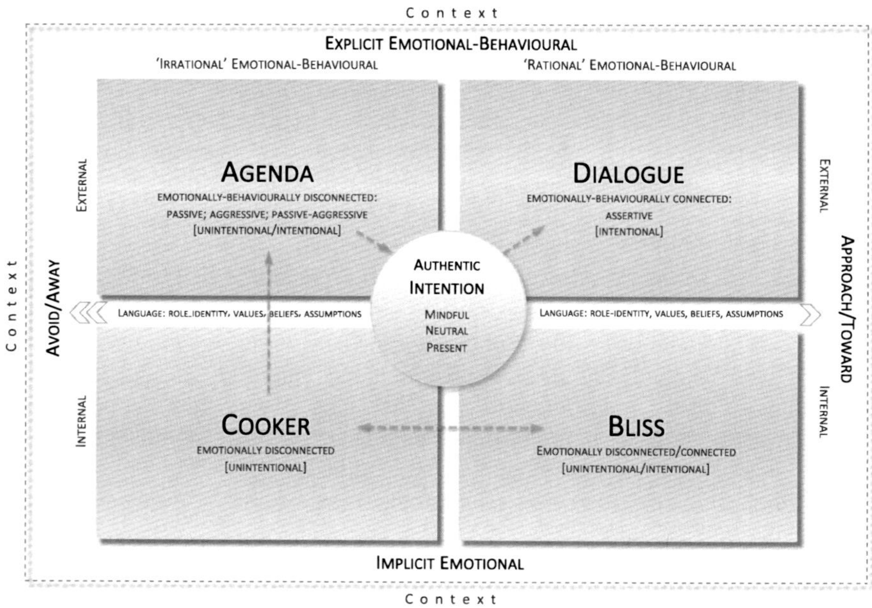

Fig. 1 The Authentic-intention Model (AiM)

role identity/identities, values, beliefs, assumptions biases and generalisations. Through this explicit articulation, the coachee makes conscious their underlying (previously nonconscious) intentions.

The AiM (see Fig. 1) comprises five components: (1) the *context* [the work/life/social socio-economic-political contextual variables]; (2) two sets of *intention* dimensions or modes: (i) *approach/toward* and *avoid/away* [i.e., the direction of an action/reaction]; and, (ii) *implicit emotional*, and *explicit emotional-behavioural* [i.e., where the action/reaction is experienced either subjectively and internally (implicitly), or objectively and externally (explicitly)]; (3) four behavioural-dynamic *attitudes* [*Cooker*, *Bliss*, *Agenda*, *Dialogue* (explained in detail, below)]; (4) the *language* bridge —which is the point at which the articulation takes place for the interplay of the context, role identity, and social expectations/beliefs—thereby facilitating verbal access to the coachee's values, attitudes, beliefs, assumptions biases/prejudices, and the generalisations that energise their *Agenda*; and, (5) the *authentic-intention* centre, which is the point at which the coachee who is using the AiM would be *Agenda*-neutral, mindful, and present to all of the above, and, in particular, to the notion that he or she always has a choice—to either remain in *Agenda* attitude mode, or to choose to adopt the *Dialogue* attitude.

Each of the five AiM components is explained in further detail:

1. *Context* is an important component of the AiM in that it sets the stage on which the coachee's various roles are played out (e.g., work, home, or social roles). The AiM should therefore be applied with due consideration to the coachee's system- or context-specific role(s). For example, a given context might be linked to a particular role and the associated social-role expectations.

2. The two *intention dimensions* are: (i) the *approach/toward* (reward-response) dimension, and the *avoid/away* (threat-response) dimension; and (ii) the *implicit emotional* and *explicit emotional-behavioural* dimensions. *Implicit emotional* is what is thought and felt by the person (internally/subjectively), and is invisible to others, within a relational situation; and *explicit emotional-behavioural* is what is thought, felt and seen by the self and by others (externally/objectively), within a relational situation.

   The above dimensions are not psychometrically scaled at this point and are, at present, taken at face value. They are viscerally (empathically) interpreted and confirmed by the coachee and the coach. Further research would benefit this aspect.
3. The intersection of these two dimensions creates four behavioural-dynamic *attitudes* or spaces:

   (i) *Cooker* [avoid/away and *implicit emotional*; disconnected (i.e., feels unsettled) and reactive/unintentional]: On a continuum, this attitude could range from being a mild, unexpressed irritation or frustration, to being an unexpressed inner rage. This can be seen as a degree of threat-response that evokes overall cognitive, emotional, and physiological dissonance and displeasure.
   (ii) *Bliss* [approach/toward and *implicit emotional*; either connected (i.e., feels settled) or disconnected, but largely inactive (disinclined to take action)]: This attitude could range from being an inner contentment and joy, to fantasising (escaping) and thus not being present. This can be seen as a degree of reward-response that evokes cognitive, emotional, and physiological pleasure.
   (iii) *Agenda* [avoid/away and *explicit emotional-behavioural*; disconnected and reactive]: This attitude is an outwardly expressed reactive response, and could encompass being passive, aggressive, and passive-aggressive. This is experienced (relationally) as a degree of threat-response and evokes cognitive, emotional and physiological dissonance, discomfort and displeasure.
   (iv) *Dialogue* [approach/toward and *explicit emotional-behavioural*; connected and pro-active]: This attitude requires a consciously intentional self-regulated (managed) approach by the individual coachee, within each relational context. This requires that the coachee displays the ability to regulate and manage his or her 'pushed buttons' and 'knee-jerk' reactions, in an adult-to-adult as opposed to a parent-to-child or child-to-parent ego state behavioural mode (Berne 1964).

4. *Language* is essential to the AiM, in that it is used to bridge (by explicitly articulating the underlying role identities and belief structures) the internalized (subjective, nonconscious) reactive and un-self-regulated *implicit emotional* response zone with the externalized (objective, conscious) self-regulatable *explicit emotional-behavioural* response zone. Lieberman et al. (2007), in their neurocognitive study of emotional-affect labelling, found that explicitly putting feelings into words had the effect of slowing down limbic brain activity and calming emotional affect.

   Role identities refers to who (which role) the coachee is being or 'enacting', in a given space and time, within their specific work or life context. The Berne (1964) ego-state behavioural model provides a valuable tool for coachees to recognise and acknowledge, both conceptually and behaviourally, the consequences (affects and effects) that their ego-state role has on others' context-specific social-role expectations.

Following on from this is the *languaging* of the belief system that is associated with each *role identity*—in particular, the languaging of the social expectations and norms as well as the incumbent rules and regulations that are linked to each role.

As an example, the 'should/should not' and the 'must/must not' (*avoid/away*) language patterns that coachees present during coaching sessions are directly indicative of their belief system around their own authorisation (or de-authorisation) to take ownership of specific actions. It is important for the coachee to become aware of these belief systems and language patterns, in that they provide access to their nonconscious and often self-censored behaviours, which are often linked to specific or multiple work and life roles. Given this, coaches could apply the AiM to facilitate their coachees' awareness toward shifting the direction of their languaging from a nonconscious *avoid/away* to a conscious *approach/toward* direction.

5. The *authentic-intention* centre is the *Agenda*-neutral, mindful and presence 'hub' of the AiM. It would not be possible to navigate or to apply the model without being present to the AiM components and the related behavioural dynamics (this aspect is discussed in further detail in the *Mindfulness and Triple-Loop Learning* section, below).

In summary, it is the coaching psychologist's task to facilitate the process that will ideally enable coachees (and their senior leader-managers) to recognize, acknowledge and to articulate the disconnects and the connects between their invisible *implicit emotional* and their visible *explicit emotional-behavioural* actions. The coach would achieve this by supporting coachees to explicitly articulate their underlying intentions that are manifest in outwardly expressed, reactive *Agendas*.

6 Mapping the Underlying Theories onto the AiM

There are four key domains that are introduced, below, that are intended to provide the theoretical, conceptual and psychological foundation for the AiM: (1) *Authentic Leadership theory* (Avolio and Gardner 2005; Gardner et al. 2006; Harter 2002; Susing et al. 2011; Wood et al. 2008); (2) *Self-Determination theory* (Deci and Ryan 2000; Ryan 2009); (3) *Approach-Avoidance Motivation and Trust theories* (Elliot 2006; Dirks and Ferrin 2002; Rousseau et al. 1998); and, (4) *Mindfulness and Triple-Loop Learning theories* (Brown and Ryan 2003; Kabat-Zinn 2003; Romme and Van Witteloostuijn 1999; Scharmer 2000).

It is important to note that this is not a definitive list; however, it encompasses the theoretical grounding—through having engaged with leader-manager coachees, using the AiM, over the years. Each of the abovementioned four key domains are discussed in detail, below.

6.1 Authentic Leadership

Authenticity, in this chapter, is discussed within the context of authentic leadership development, using coaching as an intervention.

The concept of *authenticity* is articulated, from its Greek philosophy roots, as "to thine own self be true" (Harter 2002, p. 382).

However, the aim of authentic leadership is not only to be true to oneself, but also to be authentic in one's relationship with others. Leadership cannot take place in a vacuum because it is essentially relational (Avolio and Gardner 2005). Thus, a core prerequisite of authentic leadership development, within the organizational context, is to grow the knowledge, skills, and attitudes that are required to establish authentic, trustworthy relationships.

To better understand authentic leadership, it is useful to explore the construct of authenticity in greater depth. In her highly informative chapter on authenticity, Harter (2002) states that "authenticity involves owning one's personal experiences, be they thoughts, emotions, needs, wants, preferences, or beliefs" (p. 382).

Harter (2002) establishes various perspectives on authenticity, one of them being the developmental perspective. Relational authenticity begins in early childhood, particularly via the spoken acknowledgments and validations we receive from our parents and/or significant caregivers. We learn to either accept our true self, or we become alienated from our true self by developing a false self, in order to obtain the approval that we seek from our caregivers. To obtain validation, we learn to comply with our caregivers' conditions and expectations.

These expectations are usually determined by societal and cultural norms, and manifest through our caregivers' interpretations and validations (i.e., an *approach/towards* response) or disapprovals (i.e., an *avoid/away* response) of our emotions. We are either taught to value our own individuality unconditionally, and thus we develop a true self, or we realize that complying with our caregivers is more valuable for us, in that we can avoid their disapproval, so we adapt to this conditionality by developing a false self, or a compromised self.

Harter (2002) explains that amongst adolescents, higher levels of reported true-self behaviour are correlated with their having received unconditional support and validation from parents and peers. Higher levels of reported false-self behaviour are, however, correlated with their receiving (or being 'awarded') support and validation on conditional terms, with the boundaries of these conditions being set up externally by parents/caregivers and peers. In humanist or Rogerian terms (Rogers 1951, in Harter 2002), true-self behavioural competence can be thus be facilitated through our (the coach's/clinician's) employment of empathic listening with unconditional positive regard. In AiM terms, this would constitute an *approach/toward* attitude or response.

Similarly, Horney (1950) (in Harter 2002) referred to the cause of neuroses as emanating from the alienation of our real self from our imagined or ideal self; that is, the ideal self being based on our underlying intention to seek approval by acting-reacting as we believe we 'ought to'—according to socio-cultural rules and expectations that are external to our personal values, beliefs, thoughts and feelings. In AiM terms, this would constitute an *avoid/away* attitude or response.

This is supported by Riesman (1950) (in Harter 2002) who found that inner-directed and self-determining individuals (with an internal locus of control) were more true or authentic to themselves, while those individuals who were outer-directed (with an external locus of control), and who gave in to societal expectations, were less authentic.

Finally, to emphasise the importance of the relational nature of authenticity, Harter (2002) explains that the formation of our true self is an ongoing process that occurs within relational situations and contexts, through *mutually empathic* interactions. She asserts that "genuine empathic exchange and relatedness bring clarity and authenticity to the self" (p. 389). Being mutually empathic refers to our ability, within a relational context, to achieve a balance between being self-focused and other-focused—and this is reportedly linked to providing optimal mutual validation, which leads to greater authenticity and well-being in the form of self-esteem and cheerfulness (Miller 1986, in Harter 2002). In AiM terms, being mutually empathic would constitute having an *approach/toward* relational attitude or response.

Definitions of Authentic Leadership

Walumbwa et al. (2008) define authentic leadership as "a pattern of leader behaviour that draws upon and promotes both positive psychological capacities and a positive ethical climate, to foster greater self-awareness, an internalized moral perspective, balanced processing of information, and relational transparency on the part of leaders working with followers, fostering positive self-development" (p. 94).

Harter (2002) states that authenticity is "owning one's personal experiences, be they thoughts, emotions, needs, preferences, or beliefs, processes captured by the injunction to 'know oneself'" (p. 382).

Wood et al. (2008), in their personality theory of authenticity, provide the following elements within their Authenticity Scale: (i) *Authentic Living* (being true to oneself and living in accordance with one's values and beliefs); (ii) *Accepting External Influence* (the extent to which one accepts the influence of others, and the belief that one has to conform to other's expectations); and, (iii) *Self-Alienation* (the mismatch between conscious awareness and actual experience).

According to Harter (2002) and Wood et al. (2008), people are more authentic when they perceive themselves as being accepted unconditionally, by others. Wood et al. (2008) found that authenticity is correlated with self-esteem, and that authenticity appears to be one of the strongest predictors of both subjective and psychological well-being. In addition, authentic people tended to be more extraverted, agreeable, conscientious, open, and less neurotic—with reference to the five-factor model of personality (Goldberg 1993).

Authentic leadership development "involves ongoing processes whereby leaders and followers gain self-awareness and establish open, transparent, trusting and genuine relationships, which in part may be shaped and impacted by planned interventions such as training" (Avolio and Gardner 2005, p. 322). Also, leadership cannot exist in a vacuum: In order that an organization fulfills its vision and strategic objectives, it is just as important that it develops authentic followers in parallel with the development of its authentic leaders.

Gardner et al. (2006), defining authenticity from an *authentic leadership theory* perspective, discuss four fundamental components of authenticity, as per their Authentic Leadership Questionnaire (ALQ). These leadership factors and the related characteristics are: (i) *Self-Awareness* (how one derives and makes meaning of the world; understanding one's own strengths and weaknesses); (ii) *Internalised Moral Perspective* (an internalised and integrated form of self-regulation that is guided by internal standards and values, rather than external pressures); (iii) *Balanced Processing* (objectively analysing all relevant data before deciding or reacting); and, (iv) *Relational Transparency* (presenting one's authentic self to others; the ability to be vulnerable).

Within this chapter, authenticity is referred to and is applied within the context of authentic leadership development, and, specifically, via coaching for authentic leadership. In particular, and with reference to the AiM coaching model, this encompasses the notion and understanding of *authentic intention*. Therefore, for the purpose of this chapter, a working definition would be articulated as follows:

Authentic intention is the point at which coachees ideally become *Agenda*-neutral, mindful, and present to their *avoidance/away Agenda attitude* (refer to Figure 1). It is here that coachees would recognise that they possess the option to choose to self regulate—by explicitly articulating and re-framing their previously unarticulated (and possibly nonconscious) beliefs, in order to achieve an *approach/toward Dialogue* attitude.

Authenticity and Well-Being in Coaching

There is much convergence in Susing et al.'s (2011) paper with the other research findings discussed in this section—particularly with regard to the evidence-based coaching constructs of well-being and optimised functioning. In particular—and explicitly acknowledging the relevance and centrality of authenticity within coaching—they discuss Wood et al.'s (2008) Authenticity Scale, which they confirm represents a direct measure of authenticity. These reported outcomes include: subjective and psychological well-being; self-esteem and life satisfaction; individuals who are seen as being authentic tend to be perceived as being credible leaders; also, social skills (relationships) and personal performance correlate significantly with authenticity and can be predicted via authenticity measures.

Susing et al. (2011) also refer to the following researchers, in terms of their respective findings of the attributes of *authenticity*, as related to the psychology of the coaching process: Self-awareness and self-regulation are fundamental to achieving authenticity and are correlated with psychological well-being (Gardner et al. 2005). Self-awareness provides coachees with a process tool that they can use to both recognize and to change their own behaviour (Allan and Whybrow 2007). Self-regulation is essential for the coachee's self-directed (but coach-facilitated) learning, as incorporated within the Association for Coaching's definition of coaching (AC 2015), which is quoted in Grant (2012, p. 148). And also, authentic behaviour is seen as arising from an internal locus of control, while inauthentic behaviour has an external locus of control that is triggered from a source external to the coachee (Ryan and Deci 2004).

Susing et al. (2011) also make reference to Sheldon and Elliot's (1998, 1999) Self-Concordance Model—the theory being that a high concordance between a coachee's goals and core values is correlated with his or her sustained effort and higher levels of well-being. This particular aspect of congruence, in relation to applying the AiM for coaching, is discussed in further detail, below.

Authentic Leadership, Related to Coaching and the AiM

It is asserted that when entering into a (leadership-development) coaching relationship, the coaching journey would ideally begin with the coach supporting the coachee to take ownership of the coachee's role in, and shared responsibility of, their personal and interpersonal (relational) experiences.

It is also asserted that *being* (i.e., intrapersonal awareness, self reflection) is mostly transformational and is inherently linked to intrinsic motivation. Conversely, *doing* (i.e., interpersonal awareness, activity) is mostly transactional and is inherently linked to extrinsic motivation. It is incumbent on coachees (via the coaching process) to become intrinsically motivated, in order to establish and clarify their identities, to connect emotionally to their visions, values and goals, and to believe in their *being* the role of the authentic leader.

In accordance with the abovementioned definitions, understanding and outcomes of authentic behaviour, with the underlying assumptions of the AiM model, and from evidence-based coaching-practitioner experience, coaching for authentic leadership encompasses the following attributes (amongst others): The expectation (of our peers, colleagues, families and friends) that we be congruent – that is, to congruently live and to model our espoused values, attitudes, beliefs, behaviours and morals (ethics). In this regard, it appears that authentic leaders – whose intrinsic and espoused leadership values, attitudes, beliefs, behaviours and morals are congruent – are being inherently 'transformational'. Given the above, the understanding is that authentic leaders are required to know and to regulate (transform) themselves first, in order that their followers may begin to know and to regulate (transform) themselves, thereby becoming authentic followers. Given this, the capacity and the skills for continuous self-awareness and self-regulation (that is, to know and to regulate oneself) are essential to being an authentic leader.

It is also important to note that authenticity is not a short-term, superficial, operational action, activity or goal (that is external/distal to ourselves, in time and space), so we cannot 'do' or achieve authenticity. Authenticity, and values-based authentic leadership, is a longer-term, deeper, aspirational and integral part of our identity and of our deeply-held values – which are ideally congruent with our life's philosophy and valued end-state – which has personal meaning to which we are emotionally connected (Gardner et al. 2005). These qualities and attitudes are ideally consistent and evident across our multiple work and life roles; it is who we are *being* (internally/proximally), moment by moment, within each of our roles.

If we consider *self-awareness* and *self-regulation* in relation to the AiM process, the coachee's ability to demonstrate these two qualities is necessary in order to: (i) recognize when they are in *avoid/away* mode, and (ii) recognize and access, via *languaging*, the AiM's *implicit emotional* intention (the *Cooker* attitude), before it is able to reach the *explicit emotional-behavioural* (the *Agenda* attitude). Paying attention to this, while in the *authentic-intention* centre, and by explicitly labelling/naming the emotion, it has been shown, in a neurocognitive study of emotional-affect labelling (i.e., putting feelings into words), to slow down and to calm limbic brain activity and the emotional affect (Lieberman et al. 2007). This is directly linked to our ability to self-regulate and to control ourselves.

> The awareness component refers to having awareness of, and trust in, one's motives, feelings, desires, and self-relevant cognitions. It includes, but is not limited to, being aware of one's strengths and weaknesses, trait characteristics, and emotions. (Kernis 2003, p. 13)

Therefore, without *self-awareness* and *self-regulation*, our relational dynamics would border on (varying degrees of) emotional loss of control, which is usually followed by a lowering of both credibility and relational trust for the leader-manager role.

Self-Determination Theory (*SDT*) considers both the goal content (the 'what', or the outcome) as well as the regulatory processes that we undertake (the 'why') in order to achieve our goals as we attempt to satisfy our basic psychological need for *competence*, *autonomy* and *relatedness* – to be able to self-determine and assert our free will.

If these needs are thwarted or compromised, this could "lead to specifiable patterns of behaviours, regulations, goals, and affects that do not represent the optimal development and well-being that would occur in supportive environments but which would have had some adaptive value under adverse conditions" (Deci and Ryan 2000, p. 254). These authors also found that needs that are not satisfied – i.e., needs that remain deprived or thwarted – can be linked to various forms of psychopathology.

Definition of Self-Determination Theory

Self-Determination Theory is a composite of five mini goal theories (Ryan 2009): Cognitive Evaluation Theory (CET), Organismic Integration Theory (OIT), Causality Orientations Theory (COT), Basic Psychological Needs Theory (BPNT), and Goal Contents Theory (GCT). SDT asserts that human motivation is grounded in our innate and universal psychological need for and tendency toward achieving *competence*, *autonomy*, and *relatedness* – and satisfying these three needs is instrumental to our development and well-being. However, Deci and Ryan (2000) clarify that these needs are not the only or all-encompassing determinants of our behaviour.

Extrinsic rewards and punishments – which on some level control, regulate and compromise our will, our integrity, and our need for *autonomy* (i.e., our ability to self-organize and self-regulate our own actions; our internal locus of control) – tend to undermine rather than optimise our well-being. Ryan (2009) refers to, external regulation as being "the least autonomous form of extrinsic motivation and integrated regulation the most autonomous (para. 7)." This relates to the above discussion on authenticity, with regard to authenticity being linked to an internal, rather than to an external, locus of control.

Self Determination, Related to Coaching and the AiM

Given the above, the following is asserted: When human beings are in *Agenda*-attitude mode, i.e., *avoid/away* (e.g., reactive, aggressive, and/or passive-aggressive) and our behaviour is externalised (in AiM terms), this evokes a conflict-inflating attitude for all relational parties, which compromises *competence*, *autonomy* and *relational* need attainment. This, in effect, entrenches a compounded defensive, protective, determined, inflexible and reactive position within each of the individuals involved.

Conversely, being in *Dialogue*-attitude mode, i.e., *approach/toward* (e.g., proactive, assertive, with a 'neutralised *Agenda*'), and our behaviour is being externalised (in AiM terms), this evokes a conflict-deflating attitude for the individuals involved, which contributes to the attainment and fulfilment of *competence*, *autonomy* and *relational* needs.

This, in accordance with the SDT of motivation, is positively linked to and is likely to increase our intrinsic motivation, and thus optimise our sense of *autonomy*, our *competence*, our *relational* need attainment, and thus our overall well-being.

It is, therefore, incumbent on each of us, within our respective organizational, team and interpersonal contexts, to have the ability to create and/or manage our relational socio-cultural conditions, in real time. Support for each other's autonomy leads to enhanced quality of relational interaction (Deci et al. 2006).

It is worth noting that, according to Ryan (2009), SDT emphasizes the role of *mindfulness* in self-regulation and wellness, due to the finding that autonomy is facilitated by reflective awareness (discussed in Sect. 6.4, below).

6.2 Approach-Avoidance Motivation and Trust

In the conceptualisation and application of the AiM, it is asserted that the underlying theoretical constructs of *approach-avoidance motivation* (Elliot 2006) and *trust* (Rousseau et al. 1998) are linked by a common evolutionary or survival component. Human behaviour constitutes movement (i.e., it is energised) in one of two ways: either *toward* a 'reward' stimulus, or *away* from a 'threat' stimulus.

Definitions of Approach-Avoidance Motivation and Trust

Approach-Avoidance Motivation: Elliot (2006) defines *approach motivation* as "the energization of behaviour by, or the direction of behaviour toward, positive stimuli (objects, events, possibilities)", and avoidance motivation as "the energization of behaviour by, or the direction of behaviour away from, negative stimuli (objects, events, possibilities)." (p. 111)

Elliot (2006) goes on to explain that the core premise of *approach-avoidance motivation* is that it is a core (primal) and consistent phenomenon across all life forms, and it is essential to optimal environmental and contextual adaptation and survival. "Both approach and avoidance motivation are part of our evolutionary heritage, and we certainly cannot survive, either physically or psychologically, without both types…, and avoidance motivation is undoubtedly adaptive in some instances" (Elliot 2006, p. 114).

The core element of Elliot's (2006) research – and a central premise for the AiM – is his assertion that human beings "automatically evaluate most, if not all, encountered stimuli on a positive-negative dimension…, and that these evaluations instantaneously evoke approach and avoidance behavioural predispositions (p. 113)." This, in particular, ties up with the previously mentioned *AiM assumptions*, *'f' and 'g'*.

Elliot (2006) states that "avoidance motivation is designed to facilitate surviving, whereas approach motivation is designed to facilitate thriving" (p. 115). We are evolutionarily programmed to move *away* efficiently, in order to ensure survival, so we tend to distrust others instinctively, in order to protect ourselves against possible danger. Thus, the building of trust (moving *toward*) is a more cumbersome and a less efficient process, and we approach interpersonal relationships with caution. Further investigation relating the above to personality differences would be valuable.

Avoid or *away* (incorporating fight, flight and freeze responses, according to the AiM) can then be associated with the following: the negative, threat, fear, pain, dissonance/discomfort, avoidance of being vulnerable, exclusion, and being closed to the unknown (amongst others). Conversely, *approach* or *toward* can be associated with the following: the positive, reward, love, inclusion, being open to being vulnerable, being open to discomfort/dissonance as well as to the unknown (amongst others). Given the above, while *avoid/away* is largely an unconscious knee-jerk or reactive 'irrational' paleomamallian/emotional brain reaction (MacLean 1990), *approach/toward* seems closer to being a conscious 'rational' neocortical decision-making process.

It must, however, be emphasized that *approach-avoid* is not a simplistic cause-and-effect or a one-way process: Humans are complex and we have the capacity to consciously decide to choose to *approach* – but perhaps this can occur only once we consciously recognize and acknowledge that we are experiencing *avoidance* mode. In order to achieve this decision-making state, it is necessary for humans to consciously self-regulate and to develop their ability to shift their state from emotional-reactivity to cognitive-intentionality.

An *approach-avoid* paradox exists, however, in that we have the ability to approach when we actually desire or intend to avoid, and also to avoid when we intend to approach. In other words, *approach/toward* goals may arise as a result of underlying *avoid/away* motivation, e.g., from the fear of rejection or failure (Elliot and Church 1997). Elliot (2006) states that this "allows individuals with aversive dispositional tendencies to cope with them in an adaptive manner by channelling them toward appetitive possibilities" (p. 114). Also, we have a tendency toward going into survival mode, regardless of whether there is a threat or danger; which invariably leads to lost opportunities for growth and development. However, if we overuse *avoid/away* motivation, this could lead to our inadvertently sabotaging our plans and desires, which could then negatively impact on our well-being (Elliot 2006).

Trust: Rousseau et al. (1998) define trust as "a psychological state comprising the intention to accept vulnerability based upon positive expectations of the intentions or behaviour of another" (p. 395).

Dirks and Ferrin (2002) also subscribe to this definition in their meta-analytic study of trust in leadership. Specifically, they discuss overall trust as encompassing a combination of two dimensions or forms of trust: (1) *Cognitive*: expressed through an individual's belief/expectation in their leader-manager's (the referent's) reliability, honesty, fairness, predictability and integrity, amongst others – i.e., the referent's character or trustworthiness; and (2) *Affective*: expressed via an individual's belief/perception of their referent's intention to care and show concern for the individual's welfare – i.e., referring to the socio-emotional, rather than just the economical or transactional, quality of their relationship.

Given this, it is asserted that the above definitions and the explanation of the cognitive and affective dimensions of trust, which make reference to the expectations and perceptions of an individual, link directly to the initial explanation that we instinctively and immediately pay attention to the *underlying intentions* of others, within our relational contexts.

A note on Cognitive Dissonance: Egan et al. (2007) write about our evolutionary link to cognitive dissonance. If our trust is compromised (if we perceive the underlying intentions and actions of another as being inconsistent with our perceptions and expectations), then this establishes within us a state of psychological anxiety and discomfort, or cognitive dissonance. Our immediate reaction to this inconsistency would be to move *away*, in order to reduce this discomfort. We achieve this by either changing our actions and cognitions, or by rationalising and inserting new cognitions (Festinger and Carlsmith 1959). This is significant for coaching with the AiM, as discussed below.

Taken on face value, the *approach-avoidance motivation* and *cognitive dissonance* theories appear to be complementary and mutually supportive.

Approach-Avoidance Motivation and Trust, Related to Coaching and the AiM

Within the context of coaching, the predominance of the *avoid/away* motivation within coachees appears to be the common-denominator coachee characteristic, and also the underlying reason (the driver) for the request for a coaching intervention. Many coaching sessions' overriding objective is for the coach to facilitate a shift in the coachee's framework, from an *avoid/away* motivation to an *approach/toward* motivation.

The salient aspects of the above definitions, for the AiM, are the coachee's behavioural intention and willingness to trust, i.e., to be vulnerable, in concert with his or her 'positive' expectations and perceptions of the underlying intentions and actions of others. If a positive expectation of others is thwarted (due to an unexpected or 'negative' reaction from the other), then the former intention and willingness to be vulnerable will be compromised or reversed (via an *avoid/away* fight-flight-freeze, coping, defense or survival response). This also relates to SDT in that our functioning and well-being are compromised when our fundamental needs for *competence*, *self-determination (autonomy)*, and *relatedness* are not met (Deci and Ryan 2000).

With regard to approach-avoidance motivation and its relation to the *languaging* aspect of the AiM (discussed in Sect. 5.2, above): The AiM is used to guide the coaching process with regard to the re-framing of a coachee's language patterns (incorporating their belief systems, assumptions and behaviours). The objective, within a coaching session, is to re-route the coachee's languaging from an nonconscious (often de-authorised and disempowered) *avoid/away* direction, to a conscious (self-authorised and empowered) *approach/toward* direction.

6.3 *Mindfulness and Triple-Loop Learning*

As mentioned previously, according to SDT, individual autonomy (self-regulation and well-being) is enabled in accordance with our capacity for *reflective awareness* and *mindfulness* (Ryan 2009). However, whenever our awareness is diminished our capacity for self-regulating our own actions, and thus our functioning and overall well-being, is compromised (Deci and Ryan 2000).

Definitions of Mindfulness and Triple-Loop Learning

Mindfulness: Kabat-Zinn (2003) provides an operational working definition of mindfulness as being "the awareness that emerges through paying attention on purpose, in the present moment, and nonjudgmentally to the unfolding of experience moment by moment" (p. 145).

Brown and Ryan (2003) define mindfulness as an attribute of consciousness, "the state of being attentive to and aware of what is taking place in the present" (p. 822). They go on to differentiate between the *awareness* and *attention* components of consciousness: awareness being the background of consciousness, and attention being the process of focusing conscious awareness. Awareness and attention are interconnected, in that "attention continually pulls 'figures' out of the 'ground' of awareness, holding them focally for varying lengths of time" (Brown and Ryan 2003, p. 822).

Triple-loop learning: Peschl (2007) describes triple-loop learning as such: "While classical learning strategies focus on changes in the domain of knowledge and the intellect, the triple-loop approach also includes changes on the existential level and in the domain of the 'will/heart'" (p. 138). Romme and Van Witteloostuijn (1999) explain the systemic levels of organizational learning, leading up to triple-loop learning, as follows:

> "Single loop learning refers to making simple adaptions and taking corrective actions, whereas double loop learning involves reframing, that is, learning to see things in totally new ways. Finally, triple loop learning entails members developing new processes or methodologies for arriving at such re-framings" (p. 439).

One of the bridges that connects mindfulness and triple-loop learning is articulated through Scharmer's (2000) research on *presencing*. For him, leadership requires that we demonstrate the ability to shift the place from which we (and the system) operate. He refers to Types I and II learning: Type I is learning through *reflection* and re-enactment of past experiences (which, within the 'new economy', is no longer effective on its own); and Type II is learning by sensing and embodying (*presencing*) "from a reality that is not yet embodied in manifest experience" of the current leadership structures (Scharmer 2000, p. 6). From this, he asks: "What theories, methods, and tools will help leaders switch from the surface levels of cognition to the deeper sources of knowing (sensing and presencing)?" (p. 21). His models provide, within an organizational context, a process and tools that address this need for presencing ourselves and, in particular, to sense, to acknowledge and to embody our underlying intentions, our shared vision and purpose, and our collective will.

Scharmer (2000) uses various tools in his process of *presencing* that become useful with regard to understanding the mechanics of the AiM. In particular, he refers to our need to shift the locus of control and focus within two domains: (1) our (individual/intra-personal) *listening*, and (2) our (collective/interpersonal) *languaging*.

Firstly, this requires that we deepen our *listening* (our attention and cognition) through four sequential stages: (i) *downloading* (focus is internal [*seeing myself* through my own eyes], I reconfirm my existing mental models and expectations/assumptions); (ii) *seeing* (focus is external [*seeing you* through my eyes], I attend to all that is new or different to my existing mental models and expectations); (iii) *sensing* (focus is empathic, on your internal viewpoint [*seeing you through your eyes*], dialogue happens at this level, when I humanize and, briefly, become you); and then, (iv) *presencing* (the focus on 'me-you' and our 'internal-external' boundaries is collapsed; we attend to that which is beyond the intra- and interpersonal, beyond our existing mental models and assumptions, toward that which is yet to emerge and to become). Or, as Scharmer (2000) puts it, "passing over the threshold of emptiness: letting go and surrendering to what wants to emerge" (p. 33).

Secondly, according to Scharmer (2000), we are required to shift our field of *language* (our modes of conversation) through the following four fields, in order to transform the place where the conversation comes from: (i) *talking nice* (being polite; as per the *downloading*, above, repeating old rules by making use of existing models); (ii) *talking tough* (debating, advocating our own views and adapting the rules, the language, that helps to say what we are thinking – make explicit that which is implicit – i.e., regarding the real issues); (iii) *reflective dialogue* (inquiring about and questioning the underlying assumptions of that which we advocate, acting then reflecting; intuiting the rules; being open to the possibility of unseen/unknown realities that could emerge); and, (iv) *generative dialogue* (presencing, action and reflection are one; generating new rules; being empty of and releasing all our knowing, assumptions and expectations [the 'I', 'you' dynamic becomes 'we']; being present to what is and what could be; and also giving power to that which is in the process of emerging, through the act of articulation).

It is at this fourth level of presencing and generative dialogue that we approach the concept and articulation of the AiM's *authentic-intention* centre – the neutral, mindful and presence 'hub' of the coaching model. If one were to draw parallels, Csikszentmihalyi's (1997) theory of *Flow* could possibly also be viewed in the same light (within the context of using the AiM within a coaching conversation); however, further research would be required to confirm this assertion.

Mindfulness and Triple-Loop Learning, Related to Coaching and the AiM

In relation to the previously mentioned *AiM assumptions* (in particular, *assumption 'g'*), it would be imperative that authentic, intentional leader-managers be continuously mindful and present so as to recognize and manage the multiple behavioural dynamics (particularly covert tensions) that are present within their day-to-day interpersonal interactions.

It is therefore incumbent on these leader-managers to process and reflect on each of these awareness opportunities, so as to intentionally and consciously deepen their learning – i.e., to shift this awareness from a (cognitive) conscious-competence level to the more integrated (visceral/kinaesthetic) unconscious-competence and habitual (triple-loop learning) level.

In this regard, the AiM provides a structured mental model to be used by the coach and coachee, to check or 'plot' the coachee's two *intention dimensions*, as explained previously: (i) the *approach/toward* and *avoid/away* dimension [the direction in which he or she is moving as each incident occurs (which may occur physically/viscerally, mentally and/or emotionally)], and (ii) the *implicit emotional* and *explicit emotional-behavioural* dimension [*implicit emotional* is what is thought and felt by the self (internal/subjective), but is invisible to others, within a relational situation; and *explicit emotional-behavioural* is what is thought, felt and seen/heard by the self and by others (external/objective), within a relational situation].

The importance of mindfulness of one's physical body, thoughts and emotions, contained within a specific contextual space and time, appears to be self-evident in this regard. It is therefore asserted that applying the model in this manner, over time, focuses, deepens and reinforces the coachee's ability and skill to become intentionally present, mindful, and *Agenda*-neutral — with reference to the AiM's *authentic-intention* centre. To illustrate, this would occur when individuals' growing presence to and mindfulness of their habitual reactions to specific and meaningful relational dynamics empowers them to intentionally (on purpose) neutralise or set aside their previously nonconscious, reactive *Agendas*.

7 Discussion

This chapter explores how theory and evidence-based practice converge to establish a theoretically-grounded understanding of authentic, intentional leadership – using the Authentic-intention Model (AiM). The AiM is a coaching model that is used within the context of authentic-leadership consulting and coaching, in order to diagnose, develop, manage and optimise values-based, authentic-leadership behaviour. It is used by coaches, in particular, to facilitate awareness of, and shifts in, relational dynamics (when coaching or facilitating individuals or teams). That is, from their displaying a nonconscious, unacknowledged and unarticulated reactive behaviour or *Agenda*, toward their displaying a consciously articulated, intentional and relational *Dialogue*. The objective is for leader-managers (coachees) to establish authentic, trustworthy, values-based, meaningful, and thus engaged and inspiring working relationships, at all levels within their organization.

Four theoretical domain groupings have been discussed to explain and articulate the AiM: (1) Authentic Leadership theory, (2) Self-Determination theory, (3) Approach-Avoidance Motivation and Trust theories, and (4) Mindfulness and Triple-Loop Learning theories. Each of these contributed in part to the conceptual, theoretical and evidence-based psychological foundation that, combined, ideally represent the essence of the AiM coaching model.

These particular theoretical domains were chosen in order to ascertain whether the evidence-based research elements of the researcher's understanding and experience correlated with the proposed theoretical foundation for the AiM. The feedback from, and benefits derived by, the coachees and their particular leader-managers, thus far, bear testament to the respective and combined findings of overall well-being. It was also necessary to understand how the AiM could best be articulated, in synthesis with the various theoretical constructs.

More specifically, the outcomes of applying this model, from an evidence-based research perspective, have culminated in the coachees reporting that they have a mental model and process that helps them to be conscious of their *approach/toward* and *avoid/away* intentions during context-specific critical incidences. Coachees, regardless of their diverse backgrounds, reported that this helps them to reduce their relational anxiety, and they believe and feel more empowered to adopt a mindful meta-position in their interaction with others. This newfound awareness and realization, that they have a choice, appears to boost their sense of autonomy and their awareness of their own capacity for self-regulation. They feel more comfortable (are in integrity with themselves) with being assertive and embracing, rather than avoiding, 'difficult conversations' with others. They also perceive themselves, and believe their co-workers to perceive them, to be more credible in their respective leadership roles. The coachees reported that the AiM provided them with a mental model and framework for being intentionally present, mindful, and for understanding how to be *Agenda*-neutral.

Coachees also felt that, as a result of being more mindful of their underlying intentions, their awareness of themselves either moving *away* or *toward* in a given situation helps to connect them to the beliefs that support their underlying values. This heightened presence and mindfulness slows down their *away* reactivity, giving them the space and time to choose (to self-regulate and to neutralise) an alternative course of action, which indirectly and inherently provides the ideal forum or critical incident for modelling authentic behaviour (i.e., to re-connect and re-align with their [now consciously] intended value and belief system, and to be authentic in terms of 'walking the walk').

The assertion, therefore, is that the trustworthiness of individual leaders can be established and optimised via their intentionality toward consistently recognising, acknowledging and engaging with their mindful, present and Agenda-neutral moments. In order to be deemed authentic, it is necessary that leader-managers engage their co-workers meaningfully and intentionally, by being able to explicitly articulate their previously underlying nonconscious intentions, so as to inspire their team toward achieving their, and their organization's, strategic visions and goals.

8 Conclusion and Future Research

In accordance with the author's evidence-based findings, and given the abovementioned authenticity, self-determination, approach-avoidance motivation, and mindfulness theories, the AiM ideally addresses and enhances coachees' overall work-related well-being. It provides a mental model and framework with which coaches are able to observe and assess the approach-avoid status of their coachees' underlying intentions — via their verbal and non-verbal languaging [verbal content (topic, word choice), emotion (tone), and physicality (body language)]. Coaches are then able to choose and phrase their coaching questions accordingly, in the moment, with theoretically-grounded purpose and intentionality.

One of the questions remaining is whether, after the coaching intervention, the individual coachees are willing and inspired enough to sustain the application of the model and the focused mindfulness that they have achieved. As reported by the coachees who returned for further coaching, additional coaching sessions are generally required in order to re-presence the coachee to their current situation, to ascertain the behavioural-dynamic shifts that have taken place in the interim, and to re-align accordingly, using the principles of the AiM.

This chapter represents a theoretical exploration and interpretation based on evidence-based application and experience using this model, with various coachees and over a period of time. Further research would ideally be required to establish the psychometric scales and properties needed to quantify and to verify the assumptions and said theories. It would also be useful to use this model to research intra- and inter-team dynamics, in addition to the individual application. The possibility of exploring this model across an organizational-culture context may also prove valuable.

From a diversity perspective, the coachees' perceptions of intentionality, across their specific cultures, appears to be consistent. Humans react in the same way when exposed to the same stimulus. However, this is context-specific, in that our contexts (e.g., work or home), and in particular, the situational/social-role expectation within each of these contexts, is an important factor to consider. We are expected to be 'professional' at work and informal at home, therefore the roles and role-dynamics may differ – further research would be required.

This chapter looks at leadership in corporate organizations specifically – which in all likelihood has some overlap and differences with the social expectations and dynamics of community or tribal leadership. Whether there is a consistent definition, meaning, understanding, perception and expectation of inter-contextual leaders may also be worthy of further research.

Recognizing, acknowledging and articulating our underlying intentions takes vision and the will to see the deeper meaning, in order to align our individual values to the 'bigger picture' takes an abundance attitude, which requires personal courage and mindful, present and *Agenda*-neutral intentionality.

References

Allan, J., & Whybrow, A. (2007). Gestalt coaching. In S. Palmer & A. Whybrow (Eds.), *Handbook of coaching psychology: A guide for practitioners* (pp. 133–159). New York: Routledge Publishers/Taylor & Francis Group.

Association for Coaching (AC). (2015). *Association for coaching definition of coaching*. Retrieved August 14, 2015, from: www.associationforcoaching.com/pages/about/coaching-definitions

Avolio, B. J., & Gardner, W. L. (2005). Authentic leadership development: Getting to the root of positive forms of leadership. *Leadership Quarterly, 16*, 315–338.

Berne, E. (1964). *Games people play – The basic hand book of transactional analysis*. New York: Ballantine Books.

Brown, K. W., & Ryan, R. M. (2003). The benefits of being present: Mindfulness and its role in psychological well-being. *Journal of Personality and Social Psychology, 84*(4), 822–848.

Csikszentmihalyi, M. (1997). *Finding flow: The psychology of engagement with everyday life*. New York: Harper Collins.

Deci, E. L., & Ryan, R. M. (2000). The "what" and "why" of goal pursuits: Human needs and the self-determination of behaviour. *Psychological Inquiry, 11*, 227–268.

Deci, E. L., La Guardia, J. G., Moller, A. C., Scheiner, M. J., & Ryan, R. M. (2006). On the benefits of giving as well as receiving autonomy support: Mutuality in close friendships. *Personality and Social Psychology Bulletin, 32*(3), 313–327.

Dirks, K. T., & Ferrin, D. L. (2002). Trust in leadership: Meta-analytic findings and implications for research and practice. *Journal of Applied Psychology, 87*(4), 611–628.

Egan, L. C., Santos, L. R., & Bloom, P. (2007). The origins of cognitive dissonance: Evidence from children and monkeys. *Psychological Science, 18*(11), 978–983.

Elliot, A. J. (2006). The hierarchical model of approach-avoidance motivation. *Motivation and Emotion, 30*(2), 111–116.

Elliot, A. J., & Church, M. A. (1997). A hierarchical model of approach and avoidance achievement motivation. *Journal of Personality and Social Psychology, 72*(1), 218–232.

Festinger, L., & Carlsmith, J. M. (1959). Cognitive consequences of forced compliance. *Journal of Abnormal Psychology, 58*(2), 203–210.

Gardner, W. L., Avolio, B. J., Luthans, F., May, D. R., & Walumbwa, F. (2005). "Can you see the real me?" A self-based model of authentic leader and follower development. *The Leadership Quarterly, 16*, 343–372.

Gardner, W. L., Avolio, B. J., & Walumbwa, F. (2006). *Authentic leadership theory and practice: Origins, effects and development*. Amsterdam: Elsevier JAI Press.

Goldberg, L. R. (1993). The structure of phenotypic personality traits. *American Psychologist, 48*(1), 26–34.

Grant, A. M. (2012). An integrated model of goal-focused coaching: An evidence-based framework for teaching and practice. *International Coaching Psychology Review, 7*(2), 146–165.

Harter, S. (2002). Authenticity. In C. R. Snyder & S. J. Lopez (Eds.), *Handbook of positive psychology* (pp. 382–394). London: Oxford University Press.

Horney, K. (1950). *Neurosis and human growth*. New York: Norton.

Jung, C. G. (1961). *Memories, dreams, reflections*. New York: Random House, Inc.

Kabat-Zinn, J. (2003). Mindfulness-based interventions in context: Past, present, and future. *Clinical Psychology: Science and Practice, 10*(2), 144–156.

Kernis, M. H. (2003). Toward a conceptualization of optimal self-esteem. *Psychological Inquiry, 14*(1), 1–26.

Lane, D. A., & Corrie, S. (2009). Does coaching psychology need the concept of formulation? *International Coaching Psychology Review, 4*(2), 195–208.

Lieberman, M. D., Eisenberger, N. I., Crockett, M. J., Pfeifer, J. H., & Way, B. M. (2007). Putting feelings into words: Affect labeling disrupts amygdala activity to affective stimuli. *Psychological Science, 18*, 421–428.

MacLean, P. D. (1990). *The triune brain in evolution: Role in Paleocerebral functions*. New York: Plenum Press.

Miller, J. B. (1986). *Toward a new psychology of women* (2nd ed.). Boston: Beacon.

Peschl, M. F. (2007). Triple-loop learning as foundation for profound change, individual cultivation, and radical innovation. Construction processes beyond scientific and rational knowledge. *Constructivist Foundations, 2*(2–3), 136–145. Boston: Houghton Mifflin.

Riesman, D. (1950). *The lonely crowd*. New Haven, CT: Yale University Press.

Rogers, C. (1951). *Client-centered therapy*. Boston: Houghton Mifflin.

Romme, A. G. L., & van Witteloostuijn, A. (1999). Circular organizing and triple loop learning. *Journal of Organizational Change Management, 12*(5), 439–453.

Rousseau, D. M., Sitkin, S. B., Burt, R. S., & Camerer, C. (1998). Not so different after all: A cross-discipline view of trust. *Academy of Management Review, 23*, 393–404.

Ryan, R. (2009, June). Self-determination theory and wellbeing. *Wellbeing in developing countries research review, 1*. Retrieved August 14, 2015, from: http://www.welldev.org.uk/wed-new/network/research-review/Review_1_Ryan.pdf

Ryan, R. M., & Deci, E. L. (2004). Autonomy is no illusion: Self-determination theory and the empirical study of authenticity, awareness, and will. In J. Greenberg, S. L. Koole, & T. Pyszczynski (Eds.), *Handbook of experimental existential psychology* (pp. 455–485). New York: Guilford Press.

Scharmer, C. O. (2000, October). *Presencing: Learning from the future as it emerges*. Paper presented at the MIT Sloan School of Management, OSG.

Seligman, M. E. (2002). *Authentic happiness: Using the new positive psychology to realize your potential for lasting fulfillment.* New York: Free Press.

Senge, P. M. (1990). *The fifth discipline: The art & practice of the learning organization.* New York: Doubleday.

Sheldon, K.M., & Elliot, A.J. (1998). Not all personal goals are personal: Comparing autonomous and controlled reasons for goals as predictors of effort and attainment. *Personality and Social Psychology Bulletin, 24*(5), 546–557.

Sheldon, K.M., & Elliot, A.J. (1999). Goal striving, need satisfaction, and longitudinal well-being: The self-concordance model. *Journal of Personality and Social Psychology, 76*(3), 482–497.

Susing, I., Green, L. S., & Grant, A. M. (2011). The potential use of the Authenticity Scale as an outcome measure in executive coaching. *The Coaching Psychologist, 7*(1), 16–25.

Walumbwa, F. O., Avolio, B. J., Gardner, W. L., Wernsing, T. S., & Peterson, S. J. (2008). Authentic leadership: Development and validation of a theory-based measure. *Journal of Management, 34*(1), 89–126.

Wood, A. M., Linley, P. A., Maltby, J., Baliousis, M., & Joseph, S. (2008). The authentic personality: A theoretical and empirical conceptualization and the development of the Authenticity Scale. *Journal of Counseling Psychology, 55*(3), 385–399.

Appreciative Inquiry Coaching in a Multi-cultural Context

Freddie Crous and Chantelle Christine Blandin de Chalain

Abstract Appreciative Inquiry (AI) was developed as a participative action research approach to organization development and change. It may, however, be argued that even though every Appreciative Inquiry addresses a particular change agenda it may also be regarded as a form of coaching. Those participating in an AI are inevitably coached towards inculcating this transformational process into their lives/work, often in an oblique manner. Nevertheless, because of Appreciative Inquiry's dialogic nature (as opposed to being diagnostic) embedded in social constructionism coaches, committed to working conversationally, have been able to apply AI with great success. It is, not only because of its emphasis on the relational and conversational, but also because of being unconditionally positive, that Appreciative Inquiry can be constructively applied in a multicultural context. This chapter is presented in the format of a conversation between the two authors. Apart from its origins and underlying principles two compelling case studies are presented.

Keywords Positive psychology • Appreciative inquiry • Multi-cultural • Coaching

1 Introduction

In essence, Appreciative Inquiry is about conversations for transformation (cf. Bushe and Kassam 2005). We, the authors, have therefore decided to present this chapter in the form of an inquiry. Chantelle Blandin de Chalain is a business consultant and busy with her Masters in Industrial/Organizational Psychology who wanted to know more about Appreciative Inquiry as a coaching method. She

F. Crous (✉)
University of Johannesburg, Johannesburg, South Africa
e-mail: fcrous@uj.ac.za

C.C.B. de Chalain
Optentia Research Focus Area, North-West University, Vanderbijlpark, South Africa
e-mail: chantellecrose@gmail.com

L.E. van Zyl et al. (eds.), *Coaching Psychology: Meta-theoretical perspectives and applications in multicultural contexts*, DOI 10.1007/978-3-319-31012-1_8

approached Freddie Crous, a professor of Industrial Psychology, who uses Appreciative Inquiry extensively for teaching, research, consulting and coaching.

Appreciative Inquiry was initially developed as a positive action research approach to organization development and change (Cooperrider et al. 2003), but now is applied in a range of contexts inside and outside of the organizational context. It may, however, be argued that even though every Appreciative Inquiry addresses a particular change agenda, in general it can be regarded as a form of coaching. Those participating in an Appreciative Inquiry are inevitably, by default, coached towards inculcating this transformational process into their lives and work. Nevertheless, in particular because of Appreciative Inquiry's dialogic (Bushe and Marshak 2009), discourse-centered (Grant and Mershak 2011) nature (as opposed to being diagnostic) which is embedded in social constructionism (Gergen 2009), those coaches who are committed to working conversationally, have been able to adopt and apply the approach with great effect.

Given its emphasis on the relational and conversational, and the fact that it is unconditionally positive (Ludema et al. 2001). Appreciative Inquiry can be constructively applied in a multicultural context: differences are appreciated and inclusivity is encouraged. To make sense of this approach and its application as a method for coaching lived experiences, the rest of the chapter will be mainly about the application of Appreciative Inquiry in both a diverse community and as a coaching method in an organisational context. An electronic conversation between the two authors is presented. By making use of this approach the interviewee was given ample time to consider his answers and to substantiate them with references, should the interviewer want to further explore the underlying theory.

CB: Appreciative Inquiry is a very abstract concept. What does it mean?

FC: Cooperrider and Whitney (2005 p.7) answered this question by defining both words as *action* verbs:

Ap-pre'ci-ate, v., 1. Valuing; the act of recognising the best in people or the world around us; affirming past and present strengths, successes and potentials; to perceive those things that give life (health, vitality, excellence) to living systems. 2. To increase in value – for example, the economy has appreciated in value. Synonyms: value, prize, esteem, and honour.

In-quire', v., 1. The act of exploration and discovery. (2) To ask questions; to be open to seeing new potentials and possibilities. Synonyms: discover, search, systematically explore, and study.

CB: Why the emphasis on action?

FC: Appreciative Inquiry was developed as a challenge and a positive alternative to the traditional action research approach to organization development and change (Crous 2008).

CB: Please remind me what the traditional action research model essentially is about.

FC: The traditional model suggests that without the identification and diagnosis of a particular problem and feedback about it, no change is possible (Crous 2008).

CB: Intuitively this makes sense to me. In what way is Appreciative Inquiry different?

FC: To recognize the profoundness of Appreciative Inquiry as an alternative way of approaching (organization) development and change, the story of its originator needs to be told. Watkins et al. (2011) describe how, in 1980, with the traditional action research model for organization development as roadmap, a 24-year-old doctoral student, David Cooperrider, from the Weatherhead School of Management at Case Western Reserve University, was asked by the board of the Cleveland Clinic to research what was wrong with the human side of this hospital. He was eager to do the study as he wanted to assist in helping to make one of the world's best hospitals function even better. However, Cooperrider soon became discouraged. What he found was that focusing on problems and giving feedback about those problems to the hospital staff was energy depleting, both the respondents and for him as the researcher. Cooperrider soon discovered that the approach he was following was counter-productive in that it created discomfort and ultimately resistance amongst those to whom he applied the problem-centered method. He became aware that the more problems were highlighted, the more dispirited and discouraged the hospital workers became, and this, in turn, gave way to blaming and defensive behaviour (Crous 2008).

CB: Did Cooperrider abandon the project?

FC: No. He refused to give up, because something had caught his eye which excited him: healthy practices in that very same hospital, such as high levels of cooperation, innovation and organizational effectiveness (Watkins et al. 2011). Given the nature of his problem-centered question: "What is wrong with the human side of the Cleveland Clinic?", these observations sadly fell outside the scope of his research, which seemed to emphasise to him the limitations of the traditional action research model. As far as Cooperrider was concerned, the model weakened the capacity of both researchers and practitioners to produce generative theory (cf. Gergen 1982, 2009) that would inspire imagination, commitment, and enthusiastic dialogue – factors without which fundamental organizational change would be difficult to accomplish. As people inquire about what is wrong with their organizations, i.e., thereby amplifying inter-organisational weakness and differences, they spawn vocabularies of deficits. Ironically, those vocabularies may aggravate the very conditions they are hoping to ameliorate. Cooperrider came to the conclusion that, given the disheartening experience of working with the classical action research model, he simply could not continue with his work. Yet still he refused to throw in the towel. He subsequently took the bold step of moving away from a root cause analysis of failure, to an analysis of the root causes of success. Later, in his report to the hospital board, he would refer to his approach as an *Appreciative Inquiry* (Watkins et al. 2011).

Cooperrider's thinking was challenged by the work of Ken Gergen, arguably the world's foremost scholar on social constructionism. Gergen's (1982) work challenged Cooperrider not to accept the problem-solving approach to change as the only 'truth', but rather to challenge it. In a later work, Ken Gergen and his wife Mary (Gergen and Gergen 2004, p.12), in turn reflected on problems by stating that "problems don't exist in the world for all to see; rather we construct worlds of 'the good' and deem those events that stand in the way of achieving what we value as 'a problem'. Could all that we construct as 'problems' not be reconstructed as 'opportunities'? By the same token as we speak together, we could also bring new worlds into being?"

One of the most important insights which Cooperrider arrived at, was that "human systems move in the direction of what they [humans] persistently ask questions about" (Haslebo and Haslebo (2012 p. 206). Thus, questions about problems invariably steer the conversation in the direction of what is problematic. Questions about strengths, high points, innovations and possibilities, on the other hand, tend to direct the conversation towards positive ideas and practices (Haslebo and Haslebo 2012).

CB: How did Cooperrider and the practitioners who began applying his thinking, go about implementing this insight?

FC: They developed a structured process (cf. Cooperrider et al. 2003a, b): Before commencing with the Appreciative Inquiry process, a topic is chosen and framed or defined in affirmative terms. This may be referred to as the *Define* phase. The first phase of the actual Appreciative Inquiry is referred to as the *Discovery* phase, where the aim is to discover the system's (i.e., individual's, team's, group's, organization's, community's) key strengths by appreciating the 'best of what is in the system'. Core to this phase is the use of unconditional positive questions (aligned to the affirmative topic) for (a) conducting interviews in pairs, (b) extracting themes from the stories shared in small groups, and (c) democratically voting for, selecting and capturing those themes that represent the 'positive core' of the system. Inspired and grounded by this core of strengths, the *Dream* phase is about envisioning 'what might be'. In small groups a preferred future is co-constructed and captured, and may even be enacted. To help realize this dream, a *Design* phase is introduced. In small groups, provocative propositions or possibility statements are designed or formulated in healthy terms – this, to construct an architecture which will give way to the *Delivery* of the dream, the final phase of any Appreciative Inquiry. This phase is also sometimes referred to as the *Destiny* or *Do* stage, as actions are identified and put into motion.

CB: The fact that each phase starts with a 'D' makes it easy to remember. Have you ever applied this process in a multicultural context?

FC: I have. It all started with a call from a friend, Rita Kellerman.

> "Did you hear what has happened to Gerrie's wife?"
> "No", I said.
> "She was killed a few days ago by one of their workers during a labour dispute."

Gerrie[1] was the owner of the local pub situated on the main road in Stanford, a quant village in the Overberg area of South Africa's Southern Cape. Outside the front door is an old traffic light – a green light usually indicates that the pub is open

---

[1] Not his real name.

for business. But following this fateful day, Gerrie switched off the green light for the last time.

The village, which is normally peaceful and bucolic, became tense as racial tensions flared up. Some townswomen got together, knowing that action had to be taken.

> "We need something restorative for our town," one of them remarked to Rita, who was a holiday resident at that time.
>
> "I know of somebody who might be able to help us," Rita replied. "I know he uses a method for positive change, called Appreciative Inquiry."

That is how my name entered the equation. I agreed to facilitate at a gathering of townsfolk, and the upcoming public holiday, 1 May (Worker's Day), was selected.

A local organizing committee was formed to start preparing for the Appreciative Inquiry by securing a venue. The Dutch Reformed Church hall (across the road from Gerrie's pub) seemed a suitable location. Business-owners were approached to sponsor the food and drinks for the day. Posters were printed and put up throughout the community, inviting every resident of Stanford and surroundings to attend. For days a volunteer drove a bakkie (utility vehicle), with a loudspeaker attached to its roof, around the residential areas, inviting everyone to the upcoming event.

I began preparing for the day by drafting a protocol. Despite being mindful of the fact that a life had been taken, I nevertheless wanted the Appreciative Inquiry to be a life-giving experience (cf. Cooperrider et al. 2003a, b). I chose to frame the affirmative topic as "A life worth living in Stanford", a play on the title of the book *A life worth living*, edited by Csikszenthihalyi and Csikszenthihalyi (2006). The theme was made inclusive for the various language groups in the community, and to this end Afrikaans and Xhosa translations were also used:*'n Lewe van waarde in Stanford* and *Ubomi bam ndithanda ukubuphila eStanford.*

For guidelines on the unconditional positive questions which I crafted, I searched Case Western Reserve University's *appreciative inquiry commons* website (www.appreciativeinquirty.cwru.edu), an open search website abundant with rich information, samples and case studies about the approach. Thereafter, I emailed the final document to the local organizing committee for translation into Afrikaans and Xhosa, before making printouts.

On my arrival at the church hall on the designated day I was greeted by Nelva, a former student, who handed out the protocols and took down the names of the participants.

Upon peeking into the hall I was somewhat concerned about the sight that greeted me: there were white people (mostly senior citizens) and a few people of colour, but no black people. When I shared my concern with a woman next to me, her response was: "What did you expect, this is a *Dutch Reformed Church hall*! Black people will never come here."

CB: So why was the venue such an issue?

FC: Well, the Dutch Reformed Church once was the 'spiritual home' of the all-white Nationalist Party, which had been responsible for institutionalising apartheid.

CB: So did you have to change location?

FC: No. A member of the local organizing committee indicated that the issue of the venue had indeed been discussed with representatives from the black community; they had agreed to the choice of the church hall, since it was the largest venue in the village. It transpired that the black attendees' transport had arrived late. Soon the hall was packed with people of various ages, races, classes, and languages. In total, 180 people attended.

CB: With speakers of different languages in attendance, did this represent a challenging in terms of facilitating the Appreciative Inquiry?

FC: The issue of language almost derailed the process. The protocol had been written in three languages (Afrikaans, English, and Xhosa), but I had assumed that all participants would be able to converse in basic English. I was wrong. A large number of people spoke only Afrikaans; some only spoke Xhosa, and many English-speakers did not speak or even understand Afrikaans or Xhosa. It appeared to be an insurmountable obstacle.

CB: So how did you overcome this barrier?

FC: The day was saved by a young, black journalist from a regional newspaper who was fluent in all three languages. In the end I facilitated the Appreciative Inquiry process in Afrikaans and in English; he translated whatever I said into Xhosa. Some policemen who attended were multilingual, and they joined the process by acting as translators.

CB: I would be interested to hear what questions you crafted for the Discovery phase of the Appreciative Inquiry.

FC: The specific questions for the conversations in pairs were the following:

1. Describe a peak experience you've had with friends, family or anybody else from the Stanford community that makes you think, "Yes! This is why I choose to live in Stanford."/*Omskryf enige hoogtepunt waarvan jou vriende, familie of mede-inwoner van Stanford deel was, wat jou laat voel*: "*Ja*! *Dis hoekom ek verkies om in Stanford te woon*."/Chaza into enkulu osele ukhe weyenza nabahlobo bakho, isisalwana okanye naye nawuphi na umntu apha eStanford ekwenza uthi "Henke! Yhigo lento ndakhetha ukuzohlala apha."
2. What makes Stanford unique, i.e., without it our town would just not be the same?
3. Given your unique strengths, how could you contribute to our community?
4. Tell me about a time when you or somebody you know courageously chose to collaborate and the results were profoundly positive.
5. What wishes do you have to make Stanford an even greater town to live in?

For a more diverse experience, each participant was asked to interview someone from another racial/language group. Thereafter they had to change roles: the initial interviewer became the interviewee. The participants were asked to listen attentively to one another and to capture the essence of each answer which a particular question provoked. Thereafter, each participant had to share in a small group what s/he considered to be the most compelling story or quote obtained from the person interviewed. I reminded the participants that this was an ideal opportunity to enact *ubuntu* (cf. Tutu 2010), i.e., to show respect and dignity in retelling the story of the person they had interviewed, to a larger audience. The aim was for the interviewee to be recognized or acknowledged as a person, thanks to the interviewer telling his/her story (Figs. 1 and 2).

The rest of the small group had to collectively decide on a theme for each story. This was captured by a scribe (a volunteer) on flip chart paper. Thereafter the papers were posted next to each other along the length of the church hall wall. The participants subsequently voted for those themes which, in their view, best expressed why Stanford was a great place to live in.

CB: I would be interested to hear which themes were the most popular!

FC: The themes that drew the most energy were the following (the number of votes which each drew appears in brackets):

Caring	(21)
Overcoming fear	(46)
Collaborating to solve problems	(36)
Colour-blind sport	(32)
Respect for tradition	(22)
Beauty of Stanford	(101)
Sharing skills	(105)
Teach each other about community	(42)

Fig. 1 Discovering what makes life worth living in Stanford

Fig. 2 Interviews in pairs

These themes were taken to represent the positive core of the inhabitants of Stanford.

For the Dream phase, participants had to consider and discuss (in small groups) the following question:

> *Imagine our townsfolk full of support for each other.*
> *What will Stanford look like? (What are the main activities that will make Stanford a flourishing community?*

To express their dream for their village, a young man who works in the Stanford post office, but who is also active in community development, asked for volunteers to join him on-stage, from where he would lead the group in song and dance. Soon he had everyone in the hall dancing and singing.

We then broke for our sponsored lunch, which inadvertently became something of an amusing event. The mourners in a funeral procession, which happened to pass by, joined us for a quick bite before proceeding on their way. Luckily there was more than enough food for all.

CB: So after breaking bread together, how did you start on the Design phase?

FC: We did not have much time left, so I opted to integrate the Design and Delivery phases. Each participant was given a large white pebble and requested to write on it with a black marker. Mindful of and inspired by their collective positive core and their dream for Stanford, I asked them to make a personal commitment to their village, which would make life worth living for all the inhabitants. Each of these written commitments revealed that the participants were dedicated to working together to ensure that all Stanford's inhabitants would live safely, in peace and harmony, by caring for one another, developing their community and sustaining the environment. (The pebbles were later stacked in a public space as a reminder of the significance of that day.)

The floor was declared open for those who wished to share their commitments with the group.

CB: Which commitment touched you most?

FC: I recall a retired tradesman standing up and offering young black people without employment the opportunity to be trained by him. That made me realize that if a single individual's offer came to fruition, the day would have been worthwhile.

CB: So the Stanford Appreciative Inquiry was a success?

FC: I would think so. It helped to alleviate racial/interpersonal tensions. However, the local organizing committee, inspired by their experience of the Appreciative Inquiry, wanted to take some kind of action that would truly benefit Stanford as a whole, along with all its communities. What I gathered was that, with the help of an architect from the Netherlands, they envisioned a green project aimed at making the village more self-sustainable.

It did not get off the ground, though.

CB: What was most significant for you about this experience?

FC: It was a profoundly moving and humbling experience. The appreciative awareness that developed as the day progressed, and which gave way to a cooperative awareness, enabled the different groups to transcend their cultural differences, to create a sense of unity (cf. Cooperrider and Sekerka 2003).

I've also come to realize that no matter what the change agenda of an Appreciative Inquiry is, the appreciative inquirer invariably becomes an appreciative inquiry coach by facilitating the internalization of the process. In effect, it becomes a way of being for some of those who participated in the inquiry.

CB: I appreciate your sharing this amazing experience with me. Now, to move on to coaching: Does one refer to Appreciative Coaching or Appreciative Inquiry Coaching?

FC: Both terms are used. My advice would be to keep in mind that this kind of coaching is rooted in the Appreciative *Inquiry* approach and philosophy.

CB: What are the underlying principles of Appreciative Inquiry Coaching?

FC: When coaching, I am mindful of the core principles of Appreciative Inquiry (Cooperrider et al. 2003a, b; Whitney and Trosten-Bloom 2003). In the context of coaching, the *constructionist* principle suggests that knowledge is generated during the coaching conversation. It is the outcome of the relationship which develops between the coach and the coachee. More specifically, as the conversation between the coach and coachee progresses, new knowledge is co-created. Language is as vital in helping coachees to 'recreate' themselves. For Appreciative Inquiry Coaching, the constructionist principle is central to all aspects of its practice (Orem et al. 2007). The aforementioned authors emphasize that three fundamental assumptions of Appreciative Inquiry are connected to this principle:

(1) every system (in this case, the coachee) has something that works well or works right, and as such gives it 'life' (Cooperrider et al. 2003a, b). It is through appreciative questions that the coachee discovers what makes him/her alive, successful and effective. Discovering these strengths may be the starting point for creating positive change; (2) the (emotional) language used, creates reality. The coach may, therefore, by asking certain questions, steer the conversation in either a positive or a negative direction. This suggests that (3) whatever is focused on will become (the coachee's) reality. Whitney et al. (2002) remind us that people tend to move in the direction of the images they hold of the future. These images are informed by the conversations people have with others (and themselves), as well as the stories they tell. Conversations and stories, in turn, are informed by the questions which people ask. Therefore, the questions we ask can be deemed *fateful*, in that they have a profound impact.

CB: How does one apply the other Appreciative Inquiry principles to coaching?

FC: The principle of *simultaneity* reminds me that the aim of the coaching session is, in essence, not to diagnose and then 'fix' the coachee by means of interventions. Rather, the appreciative coaching conversation *is* the intervention. From Cooperrider et al. (2003a, b) one may infer that the seeds of change are embedded in the conversation. The coach articulates the questions which give way to what is 'discovered' (the data). The exploration and discussion of this 'data' open up the possibility to imagine and construct a desirable future (Orem et al. 2007).

For me, the third principle, the *poetic*, relates to the notion of poetic activism (Gergen 2009), suggesting that the appreciative coaching conversation should be generative, challenge the coach (and coachee) to spark the conversation, establish alternative ways of understanding and create new images of possibility. Helping the client to share stories of when they are or were at their best may be more powerful in the process of achieving positive change, than focusing on the challenge they are struggling with. The coachee is invited to re-story, re-author and reframe his/her past and present, and even re-imagine their own future.

So, the coachee discovers that s/he has the freedom to choose how to interpret or write their life story. The idea of freedom links to one of the emergent principles of Appreciative Inquiry (Gordin 2008; Whitney and Trosten-Bloom 2003), namely that of *free choice*, which suggests that the coachees recognizing that they are free to choose how to view and enact their life, is liberating. Free choice liberates power. When coachees discover their personal power and strengths, they are free to choose how to craft their job (Wrzesniewski 2003) or life in such a way that they can align their strengths to action possibilities and opportunities resulting in optimal experiences and performance.

The poetic principle is related to two more emergent principles, namely *enactment* and *wholeness*. In terms of the enactment principle, once coachees know what they want, they are encouraged to try out behaviour that is aligned with this new personal knowledge. The challenge for each coachee is, in the words of Gandhi, to "be (enact) the change we want to see". This enactment principle has its origins in

William James' '*as if*' principle, which entails that 'if you want a quality, [you should] act *as if* you already have it' (cf. Wiseman 2012).

According to the emerging wholeness principle, wholeness brings out the best in people (Orem et al. 2007). Coachees become 'whole' as they discover, through the coaching conversation, that their lives can be viewed from new and different angles, which presents a richer picture of each individual. Coachees become whole when they grasp that they are part of a bigger 'whole' or an interconnected web of relationships which are embedded in a context of ever-expanding patterns.

Another core principle to be considered is the *anticipatory* principle. Cooperrider (1999) wrote a chapter 'Positive image, positive action', suggesting that the respective coachees' image of their future guides their present actions. I take heed of the reminder by Orem et al. (2007, p.74) that "[a]ppreciative coaches are especially attuned to nurturing their clients' positive expectations and encouraging them to anticipate and be proactive about the future".

The final core principle to be considered is the *positive*. This principle suggests that the Appreciative Inquiry Coaching conversation should be steered by unconditional positive questions (cf. Ludema et al. 2001), since positivity not only acts as an antidote against negativity (Cooperrider et al. 2003), but also *broadens* people's through-action repertoires and *builds* enduring personal and social resources from which the coachee will be able to draw on in future (Fredrickson 2003).

CB: Please tell me about a time when you had to facilitate an Appreciative Inquiry Coaching session in a multicultural context.

FC: Before doing so, I want to take you back many years to when, in the prime of my life, I was faced with a life-threatening disease. I went into chronic renal failure, and since my kidneys stopped functioning I had to receive dialysis 4 h a day, three times a week, just to stay alive. After 8 months of incessant hospital visits my brother, Dawie, was declared fit to donate a kidney to me. For this unconditional act of love I will be grateful to him as long as I live. During a conversation before we left the hospital, the attending nephrologist mentioned that the transplanted kidney was functioning so well that I might eventually outlive my brother.

However, because of our tissue being only 50 % compatible, I have to take immunosuppressives for the rest of my life, to guard against organ rejection. This kind of therapy has severe side-effects, one of which is the development of cancerous tumors. The specialist tried to comfort me by saying I would most probably not die from a kidney-related disease, but from a tumor. "Don't worry," he said. "This won't happen soon, perhaps 30 years from now."

During my time on dialysis I was strangely elated, experiencing an intense appreciation for life and being grateful for being alive. I chose not to lie down, but to sit *upright* when being dialysed. Gradually, as I was able to return to work and get on with my life post-transplant, these positive emotions waned. So when (believe it or not!) I was diagnosed with a cancerous tumour 3 years (not the predicted 30 years) after the transplant, I promised myself I would never take life for granted again. As a reminder, I decided to develop a visual brand which would

Fig. 3 A metaphor logo representing optimal living

reflect an 'UP' or positive state of mind. The book *Metaphors we live by* (Lakoff and Johnson 1980) led me to realise that UP is the embodied root metaphor for everything that is positive in life (Crous 2007). Informed by this realisation I conceptualized a logo/metaphor by which to live optimally (see Fig. 3). The UP font design is the product of a graphic design, whereas the figure superimposed onto the word UP is my own work.

This design has been quantitatively and qualitatively validated for use as an associative projective technique for positivity (Meiring, 2010; Osher 2014), but also as a technique for enacting positivity (Langa, 2009).

From an evolutionary perspective, assuming an upright posture may be regarded as the key development in human evolution. Therefore, having to rise up – to originate (Latin: *oriri* = to rise) – beginning to walk tall (being bipedal) is arguably the most basic, but also the most profound human act (Lieberman 2013). Moreover, from an embodied cognition perspective (Lakoff and Johnson 1980, 1999), this physical act has been psychologically internalized – the physical became the scaffold for the psychological – as the mind has become spatially oriented to frame (crudely, yet potently) whatever is healthy, strong, and good (i.e., positive) as UP, and everything that is unhealthy, weak, and bad as DOWN. UP may therefore be regarded as the root metaphor for everything that is positive (Crous 2007). As such, it may be postulated that the coachee's most basic (unconscious) need or expectation is to be coached towards UPness – to originate towards optimal living and work. But how is UPness sustained? The youthful image of the figure may provide an answer, as it incorporates an evolutionary development subsequent to humans having become bipedal, namely neoteny (juvenilization, i.e., the retention of youthfulness) (Gould 1980). In general, developmental biologists agree that humans retain certain physical juvenile traits into later adulthood, i.e., as a species we never truly grow up, despite growing older. It has been suggested that this phenomenon has been internalised psychologically (Crous 2007). Youthful attitudes and behaviours such as playfulness, curiosity, and especially relational traits such as affection, sociality and cooperation, are retained. These traits suggest that at a fundamental level, humans retain the ability to renew themselves, they are able to deal with change, and they stay open to and are appreciative of others, meaning neoteny generates UPness.

The UP metaphor/logo proved to be of great help once when I had to coach for optimal experience and performance in a multicultural context. Bushe and Kassam (2005) suggest that for an Appreciate Inquiry to be transformational, it needs to work with a metaphor.

I was approached by the CEO of a company which supplies heavy machinery to the mining sector. Despite being financially strong, the organization was plagued by high levels of negativity. His request was for me to assist the entire workforce (in excess of 100 employees, largely representative of the multi-cultural make-up of the South African population) in changing their negativity into a culture of positivity.

By using the logo we branded (or defined) the organization as an 'UP' company. I facilitated multiple appreciative inquiries across the organization, to investigate what it means to perform 'UP' as a leader, manager or worker. This was followed up with a number of individual 'UP' Appreciative Inquiry coaching sessions, where I guided coachees through the Appreciative Inquiry process. Individual coachees were asked to define what UP meant for them, with a view to discovering their UP qualities and how to employ them not only for their own benefit, but also the organization. They were invited to dream of an UP future with opportunities and possibilities; to design a personal UP value propositions for themselves, followed by the opportunity to design UP action plans. Finally, they had to make commitments, offerings and requests for support in such a way that would allow them to perform in an UP manner. (Not every coachee went through all the phases. For some the design phase was adequate; for others it was an iterative process moving forwards and backwards between the phases). It was as if individuals were able to transcend those differences (cultural and otherwise) that were experienced as divisive, moving towards a common UP future.

CB: How did you align UP with the Appreciative Inquiry principles?

FC: Guided by the constructionist principle, the coaching conversations were structured around UP as a metaphor for guiding stories and knowledge about optimal experiences and performance at work. Even those coachees whose mother tongue is not English were able to grasp the essence of UP. In terms of simultaneity, conversing about and playing with the notion of UP brought a lightness and positivity to the conversations, immediately sparking new ideas and actions to be considered. The CEO himself discovered that he lacked positivity in his interactions with employees, that he was quick to identify their mistakes or to point them out. He subsequently decided that, rather than constantly aiming to catch employees out when they err, he would catch them in the act of performing UP behaviours, and would show them appreciation for it. In line with the poetic principle, UP as metaphor allowed for a wide range of interpretations and generated a number of fresh insights and instances of meaning making throughout the coaching process, freeing coachees to construct dreams and actions which are aligned to their strengths and aspirations (the free choice principle). By branding UP throughout the organization, coachees came to realize that they were part of something bigger (wholeness principle). Yet, individual coachees were able see the possibility of themselves becoming UP leaders, managers or workers, and having an UP impact on others. Imagining a preferred UP future for themselves visibly influenced the coaches in that it grew their optimism and confidence (the anticipatory principle). Coachees were subsequently able to enact UP during every one of the Appreciative Inquiry coaching phases (enactment principle), and as far as the positive principle is concerned, UP = positivity!

CB: Did this specific approach to Appreciative Inquiry coaching contribute on a cross-cultural level?

FC: As the root metaphor for positivity, the UP-logo, in an unconscious way (cf. Lakoff and Johnson 1999) oriented the employees (irrespective of their differences) towards more constructive behaviour. For them, the logo became the common symbol for optimal experience and performance. During the time of the Appreciative Inquiry initiative, the coachees were able to transcend their differences, to the point where they collaboratively found ways to work together towards establishing an UP culture in their organization. What made this initiative unique was that despite the individual coaching being one of a number of Appreciative Inquiry interventions, it afforded me the opportunity to work appreciatively on a group and an individual level, where I was able to observe the organization adopting a culture of greater inclusivity.

Both case studies presented were provocative, mainly because of the affirmative topic choices for the respective Appreciative Inquiries. For the first one the topic of a tragedy that almost tore a multi-cultural community apart was reframed as an invitation towards co-creating a life worth living in their beautiful village. For the second case, a metaphor-logo was chosen suggesting to workers, coming from different backgrounds, the possibility of co-creating a thriving organizational culture. As Whitney et al. (2002) indicated, the topic choice is fateful because it provides the scope for the questions to be crafted, which will inform the conversations and stories, which in turn will inform images of the future. Human systems – individuals and organizations – move in the direction of the images they hold of the future.

References

Bushe, G. R., & Kassam, A. F. (2005). When is appreciative inquiry transformational? A meta-case analysis. *Journal of Applied Behavioral Science, 41*(2), 161–181.

Bushe, G. R., & Marshak, R. J. (2009). Revisioning organization development: Diagnostic and dialogic premise and patterns of practice. *Journal of Applied Behavioral Science, 45*(3), 348–368.

Cooperrider, D. L. (1999). Positive image, positive action: The affirmative basis of organising. In S. Srivastiva, & D. L. Cooperrider (Eds.), *Appreciative management and leadership: The power of positive thought and action in organisations* (Rev. ed.). Euclid: Lakeshore Communications.

Cooperrider, D., & Sekerka, L. E. (2003). Towards a theory of positive organizational change. In K. S. Cameron, J. E. Dutton, & R. E. Quinn (Eds.), *Positive organizational scholarship: Foundations of a new discipline*. San Francisco: Berrett-Koehler Publishers.

Cooperrider, D. L., & Whitney, D. (2005). *Appreciative inquiry: A positive revolution in change*. San Francisco: Berrett-Koehler.

Cooperrider, D. L., Whitney, D., & Stavros, J. M. (2003). *Appreciative inquiry handbook*. Bedford Heights: Lakeshore.

Cooperrider, D., Silbert, J. H., Mann, A. J., & Whitney, D. (2003). *Positive family dynamics: Appreciative inquiry questions to bring out the best in families*. Chagrin Falls: Taos Institute.

Crous, F. (2007). *UP: Branding the positive*. Inaugural professorial lecture, Johannesburg: University of Johannesburg.

Crous, F. (2008). From action research to appreciative inquiry: A paradigm shift in organisation development and change. In C. van Tonder & G. Roodt (Eds.), *Organisation development: Theory and practice*. Pretoria: Van Schaik.

Csikszenthihalyi, M., & Csikszenthihalyi, I. S. (2006). *A life worth living: Contributions to positive psychology*. Oxford: Oxford University Press.

Fredrickson, B. L. (2003). Positive emotions and upward spirals in organisations. In K. S. Cameron, J. E. Dutton, & R. E. Quin (Eds.), *Positive organisational scholarship: Foundations of a new discipline*. San Francisco: Berret-Koehler.

Gergen, K. J. (1982). *Toward transformation in social knowledge*. Thousand Oaks: Sage.

Gergen, K. J. (2009). *An invitation to social construction* (2nd ed.). London: Sage.

Gergen, K. J., & Gergen, M. (2004). *Social construction: Entering the dialogue*. Chagrin Falls: Taos Institute.

Gordin, S. (2008, March). Appreciative inquiry coaching. *International Coaching Psychology Review, 3*(1), 17–29.

Gould, S. J. (1980). *The panda's thumb*. New York: W.W. Norton.

Grant, D., & Mershak, R. J. (2011). Toward a discourse-centred understanding of organizational change. *Journal of Applied Behavioral Science, 47*(2), 204–235.

Haslebo, G., & Haslebo, M. J. (2012). *Practicing relational ethics in organisations*. Chagrin Falls: Taos Institute Publications.

Lakoff, G., & Johnson, M. (1980). *Metaphors we live by*. Chicago: Chicago University Press.

Lakoff, G., & Johnson, M. (1999). *Philosophy in the flesh: The embodied mind and its challenges to western thought*. New York: Basic Books.

Langa, L.L. (2009). *Optimal work experience: an embodied experience*. Unpublished Masters dissertation. Johannesburg: University of Johannesburg.

Lieberman, D. (2013). *The story of the human body*. London: Penguin.

Ludema, J. D., Cooperrider, D. L., & Barrett, F. (2001). Appreciative inquiry: The power of the unconditional positive question. In P. Reason & H. Bradbury (Eds.), *Handbook of action research: Participative inquiry and practice*. London: Sage.

Meiring, E. (2010). *Validating the positivity projective technique*. Unpublished Masters dissertation. Johannesburg: University of Johannesburg.

Orem, S. L., Binkert, J., & Clancey, A. L. (2007). *Appreciative coaching: A positive process for change*. San Francisco: Jossey-Bass.

Osher, M. A. (2014).The *positivity projective technique in relation to major positive psychology constructs*. Unpublished master's dissertation. Johannesburg: University of Johannesburg.

Tutu, D. (2010). Foreword. In D. Gluckstein (Ed.), *Dignity. Photographs by Dana Gluckstein*. Brooklyn: PowerHouse Books.

Watkins, J. M., Mohr, B., & Kelly, R. (2011). *Appreciative inquiry: Change at the speed of imagination* (2nd ed.). San Francisco: Pfeiffer.

Whitney, D., & Trosten-Bloom, T. (2003). *The power of appreciative inquiry: A practical guide to positive change*. San Francisco: Berrett- Khoeler.

Whitney, D., Cooperrider, D., Trosten Bloom, A., & Kaplin, B. S. (2002). *Encyclopedia of positive questions: Using appreciative inquiry to bring out the best in your organisation* (Vol. 1). Euclid: Lakeshore Communications.

Wiseman, R. (2012). *Rip it up*. London: Macmillan.

Wrzesniewski, A. (2003). Finding positive meaning in work. In K. S. Cameron, J. E. Dutton, & R. E. Quinn (Eds.), *Positive organizational scholarship: Foundations of a new discipline*. San Francisco: Berrett-Koehler.

An Archetypal Approach to Coaching

Daniel Hercules du Toit

Abstract The purpose of this chapter is to motivate the utilization of Jungian depth psychology as an approach towards coaching through (a) positioning archetypal psychology as a paradigm, (b) providing an overview of archetypal psychological constructs, and (c) to indicate how archetypal coaching can be utilized for aiding the coachee in dealing with irrationality and to facilitate personal growth. Archetypal psychology, as coaching approach, works at its best when dealing with irrational behaviour and reactions, and also for personal growth. Archetypal psychology provides an approach to stimulate true growth and awareness. This approach can be used for individual coaching and adds specific insights for group coaching by approaching the group as an "individual" with a personality, a shadow and possible neuroses. One of the main aims of coaching, is to facilitate sustained behavior change. An archetypal approach addresses behavioural problems at its roots. By changing the root cause of problematic behavior, chances of bringing about sustained behavior change are better than when only looking at the behavior without considering its unconscious drivers. This chapter will position archetypal psychology within the tradition of coaching, (as opposed to its clinical applications) through comparisons with traditional coaching approaches. Flowing from this, the chapter will highlight the profile of the coach likely to utilize archetypal psychology as a paradigm for coaching. The main constructs relating to Jungian archetypal psychology, such as the unconscious, complexes, archetypes, persona, shadow, anima/animus and individuation will be discussed as it relates to the coaching process to assist the coachee in dealing with irrational behaviour and to foster personal growth. Archetypal psychology provides unique methods and models for assisting coachees to deal with irrational behaviour, such as anger outbursts, shyness/withdrawal, and conflict avoidance as well as methods to change reactions and habits, such as fear of presentations or even to aid the coachee to stop smoking. Methods to managing irrational beliefs and behaviour will be discussed. Finally, we postulate the use of Jung's three-stage model (nurturing stage, adaptating stage and integrating stage) of individuation as a mechanism to aid in personal growth. Specific coaching strategies

D.H. du Toit (✉)
Optentia Research Focus Area, North-West University, Vaal Triangle Campus, Vanderbijlpark, South Africa
e-mail: danie.dutoit@nwu.ac.za

L.E. van Zyl et al. (eds.), *Coaching Psychology: Meta-theoretical perspectives and applications in multicultural contexts*, DOI 10.1007/978-3-319-31012-1_9

to facilitate change will be presented and discussed. The chapter will conclude with applying these concepts in transcultural coaching.

Keywords Archetypal psychology • Personal growth • Irrationality • Jungian coaching • Individuation • Higher levels of awareness

1 Introduction

It might seem strange to even consider an archetypal approach in coaching. Just the words "archetypal" and "depth psychology" already brings images to mind of clinical therapy for treatment of childhood wounds, whereas coaching is usually seen as more action oriented partnering with clients to address issues such as leadership, emotional intelligence, change and conflict management, which is usually seen as having nothing to do with the unconscious or archetypes. Or does it? Very often even highly intelligent people are unable to change behavior patterns, even if they want to and grasp the negative consequences of their behaviour. They know that they should change, but are unable to. Archetypal psychology, as coaching approach, works at its best when dealing with irrational behaviours and reactions, and also for personal growth. Archetypal psychology provides an approach to stimulate true growth and awareness. This approach can be used for individual coaching and adds specific insights for group coaching by approaching the group as an "individual" with a personality, a shadow and possible neuroses. This approach draws on the deep and rich history of depth-psychology for the benefit of the coachee.

The question inevitably arises: Is archetypal psychology applicable at all in a coaching situation? Should it not remain in the domain of clinical therapy? In general, coaching is more focused on growth than therapy and coaches are often more skilled at dealing with spiritual issues such as meaning of life than therapists or counselors (Schuster 2013). Both coaching and therapy sometimes ignore unconscious aspects. Jung (1959) originated archetypal psychology. He was the first to move from therapy for "sickness" to therapy for growth. Because this psychology is aimed at enhancing wellness, success and meaning, it has similar goals to coaching and is thus a useful approach.

In many paradigms, the development of people is based on the assumption that people learn from experience. People learn as they make mistakes and experience hardships (McCauley et al. 1998). For example, the most important developmental intervention for a young fledging corporate leader is seen as serious responsibility early in his/her career. Through making mistakes, he/she should learn and not repeat the same mistakes. A sad reality of life is that people, even very intelligent people, sometimes repeat the same mistakes again and again. To illustrate, consider how difficult it is to break a bad habit. At a conscious level, one know of no single rational reason to continue with a bad habit, but still it is very difficult to break. Think of habits such as smoking, traffic rage and procrastination. Addiction is, of course even more difficult. Even addictions where no chemical dependency is involved, such as gambling and pornography addictions are extremely difficult to break. The reason why it is so difficult for a human being to break a habit could be explained by the power of the unconscious mind.

The unconscious mind works with different principles than the conscious mind. Whereas the conscious mind functions on linear, cause-effect principles and logic, the unconscious mind functions mainly with associations. Think of the impact of watching a sad scene in a movie on television. Logically, the person who watches the movie knows that he/she is watching electronic signal transmitted to his/her television set, which his/her television set receives, configures the signal into images and sounds depicting a fictitious story, acted by actors whom he/she is unlikely to know. Yet, people allow the movie to touch them and they may react emotionally to the scene because the scene resonates with something in their own emotional history. An aware, well-integrated person's conscious, cognitive mind can impact the unconscious and emotional minds. His/her thinking will guide his/her feelings. An unaware person may be either totally cut off from his/her emotions, or may be inappropriate in the expression of emotions. Think of the tough, patriarchal father who seems to be without emotions, yet may be only able to cry and not be able to utter any words at his daughter's wedding.

Archetypal coaching aims at creating awareness to ultimately, by creating a healthy dialogue between the conscious and unconscious minds, increase the coachee's ability to positively harness his/her emotions. Beck (2012) uses the term "therapeutically informed coaching" to indicate coaching that takes cognizance of the unconscious mind. Whereas more traditional types of coaching would work to align thoughts, motives and behavior, as well as check effectiveness of actions in attaining goals (Schuster 2013), the archetypal approach work on root causes, gaining greater awareness and shift the way of thinking of the coachee. Though the central construct of this chapter is archetypes, as described by Carl Jung, the contribution of his predecessors, such as Freud and the more recent contributions of the post-Jungians are also be utilized as it applies to coaching.

2 Main Constructs of Archetypal Psychology

Coaching is often described as more "Jungian" than "Freudian", meaning that Jung's view of the unconscious is followed more often than Freud's (Schuster 2013). Freud viewed the unconscious as containing repressed personal traumas and unresolved personal conflicts. Jung took the construct further and stated that the unconscious also has a collective aspect, aspects all human beings share. He believed that the unconscious also contains creative energy and that the energy should be balanced. Though coaches often shy away from dealing with personal repressed issues, these often impact on behavior. If a manager shows poor emotional intelligence, it could easily be driven by personal complexes. His/her actions are not driven by external realities, but by internal unresolved issues. Coaches should thus not ignore the personal unconscious, though the focus here is more on the collective unconscious, represented by archetypes.

An example would be the very old idea of the need for a strong leader to rise up when a group is suppressed and in trouble. The belief is that a single, strong leader would be able to deliver the tribe from its problems. If one think of the hope board members have that a single CEO could deliver a company from its problems, it accounts for the remuneration boards are prepared to pay a "savior" CEO (and also, of cause the ease with which they fire a CEO if the company does not perform, i.e., he/she was not a savior).

The main constructs of Jungian depth psychology, such as the unconscious, complexes, archetypes, persona, shadow, anima/animus and individuation will be discussed next, as it relates to the coaching process to assist the coachee in dealing with irrational behaviour and to foster personal growth.

2.1 Unconscious

The unconscious or the unconscious mind refers to that part of the person which is hidden and unknown to the person him/herself. The unconscious is less in contact with the outer world, especially if there is not a healthy dialogue between the unconscious and the conscious minds; the person is then called "unaware". In archetypal coaching "unaware" does not refer to being unaware of the external world and its demands, but being unaware of the internal world and its needs. The unconscious creates patterns of adaptation as it sees fit at the time to protect the person. The unconscious always strives to act in the best interest of the person, but because it is less attuned to the outside world, often does not realize that defense patterns have become outdated and even dysfunctional. The unconscious is powerful and could maintain dysfunctional patterns despite evidence that they have become dysfunctional. Archetypal coaching concerns itself with making the person conscious of these patterns and then changing these patterns to more aware, functional reactions and behaviours.

A person's unconscious is divided into the personal unconscious and the collective unconscious. The personal unconscious contains individual unconscious material; aspects such as complexes. The personal unconscious is fed by the collective unconscious, which contains universal aspects, such as archetypes.

2.2 Complex and Archetype

The complex contains personal repressed material, such as the traumas that the person has experienced. Complexes thus contain unresolved personal issues, which cause the person to regress to earlier life stages (Freud 1950). If the coach ignores personal complexes, he/she might find that the coachee "inexplicably" does not utilize the insights gained during coaching sessions, but reverts back to previous behaviours. Archetypes refer to patterns of instinctual behaviour (Jung 1959). These patterns are innate and universal to all human beings. Whilst the complex contains personal repressed material, the archetype contains collective repressed material. Archetypes emerge as patterns of behaviour, of which the person him/herself is unconscious. He/she will come up with many reasons and excuses to justify his/her archetypal behavior.

Complexes and archetypes are closely linked and often difficult to differentiate. Archetypes are usually activated by external events and often manifest through a complex. For example, often with changes in organizations, archetypes are activated and some employees' reactions are inappropriate in terms of the change. The complex that could be activated by moving office could be a fear complex: fear that routines and known interactions might be lost after the change. It could at an archetypal level activate various possible archetypes: the archetype of the orphan, where the person feels thrown out of his/her known world and experience emotions of being abandoned. The person might then use the (inappropriate) language of the orphan and might say in coaching: "I have always given this organization my everything (I have been a good child) and now they just throw me out of my office (rejected by projected mother qualities of the organization)" or "I just do not even want to go to work anymore (loss of meaning, feeling rejected/unappreciated/disempowered)". If the coach recognizes the archetypal feeling tone of what the coachee says, he/she can also use appropriate language, acknowledge the emotions activated by the event and guide the coachee to gain insight and react appropriately in a mature manner. The coach could, for the above example, use the language of the orphan to get the coachee to understand the immaturity of his/her reaction.

2.3 *Self and Ego*

The ego can be described as a person's conscious mind (Jung 1959). The ego is his/her connection to the outer world. When a person becomes "ego-inflated", he/she thinks that the conscious mind, being in the external world, is all there is. He/she then ignores the richness of their unconscious mind. The self encompasses the whole person, both conscious and unconscious minds. The self thus includes the ego. The self is the center of the whole person, including the archetypal system of the unconscious. The self strives towards wholeness and integration of the personality. The self also has an ordering function (Kalsched 1996); it integrates the archetypal contents to create meaning. If a person does not have a healthy dialogue between his/her ego and self, the person might become ego-driven and his/her life will lack meaning. The self needs the ego to remain in contact with the external world; otherwise incorrect beliefs of the unconscious mind about the outside world are not tested against objective reality.

In coaching, the coach can assist the coachee to establish a healthy dialogue between the conscious and unconscious minds. Many leaders in organizations are ego-inflated and not attuned to their unconscious minds. Though they may achieve outer success, real meaning is often absent. If such a person is, for instance, faced with losing his/her job, his/her world crumbles because of the belief that the outer world is all there is. In such a case, the coach can assist the coachee to become more of his/her full self, not just the ego. The coach can assist the coachee to realize that he/she is more than his/her role and function in an organization.

2.4 Persona

The persona can be described as the image of how the ego projects itself to the outer world. The persona is often described as a mask. A real mask hides part of a person's face, but the mask also reveals some of who the person is with its shape and colours. The persona, like a real mask, hides some aspects of the person, but also reveals part of the person as the person chooses to show him/herself to the world. The persona is often formed and shaped by how a person believes he/she is expected to be by others.

If a person is very unaware and did not experience personal growth, he/she might believe that how he/she portrays him/herself to the outside world is all that he/she is; that the persona is the only or most important aspect of him/herself. Such a person is without much depth and facets. Handy (1995) described someone who is only what he/she portraits to the world as an empty raincoat. An empty raincoat in this sense symbolizes the emptiness of a person who became his/her mask, without the depths of other aspects of internal life.

2.5 Shadow

Shadow is the first, most accessible layer of the unconscious. Jung (1959) said that, unlike the deeper layers, it is possible to access shadow issues with some introspection. The shadow contains aspects of the person that he/she finds unacceptable in him/herself. Shadow is thus the opposite of ego. Because these aspects are not accepted, the person denies their existence and represses them into the unconscious mind. A person would usually be overly sensitive regarding such aspects. These aspects might be very obvious to others, but unknown to the person him/herself. As a result, one often gets "secrets", which others will openly discuss, except when the person is present. A leader might, for instance believe that he/she is very patient and might state that his/her strength is being patient. Team members might experience the leader as extremely impatient, and might discuss the leader's impatience amongst themselves, but no one will dare pointing it out to him/her, as he/she is likely not to accept the feedback and hold a grudge against the person who dared to point it out. The leader might even invite feedback, but team members often know that it is not wise to point out some shadow issues. An anonymous 360° feedback instrument sometimes serves the purpose to force a leader to confront his/her shadow aspects.

People often project their shadow issues onto others; a person who lacks self-confidence, might gossip about a confident person and call the person arrogant and self-centered. Shadow projections often involve same sex projections. That which a person does not own in him/herself yet, becomes difficult to tolerate in others. People see others not as they really are, but as the person him/herself is.

Groups can also have shadows. Just like an individual has parts in him/herself that he/she does not accept, so does the group. The process through which the group projects its shadow side is called "scapegoating" (Coleman 1999). In early societies, such as described in the Christian Old Testament Bible, there were rituals to "cleanse" the people. At the time, the scapegoat was a literal goat. The goat was per definition completely innocent. The goat then carried the sins of the people and was sent off into the desert or even slaughtered. The projecting of sins onto the scapegoat made people feel innocent and united them in the act of slaughtering the innocent goat. This primitive, unaware process still plays itself out as soon as a group forms. One can see this phenomena in its most archetypal pure form amongst primary school children: otherwise perfectly well behaved children could brutally mock and ridicule a child who is different. The difference becomes criminalized and judged. The difference, be it to be fatter, slimmer, have red hair, have freckles, be good (or bad) at mathematics, becomes the bases to differentiate the child and becomes the excuse to scapegoat the child. All the others agree that the difference is "bad" and therefore, they feel cleansed and innocent if they pick on the scapegoat, and because all agree, it builds the team's cohesion. The scapegoat cannot protest or argue, the power of the group dynamics would not tolerate giving the scapegoat a fair chance. Though scapegoating, as described so far, seems like a primitive or childish act, it is however, alive and well in organizations amongst supposedly sophisticated people who one would think should know better. There is a growing incidence and focus on "bullying" (Agervold 2007), which is often a form of scapegoating. In many organizations, there is a tendency amongst colleagues to openly make devaluing remarks about some departments, often the Human Resources, Information Technology or Marketing department, which all but the scapegoats agree on. The primitive projection of shadow, i.e. scapegoating, is a reality in today's organizational life.

Team coaching is becoming a common practice in many organizations. Team coaching provides opportunities to create awareness of the devastating power of scapegoating. The best way to counter, or at least limit scapegoating, is to create awareness of how it functions. A team unaware to the extent that scapegoating is rife, is unlikely to reach maturity in other aspects. Because the coach is not part of the team, he/she often is one of the only people empowered to challenge the team with its shadow side. Individual coaching can assist the person who is scapegoated to gain insight into the process and he/she often finds it of use to have confirmed that he/she truly is innocent and is devalued by being scapegoated.

2.6 Anima/Animus

The anima was first used to describe the suppressed, unconscious feminine aspects of men and the term animus referred to the suppressed, unconscious masculine aspects of women (Jung 1959). Post-Jungians used the term anima to refer to the repressed, unconscious feminine aspects in both men and women and the animus as the repressed, unconscious masculine aspects in both men and women (Samuels 1985). Having said that, men still have more anima issues than women and women more animus issues than men. The anima/animus is seen as deeper in the unconscious than the shadow, and thus more difficult to access and to integrate. A man with an unintegrated anima will focus only on goal achievement and results. He will usually find it very difficult, and thus avoid, dealing with relationship issues and ambiguity, when the answers are not clear-cut. Such a man often neglects his family and himself. His repressed feminine side might manifest in inappropriate, often destructive ways of relating to women in his search for his inner feminine side. In the business world, such a man might be seen as overly tough, unable to care for people and unable to build a productive team. A woman with an unintegrated animus will often not be goal directed and unable to organize her life and focus on achieving results. She might appear disorganized and unable to take independent action. Such women often allow abusive relationships to continue, because she lacks the willpower and assertiveness to take decisive action.

Anima/animus awareness is difficult to address during coaching. It usually manifests as compulsiveness, and usually with a person of the opposite sex. It might also manifest as projections, also usually onto members of the opposite sex; whereas shadow projections are usually onto members of the same sex. Women in senior positions in organizations are often characterized by a lack of anima: because most organizations value animus-driven behaviour, women often see it as better for their careers (and survival) to leave their feminine sides behind when they enter the organization. The tragic consequence is that organizations lose out on women's unique contributions, such as truly building teams, building relationships, as well as caring about people and the environment. Because the anima/animus is "deep" in the unconscious mind, accessing it is not easy. The coachee will usually have good reasons, actually excuses, for the irrational behavior rooted in the anima/animus.

2.7 Individuation

The aim of individuation is personal growth. Though the construct "individuation" is at a superficial level similar to Rogers (1961) and Maslow's (as cited in Schott 1992) much better known construct "self-actualization", it is a totally different construct. Individuation is about growth, like self-actualization, but there the similarity ends. Individuation emphasizes the interaction of the various aspects of the personality. Individuation is about establishing a healthy dialogue between the conscious and unconscious minds and also between the various elements (ego, self, shadow and anima/animus) of the unconscious mind. Individuation also emphasizes the individual's responsibility towards his/her community. The individual is thus encouraged to grow and develop to his/her fullest potential *whilst remaining meaningfully connected* (Jung 1948). This aspect of individuation not only resonates well with Africa's "Ubuntu" principle but also lays the foundation for a different way of leadership development. For the coach utilizing archetypal psychology, individuation of the coachee will be the ideal goal of coaching.

The process of individuation is not a neat, linear process. It is a continuous movement of temporary identification with unconscious images in order to make them conscious and then dis-identifying with the image and reflect on the image (Stein 1998). In this way the person obtains psychological distance from the archetypal images and will thus not get caught in archetypal patterns. In coaching, the coach can facilitate this process and thus integrate archetypal material.

According to Stein (2006), it is possible to differentiate between three stages of individuation:

Stage 1: Nurturing Stage During this stage, the base for lasting relationships, self-esteem and self-confidence are emphasized. During this stage, the person must experience being accepted as he/she is and allowed to take risks in a safe environment. If this stage is not completed successfully, the person will not be able to grow, because he/she will be fixated on immature activities. Behaviour such as self-sabotage, exaggerated fear of failure, inability to build relationships and high need for acceptance and approval are indicators to the coach that this stage was not completed successfully.

Stage 2: Adapting Stage During this stage, the person takes on the challenges of the world. He/she learns to take care of him/herself and leaves the nurturing protection of the real or substitute mother. The person becomes independent and self-sufficient. The person is bound to experience some anxiety, because he/she is entering unknown territory. If the anxiety is introduced in moderate amounts and the person experiences mastering of challenges, his/her self-confidence grows and the anxiety decreases. During this stage, the person comes to terms with mainly "shadow" issues. Du Toit (2011) found that many managers are stuck in this stage: they are forever looking for new challenges and often cannot even imagine moving to the next stage. If a person keeps exerting large amounts of energy to attain goals, it could lead to burnout and being less effective, particularly if the person is functioning on a senior managerial level.

The leader who has not completed the developmental tasks of this stage successfully, could be identified by an inability to disconnect from his/her team. This may be seen in an inability to evaluate performance objectively and unawareness of groupthink. He/she may also be ego-inflated to the extent that he/she may see him/herself as a super strong hero, even above laws and rules. This leader may also have many "blind spots", which are issues other people are aware of but the leader him/herself is completely unaware of. This leader may treat people in an inhumane way and be over-anxious about his/her performance.

Stage 3: Integrating Stage During this stage of individuation, the search for meaning comes to the fore. The person becomes centered and whole. He/she has a long term perspective and is able to see trends and predict future events, systems thinking starts to develop (Kets de Vries 2006). During this stage, the anima and animus becomes more integrated with the self.

Indications for the coach that the developmental tasks of this stage are not mastered are: over-involvement in detail; intolerance for ambiguity and complexity; inability to cope with chaos; lack of meaningfulness in his/her life; feels fragmented and tries to control everything.

Though these three stages can be differentiated and follow each other more or less as described, there are obviously overlaps and temporary regression to earlier stages. Full individuation can also never be achieved. These stages take place in a cyclical way (Du Toit 2011) and in a lifetime a person could go through these stages many times, every time achieving a higher level of individuation.

The coach could guide a person through these stages and could thus accelerate the maturation of the person. If the coachee is a manager, the coachee could also shift the perspective of the coachee to see the individuation of his/her team members as one of his/her prime tasks as a manager.

3 Utilization of Archetypal Psychology in Coaching

A coach utilizing archetypal psychology should have some understanding of causes of behaviour, and have some training in archetypal psychology. The coach with an understanding of archetypal psychology should also be able to have some insight into the coaching process itself; e.g., he/she should be more aware of transference and projection between him/herself and the coachee. If the coach him/herself is unaware of the dynamics of the coaching process itself, he/she could easily misunderstand these processes, which are unconscious for the coachee as well. Depth psychology provides unique methods and models for assisting coachees to deal with irrational behaviour, such as anger outbursts, shyness/withdrawal, and conflict avoidance as well as methods to change reactions and habits, such as fear of presentations or even to aid the coachee to stop bad habits, such as smoking.

The coach with an understanding of archetypal psychology has insight into unconscious processes and could thus harness the coachee's strengths. For example, Schuster (2013) states that coaches often equates low confidence, low self-esteem and shyness with introversion. If the coach's point of departure is that "introversion" is the problem, the interventions will be very different than when the coach understands the strengths of being an introvert.

One of the main competencies of an organizational coach, is the ability to facilitate sustained behavior change in the work context (Brotman et al. 1998). To bring desired change, the habitual self-defeating scripts must be identified (Koortzen and Oosthuizen 2010). These "scripts" refer to destructive patterns of behaviour which the coachee are unaware of and/or unable to break, even if he/she is aware of it and even when told repeatedly that these behaviours could cause derailment. Insight into the problem is usually only the starting point and not enough to bring change. For example, a person who wants to stop smoking knows all the facts: he/she knows the health, financial and social advantages to stopping, wants to stop, sees a clear picture of him/herself as a non-smoker, but still find it extremely hard not to continue the very simple pattern of smoking. To break more complex patterns, such as shyness, or loosing ones temper is much more complex, often with strong unconscious forces maintaining the pattern.

The origin of these patterns is usually personal repressed experiences. These personal experiences which form the roots of these patterns are often grounded in collective, archetypal sources. Freud said that the personal unconscious is like a pit, with the repressed traumas and experiences are seen as below the surface, in the unconscious (Freud 1950) (unconscious material is often symbolically described as the depths below the surface of water). Jung agreed with the view of the personal unconscious, but added that all the personal unconscious minds are linked; which he described as an underground river linking all the individual pits. The same source thus feeds personal unconscious minds (Jung 1959). These similar archetypal contents can be seen in the universal images people share, such as the idea of a witch, a wise old man, a clown or a divine child. The counter-productive behaviour patterns that people are trapped in oftentimes have such archetypal themes; these patterns thus could be like rituals. An example of such an archetypal pattern could be a leader who cannot move away from an autocratic managerial style. He/she might seem like the old king in a fairy tale who cannot change his ways and his kingdom suffers famine due to his inability to adapt. Many managers' team members suffer and cannot grow and develop (seem to live in a desolate land of starvation) due to the manager's inability to change. The coach can thus use the imagery of fairy tales to assist the coachee to gain insight into his/her counter-productive behaviour patterns.

In the archetypal approach, "awareness" is heavily emphasized. This awareness goes beyond just understanding behaviour and the negative impact of the behaviour. The coachee needs to understand his/her own emotional reality. During trauma and crises, a person sometimes makes promises to him/herself which make perfect sense at the time. For example, if a person gets cheated on by someone he/she deeply loves, the person might promise him/herself never to fall in love again, in order to never get hurt again. Often, these decisions lead to entrenched behaviour patterns which are never re-evaluated. Because these decisions were often taken after a traumatic event, they may be linked to an unconscious complex, which we know can be rooted in archetypal material. These "decisions" thus play a pivotal part in archetypal patterns. These patterns become unconscious and the person may defend the consequential behaviour as if it was a core value. Therefore the decision that initially was intended to protect the person, later can have a limiting and negative effect. The coach needs to make the coachee aware of out-dated decisions and the necessity of reflection and renewal. For example, if a person is treated very unfairly in his family of origin and by others, he might decide to never in his life treat anyone unfairly. Suppose then the person becomes an artisan and in his work fairness is the main "value" that guides his decisions, it might serve him well. Even if the person is promoted to the position of foreman, he might still be successful if he strives to be fair with his direct reports and the people he renders a service to. Suppose this person then gets promoted to a managerial position and still strives to be in the first place fair, he is likely to be unable to respond to the complexity and nuances of situations and thus fail as a manager. This is obviously not to say that a manager should be blatantly unfair, but other principles, such as efficiency and urgency, should foremost guide his decisions rather than fairness. He will often believe that his coach and manager do not fully understand the situation, even when he is told that his career might be derailed if he does not change. The coach assists the person to become aware of outdated archetypal patterns and replace them with more helpful beliefs and behaviours without sacrificing core values.

When the coach follows an archetypal approach, the coach is unlikely to take on the role of an all-knowing expert who is the coach because of his/her superior knowledge. The coach takes on the stance of "not knowing" and explores options with the coachee. The coach would not strive to be a role model for the coachee, as the coachee is encouraged to discover his/her own ideal self, not copy any role model. The following cartoon illustrates this point (Fig. 1).

More awareness does not necessarily lead directly to more happiness. "Blissfully unaware" people can sometimes be happy. The more aware person does have insight into his/her own reactions and is thus more capable of regulating his/her reactions in the long run. True personal growth, individuation, needs a high level of awareness. For the coach who follows the archetypal approach, creating higher levels of awareness in the coachee will be a key coaching objective.

4 Intercultural Coaching

Many coaches are coaching across cultural boundaries, which cause its own challenges. Coetzee (2012) found that the inter-cultural awareness levels of coaches vary greatly; she also found coaches who were unaware of their own unawareness of their cultural biases. No integrated models for dealing with inter-cultural differences are currently used by coaches. Existing models, and theory on inter-cultural coaching, are practice based and a theoretical; robust empirical research is lacking (Hamlin et al. 2007). Though culture is important, Lowman (2007) points out that culture sometimes is relevant and sometimes not. Though culture is important, it does not account for not explain individual differences. Some of the models applied in the coaching world will be discussed next, also for their possible applicability from an archetypal perspective. As stated, the inter-cultural coaching theory needs further research, an integrated inter-cultural coaching from an archetypal, or depth psychology, perspective does not exist yet.

"The first step toward enlightenment is disillusionment."

Fig. 1 The first step toward enlightenment is disillusionment (Twohy 2008)

Hofstede (1980, 2001) identified five dimensions which describe cultural differences between countries and between organizations. The dimensions are:

- Power distance: the degree of perceived inequality between members
- Collectivity/individuality: the emphasis being on the individual member or on the membership of the group
- Masculinity/femininity: if masculinity is emphasized, formal structures, goals achievement and internal competition is usually encouraged, whereas femininity refers to emphasis on the "softer", people side and aspects such as caring, inclusivity and team cohesion are emphasized.
- Uncertainty avoidance refers to the extent to which members are threatened by the unknown and avoid uncertainty.

These dimensions have face validity and appear easy to use. They have been widely accepted and have made their way into coaching sessions. Many coaches use these dimensions in preparing coachees for inter-cultural assignments, but also to understand differences between individuals. For the coach with an archetypal approach, these dimensions in themselves could be unconscious archetypal patterns. Awareness of these patterns can in itself challenge a coachee's unconscious assumptions. The archetypal coach is likely to utilize the dimensions themselves slightly different than other coaches: The coachee's reaction to (and need for) power distance is likely to be explored, rather than to just accept and adapt to it as a cultural phenomena. The archetypal coach would approach collectivism/individualism not as "either or", but view he individuation of the individual as developing in his/her own unique way, whilst remaining meaningfully connected to the collective. The masculinity/femininity resonates with the archetypal constructs anima/animus. The exploration and integration of these are seen as difficult, but an integral part of the individuation process. Regarding the dimension uncertainty avoidance, the archetypal approach would seek to understand the underlying factors which might lead to excessive avoidance of uncertainty or the taking of uncalculated risks.

Apart from Hofstede's (1980, 2001) dimensions, other intercultural models and theories also made their way into the coaching arena. Schein (1969) differentiated three levels of a culture. He likened a culture to an iceberg: On the surface, the culture manifest in artifacts and behaviours. Below the surface, the artifacts and behaviours are influenced by attitudes and at a deeper level, the attitudes are influenced and shaped by fundamental assumptions and beliefs. Schein's model resonates well with the archetypal approach: change and understanding of inter-cultural issues need to be addressed "below the surface", in other words, on an unconscious level, and not only on a behavioural level. Archetypal coaches also know that metaphoric iceberg, just like real iceberg, sometimes tip over and shadow issues surface at unexpected and inconvenient times. The coach who ignores unconscious issues, might be taken by surprise and not understand the surfacing of unconscious material, which is usually hidden.

Gilbert and Cartwright (2008) described a culture in terms of a field of influence in which the individual functions. The individual is thus influenced by the culture, usually at an unconscious level. The individual might follow the prescriptions of the culture without being aware of it. The archetypal approach is about creating awareness of this "field of influence" to enable the individual to make conscious choices. By being aware of cultural influences on others, a better understanding of the intercultural differences becomes possible.

The archetypal approach, with its emphasis on awareness, could assist coaches to be open to their own biases and intercultural misunderstandings. Some of the basic premises of coaching, such as that the goal of coaching should be to increase the coachee's internal locus of control, coach the person to be more assertive or towards more independent decision making, comes from a Western worldview. These goals might be in conflict with the culture in which the coachee functions. If the coach is aware of his/her own assumptions, it becomes possible to have greater inter-cultural sensitivity and respect the coachee's field of influence.

Fig. 2 Inscription in a church in Rwanda where hundreds of refugees were killed in 1 day during the 1994 genocide. The inscription loosely translated means: "If you knew yourself and you knew me, you would not have killed me"

Drawing from the results of global research on inter-cultural coaching, Abbott et al. (2013) talks about cultural intelligence (CQ), which refers to being intelligent about inter-cultural differences. They also mention that a global mindset is required of coachees that functions in global organizations. They identified a set of psychological, intellectual and social competencies required. The cognitive functioning includes global business savvy and the ability to deal with complexity; the psychological competence refers to passion for diversity, thirst for adventure and self-assurance whilst the social competencies are intercultural empathy, inter-personal impact and diplomacy.

The archetypal approach to inter-cultural coaching can be summarized by an inscription in the Ntarama church in Rwanda, where hundreds of people were massacred in 1 day during the 1994 genocide. Loosely translated, the inscription reads: "If you knew yourself and you knew me, you would not have killed me". The coach who does not know him/herself and does not have true empathy for the other person, can never truly understand inter-cultural differences nor truly respect the "otherness" of the coachee from a different culture (Fig. 2).

5 In Closing

This chapter endeavored to position archetypal psychology as a possible approach in coaching. Its advantages and some basic principles were highlighted. It needs to be stressed that it is not an easy approach and definitely not a "quick fix". The coach that utilizes this approach needs a through grounding in depth psychology, particularly in Jung's analytical psychology.

References

Abbott, G., Gilbert, K., & Rosinski, P. (2013). Cross-cultural working in coaching and mentoring. In J. Passmore, D. B. Peterson, & T. Freire (Eds.), *The Wiley-Blackwell handbook of the psychology of coaching and mentoring* (pp. 483–500). Retrieved from http://ir.nmu.org.ua/bitstream/handle/123456789/144889/cfdaf6e32f456ab57cc53be33169b53f.pdf?sequence–1#page=312

Agervold, M. (2007). Bullying at work: A discussion of definitions and prevalence, based on an empirical study. *Scandinavian Journal of Psychology, 48*(2), 161–172. doi:10.1111/j.1467-9450.2007.00585.x.

Beck, U. (2012). *Psychodynamic coaching focus and depth*. London: Karnac Book Ltd.

Brotman, L. E., Liberi, W. P., & Wasylyshyn, K. M. (1998). Executive coaching: The need for standards of competence. *Consulting Psychology Journal: Practice & Research, 50*(1), 40–46. doi:10.1037/1061-4087.50.1.40.

Coetzee, Y. (2012). *Intercultural experiences of South African business coaches*. Master's thesis, North-West University, Vanderbijlpark.

Coleman, A. (1999). *Up from scapegoating*. New York: Vintage Books.

Du Toit, D. H. (2011). *A Jungian perspective on the psycho-social maturity of leaders*. Doctoral dissertation, University of Johannesburg, Johannesburg.

Freud, S. (1950). *Collected papers, 1(7), (6th impression)*. London: Hogarth Press and the Institute of Psycho-analysts.

Gilbert, K., & Cartwright, S. (2008). Cross-cultural consultancy initiatives to develop Russian managers. *Academy of Management Learning and Education, 7*(4), 504–518.

Hamlin, R. G., Ellinger, A. D., & Beattie, R. S. (2007). Coaching at the heart of managerial effectiveness: A cross-cultural study of managerial behaviours. *Human Resource Development International, 9*(3), 305–331. doi:10.1080/13678860600893524.

Handy, C. B. (1995). *The age of unreason* (2nd ed.). London: Random House.

Hofstede, G. (1980). Motivation, leadership, and organization: Do American theories apply abroad? *Organizational Dynamics, 9*(1), 42–63. doi:10.1016/0090-2616(80)90013-3.

Hofstede, G. (2001). Culture's recent consequences: Using dimension scores in theory and research. *International Journal of Cross Cultural Management, 1*(1), 11–30. Retrieved from http://ccm.sagepub.com.nwulib.nwu.ac.za/content/1/1/11.full.pdf+html

Jung, C. G. (1948). *The integration of the personality* (5th ed.). London: Kegan Paul.

Jung, C. G. (1959). Concerning the archetypes, with special reference to the anima concept. *Collected Works, 9*(Part I), 54–72.

Kalsched, D. (1996). *The inner world of trauma: Archetypal defences of the personal spirit*. London: Routledge Publishers.

Kets de Vries, M. F. R. (2006). *The leadership mystique: Leading behavior in the human enterprise* (2nd ed.). London: Prentice Hall.

Koortzen, P., & Oosthuizen, R. (2010). A competence executive coaching model. *South African Journal of Industrial Psychology, 36*(1), 1–11. doi:10.4102/sajip.v36i1.837.

Lowman, R. L. (2007). Coaching and consulting in multicultural contexts: Integrating themes and issues. *Consulting Psychology Journal: Practice and Research, 59*(4), 296–303. doi:10.1037/1065-9293.59.4.296.

McCauley, C. D., Moxley, R. S., & Van Velsor, E. (Eds.). (1998). *The center for creative leadership: Handbook of leadership development*. California: Jossey-Bass Publishers.

Rogers, C. R. (1961). *On becoming a person: A therapist's view of psychotherapy*. Boston: Houghton Mifflin Company.

Samuels, A. (1985). *Jung and post-Jungians*. London: Routledge Publishers.

Schein, E. (1969). The mechanisms of change. In W. G. Bennis, K. D. Denne, & R. Chin (Eds.), *The planning of change* (pp. 98–108). New York: Holt, Rinehart and Winston.

Schott, R. L. (1992). Abraham Maslow, humanistic psychology, and organization leadership: A Jungian perspective. *Journal of Humanistic Psychology, 32*(1), 106–120.

Schuster, J. (2013). *Therapy, depth psychology and executive coaching: Where and how do they meet?* [Adobe Digital Editions Version]. Retrieved from http://www.evocateurblog.com/wp-content/uploads/2013/12/Coaching-and-Therapy-Article-For-Download.pdf

Stein, M. (1998). *Jung's map of the soul: An introduction*. Chicago: Open Court.

Stein, M. (2006). Individuation. In R. K. Papadopoulos (Ed.), *The handbook of Jungian psychology: Theory, practice and applications*. London: Routledge Publishers.

Twohy, M. (2008). *"The first step to enlightenment is disillusionment." – New Yorker Cartoon*. Retrieved from http://www.art.com/products/p15063313190-sa-i6845919/mike-twohy-the-first-step-toward-enlightenment-is-dissillusionment-new-yorker-cartoon.htm

Systemic Thinking and Transcultural Approaches in Coaching Psychology: Introducing a New Coaching Framework

Claude-Hélène Mayer and Rian Viviers

Prefer what is positive and multiple,
difference over uniformity,
flows over unities,
mobile arrangements over systems.
Believe that what is productive
is not sedentary but nomadic.

(Michel Foucault)

Abstract Coaching in organizations has become a prominent tool to address challenges experienced by individuals and teams. Different approaches in coaching are used, such as individual, team or business coaching. Certain approaches to coaching, such as psychological coaching, aim to increase optimal functioning, wellbeing and mental health for personal growth and development. The effect of psychological coaching in organizations has been empirically researched and discussed in the literature. In today's organizations, coaching is a well-established domain in theory and practice. However, studies show that transcultural (In this chapter the authors refer to the concept of "transculturality" due to the fact that the coaching framework presented is based on a "transcultural" approach. "Transculturality" refers to a world view which is based on the notion of hybridity and blurring spheres of cultures which are interconnected, mixed and integrative (Welsch W. Kultur aus transkultureller Perspektive. In Treichel D, Mayer C-H (eds) Lehrbuch Kultur. Lehr- und Lernmaterialien zur Vermittlung kultureller Kompetenzen. Münster, Waxmann, pp 149–157, 2011). In transcultural settings, culture is viewed as a dynamic and "active factior" (Welsch W. Transculturality –

C.-H. Mayer (✉)
Department of Indsutrial and Organisational Psychology,
University of South Africa, South Africa
e-mail: claudemayer@gmx.net

R. Viviers
University of South Africa, Pretoria, South Africa

L.E. van Zyl et al. (eds.), *Coaching Psychology: Meta-theoretical perspectives and applications in multicultural contexts*, DOI 10.1007/978-3-319-31012-1_10

the puzzling form of cultures today. In Featherstone M, Lash S (eds) Spaces of culture: city, nation, world. Sage, London, pp 194–213, 1999, 2003) that is inclusive and the opposite of exclusive, homogene and fixed.) organizational contexts require particular systemic and transcultural perspectives to adequately address the challenges of individuals, teams and the organizations within their local and global contexts. Yet these systemic and transcultural approaches have hardly been explored in coaching transcultural organizations. The aim of this chapter is to show that systemic thinking and transcultural approaches in coaching psychology can provide a sound theoretical base and practical intervention method for psychological coaching within globalized and transcultural organizational contexts. A new coaching framework is introduced that is based on three phases: the input, the process and the output. Within these phases systemic and transcultural approaches and aspects are discussed, the profile of a coach is presented, and practices and interventions are explored. Recommendations are made for theory and practice.

Keywords Systemic thinking • Trans-cultural psychology • Coaching model

1 Introduction

For organizations, the question of developing healthy, non-toxic work environments has gained interest (Rothmann and Cilliers 2007). It has been pointed out that psychological attributes – which include individuals' ability to adapt and deal proactively with work challenges in global, transcultural and highly dynamic work contexts – have a significant impact on individuals' development (Savickas 2011). Coaching has become a prominent tool (Fig. 1) to develop these psychological attributes in individuals, teams and organizations, aiming at increasing mental health and wellbeing within organizations and transculturally, bridging potential cultural divides (Mayer and Boness 2013a).

There is an ongoing discourse in theory and practice on the question of theoretical approaches and practical interventions that contribute to positive and healthy organizational development, stress reduction, individual growth and organizational effectiveness (Biron et al. 2014). Coaching, as a strategy to develop individuals and organizations from a positive psychological perspective has only recently attracted interest (Biron et al. 2014; Mayer 2011). At the same time, it has been pointed out that coaching need to focus on intercultural settings, culture-sensitive coaching practices and interventions to increase its contribution to individual and organizational development (Nazarkiewicz and Krämer 2012).

Focusing on the question of what keeps people healthy in global-oriented and transcultural organizations, recent research has highlighted that particular systemic (Schwemmle and Schwemmle 2012) and transcultural approaches in coaching psychology (Von Schlippe et al. 2003) in organizations can support individual and organizational development across cultures on a theoretical, as well as on a practical base (Mayer 2011).

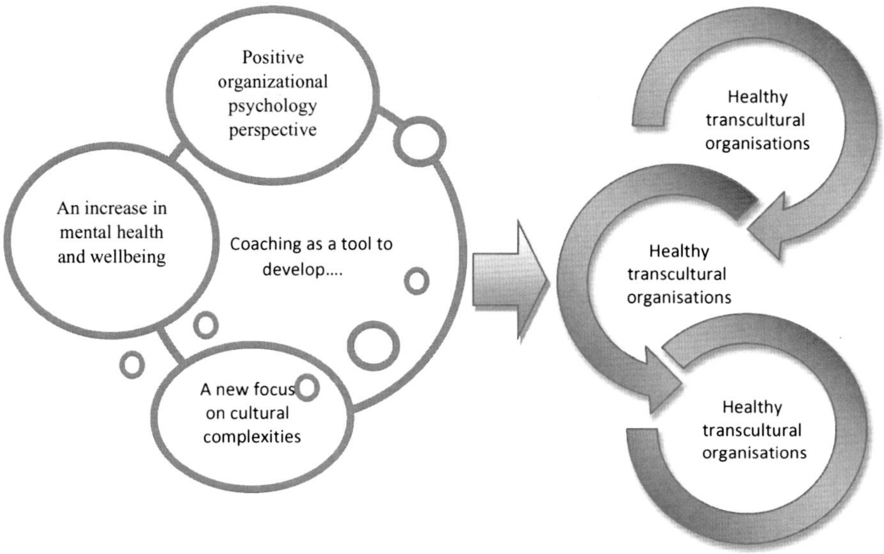

Fig. 1 Coaching as a developmental tool

The aim of this chapter is to introduce a specific phase-based coaching framework which has been developed particularly for transcultural organizational settings. The coaching framework is based on theoretical systemic thinking approaches (Bateson 1985, 1987; Luhmann 2000; Maturana 1998; Maturana and Varela 1990), as well as theories of transculturality (Lloyd and Härtel 2003). The content of this chapter is based on a critical review of the relevant literature that led to the development of the coaching framework which includes the input (theoretical approaches), the process (competences, approaches, the profile of the coach, and interventions) and the output (competence), which is to develop optimally functioning individuals within healthy organizations through the four systemic layers of the individual, the team, the organization and the environment.

2 The Frame: Coaching Psychology Within the Positive Psychology Paradigm

Coaching has become a prominent intervention in organizations and organizational staff development, not only to develop managerial wisdom, but also to cope with a dynamic and complex work environment (Bennett and Bush 2009).

The concept of coaching originated in the 1940s (Lowman 2002) and has been described as a specific form of consultancy (Deutscher Bundesverband für Coaching 2014) that has an impact on leadership behaviour and the ability to inspire and influence followers (Kampa-Kokesch 2002). Williams (2003, p. 38) notes that coaching has its fundamental roots in Maslow's (1968) work, "providing the framework for modern life coaching as it is practiced today." Since Maslow (1968) recognized that humans are naturally health-seeking, that they pursue self-actualization, creativity, curiosity and playfulness – particularly as soon as obstacles to personal growth are removed or resolved – Maslow's basic assumptions built the foundation of contemporary coaching concepts.

During the past decade, the literature on coaching has expanded, focusing on coaching in organizations (Rosinski 2011), managerial coaching (Levinsky 2000; Mayer 2011; Mayer and Boness 2013a; Rückert 2001); and coaching in therapeutic settings (Besser-Siegmund and Siegmund 2003; Mayer 2012). Peltier (2001, p. xv), differentiates between mainly two forms of organizational coaching, namely "executive coaching" and "management coaching". In both forms, the coach supports the individual in uncovering the unconscious and exploring conscious psychological processes on a cognitive level, whilst producing awareness of hidden defence mechanisms that may be hindering the individual from reaching goals and which may be producing undesirable results (Peltier 2001). The concept of executive coaching has only recently been explored more in depth and has been defined as an integration of various coaching models (Kampa-Kokesch and Anderson 2001) which may potentially enhance developmental change (Laske 1999) as well as individual and organizational performance (Olivero et al. 1997). However, certain coaching approaches such as business or strategy coaching aim at enhancing individual behaviour or/and organizational processes (Bluckert 2005).

Coaching practices in organizations range from executive coaching (Hillary 2003) to neuro-semantic coaching (Hall and Duval 2004) and from solution-focused coaching to coaching for self-actualization purposes. However, it seems to be common sense that recent coaching models are based on interdisciplinary approaches that often strive for solution-orientation (Greene and Grant 2003), an increase in self-awareness, the development of self-esteem and intrapersonal self-understanding, as well as the improvement of intra- and interpersonal communication practices (Mayer 2011). Consequently, executive and managerial coaching in organizations is founded on "a formal, ongoing relationship between an individual or team with managerial authority and responsibility in an organization; and a consultant who possesses knowledge of behaviour change and organizational functioning" (Mayer 2011, p. 113).

Techniques that are used in coaching processes vary according to the focus of the coaching process, the coaching approach, the socio-cultural context and the personality and preferences of the coach and the coachee. According to Rückert (2001), coaching techniques often include practices such as working with success factors, relaxation techniques, developing constructive new behaviour patterns through brainstorming, techniques used in change management processes, time management, optimization of personal expression, work attitudes, body work techniques, the exploration of communication, as well as mental restructuring techniques.

Across these coaching approaches and contexts of coaching psychology, coaching has increasingly been researched from a positive psychology research perspective to improve the facilitation of optimal functioning (Kauffman and Scoular 2004; Linley 2004) as well as health and wellbeing (Mayer 2011). It is assumed that the positive psychology paradigm (Lopez and Snyder 2003) that is applied in coaching processes increases health and wellbeing in organizations (Mayer 2011), learned resourcefulness (Rosenbaum 1990), as well as emotional intelligence (Goleman 1995).

Coaching processes have been found to be helpful in strengthening health and well-being within individuals and organizations and have been shown to reduce stress (Krause and Mayer 2012; Mayer and Boness 2013b). According to Rosinski (2011, p. 49), characteristics of coaching include the "belief in a vast human potential and the value of striving to unleash that potential", as well as in the ability of individuals to be resourceful and capable of (re-) activating personal resources. Besides these basic and fundamental characteristics, the aims of coaching can be multifarious and the reasons for individuals, groups, teams or organizations to undergo coaching processes are manifold. However, coaching basically seeks to support individuals in improving themselves to reach their goals. Therefore, coaching usually aims at developing individuals to attain personal success and clearly defined achievements, whilst strengthening their mental health and wellbeing. According to Rückert (2001), coaching in the professional context is used to define goals, to achieve these goals, to develop solutions, make adequate decisions, increase motivation and develop skills and competences. Beyond these individual and team development aspects, coaching also aims at "facilitating organizational development" in terms of organic organizational growth (Rosinski 2011, p. 51). Bluckert (2005) highlights that coaching in organizations includes business and strategy development on the one hand and psychology and human behaviour development and process improvement on the other hand.

Coaching processes in organizations have to deal with individual, social and cultural complexities, as well as with issues around hierarchies, decision-making, varying individual, team and organizational interests and development potential, in addition to cultural diversity issues (Mayer and Vanderheiden 2014). It is argued in this chapter that systemic and transcultural approaches in coaching can help to deal with these demands and provide applicable ideas to understand these complexities and simplify and split them into themes or trends in order to deal with the issues adequately and that more effective action can be taken. Therefore, theoretical approaches to systemic thinking and transculturality in organizations will be introduced in the following section.

3 Input

Figure 2 provides an overview of the factors that are considered in input phase I: How the individual, team, organization and finally the environment are being influenced by systemic premises, as advocated by Ludewig, Maturana, Luhmann and Bateson.

3.1 Input I: The Premises of Systemic Thinking

A basic characteristic of a system is the interconnectedness and the relations of elements, subsystems and processes. These relations are primarily determined by the assumption that the whole is greater than the sum of its parts and that holistic

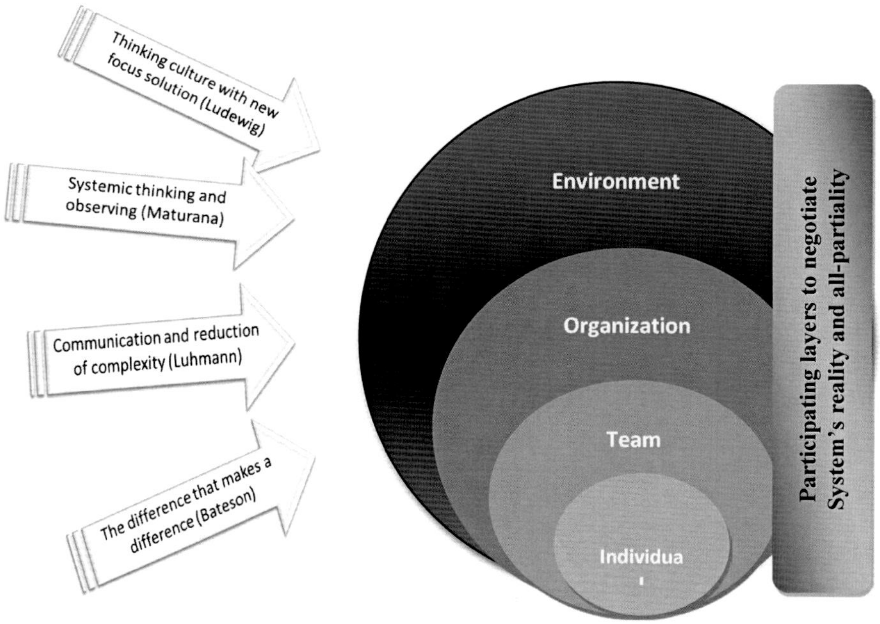

Fig. 2 Systemic premises to system's reality

approaches can lead to adequate solutions. The term "system" defines the totality of elements and their inter-relationship (Von Bertalanffy 1968, p. 55). These elements interact and communicate with each other and thereby create a sense-making and purposeful unit, the system (Meer 2008). A system demarcates its boundaries through rules and regulations, through its organization and structure.

As organizations are defined as complex adaptive systems, coaching that is based on systemic thinking is an appropriate approach to meet organizational challenges. Biological (Maturana 1998; Maturana and Varela 1990) and sociological (Luhmann 2001) assumptions have led towards an increase in systemic thinking in coaching processes and have influenced system theories (Ludewig 2005).

Maturana (1998), as one of the first scientists to study systems in depth, emphasizes that the functional and operational, closed nervous systems of human beings do not differentiate between internal and external triggers, perceptions and illusions. These nervous systems are viewed as being reproductive, autopoietic and autonomous. Thus, the concept of observation is essential in systemic thinking. For Maturana (1998) "observing" means to differentiate. If there is no possibility of differentiating, there is no cognitive (re-)cognition. That means that there is no construction of reality. Luhmann (2001), who uses Maturana's scientific findings, applies them to social systems. He highlights that social systems are based on communication and that communication contributes to the reduction of certain systemic complexities whilst creating new forms of complexities which are easier for a human being to understand and to manage. Communicated complexities are at the same time more meaningful to human beings than other complexities, such as the impenetrability, incalculability and unpredictability of systems which will be discussed in Sect. 3.2. One possibility, according to Luhmann's (2001) communication is the anthropological approach towards reducing the double contingency of impenetrability and incalculability. The problem of the incomputability of systems needs to be approached in a human way. One possibility, according to Luhmann (2001), could be to use systemic thinking approaches to reduce the complexities of reality and to make them comprehensible for the observer and the observed.

Ludewig (2005) emphasizes that systemic thinking is a kind of thinking culture ("Denk-Kultur"). This thinking culture responds to the question of how individuals construct their realities within social systems, which premises they prefer and which possibilities they see to question these premises (Ludewig 2005; Von Schlippe and Schweitzer 2003). Systemic thinking aims at accentuating the focus of a problem in a new way, to present a specific methodology to work with high complexities and to change from a problem-centred approach towards a solution-centred approach (De Shazer 2004).

Thereby, systemic thinking is always based on the world of experience of the individual – the observer and/or the observed – and therefore is always defined as subjective (Bateson 1987). In contrast to the sociological systems theory of Luhmann (2000), Ruesch and Bateson (1995, p. 305) view the acting individual as an element of the system: the social system is built out of "participating individuals" who negotiate the system's reality. However, according to Ruesch and Bateson (1995), communication happens on four different layers: on the intrapersonal level (what is going on within one person), the interpersonal level (what is going on between two or more persons), the level of group processes (interactions between many people) and the level of cultural processes (interactions between large groups, cultural groups and/or in society as a whole). According to Bateson (1987), it is the "difference that makes a difference", whereby the difference is part of the observer's construction of reality and not an objective fact. That means that within the system the processes observed are always a construction of the person who interacts and the person who observes.

This form of systemic thinking is related to the basic principle of the ethical imperative of Von Foerster (1995) who advises that actions should always aim at increasing the quantum of possibilities. Actions are defined as meaningful if they expand the possibilities of choice. Accordingly, actions such as right-wrong judgements, or actions that are prohibited due to individual or societal taboos, might limit the possibilities and are therefore rejected in systemic thinking. Furthermore, systemic thinking approaches are shaped by the concept of all-partiality. This means that all elements of a system need to be empathetically accepted before change can be introduced and high levels of subjective well-being can be reached (Mayer 2011).

In the following section, the basic assumptions of systemic thinking in coaching processes will be addressed.

3.2 *Input II: Basic Assumptions of Systemic Thinking in Coaching Processes*

Systems are characterised by impenetrability, incalculability and unpredictability (Kirchmayr-Kreczi 2001) and are therefore described as a "black box", meaning that "the only conceivable way of unveiling a black box, is to play with it" (Thorn 1984, p. 298). In systemic thinking it is assumed that one can never say how, for example, a coaching intervention will play out within its elements and its subsystems. The impenetrable streams of problems – defined in the way that a coach, for example, will never be able to impenetrate the system in its entire complexity –, decision-making processes and solutions that exist in systems usually lead to unpredictable decisions (March and Olsen 1976). This impenetrability and incalculability of systems can, according to Becker et al. (1988), only be addressed through "revisions of rationality". Therefore, to provide for the great and unpredictable complexity within organizations, systemic coaching needs to address, with adequately complex interventions, the development of multiple and various decision-making approaches on the basis of systemic premises and assumptions such as circularity. March and Olsen (1976) highlight the concept of the "rationality of arbitrariness", such as circularity, solution-orientation (Bamberger 2001; De Shazer 2004), resource-orientation and growth-orientation to explore the system's complexity, without preferring a certain way of addressing themes and topics in systemic coaching. Through systemic coaching, rationalised myths, power-related influences and individual as well as organizational aims are addressed and questioned to explore the interplay of actors and actions and – if needed – to reconstruct it. Further systemic concepts include the orientation towards narrations, phenomenology, symbolism and experiences (Bartussek 2007; Wienands 2003).

In systemic coaching, circularity is one of the main concepts used, based on the assumption that human behaviour, feelings and thoughts are part of a socially and psychologically constructed reality. Selvini-Palazzoli et al. (1981) work with the reconstruction and questioning of personal, subjective and socially reconstructed realities. By using this approach, the coach is not seen as an expert (Scheinecker 2007). It is rather the coachee who is defined as the expert for his own solutions (Bamberger 2001). By responding to circular questions, thoughts and statements of the coach, the coachee increases awareness of his/her own processes and becomes an expert to deal with him-/herself and his/her own challenges (Simon and Rech-Simon 2007).

At the moment there are few empirical research findings that refer to the efficiency and effectiveness of systemic coaching approaches in transcultural and global organizations (Cottrell and Boston 2002). Systemic coaching in a transcultural context always needs to be highly context-specific and experiences on a practical as well as on a theoretical and/or empirical level cannot just be transmitted into other systems (Brunner 2002, p. 239). Systemic transcultural coaching requires manifold resources to be implemented, specific organizational and coaching analysis and the creation of system-specific approaches to deal with the challenges.

Generally, systemic coaching is founded on a solution-focused approach, considering the assumption that "Problem talk creates problems, solution talk creates solutions" (Von Schlippe and Schweizer 2003, p. 35). The focus on solutions and how solutions can be supported (Bamberger 2001) leads to more solutions, whilst the focus on problems can easily lead to a problem trance and an increase in problems. According to De Shazer (1989), the focus on solutions and constructive actions establishes cooperation and trust between the coach and the coachee. The main task of the coach is then to be an observer and supporter of the constructive solutions the coachee implements (De Shazer 2004). Scheinecker (2007) indicates that solutions are stimulated through the analysis and perception of differences, the search for resources, future-orientation, acknowledgement and respect, as well as cooperative actions and the retention of respect towards the coachee.

Solution-orientation is highly interconnected with the resource focus in systemic coaching. Flückinger and Wüsten (2008) define resources as "something that can be used for support or help". According to the Farlex dictionary (2010) resourceful individuals can usually cope with challenging situations and know that they have the ability to deal with difficult situations effectively. In systemic coaching processes, the coachee focuses on his/her resources and thereby increases personal growth, wellbeing and a coherent identity (Mayer 2007) through the focus on resources, feelings, thoughts and behaviour change towards a positive life approach and individual growth (Satir 2001). According to Satir et al. (2007), the core aims of an internal individual development process need to include the promotion of the self-worth of a personality, honest and direct communication and an increased self-esteem that is stimulated through non-violent, respectful and positive relationships. Systemic approaches can support the coachee during the coaching process to further improve his/her communication skills, to achieve personal growth and encouragement towards building congruent communication patterns within daily interactions (Satir 2004).

Figure 3 provides a diagrammatic perspective of the basic assumptions of systemic thinking in coaching processes.

In using these systemic approaches, one important consideration is to always see the system as a whole (Luhmann 2000). This is particularly important when the complexity of the individual or the organizational system is interfused with various cultural and transcultural aspects which need to be acknowledged and respected as a part of the whole (Mayer 2011). Recent studies in organizations prove that systemic thinking approaches are effective and meaningful when it comes to systemic coaching practices (Neuvians 2011; Tuckermann 2012), also in transcultural contexts. But how are culture and transcultural aspects viewed in coaching psychology?

3.3 Input III: Transcultural Aspects in Coaching Psychology

Transcultural approaches in coaching psychology aim at understanding systems, such as individuals, groups and organizations, across cultures and improving transcultural competences. Culture is viewed as learnable, dynamic and changeable. It is

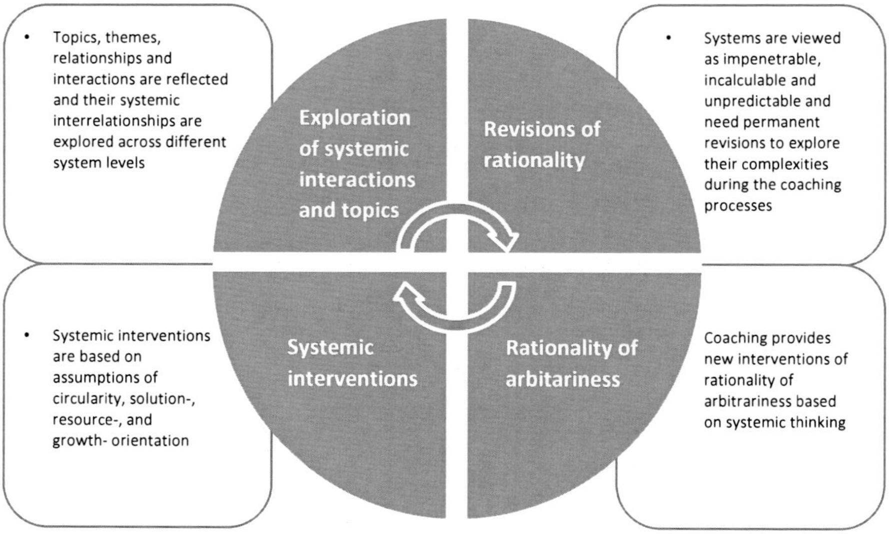

Fig. 3 Basic assumptions of systemic thinking in coaching processes

defined as a general, complex system that has an impact on the perceptions, thoughts, feelings and actions of human beings (Bhugra and Becker 2005). Culture therefore provides the framework for evaluating (systemic) relationships, value concepts and the positioning of the self within its systemic framework (Mayer and Viviers 2014a). It determines a kind of social order within a system (Durant 1981) and constructs a pattern of meaning and systems which is, according to Geertz (1987), drawn from ideologies, religion, sciences and arts to provide orientation to individuals within broader systems, such as groups, organizations or the society. However, Welsch (2011) emphasises that culture is a construction of the interplay of individual, social and societal concepts, thoughts, perceptions, meaning-making, emotions and world views (Eckersley 2007) which is dynamically reconstructed within the interplay of all of its systems' actors and their concepts. Culture is seen as contributing to the acceleration, simplification and improvement of transcultural competence and learning within social groups or societies (Herbrand 2002).

Recently, research has focused on coaching across cultures (Radice von Wogau et al. 2004; Fischer and Grothe 2007; Grothe and Straub 2008; Radice von Wogau 2004; Von Schlippe et al. 2003), cross-cultural psychology (e.g. Berry et al. 2008) and therapy with migrants (Radice von Wogau et al. 2004). Research on culture and coaching has mainly focused on the difficulties of coaching migrants, the various constructions of realities and cultures, experiences of marginalization and the development of intercultural competences in coaches in European contexts (Radice von Wogau et al. 2004). Other authors emphasize primarily the challenges coaches

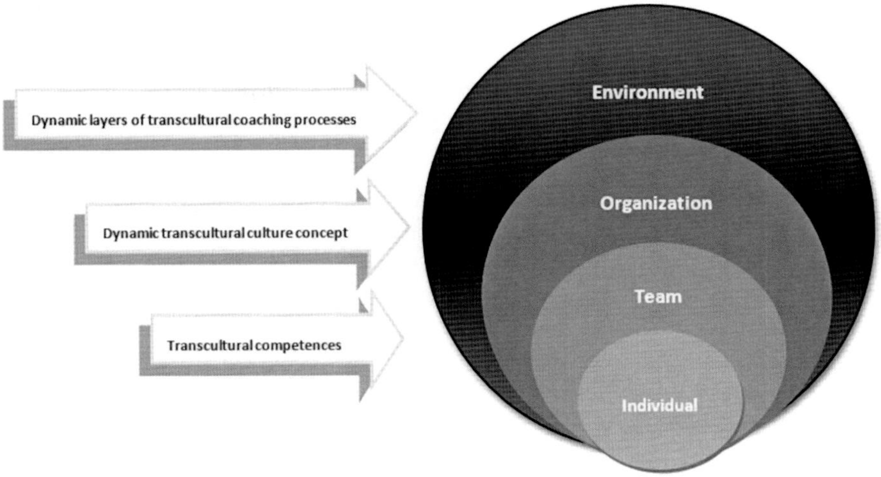

Fig. 4 Transcultural aspects in organizational coaching settings

experience in multicultural or transcultural contexts (Von Schlippe et al. 2003), such as the joining process, the management of certain topics (e.g. flight, addiction, migration) or bicultural couples. With regard to cultural aspects, Rosinski (2011) emphasises that cultural concepts and cultural dimensions such as high-context versus low-context, direct versus indirect, effective versus neutral and formal versus informal (Rosinski 2011, p. 153), and psychological models, such as the Johari window (Rosinski 2011, p. 145) can be used to refer to transcultural aspects in coaching processes (Fig. 4).

Steixner (2009, p. 83) emphasises that coaching across cultures "identifies and develops transcultural competence as a key to success in the international and globalised work environment". Transcultural coaching appears to be a key developmental intervention which increases transcultural, social, strategic and professional competences. It is considered an important integrative tool (Steixner 2009, p. 84). Steixner (2009, p. 86) asserts that transcultural coaching should contribute to developing transcultural competences, reflecting cultural identity aspects and identification with cultural differences, as well as transcultural learning processes. Coaching in transcultural and global organizations thus needs to focus on the general and specific culture competences of the selected cultural context which are present within the system. Transcultural coaching should employ person-centredness, as well as practical approaches to the organization and to work, to focus on developing the ability to increase "self-management" (e.g. self-consciousness, trust and stress resilience), "difference management" (e.g. openness, interest and tolerance) and "integration management" (e.g. flexibility, ambiguity tolerance and complexity reduction) (Steixner 2009, p. 95).

4 The Process

4.1 The Process: Systemic Transcultural Competences and Approaches in Transcultural Systemic Coaching

Practical coaching approaches (e.g. Rosinski 2011) often focus on personal development within the cultural and organizational framework by using specific transcultural communication models and checklists which refer to cultural dimensions (national and organizational), cultural differences, ethnocentric and ethno-relative approaches to cultural issues, and cultural orientation frameworks (Hofstede 1985; Rosinski 2011).

Transcultural coaching should explicitly acknowledge the issue of culture as its scope of application (Rathje 2007). It involves topics which emerge directly from the transcultural intra- and/or inter-organizational interaction within or between organizations, or an organization's elements, and the environment. Core areas of transcultural coaching in organizations include (Rathje 2007, p. 802; Wiegner and Rathje 2009, p. 132) human resource management, external business communication, internal business communication, support of internationalization processes and organizational development.

Von Schlippe and Schweitzer (2003) who developed a "travel guide" to multicultural systemic practices, emphasise that coaches need to pay attention to the topics of culture, migration, systemic constellations and language during coaching processes. To address these topics, transcultural competences on the part of coaches are needed (Grothe and Straub 2008). These competences include sensitivity towards the cultural system by using a systemic transcultural competence approach (Lanfranchi et al. 2004).

Part of systemic transcultural competence is gaining in-depth knowledge of the coachees' language competencies, similarities and differences in the meaning of words, body image, expectations of the coaching process, the management of stereotypes and prejudices – and the reflections of coachees (Geiger 2001), the overcoming of language barriers and building of relationships, trust and joining across cultures (Eberding 2004). The migration history, concepts of culture and gender and the development of the coach and the coachee are also important aspects of the coaching process (Radice von Wogau 2004). However, Hegemann (2004) also emphasises other topics to consider in coaching processes, such as health and sickness, social roles, familial life cycles, cultural traditions, life realities, the concept of all-partiality, and trust-building processes. If these are not considered in transcultural coaching practices, cultural differences and linguistic discordance may increase misunderstandings (Flores 2005), non-compliance and fear, and lead to a limited rapport between the coach and the coachee (Ramirez 2003).

Von Schlippe and Schweitzer (2003) highlight seven consecutive sets of aspects/phases which have to be observed by coaches who find themselves in systemic coaching practices in transcultural contexts: (1) Joining and affective approaches, expectations, stereotypes and the role of the translator (2) Empathy, engagement and challenges (3) First contact, genogram reframing, questions and sculptures, acknowledging and self-care (4) Cultural rituals, stories, idioms and treasures of

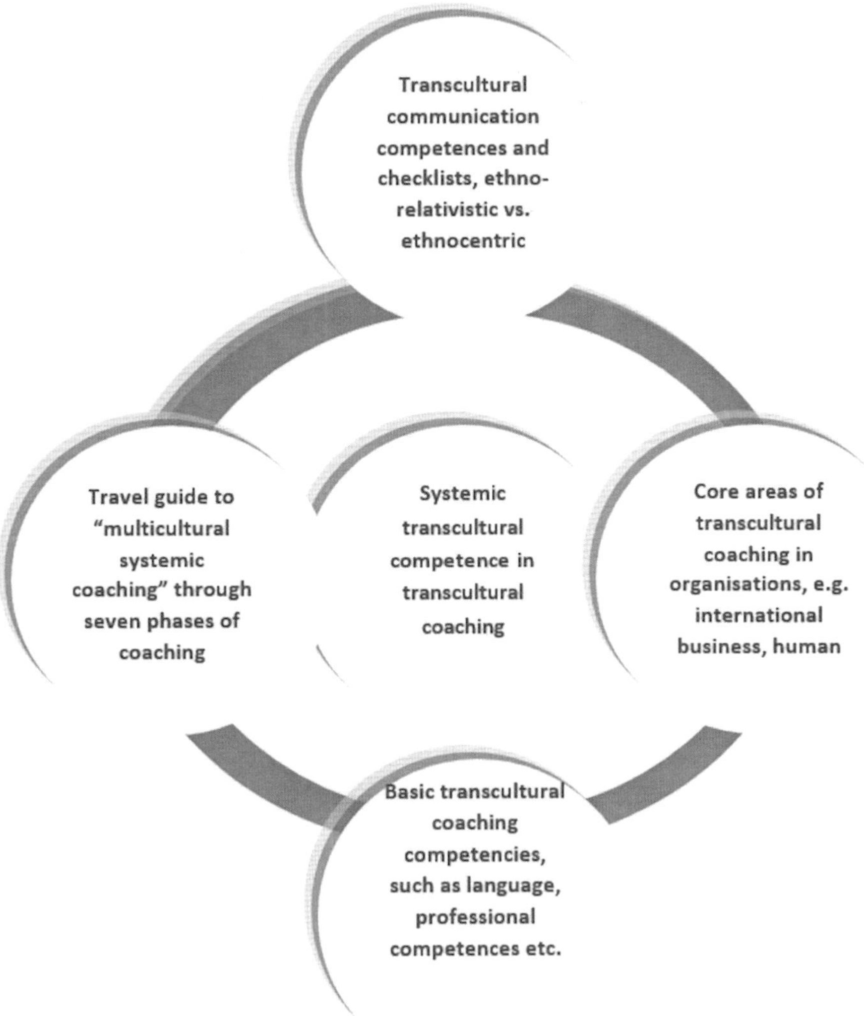

Fig. 5 Systemic transcultural competences and approaches in transcultural systemic coaching

cultures (5) The view of the observer, live supervision and the reflecting team (6) Crises, taboos, secrets and courage; and (7) The farewell. These phases can only be considered when both coaches and coachees communicate in a "culturally adequate and effective manner" (Grothe and Straub 2008, p. 60). Empathy (Gudykunst 2005; Martin and Hammer 1989), bilingualism (e.g. Redmond 2000) and transcultural experience (Martin 1987) appear to be of particular importance to transcultural communication.

Figure 5 is a depiction of systemic transcultural competences that a coach should acquire and strive for in the pursuit to become an effective transcultural coach.

In view of the described challenges of transcultural coaching processes, the transcultural systemic coach needs to have a certain profile to deal with transculturality in organizations in a system-oriented manner.

4.2 The Process: The Profile of a Transcultural Systemic Coach

The coach in systemic coaching is seen as an observer who is part of the construction of the reality (Von Foerster 1995) – therefore the reality is always the reality of the observer (Von Glaserfeld 1987). In coaching processes, the reality is invariably defined by the interplay of the constructions of the observer and the observed, and the negotiation and interplay of the worlds of the observer and the observed.

Because of these basic systemic assumptions, the establishment of the relationship of the coach and the coachee is of primary importance for the coaching process (Grothe and Straub 2008). Aspects such as self-disclosure and self-revelation on both sides are significant to establishing the relationship. Shared experiences during the coaching process increase (mutual) acceptance (Grothe and Straub 2008), the interest of the coachees and the opportunities for self-expression. The physical and social setting of the counselling premises, the "quick-into action" and "enactment assistance" (real, visible and prompt help from the coach) and, finally, the consideration of gender and language also have facilitating roles.

The coach's skills primarily consist of a specific communication style that includes communication techniques, such as active listening. Cilliers (2000) points out that these techniques should be connected with a client-centred coaching approach based on Carl Roger's operationalized ways of active listening, whilst communicating the core dimensions of empathy, respect, honesty and openness, as well as realness. Both – the communication techniques as well as human core dimensions – lead to a positive relationship between the coach and the coachee and to an experimental encounter of the other (Sanford 2002). Therefore, the coach has to display transcultural competences and be flexible and spontaneous in order to assess the moment-to-moment reality that prescribes the appropriate role of a coach. The coach needs to apply his/her various roles as a diagnostician or prescriber, a content expert and a process coach to be effective and successful (Schein 2000). At the same time, the cultural background of the coach should be considered and reflected constantly in the transcultural coaching processes, as his/her background will influence the coaching process, the interactions and the value systems created within the coaching system. Therefore, the coach must be able to self-reflect on his/her actions and thoughts constantly. Transcultural competences can help to understand and manage transcultural coaching situations and give meaning to the communication or interaction displayed by the coach and the coachee. Lloyd and Härtel (2003) emphasize that transcultural competences are needed to realize the potential synergies in communication across cultures. Transcultural competences generally include "empathy, flexibility, cross-cultural awareness, and managing stress", while some other definitions highlight respect and attitudes, technical skills, foreign language proficiency, knowledge and comprehension, desired external outcomes (such as effective and appropriate communication and behaviour), desired internal outcomes (such as an informed frame-of-reference shift), flexibility, and having an ethnorelative view (Deardorf 2012). Lustig and Koester (2003) emphasize that transcultural competences are rather the ability to cope with intercultural situations. Lloyd and Härtel (2003) complement these perspectives on transcultural competences by pointing out that the following aspects form part of transcultural competences: dissimilarity openness, emotion management skills, transcultural communication competences, tolerance for ambiguity, cultural understanding, information processing skills, conflict management and self-management skills. Deardorf (2004, p. 13) mentions that all definitions include "more than knowledge of other cultures, since knowledge alone is not enough to constitute intercultural competence. Intercultural competence also involves the development of one's skills and attitudes in successfully interacting with persons of diverse backgrounds."

The optimal profile of the coach in transcultural contexts would include a high level of the described transcultural competences, as well as language competences and a well-developed ability to reflect on the perceptions, concepts, feelings and behaviour of the self and others in interactions. Coaches in transcultural settings should therefore have various language competencies and be able to use certain communication techniques, transcultural skills and a coachee-centred approach. Coaches should also be abreast of the various systemic intervention practices which can be used and adapted across cultures and adhere to professional ethical considerations at all times. Selected interventions will be presented in the following section.

Figure 6 shows the concepts that are integrated in the profile of a systemic transcultural coach.

4.3 *The Process: Practices and Interventions in Systemic Transcultural Coaching Processes*

According to Ludewig (2005), systemic practices are defined as the application of systemic thinking in the professional interactions of individuals to manage, clarify, resolve and transform their personal, social and organizational realities and problems (Ludewig 2005, p. 16). The theory and practice of systemic interventions are based on three concepts (Ludewig 2005, p. 17): the effect of personal normative constructs on the human being; the biological autonomy of the individual (Maturana 1998); and the understanding of communication as an open, at any time changeable, socio-systemic process (Luhmann 2001).

Systemic practices include specific interventions and tools in coaching processes, such as communication techniques, including active listening, reframing or

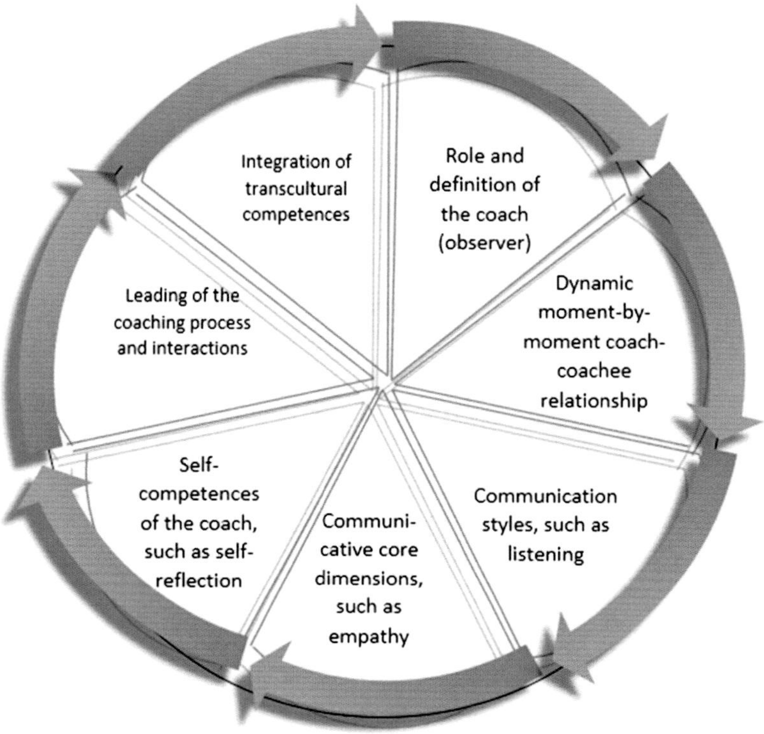

Fig. 6 The profile of a transcultural systemic coach

circular questioning, positive connotation techniques, paradox interventions, but also humorous or provocative communication techniques (Groth 1999; Kolbeck and Nicolai 1996; Simon and Rech-Simon 2007; Von Schlippe and Schweitzer 2010). With regard to questioning, circular questions aim to explore the relationships of the coachee with individuals or groups in his/her environment. It also aims to explore hierarchical constructs and differences in relationships and thereby contributes to understanding the world of the coachee. One specific form of question that asks about the impact of miracles in the life of the coachee (De Shazer 2004) introduces a reframing of the perceptions of the coachee of the world and his/her understanding of relationships in the world. It focuses on the future change that might be the aim or a subaim of the coaching process and strives to introduce new developments within the coachee. Through the miracle question, the reframing happens, shifting the situation of the coachee into another light – into the light of positive psychology constructs and also the salutogenic paradigm.

By means of these various interventions, the coach tries to build hypotheses (according to Selvini-Palazzoli et al. 1981) about the coachee's life, topics of thoughts and topics of interests, values, behavioural patterns etc, to increase comprehensibility, to question traditional patterns of behaviour and to create something new through the interaction of the coachee and the coach. In addition to this, methodological interventions in systemic coaching also include working with genograms, organograms and system constellations. These interventions focus on the construction of the relationships and the systems an individual lives and works in, and are informative of the connections and interrelationships which are part of the solutions to the problems. Many of the interventions that resulted from systemic coaching processes have been empirically tested (Schweitzer and Grünwald 2003) and their efficiency has been described (Von Sydow et al. 2007).

Systemic interventions aim to explore new and alternative views, expand perceptions and action possibilities, introduce new behavioural options and problem-solving approaches, clarify relationships, change behavioural patterns, and to refrain from making certain topics taboo (Clement 2009; Stierlin 1988). Since systemic interventions work with the exchange of rules and regulations which are viewed by the coachee as normal or as the norm, the coach opens new ways of communicating and of understanding the messages of another person (Bateson 1985). This can be particularly helpful in transcultural communication situations where there might be differences in assumptions about the norm that is valid within a certain situation. According to Bateson (1985), the increased consciousness and the change of rules and regulations lead to a deepened understanding of experiences, as well as of individuals and their positioning within systems. Bateson's (1985) ideas of communicating then leads to the breaking up of the constructed simplification mechanisms of daily communication routines which have been built up through cause-and-effect thinking. Systemic coaching approaches can support the understanding of system-specific information, thought styles or culture-specific behaviour which are based on the constructed history of the system, and give insight into the hierarchies that are prominent limitations or factual constraints. This system-specific information can be particularly well explored in systemic interventions, such as systemic constellation work (Mayer and Viviers 2014a, b). Constellation work, as a systemic intervention method, has been applied in various cultural settings in Germany, the US (Cohen 2004) and Australia (Rogers 2010), as well as in African contexts (Mahr 2004; Meyburgh 2009). However, the method has hardly been empirically researched as a transcultural intervention method, although it has been emphasized that constellation work has the potential to be successfully introduced in various cultural settings when working with individuals and groups across cultures (Mayer and Viviers 2014b).

5 The Output

The output phase of the framework refers to the ultimate goal for any coaching intervention, namely to achieve the set purpose of the coaching intervention. As coaching entails the enrichment of an individual, team, organization or environment through growth facilitation and developmental initiatives, optimal human functioning (Walsch 2014), growing human potential (Whitmore 2010), or mastery (Vella and Perlman 2014) can be strived for. The output phase of this proposed coaching framework therefore strives for attaining final optimal functioning but relies on the effective handling by both the coach and the coachee of the preceding input and process phases. The output phase therefore reflects the successful achievement of goals set as initial aims at the commencement of the coaching contract. (Also refer back to Fig. 1 that provides a diagrammatic depiction of coaching as a developmental model.)

6 Introducing a Systemic and Transcultural Coaching Framework

A systemic and transcultural coaching framework needs to take all of the above-mentioned approaches and aspects into account, whilst seeing them as being dynamic and in a dynamic relationship with the various systemic layers of the organizational system, such as the individual, the team, the organization and the environment. It is also important to keep in mind that this framework is phrased within the positive psychology paradigm and that the individual elements of the framework relate to this paradigm.

The coaching framework introduced in this chapter consists of three phases – the input, the process and the output phases which all deal with the various systemic layers during all of three phases of coaching. Figure 7 shows that these phases form a natural flow and allow transition from one element to the next. The direction of the

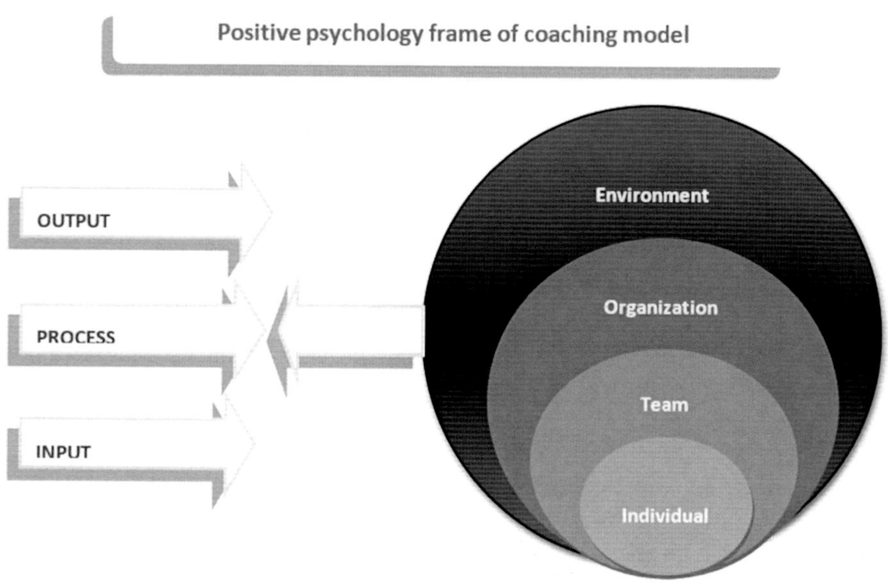

Fig. 7 The phases in coaching

flow is clockwise, with elements contributing to each other to shape and contextualise the next phase.

The input phase consists of two approaches: (1) The systemic thinking approach, and (2) The transcultural approach.

The systemic thinking approach is fed firstly by the basic assumptions of systemic thinking as explained in the theory (see Fig. 3). In collaboration and in interaction with the assumptions are the premises of systemic thinking as advocated by Ludewig, Maturana, Luhmann and Bateson (see Fig. 2). Together these assumptions and premises sculpture the foundation of the systemic approach.

The transcultural approach relies on the transcultural aspects as captured in Fig. 4 and refers to aspects such as the dynamic layers of transcultural coaching processes, dynamic transcultural concepts, and transcultural competences. Together, the perspectives of the systemic thinking approach and the transcultural approach form the input phase of the framework, which leads to the process phase.

The process phase has three elements and reflects the different integrated viewpoints of the input phase, in other words, of the systemic and transcultural approaches. It allows for a dynamic integration of the systemic and transcultural approaches so as to achieve systemic transcultural competences (see Fig. 5). These competences embody the profile of a transcultural coach (Fig. 6) who would promote transcultural coaching practices and interventions. The "shaping" of a transcultural coach in the process phase can be viewed as the establishment of a coach with new enhanced skills – someone who takes cognisance of the systemic and transcultural perspectives in coaching practices and interventions. This phase naturally flows into and results in the outcome phase.

The outcome phase reflects the contribution of the advanced skills of the systemic transcultural coach. In the introduction of this chapter, the goal and purpose of coaching was explained. Whatever purpose coaching might have for an individual, team, organization, or on the environmental level (see Fig. 2), the ultimate goal of coaching remains to provide a tool for the facilitation of optimal functioning. A competent systemic transcultural coach can therefore facilitate growth, development and optimal functioning for individuals or teams in organizational contexts, and also expand his/her impact to facilitate the optimal functioning of an organization as such. Such multiple inputs can eventually have a positive impact on the environment, which can facilitate optimal functioning in the broader human context.

Figure 8 provides an integrated, contextualised view of the systematic layers that constitute the three coaching phases in the framework.

The input phase refers to those intangible aspects (systemic thinking; assumptions and thinking approaches; transcultural aspects) that need to be considered/kept in mind to allow for the process phase (systemic transcultural competence leading to a specific transcultural profile that enables impactful practices and interventions) to be effectively sculptured. These input and process phases finally culminate in the output phase that reflects the achievement of the primary goal, namely optimal functioning within various contexts.

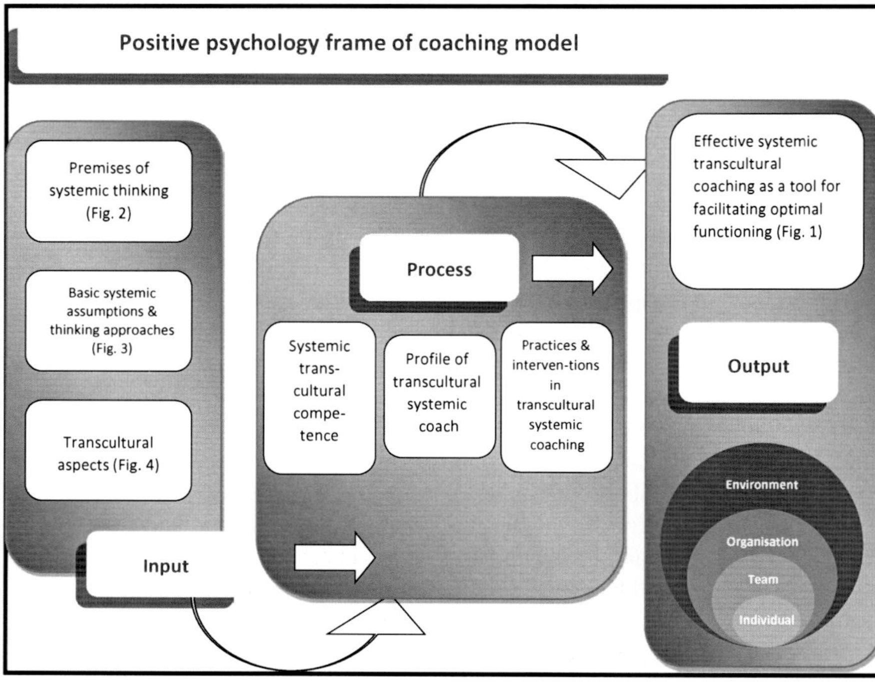

Fig. 8 The transcultural systemic coaching framework

7 Conclusions, Implications and Recommendations for Theory and Practice

This chapter aimed to introduce systemic and transcultural perspectives in coaching psychology by presenting grounded theoretical approaches, a profile of a transcultural systemic coach, and practical intervention methods for coaching in organizations. Based on the discussed perspectives, a transcultural systemic coaching framework is proposed – one which includes the specifics of systemic approaches and transcultural contexts to cope with the challenges of contemporary organizations.

Systemic and transcultural approaches should be recognized concepts in (transcultural) coaching psychology which reaches beyond causal-lineal approaches and interventions. Doing so makes it possible to respond adequately to organizational, global and transcultural complexities, whilst allowing optimal functioning of the individual, the team, the organization and the environment. The systemic and transcultural coaching framework takes systemic and transcultural aspects in coaching psychology into account and implement these across the various layers of the organizational system.

On a practical level, coaches should be trained in systemic, non-causal and nonlinear thinking approaches in coaching processes in order for them to be able to perceive and recognize the complexity of systems' phenomena and to support systemic problem-solving interventions. This is particularly important as research shows that non-systemic approaches are used in 90 % of coaching in organizations (Groth and Wimmer 2004). These might not be adequate to respond to the growing individual, organizational and global complexity in transcultural contexts.

8 Chapter Summary

This chapter introduced the theoretical approaches of systemic thinking and transculturality within the positive psychology framework of coaching psychology. It also sketched the profile of a systemic and transcultural coach, and proposed intervention methods such as constellation work which contribute to the transcultural systemic coaching framework presented.

In this chapter, it is argued that systemic thinking and transcultural approaches can support the effectiveness of coaching by providing tools and interventions to grasp complex issues, themes and relationships and their interlinkages across various systems and layers in individuals and organizations. The framework introduced suggests three phases in coaching, namely the input, process and output phase to deal with the expected complexity of coaching psychology processes to increase optimal functioning and mental health and well-being on various systems layers.

References

Bamberger, G. (2001). *Lösungsorientierte Beratung*. Weinheim: Beltz Psychologie Verlags Union.

Bartussek, W. S. (2007). Aus der Quelle schöpfen – intuitive Methoden in der Organizationsentwicklung. Ein Weg zu mehr Feinfühligkeit und Tiefe. In R. Ballreich, M. W. Fröse, & H. Piber (Eds.), *Organizationsentwicklung und Konfliktmanagement. Innovative Konzepte und Methoden* (pp. 125–138). Zürich: Haupt.

Bateson, G. (1985). *Ökologie des Geistes. Anthropologische, psychologische und epistemologische Perspektiven*. Frankfurt: Suhrkamp Taschenbuch Wissenschaft.

Bateson, G. (1987). *Geist und Natur. Eine notwendige Einheit*. Frankfurt: Suhrkamp.

Becker, A., Küpper, W., & Ortmann, G. (1988). Revisionen der Rationalität. In W. Küpper & G. Ortmann (Eds.), *Mikropolitik, Macht und Spiele* (pp. 89–113). Opladen: Westdeutscher Verlag.

Bennett, J., & Bush, M. W. (2009). Coaching in organizations. Current trends and future opportunities. *OD Practitioner, 41*(1), 2–7.

Berry, J. W., Poortinga, Y. H., Segall, M. H., & Dasen, P. R. (2008). *Cross-cultural psychology. Research and applications* (2nd ed.). Cambridge: Cambridge University Press.

Besser-Siegmund, C., & Siegmund, H. (2003). *Coach yourself – Persönlichkeitskultur für Führungskräfte*. Paderborn: Jungfermann Verlag.

Bhugra, D., & Becker, M. A. (2005). Migration, cultural bereavement and cultural identity. *World Psychiatry, 4*(1), 18–24.

Biron, C., Burke, R. J. M., & Cooper, C. L. (2014). *Creating healthy workplaces. Stress reduction, improved well-being, and organizational effectiveness* (2nd ed.). Farnham: Ashgate Publishers.

Bluckert, P. (2005). The similarities and differences between coaching and therapy. *Industrial and Commercial Training, 37*(2), 91–96.
Brunner, E. J. (2002). Von Gemeinsamkeiten und Unterschieden in der Familientherapie und der Systemischen Organizationsberatung. *Systhema, 16*, 239–248.
Cilliers, F. (2000). Facilitation skills for trainers. *Journal of Industrial Psychology, 26*(3), 21–26.
Clement, U. (2009). *Instrumente der Interventionen in der systemischen Beratung*. Unpublished document, therapy course, Göttingen, Germany, September 2009.
Cohen, D. B. (2004). *Bert Hellinger's family constellation method and its place in the psychotherapeutic tradition*. Unpublished master's thesis, Saybrook Graduate School and Research Center, San Francisco.
Cottrell, D., & Boston, P. (2002). Practitioner review: The effectiveness of systemic family therapy for children and adolescents. *Journal of Child Psychology and Psychiatry, 43*(5), 573–586.
Deardorf, D. K. (2004). *The identification and assessment of intercultural competence as a student outcome of internationalization at Institutions of Higher Education in the United States*. Doctoral dissertation, North Carolina State University, Raleigh.
Deardorff, D. K. (2012). Framework: Intercultural competence model. In K. Baardo & D. K. Deardorff (Eds.), *Building cultural competence. Innovative activities and models* (pp. 45–52). Sterling: Stylus.
De Shazer, S. (1989). Wege der erfolgreichen Kurzzeittherapie. Stuttgart: Klett-Kotta.
De Shazer, S. (2004). *Der Dreh. Überraschende Wendungen und Lösungen in der Kurzzeittherapie*. Heidelberg: Carl Auer.
Deutscher Bundesverband für Coaching. (2014). *Coaching*. Retrieved from http://www.dbvc.de/cms/index.php?id=361
Durant, W. (1981). *Kulturgeschichte der Menschheit*. Frankfurt: Ullstein.
Eberding, A. (2004). Bedeutung der Sprache in der systemischen Beratung und Therapie. In J. Radice von Wogau, H. Eimmermacher, & A. Lanfranchi (Eds.), *Therapie und Beratung von Migranten. Systemisch-interkulturell denken und handeln. Praxishandbuch* (pp. 92–102). Beltz: Weinheim.
Eckersley, R. M. (2007). Culture, spirituality and health: Looking at the big picture. *Medical Journal of Australia, 186*(10), 54–56.
Farlex Dictionary. (2010). Retrieved from http://www.thefreedictionary.com/resource
Fischer, C., & Grothe, J. (2007). Interkulturelle Kommunikation in der Gesundheitsversorgung: Konturen eines Praxis- und Forschungsfeldes. Handlung Kultur Interpretation. *Zeitschrift für Sozial und Kulturwissenschaften, 16*(2), 219–263.
Flores, G. (2005). The impact of medical interpreter services on the quality of health care: A systematic review. *Medical Care Research and Review, 62*, 255–299.
Flückinger, C., & Wüsten, G. (2008). *Ressourcenaktivierung. Ein Manual für die Praxis*. Bern: Huber.
Geertz, C. (1987). *Dichte Beschreibung. Beiträge zum Verstehen kultureller Systeme*. Frankfurt: Suhrkamp.
Geiger, H. J. (2001). Racial stereotyping and medicine: The need for cultural competence. *Canadian Medical Association Journal, 12*, 1699–1700.
Goleman, D. (1995). *Emotional intelligence: Why it can matter more than IQ*. London: Bloomsbury.
Greene, J., & Grant, A. (2003). *Solution-focused coaching*. London: Momentum.
Groth, T. (1999). *Wie systemtheoretisch ist ,Systemische Organizationsberatung'? Neuere Beratungskonzepte für Organizationen im Kontext der Luhmannschen Systemtheorie* (2nd ed.). Münster: LIT-Verlag.
Groth, T., & Wimmer, R. (2004). Konstruktivismus in der Praxis: systemische Organizationsberatung. In F. von Ameln (Ed.), *Konstruktivismus* (pp. 224–244). Tübingen: A. Franke Verlag.
Grothe, J., & Straub, J. (2008). *Cultural differences and intercultural communication in psychosocial counselling: Reflections on changes within social work practice*. Universidad de Huelva, Portularia: Revista de Trabajo Social.
Gudykunst, W. B. (2005). *Theorizing about intercultural communication*. Thousand Oaks: Sage.
Hall, L. M., & Duval, M. (2004, January). Neurosemantic coaching. *HR Future*, 4–7.

Hegemann, T. (2004). Interkulturelle Kompetenz in Beratung und Therapie. In J. Radice von Wogau, H. Eimmermacher, & A. Lanfranchi (Eds.), *Therapie und Beratung von Migranten. Systemisch-interkulturell denken und handeln. Praxishandbuch* (pp. 79–91). Weinheim: Beltz.

Herbrand, F. (2002). *Fit für fremde Kulturen: Interkulturelles Training für Führungskräfte*. Bern: Haupt Verlag.

Hillary, D. (2003, October). Executive coaching. *HR Future, 10–11*.

Hofstede, G. (1985). *Culture's consequences: International differences in work-related values*. Beverly Hills: Sage.

Kampa-Kokesch, S. (2002). Executive coaching as an individually tailored consultation intervention: Does it increase leadership? *Dissertation Abstracts International, 62*(7), 3408.

Kampa-Kokesch, S., & Anderson, M. Z. (2001). Executive coaching. A comprehensive review of literature. *Consulting Psychology Journal: Practice and Research, 53*(4), 205–228.

Kauffman, C., & Scoular, A. (2004). Toward a positive psychology of executive coaching. In P. A. Linley & S. Joseph (Eds.), *Positive psychology in practice* (pp. 287–302). Hoboken: Wiley.

Kirchmayr-Kreczi, J. (2001). *Systemisches Denken und Handeln – Grundlagen*. Retrieved from www.jkk-kommunikation.at

Kolbeck, C., & Nicolai, A. (1996). *Von der Organization der Kultur zur Kultur der Organization*. Marburg: Metropolisverlag.

Krause, C., & Mayer, C. H. (2012). *Gesundheitsressourcen erkennen und fördern. Ein Trainingsprogramm für pädagogische Fachkräfte*. Göttingen: Vandenhoeck & Ruprecht.

Lanfranchi, A., Radice von Wogau, P., & Eimmermacher, H. (2004). Zugang von Migrantinnen zu den Sozial- und Gesundheitssystemen. In J. Radice von Wogau, H. Eimmermacher, & A. Lanfranchi (Eds.), *Therapie und Beratung von Migranten* (pp. 104–120). Weinheim: Beltz.

Laske, O. E. (1999). *Transformative effects of coaching on executives' professional agenda*. Arbor: University of Michigan.

Levinsky, R. (2000). Stay in the game. *Black Enterprise, 30*(9), 117–124.

Linley, P. A. (2004). *Coaching psychology: The positive psychological foundations*. Unpublished paper presented at the International Positive Psychology Summit. Washington, DC.

Lloyd, S., & Härtel, E. J. (2003). *The intercultural competencies required for inclusive and effective culturally diverse work teams*. Melbourne: Monash University.

Lopez, S. J., & Snyder, C. R. (2003). *Positive psychology assessment. A handbook of models and measures*. Washington, DC: APA.

Lowman, R. L. (2002). *The handbook of organizational consulting psychology*. San Francisco: Jossey-Bass.

Ludewig, K. (2005). *Einführung in die theoretischen Grundlagen der systemischen Therapie*. Heidelberg: Carl Auer.

Luhmann, N. (2000). *Organization und Entscheidung*. Opladen: Westdeutscher Verlag.

Luhmann, N. (2001). *Soziale Systeme. Grundriss einer allgemeinen Theorie*. Frankfurt: Suhrkamp.

Lustig, M. W., & Koester, J. (2003). *Intercultural competence: Interpersonal communication across cultures*. Boston: Allyn & Bacon.

Mahr, A. (2004). *Family constellations: Failure, evil, and guilt as sources for loving dedication and compassionate strength*. Retrieved from http://www.collectivewisdominitiative.org/papers/mahr_constellations.htm

March, J. G., & Olsen, J. P. (1976). *Ambiguity and choice in organizations*. Bergen: Universitetsforlaget.

Martin, J. N. (1987). The relationship between student sojourner perceptions of intercultural competencies and previous sojourn experience. *International Journal of Intercultural Relations, 11*, 337–355.

Martin, J. N., & Hammer, M. (1989). Behavioral categories of intercultural communication competence: Everyday communicators' perceptions. *International Journal of Intercultural Relations, 13*, 303–332.

Maslow, A. (1968). *Toward a psychology of being*. New York: D. Van Nostrand Company.

Maturana, H. R. (1998). *Erkennen: Die Organization und Verkörperung von Wirklichkeit* (2nd ed.). Braunschweig: Vieweg.

Maturana, H., & Varela, F. J. (1990). *Der Baum der Erkenntnis*. München: Goldmann.

Mayer, C. H. (2007). Ressourcen interkultureller Identitäten. In C. Krause, N. Lehmann, F. Lorenz, & T. Petzold (Eds.), *Verbunden gesunden – Zugehörigkeitsgefühl und Salutogenese* (pp. 251–262). Heckenbeck: Verlag Gesunde Entwicklung.

Mayer, C. H. (2011). *The meaning of sense of coherence in transcultural management*. Münster: Waxmann.

Mayer, C. H. (2012, December). 'Slimming down…' A case illustration on coaching hypnosis and weight loss, *International Journal of Mentoring and Coaching, X*(2), Retrieved from http://www.emccouncil.org/eu/en/journal/journal_library

Mayer, C. H., & Boness, C. (2013a). Systemisches Denken als Grundlage salutogener Organizationsberatung. *Klinische Verhaltensmedizin und Rehabilitation, 26*(2), 168–178.

Mayer, C. H., & Boness, C. M. (2013b). *Creating mental health across cultures. Coaching and training for managers*. Lengerich: Pabst Publishers.

Mayer, C. H., & Vanderheiden, E. (2014). Einführung: Interkulturelle Öffnungsprozesse gestalten. In E. Vanderheiden & C.-H. Mayer (Eds.), *Handbuch interkulturelle Öffnung. Grundlagen, best practice, tools* (pp. 21–26). Göttingen: Vandenhoeck & Ruprecht.

Mayer, C. H., & Viviers, A. (2014a). "Following the word of God": Empirical insights into managerial perceptions on spirituality, culture and health. *International Review of Psychiatry, 26*(3), 302–314.

Mayer, C. H., & Viviers, A. (2014b). *Principles and resonance phenomena in constellation work. South African constellation facilitators' perspectives*. Unpublished document, Department of Industrial and Organizational Psychology, University of South Africa, Pretoria.

Meer, A. (2008). *Informatikprojekte in komplexen Systemen*. Retrieved from http://www.ehealthsummit.ch/downloads/2008_referate/Meer_Andreas_SEHS2008.pdf

Meyburgh, T. (2009). *Hellinger in South Africa: A story of the Zulu origins of family constellations*. Retrieved from http://tanjameyburgh.co.za/hellinger-in-south-africa-a-story-of-the-zulu-origins-of-family-constellations

Nazarkiewicz, K., & Krämer, G. (2012). *Handbuch interkulturelles Coaching. Konzepte, Methoden, Kompetenzen kulturreflexiver Begleitung*. Göttingen: V&R.

Neuvians, N. (2011). *Mediation in Familienunternehmen. Chancen und Grenzen des Verfahrens in der Konfliktdynamik*. Wiesbaden: Gabler.

Olivero, G., Bane, K. D., & Kopelman, R. E. (1997). Executive coaching as a transfer of training tool: Effects on productivity in a public agency. *Public Personnel Management, 26*(4), 461–469.

Peltier, B. (2001). *The psychology of executive coaching theory and application*. New York: Taylor and Francis.

Radice von Wogau, J. (2004). Systemische Theorie in interkultureller Beratung. In J. Radice von Wogau, H. Eimmermacher, & A. Lanfranchi (Eds.), *Therapie und Beratung von Migranten. Systemisch-interkulturell denken und handeln. Praxishandbuch* (pp. 45–63). Weinheim: Beltz.

Radice von Wogau, I., Emmermacher, A., & Lanfranchi, A. (2004). *Therapie und Beratung von Migranten. Systemisch Denken und Handeln*. Weinheim: Beltz Verlag.

Ramirez, A. G. (2003). Consumer–provider communication research with special populations. *Patient Communication and Counseling, 50*(1), 51–54.

Rathje, S. (2007). Interkulturelles Consulting. In J. von Straub, A. Weidemann, & D. Weidemann (Eds.), *Handbuch interkulturelle Kommunikation und Kompetenz* (pp. 800–808). Stuttgart: Verlag J.B. Metzler.

Redmond, M. V. (2000). Cultural distance as a mediating factor between stress and intercultural communication competence. *International Journal of Intercultural Relations, 24*(1), 151–159.

Rogers, D. E. (2010). *The role of place in personal and systemic transformation*. Project paper to the faculty of Saybrook University, Master of Arts in Organizational Systems, March 16 2010. Sydney.

Rosenbaum, M. (1990). *Learned resourcefulness: On coping skills, self-control and adaptive behaviour*. New York: Springer.

Rosinski, P. (2011). Global coaching for organizational development. *The International Journal of Coaching in Organizations, 8*(2), 49–66.

Rothmann, S., & Cilliers, F. V. N. (2007). Present challenges and some critical issues for research in industrial/organizational psychology in South Africa. *SA Journal of Industrial Psychology, 33*(1), 8–17.

Rückert, H. (2001). *Coaching. So spornen Manager sich und Andere zu Spitzenleistungen an*. Landsberg: Verlag moderne industrie.

Ruesch, J., & Bateson, G. (1995). *Kommunikation: die soziale Matrix der Psychiatrie*. Heidelberg: Carl Auer Systeme.

Sanford, R. (2002). What are the distinguishing characteristics of the group facilitator in a person-centered way of being? *Renaissance*, Summer and Fall, 37–38.

Satir, V. (2001). *Meine vielen Gesichter. Wer bin ich wirklich?* (5th ed.). München: Kösel.

Satir, V. (2004). *Kommunikation, Selbstwert, Kongruenz. Konzepte und Perspektiven familientherapeutischer Praxis*. Paderborn: Junfermann.

Satir, V., Banman, J., Gerber, J., & Kierdorf, T. (2007). *Das Satir-Modell: Familientherapie und ihre Erweiterung*. Paderborn: Junfermann.

Savickas, M. L. (2011). *Career counseling*. Washington, DC: American Psychological Association.

Schein, E. H. (2000). Coaching and consultancy. In M. Goldsmith (Ed.), *Coaching for leadership* (pp. 17–25). San Francisco: Jossey-Bass.

Scheinecker, M. (2007). Lösungsfokussierte Beratung bei Konflikten in Unternehmen. In R. Ballreich, M. W. Fröse, & H. Piber (Eds.), *Organizationsentwicklung und Konfliktmanagement. Innovative Konzepte und Methoden* (pp. 345–359). Zürich: Haupt.

Schweitzer, J., & Grünwald, H. (2003). SYMPA – Vorschau auf ein Großexperiment zur systemischen Therapie und Forschung in der Akutpsychiatrie. *Systeme, 17*(1), 36–46.

Schwemmle, M., & Schwemmle, K. (2012). *Systemisch beraten und steuern. Methoden und Best Practices in Change Management und Führungsteamentwicklung*. Göttingen: V&R.

Selvini-Palazzoli, M., Boscolo, L., Checcin, G., & Prata, G. (1981). Hypothetisieren, Zirkularität, Neutralität. Drei Richtlinien für den Leiter der Sitzung. *Familiendynamik, 6*, 123–139.

Simon, F., & Rech-Simon, C. (2007). *Zirkuläres Fragen*. Heidelberg: Carl Auer Verlag.

Steixner, M. (2009). "Fine-tuning" durch interkulturelles Coaching. *Interculture Online, 8*(9), 83–110.

Stierlin, H. (1988). *Das Tun des Einen ist das Tun des Anderen: Eine Dynamik menschlicher Beziehungen*. Frankfurt: Suhrkamp.

Thorn, R. (1984). *Mathematical models of morphogenesis*. Chichester: Ellis Horwood.

Tuckermann, H. (2012). *Einführung in die systemische Organizationsforschung: Forschung begleitender Fallstudien*. Heidelberg: Carl Auer.

Vella, S., & Perlman, D. (2014). Mastery, autonomy and transformational approaches to coaching: Common features and applications. *International Sport Coaching Journal, 1*(3), 173–179.

Von Bertalanffy, L. (1968). *General system theory: Foundations, development, applications*. New York: Braziller.

Von Foerster, H. (1995). *Wissen und Gewissen. Versuch einer Brücke*. Frankfurt: Suhrkamp.

Von Glaserfeld, E. (1987). *Wissen, Sprache und Wirklichkeit. Arbeiten zum radikalen Konstruktivismus*. Wiesbaden: Carl Auer.

Von Schlippe, A., & Schweitzer, J. (2003). *Lehrbuch der systemischen Therapie und Beratung*. Göttingen: Vandenhoeck & Ruprecht.

Von Schlippe, A., & Schweitzer, J. (2010). *Systemische Interventionen* (2nd ed.). Göttingen: Vandenhoeck & Ruprecht.

Von Schlippe, A., El Hachimi, M., & Jürgens, G. (2003). *Multikulturelle systemische Praxis. Ein Reiseführer für Beratung, Therapie und Supervision*. Heidelberg: Carl-Auer.

Von Sydow, K., Beher, S., Retzlaff, R., & Schweitzer-Rothers, J. (2007). *Die Wirksamkeit der Systemischen Therapie & Familientherapie*. Göttingen: Hogrefe Verlag.

Walsch, W. B. (2014). Counseling psychology and optimal human functioning: An introduction. In W. B. Walsh (Ed.), *Counseling psychology and optimal human functioning* (p. vii). New York: Routledge.

Welsch, W. (1999). Transculturality – The puzzling form of cultures today. In M. Featherstone & S. Lash (Eds.), *Spaces of culture: City, nation, world* (pp. 194–213). London: Sage.

Welsch, W. (2003). Rolle und Veränderungen der Religion im gegenwärtigen Übergang zu transkulturellen Gesellschaften. In D. C. Siedler (Ed.), *Religionen in der Pluralität – Ihre Rolle in postmodernen transkulturellen Gesellschaften: Wolfgang Welschs Ansatz in christlicher und islamischer Perspektive* (pp. 13–47). Berlin: Conference Proceedings.

Welsch, W. (2011). Kultur aus transkultureller Perspektive. In D. Treichel & C.-H. Mayer (Eds.), *Lehrbuch Kultur. Lehr- und Lernmaterialien zur Vermittlung kultureller Kompetenzen* (pp. 149–157). Waxmann: Münster.

Whitmore, J. (2010). *Coaching for performance: Growing human potential and purpose: The principles and practice of coaching and leadership*. Boston: Nicholas Brealey Publishing.

Wiegner, S., & Rathje, S. (2009). Interkulturelles Consulting zwischen Wunsch und Wirklichkeit – eine Marktstudie. *Interculture Journal Online Zeitschrift für Interkulturelle Studien, 8*(9), 131–149.

Wienands, A. (2003). Zur Verwendung der systemischen Familienskulptur in der Arbeitsweise von Peggy Papp, Virginia Satir sowie Fred und Bunny Duhl. *Zeitschrift für Systemische Therapie, 21*(3/4), 155–169.

Williams, P. (2003). Coaching versus psychotherapy. The great debate. *The International Journal of Coaching, 2*(1), 38–39.

Part III
Meta-theoretical Perspectives and Applications Within Multi-cultural Contexts

The Coach as a Container in the Team Coaching Process

Gail Wrogemann

Abstract The objective of this chapter is to illustrate the essential nature of the role of the team coach in holding and containing an interactional learning space for teams in transformation, such that in-depth and sustainable change can take place. In organizations, the container mechanism is held by different groups – sometimes a management group – and in a learning space it could be held by the coach, consultant, or facilitator. The structure of the methodology is in itself a container. A container refers to a capacity or structure which can hold anxieties and uncomfortable feelings while they are considered or processed, or while other essential work is done. The containing role the coach takes up is a conscious one and has direct implications for the ability of teams to change in ways that improve performance. This research explores the role of coach, as container, using projective identification as a key communications process, from the perspective of an eclectic depth-psychology approach. Using three case studies from various different cultural contexts, this containing process is highlighted and analysed from a systems psychodynamic approach and a somatic systemic theoretical perspective. Psychological strategies, approaches, techniques and coaching practice guidelines are described in their application in these teams and their complex organizational settings. Patterns and themes across these wider systems are identified. Issues of safety, splitting, belonging and conscience, and power and authority were identified. The construct of projective identification is illustrated as one of the primary containing mechanisms used.

Keywords Somatic systemic approach • Constellations • Container mechanism • Systems psychodynamics • Object relations theory • Good enough coach • Complexity • Systems transformation

G. Wrogemann (✉)
Industrial Psychologist, Team and Systems Coach,
Systems Consultant, Johannesburg, South Africa
e-mail: gcwrogemann@mweb.co.za

L.E. van Zyl et al. (eds.), *Coaching Psychology: Meta-theoretical perspectives and applications in multicultural contexts*, DOI 10.1007/978-3-319-31012-1_11

1 Theoretical Background

Theoretical perspectives of this study includes the perspectives and principles from somatic systemic approaches and constellations thinking, systems psychodynamics including Wilfred Bion's study of group relations, Melanie Klein's object relations theory and open systems theory. A brief overview of each follows, as related to organizational development and the mechanisms of containment. These three depth perspectives and the open systems perspective are considered as a robust enough foundation to allow for research and reporting in these multicultural contexts.

1.1 A Somatic Systemic Approach

This approach has developed over time from various theories and therapeutic models for example, Gestalt theory, Milton Erikson's work, Virginia Satir, Eric Berne, Murray Bowen and Family Systems theory, Boszormenyi-Nagy and contextual therapy, psychodrama methodologies, transgenerational theory, Taoist philosophy, and existential phenomenology. This theoretical basis and methodology encompasses an approach that can be useful for understanding interactions and interrelationships between parts of a system (Horn and Brick 2005). The constellations methodology grew specifically in family systems work, and reflects on interactions between family members, across immediate family units and across generations. The methodology and principles can also be used to understand other systems – business, social, community, family business systems – precisely because it simplifies the inherent complexity and because the principles observed in family systems can to some extent be seen in other systems (Horn and Brick 2005).

One aspect of this approach is taken from constellations work, a primary premise of which centres around the idea of conscience. According to Hellinger (1998) conscience can be described as a felt sense of belonging to a particular system; "as a perceptual organ for systemic balance that helps us to know whether or not we're in harmony with our reference system." (Hellinger 1998, p. 207). Therefore, a somatically orientated methodology such as constellations is profoundly suited to the emergence and observation of the dynamics of conscience. Schneider (2007) indicates that in this way we can observe some of the related constellations principles of belonging, exchange and order in action. The containment process and projective identification as an often unconscious communications process was effectively highlighted through use of a somatic methodology.

1.2 The Systems Psychodynamic Perspective

From a systems psychodynamic perspective, the application of psychoanalytic constructs to formal organizations allows insight beyond general psychological constructs to more organizationally relevant issues. Concepts such as authority, work roles, autonomy, dependency, and identity issues that arise in the workplace can be considered in depth. This approach describes the impact of conscious and unconscious behaviour of the individual, group or organizations, and how influences of early infancy - relationships and psychosocial mechanisms – can be seen in group relationships in the workplace (Cilliers and Koortzen 2002; Stapley 2006). Ruppert (2008) indicates that persistent conflict between co-workers or management and staff is likely to reflect earlier patterns of personal bonding from the family of origin. Thus unresolved family dynamics, needs and conflicts can play out at work. Wilfred Bion (Stokes 1994) considered how these dynamics played out and whether they were constructive or not. Bion's idea of sophisticated and basic assumption groups refers to on-task and off-task behaviour. Off task or anti-task behaviours are defences against the anxieties of conflict arising from unresolved internal dynamics. Anti-task behaviours are attempts to get needs met. A focus in this perspective, is thus on the basic assumptions of anti-task behaviour of dependency, fight/flight, pairing, one-ness vs. me-ness (Cilliers and Koortzen 1997). The containment of these anxieties and anti-task behavioural defences can be taken up by a group in an organization – whether they be an appropriate group or not. Containment could be reciprocal between two work groups within an organisation (Cooper and Dartington 2004); the "...container allows the intra-psychic and interpersonal tension and uncertainty to be continually processed *through the medium of relationships*." (p. 149).

1.3 Melanie Klein's Object Relations Perspective

Melanie Klein's object relations work provides insight here. Her work has contributed to understanding early processes of "... dividing feelings into differentiated elements called splitting." (Halton 1994, p. 13). By splitting emotions, children gain relief from internal and painful conflicts of love and hate for a caretaker, the mother for example. With the realization that the mother is actually one person both to be loved and hated, there is a remorse (and subsequent reparation) about the damage that the child might have caused. If the guilt about the hating is overwelming, reparative activities will be inhibited and the child will attempt to contain this for him or herself by splitting and projecting the painful feelings onto another. This projection is sometimes done via fairy tales such as the sly fox, or the jealous sister (Halton, 1994). If though, the remorse can be managed, and the reparation is enough, the child will integrate the 'good' and the 'bad' parts. The process of integrating split off parts can be allowed to occur via effective containment mechanisms.

1.4 Open Systems Theory

The premises of open systems theory (Von Bertalanffy 1972), is a valuable consideration in gaining understanding of the complexity of systems. Some of these are: the survival of a system depends on continuous interaction within itself and the environment, survival requires growth, a change in one part of the system requires a change in another part, parts are interdependent on each other, systems strives for balance, the whole is more than the sum of the parts, boundaries are permeable and need to be managed, the system comprises sub-systems which interact, and this system is by definition a subsystem of a broader system. According to Konigswieser and Hillebrand (2005), this biological application of systems theory has subsequently been broadened by contributions from other fields such as the social sciences, psychology and information theory. This development has contributed to theories of complexity and specifically complex adaptive systems and the use of the system itself to learn and grow (Tomaschek and Strobel 2010).

Roberts (1994a) indicates that a number of open systems can operate as part of complex organisms, whilst each performs its specialist functions. This thinking was applied to organizations by Rice and Miller at the Tavistock Institute of Human Relations – their model puts forward a framework for studying the relationships between parts of the organizations and the whole, and also across different organizations and their environments. Since organizational systems and teams are of increasing complexity (Lawton-Smith 2011), the potential for increasing anxieties and defences, specifically projective identification, arises.

These four perspectives together provide useful foundations with which to understand the role of coach as container, and specifically the conscious use of a projective identification process in the communications process between a client and coach. A somatic systems and constellations approach allows us to investigate the process of belonging and systems of conscience in teams and how allegiances and loyalties can prevent teams moving through transformation. These ideas give insight into conflicts of conscience which can manifest in cycling behaviour, frustrations and conflicts which can be experienced in teams, but also possibly in the wider organizations, as entrenched and immovable. The systems psychodynamic approach allows a useful diagnostic process to reflect on constructs such as team identity, authority and authorisation, and highlights recognition of task and anti-task behaviours which could be outcomes of mentioned conflicts of conscience and loyalties. For example, team identity could become stagnant due to the conscience of that team in relation to another. Melanie Klein's work is a key perspective allowing deep understanding of the projective identification communication process between coach and teams. This approach is helpful when considering the extent of safety and containment needed whilst working through significant transformation processes. Open systems theory introduces key principles of interdependencies of parts in relation to wholes, and the organic and complex nature of systems of individuals, teams, organizations and communities. Critically, the nature and depth of these perspectives allow application to multicultural contexts. In fact, they are most suited to allow the coach to work with the dynamics of the systems without bias, (at least being aware of bias) and beyond the limitations of the right and wrong of cultural boundaries.

This complexity and the dynamic interactions across systems, make the process of conscious containment an essential one in any organizational transformation or development process. The containment is a structure which 'holds' the uncertainty, fears, unknowing and anxieties in the development or change of a team identity or self-reference structures.

2 The Idea of Containment

The depth-psychological perspectives introduced above allow comprehensive exploration into the essential role a container mechanism plays in systems resolution in a systems transformation process. In these cases, resolution is on a systemic level, meaning it is powerful enough to affect change in other parts of the system. A discussion of the mechanism of the container follows.

2.1 The Coach as a Container

A point to note: The term 'coach' is used here to reference the role of coaching psychologist and as a psychologist in the consultancy to organizational development. The Somatic systemic approach, constellations work, as well as the Systems Psychodynamic approach refers to the person managing group processes as facilitator and consultant respectively. Hence when referring to the literature – these terms are used. According to Hawkins and Smith (2006), an organizational development consultant may be taking up the role of coach, mentor or facilitator depending on what is needed for the transition. Thus in the actual work processes described, the role of coach is referred to, however at times the role of consultant was taken up in the designing of various processes and negotiating project scope with clients.

The role of coach in containing, could be given more attention in team optimization processes. There are many variables that need consideration if the coach, as container, is able to work effectively for the system. Importantly conditions need to be considered as to what will allow the client group or team to feel safe enough to enable a transformative process (Schneider 2007). The sense of certainty of safety, in part, is what will allow the defences to loosen (Lee 2010) and a shift to take place. In this respect, the coach has to align completely to the client's pace, and not progress further than the client is able, but not to hold back such that no opportunities for transformation emerge (Ulsamer 2003).

A relationship is built between the organization, the team and the coach or coaches, and thus the container mechanism and defences such as projection could emerge almost immediately. As such teams would tend to look to the coach with both hope and fear. A conscious hope that the underlying difficulty would be brought to the surface and resolved, and also a fear, perhaps unconscious, of precisely that which might emerge (Halton 1994). These conflicting and possibly unconscious responses from clients need to be internally managed by the coach.

Basic business issues need to be considered, thus other aspects of containing include the selection of the coach, contracting, accurate assessment of needs and emotional capacities of individuals and groups, and clearly outlining the business context, as well as the business and coaching contract. Recognition of the coach's own valence, and thus taking part in supervision are also key processes. This level of work cannot be undertaken without adequate self-care, growth and supervision (Roberts 1994c).

Another consideration for the coach who works systemically, and as an effective container is, according to Konigswieser and Hillebrand (2005) the need to be able to be not objective – as coaches or consultants become part of the system as soon as they observe or try to understand or initiate change within the system. Knowing that conflicts and resistance are symptoms that can lead to wisdom and the opportunity for development, is an important idea to keep in mind. "Things are the way they are." (Konigswieser and Hillebrand 2005, p. 40). The identification of the 'bad' in the 'good' and the 'good' in the 'bad' leads a coach to not idealize or denigrate the experience (Stapely 2006). In this way, such an approach can be applied across multiple cultural contexts, since the therapeutic posture (Hellinger 1998), is one where the coach steps outside reliance on current personal culturally specific views.

From a purely constellations perspective, the coach's role in understanding relationship systems takes on further and deeper considerations. According to Hellinger (1998) all relationship systems are part of wider contexts, of larger wholes. "When you see people in their larger contexts, your perceptions of freedom of choice, personal responsibility, and good and evil change." (Hellinger 1998, p. 211). If you want to work systemically, the author indicates that the facilitator (coach) must find a position beyond moral judgement and beyond a position of moral superiority. This is an essential stance in the ability to work in multi-cultural settings – an awareness of moral stance and judgement of the coach that could affect the safety of the container mechanism.

2.2 *Projective Identification as a Communications Process in the Containing Process*

The process of projective identification is a key component in the communication process between coach and client, according to Moylan (1994). Roberts and Brunning (2008) indicate that this is a crucial source of information about the disturbance in the system and importantly, a communication about fears and requests for protection from someone perceived as stronger. According to (Cilliers 2005, p. 25; Dimitrov 2008) projective identification is an interaction whereby unwanted feelings and experiences are split off and projected onto others, individuals or groups, who then identify with these projections (Roberts 1994b). These individuals or groups, who could be blamed or scapegoated, may have a valence for receiving and carrying these specific projections. They thus contain the unwanted or uncomfortable feelings on behalf of the system. In an organisation, a team or individual might deny that a conflict or an unresolved dynamic exists, and attempt to contain the anxiety generated by rejecting it and recognising it in an other (projection). If this person (team or group) begins to believe this about themselves, and identify with the projection (projective identification), this could have consequences for their perceptions of themselves and their capabilities (Cilliers and Koortzen 2002).

This process is part of natural communication structures and human experience. Molyan (1994) indicates that for babies the only way they can communicate their distress is to cry. Adults tend to become agitated when a baby is crying and this alerts them to the distress of the baby because they feel it too. She calls this communication process *projective identification* in that "… the baby projects the feelings it cannot manage onto the mother, so that – through feeling them herself – she can process them on the baby's behalf." (p. 52). In the same way, when an individual, group or organization does not have the emotional literacy skill to interpret and understand for themselves what is happening in the system, or if the anxiety is too high – either way the dynamics could be unconscious – this can default to the coach to contain. Further, as Roberts and Brunning (2008) indicate, different organizational groups could take up this projective identification communications process and it can become so much a part of their role, that they themselves or others are not consciously aware of this.

The role of the coach as a container is thus an active one, and includes communication processes such as projective identification. This process thus involves constantly formulating hypotheses about the dynamics of a particular situation, testing assumptions, re-evaluating assumptions, being aware of what is surfacing and how dynamics might surface, and taking on board what is required for a good solution (Ruppert 2008).

The focus of this research was on assessing the containing mechanism used by the coach, which was the communication process of projective identification. Further, this was used in such a way that effective team integration and transformation could initiate and sustain within a wider systems and multicultural context. Some background to the idea of containing is important to note.

2.3 Children and Containing

According to Roberts and Brunning (2008) babies and children learn to manage anxieties in interaction with caretakers who attend to their needs at age appropriate times and ways. This gives a sense of security and of being understood. Anxiety is projected onto the caretaker (container) who is hopefully able to manage this constructively. Jaques (1953) refers to how individual members use institutions as mechanisms of defence against anxiety. The implications of these early experiences and interpretations are thus carried into organizational life.

2.4 *Organizations and the Container*

In organizations, the containing mechanism could be held by different groups or teams – sometimes a management group or a particular department, and in a learning space it could be held by the coach, consultant, or facilitator.

In the organization, the ideal is that management would be able to create a good enough container such that both conscious and unconscious anxieties are contained enough so employees can think and act effectively. This means that anxieties are contained sufficiently and the primary task of the organizations can be continued. The outcome of the management group holding this container effectively is that staff would not attempt to contain anxieties inappropriately though other groups or via counterproductive defence mechanisms, according to Roberts and Brunning (2008).

Thus, projections can be constructive or destructive to the system (and task), and they can be conscious or unconscious. Containing anxiety can therefore be a process of using projection (and projective identification) in a useful and effective way.

The containing role could be held by a group that is expected to do so. However, this might be felt to be unsafe (by either party) and then the containing could be picked up by another group. If a group that is expected to take up the role of container is not able to do so for whatever reason, this could lead to blame or scapegoating as a result of the unfulfilled expectations (Lee 2010). Individuals or groups might be resentful because then they have to do tasks they perceive should be done by others. This could lead to a reaction of shame, as a group might be trying to contain themselves without support, and then blaming themselves for being inadequate. Such a process can lead to splitting and the emergence of other defence mechanisms (Roberts and Brunning 2008). A marketing department for example, could take up the role of communication and then find themselves responsible for areas of internal communications. Or if a management team is not experienced as competent, containment might be sought from another group, perhaps from customers. The results of attempts of not finding appropriate containers could lead to ineffective coping mechanisms, in this example collusion of the staff and customer against the management.

Who holds the role of container and how, has implications for on task behaviour, work flow and constructive relationships, and an ability to manage the demands of changing environments.

2.5 *Organizations and 'ineffective' Containing*

Considering family systems (specifically from a constellations perspective), if a child has not learnt how to rely on others, they might not have learnt how to take, create, or recognize a safe enough or good enough container for themselves (Roberts and Brunning 2008). Thus as adults, they could attempt to partner with authority groups or individuals that are ultimately ineffective containers and who undermine the primary task of an organization. Thus the attempt to create or seek a container can lead to selecting inappropriate individuals or groups, and then coping with anxiety by blaming those who will not (either appropriately or not) take up this role. Alternative attempts are in creating an organization-in-the-mind picture (in conjunction with others) that will contain the anxiety. Often this internal image is not helpful and is itself based on upsetting experiences or conflicts, and requires various defences to be in full operation. However, as indicated above, this is not necessarily considered wrong, but can be a useful way of containing difficult experiences at a particular time, perhaps for a transitional time. Dimitrov (2008 p. 30) indicates that "By attending to these unconscious dynamics, the organizational psychodynamics seeks to provide a sense of containment for individual and organizational anxieties and defences so that a determination about which pressures to consider is [constructively] related to the primary task and not to unconscious defences or fantasies." In this way, containment can be held by the culture or the organization-in-the-mind.

3 Research Design

3.1 Research Approach

This research is within a qualitative research paradigm – the approach was investigative, exploratory and to some extent explanatory.

3.2 Research Strategy

The research design and strategy included the selection and analysis of data from the three cases, with the team as units of analysis. The focus was on how the coach as container for the communication process of projective identification within these three different contexts, allowed a process of systems transformation to initiate and sustain within these teams. These findings have been integrated into a research hypothesis and then used as a basis for further recommended research and application.

The three case studies were taken from three different clients, and were subjectively selected for the research according to the following criteria: the depth of change these teams were experiencing, common themes and dynamics experienced across the teams, process and depth of information collected, application to the research question, and the application of the methodology.

3.3 Research Method

Research Setting

At about the halfway point through the change programme and process, the coaches had planned to run a large group process (somatic systemically based) with some of the stakeholders involved. The objective of this process was to surface and resolve some core issues that were still deeply held in these systems. In all three cases, the teams who attended were from the management and staff levels of the organizations.

The coaches had considered what needed to be in place so that a process such as this would be effective. The relationship in the teams, and between the coaches and the teams, was assessed and considered as stable with enough trust that had been created for the teams to work in this way. The teams had been exposed to personal mastery and leadership development training, and team coaching, and were applying the skills effectively. An appropriate level of safety, an essential component of the containing mechanism, had been developed within the teams, and between the teams and the coaches, such that effective and transformative work could be done. The necessary conditions that needed to be in place for a further step in group awareness, and thus transformation were at an acceptable level.

Researcher Roles

Two coaches were involved in the team coaching processes. Thereafter one of the coaches spent time bringing the data together for further analysis for this research in the light of the research question.

Sampling

The depth of information gathered from these clients was considered sufficient for the purpose of this study and these three cases were considered to have the richest data to illustrate the coach as container. Johnson and Waterfield (2004) indicate that samples need to be sufficient to generate depth rather than breadth, and may therefore comprise only a small number of participants. Purposive sampling and convenient sampling were thus employed to include the information-rich cases that would incorporate data relevant to the research question. The three case studies were from a cluster of three township schools, a telecommunications organization, and a community organization.

Data Collection Method and Recording of Data

Data collection was done from detailed notes made by the coach immediately after the interventions, and by the assistant coach during the process. Comprehensive notes were also taken by both coaches during discussions and sessions over the time of the entire transformation process. Notes from each were compared and augmented. Comprehensive notes were also taken during debrief and discussion sessions held after these sessions. Data came from observations of the teams and their interactions before, during and after sessions, from individual sessions and conversations, as well as from the planning and strategy group discussions conducted in preparation for the specific interventions.

Data Analysis

The framework for both the data collection and analysis was from the position of a psycho-social approach to research. This implies the use of a cluster of points of data collection which are all aimed at researching beneath the surface dynamics (Clarke and Hoggett 2009) and that are essential in realizing and resolving. This approach emphasizes the value of the subjectivity of the researcher and the usefulness of a synthesis of methods that include psychoanalytic tools of interpretation. The application of simple and double hermeneutics was employed to deepen the understanding of the experiences of the client but also of the reciprocal reactions and unconscious communications between client and in this case the coaches (Clarke and Hoggett 2009). This includes the idea that the unconscious plays a "significant part in the generation of research data and the construction of the research environment." (Clarke and Hoggett 2009, p. 4). The data was analysed according to a theme of integration and according to processes of condensation and abstraction of data to meaningful units (Graneheim and Lundman 2004).

Data was analysed post interventions, however much of the analysis became part of the intervention itself – part of the client and consultant developmental learning process. According to Clarke and Hoggett (2009) some researchers indicate that in this way the researcher's (and client's) here and now experience of defences make the data analysis subjective. The aspect of triple hermeneutics (linked to the concept of valency) was very much considered as this is precisely the process of the evolutionary learning nature of the containers as discussed. Consultations with subject matter experts was a core component of the analysis as well as a series of supervision sessions for both coaches, separately and together, after which data was considered, assessed and analysed.

Strategies Employed to Ensure Quality of Data

Data was analysed after extensive discussions with clients, subsequent to reports submitted and discussions within the coaching partnerships. This then took some measure against the potential for 'wild analysis' that Clarke and Hoggett (2009) warn against. Thorough analysis was done with experts to assess these case studies within the fields of systems psychodynamics and somatic systemic work. Further, the experience of the coach as psychologist, specialist in the above two approaches and extensive supervision time spent analysing and interpreting the data in the context of client and self, added to the quality of data. This was essential in recognizing and articulating the projective identification process and what was taken up by the coaches.

Respondent validation which assists to establish dependability of data (Johnson and Waterfield 2004) was gained via collaborative agreement on interpretation and relevance of dynamics highlighted as well as the resolution process of dynamics for the teams concerned. This collaboration was part of the assessment of the impact for the teams on engagement processes with their wider systems, and an important key to the resolutions mentioned.

The ethical considerations of working this way in a corporate setting were carefully considered and discussed with the clients. They needed to be aware of the depth of information that would be surfaced and how they would work with and relate to colleagues after working with some vulnerability during these processes. A key point here was that no one individual was focused on as the problem, or as perpetuating a particular dynamic. All the themes that emerged were worked with from a team perspective only. Individual learning was encouraged but rather as a separate and internal process, and not in the team format. Confidentiality within the team processes was spoken about and agreed. Informed consent was gained in the use of the field notes for research studies. As Newman et al. (2002) indicate, cognisance needs to be taken of the complexity of the organizational settings and how the outcomes of the interventions could be reported on. This was noted and discussed with the contracting partners within the organizations.

4 Findings

The findings are reported according to three dominant themes that emerged from the interventions, with a subsequent discussion exploring these themes further. The research focus is to explore the role of the coach, as container, using projective identification as a key communication process, from the perspective of an eclectic depth-psychology approach. The following three themes organized into 'findings' and then a discussion, reflect the growth and developmental process of these teams – moving from splitting and projecting uncomfortable experiences, and the coaches containing these experiences via projective identification, to the process of the teams integrating these experiences and dynamics.

4.1 Theme 1: Recognition and Management of Anxiety and the Process by Which the Teams Were Currently Containing Themselves

The findings across all three organizations, indicated the numerous fragmentations and splits – between old and young, those talking about the future and those talking about the past, staff and management groups, inferiority and superiority, leadership and followership. Groups and individuals had split off and disowned unacceptable parts of themselves and their departments and had projected these onto other departments who then at times, strongly identified with these. The anxieties that these teams were experiencing were managed by the defensive process of splitting.

In one team, there were many questions about the impact and systemic cause of the traumatic events that had taken place and were still taking place in the organization. This was reflected in the splits, some of which surfaced during the intervention, and could be identified across departments. In this particular department the roles and themes of leadership, authority, obstruction, solution, clarity, theft and fraud were segmented and held by different teams. This particular team felt that certain subordinates were not stepping into their authority, and were constantly asking for help on an array of issues that should have been done independently. The leadership felt frustrated, though, about not being able to assist as much as they wanted. However, they did not think it was appropriate to help as much as was requested. The subordinates kept asking, and they felt guilty for not assisting. The process was investigated with one of the team members as a starting point. This revealed the transference of aspects of a relationship between this team member and father – and the guilt experienced in relation to the father – to the relationship between the client and subordinate. This dynamic was commonly experienced by other members of the team.

In another organization, the group process had two parts – a group process to reflect education during the apartheid years, and a second group process to reflect post-apartheid education, as it pertained to these township-based schools. One of the pivotal processes occurred in the first group process, where the representative for the theme of superiority looked around at all the other representatives, and then looked at the coach, and said in a loud but hushed whisper, "What would happen if they knew how fragile I am." The impact was electric – people froze and stared at the representative in amazement and fury. This process highlighted a key split of inferiority and superiority.

The containment from the coach for all three clients was specifically called on in the emergence of previously unnamed anxieties managed by defences of splitting, displacement and scapegoating, via the projective identification process. In some ways, most did not know what was bothering them or their system, they were just aware of the conflicts around them and the betrayals they were experiencing. Initially, they were not necessarily open to hear solutions; they just wanted the problems to go away.

4.2 Theme 2: The Effective Use of Projective Identification

With regards to this theme, taking up the role of coach took on specific significance particularly given that work was being done within wider social structures (as related to one team situation) in which the organizations itself had become a container for social anxiety. Such a situation creates a layer of complexity that needs to be consciously managed (Obholzer 1994; Cilliers and Terblanche 2010). Many times during the process there were deeper levels of realizations that "we, as coaches, can't fix it" – and that unconsciously we were trying and trying too hard – then also expecting (and hoping) that after the intervention, many more things will be better than reasonable to expect. Many times we took on the role of the 'nice' consultants who understood and were 'tough' enough to manage whatever was thrown at us.

The teams went through a variety of processes in relation to the coaches – from open arms welcoming, to complaining and attacking, to criticizing and blaming aspects of the process, to deeply working and committing themselves wholeheartedly. After many sessions, the coaches walked away feeling angry, drained, at loss, taken advantage of, and feeling unfairly treated.

Recognition of the coach's valence for wanting a good and successful outcome, needing to achieve and make the project work, and the awareness of wanting, to some extent, to take the hardship away, was essential and relevant to the transformations the organizations subsequently experienced. Once these recognitions were arrived at, the projections could be more clearly identified, and thus more consciously held. It was at such points either during discussions, sharing of insights or specifically during some of the group process methodologies, that these themes became recognisable by and tangible to the clients.

4.3 *Theme 3: Owning the Projection*

In one process, when the representative for superiority said "What if they knew how fragile I was." – this comment was made to the coach. On hearing this, and in the discussion afterwards, the team realized that they were also the strong ones. They saw the 'weak' side of superiority and the 'strong' side of inferiority, (and how they had projected these onto other groups – superiority onto the department of education and inferiority, and an associated incapability, onto the children). Thus, the insight was in realizing how, through their identification with themselves as inferior, they had aligned to other township schools to belong to these so-labelled underperforming schools.

In another case study, the belonging was sought in relation to the father. The guilt experienced in moving away from the father, is projected onto the relationship with the staff. Since it seemed as if the father was emotionally unavailable and perceived in need of support, the process of maturing and moving away from the father, created overwhelming guilt. However, the guilt experienced in the maturing process is a healthy guilt, and in fact is the price of growth (Hellinger 2006). However the connection with the father was experienced as tenuous, thus the guilt was experienced as part of a further exclusion from the father. The resolution of the dynamic entailed an awareness of the longing for connection and belonging to the father and a related taking up of adequate internal authority.

In all three studies, the process of projective identification, whereby the coaches 'held' these anxieties on behalf of the groups, was a constructive communication process. It created safety in the group process, and allowed the groups to relieve the pressing anxieties enough to reflect and consciously consider how they wanted to change, and further to understand the fears and consequences of integration.

5 Discussion

The following discussion unpacks the above findings with regard to the container and the process of projective identification in the context of this research. The focus was on highlighting the container mechanism of the coach, in order for effective team integration and then transformation to initiate and sustain within a wider systems multicultural context.

5.1 Theme 1: Recognition and Management of Anxiety: The Process by Which the Teams Were Currently Containing Themselves

According to a case study in Roberts (1994d), the process of splitting can lead to groups not taking responsibility for parts of a task deemed to belong to other groups. In that study, this led to certain groups being weighed down by having to be more rigid about certain areas of operation. This was the situation in these teams as well. As an example, staff in one team, had projected respect and good management of interpersonal relations onto management, and then did not take responsibility for sorting out even the smallest interpersonal conflicts. Young staff members projected the traditions and 'older' ways of doing things onto the older staff members, and then did not take responsibility for integrating past successes and experience into current behaviours. Older staff took this up quite strongly and did come across as always looking back, bringing up past incidences, and not planning, strategizing or having any excitement or interest in future planning and goals. In another team, the staff seemingly refused to take up any leadership authority on tasks, even those that were within their expected delivery. This clear splitting process reflected the extent of the anxieties within these systems.

Obholzer (1994) refers to three layers of anxiety that need to be understood in a change process – first by the consultant and second by the client. Firstly, personal and primitive anxiety, secondly anxiety arising from the nature of work, and thirdly, the anxiety stemming from the containing function of institutions. The emergence of these layers of anxiety will occur during the intervention process. Knowledge and consideration of these is what the consultant, in this case the coach, needs to contain. The role of the coach in this regard could be articulated in the following way: someone who initiates a process of collaboration with a client (individual, team or organization) to raise awareness of unconscious processes, to clarify primary task and authority structures, to support the client to learn through reflective exploratory discussions in order for effective transformation to be initiated and sustained. Once the coaches began to create such a relationship and interchange, the sustainability of change and transformation in these systems emerged. In fact, one of the key transformation points occurred in one team soon after the coaches, stepped fully into the 'inferiority' of the system – and introduced a section of the day with a very real and personal check in of an area of life where the experience was of inferiority, threat and anxiety. The team's recognition of themselves in the coaches – was a key prompt for their stepping into the 'opposite' role of superiority, and thus a process of integration of the two polarities was begun.

Moylan (1994) indicates that the defence of projection and projective identification is indicative of the difficulties with which some groups need to cope and a way to avoid the emotional pain by identifying with the projection from others. In this way the source of the problem is not located, creative solutions not found and thinking remains confused. In these cases the coach took up this process of projective identification in order for the team to remove it from their psyche so as to then be able to consider it, and subsequently integrate the splits. This was a critical component in the process and an effective use of projective identification as a communication process with the teams and thus an avenue of healing and transformation.

5.2 Theme 2: The Effective Use of Projective Identification

The valence of the coaches seemed to be in stepping into, and using, the basic assumption of fight, and also pairing (as there were mostly two coaches on site). Halton (1994) refers to this as the sophisticated use of the basic assumptions mentality, where Bion's basic assumptions are used in a constructive and effective way. It was as if the coaches re-awakened the fight and hope in the teams, so that they could reflect and then take effective action.

A situation to be alert to is one where over the time of a team process the effective use of the basic assumptions by the coaches is undermined. In such a case, the dependence of teams on the coaches could continue. A coach might have a valence to step into and *continue* to stay in a container role, even if this is not expected or effective (Rioch 1975). Since this valence is sometimes based on an unconscious need of the coach, the process can create an unhealthy dependency. The valence of individuals or groups (in this case a coach) to pick up particular containing processes, such as always managing structure in meetings, could be an attempt to contain their own anxiety, and for a time this might be useful for the group. This is an example of the sophisticated use of a basic assumption (Stokes 1994).

As part of the process of effective containing (in order to allow transition and transformation), the idea of a 'good enough' coach needs to be considered. Taking up the process of projective identification includes taking up to some extent, the doubts, fears, hopes, and expectations of the system. In order for the coach to stay at once involved and objective, there needs to be a key part of the self, that which stays untouched by the fear of failure, and the hope of success. This is the knowing of being 'good enough'; staying in a space of complete focus and knowing (of no doubt) and allowing the process to unfold. This concept of 'good enough' can be seen in many roles, especially those of containment (as discussed here) – from the 'good enough' mother, the 'good enough' leader, and the 'good enough' department (Obholzer 1994).

This can be difficult to remain present to. Speck (1994, p. 99) describes how carers are "…expected to be available and nice at all times, remaining calm, pleasant, able to receive and contain anything 'dumped' on to him." Yet this cannot be the case. In many of the team processes, the projections were powerful, and the coaches felt these clearly as anger, guilt and an experienced internal persecution.

An aspect of the learning was the realization of being good enough, a good enough coach, in holding this container for the process of healing in the teams. "Out of the working through of the depressive position, there is a further strengthening of the capacity to accept and tolerate conflict and ambivalence. One's work need no longer be experienced as perfect… inevitable imperfection is no longer felt as bitter persecuting failure. Out of this mature resignation comes … true serenity, serenity which transcends imperfection by accepting it' (Jaques in Speck 1994, p. 100).

An observed dynamic was the client teams' containing of themselves by alternating between feelings of guilt at their exclusions of the coaches (and projections) and then feeling the need to make reparation. This seemed like a continual see-saw, which the coaches experienced many times in relation to the teams. It was in recognizing and unpacking this that the coaches clarified what the experience was and could hypothesise about this experience. Only once this clarity emerged, part of the process could be managed. Then the teams started to more clearly understand their process. Thus the anxiety was contained and essentially not mimicked as a defensive strategy, similarly described by Lee (2010). Another defensive strategy of the coach could also be in trying too hard, or feeling pity for the client. Not only does this reduce the effectiveness of the coach, and the container, this also strengthens the client's own feeling of self-pity (Ulsamer 2003). This could mean the container is not safe and thus the client avoids reality, refocuses on the problem issues, and refuses to take up their own authority. The danger is that the coach can leave with the feeling of all powerful and 'bigger' than the client. A good internal sentence for the coach, in this case, could be "I am not that good."

There is thus no moral stance about the right or wrong way that the teams 'should' have done things (Hellinger 1998). The coaches allowed the safety of the container to encourage and support the transformation to continue. Hence such a containing process is a key component to be applied across many different contexts, groups and situations. In this regard the coaches needed to, and were able to, work beyond a localised context or restricted view of personal and current group cultural contexts.

Hellinger (1998) indicates that as a consultant he can risk a lot when he knows that what he says will be evaluated against the client's own experience – then he knows that this is a partnership in investigating experience. If clients are thus centred, he knows that there will be less chance that they will alienate themselves, using defence mechanisms, from the learning. In this way, coaches need to be in a process of projective identification, clearly using the valance for the process and trusting the client to work through their transformation. However, this was not without its risks of being seduced by the systems' apparent need of the coach and the role.

5.3 Theme 3: Owning the Projection

Consultants cannot provide the teams or individuals with the belonging they need (Obholzer 1994), and thus the identification and containing must end. The places where the teams belong are to their own organizations, to other collaborating teams, to families and communities. Perhaps in seeking own belonging (a possible valence) the coaches could have been lured into an attempt to make the consultant space the final step in this seeking process, as if the consultancy space is the space that the clients' are seeking. This repeating theme (of seeking belonging) can be a particularly alluring one to attempt to solve, as many of the children in the schools (of the one case study) are desperately seeking safe places of belonging, either physical or emotional, as many of their parents or primary caretakers are absent.

The transformation process allowed a new identity to be created that included constructive aspects of superiority – not in a judgemental and destructive way – but more so in the way of self-confidence and choice. The fact that the representative of superiority suddenly looked uncertain as she spoke was in itself a recognition of the 'shadow' side of the superiority. This indicated the 'weak' side of the superiority, as much as the shadow of their inferiority could indicate strength and lead them to their power. The resolution of this was seen a few times in interaction with this team – in their behaviour. The team had thus moved into a more integrative, depressive position, from a paranoid-schizoid position of superiority and inferiority, of privilege and disregard, of authorization and de-authorization, to been able to make clear choices rather than experiencing processes as being forced onto them.

Using the constellations thinking as a framework, and the experiencing of the constellations methodology, meant that new identities could be considered. In all three case studies, this process required an internal shift in perspective. In case one - away from a feeling of inferiority and being grouped with (or belonging with an other). In case two – the shift was from attempting to alleviate the guilt of moving away from the father and then not taking up adequate authority with their teams, and in case three – from staying in the known (and unintegrated) roles of young and old. This means an internal movement away from innocence to the 'guilt' of the new, and thus an opportunity to create a new identity.

Organizations are complex and dynamic social systems which are formed by highly complex interdependencies made up of information flow (and material flow) and social phenomena of power, ideology, conflicts and relations. They are created by people in interaction, in communication. Thus transformation can occur when individuals and teams – clients and coaches – gain a higher awareness of these complex interactions (Tomaschek and Strobel 2010), and consciously and actively enter this communication space. In this way, interactions can be understood and engaged to allow transformation to take place.

6 Conclusions, Limitations and Recommendations

6.1 Conclusions

The understanding and effective use of the container mechanism has great value in systems transformation. This study focused on projective identification as a communications process between coach and client, which formed part of the containing mechanism. This process allowed the anxieties of the clients to be 'held' such that an integration and resolution of the causes of these anxieties could be achieved.

From a family systems and constellations perspective, it is understood that children rely on a container, a caretaker, and containing process, (upbringing), in order to hold anxieties and to create a sense of security while the child grows and changes. Learning about this containment process is carried into life and into organizational life. Psychodynamic theory gives an understanding of how anxieties are effectively or ineffectively contained in the organizations, and how ineffective containment can lead to anti-task behaviour. Open systems theory explains how this anti-task behaviour and splitting process could manifest across connected systems. This dynamic of attempting to find appropriate containers for anxieties could itself play out across systems in a parallel process. The organizations or management team is normally an appropriate container, however at times this containing function is rejected by that group or containing is found elsewhere. This might ultimately be constructive for a period of time. Family constellations give good insight into the containing process, and how at times, the child attempts to be the container as opposed to taking the caretaker as container. This has implications in the playing out of the valence in picking up appropriately or inappropriately (or rejecting) a containing role in an organizations. The somatic systemic and constellations thinking and methodology was used as an effective container for holding the anxieties and discomfort in teams whilst they processed and integrated projections of split-off aspects of themselves. Finally, the coach is an essential component of this containment mechanism, as the safe receptacle of anxieties and emotions from the teams such that these can be thought about, reconsidered, felt and finally owned. The stance and approach from the coach and principles underlying the process allow wide application to different contexts, cultures, groups and group psychological structures.

In all three cases, the container provided by the coach (and methodologies) allowed deep transformation to take place. For one client (team), a pivotal component was in taking back their rejected power (reflected as superiority) and giving back their introjected powerlessness (reflected as inferiority). The process also allowed them to understand their current team identity based on allegiance to inferiority. For another client, the methodology created a time line within which they could reflect on the many difficulties and successes that they had lived through and the splits could be observed more objectively and outside of self. The objective reflection of this allowed a deep level of integration to take place in the team psyche. For the third client, the learning was in being able to reflect on the parallels between a family system and a work system, and the underlying emotion (guilt) which kept ineffectual workplace relational dynamics in place. The coach held a coaching process and structure within which these uncomfortable emotion and relational dynamics could be resolved.

Working with teams in processes of deep transformation requires many parameters to be in place. An aware, healthy and strong container is one such parameter – and the author proposes that the coach or consultant is a container as is the methodology or particular tool of learning. Then the definition of a good enough container needs attention. This requires an assessment of the interactions and reciprocal dynamics taking place within the client systems, between the client and coach systems, and in the ability of the coach and methodology to 'hold' a continual communication process such that defences are recognized and anxieties reduced.

In these three cases, the depth of change was recognised by the effective actions that were taken after the processes were run. Client one planned some effective management strategies and took charge of processes with other organizations which they had not done before. Their attitude and engagement with many other stakeholders exponentially improved and allowed greater collaboration with many related teams. This particular team showed a significant change in their ability to engage with groups they had considered 'superior' to them. They also engaged with the coaches in their roles as consultant more constructively. They had engaged with the role of coach in the group process and then had transferred this learning to the consultant. Client two had some remarkable successes of collaboration, constructive debate (versus destructive conflicts) and were at ease with each other. Client three reported immediate improvement in the dynamics and relationship interactions in their departments as well as with external stakeholders.

The methodologies and underlying perspectives, and the systems psychodynamics approach are well placed to provide the kind of insight needed to reflect on the extent of defences and anxieties experienced.

6.2 Limitations

Limitations of the research could include the subjective nature of the sampling of the clients, the fairly limited peer input into data analysis and the somewhat subjective nature of the interpretation.

Not all client situations are suited to this level of work. At times, more linear and mechanistic approaches are suitable, are more in the client's reference point and would be more effective in achieving the results being sought.

6.3 Recommendations

The continual training and openness to learning of consultants and coaches is key if they wish to enter this field. The process of good enough containment requires self-awareness, training and experience. Using a defence such as projective identification adequately, requires use of an active process of taking up projections, recognizing them, recognizing the valence for them, defining them for the clients (as appropriate) and allowing the clients to subsequently project these feelings to the appropriate container. The tendency for coaches is to not let go, at which time, change in the system with that coach or consultant stalls. Either the system will revert to its initial position, or they might have realised enough to continue.

Building relationships with clients as partnerships could also be considered a container in a change process. Perhaps more focus needs to be made here, so that neither client nor coach resorts to defences in response to learning, but work together using emerging defences as learning and change opportunities. If we consider a symptom as the emergent wisdom in a growth process, attention on this is critical.

Further research could be done around the application of both the somatic systemic approaches, constellations thinking and methodolgies, and systems psychodynamic perspectives – particularly in change management and organizational development processes. These approaches might give these types of interventions even greater oportunity for success.

Some guiding questions that were held in the minds of the coaches, both before and during the intervention process, were: How were the teams containing themselves, and who held the anxiety of the system? How and why did this feel safe? What was the outcome of this containment process? What would assist the group to feel safe enough to enter the change space and what would good-enough coaching look like for them in order for this to occur? These were useful guiding anchors for the coaches within the actual group processes.

Acknowledgements Acknowledgements are due to our clients who worked with us and were open to significant change, as well as my business partners and fellow coaches.

References

Cilliers, F. (2005). Executive coaching experiences: A systems psychodynamic perspective. *South African Journal of Industrial Psychology, 31*(3), 23–30. doi:10.4102/sajip.v31i3.205.

Cilliers, F., & Koortzen, P. (1997). *Introduction to group behaviour and processes*. Pretoria: Centre for Industrial and Organizational Psychology.

Cilliers, F., & Koortzen, P. (2002). The psychoanalytic approach to team development. In R. L. Lowman (Ed.), *Handbook of organizational consulting psychology* (pp. 260–284). San Francisco: Jossey-Bass.

Cilliers, F., & Terblanche, L. (2010). The systems psychodynamic leadership coaching experiences of nursing managers. *Health SA Gesondheid, 15*(1), Art #457, 9 pages. doi:10.4102/hsag.v15i1.457.

Clarke, S., & Hoggett, P. (2009). *Researching beneath the surface. Psycho-social research methods in practice*. London: Karnac.

Cooper, A., & Dartington, T. (2004). The vanishing organization: Organizational containment in a networked world. In C. Huffington, A. Armstrong, W. Halton, L. Hoyle, & J. Pooley (Eds.), *Working below the surface. The emotional life of contemporary organizations* (pp. 127–150). London: Karnac.

Dimitrov, P. L. (2008). *Organizational psychodynamics*. Unpublished lectures.

Graneheim, U. H., & Lundman, B. (2004). Qualitative content analysis in nursing research: Concepts, procedures and measures to achieve trustworthiness. *Nurse Education Today, 24*, 105–112.

Halton, W. (1994). Some unconscious aspects of organizational life: Contributions from psychoanalysis. In A. Obholzer & V. Z. Roberts (Eds.), *The unconscious at work* (pp. 11–18). New York: Routledge.

Hawkins, P., & Smith, N. (2006). *Coaching, mentoring and organizational consultancy: Supervision and development*. England: Open University Press.

Hellinger, B. (1998). *Love's hidden symmetry*. Arizona: Zeig, Tucker and Co.

Hellinger, B. (2006). *No waves without the ocean: Experiences and thoughts*. Heidelberg: Carl-Auer.

Horn, K. P., & Brick, R. (2005). *Invisible dynamics. Systems constellations in organizationss and business*. Heidelberg: Carl-Auer.

Jaques, E. (1953). On the dynamics of social structure: A contribution to the psycho-analytical study of social phenomena. *Human Relations, 6*(1), 3–24. doi:10.1177/001872675300600101 February.

Johnson, R., & Waterfield, J. (2004). Making words count: The value of qualitative research. *Physiotherapy Research International, 9*(3), 121–131.

Konigswieser, R., & Hillebrand, M. (2005). *Systemic consultancy in organizationss: Concepts – tools – innovations*. Heidelberg: Carl-Auer.

Lawton-Smith, C. (2011). Organizational psychology models in coaching supervision. In T. Bachkirova, P. Jackson, & D. Clutterbuck (Eds.), *Coaching & mentoring supervision: Theory and practice* (pp. 155–166). England: Open University Press.

Lee, G. (2010). The psychodynamic approach to coaching. In E. Cox, T. Bachkirova, & D. Clutterbuck (Eds.), *The complete handbook of coaching* (pp. 23–36). London: Sage Publications.

Moylan, D. (1994). The dangers of contagion: Projective identification processes in institutions. In A. Obholzer & V. Z. Roberts (Eds.), *The unconscious at work* (pp. 51–59). New York: Routledge.

Newman, J. L., Robinson-Kurpius, S. E., & Faqua, D. R. (2002). Issues in the ethical practice of consulting psychology. In R. L. Lowman (Ed.), *Handbook of organizational consulting psychology* (pp. 733–758). San Francisco: Jossey-Bass.

Obholzer, A. (1994). Authority, power and leadership: Contributions from group relations training. In A. Obholzer & V. Z. Roberts (Eds.), *The unconscious at work* (pp. 39–50). New York: Routledge.

Rioch, M. J. (1975). The work of Wilfred Bion on groups. In A. D. Colman & W. H. Bexton (Eds.), *Group relations reader 1* (pp. 21–33). Jupiter: The A.K. Rice Institute.

Roberts, V. Z. (1994a). The organization of work: Contributions from open systems theory. In A. Obholzer & V. Z. Roberts (Eds.), *The unconscious at work* (pp. 28–38). New York: Routledge.

Roberts, V. Z. (1994b). Till death us do part: Caring and uncaring in work with the elderly. In A. Obholzer & V. Z. Roberts (Eds.), *The unconscious at work* (pp. 75–83). New York: Routledge.

Roberts, V. Z. (1994c). The self-assigned impossible task. In A. Obholzer & V. Z. Roberts (Eds.), *The unconscious at work* (pp. 110–118). New York: Routledge.

Roberts, V. Z. (1994d). Conflict and collaboration: Managing intergroup relations. In A. Obholzer & V. Z. Roberts (Eds.), *The unconscious at work* (pp. 187–196). New York: Routledge.

Roberts, V. Z., & Brunning, H. (2008). Psychodynamic and systems-psychodynamic coaching. In S. Palmer & A. Whybrow (Eds.), *Handbook of coaching psychology: A guide for practitioners* (pp. 253–277). Sussex: Routledge.

Ruppert, F. (2008). *Trauma, bonding and family constellations: Understanding and healing the injuries of the soul*. Frome: Green Balloon Publishing.

Schneider, J. R. (2007). *Family constellations: Basic principles and procedures*. Heidelberg: Carl-Auer.

Speck, P. (1994). Working with dying people on being good enough. In A. Obholzer & V. R. Roberts (Eds.), *The unconscious at work* (pp. 94–100). New York: Routledge.
Stapley, L. F. (2006). *Individuals, groups, and organizations beneath the surface*. London: Karnac.
Stokes, J. (1994). The unconscious at work in groups and team: Contributions from the work of Wilfred Bion. In A. Obholzer & V. R. Roberts (Eds.), *The unconscious at work* (pp. 19–27). New York: Routledge.
Tomaschek, N., & Strobel, M. (2010). Conscious organization. The Augusburg school on innovation coaching for higher performance, agility and innovation in business. In S. Schloemer & N. Tomaschek (Eds.), *Leading in complexity: New ways in management* (pp. 118–130). Heidelberg: Carl-Auer.
Ulsamer, B. (2003). *The art and practice of family constellations*. Heidelberg: Carl-Auer.
Von Bertalanffy, L. (1972). General system theory – A critical review. In J. Beishon & G. Peters (Eds.), *Systems behaviour* (pp. 29–49). London: Harper & Row.

Relationship Among Emotional Intelligence, SOAR, and Team-Based Collaboration: Implications for a Strengths, Opportunities, Aspirations, and Results (SOAR) Based Approach to Coaching Psychology

Matthew L. Cole and Jacqueline M. Stavros

Abstract The aim of this chapter is to provide a theoretical overview of SOAR, a strengths-based framework with a whole-system (stakeholder) approach to strategy that focuses on strengths, opportunities, aspirations, and results, and to consider implications for its use within coaching psychology research and practice. We first present the results of an empirical study in which SOAR was found to mediate the relationship between emotional intelligence (EI) and team-based collaboration among team leaders but not team members. In finding that SOAR differentially mediated the EI-collaboration relationship in team leaders rather than team members, we suggest that SOAR may help a coach create a reservoir of positivity to support new ideas, innovations, and the best in people to emerge and thrive. We discuss how a SOAR-based coaching process may facilitate a coach's ability to promote performance enhancement through a results-oriented approach focusing on the coachee's strengths, opportunities, and aspirations.

Keywords Coaching psychology • Emotional intelligence • Collaboration • SOAR • Teams • Leadership • Mediation analysis

1 Introduction

Organizations in the twenty-first century are increasingly turning to work teams to meet the competitive challenges of the global marketplace (Zaccaro et al. 2001). With globalization, multicultural teams made up of diverse team members from different national backgrounds and cultures are becoming the norm (Brett et al. 2006;

M.L. Cole (✉) • J.M. Stavros
College of Management, Lawrence Technological University,
Southfield, MI, USA
e-mail: mcole@ltu.edu; jstavros@ltu.edu

L.E. van Zyl et al. (eds.), *Coaching Psychology: Meta-theoretical perspectives and applications in multicultural contexts*, DOI 10.1007/978-3-319-31012-1_12

Earley and Mosakowski 2000; Moukarzel and Steelman 2015). Organizational supervisors and managers are looking for ways to increase the effectiveness of their work teams, and a fundamental characteristic of teams that impacts their effectiveness in meeting target goals and objectives is team-based collaboration (Romero et al. 2009).

Team leaders play a critical role in facilitating the development of collaborative relationships among team members (Gratton and Erickson 2007; Sarin and McDermott 2003). Where leaders were once seen to control, plan, and inspect the overall running of a team, leadership roles are now seen to also motivate and inspire others, to foster positive attitudes among team members, and to create a sense of contribution, importance, and collaboration among team members (Palmer et al. 2001). This leadership role helps team members transcend their self-interests and collaborate via communication, compromise, and integration (Joshi et al. 2009).

Behind every leader is a successful coach (Hawkins 2014), and while coaching is one of the most effective leadership styles, it is also one of the most overlooked (Goleman 2000). An essential ingredient for high-impact coaching is emotional intelligence (EI), i.e., ability to recognize and manage the emotions of self and others (Neale et al. 2009). Awareness and management of emotions in self and others are essential EI abilities that are also the foundation for specific capabilities of leadership (Goleman 1998, 2000; Xavier 2005). Research by McClelland (1998) found that leaders with strengths in these EI abilities were far more effective than those who lacked such strengths. In a team setting, the leader acts as the team's emotional guide, and emotionally intelligent leadership inspires and stimulates passion and enthusiasm in team members while helping them to remain motivated and committed to the team's goals and objectives (Goleman et al. 2002). Effective team leaders are said to "…prime good feelings in those they lead. They create emotional resonance – a reservoir of positivity that frees the best in people" (Goleman et al. 2009, p. 9). This reservoir of positivity demands bringing EI to bear and is the essence of positive abundance which is at the core of positive psychology.

Positive psychology is a field of research and applied psychology that aims to use scientific psychological research to enhance the conditions and experiences that create well-being and happiness for individuals, teams, and organizations (Law 2013; Linley 2008; Seligman 2003, 2011). Research over the last 10 years suggests that positive psychology is important because focusing on well-being and happiness leads to optimal functioning, development, and performance (Biswas-Diener 2010). According to Seligman (2011), "Well-being theory has five measurable elements (PERMA): positive emotions (of which happiness and life satisfaction are all aspects), engagement, relationships, meaning, and achievement" (p. 24). Positive psychology assumes that individuals have the capacity for personal growth by developing strengths and building on positive emotions (Van Zyl and Stander 2013). Positive psychology is important for coaching teams because it cultivates positive relationships and interactions in the team (Leung et al. 2014).

Growing out of the theory and practice of appreciative inquiry (AI) and positive psychology is SOAR (strengths, opportunities, aspirations, and results). SOAR is a generative and strengths-based framework for strategic thinking, planning, and leading that allows a team "to construct its future through collaboration, shared understanding, and a commitment to action" (Stavros and Hinrichs 2009, p. 1). At the heart of the SOAR framework is an inclusive approach that encourages team members to frame strategy from a strengths-based perspective utilizing the team's unique strengths, assets, networks, resources, and capabilities (Cooperrider et al. 2008).

The purpose of this chapter is to consider a SOAR framework for coaching psychology. We begin with a theoretical overview of SOAR, reviewing its development from the theory and practice of both AI and positive psychology. Next, we present the results obtained from empirical research we conducted in which SOAR was found to be the mechanism of action by which EI has a positive impact on team-based collaboration. Specifically, we investigated SOAR as a mediator of the positive impact that awareness and management of emotions has on team-based collaboration in a sample of team leaders versus team members. In finding that SOAR differentially mediated the EI-collaboration relationship in team leaders rather than team members we suggest that a SOAR framework for coaching psychology may facilitate a coach's ability to promote performance enhancement through a results-oriented approach focusing on the coachee's strengths, opportunities, and aspirations.

2 The SOAR Framework

An effective team is a group of people who collaborate in support of a common vision and aspirations (Katzenbach 1998). Collaboration is especially important for team effectiveness when collaborative strategies are inclusive and draw upon the collective expertise of diverse team members (Shaw and Lindsay 2008). A collaborative strategy that provides a framework for members of a team, group, or department to approach strategic thinking, planning, and leading from a profoundly positive and inclusive approach is SOAR (Stavros and Cole 2013; Stavros and Hinrichs 2009).

SOAR is a "strengths-based framework with a participatory approach to strategic analysis, strategy development, and organizational change" (Stavros and Saint 2010, p. 380). SOAR integrates AI with a strategic planning framework to create a transformational process that inspires organizations and stakeholders of the organization to engage in results-oriented strategic planning efforts (Stavros et al. 2003). AI "is a collaborative search for the best in people, their organizations, and the world around them. It involves the discovery of what gives life to a living system when it is most effective, alive, and constructively capable in economic, ecological, and human terms. AI involves the art and practice of asking unconditional positive questions that strengthen a system's capacity to apprehend, anticipate, and heighten its potential," (Cooperrider et al. 2008, p. 3). SOAR integrates positive psychology through its focus on positive deviance, the tendency to move toward positive energy and away from negative energy, and embracing values of appreciation, collaboration, virtuousness, vitality, and meaningfulness (Cameron et al. 2003; Cameron and Spreitzer 2012). SOAR builds on AI and positive psychology to create a strategic

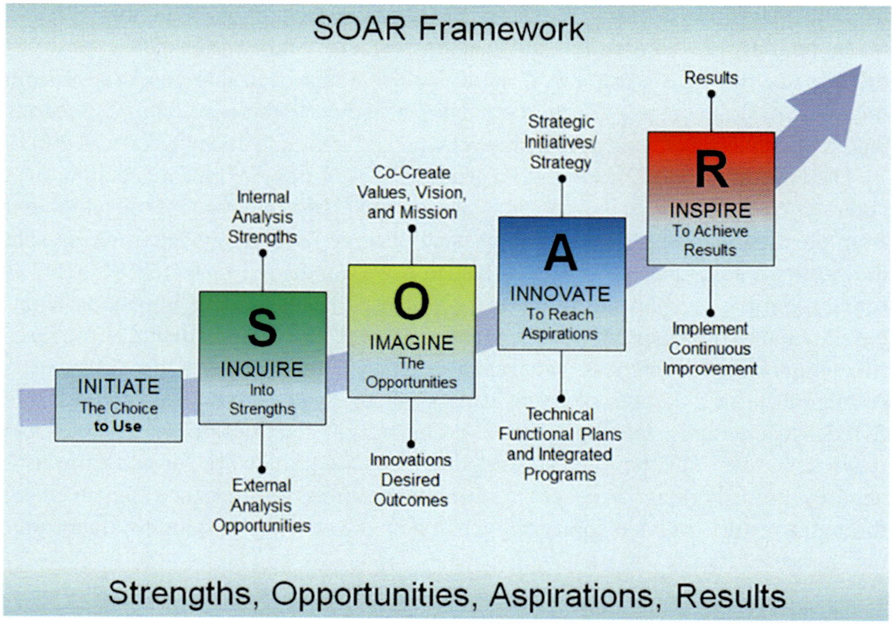

Fig. 1 The SOAR framework (Adopted from Stavros et al. 2007)

framework that enables discovery of the team's collective positive characteristics by appreciating the value of each team member.

As shown in Fig. 1, the SOAR framework transforms alternative approaches to strategic thinking to emphasize Strengths, Opportunities, Aspirations, and Results (Stavros and Hinrichs 2009). Applied to a team, SOAR-based strategic thinking enables issues to be framed from a solution-oriented perspective that is generative and focused on individual and team strengths, opportunities, aspirations, and desired results to build a positive future (Stavros and Wooten 2012). As a framework for strategic thinking and planning, SOAR describes the elements and activities that team members and team leaders should follow in their collaborative strategic thinking and planning (Stavros et al. 2007).

2.1 *Linking the SOAR Framework with Emotional Intelligence and Team-Based Collaboration*

The SOAR framework is inherently team-oriented and collaborative and seeks to involve all individuals having a perspective and stake in the teams' performance. Teams that adopt SOAR will begin with an inquiry into what works well for the team and its members followed by inclusive discussions of individual and team strengths, opportunities for growth, aspirations, and desired results. With open

Table 1 Strategic inquiry-appreciative intent: Inspiration to SOAR

Planning processes	SOAR elements	SOAR activities
Strategic inquiry	Strengths	What are we doing well?
		What are our greatest assets?
	Opportunities	What are the best possible market opportunities?
		How do we best partner with others?
Appreciative intent	Aspirations	To what do we aspire?
		What is our preferred future?
	Results	What are the measurable results?
		What do we want to be known for?

discussions of strengths, opportunities, aspirations, and results teams are better able to design strategies and methods to meet team objectives, define performance metrics aligned with team goals and objectives, and discover new and profitable opportunities. The SOAR approach to teamwork promotes individual and team freedom to imagine an innovative and creative future that is dynamic and enabling of positive outcomes. It is important to recognize the distinction of SOAR as its focus remains to identify and build on strengths and opportunities, rather than weaknesses and threats. The core SOAR questions are:

Strengths: What are our best capabilities?
Opportunities: What are the three best opportunities that leverage our strengths?
Aspirations: What do we care deeply about? Who should we become? Why?
Results: How do we know we are succeeding?

When applied to teams, SOAR may facilitate a collaborative process of dialogue and positive information exchange that may lead the team to consider what and where the team wishes to be in the future when the team is at its best. Table 1 depicts the specific activities within the SOAR framework that act as enablers for successful team performance (Stavros et al. 2003).

Since SOAR depends on the interaction of team members dialoguing in the strategic process, it may be appropriate to suggest that team members be emotionally intelligent in their exchange of ideas. Emotional intelligence (EI) represents a set of competencies for identifying, processing, and managing emotions (Zeidner et al. 2008). These EI competencies include perceiving emotions, accessing and generating emotions so as to assist thought, understanding emotions and emotional knowledge, and reflectively regulating emotions so as to promote emotional and intellectual growth (Mayer et al. 2004). Mayer and Salovey (1997) consider four EI competencies as particularly important for diverse and multicultural teams: awareness of one's own emotions (self-awareness), awareness of the emotions of others (other-awareness), management of one's own emotions (self-management), and management of the emotions of others (other-management). Furthermore, EI is generally considered to be a value added competency to various aspects of individual and team-based performance, namely collaboration (Jordan and Troth 2004).

Modern business cultures reflect accelerated changes in globalization characterized by an increasingly diverse and multicultural workforce. Many organizations today are making use of work teams as a basic structural unit, and the effects of cultural diversity on team performance have understandably received attention (Pieterse et al. 2013; Simons et al. 1999). Research on teamwork suggests that a collaborative team culture encourages team members to work together towards accomplishing team-based tasks (Romero et al. 2009). Linking EI with SOAR, team members are invited to share their perceptions, ideas, goals, and vision for the future, and the key EI competencies of emotional self-awareness, self-management, other-awareness, and other-management may benefit from SOAR-based thinking. Specifically, EI and SOAR may be particularly helpful for supporting collaborative environments in teams because team members are essentially given the permission to share and express their emotions rather than suppress them, and once positive emotions are shared, they begin to reverberate in a contagious way through the team leading to increased team performance (Cameron 2013). For teams, a shared set of values, vision, mission (purpose), and respect for each other's roles is necessary to achieve collaborative results, and the manifestations of EI, SOAR, and team-based collaboration are exemplified in self-reflection, mutual understanding, and a consideration for the collaborative team as a whole. As team members exchange ideas, aspirations, and desired results, they share a vision for the future with energy, vitality, and commitment (Stavros and Hinrichs 2009).

When individuals in a team have difficulty functioning in a collaborative environment or need support to increase their EI competencies, team leaders can have a strong impact on team performance by influencing the emotional climate of the team (Hawkins 2014). Team leadership is intrinsically an emotional process, and research suggests that team leaders with high EI obtain results from others that are beyond expectations while developing and using talents crucial for team effectiveness (Chen et al. 1998). Effective leaders steer their own feelings, acknowledge the feelings of others concerning their work culture, and intervene effectively to enhance morale.

When used by team leaders to influence a team's emotional climate, the SOAR framework has the potential to build strong and dynamic relationships among team members as they begin to understand the importance of working collaboratively to develop strategy, measurable objectives, and methods to achieve a visionary future based on strengths, opportunities, aspirations, and results. To consider the implications of the SOAR framework for coaching, we conducted empirical research that investigated the associations among EI, SOAR and team-based collaboration in a sample of team leaders and team members. We found that SOAR differentially mediated the EI-collaboration relationship in team leaders rather than team members. We discuss how a SOAR framework for coaching psychology may create a reservoir of positivity, generative action, new ideas, innovations, and the best in people to emerge (Bushe 2007, 2013; Goleman et al. 2009; Stavros 2013), thereby facilitating strong performance in the coachee via the coach's ability to inspire strengths, opportunities, aspirations, and results (Mosteo et al. 2016).

3 Research Study of SOAR as a Mediator of Team-Based Collaboration

3.1 Research Design

A sample of 308 professionals either actively working in teams or who had recent experience working in teams completed a self-report survey that measured EI, SOAR, and team-based collaboration. Approximately 49 % of the sample was female, 52 % was between the ages of 45 and 64, 75 % was white, and 70 % had a graduate degree (master's or doctoral). Participants were asked to identify their role when working in teams, and 56.8 % of the sample identified themselves as serving a team leadership role ($n = 175$), whereas 35.1 % of the sample identified themselves as a team member ($n = 108$). In accordance with U.S. federal requirements, approval to conduct research with human participants was obtained from The Lawrence Technological University Institutional Review Board (IRB).

EI was measured by the 16-item "WEIP-S" (Work Group Emotional Intelligence Profile-Short Form; Jordan and Lawrence 2009) to establish areas of respondent competency in four EI abilities helpful for understanding how EI works in teams (Mayer and Salovey 1997): SA = Self-Awareness; SM = Self-Management; OA = Other-Awareness; OM = Other-Management. SOAR was measured by the 12-item SOAR Profile (Cole and Stavros 2013, 2014), a self-report index of SOAR-based strategic thinking as measured by four elements: ST = Strengths; OP = Opportunities; AS = Aspirations; RE = Results. Team-based collaboration was measured by the 9-item Team Collaboration Questionnaire, an original measure of collaborative activity among teams, adapted from Aram and Morgan (1976), and Rahim (1983a, b) that measured three factors: IN = Integrating; CP = Compromising; CM = Communication. Participants rated both the EI and the Collaboration items using a 7-point Likert scale (1 = strongly disagree, 7 = strongly agree); SOAR items were scored using a 10-point Likert scale (1 = never, 10 = always).

Figure 2 presents the study model in which EI as the independent variable (IV) is predicted to impact the dependent variable (DV), team-based collaboration. In consideration of a variable that could mediate the indirect effects of EI on collaboration, SOAR was tested in the model as a mediator (MED). To investigate the differential relationship among EI, SOAR and collaboration in team leaders versus team members, team role was tested in the model as a moderator (MOD) of the EI-collaboration relationship, and the differential mediation of the EI-collaboration relationship by SOAR was tested as a function of team role. According to Baron and Kenny (1986), mediating variables speak to how or why effects occur between the IV and the DV, whereas moderating variables address when or under what conditions the relationship between the IV and the DV is more likely to occur. Team role as a moderator of the relationship between EI and collaboration was tested according to simple slopes analysis (Aiken and West 1991; Dawson 2014). To test if SOAR mediated the relationship between EI and collaboration, a mediation path model using structural equation modeling (SEM) with bootstrapped confidence intervals

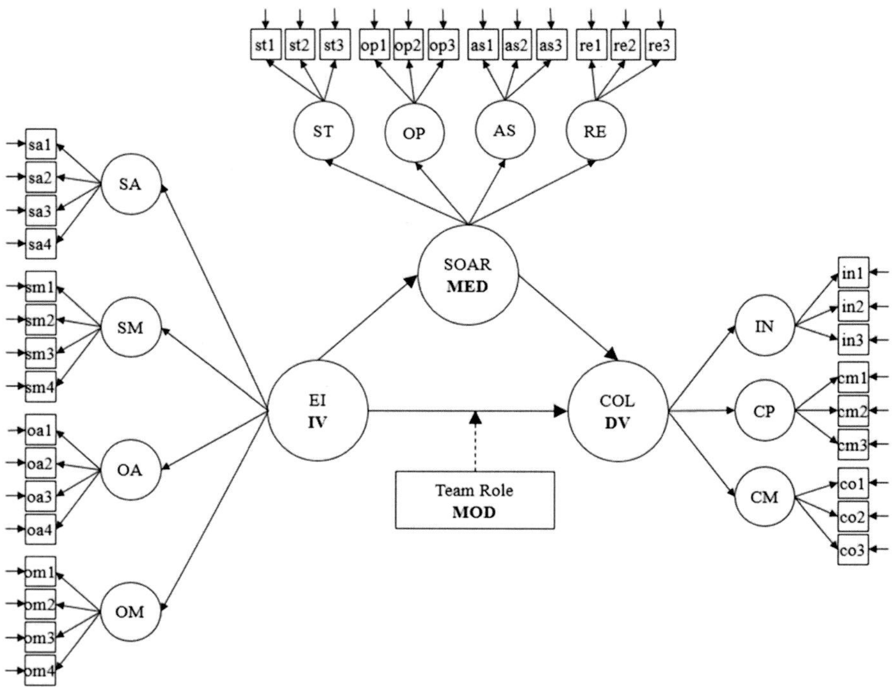

Fig. 2 Study model: SOAR as a mediator of the relationship between emotional intelligence and team-based collaboration as function of team role (leaders vs. members). *IV* independent variable, *MED* mediating variable, *DV* dependent variable. See Table 2 for abbreviations of study variables

(5000 bootstrapping samples) estimated the indirect effect of SOAR on the relationship between EI and collaboration in team leaders versus team members (Cheung and Lau 2008; Preacher and Hayes 2008). Minitab version 17 was used for descriptive and inferential quantitative statistical analysis and M*plus* version 7 was used for SEM.

3.2 Results

The psychometric properties of the WEIP-S, the SOAR Profiles, and the Team Collaboration Questionnaire were evaluated using Cronbach's alpha estimates of internal consistency reliability, and confirmatory factor analysis (CFA) estimate of construct validity. Alphas for each study variable in all participants, in team leaders, and in team members, are presented in Tables 2, 3, and 4, respectively; all values were acceptable, and ranged from 0.721 to 0.927. Tests of model fit for the CFA in all participants, team leaders, and team members were supportive of construct validity according to chi-square/df ratio less than 2, RMSEA <0.08, CFI >0.900, and all factor loadings significant at $p < 0.05$ (data not shown).

Table 2 Intercorrelations between study variables in all participants

Var	EI	SA	SM	OA	OM	SO	ST	OP	AS	RE	CO	IN	CP	CM
EI	0.893													
SA	0.75*	0.888												
SM	0.66*	0.31*	0.805											
OA	0.74*	0.33*	0.33*	0.886										
OM	0.79*	0.40*	0.46*	0.52*	0.903									
SOAR	0.45*	0.29*	0.19*	0.41*	0.42*	0.855								
ST	0.34*	0.21*	0.15*	0.30*	0.32*	0.80*	0.749							
OP	0.42*	0.23*	0.24*	0.36*	0.41*	0.77*	0.54*	0.795						
AS	0.37*	0.31*	0.09	0.33*	0.32*	0.75*	0.47*	0.44*	0.850					
RE	0.21*	0.10	0.09	0.23*	0.20*	0.69*	0.47*	0.40*	0.23*	0.790				
COL	0.49*	0.24*	0.56*	0.31*	0.40*	0.43*	0.38*	0.39*	0.18*	0.38*	0.853			
IN	0.45*	0.22*	0.58*	0.23*	0.37*	0.34*	0.33*	0.31*	0.10	0.30*	0.82*	0.909		
CP	0.30*	0.13*	0.30*	0.26*	0.23*	0.32*	0.24*	0.25*	0.18*	0.29*	0.78*	0.37*	0.849	
CM	0.45*	0.26*	0.50*	0.24*	0.39*	0.38*	0.36*	0.39*	0.14*	0.31*	0.79*	0.68*	0.34*	0.721

Scores along the diagonal are Cronbach's alpha measures of internal consistency reliability for each of the following study variables: *EI* Emotional Intelligence, *SA* Self-Awareness, *SM* Self-Management, *OA* Other-Awareness, *OM* Other-Management, *SOAR* SOAR Framework, *ST* Strengths, *OP* Opportunities, *AS* Aspirations, *RE* Results, *COL* Collaboration, *IN* Integrating, *CP* Compromising, *CM* Communication. All other scores are Pearson product-moment correlation coefficients. $^{*}p<0.05$ significant correlation (two-tailed)

Table 3 Intercorrelations between study variables in team leaders

Var	EI	SA	SM	OA	OM	SO	ST	OP	AS	RE	CO	IN	CP	CM
EI	0.879													
SA	0.73*	0.896												
SM	0.60*	0.20*	0.736											
OA	0.73*	0.30*	0.27*	0.891										
OM	0.76*	0.34*	0.46*	0.46*	0.899									
SOAR	0.45*	0.28*	0.25*	0.35*	0.40*	0.841								
ST	0.32*	0.14	0.15*	0.28*	0.34*	0.80*	0.748							
OP	0.43*	0.24*	0.34*	0.26*	0.42*	0.71*	0.47*	0.770						
AS	0.39*	0.31*	0.15*	0.29*	0.32*	0.77*	0.52*	0.40*	0.841					
RE	0.19*	0.11	0.12	0.18*	0.12	0.68*	0.43*	0.34*	0.26*	0.778				
COL	0.38*	0.17*	0.46*	0.22*	0.32*	0.45*	0.35*	0.40*	0.23*	0.38*	0.831			
IN	0.40*	0.13	0.51*	0.20*	0.39*	0.39*	0.31*	0.42*	0.18*	0.30*	0.81*	0.891		
CP	0.21*	0.08	0.25*	0.18*	0.14	0.30*	0.24*	0.20*	0.19*	0.28*	0.81*	0.41*	0.835	
CM	0.35*	0.21*	0.36*	0.15	0.30*	0.40*	0.31*	0.41*	0.16*	0.36*	0.74*	0.61*	0.33*	0.750

Scores along the diagonal are Cronbach's alpha measures of internal consistency reliability for each of the study variables. See Table 2 for abbreviations. All other scores are Pearson product-moment correlation coefficients. *$p < 0.05$ significant correlation (two-tailed)

Table 4 Intercorrelations between study variables in team members

Var	EI	SA	SM	OA	OM	SO	ST	OP	AS	RE	CO	IN	CP	CM
EI	0.890													
SA	0.79*	0.887												
SM	0.68*	0.42*	0.820											
OA	0.73*	0.36*	0.31*	0.858										
OM	0.77*	0.41*	0.40*	0.53*	0.880									
SOAR	0.44*	0.30*	0.11	0.46*	0.42*	0.866								
ST	0.35*	0.29*	0.14	0.31*	0.28*	0.80*	0.747							
OP	0.39*	0.21*	0.15	0.44*	0.38*	0.84*	0.63*	0.812						
AS	0.35*	0.30*	0.01	0.36*	0.33*	0.72*	0.39*	0.47*	0.860					
RE	0.23*	0.09	0.05	0.28*	0.26*	0.69*	0.51*	0.47*	0.19*	0.807				
COL	0.63*	0.35*	0.69*	0.42*	0.47*	0.40*	0.42*	0.36*	0.13	0.36*	0.884			
IN	0.50*	0.31*	0.66*	0.28*	0.30*	0.27*	0.36*	0.20*	0.02	0.30*	0.84*	0.927		
CP	0.50*	0.26*	0.41*	0.43*	0.42*	0.37*	0.29*	0.33*	0.20*	0.32*	0.76*	0.36*	0.868	
CM	0.54*	0.30*	0.64*	0.30*	0.44*	0.35*	0.40*	0.36*	0.10*	0.26*	0.86*	0.73*	0.43*	0.777

Scores along the diagonal are Cronbach's alpha measures of internal consistency reliability for each of the study variables. See Table 2 for abbreviations. All other scores are Pearson product-moment correlation coefficients. *$p<0.05$ significant correlation (two-tailed)

Table 5 Mean and SD of study variables in all participants, team leaders, and team members

	All participants		Team leaders		Team members	
Var	M	SD	M	SD	M	SD
EI	5.32*	0.79	5.43	0.71	5.19	0.83
SA	4.76	1.36	4.78	1.29	4.72	1.43
SM	5.95	0.84	6.00	0.73	5.94	0.90
OA	5.10**	1.11	5.28	1.06	4.87	1.13
OM	5.47**	0.99	5.66	0.89	5.23	1.03
SOAR	7.85	1.03	7.92	0.94	7.72	1.16
ST	7.86	1.24	7.90	1.21	7.78	1.30
OP	8.40	1.25	8.51	1.06	8.20	1.51
AS	6.99	1.67	7.03	1.54	6.91	1.84
RE	8.13	1.37	8.20	1.30	8.02	1.48
COL	5.86	0.73	5.92	0.67	5.76	0.83
IN	6.19	0.86	6.26	0.76	6.06	1.01
CP	5.36	1.12	5.41	1.11	5.33	1.13
CM	6.03*	0.77	6.11	0.67	5.89	0.91

See Table 2 for abbreviations. $^{*}p<0.05$ $^{**}p<0.01$ significant difference between team leaders and team members according to independent samples t test (two-tailed)

The intercorrelations between the study variables in the full sample, in team leaders, and in team members are presented in Tables 2, 3, and 4, respectively. Table 5 presents the mean and standard deviation of the study variables, along with results of independent samples t tests testing differences in mean scores between team leaders and team members. Results found higher mean scores in team leaders vs. team members across all study variables, with significantly higher scores in team leaders compared to team members for the EI variable and its factors other-awareness and other-management and for the communication factor of team-based collaboration.

As shown in Fig. 3, team role moderated the EI-collaboration relationship when EI was low. Figures 4–7 show the results of mediation path models using SEM (1, 2, and 3 asterisks reflect significant paths in the model at the 0.05, 0.01, and 0.001 levels of statistical significance, respectively). Figures 4 and 5 show that while EI was found to be a significant predictor of team-based collaboration in both team leaders and team members, a significant indirect effect of EI to collaboration through SOAR was found only in team leaders. Figures 6 and 7 show that the opportunities and results elements of the SOAR framework functioned as multiple mediators of team-based collaboration in team leaders rather than team members. Taken together, results suggest that team leaders compared to team members have higher team-based collaboration when EI is low, with SOAR helping to explain how EI impacts team-based collaboration in team leaders rather than team members. The implications of these results for team coaching are discussed.

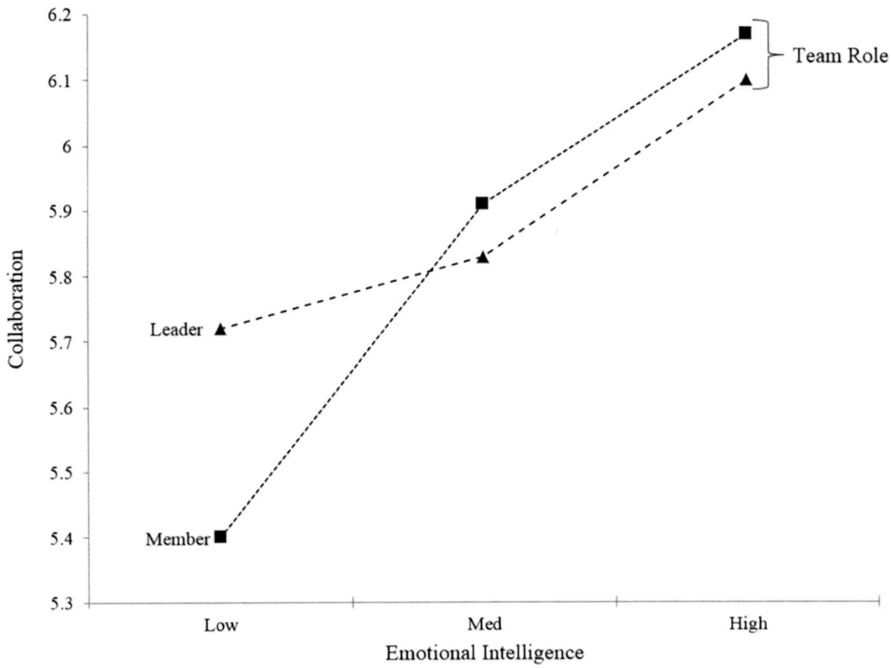

Fig. 3 Test of team role as a moderator of the EI-collaboration relationship

4 Discussion

Successful coaching in the modern international and multicultural business climate is beginning to appreciate strength-based approaches that focus on diversity and things that the coachee does well (Mosteo et al. 2016; Rosinski 2003). Such an approach enables flexibility and fluidity in the coaching process and helps the coach appreciate the diversity of strengths that characterizes the coachee. The application of strengths to coaching psychology has received considerable attention in support of the application of coaching psychology to nurture an individual's natural abilities, well-being, and performance resulting in benefit for individuals, teams, and organizations (Linley and Harrington 2006; Palmer and Whybrow 2005). Individuals working in teams who are coached by a coach who appreciates the collective strengths and capabilities of all team members may flourish and achieve extraordinarily positive performance (Cameron 2013). Furthermore, coaches should be competent in facilitating group learning processes and in teaching skills to help coachees develop dynamic collaborative relationships based on awareness and management of emotions in themselves and others (Stout-Rostron 2014).

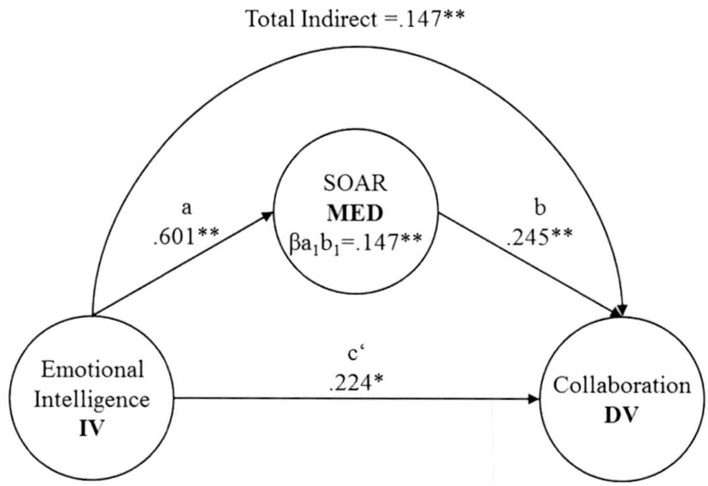

Fig. 4 Test of SOAR as a mediator of the EI-collaboration relationship in team leaders

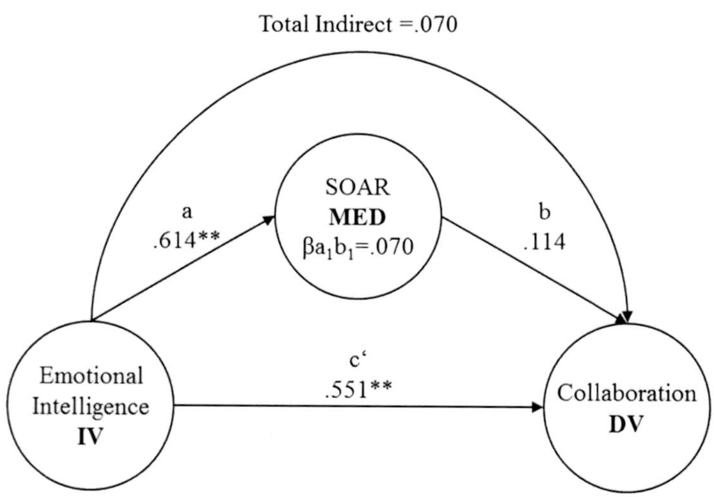

Fig. 5 Test of SOAR as a mediator of the EI-collaboration relationship in team members

5 Implications for Practice and Recommendations

Our research on the relationship among EI, SOAR and team-based collaboration has at least three implications for the use of a generative approach for team coaching that stresses strengths, opportunities, aspirations, and results. Firstly, SOAR has been developed from the theory and practice of AI and positive psychology. The AI approach focuses on the positive aspects of the team and how to seek solutions.

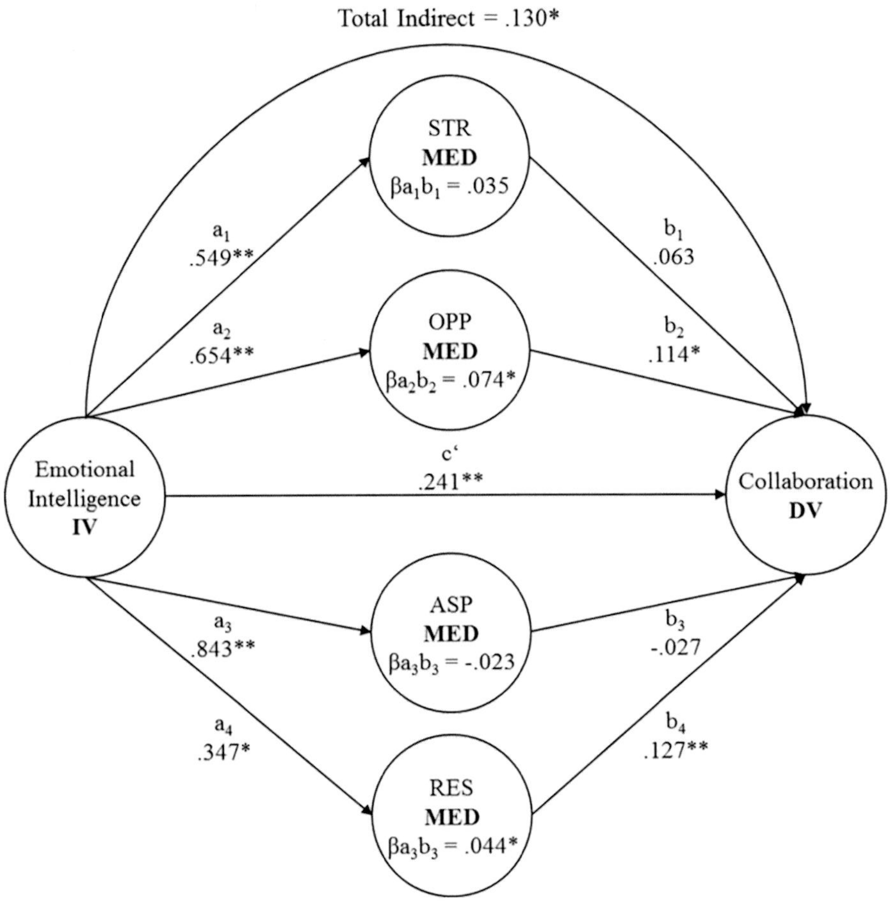

Fig. 6 Test of strengths, opportunities, aspirations, and results as multiple mediators of the EI-collaboration relationship in team leaders

The AI approach encourages the team to "envision a different way of functioning from its current patterns and create new values and beliefs that enable the team to plot a new course" (Dyer and Dyer 2010, p. 339). Since positive psychology stresses optimism and a focus on strengths (like AI), coaches who use the SOAR framework will be well-positioned to create an optimistic and strengths-based climate for the coachee, regardless of whether or not the coachee is working in teams. For example, a coach would seek to create a climate in which the coachee has clarity about his/her unique role and benefit to themselves, the team, the organization, etc. The benefit of such a climate is that the coachee might be highly motivated and more likely to be successful — as measured by time to complete task, team member satisfaction, organizational profit, etc. (Driver 2011). Regarding team member satisfaction in particular, team coaching that stresses strengths rather than weaknesses

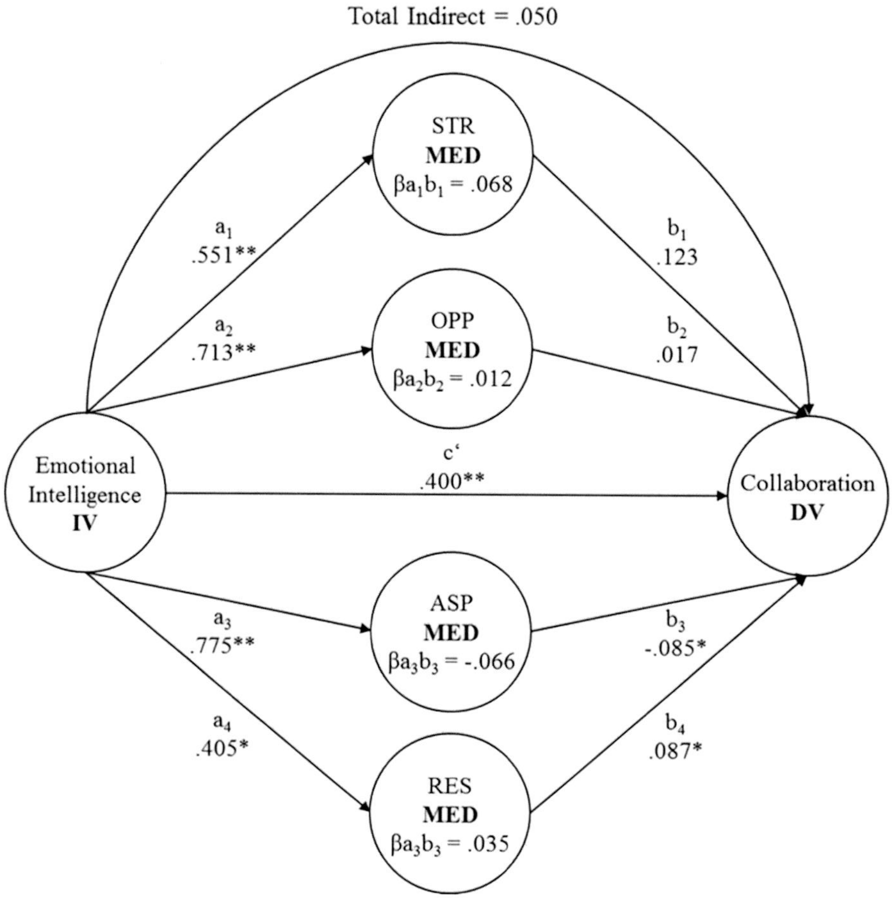

Fig. 7 Test of strengths, opportunities, aspirations, and results as multiple mediators of the EI-collaboration relationship in team members

significantly reduces team members' susceptibility to depression as the team members direct their attention towards positive emotions rather than a cycle of negative thinking (Seligman and Csikszentmihalyi 2000; Seligman et al. 2005).

This implication of SOAR to coaching involves AI's contribution to SOAR as an alternative to the traditional problem-solving approach of finding what is 'wrong' with an issue. As such, SOAR generates solutions to either correct existing problems or enhance things that are not working as efficiently as they could through AI's emphasis on seeking what is 'right' with an issue and using that as a force for change (Passmore and Hain 2005). The AI characteristics of SOAR applied to coaching, for example, would involve movement toward what the coachee is doing right, thereby providing a structure for creating a desired future characterized by flourishing and success (Watkins and Cooperrider 2000).

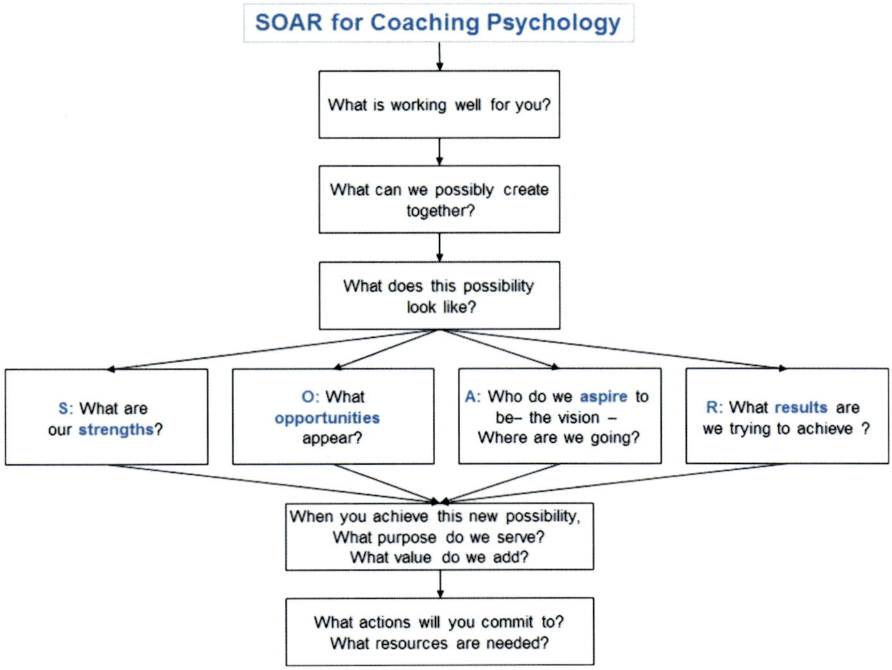

Fig. 8 SOAR framework for coaching psychology

Secondly, the four elements of the SOAR framework provide coaches with an architecture for engaging the coachee in a strategic thinking and dialogue process to help shape strategy and strategic processes. Figure 8 below exemplifies how the SOAR elements of strengths, opportunities, aspirations, and results may facilitate the coaching process. For example, the coachee is first invited to have an open conversation about his/her current environmental climate ("What is working well for you?"), current ideas for creative solutions or innovations ("What can we possibly create together?"), and current possibilities that would benefit from creative solutions or innovations ("What does this possibility look like?"). Next, the coachee is guided to engage in a collaborative and inclusive conversation on any individual, team, and/or organizational strengths as they relate to possibilities for solutions or innovations ("What are our strengths as they relate to this possibility?"), opportunities that would benefit from solutions or innovations ("What opportunities appear ?"), aspirations of a future the coachee desires ("Who will we be – the vision – where are we going?"), and measurable results indicating progress towards a goal or objective that the coachee wants to complete ("What are we trying to achieve?"). The SOAR coaching framework would conclude with appraisal of the coachee's behavior ("Who are we – what purpose do we serve – what value do we add?"), and a plan for the next strategic dialogue ("What actions will you commit to? What resources are needed?").

Thirdly, results of our research on the interrelationships among EI, SOAR, and team-based collaboration in team leaders versus team members illustrate that the SOAR framework is important for how awareness and management of emotions of oneself and others promotes a whole system and inclusive approach to collaboration. Use of the SOAR profile, for example, would offer coaches the opportunity to help themselves and their clients gain self-awareness and other awareness about their natural capacity for SOAR-based strategic thinking, planning, and leading (Cole and Stavros 2013, 2014). Regarding awareness of emotions, truly masterful coaches routinely engage in examining their own empathic stance, their range of feelings, etc., and this self-awareness creates the possibility of powerful breakthrough moments connecting coach with client (Law 2013).

In a team context, awareness of emotions is important for the team coach because helping team members acquire the ability to "step into the shoes" of another person on the team long enough to perceive situations from their perspective is essential for appreciating different cultural perspectives with respect to work norms, gender differences, differences in decision making styles, and other sources of diversity that characterize today's multicultural teams. Other-awareness encourages the emergence of a shared team identity which supports team-based collaboration (Lisak and Erez 2015). Other-awareness is also important for the coach, especially with regards to strengths, since individuals often take their strengths for granted.

Results of our study suggest that the aspirations and results elements of SOAR were found to be the significant multiple mediators of team-based collaboration in team leaders. If applied to coaching, these results suggest that coaches may be able to facilitate positive collaborative engagement among coachees by encouraging aspirational visioning of a positive future, and by asking coachees to define measurable results for individual, team, and/or organizational success. Furthermore, coaches should aim to manage emotions in coachees by using the SOAR framework to explore strengths-based opportunities and possibilities, clarify aspirational goals and measurable results, and develop the capacity for SOAR-based leadership to emerge.

Emergent leadership has received interest over the past 10–15 years due to the increase in self-managing work teams and the consequent need for leadership to emerge from within teams, alleviating the need for external team leaders (Pescosolido 2002). Use of the SOAR framework for team coaching, in particular, has the potential to develop emergent leaders who are managers of the team's emotional state. Research suggests that emergent leaders who are successful at influencing team member behaviour and team performance have the ability to manage the team's emotional state through communication, empathy, modeling of appropriate emotional responses, and the creation of shared understanding and trust among team members (Lisak and Erez 2015; Wolff et al. 2002). Additionally, application of the SOAR framework for team coaching may help emergent leaders in teams understand how they are influencing overall team processes in addition to each individual team member through SOAR's whole system perspective.

Finally, in addition to supporting awareness and management of SOAR-based capacity, the SOAR Profile may also help coaches and their clients understand their natural capacity for embracing a whole systems and inclusive approach to SOAR-based strategy and strategic thinking, planning, and leading (Stavros et al. 2007). This has implications for coaching psychology in a team or organizational context since team members who think strategically from a SOAR-based perspective are more likely to inquire into the team's/organization's positive strategic core. SOAR's positive approach embraces team and organizational diversity and leads to group changes based on images of the best possible future as articulated and visualized by the team and organization members (Cooperrider et al. 2008). When positive factors are given attention, individual and team performance tends to flourish (Fredrickson 2010). Kim Cameron's (2012) work in positive leadership suggests that this focus on positive outcomes leads to "thriving at work, interpersonal flourishing, virtuous behaviors, positive emotions, and energizing networks" (p. 2).

6 Conclusion

The aim of this chapter was to provide an overview of the potential efficacy of using the SOAR framework for coaching psychology. We began the chapter with a description of SOAR as a strengths-based framework for strategic thinking, planning, and leading that was developed from the theory and practice of AI and positive psychology. We then provided results of an empirical study in which SOAR differentially mediated the relationship between emotional intelligence and team-based collaboration in team leaders rather than team members. The contribution of the SOAR framework to coaching psychology is that SOAR has the potential to promote the positive effects of coaching through a whole system and inclusive approach based on strengths, opportunities, aspirations, and results.

References

Aiken, L. S., & West, S. G. (1991). *Multiple regression: Testing and interpreting interactions.* Newbury Park: Sage.

Aram, J. D., & Morgan, C. P. (1976). The role of project team collaboration in R&D performance. *Management Science, 22*(10), 1127–1137.

Baron, R. M., & Kenny, D. A. (1986). The moderator – Mediator variable distinction in social psychological research: Conceptual, strategic, and statistical considerations. *Journal of Personality and Social Psychology, 51*(6), 1173–1182.

Biswas-Diener, R. (2010). *Practicing positive psychology coaching: Assessment, activities, and strategies for success.* Hoboken: Wiley.

Brett, J., Behfar, K., & Kern, M. C. (2006). Managing multicultural teams. *Harvard Business Review, 84*(11), 89–96.

Bushe, G. R. (2007). Appreciative inquiry is not about the positive. *OD Practitioner, 39*(4), 33–38.

Bushe, G. R. (2013). Generative process, generative outcome: The transformational potential of appreciative inquiry. In D. L. Cooperrider, D. P. Zandee, L. N. Godwin, M. Avital, & B. Boland (Eds.), *Organizational generativity: The appreciative inquiry summit and a scholarship of transformation* (Vol. 4, pp. 89–113). Bingley: Emerald.

Cameron, K. (2012). *Positive leadership: Strategies for extraordinary performance*. San Francisco: Berrett-Koehler Publishers.

Cameron, K. (2013). *Practicing positive leadership*. San Francisco: Berrett-Koehler Publishers.

Cameron, K. S., & Spreitzer, G. (2012). Introduction: What is positive about positive organizational scholarship. In K. S. Cameron & G. Spreitzer (Eds.), *The Oxford handbook of positive organizational scholarship* (pp. 1–14). New York: Oxford University Press.

Cameron, K. S., Dutton, J. E., & Quinn, R. E. (2003). *Positive organizational scholarship: Foundations of a new discipline*. San Francisco: Berrett-Koehler.

Chen, W., Jacobs, R., & Spencer, L. M. (1998). Calculating the competencies of stars. In D. Goleman (Ed.), *Working with emotional intelligence* (pp. 377–380). New York: Bantam Books.

Cheung, G. W., & Lau, R. S. (2008). Testing mediation and suppression effects of latent variables: Bootstrapping with structural equation models. *Organizational Research Methods, 11*(2), 296–325.

Cole, M. L., & Stavros, J. M. (2013, March). *Creation of the SOAR Profile: An innovative tool to evaluate strategic thinking capacity*. Poster session presented at the meeting of Research Day 2013, Lawrence Technological University, Southfield.

Cole, M. L., & Stavros, J. M. (2014, April). *Psychometric properties of the SOAR Profile*. Paper session presented at Lawrence Tech Research Day 2014, Southfield.

Cooperrider, D., Whitney, D., & Stavros, J. (2008). *Appreciative inquiry handbook: For leaders of change*. Brunswick: Crown Custom Publishing.

Dawson, J. F. (2014). Moderation in management research: What, why, when and how. *Journal of Business and Psychology, 29*, 1–19.

Driver, M. (2011). *Coaching positively: Lessons for coaches from positive psychology*. Berkshire: Open University Press.

Dyer, G., & Dyer, J. (2010). Team building and the four Cs of team performance. In W. Rothwell, J. Stavros, R. Sullivan, & A. Sullivan (Eds.), *Practicing organization development: A guide for leading change* (pp. 329–344). San Francisco: Wiley, Jossey-Bass Publishers, Inc.

Earley, P. C., & Mosakowski, E. (2000). Creating hybrid team cultures: An empirical test of transnational team functioning. *Academy of Management Journal, 43*(1), 26–49.

Fredrickson, B. (2010). *Positivity: Groundbreaking research to release your inner optimist and thrive*. Oxford: Oneworld.

Goleman, D. (1998). The emotional intelligence of leaders. *Leader to Leader, 1998*(10), 20–26.

Goleman, D. (2000, March–April). Leadership that gets results. *Harvard Business Review, 78*(2), 78–90.

Goleman, D., Boyatzis, R., & McKee, A. (2002). The emotional reality of teams. *Journal of Organizational Excellence, 21*(2), 55–65.

Goleman, D., Boyatzis, R., & McKee, A. (2009). Primal leadership. *Leadership Excellence, 26*(10), 9–10.

Gratton, L., & Erickson, T. (2007). 8 ways to build collaborative teams. *Harvard Business Review, 85*(11), 100–109.

Hawkins, P. (2014). *Leadership team coaching: Developing collective transformational leadership* (2nd ed.). London: Kogan Page Limited.

Jordan, P. J., & Lawrence, S. A. (2009). Emotional intelligence in teams: Development and initial validation of the short version of the Workgroup Emotional Intelligence Profile (WEIP-S). *Journal of Management & Organization, 15*, 452–465.

Jordan, P. J., & Troth, A. C. (2004). Managing emotions during team problem solving: Emotional intelligence and conflict resolution. *Human Performance, 17*, 195–218.

Joshi, A., Lazarova, M. B., & Liao, H. (2009). Getting everyone on board: The role of inspirational leadership in geographically dispersed teams. *Organization Science, 20*(1), 240–252.

Katzenbach, J. R. (1998). *Teams at the top*. Boston: Harvard Business School Press.

Law, H. (2013). *The psychology of coaching, mentoring and learning* (2nd ed.). Oxford: Wiley.

Leung, K., Ang, S., & Tan, M. L. (2014). Intercultural competence. *The Annual Review of Organizational Psychology and Organizational Behavior, 1*, 489–519.

Linley, A. (2008). *Average to A+*. Coventry: CAPP Press.

Linley, P. A., & Harrington, S. (2006). Strengths coaching: A potential-guided approach to coaching psychology. *International Coaching Psychology Review, 1*(1), 37–46.

Lisak, A., & Erez, M. (2015). Leadership emergence in multicultural team: The power of global characteristics. *Journal of World Business, 50*, 3–14.

Mayer, J., & Salovey, P. (1997). What is emotional intelligence? In P. Salovey & D. Sluyter (Eds.), *Emotional development and emotional intelligence: Implications for educators* (pp. 3–31). New York: Basic Books.

Mayer, J., Salovey, P., & Caruso, D. (2004). Emotional intelligence: Theory, findings, and implications. *Psychological Inquiry, 15*(3), 197–215.

McClelland, D. (1998). Identifying competencies with behavioral-event interviews. *Psychological Science, 9*, 331–339.

Mosteo, L. P., Batista-Foguet, J. M, Mckeever, J. D., & Serlavós, R. (2016). Understanding cognitive-emotional processing through a coaching process: The influence of coaching on vision, goal-directed energy, and resilience. *The Journal of Applied Behavioral Science, 52*(1), 64–96.

Moukarzel, R., & Steelman, L. A. (2015). Navigating multicultural teams: A road map to feedback across cultures. In J. L. Wildman & R. L. Griffith (Eds.), *Leading global teams* (pp. 169–192). New York: Springer.

Neale, S., Spencer-Arnell, L., & Wilson, L. (2009). *Emotional intelligence coaching: Improving performance for leaders, coaches and the individual*. London: Kogan Page Limited.

Palmer, S., & Whybrow, A. (2005). The proposal to establish a Special Group in Coaching Psychology. *The Coaching Psychologist, 1*, 5–12.

Palmer, B., Walls, M., Burgess, Z., & Stough, C. (2001). Emotional intelligence and effective leadership. *Leadership and Organization Development Journal, 22*(1), 5–10.

Passmore, J., & Hain, D. (2005). Appreciative inquiry: Positive psychology for organizational change. *Selection and Development Review, 21*(5), 13–17.

Pescosolido, A. T. (2002). Emergent leaders as managers of group emotion. *The Leadership Quarterly, 13*, 583–599.

Pieterse, A. N., Van Knippenberg, D., & Van Dierendonch, D. (2013). Cultural diversity and team performance: The role of team member goal orientation. *Academy of Management Journal, 56*(3), 782–804.

Preacher, K. J., & Hayes, A. F. (2008). Asymptotic and resampling strategies for assessing and comparing indirect effects in multiple mediator models. *Behavior Research Methods, 40*(3), 879–891.

Rahim, M. A. (1983a). A measure of styles of handling interpersonal conflict. *Academy of Management Journal, 26*, 368–376.

Rahim, M. A. (1983b). *Rahim organizational conflict inventory—II: Forms A, B, and C*. Palo Alto: Consulting Psychologists Press.

Romero, D., Galeano, N., & Molina, A. (2009). Mechanisms for assessing and enhancing organizations' readiness for collaboration in collaborative networks. *International Journal of Production Research, 47*(17), 4691–4710.

Rosinski, P. (2003). *Coaching across cultures*. London: Nicholas Brealey.

Sarin, S., & McDermott, C. (2003). The effect of team leader characteristics on learning, knowledge application, and performance of cross-functional new product development teams. *Decision Sciences, 34*(4), 707–739.

Seligman, M. E. P. (2003). *Authentic happiness*. London: Nicholas Brealey.

Seligman, M. E. P. (2011). *Flourish: A visionary new understanding of happiness and well-being*. New York: ATRIA Paperback – A Division of Simon and Schuster, Inc.

Seligman, M. E. P., & Csikszentmihalyi, M. (2000). Positive psychology: An introduction. *American Psychologist, 55*, 5–14.

Seligman, M. E. P., Steen, T. A., Park, N., & Peterson, C. (2005). Positive psychology progress: Empirical validation of interventions. *American Psychologist, 60*(5), 410–21.

Shaw, L., & Lindsay, R. (2008). Renewing focus and building capacity for enacting authentic collaboration in work rehabilitation. *Work, 30*, 215–218.

Simons, T., Pelled, L. H., & Smith, K. A. (1999). Making use of difference: Diversity, debate, and decision comprehensiveness in top management teams. *Academy of Management Journal, 42*, 662–673.

Stavros, J. M. (2013). The generative nature of SOAR: Applications, results, and the new SOAR profile. *AI Practitioner: International Journal of Appreciative Inquiry, 15*(3), 6–26.

Stavros, J. M., & Cole, M. L. (2013). SOARing towards positive transformation and change. The ABAC ODI. *Visions Action Outcome, 1*(1), 10–34.

Stavros, J. M., & Hinrichs, G. (2009). *Thin book of SOAR: Building strengths-based strategy*. Bend: Thin Book Publishing.

Stavros, J. M., & Saint, D. (2010). SOAR: Linking strategy and OD to sustainable performance. In W. Rothwell, J. Stavros, R. Sullivan, & A. Sullivan (Eds.), *Practicing organization development: A guide for leading change* (3rd ed., pp. 377–394). San Francisco: Jossey-Bass.

Stavros, J. M., & Wooten, L. (2012). Positive strategy: Creating and sustaining strengths-based strategy that SOARs and performs. In K. Cameron & G. Spreitzer (Eds.), *The Oxford handbook of positive organizational scholarship* (pp. 825–842). Oxford: Oxford University Press.

Stavros, J., Cooperrider, D., & Kelley, L. (2003). *Strategic inquiry—Appreciative intent: Inspiration to SOAR*. AI Practitioner, November, 2–19.

Stavros, J. M., Cooperrider, D., & Kelley, L. (2007). SOAR: A new approach to strategic planning. In P. Homan, T. Devane, & S. Cady (Eds.), *The change handbook: The definitive resource on today's best methods for engaging whole systems* (2nd ed., pp. 375–380). San Francisco: Berrett-Koehler Publishers.

Stout-Rostron, S. (2014). *Business coaching international: Transforming individuals and organizations* (2nd ed.). London: Karnac Books Ltd.

Van Zyl, L. E., & Stander, M. W. (2013). A strengths-based approach towards coaching in a multicultural environment. In J. H. D. Cornelius-White, R. Motschnig-Pitrik, & M. Lux (Eds.), *Interdisciplinary handbook of the person-centered approach* (pp. 245–257). New York: Springer.

Watkins, J. M., & Cooperrider, D. (2000). Appreciative inquiry: A transformative paradigm. *OD Practitioner, 32*(1), 6–12.

Wolff, S. B., Pescosolido, A. T., & Druskat, V. U. (2002). Emotional intelligence as the basis of leadership emergence in self-managing work teams. *Leadership Quarterly, 13*, 505–522.

Xavier, S. (2005). Are you at the top of your game? Checklist for effective leaders. *Journal of Business Strategy, 28*(3), 35–42.

Zaccaro, S. J., Rittman, A. L., & Marks, M. A. (2001). Team leadership. *Leadership Quarterly, 12*, 451–483.

Zeidner, M., Roberts, R. D., & Matthews, G. (2008). The science of emotional intelligence: Current consensus and controversies. *European Psychologist, 13*(1), 64–78.

Strength Coaching as an Enabler of Positive Athlete Outcomes in a Multi-cultural Sport Environment

Frederick Wilhelm Stander

Abstract The purpose of this chapter is to introduce the reader to a practical strengths based coaching model that can effectively be applied within the context of sport. The chapter is divided into four broad sections. Firstly, an overview of literature is provided pertaining to strength based coaching in sport, contextualised within the framework of Positive Psychology. Secondly, a practical model is proposed for application, drawing from an established model developed by Van Zyl and Stander (The strength based coaching model. In White J, Motching R, Lux M (eds) Theory and practice of the person-centered approach – interconnections beyond psychotherapy. Springer, New York, 2013). Thirdly, the applicability of this model within a multicultural sport environment is put forward. Finally, the author shares a practical case study, drawing from own professional experience, to illustrate the model.

Keywords Sport psychology • Strengths-based coaching • Strengths • Coaching

1 Introduction

1.1 *The Strength Based Approach in Positive Psychology*

With the introduction of Positive Psychology, a new approach has emerged in both academic literature and practice whereby the virtues, potentialities and areas of strengths of individuals have been recognized and developed through intervention (Linley et al. 2006; Seligman and Csikszentmihalyi 2000). This offers a supplementary view on the development of human potential and functioning that has, in the realm of the traditional Psychology at least, long been inclined to identify areas of deficiency, flaw or even abnormality as a first step towards bettering and rectifying

Author would like to acknowledge the Kaizer Chiefs Centre of Innovation Knowledge Project.

F.W. Stander (✉)
Department of Industrial Psychology, Optentia Research Focus Area, North-West University, Vaal Triangle Campus, Vanderbijlpark, South Africa
e-mail: ederick.stander@nwu.ac.za

L.E. van Zyl et al. (eds.), *Coaching Psychology: Meta-theoretical perspectives and applications in multicultural contexts*, DOI 10.1007/978-3-319-31012-1_13

these areas (Cravens et al. 2010). Buckingham and Clifton (2001) were part of early efforts to capture in description which has since become known as the Strength Based Approach (SBA). Compton (2005) has described this approach, emanating directly from the Positive Psychology, simply as an effort towards understanding what people excel at and then developing those areas. Linley and Harrington (2006) describes a "strength" as an inherent capacity of an individual, originating from a particular way of thinking, acting or feeling, unique to an individual; that energizes – and assists that person to perform at an optimum level and more readily achieve goals. Kaiser and White (2009) view the SBA as essential in realising the optimum potential of human beings.

1.2 Strength Based Coaching

The application of a SBA in coaching has been described by Linley and Harrington (2006) as an approach whereby the focus is on "human potential and positive client attributes as the foundation stones of any success. While it is recognized that the identification and understanding of problems and obstacles can be important, this is counterbalanced with an equal, if not greater recognition that the identification of, and playing to, clients' strengths is the goal that should guide both assessment and intervention" (p. 42). Strength based coaching refers to the identification, application and optimization of strengths through facilitative intervention aimed at enhancing well-being and increasing performance (Van Zyl and Stander 2013). In industry and academia, a SBA in coaching has been associated with various positive outcomes. MacKie (2014) established strength based coaching of executives in a large non-profit organization enhanced the extent of transformational leadership behaviours displayed by these leaders. The approach has been associated with the enhanced professional development of female entrepreneurs in Europe (Stavropoulou and Protopapa 2013). Govindji and Linley (2007) found correlation between strength based coaching and psychological well-being of graduate students.

1.3 Strength Based Coaching in Sport

Interestingly, whereas SBA in coaching in industry is still relatively new as an approach, it has long been serving the sporting community in assisting athletes to achieve levels of optimum performance (Linley and Harrington 2006). In fact, it is reported that strength based coaching as method can be largely attributed to the practice of Psychology in sport (Noble et al. 2000). This is because the athletic environment is concerned with optimal human functioning in a perpetual pursuit to gain a competitive advantage and perform at the highest possible level. Coaches and administrators are consistently looking towards creation of platforms for better performance and enable the development of athletes' strengths through psychological intervention as a means to achieve such performance (Sarkar and Fletcher 2013). This is in stark contrast to traditional training and development approaches that focus only on the deficiencies of people and address those shortcomings (Clifton and Harter 2003).

To highlight the potential value of a SBA in sport, the author conducted a study amongst 235 multicultural (individuals from various backgrounds pertaining to race, language and ethnicity) South African student football – and rugby players to investigate the role of a strength based developmental team climate and individual pro-active orientation towards strength development; both constructs measured through the Strength Use and Deficit Improvement Questionnaire (*SUDIQ*: Van Woerkom et al. in press), to predict personal and sport related outcomes of the participants. Personal outcomes included self-efficacy, measured through the generalised self-efficacy scale (Judge et al. 1998); as well as flourishing, comprising of emotional -, social- and psychological well-being and measured through the Mental Health Continuum Short Form (*MHC-SF*; Keyes 2009); here postulated as a one-factor construct. Sport related outcomes included athlete flow, known popularly as "being in the zone", measured through the Flow State Scale-2 (*FSS-2*; Jackson and Eklund 2002); as well as athlete engagement, measured through the Athlete Engagement Questionnaire (*AEQ*; Lonsdale et al. 2007). Structural equation modelling methods were applied by utilising the Mplus 7.2 programme (Muthén and Muthén 2014). Results are presented in Table 1 below.

The results above support for the use of a SBA in the context of developing athletes to achieve favourable personal and sport related outcomes. This was done amongst a multi-cultural sample of student athletes participating in South Africa's two premier sports, football and rugby; both team sports. Firstly, the effect of team strength use (TSU) was investigated. TSU has been described by Van Woerkom et al. (in press) as an approach where an organization (sport team) utilises policies, procedures and approaches that acknowledge and play to the strengths of its members. Stander and Mostert (2013) describe TSU as a culture of strength use that

Table 1 Team – and proactive individual strength use as a source of personal – and sport related outcomes

Regression relationships	β	S.E.	*P*	Result
Team strength use (TSU)				
TSU → self-efficacy	0.07	0.09	0.447	Not significant
TSU → flourishing	0.37	0.07	0.000	Significant
TSU → flow	0.31	0.08	0.000	Significant
TSU → athlete Engagement	0.07	0.07	0.348	Not significant
Proactive individual strength use (ISU)				
ISU → self-efficacy	0.42	0.08	0.000	Significant
ISU → flourishing	0.20	0.07	0.003	Significant
ISU → flow	0.41	0.08	0.000	Significant
ISU → athlete engagement	0.64	0.07	0.000	Significant

All two-tailed p-values ≤0.01

β Beta coefficient, *S.E.* Standard error, p Two-tailed statistical significance is perceived by an organization's members, in this case the players on the team. TSU is considered a job resource that assists individuals in attaining goals (Jackson et al. 2006; Karatepe 2009; Rothmann et al. 2006; Saks 2006; Stander et al. 2014). In the study above, TSU predicted flourishing of athletes, on a personal level, as well as athlete flow from the perspective of the athlete's sport specifically. Following this, the effect of proactive individual strength use (ISU) was explored. ISU is described by Stander et al. (2014) as an individual's inherent inclination to proactively develop his/her areas of strengths to attain goals. It represents a personal predisposition whereby the individual is willing to actively capitalize on his/her virtues and seek ways to develop these virtues. The results outlined above revealed that ISU predicted both favourable personal – (self-efficacy and flourishing) as well as sport related (flow and athlete engagement) outcomes.

From the perspective of coaching specifically, the results proved intriguing. Coaching is a facilitative process aimed at the development of the individual (Van Zyl and Stander 2013). It therefore would be targeted through addressing such individual's capacity for self-development through ISU within a SBA. On the other hand TSU represents a broader culture or team environment conducive towards strength use of its members. In the context of this study, ISU, which would be a key end result of an individual strength based coaching approach, was suggested as a predictor of more positive personal and sport related outcomes than TSU, supporting the premise that strength based coaching has and can be applied with value in the

Table 2 Studies in sport linking SBA coaching through mental skills training and individual developmental intervention to positive athlete outcomes

Author(s)	Key points
Gordon (2012)	Individual and small group coaching of strengths to enhance mental toughness and performance of Sri Lankan national cricket players
Gordon and Gucciardi (2011)	Adopting strength based coaching approach to enhance levels of displayed mental toughness of professional cricket players
Golby and Sheard (2004)	Advocates for individualized psychological skills training towards hardiness levels of professional rugby league players as a way to ameliorate sport performance
Durand-Bush and Salmela (2002)	Strength based coaching through mental skill training approach where positive self-talk, imagery of athlete unique skill set before competition and elaborate cognitive processes to understand the competitive environment and how the individual athlete can be most effective in such environment correlated to peak performance of Olympic and/or World Championship athletes
Gould et al. (2002)	Coaching and enhancing the psychological virtues of the individual athlete as a means of ensuring elite athletes can achieve Olympic success during competition
Dale (2000)	Coaching towards reinforcing the positive results obtained through excessive preparatory training as a means of achieving greater focus and subsequent performance amongst elite decathlon athletes
Stander et al. (in press)	Suggests individual strength based coaching as developmental intervention based on correlations established between SBA, flow and athlete engagement of student football- and rugby players

athletic environment. A number of studies within the domain of sport have established positive outcomes by adapting a SBA to coaching through mental skills training and individual developmental intervention. A summary of some of these studies are presented above (Table 2).

2 A Strength Based Coaching Model for Sport

A gap in the literature exists concerning the development of a methodical strength based coaching model that can fruitfully be applied within the sport context. This is despite the availability of extensive literature that has linked strength based coaching to positive outcomes amongst athletes. Establishing a model for strength based coaching will assist practitioners to have a frame of reference for the processes required to conduct a strength based coaching approach in sport, and will stimulate academic investigation for scrutiny and in-depth understanding of such processes.

A number of authors have proposed SBA in structured format pertaining to coaching of athletes. Examples include Gordon and Gucciardi (2011), who have outlined a valuable approach to appreciative coaching questions called the AI (Appreciative Inquiry) 4-D Cycle. This cycle explains a process of appreciative inquiry through strength based coaching questions categorized in four phases. Firstly, the athlete is guided in a process of "discovery". This entails examining the attitude and predisposition of the athlete at that time. Examples of questions during this stage include "Describe what you consider self-belief to be". The goal is to formulate a framework of what the envisioned strength based construct means in an ideal state from the perspective of the athlete. Secondly, the coach enters into a phase known as "dream". The athlete is encouraged to think about what this ideal state means to him/her on a practical level. A question could be "When you woke up your self-belief was just as you described above. How would you know?" – and "What would be different than before in your life?". Following the dream phase, the coach enters the "design" phase of the process. During this phase, the coach facilitates a progression where the athlete must develop an action plan to achieve the ideal state identified and elaborated upon during the first two phases of the process. A question can be "How will you act differently to make the dream a reality?". Finally, a phase of "Delivery" is entered into with the athlete. Here, behaviours are examined that the athlete can immediately exhibit in order to achieve the ideal state outlined. A question in this instance could be "What are the behavioural changes you must make to help you get what you want?". By immediately incorporating these behaviours, the athlete starts to actively embody the ideal state described above. This model has been proved effective in a number of studies amongst professional cricketers.

In another study, Behncke (2004) proposes a five stage model for incorporating a SBA in coaching. Firstly, a particular issue must be identified that the athlete needs to work on. Secondly, the athlete must make a firm commitment to positively address that issue. The third step relates to execution, whereby, as with Gordon and

Gucciardi's (2011) phase of delivery, positive behaviours must be exhibited by the athlete to achieve a desired end result. Fourthly, the environment must be considered and the athlete must utilize his/her strengths to actively manage with and flourish in the reality of his/her environment. Finally, generalization of strengths and new behaviours must occur. The athlete must internalize the process and make it part of his/her daily functioning in the sporting environment.

Although both the approaches outlined above provides a logical and useful structure, it is important to consolidate SBA in a coaching model that can effectively deliver results; particularly in the sport environment. To this end, the strength-based coaching model of Van Zyl and Stander (2013) provides a great platform. This model, developed through a meta-theoretical literature review, adopts an eco-systemic view of human nature, incorporating positive psychology, psycho-existentialism and the person-centred approach to achieve what Seligman (2011) has referred to as sustainable positive change of behaviour. It is these sustainable positive behaviours that are required for an athlete to (a) achieve longitudinal success in his/her sport endeavours (b) be able to perform consistently at an optimum level and (c) progress successfully from one competitive level to the next. From this perspective, an outline of the model of Van Zyl and Stander (2013) is offered below, focusing specifically on the athlete within the sporting environment. This model can be applied to both individual – and team sports.

2.1 Phase 1: Clarifying Expectations and Establishing Rapport

Van Zyl and Stander (2013) describe this phase as one in which absolute clarity on the purpose of coaching must be obtained between the coach and coachee, case in question the athlete. These authors elaborate by stating that this phase is known for the establishment of rapport; where the line manager (the actual operational sport coach within the domain of the athlete) must be involved in the process. Biswas-Diener (2010) describes this involvement as critical to lay the foundation for the entire coaching process. Gucciardi and Gordon (2009) argue that the athlete must be actively engaged and that a clear framework must be discussed. Van Zyl and Stander (2013) propose the SOLER model of Egan (2007) to achieve this rapport. This model recommend five practical techniques to engage the coachee into the coaching process, namely facing the coachee squarely, displaying body language that can be considered open and inviting, leaning towards the coachee to display interest, ensuring eye-contact is made and relaxing as to ensure a comforting climate is created for the coaching process. It must be said that this first phase is particularly important in the realm of sport; an environment that is highly structured on goal pursuits from athletes, albeit to promote such athlete from one level of competition to the next, or mastering a specific skill that will enhance the athletic competence of the participant. It is particularly true of elite athletes, where this process of clarifying expectations and establishing rapport will form part of their imagery process as a path towards envisioning the desired end-result (Mahoney and Avener 1977).

During this phase the coach must guide the athlete to explore such questions as:

- Why are we here?
- What do we hope to achieve?
- How will we go about this process?
- Do we know exactly what our end-result will look like?

The purpose of these questions is to obtain clarity in the outcomes sought through the process. The athlete must also be set at ease during this phase and be educated on the positive inclination and strength based focus of the coaching to follow. Many athletes still consider psychological process, coaching – or any developmental performance intervention as an indication of mental ill health, flaw or weakness on their part (Acharya 2010). Gee (2010, p. 386) has stated that "the unfamiliar and often esoteric nature of sport psychology appears to be impeding a large number of athletes from soliciting these important services". This can also be true of coaching in the realm of sport and hence it is very important to establish rapport with the athlete en route to an understanding by such athlete that the coaching process is aimed at a positive personal development goal or an increased performance or competence achievement. Also, with the goal directedness of athletes in mind, it will be useful to clearly document the coaching process as to harness a complete understanding over the structure of the coaching with the athlete. Here, a logbook can serve as a useful practical tool, or structuring coaching sessions in a manner that will assist the athlete with obtaining routine, such as having coaching sessions on the same time every week, or after specific events in the training regime of the athlete. This will assist the coach and coachee to regularly revisit expectations (Van Zyl and Stander 2013).

2.2 *Phase 2: Identifying and Marrying Conscious and Unconscious Strengths*

Once expectations have been clarified and rapport established, it is important to investigate the unique strengths of the athlete. This can be related to the discovery phase of Gordon and Gucciardi (2011), because often athletes will be oblivious to their unique potentialities, aspects that assist them to (a) more readily achieve their athletic goals, (b) derive greater purpose and enjoyment from their sport and (c) contribute more to their team in the case of team sport. The process of identification must be conducted through two distinct processes.

Firstly, purposeful appreciative inquiry must be conducted with the athlete through a dynamic process of conversation. Kihl et al. (2010) outline the importance of this process as stakeholder construction, as the athlete must be guided on a route of self-discovery by the coach. Important consideration must be given here to the unique circumstances of the athlete and this must be investigated on a practical level. From an individual perspective, the athlete can be probed on past experiences in his/ her sport where the athlete's unique strengths assisted him/ her to successfully reach a goal. This can be related to a competency based evaluation as proposed in the original model of Van Zyl and Stander (2013). For example, through the inquiry process, the coach may establish that, in past successes, it was the athlete's steady resolve and ability to persevere that led to such athlete being successful. This represents an important competency of the successful athlete and can now be further developed through the coaching process. Whitney and Trosten-Bloom (2003) state this appreciative inquiry process focuses on the individual's strengths as opposed to his/her shortcomings. Further, from a team perspective, the unique strengths and offerings of the athlete must also be explored. Often in team sport, informal roles are crucial to achieve success (Cope et al. 2011). Consider for example the national rugby team of South Africa, the Springboks, in their quest to claim the Rugby World Cup in France in 2007. It has been widely documented that a critical part of this team's success during this tournament was due to clarity on the unique roles (strengths) of every team member. For example, a large portion of the squad was senior players and thus had the ability to calm the team and provide leadership during critical stages of the competition, both on and off the field. These unique roles and strengths are as important as functional roles and a good understanding of them is a sign of a mature team (Cope et al. 2011). During the strength based coaching process these roles must be explored with the athlete.

Secondly, after appreciative inquiry, psychometric evaluation can assist in the exploration phase of the athlete's strengths. According to Bachkirova (2011) this is important to gather an objective account of the virtues and potentialities of the athlete. A number of strength identification measures are available to the coach, such as the Values in Action (VIA) questionnaire (Peterson and Seligman 2004), the Clifton StrengthFinder 2.0 (Rath 2002) and the Realise 2 (Linley et al. 2010). It is accepted here that the coach is a registered professional and have the required accreditation to conduct the chosen measure. By conducting the two processes highlighted above, a good understanding and rationale comparison of the conscious and unconscious strengths of the athlete can be conducted. This will assist to incorporate these strengths with the competency arsenal of the athlete (Seligman 2011).

2.3 Phase 3: Identifying Coaching Themes

Behncke (2004) states that absolute clarity must be obtained in the core issue that the athlete wishes to address. This is the starting block for the athlete. Here it is important to distinguish between functional- and developmental themes. For example, consider a golfer. Through the information obtained in phase 2 of the coaching model, it may have emerged that this particular golfer possesses the strength of courage. This strength can assist such golfer from a functional perspective, i.e. being willing to execute risky and difficult shots on the course; but also from a personal developmental context, where this virtue can assist this individual to pursue difficult and challenging tasks in the process of self-growth. The challenge of this phase of the coaching model is to effectively identify themes and group them into the categories outlined above. This will become the themes of focus during the coaching process. It evolves the coachee's understanding of his/her strengths towards a mental space where he/she can actually develop strategies to utilize these strengths effectively to address the core issues identified during this phase of the process (Seligman 2011). A good practical tool in this phase can be the design of a developmental booklet, or personal development plan (Bachkirova 2011), wherein the coaching themes are clearly articulated and which the coach and athlete can utilise as a guide in the developmental process.

2.4 Phase 4: Encouraging, Deriving Meaning, Self-Efficacy and Installing Hope

A successful sporting environment is characterized by a positive climate of encouragement (Turnnidge et al. 2014). This is also true of the climate for the strength based coaching process with the individual athlete. This phase is critical in ensuring the athlete makes the transition from awareness towards action planning. Van Zyl and Stander (2013) comment that this phase is the driver of the development of inherent potential of the coachee; and that the coach must actively encourage the athlete to utilize his/her strengths so as to derive meaning from the athletic activity and to reach sporting goals. This relates to the identification of behaviours that will embody the strengths of the athlete and thus becomes a vehicle for the athlete to realize goals (Lyubomirsky 2011). The focus here is behaviours, specifically because this can support thought-action repertoires of positive reinforcement as advocated for through the broaden-and-built theory of Frederickson (2002). When the past utilization of strength behaviours and subsequent athletic successes of the athlete is identified, confidence can be derived that this causality can be repeated and the self-efficacy of the athlete will be bolstered. Self-efficacy refers to the athlete's inherent belief that he/she can successfully reach a goal or navigate a challenge (Luszczynska et al. 2005). Barker et al. (2013, p. 228) have pronounced self-efficacy as "one of the most important psychological variables associated with sport performance". Finally during this phase, a process must be undergone where the coach attempts to, with the athlete, cultivate hope by investigating past events of achieved goals in an effort to raise optimism that such feats can be repeated in future (Seligman 2011).

2.5 Phase 5: Framing Solutions

Van Zyl and Stander (2013) specify this phase as the one during which goals must be set with the athlete and propose the model of Doran (1981) as a good guideline for such goal development. This model ascertains that goals must be specific, measurable, attainable, realistic and time-bound. In the model of Gordon and Gucciardi (2011), this is referred to as the "design" phase. In the context of sport, clear, unambiguous goals are critical towards the athlete's ability to be successful (Locke and Latham 1985). Therefore, goals must be articulated in a way that is easy to understand and will facilitate a clear understanding with the athlete; providing a frame of reference for the developmental process. Goals should also be ambitious and should stretch the athlete (Locke and Latham 1985). This is particularly true if one of the outcomes sought from the coaching process is increased performance. This phase of the strength based coaching model provides the coach and coachee with the opportunity to consolidate and explore how the identified strengths of earlier parts of the model can now be married with the set goals. It informs a clear action plan that the athlete can implement. Van Zyl and Stander (2013) remark that it may be required to also consider the developmental areas of the athlete during this phase of the coaching process so as to ensure that these areas of deficit do not derail the athlete and subsequently the strength based development process.

2.6 Phase 6: Building Strengths and Competencies

From the perspective of sport, this phase of the model can be viewed as the intervention activation phase. It is the phase that must assist the athlete to identify and start enabling working mechanisms that will allow the strengths and potentialities vested within to come alive and lead to positive outcomes (Lyubomirsky 2011). With regards to this, Meichenbaum (1985) has proposed a valuable practical model. The model is built on three stages, namely the educational stage, the acquisition stage and the practice stage. Viewing the strength based model of coaching, education must really be achieved through phase 2 and phase 3 of the model, which entails exploration of the strengths of the athletes and linking this to coaching themes. The acquisition stage encapsulates phases 4 and 5 of the strength based model, where a process of broaden-and-build (Frederickson 2002) and positively inclined thought-action repertoires; as well as ambitious and positively stated desired outcomes will set the athlete up to enter the positive state of mind.

The third stage of Meichenbaum's model, however, is of particular interest to assist the athlete in building strengths and competencies. The practice stage implies that the athlete should execute practical steps to build on strengths. This is particularly useful if increased performance was a desired outcome established; because, in the context of sport, a great platform is available for practising strengths. The author off course refers to the sport training ground here. The training ground must be used as a resource to practice the strengths of the athlete. Drawing from the earlier example of the golfer with the character strength of courage, interventions must be sought that can assist such golfer to "practice" this strength on the training pitch in order for it to be effectively translated into competition. For example, the courageous golfer can draw from his virtue on the training ground by deliberately practising trick- and difficult shots; and placing himself in simulated scenarios where he would need to execute on his character strength of courage. In a competitive environment, this strength will then come more naturally to the athlete, and will assist him to be more effective and use such strength to his advantage. It allows the mental processes of the strength based coaching model to form a systemic methodology and hence should promote performance excellence (Holliday et al. 2008). Beauchamp et al. (2012) have incorporated Meichenbaum's practice stage successfully as part of a psychological skills programme to enhance performance outcomes of Canadian Olympic Short-Track speed skaters and encourage the use of an activity log-book to capture the proposed interventions of the phase. During this phase of the strength based coaching model it is critical to follow an approach of unconditional positive regard towards the coachee (Van Zyl and Stander 2013). The coach should not enforce any interventions onto the athlete, but rather facilitate with him/her interventions with which the athlete is comfortable and which are preferred by such athlete.

2.7 *Phase 7: Empowerment*

Seligman (2011) states that empowerment is informed by the needs of the coachee as well as the environmental context in which such coachee resides. The empowerment phase calls for a mind-set geared towards teamwork, trust and collaboration between coach and athlete (Beauchamp et al. 2012). The empowerment phase expands on building strengths and competencies and is a deliberate effort to internalize these as personal resources to the athlete. From the perspective of the well-established model of the job demands-resources (JD-R) theory, personal resources include those inherent capitals that assist the individual to negotiate the challenges of his/her environment to achieve desired personal, work-related, or in the case of athletes, sport outcomes (Van den Heuvel et al. 2010). The empowerment phase is therefore an important one on the path of ensuring the strength based coaching process delivers sustainable results for the athlete. Thus, the golfer alluded to earlier will institutionalize his virtue of courage into every aspect of his relating to, functioning in and successfully operating of his game. This is vital according to Spreitzer (1995); as empowerment entails meaning, competence and control of the individual over his/her environment.

2.8 *Phase 8: Reframing*

The phase of reframing is focused on changing, enhancing and internalizing behavioural patterns (Van Zyl and Stander 2013). Mistakes must be viewed as learning opportunities (Hawkins and Smith 2007). As in line with the positive psychology, however, the strength based model implies focusing on potentialities rather on dwelling over such mistakes (Wood et al. 2011). The athlete must draw on the strengths that are now clear to him/her, internalize such strengths and now aim to translate such into behaviours. These behaviours must be aimed towards achieving gradually more difficult and pressing goals; systemically taking up a greater challenge and drawing from the strengths to make the step up to greater levels of success (Van Zyl and Stander 2013). On a practical level, the athlete can utilize this for functional competence; first during a training session, then towards a competitive scenario such as a game, then towards events of higher importance such as competition finals and ultimately towards a space where this athlete can utilise his/her strengths for sustained successes such as in tournaments and across seasons. This will assist in laying the foundation for the next phase, which is building resilience.

2.9 Phase 9: Building Sustainable Resilience

The strength based coaching model lays the foundation for sustainable resilience through what is known as the broaden-and-build theory of Frederickson (2002). This theory implies that the experience of positive emotions, facilitated through the positive framework of utilizing strengths, will expand the perspective and repertoire of thoughts and behaviours of the athlete, in turn building personal resources and ultimately transforming that athlete into a state of sustainable well-being. This is illustrated through the figure below (Fig. 1).

The below process (Fig. 1) must be facilitated by the coach with the athlete. It can be done by optimizing experiences, both positive and negative, drawing learning from mistakes and optimizing strengths to achieve desired results (Van Zyl and Stander 2013).

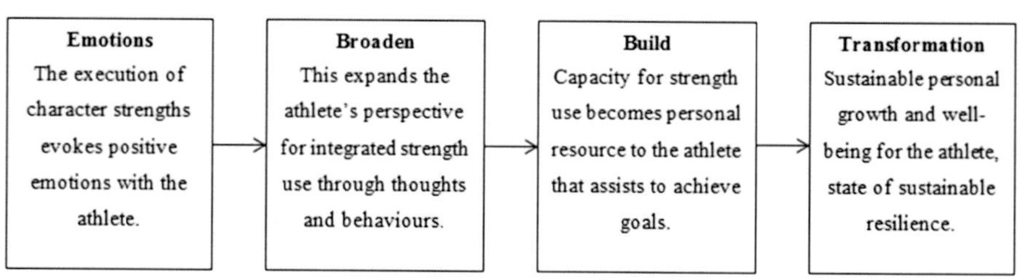

Fig. 1 How the strength based coaching model facilitates sustainable resilience through the premise of the broaden-and-build theory (Frederickson 2002)

2.10 Phase 10: Evaluating and Re-contracting the Relationship

This phase is concerned with evaluating the effectiveness of the process and to ask critical questions around whether the expectations that were set out during phase 1 of the model were met. It is also important to prepare the athlete that the coaching process is drawing to a close (Van Zyl and Stander 2013). The actual sport coach of the athlete must also be engaged during this phase as an evaluation is made over the success of the coaching process. This must also be incorporated throughout the coaching process. If there is a need for further coaching, this must be negotiated between the coach and coachee.

The strength based coaching model is depicted below (Fig. 2).

3 Coaching in a Multi-cultural Sports Environment

The domain of sport is one that is particularly diverse. Doherty and Chelladurai (2008) state that cultural differences of participants in sport are profound; and that sport represents a context where such diversity provides a platform to utilize such

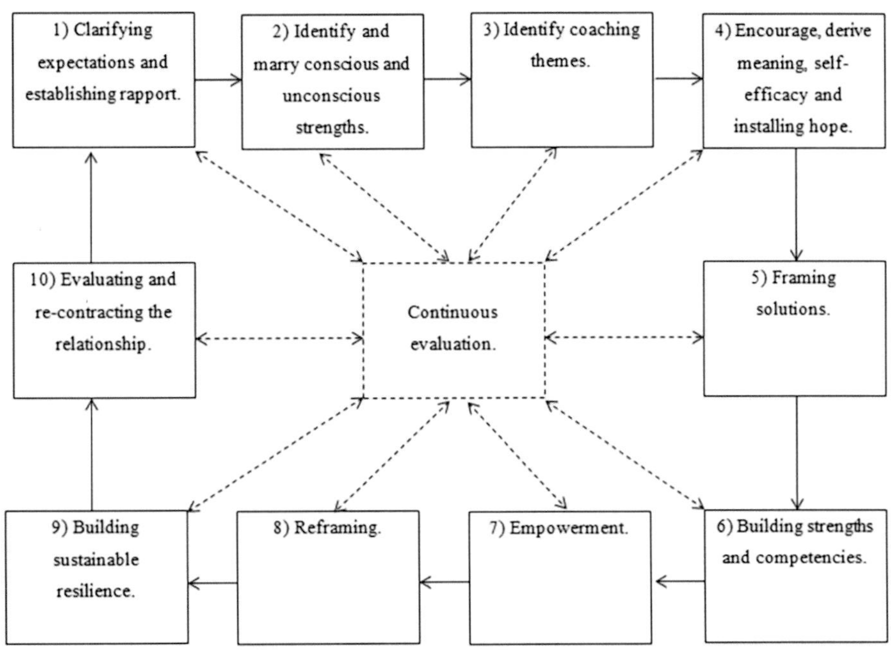

Fig. 2 The strength based coaching model (Van Zyl and Stander 2013)

diversity effectively, for example towards constructive conflict and creativity. Sport also has the ability to act as a powerful mobilizer for social redress, development and growth, transforming cultural diversity from a barrier to something of great value (Cornellisen et al. 2011). It has the ability to illuminate social ills and acts as a unifying force particularly because of its generic and universal appeal; both from the perspective of consumption of and participation in sport (Parry 2006). This is particularly true in South Africa, where sport has played a powerful role in eradicating racial and cultural divide between people (Cornellisen 2007). Consider for example the social value of such events as the 1995 IRB Rugby World Cup and the 2010 FIFA World Cup, both global tournaments that were hosted on South African soil. It is the universal appeal of sport that draws multicultural and diverse participants and hence sport has been identified as a strategic asset by government to build social cohesion (Department of Sport and Recreation 2011).

Because of the multi-cultural nature of sport and sport participation, the coach must be well equipped to deal with and be effective within this diverse environment. To assist the coach who wishes to apply the strength based coaching model with athletes, the work of Cooper et al. (2008) serves as a valuable resource in a multi-cultural environment. These authors have identified seven key themes that are of importance when consulting or coaching in a multi-cultural context. Four of these themes are directly related to the strength based coaching model and hence elaborated upon below:

3.1 Theme 1: Culture, Race and Ethnicity Matters

According to Cooper et al. (2008) culture, race and ethnic differences are very much a reality and dynamic of the coaching process and as such must be acknowledged from the onset of the engagement. Further, it is the responsibility of the coach to raise this with the coachee (Cooper et al. 2008). In the experience of the author, these multi-cultural factors must certainly be tabled and discussed between coach and athlete as it can be an invaluable tool to unlock the value of the strength based approach in particular. Consider for example the use of music in the coaching process, a tool that has long formed part of the psychological performance context of athletes and has been deliberately positioned alongside the strength based approach (Terry and Karageorghis 2006). Clearly, a generic approach to music will not suffice. The unique culture and reality of the athlete must be explored. Also, strengths and the perception of strengths may be different from one cultural group to another. The coach must acknowledge this, be sensitive thereto and explore the potential value thereof with the athlete in a manner that is natural and authentic.

3.2 *Theme 2: Use of Language Between the Coach and Coachee May Be a Challenge or an Issue When Diversity Is Greater*

Within the context of South Africa, where 11 official languages exist, this is a particularly relevant challenge that can hinder the strength based coaching process if not negotiated from the onset. Language barriers may lead to breaks in communication (Foxcroft 2004). In South Africa, it is quite often the case that both the coach and the coachee will communicate in a language that is not of their mother tongue. The challenge here is to decide on the method of communication early in the strength based coaching model, during the phase of clarifying expectations and establishing rapport. This communication must also seek clarity on language that are to be used during practical interventions of the coaching process, such as the activity – or log book (Van Zyl and Stander 2013).

3.3 *Theme 3: It Is Best to Bring Up Differences of Culture, Race, and Ethnicity Directly and into the Open*

As argued to by Cooper et al. (2008), acknowledgement of differences is a critical first step of setting up the coaching relationship. It is important to understand that the strength based coaching process that is embarked upon with the athlete represents a deeply personal journey and is an outcome-driven but also a self-exploratory intervention (Van Zyl and Stander 2013). Hence it is important to speak frankly about differences of culture, race and ethnicity at the onset of the coaching process, as to ensure these differences do not become derailing later on. It may take longer to foster trust between the coach and coachee when cultural differences exist, but this must not discourage the coach to invest proper effort in establishing proper rapport with the athlete (Cooper et al. 2008).

3.4 *Theme 4: Combining an Emic (Universal), Etic (Group), and Unique (Person) Approach to Coaching Is Recommended*

This is particularly relevant to sport, where athletes operate within contexts and have unique roles, either within their functional environment or, as in the case of team sport, their sport team (Cope et al. 2011). From the perspective of the strength based coaching model, it is important to follow the generic approach of establishing strengths, but this must be investigated with regards to the unique context of the athlete's environment and with special attention to the unique athlete at hand, albeit his/her culture, ethnicity or language. This ensures that the strength based coaching process is robust and unlocks the value it intends to.

4 Case Study

As a means of illustrating the above model, the author provides a practical frame of reference with the coaching of a young football striker of a professional club youth academy. A summarized overview of the process is provided. Only one coaching theme is outlined for illustrative purposes.

Bongani[1]*is a talented football striker from rural Eastern Cape who secured a contract at a major football club in one of the country's metropolises, far from his place of birth. He was scouted at one of the local youth tournaments in his home town. He is currently based at the club's academy headquarters and being developed to become a successful senior professional player. Coaching forms part of this process. The coach follows a structured process with Bongani. Firstly, rapport is established and the scene is set. The possible value of coaching and the developmental nature of the process are outlined. Bongani is probed on what he wishes to achieve in his football career and this is drawn to the immediate setting of the coaching process, where clear goals are set. Incorporating the work of* Cooper et al. (2008), *the diversity between coach and coachee is put on the table openly. Bongani is comfortable in English and indicates that he is willing to engage with the coach in the coaching process. He indicates that he is proud of his Xhosa heritage and the coach acknowledges this as something that will be important to incorporate into the context of the coaching sessions. Goals are set and the purpose of the coaching emerges as being improving his functional football competence as a striker. Upon exploration of Bongani's strengths through facilitative conversation, it emerges that he has strong inherent leadership capabilities. Bongani indicates that, whilst growing up in his local community in the Eastern Cape, he has always held leadership positions, albeit in school, the sport teams he was part of or as part of his group of friends. He highlights that "it has always been important to me to be a leader. I like it when people trust me to take charge". Drawing on Bongani's comments, as well as from the evidence of his community leadership positions held, leadership is identified as a strength and coaching theme and brought into the realm of his functional role as a football striker. Through the coaching process, this is re-enforced. When Bongani's team requires him to take a penalty shot and put points on the scoreboard, this is an illustration of their trust in his ability. It is an acknowledgement that he is the right man for the job, and enables his strength of leadership and willingness to take responsibility. Through the coaching process, as Bongani successfully delivers penalty kicks and goals for his team, the idea of leadership is further explored. It emerges that this trust of his team mates, coupled with his subsequent delivery of performance, greatly bolsters Bongani's confidence. This is investigated properly and discussed between coach and coachee. The coach now enters into a process of empowerment, seeking meaningful ways to develop Bongani's leadership qualities. Conversations are directed towards exploring how leadership can be developed, and how it looks like in everyday live, also in Bongani's context as part*

[1] Not real name of athlete.

of a football academy, dealing with friends and other players. The coach explores such themes as authentic leadership with Bongani and how this can assist him to develop as person and footballer. A process of reframing in entered into as a means of identifying real behaviours that can enable Bongani's strength and ensure sustainable results are achieved. Bongani must be aware of his strength of willingness for leadership, and behaviours must reinforce this. He is however guided in this process by the coach, who explores with him the need for being authentic and responsible as a leader. A long term developmental relationship is negotiated between coach and coachee. The club's endorsement of such relationship is sought.

5 Conclusion

The aim of this chapter was to put forward a strength based coaching model that could effectively be utilized within the context of sport. The chapter provided a brief overview of the potential value of following a SBA within the athletic environment, alluding to studies that supported the notion that this approach can lead to positive outcomes. A number of studies were tabled. Following the establishment of potential value, and by considering systemic approaches that have been utilized for the purpose of psychological skills training in sport through coaching, the strength based coaching model of Van Zyl and Stander (2013) was adapted for specific application in the athletic environment. The adapted model was supplemented with four key themes that was put forward as a way of ensuring this model holds applicability within a multi-cultural context, of which sport and the athletic environment is often characterised by. Finally, the author put forward a case study, drawing from experience, to illustrate a coaching theme as part of the model. The model can now be applied fruitfully by practitioners within the domain of coaching within sport, particularly from the perspective of mental skills training, psychological performance conditioning or personal development. In the context of research, the model also lays the foundation for further methodical scrutiny, particularly in view of the different phases of the model that contribute to a synergistic whole. This will further assist practitioners in understanding the SBA in coaching and applying it with systemic vigour to achieve desired results with the athletes they coach.

References

Acharya, J. (2010). Professional competence of sport psychologist. *British Journal of Sports Medicine, 44*, 1–82.

Bachkirova, T. (2011). *Developmental coaching: Working with the self*. Maidenhead: Open University Press/McGraw-Hill Education.

Barker, J. B., Jones, M. V., & Greenlees, I. (2013). Using hypnosis to enhance self-efficacy in sport performers. *Journal of Clinical Sport Psychology, 7*, 228–247.

Beauchamp, M. K., Harvey, R. H., & Beauchamp, P. H. (2012). An integrated biofeedback and psychological skills training program for Canada's Olympic short-track speed skating team. *Journal of Clinical Sport Psychology, 6*, 67–84.

Behncke, L. (2004). Mental skills training for sports: A brief review. *The Online Journal of Sport Psychology, 6*(1), 1–24.

Biswas-Diener, R. (2010). *Practicing positive psychology coaching: Assessment and strategies for success*. Hoboken: Wiley.

Buckingham, M., & Clifton, D. O. (2001). *Now, discover your strengths*. New York: Free Press.

Clifton, D. O., & Harter, J. K. (2003). Strengths investment. In K. S. Cameron, J. E. Dutton, & R. E. Quinn (Eds.), *Positive organizational scholarship* (pp. 111–121). San Francisco: Berrett-Koehler.

Compton, W. C. (2005). *An introduction to positive psychology*. Belmont: Wadsworth.

Cooper, S., Wilson-Stark, K., Peterson, D. B., O'Roark, A. M., & Pennington, G. (2008). Consulting competently in multicultural contexts. *Consulting Psychology Journal: Practice and Research, 60*(2), 186–202.

Cope, C. J., Eys, M. A., Beauchamp, M. R., Schinke, R. J., & Bosselut, G. (2011). Informal roles on sport teams. *International Journal of Sport and Exercise Psychology, 9*(1), 19–30.

Cornelissen, S. (2007). The changing political economy of global sport and the 2010 FIFA World Cup. *Politikon, 34*(3), 241–259.

Cornellisen, S., Bob, U., & Swart, K. (2011). Sport mega-events and their legacies: The 2010 FIFA World Cup. *Development Southern Africa, 28*(3), 305–306.

Cravens, K. S., Oliver, E. G., & Stewart, J. S. (2010). Can a positive approach to performance evaluation help accomplish goals? *Business Horizons, 53*, 269–279.

Dale, G. A. (2000). Distractions and coping strategies of elite decathletes during their most memorable performances. *Sport Psychologist, 14*(1), 17–41.

Department of Sport and Recreation. (2011). *Sport and recreation South Africa: Strategic plan*. Retrieved from https://www.capetown.gov.za/en/SportRecreation/Documents/2011_2015_SRSA_Stratplan.pdf

Doherty, A. J., & Chelladurai, P. (2008). Research and reviews managing cultural diversity in sport organizations: A theoretical perspective. *Journal of Sport Management, 13*(4), 280–297.

Doran, G. T. (1981). There's a S.M.A.R.T. way to write management's goals and objectives. *Management Review, 70*(11), 35–36.

Durand-Bush, N., & Salmela, J. H. (2002). The development and maintenance of expert athletic performance: Perceptions of World and Olympic champions. *Journal of Applied Sport Psychology, 14*, 154–171.

Egan, G. (2007). *The skilled helper: A problem-management and opportunity-development approach to helping* (7th ed.). Pacific Grove: Brooks/Cole.

Foxcroft, C. (2004). Planning a psychological test in the multicultural South African context. *South African Journal of Industrial Psychology, 30*(4), 8–15.

Frederickson, B. (2002). *Handbook of positive psychology*. New York: Oxford University Press.

Gee, C. J. (2010). How does sport psychology actually improve athletic performance? A framework to facilitate athletes' and coaches' understanding. *Behavior Modification, 34*(5), 386–402.

Golby, J., & Sheard, M. (2004). Mental toughness and hardiness at different levels of rugby league. *Personality and Individual Differences, 37*, 933–942.

Gordon, S. (2012). Strengths-based approaches to developing mental toughness: Team and individual. *International Coaching Psychology Review, 7*(2), 210–222.

Gordon, S., & Gucciardi, D. F. (2011). A strength based approach to coaching mental toughness. *Journal of Sport Psychology in Action, 2*, 143–155.

Gould, D., Dieffenbach, K., & Moffett, A. (2002). Psychological characteristics and their development in Olympic champions. *Journal of Applied Sport Psychology, 14*, 172–204.

Govindji, R., & Linley, A. (2007). Strength-use, self-concordance and well-being: Implications for strength coaching and coaching psychologists. *International Coaching Psychology Review, 2*, 143–153.
Gucciardi, D. F., & Gordon, S. (2009). Development and preliminary validation of the Cricket Mental Toughness Inventory (CMTI). *Journal of Sports Sciences, 27*, 1293–1310.
Hawkins, P., & Smith, N. (2007). *Coaching, mentoring and organizational consultancy: Supervision and development*. Maidenhead: McGraw-Hill International.
Holliday, B., Burton, D., Sun, G., Hammermeister, J., Naylor, S., & Freigang, D. (2008). Building the better mental training mousetrap: Is periodization a more systematic approach to promoting performance excellence? *Journal of Applied Sport Psychology, 20*, 199–219.
Jackson, S. A., & Eklund, R. C. (2002). Assessing flow in physical activity: The flow state scale-2 and the dispositional flow scale-2. *Journal of Sport & Exercise Psychology, 24*, 133–150.
Jackson, L. T. B., Rothmann, S., & Van de Vijver, F. J. R. (2006). A model of work-related well-being for educators in South Africa. *Stress and Health, 22*(4), 263–274.
Judge, T. A., Locke, E. A., Durham, C. C., & Kluger, A. N. (1998). Dispositional effects on job and life satisfaction: The role of core evaluations. *Journal of Applied Psychology, 83*, 17–34.
Kaiser, R. B., & White, R. P. (2009). Debunking an unbalanced approach to development. *Leadership in Action, 28*(5), 9–12.
Karatepe, O. M. (2009). An investigation of the joint effects of organizational tenure and supervisor support on work-family conflict and turnover intentions. *Journal of Hospitality and Tourism Management, 16*(1), 73–81.
Keyes, C. L. M. (2009). *Brief description of the mental health continuum short form (MHC-SF)*. Available: http://www.sociology.emory.edu/ckeyes/. On-line, retrieved 14 Dec 2010.
Kihl, L. A., Leberman, S., & Schull, V. (2010). Stakeholder constructions of leadership in intercollegiate athletics. *European Sport Management Quarterly, 10*(2), 241–275.
Linley, P. A., & Harrington, S. (2006). Playing to your strengths. *The Psychologist, 19*, 86–89.
Linley, P. A., Joseph, S., Harrington, S., & Wood, A. M. (2006). Positive psychology: Past, present, and (possible) future. *Journal of Positive Psychology, 1*, 3–16.
Linley, A., Willars, J., & Biswas-Diener, R. (2010). *The strengths book: What you can do, love to do, and find it hard to do – And why it matters*. Coventry: CAPP Press.
Locke, E. A., & Latham, G. P. (1985). The application of goal setting to sports. *Journal of Sport Psychology, 7*, 205–222.
Lonsdale, C., Hodge, K., & Jackson, S. (2007). Athlete engagement: II. Development and initial validation of the athlete engagement questionnaire. *International Journal of Sport Psychology, 38*, 471–492.
Luszczynska, A., Scholz, U., & Schwarzer, R. (2005). The general self-efficacy scale: Multicultural validation studies. *The Journal of Psychology, 139*(5), 439–457.
Lyubomirsky, S. (2011). *The way to happiness: Action plan for a happy life* (K. Benyovitz, Trans.). Or Yehuda: Kinneret Publishing House.
MacKie, D. (2014). The effectiveness of strength-based executive coaching in enhancing full range leadership development: A controlled study. *Consulting Psychology Journal: Practice and Research, 66*(2), 118–137.
Mahoney, M. J., & Avener, M. (1977). Psychology of the elite athlete: An exploratory study. *Cognitive Therapy and Research, 1*, 135–141.
Meichenbaum, D. (1985). *Stress inoculation training*. Elmsford: Pergamon Press.
Muthén, L. K., & Muthén, B. O. (2014). *Mplus user's guide* (7th ed.). Los Angeles: Author.
Noble, D. N., Perkins, K., & Fatout, M. (2000). On being a strength coach: Child welfare and the strengths model. *Child and Adolescent Social Work Journal, 17*, 141–153.
Parry, J. (2006). Sport and Olympism: Universals and multiculturalism. *Journal of the Philosophy of Sport, 33*, 188–204.
Peterson, C., & Seligman, M. E. P. (2004). *Character strengths and virtues: A handbook and classification*. New York: Oxford University Press.
Rath, T. C. (2002). *Measuring the impact of Gallup's strengths-based development program for students*. Princeton: The Gallup Organization.

Rothmann, S., Mostert, K., & Strydom, M. (2006). A psychometric evaluation of the job demands resources scale in South Africa. *SA Journal of Industrial Psychology, 32*(4), 87–96. doi:10.4102/sajip.v32i4.239.

Saks, A. M. (2006). Antecedents and consequences of employee engagement. *Journal of Managerial Psychology, 21*(7), 600–619.

Sarkar, M., & Fletcher, D. (2013). How should we measure psychological resilience in sport performers? *Measurement in Physical Education and Exercise Science, 17*, 264–280.

Seligman, M. E. P. (2011). *Flourish: A visionary new understanding of happiness and well-being*. New York: Free Press.

Seligman, M. E. P., & Csikszentmihalyi, M. (2000). Positive psychology: An introduction. *American Psychologist, 55*, 5–14.

Spreitzer, G. (1995). Psychological empowerment in the workplace: Dimensions, measurement and validation. *Academy of Management Journal, 38*, 1442–1456.

Stander, F. W., & Mostert, K. (2013). Assessing the organisational and individual strengths use and deficit improvement amongst sport coaches. *SA Journal of Industrial Psychology, 39*(2), 1–13.

Stander, F. W., Mostert, K., & De Beer, T. L. (2014). Organisational and individual strengths use as predictors of engagement and productivity. *Journal of Psychology in Africa, 24*(5), 403–409.

Stander, F. W., Rothmann, S., & Botha, E. (in press). *A structural model of athlete flow*.

Stavropoulou, O., & Protopapa, S. (2013). A strengths-based approach to mentoring women entrepreneurs: How to free the strengths within them. *Journal of Innovation and Entrepreneurship, 2*(13), 1–10.

Terry, P. C., & Karageorghis, C. I. (2006). Psychophysical effects of music in sport and exercise: An update on theory, research and application. In M. Katsikitis (Ed.), *Psychology bridging the Tasman: Science, culture and practice – Proceedings of the 2006 joint conference of the Australian Psychological Society and the New Zealand Psychological Society* (pp. 415–419). Melbourne: Australian Psychological Society.

Turnnidge, J., Côté, J., Hollenstein, T., & Deakin, J. (2014). A direct observation of the dynamic content and structure of coach-athlete interactions in a model sport program. *Journal of Applied Sport Psychology, 26*, 225–240.

Van den Heuvel, M., Demerouti, E., Schaufeli, W. B., & Bakker, A. B. (2010). Personal resources and work engagement in the face of change. In J. Houdmont (Ed.), *Occupational health psychology, European perspectives on research, education and practice* (Vol. 4, pp. 124–150). Chichester: Wiley.

Van Woerkom, M., Els, C., Mostert, K., Rothmann, S. JNR, De Beer, L.T. & Bakker, A.B. (in press). Following a strength-based and deficiency-based approach: The development and psychometric properties of a new scale. *Journal of Managerial Psychology*.

Van Zyl, L. E., & Stander, M. W. (2013). The strength based coaching model. In J. White, R. Motching, & M. Lux (Eds.), *Theory and practice of the person-centered approach – Interconnections beyond psychotherapy*. New York: Springer.

Whitney, D., & Trosten-Bloom, A. (2003). *The power of appreciative inquiry*. San Francisco: Berret-Koehler.

Wood, A. M., Linley, P. A., Maltby, J., Kashdan, T. B., & Hurling, R. (2011). Using personal and psychological strengths lead to increase in well-being over time: A longitudinal study and the development of the strengths use questionnaire. *Personality and Individual Differences, 50*, 15–20.

Utilizing Symbolic Expressions, Art, Myths, Dreams and Fantasies in Coaching

Daniel Hercules du Toit

Abstract The purpose of this chapter is to discuss the use, function and impact of symbolic expressions, such as art, myths, dreams and fantasies, within the coaching process from a Jungian psychology perspective. The chapter will be presented in three sections: (a) the function of art as a symbolic expression of the psyche, (b) utilizing the coachee's personal expressions during coaching and (c) utilizing the work of other artists and other medium, like film, to gain insight into the coachee's psychodynamic processes. Art as symbolic expression of inner processes will be introduced as, in its many forms, art aids in making inner processes "visible" and therefore "manageable". Though art can be used from many approaches, the Analytical Psychology approach will be followed in this chapter. Two forms of artistic expressions can be utilized during the coaching process. First, the coachee's ***own*** artistic creations/expressions could also be used to aid the coachee in delving into his/her psyche for personal growth or understanding presented issues. The coachee's own artistic creations could be utilized in the coaching process to gain insight into his/her own psyche, as well as problems and issues. The use of drawings, writing, sculpturing, composing and scrap booking as forms of self-expression will be discussed, as well as how these could be utilized in coaching. Second, utilizing art created by ***other artists*** in its many forms: paintings, music, myths, fairy tales, films, poems and stories, could be used to aid coachees to gain insight into their own psychodynamic processes. The most widely utilized art forms accompanied by examples will be discussed.

Keywords Symbolic expression • Jung • Art • Myths • Films • Music • Stories

D.H. du Toit (✉)
Optentia Research Focus Area, North-West University, Vaal Triangle Campus, Vanderbijlpark, South Africa
e-mail: danie.dutoit@nwu.ac.za

L.E. van Zyl et al. (eds.), *Coaching Psychology: Meta-theoretical perspectives and applications in multicultural contexts*, DOI 10.1007/978-3-319-31012-1_14

1 Introduction

In this chapter, the use of art in coaching will be discussed. Though art in coaching can be utilized from different theoretical approaches, the archetypal approach, as was explained in the previous chapter, is followed here. This chapter serves to illustrate the principles explained in the chapter on the archetypal approach in coaching. Because archetypal patterns are unconscious and difficult to articulate, they can best be understood and communicated through metaphors. The expression of these metaphors through various mediums will be discussed in this chapter.

This chapter is divided into two sections: the first section describes the use of artifacts created by coachees themselves. The second section deals with the utilization of existing art forms during coaching.

2 Creating Art During Coaching

Coachees tell their stories in many ways. Their "stories" represent the issues and challenges of their lives. By asking them about their dreams, particularly repeated dreams, and by listening carefully to their fantasies, the coach could already gain some insight into their unconscious lives. Dreams are usually in symbolic form and its meaning is hidden from the dreamer. Discussing dreams can bring clarity to unconscious issues. In coaching, dealing with unconscious issues, is usually referred to as "awareness" or "mindfulness". It is also important to take fantasies that coachees mention serious. In their fantasies often are the keys to necessary changes. For example, an over-worked director of companies stated to his coach that he wants to resign and start a little coffee shop in a small seaside town. On the surface, this sounds like an impractical, irrational fantasy which should be ignored. When discussing the root needs this fantasy expressed, it was not to really resign and start a coffee shop, but to have more relaxed human contact and to have a somewhat less complicated life. These needs could be addressed and some serious challenges in his life got resolved.

Apart from utilizing spontaneous manifestations of the unconscious mind, such as in dreams and fantasies, the coach could also in a more structured way gain access to the coachees' unconscious mind. The coach could encourage them to tell the stories of their lives. They are often able to tell their stories more comprehensively in symbolic expression than in words. By creating an artifact, the coachee creates a symbolic expression of a certain experience or psychological state. The symbolic expression serves the function to gain insight into the issue. Insight and awareness is the first step towards bringing change. Jung talked about "healing images" (Jung 1948). For example, if a coachee draws a mountain, he/she can, in drawing the mountain, already start gaining insight by taking a more holistic, systemic view on current challenges in his/her life, as if from a mountain top. Apart from the insight it brings, creating a symbolic image could in itself already bring healing.

The way the coach deals with the artifact that a coachee created, is by utilizing it to enter into a discussion, and the skilled coach could even enter into a dialogue with the artifact; the coach could ask questions such as:

- What is the artifact telling you?
- What question/s could you ask the artifact?

The coach will thus mainly ask probing questions to understand the artifact, and thus the coachee. It is important that the coach shows respect for the coachee's creation. The worst the coach could do is to kill the creation with ruthless interpretation.

Having said that, to utilize artistic creations in coaching, the coach must have some idea about the archetypal symbolic meaning of images, colours, tone and form. Though an image has a unique personal meaning that is specific to the person who created it, images often have archetypal roots. The coach needs to have some understanding of archetypal symbols. Sometimes the image needs to be seen as a symbolic representation, but sometimes it simply is what the coachee created, a depiction of a situation without a "deeper" meaning.

Art created by artists differ from art created by coachees. Though there are similarities, the processes and aims are very different. Art, as created by artists, and that created by coachees, are both personal expressions and the two "disciplines" influences and inform one another. The fine artist, for example, doing a painting, will often not replicate an existing image, but will draw from archetypal images in his/her unconscious mind. Even when the fine artist paints a tree, he/she paints the tree as he/she sees it, not as the tree really is. The fine artist applies the principles of his/her profession in deciding on shading, brush strokes, composition and colour. In coaching, the coachee follows his/her intuition throughout the creative process and usually does not have or need an understanding of the requirements to create a "good" work of art. Both can thus express something which grew from within themselves, and at best, neither strive to produce "pretty pictures". For the fine artist, critique of the creation is usually an accepted part of the process. Creations during the coaching process are never subjected to critique; they are respectfully utilized to gain a deeper understanding of the coachee and the coachee is encouraged to enter into a dialogue with his/her creation.

Creating art as technique is sometimes confused with projective techniques. Creating art is an expression of inner conflicts, complexes and often unconscious challenges. It is a relatively pure, totally individual expression. Such a creation differs from projective techniques in that with projective techniques, the coachee would be shown a piece of art and asked to say what he/she sees or may be asked standardized questions on the work of art. The way the coachee then explains what he/she sees is what he/she is projecting of themselves onto the work of art. Creating art is a process whereby the coachee tells his/her own story in his/her own unique way with unconscious elements coming into the open. Creating art is thus a personal symbolic expression and not a projective technique.

Next, the various different ways to utilize art will be discussed. These different ways are sometime used in combination or are offered as alternatives to coachees, acknowledging the individual differences in coachees' preferences.

2.1 Drawings and Painting

To utilize drawings or paintings, the coach encourages the coachee to create a drawing or quick painting to express the challenges or difficulties under discussion. The question arises: why would one ask the coachee to draw a picture of the issue rather than just describe it in words? Roger Whittaker's song of the 1960s might have a partial answer to this question; the song starts with the line: "If a picture paints a thousand words…" (The Kipling Society 2014). If one considers this for a second: a picture could never be fully described by even many thousands of words. A picture goes beyond what words could ever describe.

The coach using drawings and paintings need to provide some art supplies. It is preferable to have a variety of supplies to cater for individual preferences of coachees. Acrylic paint and brushes works well, but soft pastels, oil pastels, crayons and charcoal should preferably also be offered, as well as various sizes paper. The coach should give a brief demonstration of materials. In introducing art, the coach should emphasize that the exercise is not about drawing a pretty picture for others' approval. Many people carry a fear for drawing as a result of negative feedback they received on their drawings as children, which for many was the last time they drew. It is advisable to encourage the coachee to draw with his/her non-dominant hand: in other words, a right handed person is encouraged to draw with the left hand and vice versa.

The following is an example of such a drawing. This person drew this during a group session with the purpose of individual growth (Fig. 1).

The coachee is a female in her mid-twenties who has not drawn anything for many years. The instruction was to draw anything which symbolically expresses the current issues or challenges in her life (usually, the exact instruction does not really matter; the prominent issues will respond to the "invitation" and will surface. Care should be taken, however, not to be restrictive when inviting coachees to do a drawing). She drew herself without arms or legs, lying in a boat. The boat is surrounded by red flowers. In the discussion on the drawing, it transpired that she was just starting her career and her first job was mainly administrative and she found it boring. She felt that she had no say in how things were done, and because of her lack of experience, she could also not leave the job. The drawing illustrates beautifully how she felt: without arms and legs and drifting in a rudderless boat; she indeed felt that she had no impact on the direction, or even speed, of the boat. She also felt "faceless"; as if she had no identity. She indeed had some serious work identity issues. The boat is drawn very dark, representing mainly her work-life. The water is drawn calm, depicting that despite the lack of control, she was at a fairly stable period in her life; she felt secure in her job, as she felt that she was doing the required work

Fig. 1 An example of a drawing by a coachee

well. The light section around the boat also indicated that the areas of her life outside her work life, symbolically indicated by the area around the boat, are "lighter" than her work life. She is in a satisfying relationship and also has satisfying relationships with friends and colleagues, indicated by the flowers in the water.

Apart from utilizing forms in a drawing, the colours used are as important. Though one must be careful to interpret colours, and shapes, from a "dictionary" of unconscious symbols, the coach can carefully ask about the archetypal meaning of colours. Skillful questioning around colours may elicit responses that align neatly with archetypal associations around colour. Green usually indicates growth; in this instance, the artist drew herself as green, indicating that she was still experiencing personal growth. She also said that growth was one of her core personal values.

So far, the drawing was discussed in terms of the personal unconscious of the artist. As was discussed, a person's personal unconscious is grounded in the collective unconscious. In this particular drawing, the collective unconscious impacting on the personal unconscious is clearly illustrated. The artist drew herself as without hands, because in her own life, she experienced that she did not have control over her work life. On a collective level, her challenge resonates with the issue of many other people, men and women, who feel powerless in their jobs. In our culture, women in particular are still more often than men discriminated against and as a result feel powerless. Though many will argue against this statement, the relative small number of women who are Chief Executive Officers (CEO's) (Catalyst 2015) as well as the much shorter tenure of female CEO's, those who do make it to the most senior position in an organization, compared to their masculine counterparts (Bruckmüller and Branscombe 2011) support this argument. Many women who can vouch for subtle discrimination just because they are women all are indications that women in the world of work are not on equal foot with men in many organizations.

This view of women as inferior is not new and reflected in many myths and stories. This particular drawing reminds of the myth of the handless maiden. This myth's (Johnson 1995) central theme is women's inability to *do* things. Myths often capture universal archetypal truths. Johnson (1995) wrote on the myth of the handless maiden: "…this story came from a time in European history when our present attitudes were being formulated in those deep places where the collective unconscious is generating the next step in its evolution" (p. 56). It is thus not surprising that a modern woman in South Africa, with European ancestors, drew herself unconsciously as a "handless maiden". Briefly, the story line of the handless maiden myth is as follows: the story starts with a miller whose job is to grind grain for the village. The devil makes a bargain with him: he will make his mill faster, easier and more efficient if he gives the devil what stands behind the mill. The miller thought that the devil wants the tree that grew behind the mill, but was unaware that his daughter was standing behind the mill. He thus sacrificed the young feminine for technological advancement. The devil then demands that he chops off her hands, which he does. Johnson (1995) states that this bargain is still made by people today. Every time one gives up an inner "feeling" value for an outer benefit or to attain a practical goal, one enters into a "devil's bargain" (Johnson 1995, pp. 59–60). It is quiet common that people sacrifice the beautiful and feeling aspects of their lives for the sake of outer success. People easily skip their exercise, listening to music, attending a child's sport game or watching a sunset because of work demands. These are typical "devil bargains" and the feelings of meaninglessness, emptiness and guilt associated with these bargains are often the topics brought to coaching sessions. It is then useful to investigate the "devil's bargains" in their lives and look at ways to break these archetypal patterns. Possible coaching questions to probe for "devil's bargains":

- Do you sometimes sacrifice what is dear to you, for instance, to comply to job pressures?
- How do you feel about such sacrifices?
- What is the cost of these sacrifices?
- Is it worth it?
- Are alternative choices possible?

This drawing could also be utilized to understand the interplay between the mother complex and the mother archetype in this person's unconscious mind. The armless, handless, legless and feetless way she depicted herself can be seen from the viewpoint of the individual mother complex. This powerlessness usually results in regressive fantasies; a desire to return to the caring, nurturing mother, rather than become independent and face the challenges of the world. At this point, the coach could encourage the coachee to become more empowered and independent through, for instance, self-education.

From the mother archetype perspective, as was already explained, it could indicate a "negative" mother archetype: the plight of women in general who often are forced into inferiority. It could also indicate a more positive mother archetypal perspective: that of surrendering to life; believing that "mother nature" will take care of her, without exerting huge effort and taking decisive action. In a similar way, through dialogue, the coach could gain understanding of why she drew herself faceless and lying down. Once insight is gained, change can take place by focusing on the root of the behavior.

Though reference so far was to using drawing and painting for individual coaching, it can also be used for team coaching. All the team members can work together on the same drawing in order to; for instance, give a symbolic illustration of where the team is at that point in time. The team's unconscious dynamics often comes to the fore as they decide what to draw, what size paper to use, what medium to use and who draws what. If the leader of the team, for instance chose the symbolic representation, the coach as observer can see how successful the leader is in conveying his/her vision to the team. Unconscious aspects can be made known when the team discusses the drawing after completion. One executive team in a very competitive environment, for example, depicted their team as a dangerous, narrow winding road. One member drew skid marks and a road kill in the road. The skid marks, though, were drawn after the dead animal. He drew this unconsciously, but during discussions, many other team members could associate with that part of the drawing. It emerged that exactly that takes place in the team: team members would ruthlessly accuse and attack each other during meetings and only stop and think what they have said afterwards, in other words, hit the brakes after they have gone for the kill.

2.2 *Writing*

Whereas the coachee would usually make a drawing during a coaching session, writing usually takes place between sessions and is then discussed during session. The coachee is usually encouraged to keep a journal or diary of thoughts and reactions, or to write a letter to a person he/she has a difficulty with. The idea is not to give the letter to the person it is addressed to, but to express emotions and gain insight. There is also another reason for writing down what one feels: When a person is confused and unsure of his/her true view on and feelings about a challenge, formulating it into words and writing it down often brings clarity and re-instates a sense of control.

Apart from writing during troubled times to address specific issues or problems, coaches could encourage coachees to clarify their thinking by writing on a regular basis. Cameron (2002) in her writing on how a person could be more creative suggests writing one's thoughts, feelings and fears first thing every morning in what she calls the "morning pages". Writing down their thoughts, feelings, fears and the main challenges of the day ahead every day, could help coachees getting a better grip on their lives and also increase their levels of awareness of their unconscious minds.

2.3 Sculpturing, Composing, Scrap Booking and Collage

In encouraging coachees to express themselves in artistic terms, it is important to follow the coachee's natural inclinations. Some people express themselves easier in words, others in a drawing; still others could be uncomfortable with both, and prefer to express themselves in a wooden or clay sculpture. If the coachee builds metal objects for a hobby, he/she could be encouraged to build and weld together an object that symbolically represents a particular psychological state or experience. If the coachee relates to music, he/she can be encouraged to symbolically describe an emotion or event by composing a piece of music or a song. This type of expression will be applicable to very few coachees. If a coachee does scrap booking, he/she could also be encouraged to express him/herself through scrap booking. Whatever form of artistic expression the coachee feels comfortable with, could be utilized.

Whereas mediums mentioned in the previous paragraph are seldom used as artistic expression in coaching, collage building is often used. Collage building is particularly useful when the coachee feels that he/she is unable to be artistically creative. Though a collage could be built at any stage of the coaching process, it is very useful early in the process because it gives very valuable insights about the coachee. Collage building is most often used when the coachee has challenges relating to his/her personal values, purpose in life, meaning in life, identity and personal life priorities.

Usually, the coachee is asked to build the collage at home between sessions. The coachee is asked to collect a number of magazines, printed on high quality paper, aimed at addressing different interests, such as gardening, home decoration, vehicles, outdoor life, fitness and beauty. The coachee should be comfortable destroying these magazines. The coachee should set aside some relaxed time to peruse the magazines. He/she tears out any picture or word in the magazine that he/she feels that he/she can relate to. The coachee should not question why he/she relates to it at this stage, that will be done during the coaching session. Once the coachee has collected a good number of pictures, he/she should, still in a very relaxed state, start arranging the pictures on a poster size carton paper. Over a few days, the coachee should change and re-arrange the pictures until he/she feels that the important pictures are present and arranged in an acceptable way. He/she must then paste the pictures onto the carton paper. The coachee is free to add small pieces of memorabilia or do some painting between the pictures, only if they want to.

During the session, the coach then discusses the collage with the coachee. Whereas the coachee was encouraged up to this point not to cognitively analyze what he/she is doing, at this point the "feeling" decisions are brought under cognitive scrutiny. It is very important to do it very gently and respectful. This is particularly important if the coachee has a more cognitive oriented style, and has had to manage his/her intuitive decision making during the process of building the collage. Positive feedback would certainly encourage these behaviours.

Managers are often excellent at dealing with *complexity*, meaning that they must manage many conflicting variables at the same time, but less good at dealing with *ambiguity*, where the outcome and consequences of a decision is unclear (Du Toit 2011). This means that most managers are comfortable with taking rational decisions, when they can process data, evaluate benefits and risks and then take the decision. Most managers are much less comfortable taking decisions where they have to rely on their more intuitive, feeling sides. Many major decisions in life rely more on one's complete wisdom, analysis of data often cannot indicate the best decision; think of decisions such as getting married, having a child, accepting a job, where to go on vacation, what to say when a colleague lost a loved one, expanding a business and many more such decisions are taken by using one's full wisdom. Not to say that managers should not analyze data, explore cost/benefit ratios and calculate risks, but they need to become more comfortable taking decisions under uncertain conditions. This competence usually gets more and more important as a manager's area of responsibility grows. The experience of building a collage in itself is already an exercise in utilizing the intuitive function, and therefor very uncomfortable for coachees who are more comfortable with using rational reasoning.

In discussing the collage, the coach should thus start by discussing the coachee's experience of building the collage. Ask questions such as:

- Was it easy or difficult to take decisions where there was no right or wrong choice? How do you feel about the final product?
- Does the collage tell us anything about you as a person?
- Does it give us clues on your preferences?

Though there is no set sequence in discussing the collage, it is usually appropriate to start the discussion by explaining to the coachee how the process of building a collage works: One chooses pictures that reflect and represent something of one's inner world. Each picture chosen might represent some part of one's psyche. The pictures give some indication of the person's inner landscape. How they were grouped and placed on the carton paper can also be significant; often the pictures representing the most important aspects of the coachee are placed in the middle of the carton paper: aspects that are literally central to his/her life.

It is usually a good idea to discuss the general impression of the whole collage first. The coachee can be asked what impression the collage creates, looking at it objectively. The coach could ask questions such as:

- What would one think is important to the person who built this collage?
- What are the themes of most of the pictures?
- What is likely to be central to this person's life?
- What are his/her most likely strengths and weaknesses?

It is also important to note what is absent. For instance, if there are no people in the collage, or no people who appear to be intimately connected, or no natural objects like plants or animals, the possible absence of these, not only in the collage, but also in the coachee's psychic life, can be explored. Next, each picture could be discussed in terms of its meaning to the coachee. The coach should take notes throughout the process and when the discussion has exhausted most possibilities, give a summary of the insights gained from the collage. How well this works for the coachee should be discussed next, as well as aspects which need to change. In this way, the collage could give direction to the coaching process.

3 Utilizing Existing Art During Coaching

In the previous section, how a coach can utilize the artistic creations of coachees was discussed. In this section, the utilization of existing art, such as existing paintings, films, music and stories during the coaching process will be discussed. Some of these, such as myths, can be used in a continuous process, others, such as paintings and films lend themselves more to incidental use.

3.1 Paintings

Many famous artists expressed their pain, joy and challenges in their paintings. In their paintings they express what might also be unconscious to themselves. Well known Mexican artist, Frida Kahlo stated: "I paint my own reality. The only thing I know is that I paint because I need to, and I paint whatever passes through my head without any other consideration." (Souter 2006, p. 3). Frida endured severe physical pain during her lifetime due to sickness and accidents. She depicted her suffering in her paintings.

Pablo Picasso beautifully captured how he coped with very challenging circumstances during his so called "blue period". Picasso's "blue period" started when his best friend, Casagemus, committed suicide. Picasso tried before his friend's suicide to cheer him up, but was unable to do so. Picasso was in Spain when his friend committed suicide in Paris and could thus not attend his friend's funeral. The following prints beautifully illustrate how he worked through his sadness, sense of loss and guilt (Kahnweiler et al. 1976) (Figs. 2, 3, and 4).

These are only a few examples of Picasso's many paintings inspired by his friend's suicide. In the first painting, he painted his friend's body next to a candle with the bullet hole clearly visible. The second painting is about his friend's funeral. He even drew some of the people he thought or knew was at the funeral. The painting shows how Casagemus' spirit is leaving earth. The last painting was done towards the end of the "blue period". Casagemus' face and hands look peaceful. Some humour is also entering as he drew Casagemus partly in the harlequin, or clown, attire. The harlequin was important during the end of this period in Picasso's work. The harlequin is seen as a figure who brings change and transformation, not only in Picasso's work, but in many other stories and films. The harlequin says what others dare not say, thus bringing awareness. From this drawing it appears as if Picasso was starting to come to terms with his friend's death and finding some inner peace again. One could guess that he faced the truth about his friend's death and

Fig. 2 Picasso's "Death of Casagemus"

also faced the full reality of his sadness, loss and guilt. This last painting is noticeably different from the first one with the bullet mark. One can see the changes as he went through his grieving process.

During coaching sessions, prints such as these can be utilized to open a discussion on the coachee's unconscious life. If the coachee identifies with the print and in that way recognizes the expression of something in him/herself, the artist's painting could assist in accessing emotions and experiences and the coachee could feel that that part of him/herself is respected and validated. Once accepted, the print could facilitate movement towards something else.

3.2 Music

Music is probably the art form which most touches a person's heart. Music and songs expresses archetypal human conditions, desires and tragedies. The coach can utilize music to access the coachees' repressed feelings and also to bring change. For example, the coachee can be asked to visualize success whilst listening to motivating music, such as "One moment in time" by Whitney Houston. The coach has to consider, though that a coachee's experience of music is a very personal issue. The coachee's association with a particular song might bring a very different emotion from what the coach intend because of the coachee's own history and association with the song.

The coachee's level of sophistication and music taste must also be considered. A person unfamiliar with opera music is unlikely to understand and experience the

Fig. 3 Picasso's "Burial of Casagemus"

Fig. 4 Picasso's "Burial of Harlequin"

emotions and issues portrayed in opera music, whereas the opera enthusiast would appreciate and be touched by opera music. Similarly, a person who likes classical music might only experience irritation if the coach plays commercial, popular songs. Usually, songs which are not heard too often, but are also not totally unfamiliar, works best. Musicals often have songs which address serious human challenges and difficulties, as *well* as encounters with archetypal forces. *Phantom of the opera*, *Chess*, and *Les Miserables* are examples of such musicals depicting universal human themes.

3.3 Myths and Fairy Tales

Though myths and fairy tales are synonymous for most people, in Jungian psychology they are totally different constructs. In myths, a "hero" usually embarks on a journey and during the journey, encounters challenges which represent archetypal ideas. The hero often has to conquer a dragon or save a damsel in distress. Examples are the myths of King Arthur, Parsifal (popularized by Wagner's opera with the same name and the 1990s film "Fisher king" based on the Parsifal myth) and The wizard of Oz (this myth differs from most myths, in that it can be seen as representing the feminine journey. The heroine, Dorothy, in this myth is accompanied by others on her journey, whereas in most myths, the hero takes on the world alone). During the journey, the main character typically grows and gains insight before returning home.

Where in myths, the main character encounters archetypes, in fairy tales, the characters can be seen as representing archetypes *within* the main character. Characters in a fairy tale are therefor usually one dimensional and does not develop or grow: the princess is only good and beautiful, the step mother is only wicked and the prince is only handsome and brave. Sadly, many coachees who are in leadership positions, are in many respects one dimensional, like fairy tale characters. They might, for instance, build their leadership style and approach around a single value. Other organizational leaders might drive a one dimensional vision: for instance, only focusing on the financial aspect of the organization and ignoring the people side. A fairy tale about a king whose people were suffering and stagnant might bring insight for a coachee who is such an organizational leader.

Fairy tales usually start with a narrator introducing the fairy tale and giving some perspective: "long, long ago, in a faraway country…". At the end of the fairy tale, the narrator might give a final comment or even a lesson from the fairy tale.

Myths and fairy tales can be used in coaching to assist the coachee in gaining insight. Because they deal with universal truths, coachees can relate to the characters and gain insight into their own unconscious archetypal patterns. For example, consider the wife of the giant in the well-known fairy tale "Jack and the beanstalk". The wife knows that her husband is vicious; therefor she lies, hides Jack and distracts the giant. Many persons in both physically and emotionally abusive relationships can relate to the giant's wife. They spend their time, often lifetimes, being as quiet as possible, distracting and trying to sooth their partners who act like the abusive "giant".

Old myths, such as found in Greek, Celtic and African mythology contain universal truths. Many of the themes and characters found in the different old myths show remarkable similarities. Consider that theses myths developed in societies which did not have any contact with each other during the times these myths developed. The reason for these similarities are, at a level, that the myths deal with issues and life struggles which are universal in all cultures for all people. The myths also represent archetypal truths, which are universal to all human beings. Whether the characters of the myths are depicted as gods, as in Greek mythology, or as a village child in African mythology, the archetypal truths remain the same.

3.4 Films/Theatre/Opera

Films, theatre and opera often deal with universal, archetypal truths. By watching it, it could resonate with one's own archetypal images. The coach would usually ask the coachee to watch the film, or if the coachee has seen the film, or stage production or opera, it could be utilized during the coaching session. "Art" films often symbolically express archetypal struggles. Izod and Dovalis (2015) said cinema is a medium which engages people in a virtual dialogue with their own and their culture's unconscious minds more deeply than is commonly thought. They further stated that the movie theatre could be seen as a sacred space where people can encounter the archetypal to reach a deeper understanding of themselves. The coach could further develop insights and self–awareness by discussing the coachee's experiences and the part of the film which touched him/her.

Examples of films which could be utilized in coaching: Tree of Life; The life of Pi; The Fisher king; Three colours blue; Prince of Tides; Big Fish; Troy; The Gladiator and My old lady. Care should be taken not to choose a film which might offend the coachee. An example is: The unbearable lightness of being; though an excellent film to illustrate many human challenges, it is likely to offend some coachees. These films represent various very different aspects of life and encounters with archetypal patterns and forces. A simple example of how a film could be used: a senior manager in his late 40s was used to face problems and challenges by exerting massive amounts of energy to resolve them. Though it worked for him earlier in his life to attain success, it causes problems in his later life: apart from finding it difficult to sustain relationships with his loved ones, he suffered various stress-related medical problems such as high blood pressure, ulcers and a heart condition. His doctor told him that he needed to "slow down". It was difficult, almost impossible for him to even imagine not using brute force and an aggressive approach to attain results. He brought up a film in an early coaching session. He strongly resisted even considering the possibility to change. He stated that, like the main character in the film "The Gladiator", he would be happy to die fighting with his sword in his hand. This opened the possibility to discuss the values and needs of the main character of the film, which was to return home after his many battles and spend the end of his life farming and being closely connected to his family. In the film, the main character was forced to die with a sword in his hand. The coachee was confronted with his options, and the fact that, unlike the main character in the film, he was free to choose to approach life differently. He gained insight through these discussions and agreed to approach life more like a general using his wisdom to strategize than a gladiator, using force and sheer aggression. As a result, his health and relationships improved and he was more successful in his career.

In this chapter the use of art forms to explore the unconscious mind and gain understanding of archetypal patterns was discussed. Many of these art forms overlap and some could be used together. A coachee can, for example be given the option of either doing a drawing or using clay to sculpture an image. The more visual person would usually prefer a visual medium and the more kinesthetic coachee might prefer a medium he/she can feel and touch. The options and mediums to use as expressions of the psychic life are only limited by the imaginations and creativity of the coach and the coachee.

References

Bruckmüller, S., & Branscombe, N. R. (2011, January). *How women end up on the "glass cliff"*. Harvard Business Review. Retrieved from https://hbr.org/2011/01/how-women-end-up-on-the-glass-cliff

Cameron, J. (2002). *Walking in this world: Practical strategies for creativity*. London: Ebury Press.

Catalyst. (2015). *Women CEOs of the S&P 500.* Retrieved from http://www.catalyst.org/knowledge/women-ceos-sp-500

Du Toit, D. H. (2011). *A Jungian perspective on the psycho-social maturity of leaders* (Doctoral dissertation). Johannesburg: University of Johannesburg.

Izod, J., & Dovalis, J. (2015). *Cinema as therapy: Grief and transformational film.* New York: Routledge Publishers.

Johnson, R. A. (1995). *The Fisher King and the handless maiden.* New York: HarperOne Publishers.

Jung, C. G. (1948). *The integration of the personality* (5th ed.). London: Kegan Paul.

Kahnweiler, D. H., Reff, T., Rosenblum, R., Golding, J., Bowness, A., Penrose, R., Boggs, J. S., & Leiris, M. (1976). *Picasso 1881–1973.* London: Paul Elek Ltd.

Souter, G. (2006). *Kahlo* (Mega Squares Series). Hoo: Grange Books.

The Kipling Society. (2014). *The musical settings of Kipling's verse* [Adobe Digital Editions Version]. Retrieved from http://www.kiplingsociety.co.uk/settings_60.pdf

Exploring Positive Psychology and Person-Centred Psychology in Multi-cultural Coaching

Llewellyn E. van Zyl, Renate Motschnig-Pitrik, and Marius W. Stander

Abstract Positive psychology and the person centred approach have emerged as dominant perspectives utilized within multi-cultural coaching contexts owing to 'cultural neutrality'. Eclectic theorists within coaching psychology suggest that these perspectives are mutually related and complementary both in conceptualization and application (Joseph S, Murphy D. Person-centered theory encountering mainstream psychology: Building bridges and looking to the future. In: Interdisciplinary handbook of the person-centered approach. Springer, New York, pp 213–226, 2013). Though, purists in both the positive psychological and person-centred domains argue that each paradigm is mutually exclusive, unrelated and conceptually dissimilar (Robbins, Humanist Psychol 36: 96–112, 2008). As such, this chapter is aimed at contrasting eclectic and purist theorising through examining similarities and differences between positive psychology and the person-centred approach as dominant paradigm perspectives within multi-cultural coaching. Both the positive psychological and person-centred paradigms will be presented against an eclectic multi-cultural strengths-based coaching model founded in both paradigms (cf. Van Zyl LE, Stander MW. A strengths-based approach towards coaching in a multicultural environment. In Cornelius-White JHD, Motschnig-Pitrik R, Lux M (eds) Interdisciplinary handbook of the person-centred approach. Springer, New York, pp 245–257, 2013). Through the use of connective conceptual analysis (Banicki 2011), each phase of the proposed eclectic coaching model will be explored from a positive psychological and person-centred orientation to develop a clear understanding of the essential commonalities and dissimilarities of the paradigms within the multicultural coaching context.

L.E. van Zyl (✉) • M.W. Stander
Optentia Research Focus Area, Department of Industrial Psychology, School for Behavioural Sciences, North-West University, Vaal Triangle Campus, Vanderbijlpark, South Africa
e-mail: llewellyn.vanzyl@nwu.ac.za; marius.stander@nwu.ac.za

R. Motschnig-Pitrik
University of Vienna, Vienna, Austria
e-mail: renate.motschnig@univie.ac.at

L.E. van Zyl et al. (eds.), *Coaching Psychology: Meta-theoretical perspectives and applications in multicultural contexts*, DOI 10.1007/978-3-319-31012-1_15

Keywords Coachee-centred coaching • Positive psychology • Person-centred approach • Strengths-based coaching • Executive coaching • Multi-cultural environment

1 Introduction

Coaching psychology is a relatively new practice domain within the meta-contextual boundaries of general psychology (Palmer and Whybrow 2014) with the aim to actualize human potential, enhance well-being and facilitate personal/professional development (Coetzee and Van Zyl 2014; Van Zyl and Stander 2013) in both uni- and multi-cultural contexts (Passmore 2013). Any developing practice domain, such as coaching psychology, needs to demarcate its professional territory and develop domain specific theories/approaches/models (Joseph 2006). These domain specific theories/approaches/models are usually rooted in previously researched or validated theorems in its 'mother domain', whereby the application value is amended to the needs of the new practice domain. Practically, coaching psychology draws from various psychological and related approaches, applied in the context of personal/ professional development as opposed to the traditional 'disease alleviation' approach.

Two popular paradigms[1] in general psychology, positive psychology and the person centred approach, have emerged as dominant paradigm perspectives utilised within multi-cultural coaching contexts owing to 'cultural neutrality' (Van Zyl and Stander 2013). These paradigms are widely accepted within traditional psychological practice domains (such as therapy) because of their short to medium term effectiveness (Passmore 2013; Van Zyl and Stander 2013). Because, coaching psychology is a short to medium term, goal directed process (Grant 2006), focused on positive growth (Van Zyl and Rothmann 2014), these approaches naturally resonate within the coaching psychology domain. However, the inter-relationship between positive psychology and the person centred approaches have been marked by contention, tension and ambivalence amongst practitioners, researchers and theorists in various applied psychological contexts such as therapy, counselling and coaching (Waterman 2013).

Innumerable attempts in the literature have been made to reconcile these two paradigms (c.f. Froh 2004; Joseph and Linley 2004; Linley et al. 2006; Robbins and Friedman 2008; Schneider 2011; Waterman 2013). These attempts have not succeeded in reconciling the paradigms, rather they have raised yet more awareness about the incompatibilities of the paradigms despite the apparent similarities. As a consequence, more disagreements (Waterman 2013) and confusion (Schneider 2011) has been created. The confusion spills over from the discipline into the

[1] The term paradigm and perspectives are used interchangeably within this chapter.

profession, which could have various adverse consequences for the coach, and the coachee.

From the literature it is apparent that two main arguments exist: (a) an eclectic and (b) purist approach to positive psychological and person centred coaching. Eclectic theorists within coaching psychology suggest that these perspectives are mutually related and complementary both in conceptualization and application (Joseph and Murphy 2013). Positive psychology positively contributes to the person centred approach as it provides more structure and proverbial 'quick wins' in the developmental process (Van Zyl and Stander 2013). Though, purists in both domains argue that each paradigm is mutually exclusive, unrelated and conceptually dissimilar (Robbins 2008; Waterman 2013). Person centred coaches tend to believe that humanistic psychology was the forerunner of positive psychology and the most important contributor to the paradigm which focuses on many of the same concerns (Robbins 2008; Waterman 2013). In contrast, positive psychological coaches are inclined to see the person centred approach as one (amongst many) psychological foundations of positive psychology and not the most important as stipulated by purists in the person centred approach (Joseph and Murphy 2013). According to Waterman (2013), purists in the person centred approach are not pleased with the direction in which the positive psychology discipline is developing in relation to human potential development and well-being. Similarly, purist positive psychological coaches have not found it important to capitalize on all the insights and contributions of the person centred approach because they are deemed insignificant or in effective (Waterman 2013). Waterman (2013, p. 124) indicates that the main differences between the paradigms lies in its "(a) ontology, including the ways in which human nature is conceptualized regarding human potential and well-being; (b) epistemology, specifically, the choice of research strategies for the empirical study of these concepts; and (c) practical philosophy, particularly the goals and strategies adopted when conducting [coaching] interventions".

As such, this chapter is aimed at stepping out of the tight discourse between eclectic and purist theorising through taking a fresh view on similarities and differences between positive psychology and the person-centred approach as dominant paradigm perspectives within multi-cultural coaching. Banicki (2011) suggest clarification regarding complex subject matter needs to be presented against a practical problem or approach. As such, each paradigm will be presented against an eclectic multi-cultural strengths-based coaching model founded in both paradigms (cf. Van Zyl and Stander 2013) in order to conceptualize the core differences in each. Through the use of connective conceptual analysis (Banicki 2011), each phase of the proposed eclectic coaching model will be explored from a positive psychological and person-centred orientation to develop a clear understanding of the essential commonalities and dissimilarities of the paradigms. Further, this chapter aims to reveal conceptual implications and limitations of both paradigms within multi-cultural coaching. The chapter concludes by suggesting in which ways the two related paradigms are mutually beneficial, non-exclusive and applicable within multi-cultural coaching contexts.

Intriguingly, the insights we want to share through this chapter precisely match our experience as co-authors working together and coming from the realm of positive psychology on the one hand and the person centred approach on the other. While the objectives we endeavour to achieve through proposing the multi-cultural coaching model are exactly the same, the paths to get there differ significantly, based on the respective philosophical underpinning or paradigm we draw from.

2 Orientation to the Person Centred and Positive Psychology Approaches in Coaching

There is accumulating evidence that professionals aiming to promote human potential need to move away from the "medical"-, disease-oriented model towards facilitating psychological growth (Seligman 2011) and optimal development (Cilliers 2011). As individuals present with an inherent tendency to become the best they can under given circumstances (Rogers 1961), growth can happen through focusing on individual strengths, as argued, for example, by the positive psychologists Park and Peterson (2006). Complementarily, growth can happen by providing persons with a psychological climate in which their inherent tendency towards actualization can unfold optimally (Rogers 1951). In such a climate persons are provided opportunities to discover their potentials and to utilize them, for example in the organization that employs them.

One area through which personal and professional enhancement can be furthered is coaching (Cilliers 2011). Fledman and Lankau (2005) describe coaching as a professional goal directed relationship between a coach and coachee with the intent to improve the work performance of the coachee through concentrating on altering behaviour and addressing/preventing organizational problems. Coaching is conceptualized as a practical, short to medium term, goal-orientated form of personal- and professional development (Van Zyl and Stander 2013) which is in contrast to the classical or traditional medical/disease model approaches.

Cilliers (2011) argued that these "classical" or "traditional" over emphasises "correcting what is wrong" rather than facilitating optimal development, resulting in rather mechanistic approaches, leaving the coachee as human being behind (Biswas-Diener 2010). Consequently, sustainable, inherently motivated change might not happen and the manifested behaviour would be likely to reoccur (Rogers 1951; Seligman 2011). Therefore, to promote sustainable change, the coaching relationship and approach urgently need to focus on the realities and potentials of the coachee in their work environment.

According to Rogers (1951), the father of the person-centred approach, the individual (client/coachee) should be at the centre of the personal development process, and not be dictated by the process or the counsellor (coach, therapist, etc.). From this perspective, the central function of the person centred coach is to act as a facilitator for the growth-process and to aim to uncover and understand the subjective reality of the coachee (from his/her own perspective) (Carkhuff 2000; Rogers 1951). This calls for the coach to approach the process from within the coachee's reality. Since this is also a main theme in positive psychology (Seligman and Csikszentimihalyi 2000), person-centred coaching practitioners characterize their approach to coaching as being *coachee-centred*. Further, the person centred approach focuses on providing those qualities of interpersonal relationships that, if perceived, contribute to empowerment, constructive change, and creative problem solving. Strongly simplified, according to Rogers (1959, 1961) a person needs to perceive the "core conditions" of congruence, unconditional positive regard, and empathic understanding, at least to some degree, for constructive personality change to occur.

Positive psychology assumes that each individual has the capacity for personal growth, to develop strengths, build on positive emotions, and to develop sustainable resilience (Van Zyl and Stander 2013). Further, positive psychology, unlike the person centred approach, is also concerned with how individuals within organizational contexts can develop in order to enhance organizational flourishing (Biswas-Diener 2010; Seligman 2011) through various positive psychological intervention strategies (such as positive psychological coaching) targeting different levels within the organisational context (Van Zyl and Rothmann 2014). Positive psychological coaching, in particular, refers to a structured approach relating to the identification, optimization and application of individual strengths, positive behaviours/attitudes and positive emotions in order to facilitate development of individuals in organizational contexts (Van Zyl and Stander 2013). However, limited research exists on positive psychological coaching within multi-cultural environments (Cilliers 2011) as well as the boundaries between the person-centred and positive psychological paradigms within coaching psychology (Van Zyl and Stander 2013).

Both these approaches focus or rely on identifying, employing, and enhancing individual strengths and qualities (e.g. authenticity, autonomy etc.) in order to facilitate personal and professional development (Van Zyl and Stander 2013). Further, both paradigms intend to facilitate the development of interpersonal attitudes of openness to experience, unconditional positive regard, non-directivity and empathic understanding within a personal development process (Van Zyl and Stander 2013).

In order to illuminate the positive psychology and person-centred approaches to multi-cultural coaching, we briefly re-introduce the ten-phase strengths based coaching model developed by Van Zyl and Stander (2013) which is founded in the principles of both the positive psychological-, and person centred approaches. The proposed model provides the ideal context to contrast the positive psychological and person centred approaches due to its eclectic stance in the use and application of core principles of each paradigm. We proceed by presenting a brief overview of the ten-phase model as well as its components, whereby it will be attempted to contrast the positive psychological and person centred principles and consequent practices underpinning each phase. On this basis we are able to explore in which ways the positive psychological- and person-centred schools of thought relate, differ, and can potentially complement each other within the multi-cultural coaching environment.

3 The Strengths Based Coaching Model: Contrasting Paradigms

Van Zyl and Stander (2013) proposed a strengths based coaching model built upon the assumption that individuals have a capacity to grow, develop and actualize their inherent, 'untapped' potential. The model assumes that individuals have a natural inclination to engage in behaviours associated with this inherent propensity to develop and grow (Rogers 1951; Seligman 2011). Thus, human behaviour is naturally directed towards the maintenance and enhancement of their organisms (Rogers 1951). Hence, a central orientation in this model is on persons and the provision of an atmosphere or context in which enhancement rather than just maintenance is the choice. This tends to be the case when individuals feel safe and accepted rather than threatened by some external demand to change their behaviour, thinking, personal attitudes and preferences.

At its core, the model focuses on the development and application of individual strengths in order to satisfy the inherent human need for self-actualization (Van Zyl and Stander 2013). According to Peterson and Seligman (2004), personal or 'signature' strengths – from the positive psychology stance – can be defined as a universally valued set of core characteristics that attributes to good character which manifests as individual differences/traits which are relatively stable overtime and shaped by the contextual environment. The focus on the development of strengths, within the coaching environment may contribute to the development of life satisfaction and facilitate the pursuit of a meaningful life or career (Fronczak 2006; Sheldon et al. 2011; Van Zyl and Rothmann 2014).

Similarly, Van Zyl and Stander (2013) argues that the pursuit of meaningful life and career goals is brought on by a need of the coachee to execute tasks and engage in activities which are more in line with his/her strengths. Their model draws from the positive psychological assumption that individuals have a natural capacity to engage in behaviours, initiate cognitive evaluations and activate certain emotions which allows for the optimal functioning and performance in pursuit of the aforementioned goals (Linley and Harrington 2006). This appears to be in line with the person-centred perspective assuming an individual's actualizing tendency that forms the foundation through which a person has the inherent potential to become the best he/she can under given circumstances or in their environment. This potential can best be tapped when respecting the natural, biological tendency toward unfolding inherent capacities rather than imposing some external direction of development (Rogers 2008a) through the coaching process.

Flowing from these conceptual frameworks for strengths, Van Zyl and Stander (2013) states that strengths-based coaching is a short to medium term strengths focused developmental process aimed at harnessing the inner potential of a coachee in order to optimize his/her performance and to actualize his/her potential. The strengths-based approach focuses on altering the way in which the coachee thinks,

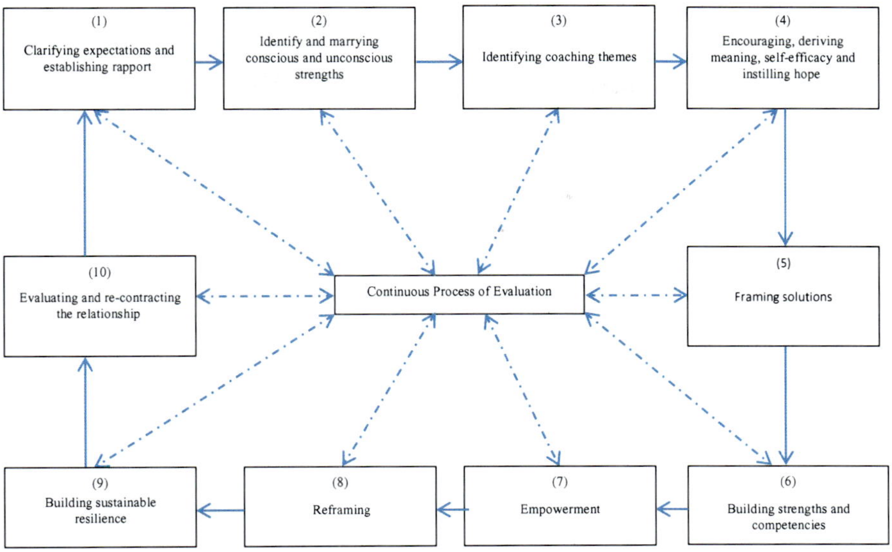

Fig. 1 The strengths based coaching model

feels and acts through building on his/her signature strengths in order to optimize performance, enhance personal well-being and to achieve live/work goals (Van Zyl and Rothmann 2014; Van Zyl and Stander 2013). These fundamental ideals are core to both the person centred and the positive psychological paradigms (Waterman 2013), even though different terminologies may be used as descriptors, such as 'strengths' (positive psychology) versus 'capacities/potentials' (person-centred) or 'natural capacity' (positive psychology) versus 'actualizing tendency' (person-centred).

Flowing from these core principles, Van Zyl and Stander (2013) developed the ten phase strengths-based coaching model (see Fig. 1). Van Zyl and Stander (2013) as well as Stander (in this book) argue this strengths-based coaching process is cyclical and rooted in the principles of continuous feedback and evaluation. As with the person-centred approach, minimal encouragement sits at the core of this model, since this acts as an indication of unconditional positive regard (Carkhuff 2000; Rogers 1978; Van Zyl and Rothmann 2014). Drawing from these, this model implies that an empowering, encouraging relationship between the coach and coachee aids the coach in order to (a) express unconditional acceptance, (b) communicate empathy, (c) project confidence, (d) reinforce the identification and utilization of strengths and inner-resources, (e) acknowledge the effort and improvement of the coachee, and (f) facilitate the successful completion of mutually identified goals during the process (Van Zyl and Stander 2013).

A key part of the model is unconditional positive regard resulting in the unhindered unfolding of the coachee's actualizing tendency and thus setting free vast resources of motivational energy to participate and engage in the growth process. Practically, this is a process in which the coach:

- feels and expresses acceptance,
- endeavours to empathically understand the coachee, their manager(s), and their environment,
- has confidence as to positive results,
- acknowledges, in particular, the strengths and resources of all persons participating in the coaching process,
- appreciates the effort and improvement of the client and attends, in particular, to the transfer of competencies acquired in the self-directed process to the work-environment,
- facilitates the implementation of decisions that are made throughout the process,
- works at empowering the coachee to remove structural/organizational barriers that hinder the process,
- knows and does not feel any resistance – optimally feels at ease and supportive of – the goals of the organization and the manager. In other words, the coach feels congruent and in no way conflicted with regard to his/her feelings toward the organization's aspired direction and coachee-centred coaching job. This entails clarity about what would happen if – as a result of coaching – the coachee would find out that it is better for them to leave the job or change to a different department or any other consequence that might be at cross with what the manager aspires.

These inherent drivers are essential to facilitate a change in the coachee's behaviour (Carkhuff 2000) which is aligned to the person-centred approach (Rogers 1951, 1961). Drawing from the positive psychological paradigm, Van Zyl and Stander (2013) argued that strengths must be evoked to aid in the sustainable change in behaviour and to overcome obstacles. As such, the pivotal challenge for the coach is to facilitate the unfolding of the coachee's inherent psychological resources that will lead to self-directed behaviour changes ensuring improved performance for the organisation and wellness for the individual (Moore and McBride 2014).

In summation, the model aims to support an effective coaching process in a manner that:

- Is strength-based – focusing on the coachee's strengths and his/her developmental potential,
- Is coachee-centred – acknowledging the coachee as part of an organization to be in the center of the coaching process. This entails a non-directive stance in which it is the coachee who drives the direction of his/her development and change,
- Provides a process structure as a tool to consider essential aspects in the coaching process,
- Considers the organizational context and a multicultural environment.

In the following sections extracts from each phase of the Van Zyl and Stander (2013) model will be provided followed by a positive psychological and person-centred interpretation.

3.1 *Phase 1: Clarifying Expectations and Establishing Rapport*

Central Goals and Tasks

According to Van Zyl and Stander (2013) the purpose of this phase is to clarify the expectations between (a) the coach/coachee, (b) coach/senior management, (c) coach/direct manager and (d) coachee and his/her direct manager, in order to establish rapport, transparency of expectations and to include the organizational context (e.g. vision/mission/strategy) into the coaching process. Importantly, this clarification process is targeted at developing the individual within his/her current role or position (Koortzen and Oosthuizen 2010), as well as within the broader organisational context (Van Zyl and Stander 2013). As such, the objective of this phase is to develop an understanding of the associative dynamics of the coachee's current work-related reality, the nature and extent of his/her role within the contextual department/organization boundary and to establish a foundation from which to approach the developmental process (Van Zyl and Stander 2013).

Consequently, Van Zyl and Stander (2013) supports Bennett (1993) and Rogers (1961) through highlighting the importance of understanding the coachee's work-related reality and interpretative framework in terms of potential gender-, generations-, values-, interactional preferences-, belief and cultural differences as well as its associative impact. As such, the coach needs to be culturally sensitivity and interoperate the coachee's messages from his/her own perspective (Bennett 1993; Van Zyl and Stander 2013). These cultural differences are optimally appreciated as opportunities which could have the potential to enrich the coaching relationship (Bachkirova 2011). Through focusing the developmental process in line with the coachee's current work-related reality and interpretive framework, the coach could capitalize on cultural specific nuances and support mechanisms emanating from cultural specific heritage. For example, Western cultures are described as being individualistic and places a high value on autonomy as a signature strength, where as in African (collectivistic) cultures social competence and relatedness strengths are valued (Smith 2006). Therefore, within multi-cultural contexts, authentic and respectful interactions are crucial to the success of the coaching process (Rogers 1961; Van Zyl and Stander 2013). Similarly, potential differences and hindrances should be expressed and clarified between the coach and coachee (van Zyl and Stander 2011), such as conflicting views on religion.

A Positive Psychology Approach to Phase 1

From a positive psychological perspective, this phase involves discovering the potential (mis)alignment between individual strengths of character (Peterson and Seligman 2004), managerial demands and organizational expectations (Van Zyl and Stander 2011) in order to develop an understanding of the coachee's current work-related reality. The function of this phase is to advocate a collective strengths-based inquiry into (a) the best of the current reality encompassing the coachee/manager/organizational interface, (b) to imagine the reality which could be, and (c) to collectively construct a compelling future where incentives, persuasion, or coercion is not needed (Lewis et al. 2008; Whitney and Trosten-Bloom 2010). The focus here is to frame questions in a positive, constructive and imaginative manner in order to stimulate thinking around what is 'right' (i.e. currently working well) rather than focusing what is 'wrong' (i.e. distracting from performance or the 'deficiency model') (Lewis et al. 2008). In this phase, the use of positively infused language is imperative, as it sets the proverbial scene and intention of the process that is to follow (Cannell 2015). Further, positively infused language communicates empathy, positive regard and authenticity which results in a stronger rapport, creating a psychologically safe environment and facilitates the coachee towards self-acceptance (Scheel et al. 2013).

A Person-Centred Approach to Phase 1

From the person-centred approach, the coachee's and their manager's intrinsic motivation to engage in the coaching process is crucial (Rogers 1961). To achieve this, the participants in the coaching process must sense that the process will be of genuine value to them. The pivotal factor for evoking motivation and engagement is the quality of the interpersonal relationships between the participants throughout the process (Rogers 1951). Therefore it is essential to allow time for establishing constructive, interpersonal relationships that will energize all involved for maximum possible psychological growth (Rogers 1959, 1961) and collaboration (Cain 2010; Motschnig-Pitrik 2014). Furthermore, if the coachee perceives the coach as a resourceful person (Barrett-Lennard 2013), having resources that extend their own, this can strengthen the motivation to engage in the coaching process.

According to the theory of the person-centred approach, an interpersonal relationship between the facilitator/coach and the client/coachee will be growth promoting under the condition that the coach succeeds in establishing and cultivating a specified but unspecific interpersonal climate based on genuineness, acceptance and empathic understanding. This *climate* is interchangeably referred to as *person-centred, facilitative, growth-promoting or constructive*. More precisely, it arises if the coach communicates his/her congruence, acceptance and empathic understanding of the coachee in such a way that the coachee can perceive these attitudes at least to some degree (Rogers 1961).

A helpful practice for gaining thorough and empathic understanding of the coachee is active listening (Rogers and Farson 1987). This way to listen is particularly important in multicultural settings, where persons can't rely on mutually identical cultural patterns, habits, norms, and expressions (Lago 2013). Hence, understanding needs to be confirmed explicitly while listening, e.g. by paraphrasing or asking questions more often than in culturally homogenous situations. In any environment, however, it is vital that the coach's understanding of the coachee (and optimally also the other participants in the coaching process) is a complex, thorough, and empathic one, including the inner world of the coachee along with his/her current work-related environment and relationships.

In the course of establishing contact and initial, constructive, collaborative relationships, it is essential to share expectations and to determine, whether all involved are moving into coherent directions. Optimally, all stakeholders involved are facilitated to develop a shared vision of the coaching intervention that includes the participants' expectations and intended outcomes of the process. This can happen either in a series of individual- and manager-coachee-coach sessions, or in facilitated small group settings, depending on the particular situation/atmosphere in the organization and on the coach's competencies of working with groups. As a result, participants' expectations and goals would best be formulated to provide a reference point to return to whenever needed.

Finally, the coaching process and the means of documentation and re-evaluation need to be agreed upon. Typically, for the latter two aspects, the coach and coachee (and potentially all participants) would provide free-text-style reflection journals in which they'd share for example significant experiences, thoughts, changes, and questions from or between the sessions (Rogers 1983; Motschnig and Nykl 2014). In a democratic environment, these could be shared and used to inform follow up sessions for increased continuity of the process. Optimally, the reaction journals would be complemented by participative designed, semi-structured questionnaires to keep track of special aspects of the coaching process, such as cultural sensitivity and competence, person-centred attitudes of the coach, or changes in the coachee's self-concept. In this way data for participatory action research could be supplied, enabling systematic, open, and continuous learning throughout the process.

3.2 *Phase 2: Identifying Conscious and Unconscious Strengths*

Central Goals and Tasks

According to Van Zyl and Stander (2013), the purpose of this phase is to initiate a process whereby the coachee's unconscious capacities/strengths are determined and merged with (a) his/her current competencies (Seligman 2011), and (b) aligned to the clarified expectations and measurable outcomes determined in Phase 1. An evaluative methodological framework such as a competency profile needs to be developed in line with the coachee's current (and future) role within the organization, which highlights the crucial performance areas associated with the position as well as the aspired outcomes (Bachkirova 2011). Finally, the coachee's individual- and team related competencies should be explored in order to draw attention to his/her currently manifested signature strengths and raise awareness of the developmental areas or potential deraillers (Van Zyl and Stander 2013).

A Positive Psychology Approach to Phase 2

Within the positive psychological paradigm, strength identification, -awareness and -utilization is key to human potential development as well as individual- (Seligman 2011) and organizational performance (Bayramoğlu and Şahin 2015). However, most individuals are not completely aware of their manifested ('know') or unconscious ('unknown') strengths (Peterson and Seligman 2004). It is therefore imperative in this phase to make the coachee aware of his/her strengths through either (a) strengths based psychometric assessments, (b) strengths based inquiry and (c) strengths based identification initiatives.

First, various self-report strengths-based psychometric instruments exists such as the VIA signature strengths inventory (VIA: Peterson and Seligman 2004) or the Strengths Finder 2.0 (SFF2.0: Rath 2007). These instruments provide a cross-culturally validated platform through which to aid the coachee in the identification and 'ranking' of personal (VIA) or professional (SF2.0) strengths. Both instruments rank self-report strengths in order of frequency of use as well as provide a classification of prevalence. The five most prevalent and highly used strengths should be used by the coach to highlight their occurrence in the life story of the coachee as well as employed as part of the personal/professional development strategies (Van Zyl and Stander 2013; Welch et al. 2014). The coachee could be presented with questions similar to 'How would you use the combination of your leadership strength and social intelligence to approach the presented problem?' in order to cognitively develop strength-based strategies aimed at personal/professional grow and/or to approach problems (Scheel et al. 2013; Welch et al. 2014).

Second, in some circumstances the results of the strengths-based psychometric assessment measures may not be readily available. As such, alternative strengths-based identification methods, such as strengths-based inquiry, need to be employed (Welch et al. 2014). Strength-based inquiry pertains to the identification of a coachee's signature strengths through conversations whereby the coachee's strength use are highlighted and accentuated (Peterson and Seligman 2004; Scheel et al. 2013). Coachees may be requested to share stories where they were at their best, where they were in a state of flow (absolute engagement) or where they felt that they were in complete control of their proverbial destiny (Scheel et al. 2013; Van Zyl and Rothmann 2014). These stories tend to highlight virtuous abilities, characteristics or talents which the coachee employed at their 'self-report proverbial best' (Scheel et al. 2013; Seligman 2011). However, strengths may also manifest as part of the coachee's personal deficits or challenges (e.g. humour employed as a mechanism to manage conflict or to ease emotional pain) (Scheel et al. 2013). Therefore, the coach needs to be fully competent in strengths-based inquiry in order to identify, highlight and re-inforce the coachee's strengths in both 'successful' and 'unsuccessful/ challenging' scenarios (Coetzer et al. 2014; Peterson and Seligman 2004; Scheel et al. 2013).

According to Peterson and Seligman (2004), the coach needs to be fully aware of the diagnostic criteria of a signature strength in order to easily identify the use of a particular strength in various contexts. Specifically, the coach needs to identify the following characteristics in the coachee's story to determine whether or not a presented ability is a strength:

1. There is a sense of ownership and authenticity when presenting with a strength
2. Feelings of excitement when displaying a strength
3. Seeking new ways to enact strengths
4. Yearning to act in accordance with the strength
5. Feeling of inevitability in using the strength
6. Feelings of invigoration rather than exhaustion when acting it
7. Creating and seeking projects which endorses these strengths
8. Intrinsically motivated to use the strength

Finally, strengths-based identification initiatives could be employed to determine strengths. These initiatives refer to objective attempts by the coach/coachee to initiate processes whereby strengths could be identified and/or exposed. These initiatives relates to aspects such as 360° Strengths Evaluations or a 360° competency assessment, whereby peers, supervisors, direct reports, friends, family and the like are requested to rate or rank the coachee's strengths. Similarly, peer strengths-based story telling could be employed whereby significant others in the coachee's life are requested to pose stories whereby they perceived the coachee to be at his/her best. These strengths-based identification initiatives aids the coach to obtain either (a) an indication of the coachee's manifest strengths or (b) relatively 'objective' evidence of the coachee's strength use as perceived by others. This may also highlight and reinforce strength use in the coachee.

Through the use of the aforementioned strengths-based identification strategies, the positive psychological coach should also aim to (a) identify strengths explicitly present in the coachee, (b) gain an understanding of the coachee's perceptions of his/her strengths, (c) raise awareness of the coachee's strengths, (d) aid coachees to overcome their focus on problems/weaknesses, and (e) emphasize culturally specific strengths, in order to subtly amplify the coachee's strengths through cognitive restructuring (Scheel et al. 2012).

A Person-Centred Approach to Phase 2

In a person-centred atmosphere, the coachee will tend to feel safe to explore his/her capacities and thus become more aware of both their strengths and weaknesses. By recognizing the coachee's talents and strengths, the coach can empathically accompany the coachee towards strengthened self-awareness and differentiation of their strong sides. This "selective empathy" builds trust and tends to motivate the coachee to stay with their strong sides and give more weight to them, in particular in the context of the coachee's work-related activities. To stay focused on the work setting, the coach may furthermore "guide his/her empathic understanding" to work-related issues. This will help to keep the coachee's exploration to relate to work situations rather than diverse other directions (that at times may be worth following, though).

If, however, the coachee comes to a point where he/she explicitly wants to explore a weakness too, an empathic coach would respect that. He/she would offer their relationship to allow the coachee to move forward in their unfoldment along the coachee's sense of what matters to him/her at the moment. In brief, the focus on strengths is considered as a helpful guideline but not an exclusive imperative.

If the coach feels that the self-exploration process could be made more effective by employing psychometric measurement and/or self-assessments by the coachee, he/she can suggest such instruments to be introduced. For example, the coach can invite the coachee to learn more about his/her strengths by suggesting to complete the Values in Action Inventory of Strengths (VIA-IS) (Peterson and Seligman 2004). Given the coachee is interested in some testing, the test results need to be discussed with him/her and their view on the results need to be received empathically and taken into account. One example of a test that tends to be worthwhile for heightening awareness of the coachee's preferred role(s) when working in teams is the Belbin teamwork test (Belbin 2010). It allows one to find out which team role(s) and functions one tends to manifest (Belbin 2010). An attractive feature of Belbin's teamwork test is that each team type is described appreciatively with strong and weak sides appearing like two sides of one coin. Instruments like Belbin's test can, in the authors view, extend the coachee's complex understanding of work-related issues that might not come up in pure active listening endeavours that lie at the core of the person-centred approach.

Another person-centred way to strengthen one's awareness of (inter)personal capacities and at the same time provide for personal growth is the participation in encounter groups, intensive, often unstructured self-experience groups (Rogers 1970; O'Hara 2013). For work- related contexts, these encounter groups could be theme-based and devoted to tackling relevant, timely themes in an organization or even across organizations while discovering interpersonal capacities. Examples of such themes are: Organizational change, collaboration in multicultural teams, managing family and work, or collaboratively exploring team's and individual's strengths.

The competence profile would typically be co-developed as a collaborative endeavour between the coach and the coachee (Cain 2010) after the coachee had sufficient opportunity to become more aware of his/her capacities as well as goals for personal and work-related development. The process would be open to be creatively complemented by whatever aspect the coachee considers important.

3.3 *Phase 3: Identifying Coaching Themes*

Central Goals and Tasks

The purpose of this phase is to develop a clear understanding regarding the current challenges in the coachee's life and to develop a strategy to build competencies (Bachkirova 2011; Seligman 2011) through integrating the information gathered in Phases 1 and 2 (Van Zyl and Stander 2013). The focus is to determine the coachee's areas of development through understanding the current challenges in his/her current work-related reality (Van Zyl and Stander 2013). As such, a deliberate attempt needs to be employed in order to reveal the coachee's (a) perceptions associated with current difficulties/challenges, (b) reasons why these exists, (c) the factors attributable to the challenges, (d) the possible consequences if these are unresolved and (e) the meaning derived from the given challenging context (Bachkirova 2011; Palmer and Whybrow 2014; Rogers 1951). Through understanding the presented problem/challenges, aligned to the coachee's strengths, a personal development strategy aligned to a personal growth or development plan could be co-developed and implemented (Van Zyl and Stander 2013).

A Positive Psychology Approach to Phase 3

Much of the criticizm relating to positive psychology pertains to the fallacy that the paradigm ignores the proverbial 'negative' conditions of the human psyche (Lopez et al. 2014). However, positive psychology doesn't shun these negative conditions (Smith 2006; Tugade and Fredrickson 2004; Van Zyl and Rothmann 2014; Van Zyl and Stander 2013), but rather suggests that these conditions need to be (a) interpreted from and (b) addressed through the use of individual signature strengths (Peterson and Seligman 2014) or competencies.

First, problems/challenges of the coachee need to be interpreted from a positive psychological perspective. Although research suggests the importance and value of strengths use (Grant and Schwartz 2011; Seligman 2011; Van Zyl and Rothmann 2014; Niemiec (2014) argues that strengths could be over/under utilized which may result in an in balance within the coachee or in relation to important relationships. Practically, presented challenges in the coachee's reality relates to the over-use of a signature strength which might have been appropriate in previous contexts (Niemiec 2014). Grant and Schwartz (2011) found the strength use may reach an inflection point whereby the experience and resultant effects turn negative.

Each character strength lies on a continuum in relation to expression (or use) ranging from over/under utilization to optimal expression (Grant and Schwartz 2011) whereby an ideal point of balance is sought between these extremes (Niemiec 2014). This argument suggests that desirable attributes, such as a coachee's signature strengths, should be cultivated in moderation. Practically speaking, when a strength is under/over utilized it is no longer considered a strength because it distracts the attainment, utilization and expression of other more appropriate strengths and counter-acts the outcomes it is intended to promote (Grant and Schwartz 2011). For example, within academic literature the well-being benefits of the signature strength 'Kindness and Generosity' (giving of one's self unconditionally, and more than one would receive) has been greatly documented (*c.f.* Lyubomirsky 2011; Lyubomirsky et al. 2005; Seligman 2011), however Flynn (2003) found an inverted U relationship between generosity and the quality, quantity and efficiency of completed work (productivity) relative to manager's expectations. As such, the coachee's presented problems/developmental areas/negative conditions should be interpreted against the strengths over/under/optimal use principle (Niemiec 2014).

Second, these problems/challenges should be addressed through capitalizing on the coachee's optimally used signature strengths. Because, individuals approach, interpret and manage situations within the bounds of their contextual strengths awareness, strength utilization should form a key part of the developmental strategy. The developmental strategy should be co-developed with the coachee highlighting (a) the competencies which need to develop in order to effectively manage the presented challenges, or highlighting the personal/professional goal the coachee wants to achieve, (b) developing an action plan for addressing presented challenge/achieving professional goal, (c) determine the desired outcome, (d) methods used to evaluate (measure) the progress (or success) of the initiative, (e) the internal (psychological strengths) and external resources required, (f) a mutually agreed deadline for completion and (g) ensure that the unique multi-cultural strengths and capabilities of the coachee is incorporated and capitalized on throughout the strategy (Van Zyl and Stander 2011).

A Person-Centred Approach to Phase 3

Based on a thorough and complex understanding of the coachee's current challenges and on the information as well as, importantly, the interpersonal relationship(s) that unfolded in the previous phases, a strategy to strengthen work-related competencies (Bachkirova 2011; Seligman 2011) is developed. Thereby the coach relies, first of all, on the coachee's actualizing tendency towards enhancement of their potentialities by trusting their sense of the situation and choice of paths to move forward. The resulting directions and goals are summarized in a personal development plan (PDP) to accompany the process as a reference (Bachkirova 2011). The PDP is viewed as a working document to be revisited and evolved on demand. Time and atmosphere permitting, the PDP is shared with the manager and he or she is kept informed about any major changes, accomplishments or burdens popping up on the way.

3.4 Phase 4: Encouraging, Deriving Meaning, Developing Self-Efficacy and Instilling Hope

Central Goals and Tasks

The purpose of this phase is to facilitate the development of the coachee's inherent potential through encouragement, the use of strengths-based meaning crafting activities and capitalising on his/her self-actualising tendency in order to enhance hope (Van Zyl and Stander 2013). From this perspective, encouragement serves as a mechanism to positively reinforce desired behaviour and to emphasize strengths use (Lyubomirsky 2011; Smith 2006). As such, encouragement is employed as a means through which the coachee's psychological resources are highlighted, and developed in order to facilitate the formulation of positive decisions and approaches (Rogers 1951). The coach could utilize encouragement in order to 'support' the manifestation of desired behaviour (e.g. strength utilisation) in order for the coachee to reframe this behaviour as a strength (Lyubomirsky 2011). The intent is to facilitate self-exploration and the reinforcement of strength use in a presented scenario through probing the coachee on strategies where he/she used the signature strengths to address the presented challenges (Niemiec 2014; Seligman 2011). The coach invites the coachee to learn from different experiences. As a result the coachee will discover alternative possibilities to use these capacities, motivating the exploration of the self and the development of self-identity. Further, the coach should initiate own self-reflective processes and practices in order to effectively process his/her own understanding of the context, the coachee and the incorporated approach.

In a nutshell, while the coach may offer instruments or interpretations addressing the over- and underutilization of strengths, his/her primary resource remains to be the interpersonal relationship with coachee and his/her genuine interest in accompanying the coachee to meet presented challenges in his/her reality. Like in the positive psychology approach, the PDP needs to be developed as a collaborative endeavour between coach and coachee (Cain 2010).

A Positive Psychology Approach to Phase 4

One of the central tendencies in applied positive psychology is to facilitate the development of self-identity through the use of strengths-based initiatives aimed at self-exploration in order to establish self-awareness (Seligman 2011). Self-awareness, in itself, should also be considered a psychological strength (Niemiec 2014) as it aids in building ego strength, manages anxiety, activates self-appreciation and promotes further engagements in obtaining self-knowledge (Scheel et al. 2012).

From a purist positive psychological perspective, the aim of this phase would be to make the coachee aware of the manifestation of strength utilization within a presented problem and to aid in reinforcing strength use in problematic situations through the use of positive reinforcement (Scheel et al. 2012). This can, however, only be achieved if the coach aims to intentionally and deliberately highlight and honours (validates) the coachee's efforts and struggles in his/her attempts to deal with the negative conditions or presenting issues (Smith 2006). Research suggests that the coachee of practitioners whom engage with validation (encouragement) and strengths-confirming initiatives achieve their coaching/therapy/counselling goals at a higher rate than those who do not engage in the practice (Niemiec 2014; Seligman 2011; Smith 2006; Weick and Chamberlain 2002).

Therefore, the aim of this phase is to systematically alter the way in which the coachee interoperates negative conditions through the use of positive reinforcement in order to aid the development of inner resources and courage to engage in positive decision making practices (Palmer and Whybrow 2014; Smith 2006). One way in which this could be achieved is for the positive psychological coach to utilize narrative psychological practices through encouraging coachees to retell their stories as survivors, rather than victims. This aids in altering the coachee's perspectives of the presented problem and establishes a sense that numerous possibilities exists to understanding the problem (Smith 2006; Van Zyl and Rothmann 2014; Van Zyl and Stander 2013) as it aids the coachee to shed the victim mentality (Desetta and Wolin 2000). This results in the establishment of hope and optimism as different perspectives to the presented problem is highlighted (Van Zyl and Stander 2013). As hope and optimism buffers against the onset of psychopathology (Peterson and Seligman 2004; Seligman 2011; Smith 2006), the positive psychological coach should aim to rekindle these positive psychological states through purposeful reflection and/or exploring other scenarios where the coachee may have felt hopeful/optimistic (Palmer and Whybrow 2014; Smith 2006).

In summation, the intention of this phase from a positive psychological perspective is to (a) encourage the continuation of change, (b) to ensure that the coachee feels part of the process or 'heard' through ensuring compliance to multi-cultural facets, (c) to advocate for a positive 'voice' in the coachee's reality evaluation framework, (d) to show appreciation for the effort the coachee is exerting in the process, (e) to validate the coachee's experiences, (f) to positively affirm the coachee's successes and to (g) positively reframe negative experiences.

A Person-Centred Approach to Phase 4

While, interestingly, the intention of this phase largely coincides with the one described in the positive-psychology approach to this phase, the description/wording of the person-centred approach to phase 4 differs substantially. Rather than "aiming to systematically alter the way in which the coachee interoperates negative conditions" or "utilizing psychological practices" the person-centred coach would stay non-directive, unconditionally accepting the coachee, and refraining from seeking to change. This is because, philosophically, the coachee is considered his or her own expert and any explicit effort to change him or her could be perceived as threat that may invoke defence mechanisms in the coachee that make his/her self-concept more rigid than flexible or changeable (Rogers 1959; Rogers and Farson 1987).

Consequently, like in the previous phases, the coach offers his/her person-centred attitudes and thus supports the coachee to accept him-/herself in their way of being. This unconditional acceptance is – paradoxically – the first step towards constructive change that is inherently motivated and self-directed (Rogers 1961). Through perceiving the safe, confirming climate in the coaching relationship, the coachee feels secure enough to open up towards any experience he/she encounters, to process it in and outside the coaching relationship and to grow from it. This free exploration of own experience and reliance on their feelings as well as rational thought will tend to render the coachee more creative to deal with new situations. Supported by a genuinely accepting and empathic coach, he/she is trusted and facilitated to find situation-specific, often unorthodox solutions to complex problems (Rogers 1961). Furthermore, the coachee will tend to reciprocate the acceptance and respect he or she is enjoying to receive from the coach and try to grant it to their environment (Rogers 1951, proposition18). This will benefit, in particular, relationships with culturally diverse colleagues whose being different will be accepted rather than combatted or devalued. All in all, the coachee will become more open-minded and up to following their personal goals and the shared vision specified in earlier phases.

To support this development, the coachee can be offered to try the experiential technique of focusing (Gendlin 1982). This entails an explicit offering to sense e.g. a problem in one's body and to find and name a referent expression or feeling. Focusing may speed up the coachee's capacity to get in touch with their feelings, to clear (inner) space for more openness, and to reduce stress and tension. In this way the whole organism including cognitions, feelings, meanings, and the body is mobilized to deal with upcoming challenges in a coordinated and united way.

3.5 Phase 5: Framing Solutions and Action Plans

Central Goals and Tasks

This phase involves developing or framing solutions and action plans to current challenges and developmental areas (Van Zyl and Stander 2013). This is done through solution-building conversations (Smith 2006), whereby the coachee is made aware of Justice and Jamieson's (2002) "accept, change or leave principle". Justice and Jamieson (2002) postulates that there are three high-level responses to most given stressors, challenges and problems, namely: (a) accepting the status quo, (b) changing oneself or changing the environment, or (c) leaving the problem situation. Solutions need to be built around one of these ideals as different developmental strategies are associated with the various outcomes. Through simplifying the available choices, the coachee might feel more in control of the process whereby the extent problem area may be minimalized in his/her mind (Van Zyl and Stander 2013). Both the coachee and the coach should collaboratively identify the current working mechanisms in the coachee's life through a process of systematic probing (Smith 2006; Stelter 2014; Yalom 1980). Through collaboration the coach and coachee generate solutions, develops strategies and commits to the change (Smith 2006). Van Zyl and Stander (2013) notes that the emphasis through this process is on coachee-coach collaboration which can be seen as an expression of mutual positive regard as well as interpersonal transparency of goals and intents.

A Positive Psychology Approach to Phase 5

In this phase, the positive psychological coach engages in solution-building conversations whereby the coachee is enlisted to aid in determining practical solutions to presenting issues (Deane et al. 2014; Smith 2006), whereby the focus is on 'how' a coachee is addressing presenting problems, rather than the actual problem (Berg and De Jong 1996; Stelter 2014). Smith (2006) argues that the positive psychological coach and coachee works collaboratively to determine strength-based strategies which aided the coachee to cope with or manage similar problems in the past and to identify available psychological and social resources to confront current challenges. The purist positive psychological coach will aim to highlight the strengths used in the past coaching experiences and reinforce the positive components thereof (Scheel et al. 2012) through structured positive psychological solutions framing interventions.

A popular positive psychological approach to frame solutions and develop action plans is to utilize an Appreciative Inquiry (AI) (Sheldon et al. 2011; Whitney and Trosten-Bloom 2003). AI is a method of personal- and organizational development which emphasizes what the individual does well (strengths) rather than addressing difficulties through a greater understanding of the derailing mechanisms (Whitney and Trosten-Bloom 2003). Appreciative inquiry is a four phase cyclical change model (called the 4D cycle) which refers to a collaborative 'inquiry' into what currently **is** working well/optimally (Phase 1 -Discovery), in order to envisage what **could** work well in the future (Phase 2 – Dream), followed by collective planning and prioritizing process that **would** work well (Phase 2 – Design) and ended off with the execution of the proposed designed strategy to achieve the preferred future state (Phase 1 – Destiny) (Lewis et al. 2008). According to Gordon (2008) the model assumes that:

- There are somethings that works well within and without the coachee;
- Where the coachee focuses attention will become his/her reality;
- Multiple realities exists as they are constructed in relation to others;
- Realities are constructed within the moment;
- Presenting questions to the coachee influences the way in which he/she thinks, feels or behaves
- Individuals are more confident in working towards a positive future, if they transpose learning which worked well in the past;

Table 1 Appreciative Inquiry focused solution generation

Phase 1 – discover	Phase 2 – dream	Phase 3 – design	Phase 4 – destiny
Establishing what currently works well and what the coachee's strengths are aligned to the desired outcome	Encourage the coachee to create images of the preferred future aligned to the desired outcome	Aiding the coachee in refocusing the dream and aligning it practical reality	Aid the coachee to align the dreams to the present
Facilitate the coachee to discover different perspectives, and approaches to the desired outcome	Inviting the coachee to be as creative as possible in determining this ideal state of functioning relating to the desired outcome	Determining which current and new/alternative behaviours the coachee needs to exert to obtain his/her dream	Facilitate the coachee to determine which immediate changes he/she can make to achieve this dream
Cultivate the coachee's belief in a more optimistic and hopeful future	Invite the coachee to present this ideal future in as much detail as possible relating to the desired outcome	Assisting the coachee to determine which physical, psychological and social resources are needed to achieve his/her dream	Aid the coachee to determine short, medium and long term goals (and strategies) for achieving the dream
	Enable the coachee to incorporate aspects which worked well in the past, as part of his/her dream state	Determining methods/approaches used in the past which may be valuable to achieving the dream	Aid the coachee to set time frames and deadlines for achieving the dreams
	Affirm the coachee's presented ideal future and the sense that it's possible to achieve	Continuously affirm the coachee's dream	
		Support realistic decisions and strategies	

- Individual, group, organizational and cultural differences should be valued
- The language people employ, structures their collective realities.

Applied to this phase of the coaching model, the coach and coachee co-constructs an action plan for the current challenges through applying the 4D model. Here 'problems' or 'areas of development' are reframed as 'desired outcomes' (Phase 1 and 2) and 'Dreams' (Phases 3 and 4). Table 1 highlights the process involved in structuring an action plan or solutions in each phase:

As mentioned in Phase 1, the implementation strategy of the action plan needs to be documented and should form part of the PDP.

Further, Scheel et al. (2012) indicates that the positive psychological coach should be cognisant of (a) barriers to the use of coachee's strengths, (b) coachee

Table 2 Contextual considerations when framing strengths-based solutions

Barriers to the use of coachee's strengths	Coachee personal characteristics	Matching the coachee's context to strengths
Some problems require more of a problem focus	Emphasize coachee's help-seeking behaviour as a strength	The types of problem will determine the use of strengths
Limitations to exclusive focus on strengths	Coachee acceptance of strengths gives coach go-ahead to work toward change	Internal problems (e.g., existential, self-esteem, low self-confidence) are more appropriate for a strengths-based approach
In crisis, first focus on problems, then move to work on strengths	Strengths are defined by coachee's ego functioning	Matching coachee strengths with a corresponding intervention approach
An elaborate strengths presentation can be detrimental to higher ego strength	Use of more flexible and sophisticated defence or coping mechanisms should be seen as a strength	Supporting coachees as experts of their lives and adopting their treatment ideas
Strength-based approaches are not helpful with narcissistic coachees	The way coachees uses strengths is an indicator of what change he/she is capable	Capitalizing on the strengths the coachee identifies
Single focus on problems leads to blindness of strengths	Knowing the coachee's strengths helps in understanding resiliency during the stress of changing	
Pushing too quickly can prevent future acceptance of strengths	Coachee's acceptance of strengths depends on developmental level	
	Coachee's willingness to try something different is a strength	
	Coachee's follow-through on the coach's suggestions and/or homework identifies strengths	

personal characteristics and (c) matching the coachee‘s context to strengths when framing solutions and determining action plans. Table 2 above presents a summary of Scheel et al.'s (2012) findings:

A Person-Centred Approach to Phase 5

Once the coachee feels safe and received in the coaching relationship and furthermore is more aware, open and sensitized, he or she can focus effort on addressing individual areas from their personal development plan. The coach will accompany the coachee in finding quite concrete action plans on how to put intentions into practice, such that outcomes can be perceived and reflected in coaching sessions and/or the reflection journals and future actions adapted in a deliberate, reflected way. Occasionally, clearing space and focusing on challenging situations can help the coachee in finding a solution path in which he/she feels united as a whole person including their personal, social and cultural feelings and thought. While in general the coachee will choose the order in which he/she wants to address areas from their PDP. In case of indifference or difficulties the coach may suggest areas to tackle first, based on his/her empathy for the coachee and the environment, and/or borrowing from the technique of appreciative inquire as described above. The process of collaborative decision making can be reflected later as a referent process: How did we proceed to make a decision? What was helpful in the process?

3.6 *Phase 6: Building Strengths and Competencies*

Central Goals and Tasks

The main function of this phase is to develop the coachee's competence through strengths identification, building and utilization activities. The coachee is encouraged to identify working mechanisms in his/her current work-related reality (Lyubomirsky 2011). These working mechanisms are usually exhibited, but supressed signature strengths (Lyubomirsky 2011; Sheldon et al. 2011). Through supporting the self-exploration process, the coach aids the coachee to highlight these suppressed strengths and encourages its use in new and challenging environments (Sheldon et al. 2011) in order to enhance personal and work-related well-being (Niemiec 2014). Further, the coachee should also focus on enhancing his/her manifested strengths and seek opportunities to apply newly developed strengths in line with the personal development strategy (Peterson and Seligman 2004) in order to develop the desired/ identified work-related competencies (Van Zyl and Stander 2013).

In addition, the coachee should also be acquainted with the Lyubomirsky (2011) the 10 %, 40 %, 50 % principle. From this perspective, well-being is determined by a biological set point, the coachee's current environment, and intentional activities aimed at developing positive affect (Lyubomirsky et al. 2005). Each one of these factors declares a fairly large amount of variance in the overall experience of positive affect (Van Zyl and Stander 2013). Lyubomirsky (2011) argues that biological set point declares 50 % of the aforementioned variance, where the current environment declares 10 % and intentional activities declares 40 %. The implication is that coachee's intentional activities has a larger effect on sustainable well-being than his/her current environment has on the experience of positive affect. Therefore establishing that the person is in control of how they feel, think and act.

A Positive Psychology Approach to Phase 6

A basic assumption of positive psychology is that people have the capacity for developing strengths in order to grow and change (Peterson and Seligman 2004; Seligman 2011) due to their self-correcting (or self-righting) tendencies (Smith 2006). Strengths develop as a result of individuals' attempts to adapt to challenging environments based on the inherent and genetically imprinted need to survive (Cilliers 2011; Peterson and Seligman 2004). As the survival instinct is genetically imprinted, it is assumed that strength development would be a life-long process as the struggle for survival is ever-present (Smith 2006). Further, Smith (2006) suggests individuals have a reservoir of manifested (known) and unexplored/unrecognized (unknown) strengths which develops as a result of an internal struggle with the self or an external struggle with the environment. As such, the role of the positive psychological coach is to support the coachee's natural strengths-development capacity and to encourage engagement in challenging scenarios to develop new or enhance known strengths (Niemiec 2014; Roarty and Toogood 2014). Further, as strengths are not contextually bound (Niemiec 2014; Seligman 2011), the coachee is also encouraged to seek opportunities outside of the work-related and coaching session whereby he/she could seek to apply these strengths. As such, an action learning approach is initiated and controlled for.

Character strengths can also be taught and affected through the engagement in deliberate interventions (Lyubomirsky 2011; Niemiec 2014; Peterson and Seligman 2004; Seligman 2011). Niemiec (2014) states that coachees could be taught how to be more courageous, gracious, open-mined, creative and prudent through various interventions such as strengths journaling, goal orientated planning, or gratitude visits. The positive psychological coach should facilitate the implementation of these interventions through creating opportunities for discovery and providing the necessary skills to practice these newly developed signature strengths (Lyubomirsky 2011; Van Zyl and Rothmann 2014).

A Person-Centred Approach to Phase 6

The central goals and tasks of this phase, namely to build strengths and competencies or in other words to unleash and the coachee's inherent constructive potential and let him or her unfold it in real-world situations are in high accord with the person-centred approach. A specific feature of the "building strengths and competencies" phase in the strengths based coaching model (Van Zyl and Stander 2013), however, is that there exist particular goals behind the coachee's self-exploration such as:

- to heighten awareness of personal strengths and competencies
- to find new ways of employing and enhancing strengths in line with the PDP
- to increase the awareness of the coachee that his/her intentional activities have a significant effect on their well-being.

It is essential that these goals are communicated such that there is transparency in the process and the coachee can better understand the selective listening for the issues named above. To clarify, selective empathic listening means that the coach selectively attends to those feelings and meanings in the coachee's utterances that are related to some focus such as emphasizing strengths. Importantly, the coachee must not feel that any goals are imposed from an external perspective and has to stay in ultimate control of the direction of their personal development (Rogers 1959). Only in being transparent regarding specific goals, the coach can stay congruent in the relationship despite having goals/strategies that exceed his/her offering of a person-centred relationship and climate for self-exploration (Rogers 1959). In any case, the coach's hidden goals or goals that conflict with the coachee's inherent direction would interfere with the coachee's inherent, directional actualizing tendency and thus with the principles of the person-centred approach.

3.7 Phase 7: Empowerment

Central Goals and Tasks

According to Van Zyl and Stander (2013), the purpose of this phase is to instil psychological empowerment within the coachee through activating existing *internal and external resources* and to promote collaboration during the coaching process. Smith (2006) indicates that empowerment is a process whereby the coach identifies, promotes and validates a coachee's competent functioning during the coaching process. Through establishing empowerment, the coachee adopts a self-guided mindset of personal responsibility and self- assurance (Kidman and Davis 2007). As such, empowerment facilitates the client from a dependence to independence stance through exploring the social origins of the coachee's behaviour and focus on the context in which it resides (Smith 2006).

For psychological empowerment to manifest, the coachee must experience a higher level of personal meaning, self-perceived competence and feel that he/she is in control the environment (Spreitzer 1995) in order to feel confident in applying strengths in new and innovative ways to overcome adversity, challenges and problems (Peterson and Seligman 2004).

A Positive Psychology Approach to Phase 7

From a positive psychological perspective, psychological empowerment refers to an intrinsic multi-dimensional motivational construct which manifests in experiences of meaningfulness, professional competence, self-determination and personal impact (Spreitzer 1995). As such the coach would need to ensure that the coachee (a) feels connected to the proverbial 'bigger picture' (meaningfulness), (b) exerts confidence in their abilities to successfully perform in a task (competence), (c) experiences a sense of control over initiating and regulating own work (self-determination) and (d) feels he/she is making a difference within the context in which he/she functions, in order to establish a sense of psychological empowerment.

A Person-Centred Approach to Phase 7

As in the previous phase, the goals as to what shall be achieved need to be transparent such as to avoid any sense of some "hidden agenda" and to include the coachee in the intended change process and let him/her co-decide on the paths how to move forward in accomplishing the PDP. This inclusion, based on the attitude of respect and empathic understanding of the coachee in his/her work environment is essential. Being trusted and met at eye-level, per se will empower the coachee and set him/her free to experiment with new behaviours. These will tend to be in part behaviours and attitudes that the coachee is receiving in the relationship and work with the coach and in part his/her own expressions of person-centred attitudes that the coachee perceives as constructive and wants to "reciprocate" in their relationships Rogers 1951). In brief, the major "force" towards empowerment will come from experiencing the genuine, real person-centred relationship with the coach in which the coachee will feel deeply understood, accepted and prized for who they are (Rogers 1978), regardless of their culture or social status.

A further aspect of empowerment might reside in "paving the path" towards constructive change by putting away hindrances that the coachee might encounter. For example, over critical or sarcastic or ironical, etc. colleagues or managers might be confronted with the effects of their behaviour or just pointed to the fact that the coachee is working hard at a better fit in the work context and that their support could be decisive for sustained benefit.

3.8 Phase 8: Reframing

Central Goals and Tasks

Van Zyl and Stander (2013) states that purpose of this phase is to alter behaviour through physically, psychologically or emotionally reframe work/life activities in order for them to be perceived as subjectively meaningful. Further, in this phase the coach aids the coachee to deconstruct and reframe the meaning they have attached to and derive from specific life/work events (Smith 2006). Here, the personal capacities and signature strengths of the coachee are viewed as the foundation from which constructive change is facilitated (Van Zyl and Stander 2013). Further, Van Zyl and Stander (2013) indicates that the coach should accompany the coachee by recognizing the efforts exerted and accomplishments achieved in the pursuit of achieving the associative goals as part of the personal development strategy. In addition, the coachee might be asked to reflect on the lessons learned from practice, as well as how these lessons affect the meaning attached to certain events (Seligman 2011).

Van Zyl and Stander (2013) further suggests that the coach may find it helpful to utilize Smith's (2006) theoretical framework on cognitive reframing, stating seven steps in which reframing tends to occur: (a) recognition, (b) acceptance, (c) understanding, (d) learning there is always choice for how to view adversity, (e) changing the meaning ascribed to an event, (f) deriving lessons from the painful event, (g) redefining ourselves around our strengths and multiple talents, and (h) taking constructive action around the new strength-based identities and perseverance.

A Positive Psychology Approach to Phase 8

The process highlighted above is completely aligned to the purist positive psychological perspective. Further, the concept of reframing is strongly associated with the concept of subjective meaningfulness as defined by Seligman (2011) and Van Zyl (2012). Seligman (2011) defines meaning as the ability of an individual to utilize and apply signature strengths in the service of a larger/greater purpose. Van Zyl (2012) defines psychological meaning as the extent towards which an individual feels connected to the larger socially constructed reality or to the proverbial 'bigger picture'. It further refers to experience of gaining a return on investment in the energy which one exerts in the pursuit of personal of professional goals (Seligman 2011). The practices associated with the search for and experience of meaning manifests differently for individuals, whereby meaning crafting or recrafting activities will differ from person-to-person (Van Zyl and Stander 2014).

Reframing refers to an intentional effort by an individual to positively alter, amend or change the meaning attached to and derived from traumatic events, negative conditions or unfulfilling work (Niemiec 2014; Van Zyl and Stander 2014). Coachees may engage in reframing activities to either: (a) take control over certain aspects of their lives to avoid negative consequences later, or (b) alter aspects relating to work/life in order to receive more positive expressions from others, or (c) to fulfil the basic human need for connectedness and acceptance by others (Kooij et al. 2015; Rogers 1959).

As noted above, the mechanisms employed to do so would differ based on the presented strengths of the coachee, the type of scenario and the availability of personal and professional resources. However, Kahn (1990) suggests three cross-culturally appropriate activities which coaches could engage in to aid the client to experience meaning: (a) increasing the challenge of activities and/or work related tasks, introducing variety and providing autonomy, (b) increasing the fit between the individual and the current role he performs within the organization, and (c) establishing rewarding and purposeful interpersonal reactions which results in experiences of self-appreciation and worthwhileness.

A Person-Centred Approach to Phase 8

In a person-centred climate in which the coach respects the actualizing tendency inherent in the coachee, changes in attitude, values, and behaviour tend to be a sign and expression of a person's development toward their optimal functioning. Such changes would typically actualize and enhance the coachee's organism, making the coachee's experience more congruent or in tune with their awareness resulting in the coachee feeling more in control of their life. The changes would not be confined to the cognitive level but affect deeper levels of the coachee's self-structure. Using person-centred terminology, the self-initiated change process is called "reorganization" of the self-structure (Rogers 1959) and is directed toward increased congruence (match) between self and experience and thus increased sense of unity and psychological well-being.

In order to increase the coachee's awareness in the reframing/reorganization process, the coachee may be invited to reflect on his/her process and the changes perceived in him-/herself and the environment. Subsequently, to increase transparency and participation, the coachee could reflect from his/her own perspective, how and whether at all, the learning relates to their personal goals and the PDP (see phase 3).

Thus, as in all phases, a primary goal is to provide a genuine, accepting, and empathically understanding climate, in which the coachee feels free to release his/her inner potential and unfold from inside towards perfection under current circumstances. More concretely, Rogers (1959, p. 218–219) describes the outcomes in personality and behaviour when, in simplified terms, perceiving a person-centred relationship. Some of the outcomes/changes are:

- The client is more congruent, more open to his experience, less defensive.
- He is consequently more effective in problem solving.
- His psychological adjustment is improved, being closer to the optimum.
- He feels more confident, more self-directing.
- He experiences more acceptance of others.
- His behaviour is more creative, more uniquely adaptive to each new situation, and each new problem, more fully expressive of his own purpose and values. (Rogers 1959, pp. 218)

3.9 *Phase 9: Building Sustainable Resilience*

Central Goals and Tasks

The purpose of this phase is to aid coachees in building resilience to buffer against the reoccurrence of similar problems in the future (Van Zyl and Stander 2013). Resilience is defined as an individual's ability to proverbially bounce back to a 'normal level of functioning' after a traumatic or stressful event (Smith 2006). Resilience is developed through understanding and utilizing the internal psychological resources (e.g. signature strengths) and external support mechanisms (e.g. social support networks) to cope with and recover from negative conditions (Seligman 2011). Van Zyl and Stander (2013) does not provide structured guidelines on the development of resilience as they argue it is multi-facetted and depended on the types of complexes manifested in the coachee's ego or through the coachee's life philosophy as embodied in his/her value system.

A Positive Psychology Approach to Phase 9

Resilience is considered a non-traditional positive psychological construct as it has roots in the traditional deficit model (Maymin and Britton 2009). Resilience is defined as an individual's capacity and ability to effectively and efficiently adapt to or recover from stressful events, adverse environments and negative conditions (Gonzales 2012). Resilience should be considered as a formative process rather than an individual personality trait (Gonzales 2012; Seligman 2011). Kuyken et al. (2009) argued that developing resilience in any psychological intervention should be an explicit goal. When resilience is established as a formative outcome of the coaching process, research suggests that both coach and coachee are expected to commit more readily to proactive strategies to use identified strengths to foster future resilience (Kuyken et al. 2009; Maymin and Britton 2009).

Although resilience building is client specific, Newman (2005), the American Psychological Association (2010) and Robertson (2012) suggests ten generic way for the coach to aid the coachee to build resilience which are:

1. to establish and maintain good interpersonal relationships with close friends/family;
2. to refrain from interpreting stressful life/work events as intolerable problems;
3. to accept things that cannot be changed;
4. to set specific, realistic and attainable goals and implement strategies for attainment;
5. to take vital decisions in adverse, negative or stressful situations;
6. to seek opportunities of self-discovery, personal-reflection and post-traumatic growth after negative conditions have expired;
7. to develop self-confidence;
8. to focus on the proverbial bigger picture in order to consider adverse work/life event or negative condition in the broader context;
9. to develop and maintain an optimistic and hopeful orientation through the experience of a negative condition through purposefully expecting positive outcomes and visualizing what is wished;
10. to take care of one's mind (e.g. meditation) and body (e.g. exercise).

A Person-Centred Approach to Phase 9

Towards the end of a coachee-centred coaching process in a person-centred climate, the coachee will tend to have assimilated a higher level of person-centred attitudes (congruence, acceptance, empathic understanding) which will empower him/her to solve complex problems more effectively. According to Rogers (1961), "the other individual [in our context the coachee] in the relationship:

- will experience and understand aspects of himself which previously he has repressed;
- will find himself becoming better integrated, more able to function effectively;

- will become more similar to the person he would like to be;
- will be more self-directing and self-confident;
- will become more of a person, more unique and more self-expressive;
- will be more understanding, more acceptant of others;
- will be able to cope with the problems of life more adequately and more comfortably." (p. 37–38).

These appear to be highly relevant moves, in particular in multicultural contexts that require a high degree of respect of otherness. According to Rogers (1959, 1961) the changes are hypothesized as being relatively permanent. Nevertheless, in for these changes to sustain more fully, the coachee benefits from experiencing a person-centred climate (Motschnig and Nykl 2014; Rogers 1970). This is why it is essential that the coaching process goes far enough that the coachee (and optimally also his/her direct manager) can themselves offer a person-centred atmosphere to others and thus unfold more of it in the organization. Additionally, the coachee may attend person-centred encounter groups (e.g. twice a year 1.5 days) to refresh their attitudes and/or build support networks with like-minded colleagues within or across organizations to cultivate person-centred attitudes. No cross cultural view.

3.10 Phase 10: Evaluating and Re-contracting the Relationship

Central Goals and Tasks

The final phase of Van Zyl and Stander's (2013) coaching model culminates in the evaluation of the coaching relationship and potential re-contracting. They argue that evaluation of the process should continue throughout the coaching intervention in order to ensure that the developmental strategy is on track. However, in the final phase of the coaching relationship, a formative evaluation process needs to be conducted to determine the effectiveness of the developmental strategy and either prepare the coachee for terminating the relationship or re-contracting for further development (Van Zyl and Stander 2013). They further argue that the evaluation process needs to be coupled with calculating the return on investment for the coaching process (Pedler et al. 2007).

Evaluated against the initial objectives set in Phase 1, both the coach and coachee needs to determine the success of the intervention (Van Zyl and Stander 2013). Further, the expectations of the other stakeholders (e.g. managing director, direct manager) needs to be evaluated against the process of the coaching intervention. In order to formally close off the coaching relationship a follow-up meeting between the coachee and his/her direct manager needs to take place in order to determine whether the expectations of the process were met (Pedler et al. 2007). In the scenarios where the expectations have not been met, or if the coachee presents a need for further intervention, a re-contracting process could be initiated (Van Zyl and Stander 2013).

A Positive Psychology Approach to Phase 10

With the exclusion of Smith (2006), no formal or informal positive psychological approach could be found relating to the evaluation and termination of a positive psychological intervention strategy, -therapeutic intervention or -coaching process. According to Smith (2006) during this phase all stakeholders honours the progress which has been made. The coach would determine whether the coachee has achieved his/her objectives, whether the changes that manifested was indeed as a result of the positive psychological coaching process and which signature strengths/environmental resources were most significant/effective in the process (Smith 2006).

A Person-Centred Approach to Phase 10

In a person-centred approach to evaluation (Rogers 1983; Standl et al. 2012), the coachee's self-evaluation would come first and guide the feedback and evaluation process. The self-evaluation can happen either as an open, free-style (oral or written) task or one guided by questions that the coach and coachee determine beforehand and the coachee is asked to respond to. Optimally, this self-evaluation by the coachee is be followed by feedback of the coach and optionally also the direct manager in a transparent session allowing all parties to share their perceptions, feelings and potential further action. As a result, a follow up plan for further development is agreed upon, potentially including a process of re-contracting. In that case, the coach, coachee and manager would explore what is needed for the expectations to be met and how each can contribute to this aim. Also, each expectation would be reconsidered whether it still holds or should better be revised to reflect the new situation and insight from the first round. This is particularly important in a multicultural environment where, for example, expectations regarding punctuality, masculinity, or ambiguity avoidance may differ considerably between coachee and manager. A two sided move instead of putting all burdens on the coachee might prove to be a good way to resolve some ongoing issues.

Since the person-centred approach sees each person continually becoming the best they can (Rogers 1980), further opportunities of personal development for the coachee would be a valuable complement to any coaching process. Even though person-centred attitudes are resilient and once acquired don't "get lost" (Rogers 1980), they need to be experienced and renewed not to get "buried under" careless, often hectic, superficial everyday conversations (Rogers 1970). Opportunities for renewal could be very simple and become part of the coaches work life, like regular open sharing session with colleagues and/or the manager. Alternatively, externally facilitated encounter groups could be offered as further means of life-long learning (Rogers 1983).

4 Reflecting on the Positive Psychological and Person-Centred Approach During the Coaching Process

4.1 *Orientation*

Through providing an interpretation of a paradigm specific approach to each phase of Van Zyl and Stander's (2013) eclectic strengths-based coaching model, the similarities, and differences of the positive psychological and person-centred approaches within this context could be highlighted. Further, a number of conceptual implications and limitations of the differences/similarities between the paradigms for multi-cultural coaching could be derived. In the following sub-sections we will attempt to highlight and discuss these similarities, differences and implications.

4.2 *Similarities Between Paradigms Within the Eclectic Multi-cultural Coaching Process*

From our contrasting discussion it is clear that both positive psychology and the person-centred approach shares fundamental features even though the wording, labels or language employed may be different (Joseph and Murray 2013). As such, a brief overview of the core similarities highlighted in this chapter between the paradigms is presented:

- Both approaches distances itself from the medical or deficit model (Joseph and Murray 2013)
- Both approaches focuses on constructive human qualities or traits within the coaching process
- Both assumes the coachee has the capacity for strength development, growth and change (Rogers 1961, 1964; Smith 2006)
- The person-centred approach aims to aid in letting the fully functioning person/coachee unfold through developing an openness to experience, to value autonomy, to reduce defensiveness, and to function authentically. These core characteristics of the fully functioning coachee are characterized as the signature strengths which the positive psychological coach aims to develop in the coachee
- Both subscribes to the self-actualizing tendency of the coachee, whereby development and growth is facilitated within the context in which he/she resides (Joseph and Murray 2013),
- Even though in a positive psychological setting this happens more explicitly and strategically, in the person-centered approach the experience of a constructive interpersonal climate is pivotal
- Within the coaching process, the coach honours/acknowledges the coachee's efforts to engage to move forward and struggles to deal with presenting issues (Rogers 1961; Seligman 2011; Smith 2006)

- Both approaches underpins the importance of understanding the coachee's current work-related reality and interpretative framework (Smith 2006)
- It is apparent that both paradigms within the multi-cultural coaching framework embodies an eudaimonic as opposed to hedonic philosophy (Robbins 2008)
- Both paradigms strives towards developing constructive capacities and resilience, as opposed to reactive intervention methods (Joseph and Murray 2013)
- Resilience is a key concept within both the positive psychological and person-centred approaches (Friedman and Robbins 2012), however it is approached from different angles in the coaching process.

4.3 Differences Between Paradigms Within the Eclectic Multi-cultural Coaching Process

In contrast to the previous section, our contrasting discussion highlights that the positive psychological and person centred approached differ fundamentally in various application areas within the eclectic multi-cultural coaching model. For simplification, the differences in paradigms are presented below.

Positive Psychology

Presented against the eclectic multi-cultural coaching model, positive psychology differs with the person-centred approach in this context in the following ways:

- The person-centred approach over-estimates the importance of growth-promoting environments (Harter et al. 1996) where the positive psychological approach acknowledges the impact of the environment on personal development but to a limited extent (Lyubomirsky 2011).
- Positive psychology places more reliance on instruments and evaluation by "external means" rather than on personal exploration.
- The positive psychological approach tends to favour quantitative intervention methodologies whereas the person-centred approach shows a preference for the qualitative (Friedman 2008).
- Coach is considered an expert in the interventions process and through the use of psychometric instruments, he/she guides/facilitates the process.
- Focus in the coaching process is on strength awareness, -identification and -utilization where positive feelings or experiences are explicitly emphasized.
- Coach excels in knowledge and competences about the effects of positive feelings and how these could be enacted.
- Coach provides structured and organized guidance through the coaching process.

- The positive psychological approach focuses more on the person-environment-fit awareness, while the person-centred approach focuses on the individual within the environment.
- The positive psychological approach is about the coach concentrating on strengths utilization contrasted to a more accepting the self.
- The positive psychological coach focusses on framing practical solutions while the person-centered approach focuses on the coachee as a whole person who is trusted to find his/her solution in a self-initiated way.
- From the positive psychological perspective, strengths and virtues are considered logically independent, as opposed to the holistic and interdependent view the person-centered approach employs. Within the person-centered approach strengths relates to a single/master, multi-facetted virtue called phronesis.
- The positive psychological coach employs a nomothetic approach towards human potential development.
- The positive psychological coach attributes resilience as a virtue which transcends the environment in which the coachee functions.
- Although the positive psychological coach does not shun or ignore the presence of negative conditions or emotions, he/she does however over accentuate the positive.

Person Centred Approach

Further, from our investigation it is evident that the person-centred approach differs significantly with positive psychology within the context of the coaching model in the following ways:

- Coach is more like a facilitator, deeply listening to the coachee as well as the manager and providing – with highest priority – a facilitative person-centred relationship based on congruence, acceptance and empathic understanding. In this climate positive change is expected to happen as a consequence of the inherent actualizing tendency.
- Coach acts as a resourceful person (Barrett-Lennard 2005) making suggestions and relying on the self-organizing potentials of the person (and organization).
- Coach excels in active listening and deep understanding of the coachee in his/her environment, making the coachee feel safe and fully received, and passing on person-centred attitudes and relationships (Rogers 1978). Coach and coachee meet each other at eye level in dealing with each other; Whenever appropriate, the organizational environment is included to increase transparency of the process and decision making. The process (=10 step) model is used as a loose guideline that can be flexibly adapted if deemed beneficial. The ultimate goal is the work-related, personal development of the coachee.
- There is more trust in the individual to sense and explore their capacities in the climate of a person centred relationship. Work with encounter groups for simultaneous discovery and growth can be a valuable complement increasing the self-experience of the coachee in a group of peers.

- Instruments are not imposed, their usage will finally be the coachee's choice. This will ensure better collaboration since there is inherent motivation to use the instrument, if the choice is self-determined. Furthermore, the coachee experiences a sense of control and co-design of his/her coaching session which lets them experience the empowerment they are actually receiving.
- Effects of interpersonal relationship and own striving are more in the foreground than "engineered" and reinforced strategies that have been found to be effective through science and "applied upon" the coachee. This implies that the whole person approach with emphasis on work-related capacities is more important than a strict strength-based approach.
- Hope, energy, unfolding and well-being tend to be released from experiencing a resourceful, enriching interpersonal relationship that confirms the coachee's direction and capacity to grow from any experience and inspires him or her to proceed with this. Sustainability is increased through reflection (Motschnig and Nykl 2014).
- When following explicit goals other that the general personal growth of the coachee, for example elaborating signature strengths, transparency is vital. The coachee must be included in knowing and co-determining the coaching agenda. In this way he/she can better understand why the coach's empathic listening might focus on certain aspects of what the coachee is sharing while leaving others unattended.
- There is more reliance on the actualizing tendency and the impact of the coaching relationship on change. The coachee is perceived as more self-determining, trusted, and participating as a collaborative partner. The coachee is left with more choices and self-direction already in the coaching process.
- Self-evaluation precedes and is prioritized over evaluation by others (Rogers 1983). Feedback is appreciated as a resource to complement self-evaluation.
- Further steps are co-decided rather that elaborated by the coach as an expert
- Ongoing development is sought to ensure moving forward. Opportunities may be self-initiated and self-organized, since the coachee wants to continue the path towards more congruence and well-being and has been empowered to take action.
- The person-centred coach adopts a non-reductive, whole person approach towards the developmental process
- The person-centred coach accepts the coachee unconditionally, as opposed to the positive psychological stance which emphasizes a prescriptive valuation during coaching
- The person-centred coach focuses on resilience in a more holistic manner in the coaching process through attributing its development to a combination of virtues, environmental and contextual factors
- The person-centred coach embraces a holistic approach through embracing the value of both positive and negative conditions within the coachee's reality. Neither the positive or negative processes nor experiences of the coachee are over or under emphasized.

Summary of Comparison

Based on the strong sides and research base of the two traditions of positive psychology and the person-centred approach, these two directions put different emphasis on certain aspects of the eclectic coaching model. In a nutshell:

- The positive psychology approach emphasizes strength-identification, psychometric measurement and cognitive strategies to evoking positive emotions and enacting the coachee's strengths.
- The person-centred approach emphasizes the development/unfolding of inherent capacities of the coachee by experiencing a growth-promoting interpersonal relationship with the coach.
- Both approaches promote the development to the coachee's well-being in a coachee-centred way rather than adopting the medical model of removing deficiencies.

Intriguingly, much in line with a strengths-based model, each approach focuses on including and enacting their strong sides ("strengths"), without contradicting the other approach. This can be derived from the "more or less" nature of the comparative description above, such as: "more reliance on instruments and evaluation" versus "more trust in the individual to sense and explore their capacities".

5 Concluding Remarks

The purpose of this chapter was to examine similarities and differences between positive psychology and the person-centred approach as dominant paradigm perspectives within multi-cultural coaching. Both paradigms were presented against an eclectic multi-cultural strengths-based coaching model founded in both paradigms (cf. Van Zyl and Stander 2013). Through the use of connective conceptual analysis (Banicki 2011), each phase of the proposed eclectic coaching model was explored from a positive psychological and person-centred orientation to develop a clear understanding of the essential commonalities and dissimilarities of the paradigms. The chapter concluded with revealing conceptual implications and limitations of this work in the multi-cultural coaching context.

In summation, both positive psychology and the person-centred approach were found to share fundamental goals, features, and the core attitude of respect, yet differ significantly in key functional areas where Positive psychology tends to focus more on the conscious level of the coachee as well as the coach. This manifests in relying more explicitly on both psychological and culturally specific strengths, their identification, measurement, and enactment as well as on explicit strategies of positive enforcement of positive (past) experience. The person-centred approach emphasizes the integration of conscious and unconscious levels of the coachee through relying primarily on the coachee's experiencing a growth-promoting, genuine interpersonal relationship in which he/she feels unconditionally accepted, valued, and deeply understood at conscious and unconscious levels. There is apparently more trust and reliance on self-organization and the coachee's inclusion into the whole process in person-centred coaching while positive psychology relies more strongly on the coach as an expert in personal development interventions including the thoughtful application of techniques, methods, instruments, etc. The chapter ends with hope for integration in the realm of coaching, which is considered to offer particular benefits for culturally diverse coachees, however will be challenging to achieve in practice. If this article has illustrated some basic differences in the practices and underlying philosophies and of the two psychological orientations in the context of coaching and also made clear that these are different paths to reach strongly resonant goals, it has fulfilled its purpose.

References

American Psychological Association (APA). (2010). *The road to resilience: Resilience factors & strategies*. Retrieved April 24, 2015, from http://www.apa.org/helpcenter/road-resilience.aspx

Bachkirova, T. (2011). *Developmental coaching: Working with the self*. Maidenhead: Open University Press/McGraw-Hill Education.

Banicki, K. (2011). Connective conceptual analysis and psychology. *Theory & Psychology, 22*(3), 310–323.

Barrett-Lennard, G. T. (2005). *Relationship at the centre: Healing in a troubled world*. Philadelphia: Whurr Publishers.

Barrett-Lennard, G. T. (2013). *The relationship paradigm. Human being beyond individualism*. Houndmills: Palgrave Macmillan.

Bayramoğlu, G., & Şahin, M. (2015). Positive psychological capacity and its impacts on success. *Journal of Advanced Management Science, 3*(2), 154–157.

Belbin, R. M. (2010). *Team roles at work*. Oxford: Butterworth-Heinemann.

Bennett, M. J. (1993). Towards ethnorelativism: A developmental model of intercultural sensitivity. In R. M. Paige (Ed.), *Education for the intercultural experience* (2nd ed., pp. 21–71). Yarmouth: Intercultural Press.

Berg, I. K., & De Jong, P. (1996). Solution-building conversations: Co-constructing a sense of competence with clients. *Families in Society: The Journal of Contemporary Social Services, 77*(6), 376–391.

Biswas-Diener, R. (2010). *Practicing positive psychology coaching: Assessment and strategies for success*. Hoboken: Wiley.

Cain, D. J. (2010). *Person-centered psychotherapies*. Washington, DC: American Psychological Association.

Cannell, L. (2015). A guided conversation among leaders in changing times. *Common Ground Journal, 12*(1), 11.

Carkhuff, R. (2000). *The art of helping in the 21st century*. Amherst: Human Resource Development Press.

Cilliers, F. (2011). Positive psychology leadership coaching experiences in a financial organisation. *SA Journal of Industrial Psychology/SA Tydskrif vir Bedryfsielkunde, 37*(1), 1–14.

Coetzee, M., & Van Zyl, L. E. (2014). A review of a decade's scholarly publications (2004–2013) in the South African Journal of Industrial Psychology. *SA Journal of Industrial Psychology, 40*(1), 1–16.

Coetzer, A., Redmond, J., & Bastian, V. (2014). Strength-based coaching: Making the case for its adoption in small businesses. *Development and Learning in Organizations: An International Journal, 28*(3), 6–9.

Deane, F. P., Andresen, R., Crowe, T. P., Oades, L. G., Ciarrochi, J., & Williams, V. (2014). A comparison of two coaching approaches to enhance implementation of a recovery-oriented service model. *Administration and Policy in Mental Health and Mental Health Services Research, 41*(5), 660–667.

Desetta, A., & Wolin, S. (2000). *The struggle to be strong: True stories by teens about overcoming tough times*. Minneapolis: Free Spirit Press.

Feldman, D. C., & Lankau, M. J. (2005). Executive coaching: A review and agenda for future research. *Journal of Management, 31*(6), 829–848.

Flynn, F. J. (2003). How much should I give and how often? The effects of generosity and frequency of favor exchange on social status and productivity. *Academy of Management Journal, 46*, 539–553.

Froh, J. J. (2004). The history of positive psychology: Truth be told. *NYS Psychologist, 16*(3), 18–20.

Fronczak, D. B. (2006). Coaching men at midlife. *Dissertations abstracts international: Section B: Sciences and engineering, 66*(10), 5710.

Gendlin, E. T. (1982) [1978]. *Focusing* (2nd ed.). New York: Bantam Books.

Gonzales, L. (2012). *Surviving survival: The Art and science of resilience*. New York: W. W. Norton & Company.

Gordon, S. (2008). Appreciative inquiry coaching. *International Coaching Psychology Review, 3*, 19–31.

Grant, A. M. (2006). A personal perspective on professional coaching and the development of coaching psychology. *International Coaching Psychology Review, 1*(1), 12–22.

Grant, A. M., & Schwartz, B. (2011). Too much of a good thing: The challenge and opportunity of the inverted U. *Perspectives on Psychological Science, 6*, 61–76.

Harter, S., Marold, D. B., Whitesell, N. R., & Cobbs, G. (1996). A model of the effects of parent and peer support on adolescent false self-behaviour. *Child Development, 67*, 360–374.

Joseph, S. (2006). Person-centred coaching psychology: A meta-theoretical perspective. *International Coaching Psychology Review, 1*(1), 47–54.

Joseph, S., & Linley, P. A. (2004). Positive therapy: A positive psychological theory of therapeutic practice. In P. A. Linley & S. Joseph (Eds.), *Positive psychology in practice* (pp. 354–368). Hoboken: Wiley. doi:10.1002/9780470939338.ch22.

Joseph, S., & Murphy, D. (2013). Person-centered theory encountering mainstream psychology: Building bridges and looking to the future. In *Interdisciplinary handbook of the person-centered approach* (pp. 213–226). New York: Springer.

Justice, T., & Jamieson, D. (2002). *The facilitator's fieldbook* (2nd ed.). New York: City Cress.

Kahn, W. A. (1990). Psychological conditions of personal engagement and disengagement at work. *Academy of Management Journal, 33*(4), 692–724.

Kidman, L., & Davis, W. (2007). Empowerment in coaching. In *Ecological task analysis and movement* (pp. 121–139). Champaign: Human Kinetics.

Kooij, D. T., Tims, M., & Kanfer, R. (2015). Successful aging at work: The role of job crafting. In *Aging workers and the employee-employer relationship* (pp. 145–161). Cham: Springer International Publishing.

Koortzen, P., & Oosthuizen, R. (2010). A competence executive coaching model. *SA Journal of Industrial Psychology/SA Tydskrif vir Bedryfsielkunde, 36*(1), 7–22.

Kuyken, W., Padesky, C. A., & Dudley, R. (2009). *Collaborative case conceptualization: Working effectively with clients in cognitive-behavioral therapy*. New York: Guilford.

Lago, C. (2013). The person-centered approach and its capacity to enhance constructive international communication. In J. H. D. Cornelius-White, R. Motschnig-Pitrik, & M. Lux (Eds.), *Interdisciplinary applications of the person-centered approach*. New York: Springer.

Lewis, S., Passmore, J., & Cantore, S. (2008). *The appreciative inquiry approach to change management*. London: Kogan Paul.

Linley, P. A., & Harrington, S. (2006). Playing to your strengths. *The Psychologist, 19*, 86–89.

Linley, P. A., Joseph, S., Harrington, S., & Wood, A. M. (2006). Positive psychology: Past, present, and (possible) future. *Journal of Positive Psychology, 1*, 3–16. doi:10.1080/17439760500372796.
Lopez, S. J., Pedrotti, J. T., & Snyder, C. R. (2014). *Positive psychology: The scientific and practical explorations of human strengths*. London: Sage Publications.
Lyubomirsky, S. (2011). *The way to happiness: Action plan for a happy life* (K. Benyovitz, Trans.). Or Yehuda: Kinneret Publishing House.
Lyubomirsky, S., Sheldon, K. M., & Schkade, D. (2005). Pursuing happiness: The architecture of sustainable change. *Review of General Psychology, 9*, 111–131.
Maymin, S., & Britton, K. (Eds.) (2009). *Resilience: How to navigate life's curves*. Charleston: Positive Psychology News.
Moore, M., & McBride, B. W. (2014). Health and wellness coaching in practice. In *Coachingpraxisfelder. Forschung und praxis im dialog* (pp. 43–51). Wiesbaden: Springer Fachmedien Wiesbaden.
Motschnig, R. (2014). Die Tendenz zur Co-Aktualisierung. [The tendency toward co-actualization: Considerations regarding the actualizing process in interpersonal relationships]. *Person, 18*(2), Facultas Universitätsverlag, 163–175. ISSN 1028-6837.
Motschnig, R., & Nykl, L. (2014). *Person-centred communication: Theory, skills, and practice*. McGraw Hill: Open University Press.
Newman, R. (2005). APA's resilience initiative. *Professional Psychology: Research and Practice, 36*(3), 227.
Niemiec, R. M. (2014). *Mindfulness and character strengths: A practical guide to flourishing*. Cambridge, MA: Hogrefe.
O'Hara, M. (2013). PCA encounter groups: Transformative learning for individuals and communities. In J. H. D. Cornelius-White, R. Motschnig-Pitrik, & M. Lux (Eds.), *Interdisciplinary applications of the person-centered approach*. New York: Springer.
Palmer, S., & Whybrow, A. (2014). *Handbook of coaching psychology: A guide for practitioners*. London: Routledge.
Park, N., & Peterson, C. (2006). Character strengths in organizations. *Journal of Organizational Behaviour, 27*, 1149–1154.
Passmore, J. (2013). *Diversity in coaching: Working with gender, culture, race and age*. New York: Kogan Page Publishers.
Pedler, M., Burgoyne, J., & Boydell, T. (2007). *A manager's guide to self-development* (5th ed.). Maidenhead: McGraw-Hill Professionals.
Peterson, C., & Seligman, M. E. P. (2004). *Character strengths and virtues: A handbook and classification*. New York: American Psychological Association.
Peterson, C., & Seligman, M. E. P. (2014). *Character strengths and virtues: A handbook and classification* (2nd ed.). New York/Oxford/Washington, DC: American Psychological Association.
Rath, T. (2007). *Strengths finder 2.0.*. New York: Gallup Press.
Roarty, M., & Toogood, K. (2014). *The strengths-focused guide to leadership: Identify your talents and Get the most from your team*. Harlow: Pearson.
Robbins, B. D. (2008). What is the good life? Positive psychology and the renaissance of humanistic psychology. *Humanistic Psychologist, 36*, 96–112. doi:10.1080/08873260802110988.
Robbins, B. D., & Friedman, H. (2008). Introduction to our special issue on positive psychology. *Humanistic Psychologist, 36*, 93–95. doi:10.1080/08873260802110947.
Robertson, D. (2012). *Build your resilience*. London: Hodder.
Rogers, C. R. (1951). *Client-centred therapy*. London: Constable.
Rogers, C. R. (1959). A theory of therapy, personality, and interpersonal relationships, as developed in the client-centred framework. In S. Koch (Ed.), *Psychology: A study of a science* (Vol. 3). New York: McGraw-Hill.
Rogers, C. R. (1961). *On becoming a person*. Boston: Houghton Mifflin.
Rogers, C. R. (1970). *Carl Rogers on encounter groups*. New York: Harper and Row.

Rogers, C. R. (1978a). *Carl Rogers on personal power*. London: Constable.
Rogers, C. R. (1978b). *On personal power*. London: Constable.
Rogers, C. R. (1980). *A way of being*. Boston: Houghton Mifflin.
Rogers, C. R. (1983). *Freedom to learn for the 80s*. Columbus: Charles E. Merrill Publishing Company, A Bell & Howell Company.
Rogers, C. R., & Farson, R. E. (1987). Active listening. In R. G. Newman, M. A. Danzinger, & M. Cohen (Eds.), *Communicating in business today*. Lexington: D.C. Heath and Company. Online: http://www.gordontraining.com/pdf/active_listening_article_rogers-farson.pdf.
Scheel, M. J., Davis, C. K., & Henderson, J. D. (2013). Therapist use of client strengths: A qualitative study of positive processes. *The Counseling Psychologist, 41*(3), 392–427.
Schneider, K. J. (2011). Toward a humanistic positive psychology: Why can't we just get along? *Existential Analysis, 22*, 32–38.
Seligman, M. E. P. (2011). *Flourish: A visionary new understanding of happiness and well-being*. New York: Free Press.
Seligman, M. E. P., & Csikszentimihalyi, M. (2000). Positive psychology: An introduction. *American Psychologist, 55*, 5–14.
Sheldon, K., Kashdan, T. B., & Steger, M. F. (2011). *Designing positive psychology: Taking stock and moving forward*. New York: Oxford University Press.
Smith, E. J. (2006). The strength-based counselling model. *The Counseling Psychologist, 34*(2), 13–80.
Spreitzer, G. (1995). Psychological empowerment in the workplace: Dimensions, measurement and validation. *Academy of Management Journal, 38*, 1442–1456.
Standl, B., Motschnig, R., & Haselberger, D. (2012). Case study on person – centred assessment in computer science. In T. Amiel & B. Wilson (Eds.), *Proceedings of world conference on educational multimedia, hypermedia and telecommunications 2012* (pp. 2343–2351). Chesapeake: AACE.
Stelter, R. (2014). Intervention theories in coaching and coaching psychology. In *A guide to third generation coaching* (pp. 45–109). Dordrecht: Springer.
Tugade, M. M., & Fredrickson, B. L. (2004). Resilient individuals use positive emotions to bounce back from negative emotional experiences. *Journal of Personality and Social Psychology, 86*(2), 320.
Van Zyl., L. E. (2012). *The development and evaluation of positive psychological interventions aimed at happiness*. Unpublished doctoral thesis, North-West University.
Van Zyl, L. E., & Rothmann, S. (2014). Towards happiness interventions: Construct clarification and intervention methodologies. *Journal of Psychology in Africa, 24*(2), 327–341.
Van Zyl, L. E., & Stander, M. W. (2011, July). *An analytical strength based approach towards coaching*. Research paper presented at the 12th annual Society of Industrial/Organisational Psychologists in conference, Johannesburg, South Africa.
Van Zyl, L. E., & Stander, M. W. (2013). A strengths-based approach towards coaching in a multicultural environment. In J. H. D. Cornelius-White, R. Motschnig-Pitrik, & M. Lux (Eds.), *Interdisciplinary Handbook of the person-centred approach* (pp. 245–257). New York: Springer New York. doi:10.1007/978-1-4614-7141-7-17.
Van Zyl, L. E., & Stander, M. W. (2014). Flourishing interventions: A practical guide to student development. In *Psycho-social career meta-capacities* (pp. 265–276). Cham: Springer International Publishing.
Waterman, A. S. (2013). The humanistic psychology–positive psychology divide: Contrasts in philosophical foundations. *American Psychologist, 68*(3), 124.
Weick, A., & Chamberlain, R. (2002). Putting problems in their place: Further explorations in the strengths perspective. In D. Saleebey (Ed.), *The strengths perspective in social work practice* (3rd ed., pp. 95–105). Boston: Allyn & Bacon.
Welch, D., Grossaint, K., Reid, K., & Walker, C. (2014). Strengths-based leadership development: Insights from expert coaches. *Consulting Psychology Journal: Practice and Research, 66*(1), 20.

Whitney, D., & Trosten-Bloom, A. (2003). *The power of appreciative inquiry*. San Francisco: Berret-Koehler.
Whitney, D. D., & Trosten-Bloom, A. (2010). *The power of appreciative inquiry: A practical guide to positive change*. San Francisco: Berrett-Koehler Publishers.
Yalom, I. (1980). *Existential psychotherapy*. New York: Basic Books.

Training Emerging Psychologists as Multi-cultural Contextual Coaches

Lené Ilyna Jorgensen, Llewellyn E. van Zyl, and Marius W. Stander

Abstract Research on the education, professional training and tuition models of emerging psychologists (or 'student psychologists') has significantly increased during the past two to three decades (Johnson WB, Kaslow N (eds). The Oxford handbook of education and training in professional psychology. Oxford University Press, New York, 2014). Various evidence-based, practitioner-scholar-, clinical-scientist- and science-practitioner models have been developed to aid in the professional training of emerging psychologists (Bell D, Hausman EM. 3 training models in professional psychology doctoral programs. The Oxford handbook of education and training in professional psychology. Oxford University Press, New York, 2014) in order to develop competence in different practice domains such as counselling/ therapy (Smith EJ. Couns Psychol 34(2):13–80, 2006), psychometric evaluation (Theron C. SA J Ind Psychol 33(1):102–117, 2007), forensic analysis (Neal TM, Brodsky SL. J Forensic Psychol Pract 14:24–44, 2014) and coaching psychology (Biswas-Diener R, Dean B. Positive psychology coaching: putting the science of happiness to work for your clients. Wiley, Hoboken, 2007). Coaching psychology has emerged as a rapidly growing practice domain (Passmore J (ed). Diversity in coaching: working with gender, culture, race and age. Kogan Page Publishers, New York, 2013) in both uni- and multi-cultural contexts (Palmer S, Whybrow A (eds). Handbook of coaching psychology: a guide for practitioners. Routledge, London), however limited scientific research exists relating to the training and development of emerging psychologists as coaches within multi-cultural environments. As such, the chapter aims to evaluate the experiences of emerging psychologists relating to an evidence-based training methodology in order to provide structured guidelines for the development of a multi-cultural coaching training programme. Through the use of an evidence-based research methodology and thematic content analysis, the chapter will present the specific strategies employed

L.I. Jorgensen (✉)
Department of Industrial Psychology, School of Human Resource Sciences, WorkWell Research Unit, North-West University, Potchefstroom Campus, Potchefstroom, South Africa
e-mail: Lene.Jorgensen@nwu.ac.za

L.E. van Zyl • M.W. Stander
Optentia Research Focus Area, Department of Industrial Psychology, School for Behavioural Sciences, North-West University, Vaal Triangle Campus, Vanderbijlpark, South Africa
e-mail: llewellyn.vanzyl@nwu.ac.za; marius.stander@nwu.ac.za

L.E. van Zyl et al. (eds.), *Coaching Psychology: Meta-theoretical perspectives and applications in multicultural contexts*, DOI 10.1007/978-3-319-31012-1_16

and methodologies utilized in the development of multi-cultural coaching competence of emerging psychologists as part of their formal academic training. The research method, data analysis and results will be presented followed by recommendations that flowed from the study.

Keywords Coaching training • Industrial psychologist as coaches • Coaching psychology • Professional development

1 Introduction

Industrial and Organisational Psychologists (IOPS) have been quite successful in securing employment the past few decades (SIOPSA 2012). This is further highlighted by Byrne et al. (2014). However, they caution that with difficult economic conditions it may become tougher for student or 'emerging' psychologists entering the job market. The Psychology Board of the Health Profession Council of South Africa recently increased pressure on universities to deliver well rounded professionals to organizations. Universities are encouraged to provide suitable practical work opportunities and even internships in order to ensure that students' are fully prepared for the workplace (HPCSA Personal Communication 2014).

One of the areas where students need to be competent is people development. In most if not all countries, people development and retention are some of the biggest business challenges. Coaching is a very important part of people development. Grant (2006) postulates that coaching psychology has the potential to promote the performance and well-being of the individual, organization and society. It is further important to take cognisance of the fact that industrial psychology is an applied discipline that preaches the science-practitioner model, training students in science and practice (Weathington et al. 2014). This chapter deals with the training of future industrial psychologists as people developers, with a specific focus on coaching psychology.

Although coaching and coaching psychology has emerged as a rapidly growing practice domain (Abbott et al. 2013; Grant and Cavanagh 2007) in both uni- and multi-cultural contexts (Palmer and Whybrow 2014), limited scientific research exists relating to the training and development of coaches within multi-cultural environments (Egan and Hamlin 2014). Stein et al. (2014) postulate that coaching education has entered an era of greater influence with a focus on how to prepare coaches to be competent. Research on the education, professional training and tuition models of emerging psychologists (or student psychologists) has dramatically accelerated during the past two to three decades (Byrne et al. 2014; Johnson and Kaslow 2014; Tett et al. 2013). Various models, including, evidence-based, practitioner-scholar-, clinical-scientist- and science-practitioner models have been developed to aid in the professional training of emerging psychologists (Bell and Hausman 2014). These models are mainly used in an effort to develop student competence in different practice domains of psychology. Competency in areas such as counselling and therapy (Smith 2006), psychometric evaluation (Theron 2007), forensic analysis (Neal and Brodsky, 2014a) and coaching psychology (Biswas-Diener and Dean 2007) are required in order to provide well-rounded psychology-practitioners in the field of industrial psychology.

Therefore, the chapter aims to evaluate the experiences of emerging psychologists relating to an evidence-based training methodology in order to provide structured guidelines for the development of a multi-cultural coaching training programme. Through the use of evidence-based research methodology, the chapter will present the specific strategies employed and methodologies utilized in the development of multi-cultural coaching competence of emerging psychologists as part of their formal academic training. The research method, data analysis and results will be discussed and finally recommendations will be made.

2 Training Students as People Developers

The "people development" module, combined with four other modules (well-being, scientific reasoning, applied counselling and professional industrial psychology) form the teaching part of the Industrial Psychology Masters qualification. As part of the qualification, a research dissertation contributes 50 % to the program. The philosophy behind the program is firstly that the students must focus on their own development before coaching and developing others. Secondly, the program is based on a combination of class room teaching, self-directed learning, mentoring and peer coaching where the student must through experiential learning develop the skills of a coach in a multi-cultural environment. This takes place under the guidance of a university and primary supervisor. In this process the student experience a high level of meaning while building a professional identity.

There is a need for evidence-based coaching (Grant and Cavanagh 2007) that has the potential to raise the standard and credibility of coaching (Stober et al. 2006). The program follows an evidence-based approach. The American Psychological Association (2005) defines evidence-based practice as "the integration of the best available research with clinical expertise". Poduska and Kurki (2014) stated that moving evidence-based practices from classroom to practice is a high priority for educators. Grant and Hartley (2013) are of the opinion that a program to develop coaches must be theoretically grounded and especially practical. Stober et al. (2006) are of the opinion that coaching as an emerging profession must integrate evidence from coaching specific research, related disciplines, own experience and an understanding of the uniqueness of each client. Students in such a program must be able to clearly perceive the link between theory and practice while they experience positive results over the short term.

The module is presented based on the assumption that the students are seen as adult learners. Zepeda et al. (2014) summarises the five major characteristics of adult learning as, "self-directed, motivational for the learner, problem centred, relevancy oriented and goal directed" (p. 301). In order to optimise an adult learning process it was decided to use experiential learning, self-directed learning, mentoring, peer coaching, coaching and workshops as the major methods of training.

Knowles' (1973) original work on adult learning forms the basis of this approach. Students are seen as:

(a) motivated to learn,
(b) accountable for their own learning,
(c) willing to challenge the lecturer and colleagues,
(d) learning best in a comfortable and relaxed environment,
(e) learning by doing,
(f) preferring a variety of teaching methods,
(g) learning by solving realistic problems,
(h) wanting guidance not marks,
(i) individuals that learn at different rates and methods (give them the end-results and they will decide on the how to get to the end-results),
(j) social creatures that need fun and interaction,
(k) self-disciplined and want to control their own learning,
(l) learners that will maximise their resources,
(m) having a need for positive and negative feedback,
(n) having a capacity and can only handle so much information at a time.

In support of the adult learning principles an experiential learning approached is followed. Hoover (2007) suggests that experiential learning is much more than learning by doing. Hoover (2007) further conceptualize experiential learning as "a methodology of education which has a learning impact on the whole person, including spirituality, emotion and behaviour in addition to cognitive stimulation" (Hoover 2007, p. 325). Carroll (2006) classified experiential learning as "the heart of coaching supervision" (p. 5). Students must learn from the process and content of learning. Practice sessions in workshops provide students the opportunity to apply new skills, increasing the likelihood of applying it in practice (Reed et al. 2014). Vella et al.'s (2013) research found that coaches have the need for practical training where the learner coach (student) work with the facilitator to understand the application of program content in coaching practice.

Grant's (2007) research indicated that it will take between 3 and 6 months to become a competent coach. In this study, the students attend seven full day lectures spread over 9 months as part of the module.

Martin et al. (2014) identified seven criteria's to decide on the relevance of a training method. These criteria are learning modality (seeing, hearing or doing); training environment; availability of trainer; proximity (face to face vs. distance); interaction between trainer and learner and between learners; costs and time demands (Martin et al. 2014). For this study, Table 1 summarizes the content and training methods used in the module. The following part will briefly elaborate on some of the training methods used.

Table 1 The content and methodology of the coaching training programme

Format	Title	Objective	Method	Length
Assignment 1: individual assignment	Develop a personal coaching model	Gain knowledge of coaching and mentoring	Self-directed learning	20 h (revision time added)
		Develop critical thinking skills		
		Integrate different areas of IOPS		
		Understand and apply the ethical and legal implications of the coaching process		
		Develop trust in own process		
Workshop	Session 1: music therapy	Develop an understanding of own emotional experiences	Music therapy	5 h
		Explore own and others' experiences during music therapy to develop personal insight	Reflection	
	Session 2: practical coaching workshop	Be able to understand the characteristics and principles of coaching	Small group discussions and 1:1 with lecturers	4 h
Assignment 2: group assignment	Formulate a learning and development strategy for a company aimed at leadership development	Link people development strategy with business strategy	Group work	20 h
		See development as part of bigger business picture	Networking with practitioners	
		Develop understanding for a multi-cultural environment		
		Demonstrate a sensitivity and understanding for diversity		
		Integrate different areas of IOPS		
		Create awareness of importance of profession		
		Illustrate creative thinking		
		Develop a scope of practice and competencies for the IOP as people developer		

(continued)

Table 1 (continued)

Format	Title	Objective	Method	Length
Assignment 3: group assignment	Develop a model for leadership/ management development in South Africa	Apply the principles of adult learning Ensure the transfer of learning Utilise the principles of experiential learning Utilise/manage individual learning styles	Group work Networking with practitioners	20 h
Assignment 4: class assignment	Draw up a generic competency profile of an "Industrial Psychologist as People Developer in South Africa"	Explore a variety of strategies to ensure learning Develop understanding for a multi-cultural environment Demonstrate a sensitivity and understanding for diversity Integrate different areas of IOPS Create awareness of importance of profession Illustrate creative thinking Develop a scope of practice and competencies for the IOP as people developer	Class interaction	8 h
Assignment 5: group assignment workshop	Presentation on IOPS as people developer	Explore and present a variety of strategies to ensure learning on individual and group level	Group work Networking with practitioners Facilitation and lecturers	48 h
Assignment 6: individual assignment	Develop, implement and evaluate a mentoring/ coaching/ development process	Be capable of applying the basic coaching skills to stimulate growth in a protégé	Self-directed learning	23 h
		Understand the dynamics involved in a development relationship	Mentoring	
		Learn the basic principles of coaching	Coaching	
		Gain personal insight, self-awareness and self-management	Peer mentoring and coaching	
		Understand human behaviour	Small group learning Case study Contracting with their mentor	

2.1 Self-Development and Self-Directed Learning

For their own personal development students must firstly have a session with a psychologist (clinical, counselling, or industrial) and summarize the outcome of the development discussion in a report. Students are encouraged to develop their own coaching model (based on extensive literature reviews). Grant and Hartley (2013) support this by encouraging students in a coaching program to develop personalized phrases and language that is authentic. By making the coaching process their own it will facilitate quicker transfer of learning and create personal meaning. In addition, to support the meaningfulness the students are encouraged to identify their strengths and integrate these strengths into their personal coaching model. For this purposes, Van Zyl and Stander (2013) developed a strengths-based coaching model where the protégé's unique cultural position, preferences and experience is optimised as strengths, and presented to the students as part of this module.

2.2 Mentoring, Coaching and Supervision

Students are requested to have at least one mentor/coach (supervising psychologist) that is an Industrial Psychologist. This person will assume the role of mentor, coach and supervisor for a 1 year period. Students are required to engage with their allocated supervising psychologists at least five times during the course of the year for individual sessions and be part of a peer coaching group on a quarterly basis. The students have to keep a logbook of these sessions in order to provide evidence of attendance.

The role of the ***mentor*** is to facilitate the students' own personal and professional development and growth. According to Clutterbuck (2005), the most powerful learning is often a result of a mentor-mentee relationship. If successful it can create both task and socio-emotional learning in a trustworthy situation. Bozeman and Feeney (2007) defines mentoring as "… transmission of knowledge, social capital, and psychological support perceived by the recipient as relevant to work, career or personal development…between a person whom is perceived to have greater relevant knowledge, wisdom, or experience and a person who is perceived to have less" (p. 731). Mentoring involves a one-on-one relationship between an inexperienced person and an experienced person (Martin et al. 2014), in this case a psychologist. Developing self awareness and understanding others are important outcomes of this relationship. By being a role model, Clutterbuck (2005) identified developing these two aspects as core competencies of a mentor.

Where mentoring focuses on total personal development, ***coaching*** will be more specific and task orientated. Most definitions of coaching focus on a facilitation process or set of behaviours to help individuals or groups to develop skills, improve performance and enhance personal growth (Ellinger and Kim 2014; Hamlin et al. 2008). Students must select and contract a protégé to develop during the course of this year. The mentor should aid them in the development of their protégé's and should sign off on their progress at the end of the year.

Carroll (2006) supports coaching psychology ***supervision*** to enhance learning and improve quality. He describes "supervision as a forum where supervisees think about their work in order to do it better. Coaching psychologists bring their practice to another person or to a group and with their help review what happened to learn from that experience" (Carroll 2006, p. 4). Grant and Hartley (2013) strongly recommend group supervision over time to embed skills taught. The lecturers will meet bi-monthly with small groups to enable peer coaching and playing a supervision role. A strengths-based approach allows students to firstly share successes and then concerns with the coaching process. The focus is on learning from experiences and from each other. Grant and Hartley (2013) recommend such an approach to develop self-efficacy and peer-coaching. Beattie et al. (2014) added that peer coaching play an important role in reducing stress ("a safety valve") when participants share their concerns (p. 190).

Beattie et al. (2014) further report a lack of research on *multi-cultural coaching*. Abbott et al. (2013) indicate the importance of coaches understanding the complexity and developing sophistication in multi-cultural coaching. They further stress the importance of dealing with diversity as a resource and not a problem, "... using cultural orientation as a resource for learning, with coaching and mentoring as the medium, diversity can be harnessed as a resource..." (Abbott et al. 2013, p. 493). In this module students from different cultures must work on a group assignment and analyse the learning in terms of diversity.

The main aim of this chapter is to evaluate the experiences of emerging psychologists during an academic multi-cultural coaching training module, termed, people development. The study aims to utilise an evidence-based training methodology in order to evaluate the existing experiences of the students, followed by providing structured guidelines for the development of a multi-cultural coach.

3 Research Design

3.1 Research Approach

Presented against the primary aim of this chapter, a qualitative content analytic (Duriau et al. 2007), descriptive research design (Creswell 2013) drawing from the post-positivistic paradigm (Zammito 2004) was employed. Post-positivism assumes that knowledge is developed through investigation, discussion and formative inquiry (Duriau et al. 2007; Zammito 2004) and should be interpreted through rigorous contextual evaluation based on the scientific method (Creswell 2013). Post-positivism provides for researchers' potential biases, through presenting the researcher as an instrument of analysis, rather than an object of the process (Duriau et al. 2007). The paradigm is useful for most qualitative analytic techniques such as thematic content analysis (Creswell 2013) which makes provision for the quantification of qualitative results (Coetzee and van Zyl 2014). As such, thematic content analysis was employed to evaluate a masters training programme aimed at developing emerging psychologists as multi-cultural coaches.

3.2 Research Strategy and Setting

The participants in this study were registered student psychologists with the Health Professions Council of South Africa (HPCSA) and registered for a master's degree in Industrial Psychology with a tertiary educational institution in South Africa. These students were registered for a master's degree level module relating to coaching psychology, namely people development. A census-based sampling approach was employed (Gupta and Kabe 2011), whereby all students registered for the module were invited to partake in focus groups after the final contact session (or 'class'). Three focus groups were arranged whereby a semi-structured discussion was facilitated. The data was voice recorded, thereafter the data was transcribed and analysed.

3.3 Sampling Procedure and Participation

The sample consisted out of student psychologists ($n = 17$) registered for a master's degree in industrial psychology with a tertiary education institution within Gauteng, South Africa. All participants in this study were registered for a master's level module in people development with the same institution. Table 2 provides a detailed overview of the demographics of the sample.

The majority of the respondents were single (94.12 %) Afrikaans speaking (88.24 %), white (88.24 %), females (88.24 %), between the ages of 21 and 25 years (94.12 %) with an Honours degree (94.12 %). Similarly, individuals were predominantly full time students (58.82 %) with no previous formal training in coaching psychology (94.12 %).

3.4 Data Collection Methods

The sample was divided into three focus groups with a semi-structured question brief were employed to obtain data relating to the primary research objective. Focus groups are popular to determine shared experiences (Creswell 2013). The insights produced as part of a focus group would be less accessible without the (un)conscious dynamics and interactions amongst participants. Participants' thoughts, ideas, experiences and memories are stimulated through interaction and listening to others' verbalised experiences (Lindlof and Taylor 2002). Through the use of a

Table 2 Demographics of participants

		Occurrence	Frequency (%)
Gender	Male	2	11.76
	Female	15	88.24
Age	21–25	16	94.12
	26–30	1	5.88
Race	White	15	88.24
	African	2	11.76
Language	Afrikaans	15	88.24
	English	1	5.88
	Sesotho	1	5.88
Marital status	Single	16	94.12
	Married	1	5.88
Highest level of education	Honours	16	94.12
	Masters	1	5.88
Employment status	Full time employed	2	11.76
	Part time employed	5	29.41
	Full time students	10	58.82
Previous coaching training	Yes	1	5.88
	No	16	94.12

semi-structured discussion schedule, based on the principles of programme evaluation (Owen and Rogers 1999), the researchers were able to probe interesting avenues which emerged as part of the focus group process (Creswell 2013; Lindlof and Taylor 2002). For consistency in the discussion process of the three focus groups, the following questions were posed to participants:

- What was your overall experience of the module?
- How did you personally grow and develop as part of this module?
- How did you experience the methods employed in your training as multi-cultural coaches in the coaching component of this module?
- How did the module shape your competence as a multi-cultural coach?
- What recommendations can you make for us to improve the coaching training component of the module for next years' students?

3.5 Data Recording and Analysis

The focus groups were recorded through the use of an electronic recording device and were transcribed, verbatim, onto a Microsoft Excel® spreadsheet for further analysis. Thereafter, interview transcripts were compared to the voice recordings to ensure consistency and objectivity. Thematic content analysis was subsequently employed to process the data. According to Creswell (2013), thematic content analysis provides for the exploration of large amounts of 'muted' textual data in order to identify common (or frequently occurring) properties through structured categorical organisation. First, a thorough overview of the verbatim transcripts was compiled. Second, the transcripts were perused by the researchers in order obtain a 'general feel' for the results. Third, categories, primary and secondary themes were derived through the clustering of similarly categorized or themed responses by means of a formalized coding process. Finally, the coding process was co-coded whereby the primary researchers coded the data individually and compared the findings. Thereafter incongruences were discussed and consensus reached on categories, primary and secondary themes.

3.6 Reporting Style

The findings of the thematic content analysis are presented in line with the aim of this chapter. The findings are clustered as categories whereby themes were extracted and reported non-verbatim, coupled with the most supporting responses.

4 Findings

The data of the focus groups were analysed and are reported next. From the findings five categories emerged based on the responses received from the students on the initial questions. Themes, and sub-themes, with two of the most descriptive responses by the participants are provided in order to substantiate the particular findings in this category (see Fig. 1).

The findings are provided in the following order:

Table 3:	Category 1: Overall experience
Tables 4 and 5:	Category 2: Growth and development
Table 6:	Category 3: Training methodology
Table 7:	Category 4: Competence
Table 8:	Category 5: Recommendations

4.1 Category 1: Overall Experience

The finding from the first category related to the participants overall experience of the module. The findings showed two main themes which are reported next.

From the findings it was clear that the participants found the module to be quite *challenging*. The participants agreed that although the overall experience was positive, it was a demanding experience emotionally. The participants commented on the obvious difference in the levels of learning from their honours degree year,

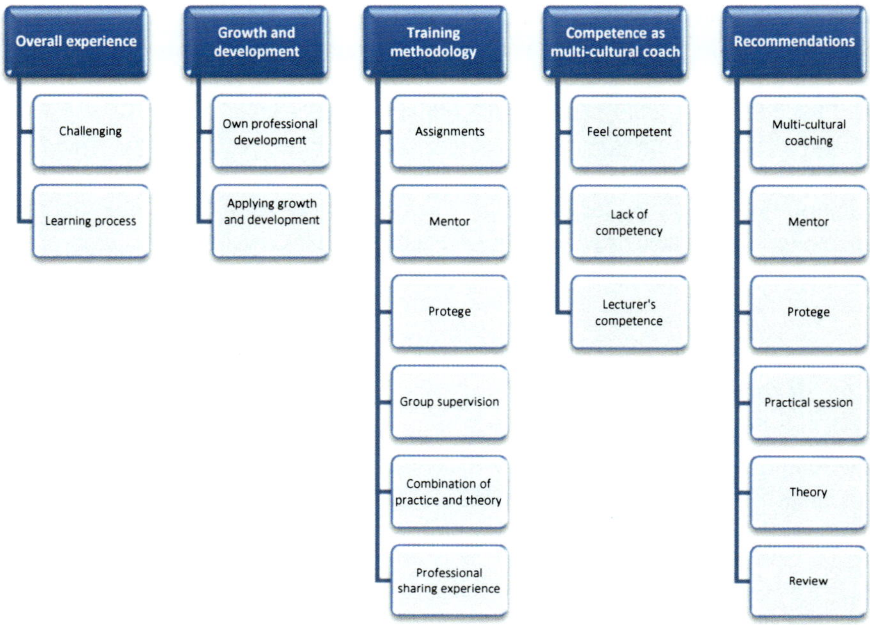

Fig. 1 Outline of findings

Table 3 Overall experience

Theme	Sub theme	Response
Challenging	Positive experience	…it wasn't easy. It is nice looking back now especially if I know what I know now I would have been less stressed out…
		It was a challenge but a good one…
	Emotional experience	…there was a lot of anxiousness about that for me, sometimes anger and even sometimes happiness because some things went wrong. So it was a rollercoaster
		… what made it so difficult was the emotional component of it. You get people that are more sensitive and they think about these things…a tough minded person… that's what made it very difficult because we sometimes allow our emotions to get to us and we take our emotions to the extreme
Learning process	Levels of learning	…A lot of learning where we digged deeper
		…Huge learning curve from honours…
	Practical application	I think I am more enlightened of what it actually entails. I will definitely be able to do it but I still like to practise…
		The module taught us to work with people in a practical manner…it was not just an assignment but the physical experience. That was the most outstanding

Table 4 Own professional development

Subtheme	Response
Growth process	For me it was good to see the impact my personality has on other people and to give myself feedback on my development areas that I need to focus on and see how it influences people
	Your personal development was challenged up to the extreme… you have to learn quickly, in my case I had to develop certain areas because it was destructive in nature for me
Self-awareness	For me to experience that self-awareness. The fact that I became self-aware through the process helped me to become more aware of others needs and emotions so I am more likely to take them in consideration now
	I did not only learn more about myself but I learned when I saw an emotion in somebody I could identify what happened… I am more aware, I am able to stand back and observe the emotions. You learn to put yourself in their shoes
Self-confidence	…the growth you can see with people that are working with you how they say they experienced you then and how they do now
	…there was a lot of growth taken place and you start to believe in yourself. You see your strengths and that you were actually able to do a whole day's activities and you were able to help and assist people in their development
Value of profession	For me as well to realise how important our role is. Now we take it serious to work with people and people's lives. We have a big impact and realise that responsibility in the future. To take responsibility for our future role. That was big for me to see what I am able to do
	That's why I love industrial Psychology, because you get the best of both worlds
Personal mastery	Once I feel comfortable even if I make mistakes then I know I am able to say it is ok, it is learning and I am human. And when I know how to deal with that
	You have to know you can do this, you have the ability to coach otherwise you can do more damage than good if you are doubtful in your ways

Table 5 Applying growth and development

Subtheme	Response
Building sensitive relations	You will have empathy because you understand their process. Also be careful to not always tell them I know what you feel because I have been through it
	…a lot of it comes in with building rapport. If you are more confident the person will also be more open to share
Apply knowledge and insight to the process	…it is our part in their life to encourage the same part of development, or to help them develop…if I see certain factors in that person's life I can guide them, and say maybe this is what I did to develop myself and how do you think you can develop yourself, utilising my view…that is how I will use my personal development for the future
	I really learned how other people see things and how they react or what their feelings are about the situation that happened. That is something that I will take with me and what I will actually apply in my own process or on somebody

Table 6 Training methodology

Theme	Subtheme	Response
Assignments	Creativity	I loved the assignment and the creativity component… I discussed it with my mentor and I used it in my coaching sessions
		I liked the fact that we were allowed to be creative, we were forced to find a protégé and then to create a model that we need to apply. If it didn't work we struggled and we have to find out from each other
	Relevance	The extend of the assignments, the way we need to engaged it was on a great strategic level and it learned us a lot on how to act in the professional world
		I actually think this module is almost the most relevant to business practice. Every assignment, every challenge we faced, is something that you will face in the industry… So it is interactive, you can challenge them and they pick your brain, you can actively engage with them
	Coaching model	In terms of developing our own model, that was a lot of fun for me, and I enjoyed developing my own…
		I went with my own process and I never used my model. I just went on what I felt and that also worked out. That is what my mentor did and I utilised that as a bases of our process and that worked out. I never used the model that I developed at the beginning of the year
	Self-reflection	…in terms of the reports that we need to do the self-reflection component is very valuable but for me it also helped me to evaluate if I am adding value to this person. Also to critically think about that as a major concern for me throughout the process was if I am adding value
		I think it is very effective especially the reports we had to write. It forced us to make sure we are on the right way and reflect on what we are doing and if we are making progress. So I think that aspect was very effective

(continued)

Table 6 (continued)

Theme	Subtheme	Response
Mentor	Valuable experience	I have learned so much from that person and I was scared at him in the beginning, I did not even think that he would become my mentor, but we just clicked like this. So many times I would just ask his advice on my process
		I think having a mentor and a protégé was a very good idea. I experienced it very well and I had a very close relationship with my mentor
	Personal growth	With my mentor he developed me on a personal, professional and as a coach, it was valuable in my own development. I can clearly see where I was and where I am now
		He (mentor) guided me through this year and now I have a better and much deeper insight on myself. As where I am today and where I was at the beginning of the year I now know more on where my developmental areas are and that will advance me in the business knowing now I am able to go out and I know what my frustrations will be and this is how I will handle it. I now have the skills and knowledge to handle myself
	Stretching comfort zone	He (lecturer) said get a mentor and go out of your comfort zone, get someone in business. And I did that and I feel that helped me, it was challenging but in the end it helped me
		That developed me on a personal level, I came aware of what is happening outside of our secure academic environment to make ourselves relevant within the professional world
Protégé	Personal growth and development	… the expectations that I had before my first meeting with my protégé and how it turned out is different because at the end it wasn't even that formal. It was a nice experience. I think I over complicated it a bit for me but there was obviously a lot of learning taking place through the whole process
		…the protégé, that was the nicest feeling ever when she really appreciate it and she told me thank you I really learned something and you really gave me some insight on something I never thought of. So that experience is something that I will always hold on to
	Responsibility	He [Lecturer] gives you options, putting the responsibility in your hands to do it. He [Lecturer] gives us advice instead of "do it"
		He [Lecturer] gave us the responsibility to go and coach a protégé. We had a real life coaching experience

(continued)

Table 6 (continued)

Theme	Subtheme	Response
Group supervision	Guidance	Also the fact that we need to have meetings with the lecturer. We talked about our protégés and he gave us advice, telling us this is what you can do. That really helped. He did not leave us to go and just coach our protégé
		…those sessions really helped us with new ideas to get your protégé where they need to go. So I think that sessions really helped you to consider other options as well
	Safe environment	.. it was also nice to me that when you (the lecturer) in the group sessions that you did something wrong, it is a safe environment to make mistakes. And the way he handled it, he wouldn't tell you are wrong, he would just tell you try this, and you don't feel bad about your mistake
		Because it was a group session, I felt at ease to know you are also struggling with this
Combination of practice and theory	Balance	And I think that session with the music therapy was such a nice environment when we talked about coaching, do you remember? We went outside and discuss it and I think it made us more comfortable to have a class session apart from the university
		I think the methods you employed this year were both theoretical and practical. You taught us the theory behind coaching and mentoring but you also put us in a practical position…
Professional sharing experiences	Related	…when the experts came to talk to us and we could understand what they went through. I think the methods that you used were good as well as the experience. It was really insightful to me because I could relate it to what I learned in the theoretical principles. What people said in practise, I could relate to it. It was good methods
		…also when they got someone to talk to us that recently started working so that we can relate to them. People who is new in the industry and only has a couple of years, maybe 2 years, of experience and they went through the same thing that we are going through now like looking for internships

noting that the standard of the *learning process* increased significantly and that more was expected of them during Masters' classes. They noted that the learning process was more on a practical level, some participants felt they needed more practise in order to feel comfortable with the coaching process. The participants indicated that the practical approach to the module was overall experienced positively.

Table 7 Competence as multi-cultural coach

Theme	Subtheme	Response
Feels competent	Self-confident	What really boosts my self-confidence was self-efficacy, seeing I can do this. That helped me a lot
		At the beginning of the year when I need to coach my protégé I was also scared. But now I am very confident
	Continuous development	I also agree I still feel that I am not there yet… I don't think coaching is something that you can do right. I don't want to be blindfolded and think this person will be the same as the next person because that is a mistake. I need to be flexible
		I want to explore the next step for me. I want to join a coaching organisation next year
Lack of competence	Trust own ability	I would say I still feel very incompetent to do it in practise now because I have that self-doubt again. I feel from my point of view I still need a lot of coaching, from my own mentor in order for me to be exceptional coach. I think it makes us still incompetent because at the end of the day you are working with a person's life
		What I need is just to get my self-confidence back. I need to work on trusting my own ability
Lecturer's competence	Practicing professional	I liked the module because the lecturer is still in practice. He is not an academic lecturer only he had new knowledge and scenarios to share…so I have learned from him
		Experience by far…he gave examples that were relevant in practice and we've learned a lot from that. That was a big positive for me. To learn from his experience. I can relate that back to similar situations I might find myself in
	Shows respect	We have discussions with him and there is respect. He actually wants your input and you get his input
		He treats us as colleagues and it is nice to experience that. It puts you in the mind-set where you take your work much more seriously
	Consistent	He always treats everybody the same
		… if he said class is till four, he won't go over the time because he knows we got somewhere to be
	Encourager	He is still excited for us. He is proud of us and it motivates us
		I was able to develop my biggest passion for Industrial Psychology…and with all his experiences he just strengthens that passion so much more. So if it wasn't for this I may not have the focus in IP as I do now
	Challenger	…he challenged us, that is what I also liked. It wasn't just textbook…
		He also picks your brain. He really challenges you to not only give a quick answer but to really reflect on what you think and then give an answer

Table 8 Recommendations

Theme	Subtheme	Response
Multi-cultural coaching	Different cultures, occupations and ages	I would have liked to coach someone with a different cultural background. I would have liked more knowledge on that and maybe if I had I will choose someone from a different culture to coach
		…on a business level especially because we are comfortable with younger people but not in the business, also people from different careers like an engineer and other cultures
Mentor	Choose mentor selectively	They must be more aware of the process and how important it is
		I just want to add to the assigning mentors; provide us with a checklist that we can give to the mentors just a few pointers that the mentors had guidelines because if you didn't give that they wouldn't know what you want out of the process
Protégé	Evaluate sessions	…maybe you or (lecturer) can sit in with me and my protégé…
		I think if you evaluate what we are doing for example… I think that would benefit the coaching process a lot and you will be able to see what we are doing and give us feedback based on that
	Feedback	I would just like to suggest that they can also write a report if they are willing to…they can share what they were feeling and how they see you as a coach
		Feedback from the coachee…
Practical session	View coaching session	I feel that I could have learned more from the module if we could have seen a real life coaching situation…to see you or (lecturer) "work your stuff"
		To see proper executive coaching…
	Feedback	…we could really benefit from more feedback. I feel we didn't get enough feedback
		…not getting feedback it would have been nice to present our work or assignments to the lecturer and let them critique it to what they think will work
Theory	More structured	A bit more structure to develop the model, like a criterion. Because when I start coaching I didn't know where to go from there
		… I missed a class in coaching skills
	Formal coaching workshop	Yes we need a more formal type of workshop. With more different practical things
		…a workshop at the beginning of the year on coaching and mentoring. An in-depth workshop, telling the students exactly what to expect and how do you run the process…
	Review	You start with the model because that gets you thinking and after the year renew your model and write a report on how you would have done it differently
		…at the beginning of the year they told us to get a paradigm and there was no paradigm in my coaching model. But after the year we can add a paradigm to our model

4.2 Category 2: Growth and Development

The findings of the second category showed two main themes. The participants commented on their own growth and development process, as well as their experience of applying growth and development during the coaching process with the protégés.

In Table 4 the subthemes that emerged from the theme *own professional development*, are reported.

The findings show that the module enabled the participants to *grow* and gain insight in themselves. The participants were confronted with their own emotions, issues and problems and had to deal with these before being able to assist their protégé's in his/her growth process. They also reported becoming more aware of their protégé's feelings. The participants became *aware* of themselves and the impact they have on their protégé's, this lead to them gaining insight, understanding and empathy for their clients.

The participants indicated that they viewed the module as a safe environment to allow themselves to grow and develop. They indicated that as they experienced their own growth and witnessed the effect on their clients, and received feedback on their development, they gained *self-confidence*.

The findings showed that the participants became aware of their important role in the profession of industrial psychology. They indicated that they gained insight in the *value of the profession*, as well as their ethical responsibility and impact in the workplace.

It is clear from the findings that as the participants learned from their mistakes, and gained insight and understanding in the coaching process, they *mastered the skills* and developed as coaches.

In Table 5 the subthemes that emerged from the second theme *Applying growth and development*, are reported.

From the findings is became clear that the participants became aware of their role in the protégé's growth and development. They reflected on how to establish and build *sensitive relations* with their clients, by being aware of the protégé's feelings, not leading during the process and by building rapport. The participants indicated that they gained more insight and understanding into the growth process of their clients, they *applied the knowledge* they learnt to assist the client to develop and grow in the coaching process. It seems that the participants drew from their own growth process in order to guide their protégés.

4.3 Category 3: Training Methodology

Next, the findings on the methodology used during the module are discussed.

The participants commented on the various methods used for training the students as coaches in this module. The results showed that the participants appreciated that they were encouraged to use their creativity with *assignments*. Although they felt challenged by the assignments, their experience was mostly that the assignments added value and was meaningful. The findings indicate that the participants felt the coaching model they had to develop was enjoyable and valuable, although some participants did not necessarily utilize the model in their own mentoring process. The participants indicated that the reports they had to write after mentoring sessions led to valuable self-reflection.

The participants indicated that the *mentor* they had to obtain as part of the module was a valuable experience. Not only did this relationship add to their growth and development but it stretched them beyond their comfort zones. The *protégé* they were required to coach in this module added to their development as a coach and also led to a sense of self responsibility and accountability which was highlighted by the lecturer. The participants indicated that they viewed the process as valuable since it was not an artificial process but a real life coaching relationship.

The participants indicated that the *group supervision sessions* with the lecturer were valuable to them and provided guidance when they needed it most. They also felt it was a safe environment to share experiences with fellow-students and gain insight from each other. The findings further showed that the participants indicated the *combination between practical and theoretical* work was balanced and valuable theory was learnt through practice. The findings show that the sessions with *professional practitioners* from the practice were insightful to the participants in order to gain knowledge on the workplace.

4.4 Category 4: Competence as Multi-cultural Coach

The fourth category of the findings related to the competence of the participants as multi-cultural coaches. Three themes emerged from the data, firstly relating to the participants' competence as coaches, secondly their lack of competence as coaches and lastly a theme referring to the lecturer's competence.

From the findings the first theme related to the participants indicating their competencies. The participants reported feeling *self-confident* as coaches after initially doubting themselves. They also added that they would continue to focus on their *future development* as coaches. The second theme related to some participants indicating *not feeling competent* yet mainly related to the lack of trusting their own abilities in the coaching process.

It is clear from the findings that the participants' reflected on the *competencies* they identified in their *lecturer*. They mainly indicated that the fact that he is involved in the business practice added to the value of the module. The participants indicated that the respect the lecturer showed towards them impacted on them and added to them even taking their work more seriously. Furthermore, the consistency the lecturer showed in the module was noted by the participants. The findings showed that the participants valued the lecture's encouragement and thus resulted in them acquiring a passion for and valuing their profession. Lastly, the fact that the lecturer challenged the participants in this module was clear in the findings.

4.5 Category 5: Recommendations

The last category related to recommendations for future training made by the participants.

From the findings it is clear that the participants initiated several recommendations to improve the module. A first theme that was identified related to the module including more *different levels of coaching*, such as more multi-cultural coaching, also knowledge on how to coach different occupations and ages. The participants also indicated that the process of assigning a *mentor* should be done more selectively. Some participants felt they were too far from their mentors, whilst others' mentors were not always available. The participants recommended that the *protégé* process should be formally evaluated by the lecturer in order to provide more guidance and feedback. Some participants also indicated that feedback from the protégé would be helpful, such as in a report format. The participants indicated that they would have preferred to view a *practical* coaching session from the experts, especially an executive coaching session. The participants further indicated that more feedback on their work during the year would have been helpful. It seems from the results that the participants required more structure in terms of the coaching process, especially so by means of a formal coaching workshop in order to acquire more *theory* and learn different coaching styles and models. Another recommendation related to reviewing their coaching models towards the end of the module, thereby being able to adapt the models and reflecting back on their work.

5 Discussion

The chapter aimed to evaluate the experiences of emerging psychologists relating to an evidence-based training methodology in order to provide structured guidelines for a proposed multi-cultural coaching training programme. Figure 2 presents an interpretation of the most frequently occurring themes extracted from the findings which acts as an overview for the components of a formal multi-cultural coaching training programme. The results indicated that the programme underemphasised the multi-cultural components of the training methodology employed and that limited attention was provided as to the development of a socio-cultural mind-set. However, the experiences associated with the training methodology employed proved to be meaningful and valuable to the participants. Below, the findings will be discussed and possible recommendations made in order to capitalize on the working mechanisms and to address the limitations of the training methodology.

Based on the experiences of the participants of the people development module, a multi-cultural coaching training programme should include three important components. The overall aim of the programme should first be to positively challenge participants to creatively design their own coaching model and coaching approach. Grant and Hartley (2013) support this finding indicating that students should be

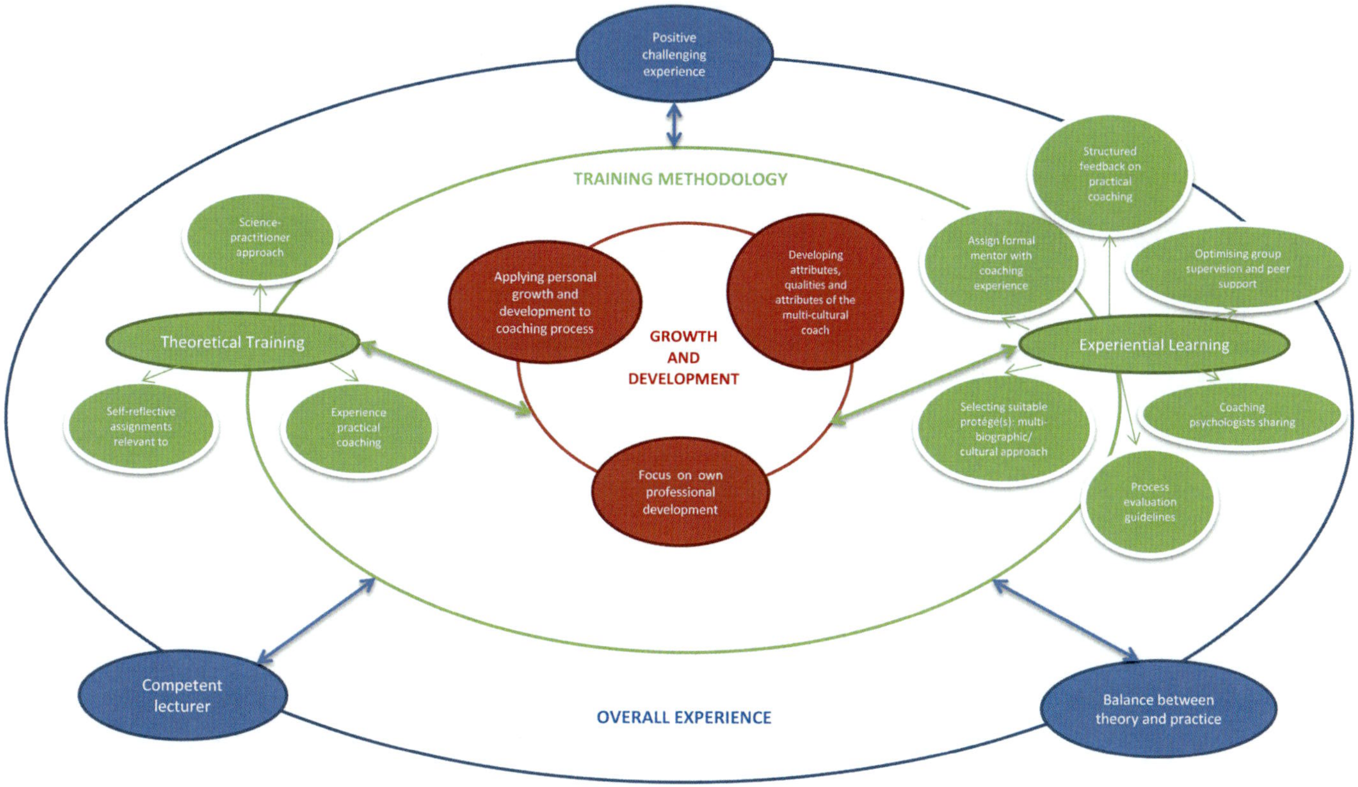

Fig. 2 Overview of a training programme aimed at multi-cultural coaching

encouraged to personalise their coaching approach. The findings further indicated that an ideal coaching training programme should include a reflective component towards the end of the training period in order to allow the students to make adjustments to their own model and approach. The programme should further include a balanced approach between coaching theory and practical application.

This finding is supported by the American Psychological Association's (2005) definition of evidence-based practice, indicating that an integration between available research and clinical expertise should take place. The programme should be presented by a competent lecturer, the findings indicate that the lecturer acts as a role model with expert subject knowledge and ability to apply coaching theory to business practice.

Second, a multi-cultural coaching training programme should lead to personal/professional growth and development taking place. An important principle of such a training programme is to allow for the students' own professional development. This finding links with Hoover's (2007) conceptualization of experiential learning, indicating that learning impact on the whole person (including spirituality, emotion and behaviour). This is an important concept for a coach who should be aware of the emotions of their protégés and be able to apply growth and development. According to Palmer and Whybrow (2014) the willingness of the protégé to grow is primary determined by the success of the interaction with and personality of the coach. While pathology, lack of motivation and follow-through by the coach has a negative impact on the development of the client, self-knowledge leads to increased coaching mastery (Drake 2009).

Furthermore, a multi-cultural coaching training programme should develop certain attributes, qualities and attitudes of the coach. The findings of this study show that after the coaching training programme the participants experienced increased self-confidence in their coaching ability and showed a development focus. Thus by enhancing their self-awareness the coach is aware of their own emotional maturity and self-actualization, and by implication, also in their clients (protégés) (see Cilliers 2000).

Third, training methods used in a coaching training programme should include a theoretical-based component and experiential learning. The findings of the study showed that the participants recommended more structured theory to be presented in a workshop format. According to Palmer and Whybrow (2014) a coaching programme should combine ideas from theoretical models coupled with practical sessions in order to develop a unique coaching approach where the models are applied to practical business challenges. Drawing from the theory behind various coaching models, the student is enabled to develop and test techniques as they practice them in a real life coaching sessions. Parilla and Hesser (1998) recommends that teaching and learning should be based on experiential learning to increase motivation of the learner and to improve long term retention of learning and leads to a greater sense of personal accomplishment. An experiential learning experience leads to knowledge being more readily accessible, and by implication easier to apply in the coaching process.

Moreover, the findings of this study showed that the participants requested more practical sessions where a coaching process can be viewed, more structured feedback and evaluation of their own coaching sessions. This finding is supported by Vella et al.'s (2013) research where coaches indicated a higher need for practical training. The ability to apply theory in practice should be based on the science practitioner approach whereby the student is trained in scientific approaches and techniques of coaching. Similarly, structured self-reflective assignments relevant to the business context should be presented to the student as part of the theoretical training, for example, developing their own coaching model based on the scientific method in relation to a given theme (e.g. leadership coaching). This enables the student to critically evaluate their own approach towards coaching. Finally, students need to be exposed to practical coaching sessions (e.g. own coaching process, role-plays, coaching simulations) in order to understand the dynamics of coaching.

Finally, in relation to the experiential learning component of the training methodology it is suggested that an ideal training programme consists of the following:

(a) Assigning a formal mentor for the coach to facilitate their own development: in this regard at least two mentors are appointed, an academic mentor and a primary mentor to formally assist the student in their coaching training.
(b) Selecting a suitable protégé from a multi-cultural and biographic position: students should acquire at least two protégés to formally assist the student in their coaching training.
(c) Optimizing group supervision and peer support;

    1. Providing structured feedback on the practical coaching process;
    2. Providing guidelines for the coach, mentor and protégé in order to evaluate the process;
    3. Encouraging practicing coaching psychologists to share their experiences with the students.

In conclusion, a multi-cultural coaching training programme should be focused on developing a science-practitioner within the coaching milieu. The programme should be comprised of both theoretical and experiential learning components in order to enhance the learning process. The theoretical component should expose the student to various coaching methods, approaches and ethics in order to aid the student in developing their own coaching approach. Further, the experiential learning component should be structured around the development of coaching competence through practical coaching training (coupled with appropriate supervision). Finally, the focus of the programme should be to facilitate the personal and professional growth of the emerging coaching psychologist.

5.1 Recommendations for Future Training of Multi-cultural Psychology Coaches

Based on the findings reported in this chapter, recommendations for future training of coaches include:

1. Multi-cultural coaching. Coaching across cultures and biographics. Students could have more than one protégé, where one is from a different cultural background.
2. Commencing with a theoretical basis and practical workshops at the onset of the module (training). Students could practice in a safe environment while they are observed by the lecturers.
3. Students observe where one or two experienced coaches simulate a real coaching session.
4. Consistent and regular feedback on the students' sessions with the protoge.
5. More, and regular feedback by using peer support (group supervision).
6. Record an ideal coaching session/s to be played during the theoretical session and or during small group sessions.
7. Allow time half way through the year for the students to adjust their coaching models and approaches, as well as at the end of the year, before submitting their finalized coaching models. More time could be spend to help students to integrate different sources of information (psychometric test results, 360° assessments, feedback from others, etc.) into the coaching process.
8. It is recommended that tertiary institutions offering Masters programmes in Industrial Psychology should consider presenting a module relating to coaching and people development.
9. Based on the results as well as the recommendations, Appendix A provides an overview of an alternative methodology to be employed to aid in this process.

6 Recommendations for Future Research

Based on the aforementioned it is lastly recommended that future research could include:

1. Studies should aim to develop a module which could be included in the training curriculum of IOP students in South Africa. Subsequently, such research could aim at evaluating such a module by means of a longitudinal approach.
2. Pre-, and post testing competency assessment of students coaching behaviours.
3. Evaluation of coaching process on "behaviour" and "results" levels. Feedback from protégés will be valuable in this regard.

7 Appendix A: Overview of Methodology to Be Employed to Train Multi-cultural Coaching Psychologists

Format	Title	Practical objective
Assignment 1: Individual assignment	Develop a personal coaching model	Students are encouraged to develop a theoretical understanding of coaching psychology applied in multi-cultural contexts through a structured assignment The assignment is structured into four sections:
		Section 1 – Academic component
		Students need to critically evaluate any five coaching models in relation to its applicability within multi-cultural contexts. The following areas need to be covered in the evaluation:
		(a) Provide an overview of coaching and coaching psychology with reference to multi-cultural contexts
		(b) Provide a theoretical discussion (systematic literature review) of each coaching model
		(c) Provide a thorough overview and discussion regarding the psychological paradigm underpinning each coaching model
		(d) Discuss the proverbial 'pros' and 'cons' of each model
		(e) Evaluate the multi-cultural applicability of each model
		(f) Give your verdict as to which coaching model would be the most appropriate for the use in multi-cultural contexts
		Section 2 – Developing a personal coaching model (working document)
		1. Flowing from the above, students need to select a scientifically validated coaching model which conforms to his/her own preferred approach, style and strengths. Through using this model as a foundation, he/she would need to develop a unique (conceptual) multi-cultural coaching model that's aligned to the aforementioned preferred approach, style and strengths. (This model will be seen as a 'working document', whereby it will evolve, adapt and develop throughout the training process)
		2. Present a visual representation of this model
		3. Indicate why/how this model will fit your strengths, preference and style and discuss its applicability to a multi-cultural coaching context

(continued)

Format	Title	Practical objective
		Section 3 – Professional ethics of coaching and practice management
		1. With reference to the legislative frameworks governing psychologists, the ethical practice guidelines of the governing bodies as well as SIOPSA's Code of Practice for Registered Psychology Practitioners in Coaching, the following areas need to be discussed:
		(a) The ethical framework for coaching psychology and how it applies to emerging (student/intern) psychologists with specific reference to:
		(i) Rights and responsibilities of stakeholders in the coaching relationship
		(ii) Representations by the coach relating to truthfulness, responsibility, integrity and dynamics of the coaching relationship
		(b) Good practices in coaching psychology with reference to:
		(i) Dealing with rights of the coachee
		(ii) Representations by the coach
		(iii) Supervision of coaching practitioners
		(iv) How notes of sessions will be managed and stored
		2. Provide the following templates which you will use for your coaching process with your coachee for Assignment 4:
		(a) Letter of informed consent for the process
		(b) Coachee intake form
		(c) Coaching log
		(d) Personal development plan
Workshop	Session 1: music therapy	1. Develop an understanding of own emotional experiences
		2. Explore own and others' experiences during music therapy to develop personal insight
	Session 2: practical coaching workshop	1. Be able to understand the characteristics and principles of coaching
Assignment 2: group assignment	Formulate a learning and development strategy for a company aimed at leadership development	The purpose of the assignment is to aid the student in developing a learning and development strategy aimed at leadership development for a given organisation. The groups for this assignment will be formed based on diversity criteria; that is, gender, race, work experience, geographical area and personality. The focus should be on creating links between various types of development strategies and the organisation's bottom line
		Section 1 – Academic component
		The following components need to be addressed in this group assignment:

(continued)

Format	Title	Practical objective
		Do an environmental and business analysis of the company (example PESTEL & BSC) with a clear indication of the business drive and strategy
		Create a scenario of the SA business environment the next 2 years and clearly indicate what challenges this will create for leaders
		Conceptualise the idea and characteristics of "Positive Organisations" and make it applicable to your company
		Define the role and competencies of a positive leader
		Within the above scenarios and challenges critically discuss the learning and development challenges facing South African companies and your specific company during the next 3 years?
		Develop a scenario of international and national trends in the Education, Training and Development of leaders/managers
		Develop a unique leadership development strategy/ model for South African leaders by integrating the above information (integrate the concept of positive psychology and wellness into your program). Present a visual representation of this model in your assignment
		The model must be an indication that you have mastered the following:
		(a) Learning and development principles
		(b) Knowledge about the next generation of learning tools and technologies which can be utilised to develop leaders
		(c) The integration of different development strategies into one model?
		(d) The creation of a training climate which will ensure continuous learning? I expect that you will be very creative and original in your ideas
		(e) The optimisation of social media in the learning process?
		(f) Measuring value add (ROI)
		Section 2 – Personal development component
		The second component relates to how the students worked together as a team within this diverse multi-cultural context. After completion of this section of the assignment the learner should be able to:
		Work effectively in a diverse team
		Organise and manage oneself and team members effectively
		Collect, analyse, organise and critically evaluate information

(continued)

Format	Title	Practical objective
		Demonstrate a sensitivity and understanding for diversity
		Explore a variety of strategies to learn more effectively as a team
		As part of the personal development report, each individual team member needs to compile a report on the following:
		Illustrate by means of a diagram your team development process that you have followed
		What team development model/strategy did you use to improve team work?
		What role did every member play in the team?
		What role did diversity play in the management of the team?
		How effective was the team? Assess the team against the criteria for effective team work. Assess the levels of trust, constructive conflict, commitment, accountability and delivering results during and at the end of the team process aligned to the multi-cultural nature of the team
		How did the team develop (from group to team) during the past 6 months?
		What happened in terms of team dynamics?
		What did you learn from the "diversity" of the team?
		What were the strengths and weaknesses of the diverse team?
		What was the leadership dynamics in the team?
		What are the strengths of every team member?
		How did you personally grow from this experience?
		Name the 5 strengths and 3 areas of development as people developer and team player for every member?
		What learning strategies worked best?
		How did you optimise social learning in this assignment?
		Recommendations for improving team work.
		Using your preferred psychological paradigm, provide an analysis and interpretation of the multi-cultural group dynamics
Assignment 4: class assignment	Draw up a generic competency profile of an "Industrial Psychologist as multi-cultural coach in South Africa"	1. Explore a variety of strategies to ensure effective multi-cultural coaching
		2. Develop understanding for a multi-cultural environment and socio-identity development

(continued)

Format	Title	Practical objective
		3. Demonstrate a sensitivity and understanding for diversity within the coaching context
		4. Create awareness relating to the importance of multi-cultural sensitivity within the coaching context
		5. Illustrate creative thinking as to the capitalisation of multi-cultural and diverse strengths
		6. Develop a scope of practice and competencies for the IOP as multi-cultural coaching psychologist
Assignment 5: group assignment workshop	Presentation on IOPS as people developer	1. Explore and present a variety of strategies relating to individual and team multi-cultural coaching strategies in order to ensure learning on individual and group level
		2. Potential topics include:
		(a) The Industrial Psychologist as developers of high-potential talent within multi-cultural contexts
		(b) The Industrial Psychologist as multi-cultural performance improvement consultant (to create a positive organisation)
		(c) The Industrial Psychologist as multi-cultural mentor (to create mature leaders)
		(d) The Industrial Psychologist as multi-cultural coach (to create competent leaders)
		(e) The Industrial Psychologist as multi-cultural team coach and mentor (to create a high performing team)
Assignment 6: individual assignment	Develop, implement and evaluate a multi-cultural coaching process	1. Register with the local governing body as a student psychologist (where applicable)
		2. Identify and contract a supervising psychologist
		3. Identify and contract two coaches (one for a similar race/age/gender as the coach and one from the opposite race/age/gender)
		4. Develop, implement and evaluate the coaching intervention
		5. Submit two quarterly reports and a final portfolio of evidence:
		(a) **Report 1**
		(i) Section A: The Protégés
		1. Biographical information of your protégés
		2. A very short psychometric report based on the above mentioned psychometric measures for both the protégés
		3. A summary of the protégés' expectations, needs, 10 strengths and 4 developmental areas
		4. Summarise your initial experience with the protégés

(continued)

Format	Title	Practical objective
		5. Briefly mention the experience working with the protégé from a different culture and mention the cultural factors which may influence your coaching process
		6. Discuss the approach which you will use in order to mentor your protégés
		7. Provide a time schedule for your future meetings
		(ii) Section B: You
		1. A short psychometric or competency based report on yourself based on the above mentioned psychometric measures
		2. A summary of your expectations, needs, 10 strengths, 4 developmental areas and your plan of action for own development
		3. 360° assessment/feedback on a People Developer competency profile from at least 3 people
		4. Summarise your initial experience with this assignment
		5. Discuss the ethical issues you might encounter in the process, and indicate how you will manage them
		6. Present a short summery of your first individual session with your supervising psychologist
		(iii) Section C: Interim feedback on the effectiveness of the coaching intervention
		1. Provide an orientation to the coaching methodology or model that will be employed (based on Assignment 1)
		2. Discuss the research method, design and evaluation/analysis methods that will be employed to determine the effectiveness of the coaching intervention
		3. Provide feedback on your baseline results
		(iv) Section D: Addendums
		1. Attach the RAW data of the psychometric instruments you used
		2. Attach your coaching log for your sessions with the protégé
		3. Attach a certified copy of your registration certificate as a student psychologist with the HPCSA
		4. Attach a signed letter from your Industrial Psychologist Mentor indicating that he/she helped you with the interpretation and feedback on the psychometric tests

(continued)

Format	Title	Practical objective
		5. Attach evidence that you have attended the first session with your academic supervisors
		6. Provide a signed document commissioned by a commissioner of Oaths (Police officer, attorney, post master at the post office etc) that confirms that you will adhere to the processes, principles and ethical guidelines as promulgated by the HPCSA (HPCSA Form 223), the SIOPSA code of practice for registered psychology practitioners in coaching as well as the Health Professions Act No 56 of 1974
		(b) Report 2
		(i) Section A: The Protégés
		1. What progress has the protégés made since your initial meeting?
		2. How are these individuals applying their unique signature strengths?
		3. What obstacles are in the protégés' way for achieving their end results?
		4. How will the protégés address these objectives?
		5. Summarise the meetings with the protégés
		(ii) Section B: You
		1. What are you currently experiencing with regards to the relationship with your mentor?
		2. What are you currently experiencing with regards to the relationship with the protégés?
		3. What challenges (problems?) are you experiencing?
		4. How are you going to address these issues?
		5. How are you applying your own unique strengths?
		6. Present a short summery of your second individual session as well as your group discussion with your supervising psychologist and academic supervising psychologists
		(iii) Section C: Interim feedback on the effectiveness of the coaching intervention
		(1) Provide feedback on your second measurement
		(2) Provide an indication as to how you would either (a) sustain the success or (b) amend your process to improve the results
		(3) Now that you are half-way through your coaching process, provide an 'updated' version of your coaching model/approach
		(iv) Section D: Addendums
		1. Attach your coaching log for your sessions with the protégé

(continued)

Format	Title	Practical objective
		2. Attach evidence that you have attended the second session with your academic supervisors
		3. Attach any relevant documentation in support of your coaching processes
		(c) Portfolio of evidence
		(i) Section A: Report 1 (Attach Report 1)
		(ii) Section B: Report 2 (Attach Report 2)
		(iii) Section C: Report 3
		1. Section C.1: The Protégés
		(a) Provide an overview of your two protégés development journeys
		(b) Discuss the ethical challenges experienced during this process and how these were managed
		(c) Discuss your experiences when working with someone from a different culture
		(d) Indicate how the professional relationship was terminated
		(e) Provide a brief psychometric report of your protégés at the end of their developmental journeys
		2. Section C.2: Final scientific evidence as to the effectiveness of your coaching intervention
		(a) Provide final scientific evidence as to the effectiveness of your coaching intervention
		(b) Based on the previous point, discuss your 'final' coaching model/approach/methodology (amended and adapted based on Assignment 1)
		3. Section D: Addendums
		(a) Attach feedback from your protégés as to his/her experience of the coaching process
		(b) Attach all (completed) coaching logs, personal development plans, client intake forms, letters of informed consent, signed informed consent forms, raw data of the psychometric assessments
		(c) A letter from you supervising psychologist indicating that you have attended at least 5 sessions
		(d) Attach evidence that you have attended all the sessions with your academic supervisors
		(e) Provide a signed document commissioned by a commissioner of Oaths (Police officer, attorney, post master at the post office etc) that confirms that you HAVE adhered to ALL the processes, principles and ethical guidelines as promulgated by the HPCSA (HPCSA Form 223), the SIOPSA code of practice for registered psychology practitioners in coaching as well as the Health Professions Act No 56 of 1974

References

Abbott, G., Gilbert, K., & Rosinski, P. (2013). Cross-cultural working in coaching and mentoring. In J. Passmore, D. B. Peterson, & T. Freire (Eds.), *The Wiley-Blackwell handbook of the psychology of coaching and mentoring* (pp. 484–500). Retrieved from http://ir.nmu.org.ua/bitstream/handle/123456789/144889/cfdaf6e32f456ab57cc53be33169b53f.pdf?sequence=1#page=312

American Psychological Association. (2005, August). *American Psychological Association policy statement on evidence-based practice in psychology* [Adobe Digital Editions Version]. Retrieved from http://www.apa.org/practice/ebpreport.pdf

Beattie, R. S., Kim, S., Hagen, M. S., Egan, T. M., Ellinger, A. D., & Hamlin, R. G. (2014). Managerial coaching: A review of the empirical literature and development of a model to guide future practice. *Advances in Developing Human Resources, 16*(2), 184–201. doi:10.1177/1523422313520476.

Bell, D., & Hausman, E. M. (2014). *3 training models in professional psychology doctoral programs* (The Oxford Handbook of Education and Training in Professional Psychology). New York: Oxford University Press.

Biswas-Diener, R., & Dean, B. (2007). *Positive psychology coaching: Putting the science of happiness to work for your clients*. Hoboken: Wiley.

Bozeman, B., & Feeney, M. K. (2007). Toward a useful theory of mentoring: A conceptual analysis and critique. *Administration & Society, 39*(6), 719–739. doi:10.1177/0095399707304119.

Byrne, Z. S., Hayes, T. L., McPhail, S. M., Hakel, M. D., Cortina, J. M., & McHenry, J. J. (2014). *Industrial and Organizational Psychology, 7*(1), 2–14. doi:10.1111/iops.12095.

Carroll, M. (2006). Key issues in coaching psychology supervision. *The Coaching Psychologist, 2*(1), 4–8. Retrieved from http://www.supervisioncentre.com/docs/kv/Key%20Issues%20in%20Coaching%20Psychology%20Supervision.pdf

Cilliers, F. (2000). Facilitation skills for trainers. *South African Journal of Industrial Psychology, 26*, 21–26.

Clutterbuck, D. (2005). Establishing and maintaining mentoring relationships: An overview of mentor and mentee competencies. *South African Journal of Human Resource Management, 3*(3), 2–9. Retrieved from http://www.sajhrm.co.za/index.php/sajhrm/article/download/70/70

Coetzee, M., & Van Zyl, L. E. (2014). A review of a decade's scholarly publications (2004–2013) in the South African Journal of Industrial Psychology. *SA Journal of Industrial Psychology, 40*(1), 1–16.

Creswell, J. W. (2013). *Qualitative inquiry & research design: choosing among the five approaches*. Thousand Oaks: Sage Publications.

Drake, D. B. (2009). Evidence in action: A relational view of knowledge and mastery in coaching. *International Journal of Evidence Based Coaching and Mentoring, 7*(1), 1–12.

Duriau, V. J., Reger, R. K., & Pfarrer, M. D. (2007). A content analysis of the content analysis literature in organization studies: Research themes, data sources, and methodological refinements. *Organizational Research Methods, 10*, 5–34.

Egan, T., & Hamlin, R. G. (2014). Coaching, HRD, and relational richness: Putting the pieces together. *Advances in Developing Human Resources, 16*(2), 242–257. doi:10.1177/1523422313520475.

Ellinger, A. D., & Kim, S. (2014). Coaching and human resource development: Examining relevant theories, coaching genres, and scales to advance research and practice. *Advances in Developing Human Resources, 16*(2), 127–138. doi:10.1177/1523422313520472.

Grant, A. M. (2006). A personal perspective on professional coaching and the development of coaching psychology. *International Coaching Psychology Review, 1*(1), 12–22. Retrieved from http://www.enhancingpeople.com/paginas/master/Bibliografia/biblio_V1/Sesion012/A%20personal%20perspective%20on%20professional%20coaching%20and%20the%20development%20of%20coaching.pdf

Grant, A. M. (2007). Enhancing coaching skills and emotional intelligence through training. *Industrial and Commercial Training, 39*(5), 257–266.

Grant, A. M., & Cavanagh, M. J. (2007). Evidence-based coaching: Flourishing or languishing? *Australian Psychologist, 42*(4), 239–254. doi:10.1080/00050060701648175.

Grant, A. M., & Hartley, M. (2013). Developing the leader as coach: Insights, strategies and tips for embedding coaching skills in the workplace. *Coaching: An International Journal of Theory, Research and Practice, 6*(2), 102–115. doi:10.1080/17521882.2013.824015.

Gupta, A. K., & Kabe, D. G. (2011). A quadratic programming approach to a survey sampling cost minimization problem. *Istanbul Üniversitesi İşletme Fakültesi Dergisi, 40*(1), 15–21.

Hamlin, R. G., Ellinger, A. D., & Beattie, R. S. (2008). The emergent 'coaching industry': A wake-up call for HRD professionals. *Human Resource Development International, 11*(3), 287–305.

Hoover, J. D. (2007). How "whole" is whole person learning? An examination of spirituality in experiential learning. *Developments in Business Simulation and Experiential Learning, 34*(1), 324–330. Retrieved from https://journals.tdl.org/absel/index.php/absel/article/download/482/446

Johnson, W. B., & Kaslow, N. (Eds.). (2014). *The oxford handbook of education and training in professional psychology*. New York: Oxford University Press.

Knowles, M. (1973). *The adult learner: A neglected species* [Adobe Digital Editions Version]. Retrieved from http://files.eric.ed.gov/fulltext/ED084368.pdf

Lindlof, T. R., & Taylor, B. C. (2002). *Qualitative communication research methods* (2nd ed.). Thousand Oaks: Sage.

Martin, B. O., Kolomitro, K., & Lam, T. C. M. (2014). Training methods: A review and analysis. *Human Resource Development Review, 13*(1), 11–35. doi:10.1177/1534484313497947

Neal, T. M. S., & Brodsky, S. L. (2014a). Occupational socialization's role in forensic psychologists' objectivity. *Journal of Forensic Psychology Practice, 14*, 24–44. doi:10.1080/15228932.2013.863054.

Owen, J. M., & Rogers, P. (1999). *Program evaluation: Forms and approaches*. London: Sage.

Palmer, S., & Whybrow, A. (Eds.). (2014). *Handbook of coaching psychology: A guide for practitioners*. London: Routledge.

Parilla, P. F., & Hesser, G. W. (1998). Internships and the sociological perspective: Applying principles of experiential learning. *Teaching Sociology, 26*(4), 310–329.

Passmore, J. (Ed.). (2013). *Diversity in coaching: Working with gender, culture, race and age*. New York: Kogan Page Publishers.

Poduska, J. M., & Kurki, A. (2014). Guided by theory, informed by practice: Training and support for the good behavior game, a classroom-based behavior management strategy. *Journal of Emotional and Behavioral Disorders, 22*(2), 83–94.

Reed, S., Shell, R., Kassis, K., Tartaglia, K., Wallihan, R., Smith, K., … Mahan, J. D. (2014). Applying adult learning practices in medical education. *Current Problems in Pediatric and Adolescent Health Care, 44*(1), 170–181. doi:10.1016/j.cppeds.2014.01.008.

Society for Industrial and Organisational Psychology of South Africa. (2012). *Annual report*. https://www.siopsa.org.za/files/SIOPSA%20Annual%20Report%202012_Final%20JE.pdf. Accessed 3 Mar 2016.

Smith, E. J. (2006). The strength-based counselling model. *The Counselling Psychologist, 34*(2), 13–80.

Stein, I. F., Page, L. J., & Maltbia, T. E. (2014). Coaching education: Coming of age. *Journal of Psychological Issues in Organizational Culture, 5*(2), 7–15. doi:10.1002/jpoc.21149.

Stober, D. R., Wildflower, L., & Drake, D. (2006). Evidence-based practice: A potential approach for effective coaching. *International Journal of Evidence Based Coaching and Mentoring, 4*(1), 1–8. Retrieved from http://ijebcm.brookes.ac.uk/documents/vol04issue1-paper-01.pdf

Tett, R. P., Walser, B., Brown, C., Simonet, D. V., & Tonidanel, S. (2013). 2011 SIOP graduate program benchmarking survey part 3: Curriculum and competencies. *The Industrial Organizational Psychologist, 50*(4), 69–90.

Theron, C. (2007). Confessions, scapegoats and flying pigs: Psychometric testing and the law. *SA Journal of Industrial Psychology, 33*(1), 102–117.

Van Zyl, L. E., & Stander, M. W. (2013). A strengths-based approach towards coaching in a multicultural environment. In J. H. D. Cornelius-White, R. Motschnig-Pitrik, & M. Lux (Eds.), *Interdisciplinary handbook of the person-centered approach* (pp. 245–257). New York: Springer. doi:10.1007/978-1-4614-7141-7-17.

Vella, S. A., Crowe, T. P., & Oades, L. G. (2013). Increasing the effectiveness of formal coach education: Evidence of a parallel process. *International Journal of Sports Science & Coaching, 8*(2), 417–430. doi:10.1260/1747-9541.8.2.417.

Weathington, B. L., Bergman, S. M., & Bergman, J. Z. (2014). Training science-practitioners: Broadening the training of industrial-organizational psychologists. *Society for Industrial and Organizational Psychology, 7*(1), 35–38. doi:10.1111/iops.12101.

Zammito, J. H. (2004). *A nice derangement of epistemes. Post-positivism in the study of science from Quine to Latour*. Chicago: The University of Chicago Press.

Zepeda, S. J., Parylo, O., & Bengtson, E. (2014). Analyzing principal professional development practices through the lens of adult learning theory. *Professional Development in Education, 40*(2), 295–315. doi:10.1080/19415257.2013.821667.

Enhancing Evidence-Based Coaching Practice by Developing a Coaching Relationship Competency Framework

Yi-Ling Michelle Lai and Almuth McDowell

Abstract This chapter takes a competence focused approach to coaching in order to outline relevant knowledge, skills and abilities (KSAs) for Coaching Psychologist to enhance coaching relationship towards positive outcomes. We commence with a comparison of relevant existing competency frameworks for coaching practitioners, such as the International Coach Federation (ICF), Association for Coaching (AC) and also the Special Group in Coaching Psychology (BPS, UK) to determine their similarities and differences. Our analysis outlines how the different models feature in terms of their development process, conceptual robustness and also how they address cross cultural issues in coaching. As a next step, we outline a rigorous role analysis to develop a comprehensive Coaching Relationship Competency Framework (CRCF), focusing furthering the effectiveness of the coaching relationship. A Systematic Review which can inform us about current knowledge as well as gaps and research trends in the field therein is essential prior primary research. The review results determined the need to focus on the coaching relationship and in particular the coach's competencies for facilitating this in an effective way. It then fed into three subsequent studies to draw up a new competence framework, which has been tested out through a pilot study. A Coaching Relationship Competency Framework with 75 behavioural indicated was identified and provided a guideline for future practice and research by spelling out (a) 'Soft Skills' which are key behaviours needed in any coaching relationship such as "listening actively", and (b) 'Hard Skills', such as "establishing mutually agreed goals", which can inform concrete coach training and development. In short, we argue that a behavioural focus and framework has much to offer by providing benchmarks for training and reflective practice. We illustrate the chapter with brief interactive exercises and reflections for practice, giving attention to cross cultures issues as appropriate. In

Y.-L.M. Lai (✉)
Organisation Studies and HRM, University of Portsmouth, Portsmouth, UK

Department of Organizational Psychology, Birkbeck, University of London, London, UK
e-mail: yi-ling.lai@port.ac.uk

A. McDowell
Organisation Studies & HRM, University of Portsmouth, Portsmouth, UK
e-mail: a.mcdowall@bbk.ac.uk

L.E. van Zyl et al. (eds.), *Coaching Psychology: Meta-theoretical perspectives and applications in multicultural contexts*, DOI 10.1007/978-3-319-31012-1_17

conclusion, the key contribution of the framework presented here is that it was designed from the outset to acknowledge the perspectives of coaches, coachees and also commissioning clients.

Keywords Evidence-based coaching • Competency framework • Coaching

1 Introduction

The role of the coaching relationship in facilitating coaching outcomes has been widely discussed and investigated since 2008 (Baron and Morin 2009; Boyce et al. 2010; de Haan 2008; Palmer and McDowall 2010; de Haan et al. 2013). However, most of the existing studies are still not adequate to confirm what the active factors are for an effective coaching relationship and how these factors could be optimized in the coaching process. This chapter presents a different approach to understand the coaching relationship by investigating essential coach's attributes and competencies facilitating an effective coaching relationship. It commences with a brief discussion on contemporary issues and challenges in the field of coaching. The diversity of coaching disciplines has shifted the research focus from examining singular coaching intervention to studying the effectiveness of coaching process. The association between the coaching relationship and coaching outcomes has been examined through several studies (Baron and Morin 2009; Boyce et al. 2010; de Haan et al. 2013), nevertheless there is no denying that more rigorous evidence is required to examine common factors for a better desired working relationship in the coaching process. A systematic review on coaching psychology was carried out to ascertain specific research topics according to existing issues in coaching filed before further any primary studies. The review results (Lai and McDowall 2014) indicated a comprehensive role analysis study to identify and validate required competencies for coaches to establish a productive coaching relationship is necessary. The detailed investigation process and results of this coaching relationship competency framework study will be summarised in this chapter.

2 Contemporary Issues in Coaching and Coaching Psychology

Given the increase in coaching application in the organisational and leadership development field, the evaluation of the impact of coaching on personal and organisational development is a key interest to organisational stakeholders and coaching practitioners (Passmore and Fillery-Travis 2011). Whilst the ultimate objective of coaching is similar to other helping interventions to facilitate positive life and behavioural change, organisations (and coaches) need to demonstrate that coaching produces positive outcomes and is worth continued investment. Thus, the promotion of evidence-based coaching to document any effects on concrete personal development or organisational-based (e.g. ROI) outcomes is essential in contemporary coaching study (Passmore and Fillery-Travis 2011).

However, some issues emerged in the development of evidence-based coaching due to the diversity of coaching disciplines. The following sections will summarise the challenges of existing coaching study and practice to explain why this SR was an essential step in the field of coaching.

2.1 The Role of Psychology in Contemporary Coaching Practice

Summarising from some leading coaching studies (Berglas 2002; Cavanagh 2006; Grant 2001; Naughton 2002; Whybrow 2008), psychological interventions are regarded bringing positive effects on coaching outcomes; however more rigorous evidence is required. The diversity of coaching disciplines (e.g. management, psychology, and education etc.) increases the difficulty in integrating existing evidence and identifying the best available knowledge for coaching practitioners to apply in their coaching sessions (Stober et al. 2006). In addition, it becomes a challenge to distinguish standardised assessment criteria for coaching professionalisation if the fundamental theoretical knowledge for professional coaching practice could not be confirmed through evidence-based research process.

Applying psychological principles in the coaching sessions are considered as one of the key elements for the enhancement of evidence-based practice (Grant 2008). Here are the rationales to support this statement: firstly, psychology is a theoretically grounded science that underpins the processes and understanding of human change (Whybrow 2008). The evidence-based coaching interventions (adopted from therapeutic models) fulfil the essential purpose of coaching, which is to facilitate a coachee's continuous learning and growth in the workplace through motivation and attitude change. For example, Simons and Cleary (2006) suggested that a high degree of self-knowledge is essential for successful leadership; coaching practitioners should integrate elements of counselling to address the influences of the coachee's past and consequent attitudes, feelings and beliefs that underpin behaviour. Secondly, psychology is a recognised academic qualification, thus coaches who apply psychological grounded principles can ensure that a coaching process is based on enforceable ethical codes and supervised by relevant governing associations (e.g. British Psychological Society). Thirdly, having proper training in psychology assists the professional coach to minimise causing harm to a coachee with so far unrecognised mental health problems (Berglas 2002; Cavanagh 2006; Naughton 2002). Though the general aim of coaching is to facilitate individual behavioural change and performance improvement in the workplace, studies indicated between 25 and 50 % of individuals who attend life coaching programmes (mainly focus on personal development goals and aspirations of individuals) may have hidden mental health issues, such as stress, anxiety and depression (Oades et al. 2005; Spence and Grant 2005). Therefore these studies indicated having a background in psychology or acquiring fundamental psychological knowledge is crucial to be able to identify if coachee has mental disorder issues and refer them to the appropriate therapeutic treatment such as counselling.

Several coaching reviews and book chapters (Bachkirova 2008; Grant 2001; Passmore and Fillery-Travis 2011; Whybrow 2008) have addressed the role of psychological principles in coaching. These papers indicated it is necessary to build on this groundwork to conduct a more in depth review, with clear review criteria which assess the quality of any primary sources, to allow us to spell out clear hypotheses for further investigation.

2.2 *The Role of Coaching Relationship for Facilitating Coaching Outcomes*

As discussed earlier, it remains a challenge for coaching researchers to examine the most effective coaching method for a positive coaching outcome due to the diversity in domains, methods and outcomes discussed earlier. Therefore coaching research has shifted its focus from examining singular coaching interventions to investigating the active ingredients in a productive coaching process (Palmer and McDowall 2010). The choice of coaching interventions usually depends on the coachee's individual development obstacles and organisational context, and should be tailored in accordance with the coachee's individual scenario. This indicates that adopting one singular coaching framework is not sufficient for the potentially complex coaching context. Therefore a contextual-model (Stober et al. 2006) of coaching which integrates various techniques might be more helpful for productive coaching outcomes. This model is expanded from the components described by Wampold (2001) for a contextual model for psychotherapy. A Contextual Coaching Approach, which aims to understand the process of coaching, including "what the common themes" are that benefit to coaching process and outcomes. Seven thematic factors for the Contextual Coaching Approach, which outline the essential elements to facilitate effective coaching outcomes, were outlined to explain why coaching relationship plays a key role in contemporary coaching practice and study (Stober et al. 2006). These seven thematic factors highlight that coaching is a collaborative process in which the coach and coachee work toward mutual goals. Hence, an "effective" and "constructive" coaching relationship is the key factor for positive coaching outcomes as most of the coaching process relies on two people's (coach-coachee) conversation and interactions.

Inheriting the Contextual Coaching Approach, de Haan (2008) transferred a concept from a meta-analysis result in psychotherapy study (Wampold 2001) to the field of coaching as both interventions share a very similar process: the essence of therapeutic and coaching process relies on sustaining interpersonal interactions between therapist/coach and patient/coachee. This meta-analysis indicated there was no significant difference in effectiveness on desired outcomes between different approaches and techniques. The working alliance (relationship) between the therapist and client was identified as the most effective ingredient for facilitating a positive therapy outcome across all approaches. Based on the aspect of 'outcome equivalence' in this study (Wampold 2001), a quality coaching relationship across the coaching engagement was inferred as the most essential common factors for positive coaching outcomes. Indeed, the age of "relational coaching" has been confirmed by means of a number of quantitative studies. These studies examined a positive correlation between the coaching relationship and results, such as coachees' self-efficacy (Baron and Morin 2009; Boyce et al. 2010; de Haan et al. 2013).

In a short summary, the coaching relationship appears as an essential role in contemporary coaching study and practice based on the result of positive correlation with coaching outcomes (e.g. self-efficacy). However the questions about what the active factors are for an effective coaching relationship and how these factors could be optimised in the coaching process have not be answered. The next section will briefly discuss these issues based upon current literature.

2.3 What Are Active Ingredients in an Effective Coaching Relationship?

As investigating active factors for an effective coaching relationship become the key focus in contemporary coaching study de Haan (2008) conducted a survey study with 71 executive coaching clients to distinguish "helpful" elements in the coaching journey and how these elements could be "optimized" to create a constructive coaching process. The study results were similar to the meta-analysis in the field of psychotherapy (Wampold 2001); an effective coaching relationship can be the key indicator for a positive outcome. In order to identify what the coach's role is in an effective coaching process; qualitative questions were included in de Haan's study (2008) to elicit effective attributes for a professional coach to generate a greater effect on coaching alliance. This study outlined three attributes of the coach, which were (a) listening, (b) understanding and (c) encouragement to facilitate coachee participants' learning and development in the coaching process. This study revealed that the coach plays a key role in initiating a harmonious relationship in the coaching journey, although the specific behavioural indicators were not identified here. Another quantitative study (de Haan et al. 2013) was carried out with 156 coach-coachee paired participants to examine the correlation between coaching relationship (*Working Alliance*) and outcomes (*Self-efficacy*). It investigated whether personality matching between coach and coachee is an influential factor in an effective coaching relationship. Though there was no strong correlation between personality matching and coaching relationship; subjective matching where the coach and client physically met each other and had an interview or trial session was recognised as the critical stage/moment to determine the effectiveness of the subsequent relationship on the coaching journey. This disclosed that the coach has the opportunity and responsibility to initiate a positive impression and relationship for the subsequent sessions. Hence, identifying and examining what attributes a professional coach should acquire to establish a constructive coaching relationship are critical steps in contemporary Coaching Psychology research.

2.4 Analysis of Existing Professional Coaching Frameworks

Summarising the previous discussion, there is a need to investigate explicit attributes for a coaching practitioner and how these link to any effects on the coaching relationship. This is a potential key step for the development of evidence-based coaching. Many governing professional associations worldwide such as the Association for Coaching (AC), The British Psychological Society (BPS), the European Mentoring and Coaching Council (EMCC) and the International Coach Federation (ICF) have developed professional frameworks in consultation with members to outline the benchmark required for those who would like to practice as a professional coach. However, certain aspects of these frameworks appear to require further validation and investigation. The defining elements presented on their published documents are summarised in Table 1.

A number of similarities and differences between these frameworks were noted following an initial content analysis. First, all of these competency frameworks were developed either by integrating previous evidence (meta-analysis) or consulting with their internal coaching experts. Second, only the framework developed by EMCC sorted their competencies into groups to differentiate different job levels (e.g. foundation, practitioner, senior practitioner etc.). Third, most of these competency frameworks tended to consider coaching as a cross disciplinary developmental activity because no specific theoretical domain was highlighted in their documents. BPS Standard Framework for Coaching Psychologist is the only one coaching guideline which distinguished the role of psychology in coaching practice. In addition, the significance of coaching relationship has been emphasised in all competency frameworks, nevertheless behavioural indicators to facilitate an effective coaching relationship could not be identified in their documents. In a brief summary, existing competency frameworks appear more like a general guidance for people who would like to practice coaching. Because the purpose and focus of these frameworks were not addressed clearly in their documents and a relatively wide range of aspects was covered (e.g. contracting ethics, coaching process and relationship).

In a brief conclusion, coaching relationship has been highlighted and examined as the key indicator for a positive coaching outcome. In addition, the coach's role and behaviours have a significant influence on coaching relationship (de Haan 2008). Though many coaching governing associations developed relevant frame-

Table 1 Summary of previous coaching competency frameworks

Association	Sources of published documents	Investigation process	Structure	Level of rating	Psychological perspective	Emphasis on coaching relationship
BPS Standard Framework for Coaching Psychology (2008)	(BPS 2008) http://www.bps.org.uk/networks-and-communities/member-networks/special-group-coaching-psychology	Meta-analysis of previous research and coaching expert's personal experiences	4 broad clusters 112 competencies	Not specifically refer to more generic coaching competencies such as listening, building rapport, managing the process	Yes	Yes
ICF Professional Coaching Core Competencies (2009)	(Griffiths and Campbell 2008) http://www.coachfederation.org.uk/	Grounded theory Approach (five coaches and nine coaching clients)	4 competency groups 11 competencies 70 behaviours	No	No	Yes
EMCC Competency Framework (2009)	(Willis 2005; Grant et al. 2010) http://www.emccouncil.org/	Developed through an extensive Europe-wide consultative process, drawing on both expert and practitioners' experiences by semi-structure interviews or questionnaires	8 competency groups	Yes (4 levels) Foundation Practitioner Senior practitioner Master practitioner	No	Yes
AC Coach Accreditation Scheme Integrated Coaching Competency Framework (2011)	http://www.associationforcoaching.com	Collected the perspectives from AC members in early 2005 Five coaching experts/practitioners (one is charted psychologist) helped to analyse and combine the data collected from the members	12 categories 74 behaviours	No	No	Yes

works for coaching practitioners to follow, they appear more like a general guideline and a relatively wide range of aspects were covered. Therefore, a comprehensive research study (including synthesising existing evidence systematically) to examine explicit attributes for the coaching practitioner to strengthen the coaching relationship built on previous psychologically based evidence (working alliance) is demanded.

2.5 A Systematic Review on Coaching Psychology

A good literature review that informs us about current knowledge as well as gaps and research trends in the field therein is essential prior to any empirical study (Gough et al. 2012); thus a systematic review which has been identified as the most rigorous approach for the enhancement of evidence-based practice (Briner et al. 2009) was conducted. This review results (Lai and McDowall 2014) indicated (1) the role psychology plays in coaching has been strengthened in this review. A total of 69 % included studies in this review investigated the associations between psychological interventions and coaching outcomes. In addition, the top five most frequently and examined psychological coaching interventions were outlined after synthesising relevant studies in this review. (2) This review enhanced the concept that coaching relationship is a key focus of coaching study and practice as one third of the included studies (44 of 141 papers) indicated coaching relationship the common factor for a positive coaching outcome. (3) This SR emphasised coaches' attributes have a significant impact on a constructive coaching relationship, five effective factors (such as building trust) and the initial coaching psychology KSAs (required knowledge, skills and attributes) were outlined to provide an overview which attributes a coaching practitioner should acquire to facilitate an effective coaching process. Therefore, this review concluded a primary study focusing on the effective attributes for coaching practitioners to establish and maintain a constructive coaching relationship is indeed required.

Therefore, following this SR results, a role analysis comprised three stage studies was carried out to identify and examine behavioural indicators for a professional coach to facilitate a better professional working relationship was carried out. The detailed research methods and results will be explained in the following sections.

3 Research Methods and Findings

3.1 Study One: The Development of Coaching Relationship Competency Framework

The first study aimed to elicit effective coach's attributes/behavioural indicators to establish and maintain a constructive coaching relationship. This study inherited the review results from the SR on Coaching Psychology. According to the Standard

Competency Modelling process (Boyatzis 2008; Shippmann et al. 2000), a variable combination and logically selected mix of multiple approaches was ranked as the top rigorous investigation method for competency modelling. Because one given method may only allow the researcher to collect limited data regardless of setting or target population. Therefore, a three-stage competency framework investigation process was formed: (a) Critical Incident Technique (CIT) (b) Thematic Analysis (TA) and; (c) Q-sorting. Also, it is essential for yielding a complete competency framework through involving multiple systematic samples of content experts to review and verify the effectiveness of identified competency framework. Table 2 summarises the research process of this study.

Critical Incident Technique

Critical Incident Technique (CIT), which was originally developed by Flanagan (1954), consists of a set of procedures for collecting direct observations of human behaviours in such a way as to facilitate their potential usefulness in solving practical problems and developing broad psychological principles (Flanagan 1954). It outlines procedures for collecting observed incidents having special significance

Table 2 Overview of the research procedures

Stages	Process and outcomes
Stage one:	
Critical incident interviews	25 interview transcripts
Stage two:	
Thematic analysis	Themes were extracted and coded from the transcripts:
Data/theme extraction	522 elements
	341 initial attributes
	278 behavioural descriptions
	76.4 % agreement level
Data review	Language errors were amended and duplicate behaviours were integrated or discarded:
	14 initial themes
	103 behavioural indicators
Stage three: Q-sorting	
1st level Q-sorting	Similar behaviours were clustered into the same groups and competencies were named:
	13 competencies
	103 behavioural indicators
2nd level Q-sorting	Behaviours were re-clustered into the identified 13 competency groups from previous step
Review of results	Q-sorting results were reviewed and amended:
Totals:	**13 competencies**
	100 behavioural indicators

and meeting systematically defined criteria. CIT has been more frequently cited by industrial and organisational psychologists than any other article over the past 40 years (Anderson and Wilson 1997) but it has been also utilised across a diverse number of disciplines, including job analysis (Kanyangale and MacLachlan 1995; Stitt-Gohdes et al. 2000), counselling (Dix and Savickas 1995; McCormick 1997) and performance appraisal (Evans 1994; Schwab et al. 1975). This study used critical incident interviews with all participants to collect their perspectives on effective coaches' attributes drawn on the specific incidents or events relevant to their coaching experiences. This stage interviewed a total of 25 participants who had relevant coaching experiences playing different roles in the coaching process. In order to collect perspectives from a diversity of angles, four groups of participants were recruited: professional external coaches, coachees, organisational stakeholders (e.g. HR and coaching programmes evaluators) and internal coaches who attended coaching leadership and develop programmes in their organisation. Table 3 provides an overview of the value that each of these groups could offer. A one-on-one interview (either face-to-face, phone or email) was undertaken and each interview averaged 40–50 min. All participants were required to recall one recent positive coaching experience and share the effective elements optimising the coaching relationship.

Thematic Analysis

Thematic Analysis (TA) method was used to extract effective attributes for a coaching psychologist from interview transcriptions in this study. TA is a method to be used with qualitative information (Boyatzis 1998). It identifies analyses and reports patterns (themes) within qualitative data and translates them into quantitative information (i.e. codes). A pattern (theme) is usually found in the information that

Table 3 Purpose of each interview group

Interview groups	Purpose of the interview
External professional coaches with a psychological background	To probe effective coaching factors through their "self-reflection" on specific coaching experiences
Coachees	To probe effective coaching factors through their experiences of specific coaching sessions to minimise the biased statements from coaches' interview only
Organisational stakeholders	To investigate coaches' attributes through their experiences in facilitating coaching sessions in their respective organisations and their expectations of coach selection because most of the coaching programmes are commissioned by coachees' companies
Internal coaches who attended a coaching training programme in the organisation	To explore whether the coaching training they attended met their needs and to probe effective coaching factors through their "self-reflection" on specific coaching experiences

describes and organises the possible observations and interprets aspects of the phenomenon. The use of TA involves three distinct stages: (a) deciding on sampling and designing issues; (b) developing themes and a code; (c) validating and using the code. TA is a flexible method which allows for a wide range of analytic options (Braun and Clarke 2008). It usually summarises the key features of a large body of data and offers a "rich description" of the data set. In addition, TA works very well in studies which seek to examine the perspectives of different groups within a topic/context (King 2004).

All interviews were transcribed word-by-word for further data extraction and coding. Subsequently, thematic analysis was used to extract and code the themes from the interview transcriptions. This stage extracted 103 behavioural indicators for further analysis.

Q-Sorting

Following the thematic analysis, two Q-sorting sessions were conducted with two coaching experts with psychological background and two post-graduate students in psychology. Q-methodology, developed in the 1930s, has been widely applied within psychology (Stephenson 1953), although Q-methodology has been increasingly used in other disciplines, such as political science, particularly in the U.S.A. (Brown 1980). Q-methodology is a technique incorporating the benefits of both qualitative and quantitative research. It involves Q-sorting, a method of data collection and factor analysis, to assess subjective (qualitative) information. In Q-methodology, participants are typically provided with a set of stimuli, usually statements, (known as the Q-sample) which they rank via a process, called Q-sorting (Van Exel and De Graaf 2005). Participants are required to systematically force-sort a set of statements based on how strongly they agree or disagree with each statement (Brewer et al. 2000; Jacobson and Aaltio-Marjosola 2001). Usually several Q-sorting sessions are conducted in a study. The Q-sorting participates were asked to cluster the similar behavioural indicators into same group and name the competencies. A total of 13 competencies underpinned by 100 behavioural indicators were outlined in this study. Table 4 provides one example of these competencies:

In order to evaluate the consistency and accuracy of this draft competency framework, Coaching Relationship Competency Framework (CRCF), a cross validation questionnaire study was carried out afterwards which will be presented in the next section.

Table 4 One example of the draft Coaching Relationship Competency Framework (CRCF)

Competencies	Definitions	Indicators
Active communication skills	Applying highly developed communication skills to understand coachees' issues, enhance motivation, facilitate change and build the rapport. Listening, responding, questioning, asking challenging questions and using body language appropriately	E.g. actively listening

3.2 Study Two: Establishing Validation Criteria: Reliability and Validity

Research Process

Study two aimed to evaluate the reliability (such as internal consistency) validity of the draft CRCF by means of a questionnaire study. Two evaluations were used in this study. First, we transferred the draft CRCF into a behavioural-based questionnaire (see Table 4 for one example) comprising 100 items which are specific and clear behavioural descriptions (e.g. asking open questions) for respondents to rate to assess an effective coach's behaviours for facilitating a constructive coaching relationship. Second, Coaching Alliance Inventory (CAI) which is modified from Tracey and Kokotovic's (1989) Working Alliance Inventory-Short Form was applied in this study to cross validate with CRCF questionnaire. According to Bordin (1979), the concept of "working alliance" is the combination of (a) a client and therapist agreement on goals (b) a client and therapist agreement on how to achieve the goals and (c) the development of a personal bond between the participants. In 1986, Horvath and Greenberg (1986) developed the Working Alliance Inventory (WAI) to specifically assess these three related dimensions which are rated by both coach and client. They stated the focus of WAI is a measure that captures both outcome variance and a clearly articulated relation with a specified body of theory. Hatcher and Barends (2006) put forward that the "working alliance" is used to refer to the quality and strength of the collaborative relationship between client and therapist; and O'Broin and Palmer (2010) transferred this concept into a coaching relationship study. They highlighted that the psychological contract is very important in the coaching relationship because it provides a "container" for the joint purposive work of coaching to take place and also ensure the clarity and transparency in the process. This conceptualisation of the psychological contract through the coaching alliance framework emphasises the collaboration, mutual influence and cooperation of both coach and coachee, and goal-focus that is the nature of coaching in the coaching relationship. The working alliance provides a medium for collaboration and co-creation as well as a space for the coachee to feel safe and accepted enough to step into new forms of behaviour and creative action (Cavanagh 2006). Therefore, the working alliance would appear to be an appropriate construct to evaluate the coaching relationship as its three core features (goal, task and bond) have been validated through a rigorous quantitative research (Tracey and Kokotovic 1989) (Table 5).

Prior to the official questionnaire launch, CRCF questionnaire and CAI were mapped to investigate their convergent and divergent validity and to determine whether they were theoretically related for a cross-validation examination. Both coaches and coachees were recruited to rate the CRCF and CAI based on their previous specific coaching experiences. The quality of coaching alliance/relationship is more likely to be assessed through subjective perspective, hence involving both key

Table 5 An example of an item taken from the WAI questionnaire

	Never	Rarely	Sometimes	Often	Very Often	Always
Statement	1	2	3	4	5	6
My client and I agree about the steps to be taken to improve his/her situation.	☐	☐	☐	☐	☐	☐

parties in the coaching process in this validation study tended to reduce the bias. A total of 107 respondents of this questionnaire study: 72 respondents were from coach groups and 35 were done by coachees.

Data Analysis

Initially, we evaluated the internal consistency of these 13 competencies, most (11 of 13 competencies) of the competencies' α values were larger than .7 (α>.7). Though the α value of two competencies (e.g. "Using Resources") was slightly lower than .7, it may not suitable to determine whether these two competencies are unreliable before further analysis because the number of items also affects the value of α (Cortina 1993). For example as the number of items on the scale reduces, α reduces. These two competencies had only two items each, thus further analysis (e.g. interclass correlation and cross-validation) was undertaken to determine which items should be retained in the final competency framework.

Second, we examined the relation between items of the CRCF and their corresponding CAI indicators. The stronger correlation between competencies and their corresponding CAI indicators, the greater effectiveness of this competency framework for establishing and maintaining a constructive coaching relationship. Almost half of the items (49 of 100 behavioural indicators) have a moderate correlation with their corresponding CAI indicators (r≥.3). In order to evaluate these items in a more rigorous way, the mean and range were also considered when screening the competencies and behavioural indicators.

According to standard competency framework modelling method (Shippmann et al. 2000), differentiating different levels of competence articulates these behavioural indicators into a set of comprehensive framework. Also, it provides competency users a benchmark to distinguish high performers from others. Therefore, these behavioural items were sorted into groups/levels through examining their means, range and correlation with CAI. Three levels of competency were defined in this study; Table 6 outlines the criteria and features of each level.

Table 6 Three levels for the CRCF

Level	Definition	Criteria
Soft skills	Items which showed both higher means and correlation are defined as a "baseline" for any coaching sessions. These behavioural indicators appear more like coach's interpersonal skills	Means ≥5.3 and Correlation with CAI ≥.30
Hard skills	Items which showed slightly lower means but significant correlation with CAI. These indicators are more relevant to coach's goal setting and process management skills	Means between 3.0 and 5.3, Correlation with CAI ≥.30
Additional behavioural indicators	Items which have minor influence on coaching relationship but could be used to support soft and hard skills	Means≥.30 Correlation with CAI <.30

Soft Skills (Mean ≥ 5.3; r. ≥ .30)

Items of which mean is equal to or larger than 5.3 and also the correlation coefficients with their corresponding CAI indicators are equal to or larger than .3 (r. ≥ .30) were defined as essential elements. These items had a stronger internal consistency and high correlation with CAI, thus they were considered as 'core behaviours' for an effective coaching relationship in this study. Seven items (e.g. listening actively) were identified as such Soft Interpersonal Skills". These behavioural indicators are more relevant to coaches' interpersonal skills to facilitate an effective coaching relationship.

Hard Skills (Mean Between 3.0 and 5.3; r. ≥ .30)

Items of which are between 3.0 and 5.3; and also the correlation coefficients with their corresponding Coaching Alliance Inventory indicator are stronger than .30 were sorted into the second group. Items in this group have less strong internal consistency than Soft Skills. It does not indicate that these items are of minor importance; they facilitate the effective coaching relationship through a constructive way. A total of 38 items underpinning six competencies were sorted into this group. The majority of these items are more associated with goal setting and process management/contracting skills (e.g. developing realistic tasks and actions and inviting coaches to share what is important to them). Referring back the ultimate purpose of coaching, coaching aims to facilitate the coachee's behavioural and performance change through an interactive process between two people (coach and coachee). It implies that successful coaching is not only about building a harmonious relationship with the coachee but also assisting the coachee to achieve the goal.

Additional Behavioural Indicators

These items had relatively weak correlation with their correspondent CAI indicators; they still had moderate significant internal consistency ($\alpha > .30$) which meant they still had a certain degree influence on supporting the Hard and Soft Skills to strengthen the coaching relationship and toward goal achievement.

In summary, a total of 75 behavioural indicators sorted into three groups/levels were retained in this competency framework for further examination by means of a quasi-experiment which will be presented in the next section. Table 7 shows the overview of CRCF.

3.3 Study Three: The Evaluation of the Coaching Relationship Competency Framework

Study three was an extension of study two to examine the effectiveness of the CRCF. A quasi-experiment was carried out to compare a group that received training based on the identified competency framework with a control group that did not receive this training. A quasi-experimental study usually occurs in workplace field settings that participants cannot be placed into various treatment conditions for practical reasons, for example the study of the effects of training in the organisation. Yet the quasi-experiment study shares two features of true experiments: entailing the use of at least two treatment conditions and the measurement of intervening and dependent variables (Stone-Romero 2002). However, one tracking diary report was combined in this study to diminish the potential threats to internal validity from quasi-experiment. The outcome measures were CRCF Questionnaire, Coaching

Table 7 Overview of CRCF

Category	Description	No. of competences	No. of behavioural indicators
Soft skills	Items which showed both higher means and correlation are defined as a "baseline" for any coaching sessions. These behavioural indicators appear more like coach's interpersonal skills	2	7
Hard skills	Items which showed slightly lower means but significant correlation with CAI. These indicators are more relevant to coach's goal setting and process management skills	6	38
Additional behavioural indicator	Items which have minor influence on coaching relationship but could be used to support soft and hard skills		30
Total			75

Alliance Inventory (CAI) and Self-Efficacy Scale (SES). A total of 26 participants were recruited and assigned into groups (experimental or control group) and roles (coach or coachee) randomly.

The research question and hypotheses of this study were as below:

Does a coach training intervention designed around the CRCF facilitate a better coaching process and results than a control group intervention?

- *Hypothesis 1*: Coaches who attend a training workshop targeting the identified Coaching Psychology Competency Framework are able to facilitate a better coaching relationship as measured by the Coaching Alliance Inventory (rated by both coaches and coachees) created in the coaching session than those who have not attended this type of training.
- *Hypothesis 2*: Coaches who attend a training workshop targeting the identified Coaching Psychologist Competency Framework are able to demonstrate more effective coach behaviours as measured by the Coach Competency Evaluation (rated by both coaches and coachees).
- *Hypothesis 3*: Coaches who attend a training workshop targeting the identified Coaching Psychologist Competency Framework will be more effective at facilitating the coachees to have a stronger confidence of self-belief level as measured by the Self-Efficacy Scale than those who have not attended this type of training.

Quantitative Data Analysis

Data analysis of this quasi-experiment was split into two major parts. The first part focused on the quantitative evaluations: Coaching Alliance Inventory (CAI), Coaching Psychologist Competency Framework Questionnaire (CRCF) and Self-Efficacy Scale (SES). It assessed the internal consistency of each measurement and compared two groups' (the group that attended the coaching training workshop, and the other group that only received a self-study training kit) results through conducting independent-sample t-tests. The second part integrated the respondents from open questions attached to the CRCF Questionnaire and diary tracking report by content analysis to investigate to what extent the CRCF-based training generated an effective coaching process.

Coaching Alliance Inventory (CAI)

The internal consistency of CAI evaluation in this study was assessed using Cronbach's alpha. The alpha value ($\alpha=.86$) was accepted because it was higher than the general cut-off point ($\alpha=.7$), It could be initially concluded that the coaching relationship of the group whose coaches had three-hours of training was preferable to the group that did not. Subsequently, an independent-samples *t*-test was conducted to compare items relating to the coaching relationship between the experimental and control groups. On average, the coaching alliance items for the experimental group had a higher mean than the control group. The significance was not very strong (all of the p values > .05), however medium-size effects (almost half of the item's r > .30) were observed. It could be initially concluded that the coaching relationship of the group whose coaches had 3-h of training was preferable to the group that did not.

CRCF Questionnaire

Coaches' behaviours in the coaching session were evaluated by the Coaching Psychologist Competency Framework questionnaire which was designed on the basis of the questionnaire study results. The internal consistency of this evaluation was very high ($\alpha = .90$). Nearly all the item means of the experimental group (35 of 42 items) were larger than the control group. This indicates coach participants who attended the training workshop demonstrated the competencies more effectively than participants who did not. The significance was not strong because only 13 of these 35 items' p values were smaller than .05. However, 62 % (26 items) of the items were between small and medium effect ($r \geq .10$). Though, the difference between two groups was not significant, it does not determine this competency framework is invalid as (a) this was one "snapshot" training and evaluation due to time restriction (b) the control group had 1 week to self-learn behavioural indicators underpinning CRCF. Therefore, we could initially infer that the CRCF did facilitate coach participants to generate a more constructive coaching relationship in this study, but further evaluation is required to contrast the differences between two groups.

Self-Efficacy Scale (SES)

Coachees' goal achievement progress in this study was assessed by a generalised Self-Efficacy Scale (SES). Self-efficacy is defined as the belief that a person is capable of accomplishing a given task (Bandura 1977). Self-efficacy has been widely applied in organisational studies, for instance organisational training and learning (Bandura 1977; Colquitt et al. 2000). It was also used as a key variable to predict the coaching outcomes in several coaching studies (Baron and Morin 2009; Brouwers et al. 2006; Grant 2008; Stewart et al. 2008). The internal consistency of SES in this study was very high ($\alpha = .95$). The *t*-test of the SES showed all of the item means of the experimental group were larger than the control group. However, half (four of eight) of their p values was >.05 which indicated that the difference in self-efficacy belief between two groups was not significant. It indicated that coachee participants, facilitated by the coaches who attend the training workshop, had stronger confidence or faith in their behavioural changes or improvement in this study. In addition, a follow-up diary open-question questionnaire designed by the main researcher to draw out the participants' perspectives which were not covered by quantitative evaluations and gather more information reflecting on the coaching process they had in this study. Nevertheless, we could not confirm the significant difference between two groups due to insufficient sample size and one snap-shot evaluation.

In summary, these three quantitative evaluations indicated that coach participants from the experimental group (who attended the training workshop) facilitated a slightly better coaching relationship and generated more productive goal achievement progress (coachees' motivation and self-belief) through demonstrating a superior CRCF than the control group. Nevertheless, the data did not show strong significance. Thus, a longitudinal study design with larger participation size which might generate a more accurate study result should be carried out in the future research.

Qualitative Data Analysis

In order to investigate how and what the exact elements/behavioural indicators generated for a constructive coaching relationship are/ were, both coach and coachee participants were asked to respond to several open ended questions after the coaching session. For example, "What did the coach do/say to make you feel you have a "good relationship" with him/her?" Several competencies were emphasised by coach and coachee participants in establishing a constructive coaching relationship and generating positive results after integrating their responses to these open questions by means of a content analysis (e.g. Active Communication Skills and Goal Focus/Goal Tracking). The viewpoints from both study groups) were aligned. Understanding the coachee's feelings and issues by applying highly developed communication skills and developing realistic plans through a collaborative process were the most effective ingredients for facilitating an effective coaching relationship.

Referring to the diary tracking report, the main challenge both groups faced was how they motivated themselves to commit to their development plans. For example, coachee participants had to manage their time effectively to fit in the development plans. In addition, being confident was also a key element in initiating the first step for behavioural changes. It took some coachee participants a certain time to adjust their mindset. The significant difference between the experimental and control group was the degree of their motivation. Coachees in the experimental group had stronger motivation and commitment to their plans. Coach participants who attended the training workshop generated more productive coaching attainment progress because they established a collaborative coaching relationship to enhance the coachees' self-motivation for change.

In a brief conclusion, the effectiveness of the CRCF was initially examined by means of a quasi-experimental study here; it did provide the coach with a professional guideline to enhance a better coaching relationship and outcomes (coachees' motivation and confidence level) in accordance with the study results. Nevertheless, there was no strong significance in the quantitative measurement as a bigger sample size and a longitudinal study design were required.

4 Discussion

CRCF is the first psychological grounded competency framework outlining explicit behavioural indicators for the enhancement of working alliance in coaching. This research investigated explicit competencies, as measured by behavioural indicators, which appear to be prerequisites for strengthening the working alliance and building an effective coaching relationship. The identified CRCF contributed the following three aspects:

1. The development of the CRCF filled a theoretical gap by identifying the explicit attributes to facilitate an effective coaching process from a Coaching Psychology perspective. As discussed earlier, subjective matching where the coach and coachee physically meet each other is a particularly critical stage for the subsequent effectiveness of the following relationship in the coaching journey (de Haan 2008). To date, no published rigorous role analysis to yield definite coach's attributes for facilitating a constructive coaching relationship. This research addressed this by identifying 75 behavioural indicators sorted into three groups for different training purposes against Standard Competency Modelling criteria (Shippmann et al. 2000). Therefore, the development of the CRCF took existing coaching knowledge a step further towards yielding KSAs for an effective coaching alliance drawn on all the relevant coaching stakeholders' perspectives (coach, coachee and client) through a rigorous role analysis. This study outcome also aligned with contemporary therapeutic relationship study findings, which indicated the quality of shared understanding of the nature of the patient's problem (called therapeutic rapport) mainly counts on physicians' active communication abilities (Norfolk et al. 2009), a comprehensive skill-based training model provided professional guidelines for physicians to follow. In essence, what people actually do effectively and actively regarding communication and rapport, whether they are coaches or physicians, makes a difference to the quality of the relationship.
2. The CRCF built on previous psychologically based evidence to draw out effective behaviours for a constructive coaching relationship. The concept of a working alliance has been recognised as the focal point for integrating three major psychological traditions, psychoanalytic, humanistic psychology and psychotherapy, in a new paradigm (de Haan and Sills 2012). A meta-analysis in psychotherapy (Wampold 2001) indicated there was no significant difference in effectiveness on desired outcomes between different and techniques. The working alliance, which emphasises relationship factors (such as mutual trust, empathy and respect) as well as links to positive outcome (clear mutual agreed goal and action plans), optimises the bond in the process of certain psychological helping interventions (e.g. counselling, therapy and coaching) and facilitates the joint purposive goal to be perfectively achieved (O'Broin and Palmer 2010). In other words, a preferable working relationship was recognised as the essential indicator toward desired outcomes in the counselling/therapy process. This "relationship" concept was transferred to coaching domain and examined by

de Haan (2008): The coaching relationship is a key common factor for an effective coaching engagement. In addition, the association between the working alliance and coaching outcomes has been examined in research (Baron and Morin 2009; de Haan et al. 2013). The content of the CRCF is consistent with the three key features of the working alliance: both interpersonal attributes (e.g. demonstrating empathy and emotional bond) and learning and facilitation skills (e.g. Goal Focus/Goal Tracking) are essential requirements for a coaching psychologist to establish a harmonious coaching process and facilitate a greater outcome. Therefore, in contrast with previous coaching relevant competency guidelines, the CRCF is the first framework that builds on psychologically proved evidence from psychoanalytic and humanistic perspectives and the transferring of theoretical concept from the working alliance into visible dimensions to be applied in a helping relationship.

In terms of methodical and practical contribution, CRCF is the first framework that has been developed and examined through a systematic and transparent process to meet the standard competency modelling criteria. In contrast with previous competency frameworks, the CRCF provides an explicit guideline (KSAs) to facilitate a greater coaching relationship, specifically focusing on *coaching alliance*. Competency items underpinning the CRCF tend to be brief and behavioural-based descriptions which are more user-friendly than previous frameworks. In addition, three differentiated groups of competencies provide a clearer guideline for coaching relevant training and development agenda. For instance, attributes under the first group which appear more likely interpersonal soft skills could be used as the baseline for fundamental coaching training as they had stronger correlations with their corresponding CAI indicators in this chapter In summary, coaching training and development is in urgent need of standardisation because it has been widely applied in the organisational and workplace learning and development field but draws on varied disciplines. Therefore the CRCF, underpinned by explicit competencies and behavioural indicators, could feed the gaps of previous competency frameworks in coach training and development design.

5 Conclusion

The value of investment in coaching intervention will continue to be a major interest for practitioners and organisational stakeholders; however the most popular evaluation methods in the contemporary coaching industry rely on coachees' satisfaction and feedback rather than any concrete outcome measurements. This sort of subjective evaluation on coaching impacts cannot truly provide evidence for decision makers to justify whether the investment of coaching should be carried on in the organisations (Grant 2007). As a researcher in Coaching Psychology, the positive impact on a coachee's work and life balance as well as learning and development is far more important than the ROI since the ultimate goal of coaching is to optimize people's potential and self-growth through systematic dialogue between the coach and coachee (Passmore and Fillery-Travis 2011). In order to yield valid and solid evidence, the development of evidence-based practice that investigates the best available knowledge or theoretical grounded interventions to apply in coaching practices has become the joint interest of researchers, practitioners and clients of coaching.

This study aimed to strengthen the evidence-based coaching practice by developing and validating a CRCF through four studies. The effectiveness of the CRCF in training and development was investigated in a pilot field experiment and the results indicate relevance for practice. Future research could build on our findings for instance using longitudinal field studies, larger and also more professional samples and also conduct investigation into how skills identified through the CRCF work in conjunction with other coaching techniques. Last but not least, it still remains to be investigated which skills coaches bring to coaching process could be developed right at the start of a coaching relationship in order to maximise effective outcomes. This study contends that a behavioural approach, using clear and evidence-based models to guide interventions and best practice, will provide a basis for such future research.

References

Anderson, L., & Wilson, S. (1997). Critical incident technique. In D. L. Whetzel & G. R. Wheaton (Eds.), *Applied measurement methods in industrial psychology* (pp. 89–105). Palo Alto: Davies-Black.

Bachkirova, T. (2008). Role of coaching psychology in defining boundaries between counselling and coaching. In Palmer S. & Whybrow A (Eds.), *Handbook of coaching psychology: A guide for practitioners* (2nd ed., pp. 351–366). London: Routledge.

Bandura, A. (1977). Self-efficacy: Toward a unifying theory of behavioral change. *Psychological Review, 84*(2), 191.

Baron, L., & Morin, L. (2009). The coach-coachee relationship in executive coaching: A field study. *Human Resource Development Quarterly, 20*(1), 85–106.

Berglas, S. (2002). The very real dangers of executive coaching. *Harvard Business Review, 80*(6), 86–93.

Bordin, E. S. (1979). The generalizability of the psychoanalytic concept of the working alliance. *Psychotherapy: Theory, Research & Practice, 16*(3), 252.

Boyatzis, R. E. (1998). *Transforming qualitative information: Thematic analysis and code development*. Thousand Oaks: Sage.

Boyatzis, R. E. (2008). Competencies in the 21st century. *Journal of Management Development, 27*(1), 5–12.

Boyce, L. A., Jackson, R. J., & Neal, J. L. (2010). Building successful leadership coaching relationships: Examining impact of matching criteria in a leadership coaching program. *Journal of Management Development, 29*(10), 914–931.

BPS. (2008). *Standards framework for coaching psychology*. Retrieved 5 January 2011, from: http://www.bps.org.uk/networks-and-communities/member-networks/special-group-coaching-psychology

Braun, V., & Clarke, V. (2008). Using thematic analysis in psychology. *Qualitative Research in Psychology, 3*(2), 77–101.

Brewer, G. A., Selden, S. C., & Facer, R. L. (2000). Individual conceptions of public service motivation. *Public Administration Review, 60*(3), 254–263.
Briner, R. B., Denyer, D., & Rousseau, D. M. (2009). Evidence-based management: Concept cleanup time? *The Academy of Management Perspectives, 23*(4), 19–32.
Brouwers, A., Evers, W. J., & Tomic, W. (2006). A quasi-experimental study on management coaching effectiveness. *Consulting Psychology Journal: Practice and Research, 58*(3), 174.
Brown, S. (1980). *Political subjectivity: Applications of Q methodology in political science.* Yale: Yale University Press.
Cavanagh, M. (2006). Coaching from a systematic perspective: A complex adaptive conversation. In D. R. Stober & A. M. Grant (Eds.), *Evidence based coaching handbook: Putting best practices to work for your clients.* Hoboken: Wiley.
Colquitt, J. A., LePine, J. A., & Noe, R. A. (2000). Toward an integrative theory of training motivation: A meta-analytic path analysis of 20 years of research. *Journal of Applied Psychology, 85*(5), 678.
Cortina, J. M. (1993). What is coefficient alpha? An examination of theory and applications. *Journal of Applied Psychology, 78*(1), 98.
de Haan, E. (2008). *Relational coaching: Journeys towards mastering one-to-one learning.* Chichester: Wiley.
de Haan, E., & Sills, C. (2012). *Coaching relationships: Relational coaching field book.* Faringdon: Libri.
de Haan, E., Duckworth, A., Birch, D., & Jones, C. (2013). Executive coaching outcome research: The contribution of common factors such as relationship, personality match, and self-efficacy. *Consulting Psychology Journal: Practice and Research, 65*(1), 40.
Dix, J. E., & Savickas, M. L. (1995). Establishing a career: Developmental tasks and coping responses. *Journal of Vocational Behavior, 47*(1), 93–107.
Evans, C. R. (1994). *Rating source differences and performance appraisal policies: Performance is in the "I" of the beholder.* Unpublished doctoral dissertation, The University of Guelph, Guelph, ON, Canada.
Flanagan, J. C. (1954). The critical incident technique. *Psychology Bulletin, 51*(4), 327–358.
Gough, D., Oliver, S., & Thomas, J. (2012). *An introduction to systematic reviews.* London: SAGE Publications.
Grant, A. M. (2001). *Toward a psychology of coaching: The impact of coaching on metacognition, mental health and goal attainment.* Sydney: Coaching Psychology Unit, University of Sydney.
Grant, A. M. (2007). Past, present and future: The evolution of professional coaching and coaching psychology. In S. Palmer & A. Whybrow (Eds.), *Handbook of coaching psychology: A guide for practitioners* (pp. 23–39). London: Routledge.
Grant, A. M. (2008). Past, present and future: The evolution of professional coaching and coaching psychology. In S. Palmer & A. Whybrow (Eds.), *Handbook of coaching psychology: A guide for practitioners* (2nd ed., pp. 23–39). London: Routledge.
Grant, A. M., Passmore, J., Cavanagh, M. J., & Parker, H. M. (2010). The state of play in coaching today: A comprehensive review of the field. *International Review of Industrial and Organizational Psychology, 25*(1), 125–167.
Griffiths, K., & Campbell, M. (2008). Regulating the regulators: Paving the way for international, evidence-based coaching standards. *International Journal of Evidence Based Coaching & Mentoring, 6*(1), 19–31.
Hatcher, R. L., & Barends, A. W. (2006). How a return to theory could help alliance research. *Psychotherapy: Theory, Research, Practice, Training, 43*(3), 292.
Horvath, A., & Greenberg, L. (1986). *The development of the working alliance inventory.* New York: Guilford Press.
Jacobson, S., & Aaltio-Marjosola, I. (2001). Strong objectivity and the use of Q-methodology in cross-cultural research. *Journal of Management Inquiry, 10*(3), 228–248.
Kanyangale, M., & MacLachlan, M. (1995). Critical incidents for refugee counsellors: An investigation of indigenous human resources. *Counselling Psychology Quarterly, 8*(1), 89–101.

King, N. (2004). Using templates in the qualitative analysis of text. In C. Cassell & G. Symon (Eds.), *Essential guide to qualitative methods in organizational research*. London: Sage.

Lai, Y., & McDowall, A. (2014). A systematic review (SR) of coaching psychology: Focusing on the attributes of effective coaching psychologists. *International Coaching Psychology Review, 9*(2), 120–136.

McCormick, R. (1997). Healing through interdependence: The role of connecting in first nations healing practices. *Canadian Journal of Counselling, 31*(3), 172–184.

Naughton, J. (2002). The coaching boom: Is it the long-awaited alternative to the medical model? *Psychotherapy Networker, 42*, 1–10.

Norfolk, T., Birdi, K., & Patterson, F. (2009). Developing therapeutic rapport: A training validation study. *Quality in Primary Care, 17*(2), 99–106.

O'Broin, A., & Palmer, S. (2010). Building on an interpersonal perspective on the coaching relationship. In *The coaching relationship: Putting people first* (p. 34). New York: Routledge.

Oades, L. G., Green, S., & Grant, A. (2005). An evaluation of a life coaching group program: Initial findings from a waitlist control study. In M. Cavanagh, A. Grant, & T. Kemp (Eds.), *Evidence-based coaching* (pp. 127–142). Bowen Hills: Australian Academic Press.

Palmer, S., & McDowall, A. (2010). *The coaching relationship: Putting people first*. London: Routledge.

Passmore, J., & Fillery-Travis, A. (2011). A critical review of executive coaching research: A decade of progress and what's to come. *Coaching: An International Journal of Theory, Research and Practice, 4*(2), 70–88.

Schwab, D. P., Heneman, H. G., & DeCotiis, T. A. (1975). Behaviorally anchored rating scales: A review of the literature. *Personnel Psychology, 28*(4), 549–562.

Shippmann, J. S., Ash, R. A., Batjtsta, M., Carr, L., Eyde, L. D., Hesketh, B., et al. (2000). The practice of competency modeling. *Personnel Psychology, 53*(3), 703–740.

Simons, L., & Cleary, B. (2006). The influence of service learning on students' personal and social development. *College Teaching, 54*(4), 307–319.

Spence, G. B., & Grant, A. M. (2005). Individual and group life-coaching: Initial findings from a randomised, controlled trial. *Evidence-Based Coaching, 1*, 143–158.

Stephenson, W. (1953). *The study of behaviour*. Chicago: University of Chicago Press.

Stewart, L. J., Palmer, S., Wilkin, H., & Kerrin, M. (2008). The influence of character: Does personality impact coaching success? *International Journal of Evidence Based Coaching and Mentoring, 6*(1), 32–42.

Stitt-Gohdes, W. L., Lambrecht, J. J., & Redmann, D. H. (2000). The critical-incident technique in job behavior research. *Journal of Vocational Education Research, 25*(1), 59–84.

Stober, D., Wildflower, L., & Drake, D. (2006). Evidence-based practice: A potential approach for effective coaching. *International Journal of Evidence Based Coaching and Mentoring, 4*(1), 1–8.

Stone-Romero, E. F. (2002). The relative validity and usefulness of various empirical research designs. In *Handbook of research methods in industrial and organizational psychology* (pp. 77–98). Malden: Blackwell.

Tracey, T. J., & Kokotovic, A. (1989). Factor structure of the working alliance inventory. *A Journal of Consulting and Clinical Psychology, 1*(3), 207–210.

Van Exel, N. J. A., & de Graaf, G. (2005). *Q methodology: A sneak preview*. Available from www.jobvanexel.nl

Wampold, B. E. (2001). *The great psychotherapy debate: Models, methods, and findings*. Mahwah: L. Erlbaum.

Whybrow, A. (2008). Coaching psychology: Coming of age? *International Coaching Psychology Review, 3*(3), 219–240.

Willis, P. (2005). *Competency research project: Phase 2 output*. London: European Mentoring and Coaching Council. Downloaded on 12 October, 2006, from:http://www.coachingpsychologist.net/Forums/showthread.php?t=47

The Future of Multi-cultural Coaching Psychology

Llewellyn E. van Zyl and Marius W. Stander

Abstract The final chapter of this manuscript focuses on determining the future direction of multi-cultural coaching psychology for both the discipline (research) and the profession (practice). Through thematic content analysis, this chapter aimed to evaluate the 17 manuscripts submitted for this specialist book in order to provide a descriptive overview of the most frequently occurring themes relating to the future direction of coaching psychology within multi-cultural contexts. A brief overview of the research method, data analysis and findings will be presented.

Keywords Coaching psychology research • Coaching psychology

1 Introduction

Coaching has emerged as a popular new discipline and area of practice within the field of psychology (Coetzee and Van Zyl 2014). With the popularization of the concept, various psychological models and approaches have been introduced to the market as a means of facilitating personal and professional development (see Biswas-Diener and Dean 2007) yet few are empirically validated (Kauffman 2006; Koortzen and Oosthuizen 2012) or grounded in psychological theory (Van Zyl and Stander 2013). Moreover, limited research and practice guidelines exist for multi-cultural environments. Those models, methodologies and approaches which have been validated empirically within multi-cultural contexts, are not consumed by the mass-market as a result of the restrictions regarding consumption/distribution imposed by scientific journals.

In order to address these problems, this manuscript attempted to provide a theoretical foundation to attend to the needs of academics, researchers, students and specialists working within the field of multi-cultural coaching psychology. The aim of this book was to synthesise empirical-research-based and theoretical perspectives

L.E. van Zyl (✉) • M.W. Stander
Optentia Research Focus Area, Department of Industrial Psychology, School for Behavioural Sciences, North-West University, Vaal Triangle Campus, Vanderbijlpark, South Africa
e-mail: llewellyn.vanzyl@nwu.ac.za; marius.stander@nwu.ac.za

L.E. van Zyl et al. (eds.), *Coaching Psychology: Meta-theoretical perspectives and applications in multicultural contexts*, DOI 10.1007/978-3-319-31012-1_18

on coaching psychology within multi-cultural contexts in order to provide a comprehensive perspective on contemporary research and practice which is accessible to researchers and practicing psychology professionals globally. The themes discussed in the various chapters provided not only context and practice guidelines to professionals coaching from a psychological perspective, but elaborated upon its complexity within multi-cultural contexts.

In order to provide researchers and practitioners with guidelines for effective coaching within multi-cultural environments, the manuscript attempted to provide applicable meta-theoretical perspectives in three primary domains. These domains also acted as the three sections of the manuscript. First, the focus was on providing context to the fundamentals of coaching psychology within multi-cultural contexts. Second, to highlight psychological approaches towards multi-cultural coaching. Finally, the manuscript aimed to provide meta-theoretical perspectives and practical applications of multi-cultural coaching psychology.

Flowing from these three broad domains, the specific aims of the book was sixfold: (a) to present psychological coaching strategies, methodologies, approaches, practice guidelines and policy implications for multi-cultural contexts; (b) to introduce new frameworks for psychological coaching practice; (c) to elaborate upon the fundamentals of coaching psychology within multi-cultural contexts; (d) to provide context to the multi-cultural competencies required for the psychologist as coach; (e) to provide new methodologies and approaches for the psychology of coaching within multi-cultural context and (f) to provide direction for future research and practice in these domains.

Although all these aims have been systematically addressed throughout the preceding 18 chapters, the future direction for research and practice within multi-cultural coaching psychology needs to be consolidated. Through thematic content analysis, this chapter aimed to evaluate the 17 manuscripts submitted for this specialist book in order to provide a descriptive overview of the most frequently occurring themes relating to the future direction of coaching psychology within multi-cultural contexts. A brief overview of the research method, data analysis and results will be presented.

2 Research Design

2.1 Research Approach

A post-positivistic qualitative thematic content analytic approach, with a descriptive research design was employed to determine themes relating to future research and practice domains of coaching psychology within multicultural contexts (Creswell 2013; Van Zyl 2013). Themes were derived from these chapters.

2.2 Research Strategy

Thematic content analysis was employed in order to determine the future research and practice domains as presented in the 17 manuscripts submitted as part of this publication. Thematic content analysis makes provision for both qualitative analysis as well as quantitative frequency clustering (Creswell 2012; Lindlof and Taylor 2002; Van Zyl 2013). Subjected to the limitations of nominal-orientated measurements, thematic content analysis allows for qualitative data to be converted into quantitative terms in order to be further processed and compared (Duriau et al. 2007). This approach allows for future replication, and is considered non-intrusive (Zammito 2004).

2.3 Sampling Procedure and Inclusion Criteria

The sample consisted out of 18 chapters submitted for publication in this manuscript. All chapters were submitted in English, made either an empirical or theoretical contribution to the field of multicultural coaching psychology and was double blind peer-reviewed (inclusion criteria). All 18 Chapters were included as part of the sample.

2.4 Data Collection Methods and Recording

The final versions of the 17 chapters were treated as sources of data for this chapter. Authors were instructed, as part of the publication brief, to ensure that a section in each chapter be dedicated to the future research trends in their research domain. Some authors provided dedicated sections to these trends, whereas other integrated the trends as part of the discussion. After peer-review, the final chapters were then collected and coded in relation to the three parts of the manuscript. The appropriate sections, or sub-sections, were then captured from each chapter on a Microsoft Excel® spreadsheet. Thereafter, the data was scrutinised in order to ensure accuracy and prepared for analysis.

2.5 Data Analysis Procedure

The data was captured on a Microsoft Excel® spreadsheet for analysis and thematic content analysis was employed to analysis the data. The best-practice guidelines for thematic content analysis, suggested by Duriau et al. (2007), was utilised in order to ensure consistency, credibility and transferability of the findings. Initially, a broad coding taxonomy was developed in order to ensure consistency in the analysis process. The coding taxonomy was refined through discussion and consultation amongst the editors and applied consistently throughout the analysis process.

Thematic content analysis was used to explore the content of the 'muted' textual data in order to determine the most frequently occurring themes in each one of the three parts or domains of this manuscript ((1) Fundamentals of multicultural coaching psychology; (2) Psychological approaches to multicultural coaching psychology (3) Meta-theoretical perspectives and practical applications of multicultural coaching psychology) through a systematic categorisation process in line with the coding taxonomy. The categorisation process flowed in three stages: (1) a thorough overview of the data conducted in order to obtain a general 'feel' for the findings; (2) thereafter primary themes were derived through clustering similar categories, ideas or themes in the responses together through a formalised coding process; and (3) the themes were co-coded individually between two researchers and findings were consolidated.

2.6 Reporting Style

The findings of the thematic content analysis are presented in line with the purpose and aim of this chapter. The findings are clustered in line with the three categories, sections or parts of the book whereby themes were extracted and reported non-verbatim. The findings are discussed in line with the results.

3 Findings and Discussion

The findings of this chapter are presented in three sections: (1) Fundamentals of multicultural coaching psychology; (2) Psychological approaches of multicultural coaching psychology; (3) Meta-theoretical perspectives and practical applications of multicultural coaching psychology, whereby appropriate themes are presented for each. Within each section, the results are discussed and interpreted.

3.1 Fundamentals of Multicultural Coaching Psychology

The findings from the first section related to the future perspectives on research and practice relating to the fundamentals of multicultural coaching psychology. The most frequently occurring themes in this section are presented in Table 1.

The findings indicated that theories and approaches specifically for coaching psychology need to be developed in order to effectively manage the developmental processes within multicultural environments. Theories should move away from the

Table 1 Future research themes within the fundamentals of multi-cultural coaching psychology

Theme	Response
Developing and evaluating the effectiveness of coaching interventions	A stronger focus should be placed on empirically validating coaching interventions
Identifying moderating and mediating factors impacting on the coaching process	Identifying the moderating factors can have strong implications for future research on coaching
	Determining the factors impacting on the effectiveness of coaching psychological processes within multi-cultural environments
Investigating relational dynamics within the coaching process	It is essential to strengthen the practitioners' understanding of relationship issues and to help them to gain insight into what happens in the working alliance with their coaching partner
	It is worthwhile to promote research that focuses on the impact of specific relational topics on the coaching outcomes
Developing ethical guidelines for multi-cultural coaching that are statutorily enforceable	More research evidence is required to identify and prescribe practices that are scientifically valid to inform coaching approaches applied during coaching sessions
	Future research should specifically examine ethical issues relating to cross-cultural coaching, a research focus that has received little attention so far
Developing coaching specific theories, methodologies and approaches unrelated to psychotherapy	Clearly, the chapter has included many references from psychotherapy research. The central statements of this chapter would even be more valuable if they could be supported by evidence from coaching research
	Coaching specific theories need to be constructed relating to the multicultural coaching psychological discipline
Training and supervision of psychological coaches within the multi-cultural context needs to be validated	Formal training and supervision methodologies associated with the development of multi-cultural coaches needs to be developed, evaluated and validated within tertiary educational institutions

application of psychotherapeutic techniques within coaching relationships, through developing specific methodologies, techniques and approaches aimed at facilitating optimal performance of the coaches (Palmer and Whybrow 2014; Passmore 2013). Ellinger and Kim (2014) noted that coaching is under-examined concept with limited coaching specific theories.

Further, the majority of the chapters indicated that a stronger focus should be placed on investigating the effectiveness of coaching psychology as a mechanism to enhance optimal functioning of individuals in multi-cultural environments. Research should focus on developing and validating coaching interventions with true experimental designs. Similarly, the findings also suggest that both mediating and moderating variables impacting on the effectiveness of coaching interventions need to be identified through empirical research (Palmer and Whybrow 2014). Through the identification of these variables coaches are able to structure more effective coaching psychological interventions. Jones et al. (2015) state that despite the growth of coaching as a development technique, limited scientific evidence exist of the benefits of coaching.

The authors indicated that research should be focused on identifying relational specific components which impacts on the coaching process, specifically within multi-cultural contexts. The findings indicate that limited research in this regard exists in both uni- and multi-cultural contexts. Consensus in literature exists with regard to the importance and value of the coaching relationship (Egan and Hamlin 2014; Gregory and Levy 2011; Gyllensten and Palmer 2007). It is postulated that the relationship between coach and coachee is a key process variable impacting on coaching outcomes (Baron and Morin 2009; Beattie et al. 2014).

The findings suggest that a stronger focus should be placed (in both theory and practice) on the ethics associated with the coaching relationship in order to de-risk the process. The findings suggest that limited research emphasis has been placed on understanding the ethical processes associated with the coaching relationship within multicultural contexts. Thompson and Dieffenbach (2015) advise that the continual examination of ethical coaching or grey areas within coaching are important, while Fillery-Travis (2015) states that contracting can be a way of ensuring transparency and appropriate ethics.

Finally, one of the authors argued that training and supervision methodologies associated with the development of psychological coaches within the multi-cultural context needs to be developed, evaluated and validated. This should facilitate the development of psychological coaches within the traditional science-practitioner model and provide further evidence of the effectiveness of supervision within these contexts (Abbott et al. 2013; Bell and Hausman 2014; Carroll 2006; Weathington et al. 2014). Lawrence and Whyte (2014) recommend that further qualitative research is needed to determine the purpose of supervision for the individual coach.

3.2 Psychological Approaches Within Multicultural Coaching Psychology

The findings from the second section relate to the future perspectives on research and practice for the psychological approaches to multicultural coaching psychology. The most frequently occurring themes in this section are presented in Table 2.

First, the findings suggest that the role which psychological ownership could play in the coaching process is under investigated (in the literature) and underutilised (in practice). Psychological ownership could be investigated as both a moderating factor and outcome of the coaching psychological process within multi-cultural environments. Research in this domain could focus on how the coaching process could be utilised to aid in the development of self-efficacy, self-identity, belongingness, and accountability as well as the management of feelings of territoriality. Peng and Pierce (2015) note that psychological ownership has been influenced mainly by

Table 2 Future research themes within the psychological approaches of multicultural coaching psychology

Theme	Response
The role of psychological ownership should be explored as part of the coaching process	To date, no research has been conducted on how psychological ownership can play a role during the coaching process
	The establishment, management and development of psychological ownership (self-efficacy, accountability, belongingness, self-identity and territoriality) could play a crucial role in the enhancement of individual well-being and organisational functioning if managed through a coaching process, yet limited attempts have been made to empirically or theoretically explore these implications
Developing new coaching psychological models and paradigms	The focus should be on developing coaching psychological models that are not built on psychotherapeutic or business coaching approaches
	Coaching psychological paradigms need to be developed as current disease orientated paradigms are not sufficient
Coaching approaches should be investigated within systems	Systemic and transcultural approaches should be recognised concepts in (transcultural) coaching psychology which reaches beyond causal-linear approaches and interventions. Doing so makes it possible to respond adequately to organisational, global and transcultural complexities, whilst allowing optimal functioning of the individual, the team, the organisation and the environment
	The systemic and transcultural coaching framework takes systemic and transcultural aspects in coaching psychology into account and implement these across the various layers of the organisational system

Western thought. This supports further research on psychological ownership in the coaching process within a multi-cultural context.

Similar to the findings in the previous section, the results indicated that new coaching psychological models and paradigms needs to be developed for the multi-cultural coaching environment. The chapters highlight that most of the current models and paradigms are focused on uni-cultural or individualistic processes and does not take into account the nuances of different cultures, ages, races and the like. The authors of these chapters believes that this is a serious limitation and could impact on the effectiveness of a coaching intervention (Van Zyl and Stander 2013; Vella et al. 2013). Schutte and Steyn (2015) postulate that research on coaching is still in its infancy and needs be scientifically synthesised and explored. Ellinger and Kim (2014) describe coaching as an under-examined and – research field.

Finally, two of the chapters highlight the need to investigate and manage coaching interventions from a systems perspective. Authors argued that coachees functions within a larger organisational system and that interventions may only be effective if the coaching process takes place within the system through viewing the participant as an individual, yet part of such a system. Motsoaledi and Cilliers (2012) found that coaching from a systems psychodynamic perspective uncover diversity dynamics.

3.3 Meta-theoretical Perspectives and Practical Applications Within Multicultural Coaching Psychology

Finally, the findings relating to the future perspectives on research and practice on the meta-theoretical perspectives and practical applications of coaching psychology within multi-cultural contexts are presented. The most frequently occurring themes in this section are presented in Table 3.

The findings suggest that six main themes were indicative in this section. First, it was believed that practical 'tools' or techniques should be developed and validated within multicultural contexts. Limited research exists on practical techniques which could be used in order to facilitate the development of the coachee (Parilla and

Table 3 Future research themes relating to the meta-theoretical perspectives and practical applications of coaching psychology within multi-cultural contexts

Theme	Response
Practical 'tools' need to be developed, validated and distributed	Limited research exists relating to the validation of individual self-administered intentional activities and/or group based coaching intervention mechanisms. The focus should be on the development of coaching psychological 'tools' (e.g. gratitude visit) which could be taught as part of formal graduate studies
Coaching should focus on the optimisation of potential	Research on coaching psychology within the multicultural context should not focus on 'correcting' deviant behaviour but should rather focus on the optimisation of individual, organisational and societal potential. Theory building initiatives should be congruently structured around this central tendency
Projective techniques should be used as part of the coaching process	Projective techniques (through the use of films, art, fairy tales etc.) are powerful instruments which could be used to facilitate the development of potential through the coaching process. These, however, have been largely underutilised and investigated in both theory and practice
Eclectic approaches to coaching should be investigated	Puristically, both the positive psychological paradigm and the person-centred approach are powerful instruments through which to facilitate well-being of the coaches. Both paradigms have enjoyed the benefit of extensive research, yet both used in isolation has its limitations. It is suggested that eclectic approaches (combining either paradigms or others) should be developed in order to capitalise on the strengths of the various paradigms within multi-cultural contexts
Multi-cultural coaching psychology should form part all training processes	It is recommended that tertiary institutions offering Masters programmes in Psychology should consider presenting a module relating to coaching and people development within multicultural contexts. Studies should aim to develop a module which could be included in the training curriculum of psychologists as coaches within multicultural contexts. Subsequently, such research could aim at evaluating such a module by means of a longitudinal analysis
Skills development of the coachee should take place at the start of the relationship	It still remains to be investigated which skills coaches should aim to develop at the start of the coaching relationship in order to maximise effective outcomes

Hesser 1998; Passmore 2013). The authors of some of the chapters indicated that these tools or techniques should then also be taught as part of the formal training of psychologists as coaches.

Flowing from this idea, one chapter indicated that projective techniques could be used as a practical tool to facilitate the development of the coachee. Projective techniques provide insight into how the coachee processes information and acts as a mechanism to investigate underlying mechanisms which influences behaviour. The use of projective techniques as part of the coaching process should be investigated empirically.

Most of the chapters indicated that coaching should be conceptualised as an intervention strategy which aims to enhance or optimise the potential of individuals, groups/teams and organisations. The chapters highlight that some of the current coaching models are aimed at rectifying deviant or abnormal behaviour in line with the requirements of the organisation. Specifically it was suggested that '[r]research on coaching psychology within the multicultural context should not focus on 'correcting' deviant behaviour but should rather focus on the optimisation of individual, organisational and societal potential. Theory building initiatives should be congruently structured around this central tendency' (Donaldson et al. 2015).

Further, the findings suggest that eclectic approaches to coaching psychology should be investigated. Here it was suggested that the strengths of various paradigms should be incorporated into an eclectic approach in order to capitalise on the respective benefits of each and to address possible limitations of others. Limited research exists regarding the positive use of eclectic styles in coaching psychology.

The findings also highlights the need for multi-cultural coaching psychology to form part of all training programmes for psychologists. As the coaching process differs from both psychotherapy and counselling, it is imperative to also train psychologists with coaching skills. It was suggested that a training module be developed and validated at an institution and that this be rolled out into all formalised tertiary educational programmes aimed at training psychologists.

Finally, it was recommended that skills training should form part of the coachee's development. However, during some coaching processes, practical skills are only transferred during the middle or end of the process. The authors of the applicable chapter indicated that skills training and transference should take place during the initial phases of the coaching process in order to enhance the effectiveness of the intervention.

4 Conclusion

This chapter aimed to determine the future direction of both the discipline and profession of multicultural coaching psychology. Through the use of thematic content analysis, this chapter evaluated the 17 manuscripts submitted for this specialist book in order to provide a descriptive overview of the most frequently occurring

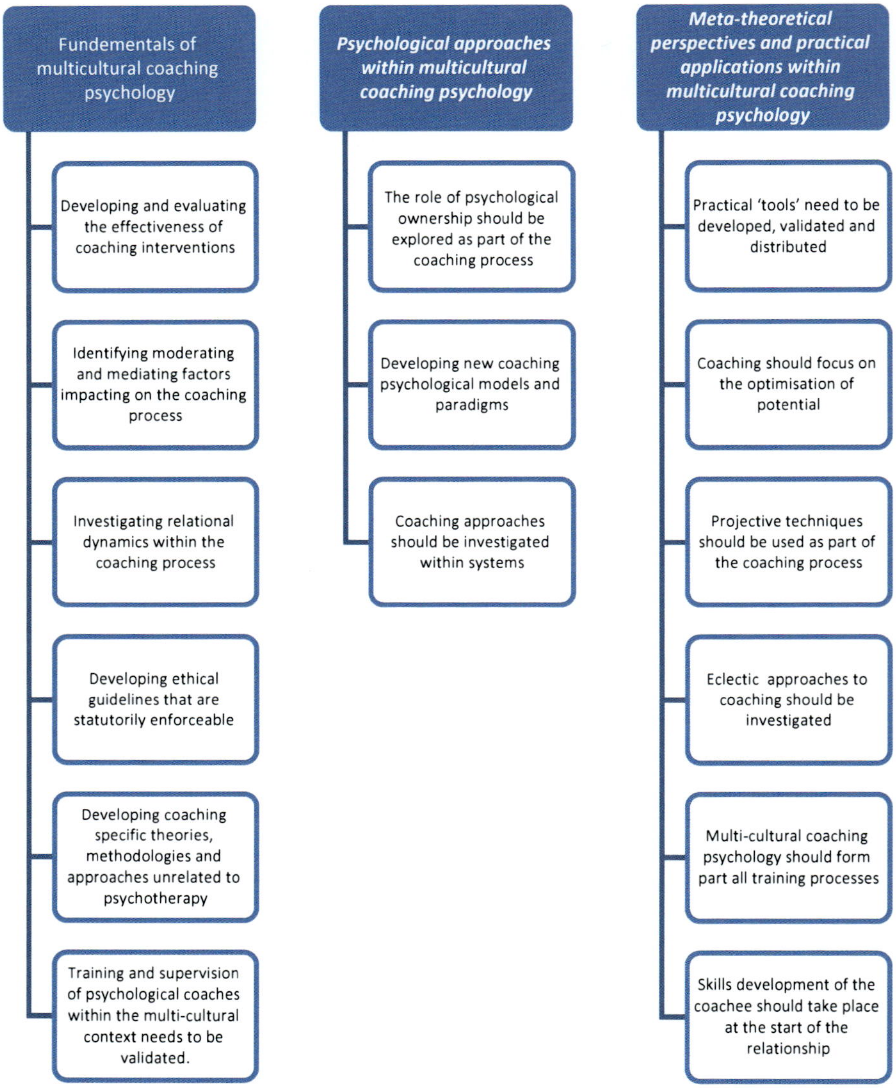

Fig. 1 Consolidated future research theme

themes relating to the future direction of coaching psychology within multi-cultural contexts. The findings showed that 15 research related themes could be structured across the three broad theoretical domains presented in this manuscript.

Figure 1 presents a graphic representation and interpretation of the most frequently occurring themes extracted from the findings and act as a foundation for possible future research themes in this area. In this chapter the findings were discussed and possible recommendations made in order to capitalise on the working mechanisms and to address the limitations of the training methodology.

References

Abbott, G., Gilbert, K., & Rosinski, P. (2013). Cross-cultural working in coaching and mentoring. In J. Passmore, D. B. Peterson, & T. Freire (Eds.), *The Wiley-Blackwell handbook of the psychology of coaching and mentoring* (pp. 484–500). Retrieved from http://ir.nmu.org.ua/bitstream/handle/123456789/144889/cfdaf6e32f456ab57cc53be33169b53f.pdf?sequence=1#page=312

Baron, L., & Morin, L. (2009). The coach-coachee relationship in executive coaching: A field study. *Human Resource Development Quarterly, 20*(1), 85–106.

Beattie, R. S., Kim, S., Hagen, M. S., Egan, T. M., Ellinger, A. D., & Hamlin, R. G. (2014). Managerial coaching: A review of the empirical literature and development of a model to guide future practice. *Advances in Developing Human Resources, 16*(2), 184–201. doi:10.1177/1523422313520476.

Bell, D., & Hausman, E. M. (2014). 3 training models in Professional Psychology Doctoral Programs. In *The Oxford handbook of education and training in Professional Psychology*. New York: Oxford University Press.

Biswas-Diener, R., & Dean, B. (2007). *Positive psychology coaching: Putting the science of happiness to work for your clients*. Hoboken: Wiley.

Carroll, M. (2006). Key issues in coaching psychology supervision. *The Coaching Psychologist, 2*(1), 4–8. Retrieved from http://www.supervisioncentre.com/docs/kv/Key%20Issues%20in%20Coaching%20Psychology%20Supervision.pdf

Coetzee, M., & Van Zyl, L. E. (2014). A review of a decade's scholarly publications (2004–2013) in the South African Journal of Industrial Psychology. *SA Journal of Industrial Psychology, 40*(1), 1–16.

Creswell, J. W. (2012). *Qualitative inquiry and research design: Choosing among five approaches*. London: Sage.

Creswell, J. W. (2013). *Qualitative inquiry & research design: choosing among the five approaches*. Thousand Oaks: Sage Publications.

Donaldson, S. I., Dollwet, M., & Rao, M. A. (2015). Happiness, excellence, and optimal human functioning revisited: Examining the peer-reviewed literature linked to positive psychology. *The Journal of Positive Psychology, 10*(3), 185–195.

Duriau, V. J., Reger, R. K., & Pfarrer, M. D. (2007). A content analysis of the content analysis literature in organization studies: Research themes, data sources, and methodological refinements. *Organizational Research Methods, 10*, 5–34.

Egan, T., & Hamlin, R. G. (2014). Coaching, HRD, and relational richness: Putting the pieces together. *Advances in developing Human Resources, 16*(2), 242–257. doi:10/1177/1523422313520475.

Ellinger, A. D., & Kim, S. (2014). Coaching and human resource development examining relevant theories, coaching genres, and scales to advance research and practice. *Advances in Developing Human Resources, 16*(2), 127–138.

Fillery-Travis, A. (2015). *Contracting within the business coaching relationship -a guide and a cautionary tale!* Discussion paper, Worldwide Association of Business Coaches, Canada.

Gregory, J. B., & Levy, P. E. (2011). It's not me, it's you: A multilevel examination of variables that impact employee coaching relationships. *Consulting Psychology Journal: Practice and Research, 63*(2), 67.

Gyllensten, K., & Palmer, S. (2007). The coaching relationship: An interpretative phenomenological analysis. *International Coaching Psychology Review, 2*(2), 168–177.

Jones, R. J., Woods, S. A., & Guillaume, Y. R. R. (2015). The effectiveness of workplace coaching: A meta analysis of learning and performance outcomes from coaching. *Journal of Occupational and Organizational Psychology*. doi: 10.1111/joop.12119.

Lawrence, P., & Whyte, A. (2014). What is coaching supervision and is it important? *Coaching: An International Journal of Theory, Research and Practice, 7*(1), 39–55.

Lindlof, T. R., & Taylor, B. C. (2002). *Qualitative communication research methods* (2nd ed.). Thousand Oaks: Sage.

Motsoaledi, L., & Cilliers, F. (2012). Executive coaching in diversity from the systems psychodynamic perspective. *SA Journal of Industrial Psychology, 38*(2), 32–43.

Palmer, S., & Whybrow, A. (Eds.). (2014). *Handbook of coaching psychology: A guide for practitioners*. London, UK: Routledge Publications.

Parilla, P. F., & Hesser, G. W. (1998). Internships and the sociological perspective: Applying principles of experiential learning. *Teaching Sociology, 26*, 310–329.

Passmore, J. (Ed.). (2013). *Diversity in coaching: Working with gender, culture, race and age*. New York: Kogan Page Publishers.

Peng, H., & Pierce, J. (2015). Job-and organization-based psychological ownership: Relationship and outcomes. *Journal of Managerial Psychology, 30*(2), 151–168.

Kauffman, C. (2006). Positive psychology: The science at the heart of coaching. In D. R. Stober & A. M. Grant (Eds.), *Evidence based coaching handbook: Putting best practices to work for your clients* (pp. 219–253). Hoboken: Wiley.

Koortzen, P., & Oosthuizen, R. M. (2012). Psychological experiences in South African society before the 2010 FIFA World Cup from the systems psychodynamic and positive psychology perspectives. *SA Journal of Industrial Psychology, 38*(2), 156–169.

Schutte, F., & Steyn, R. (2015). The scientific building blocks for business coaching: a literature review: Original research. *SA Journal of Human Resource Management, 13*(1), 1–11.

Thompson, M., & Dieffenbach, K. (2015). Measuring professional ethics in coaching: Development of the PISC-Q. *Ethics & Behavior*, 1–17. doi:10.1080/10508422.2015.106057

Van Zyl, L. E. (2013). *Research methodology for economic and management sciences*. Upper Saddle River: Pearson Education International.

Van Zyl, L. E., & Stander, M. W. (2013). A strengths-based approach towards coaching in a multicultural environment. In J. H. D. Cornelius-White, R. Motschnig-Pitrik, & M. Lux (Eds.), *Interdisciplinary handbook of the person-centered approach* (pp. 245–257). Springer: New York

Vella, S. A., Crowe, T. P., & Oades, L. G. (2013). Increasing the effectiveness of formal coach education: Evidence of a parallel process. *International Journal of Sports Science & Coaching, 8*(2), 417–430. doi:10.1260/1747-9541.8.2.417.

Weathington, B. L., Bergman, S. M., & Bergman, J. Z. (2014). Training science-practitioners: Broadening the training of industrial-organizational psychologists. *Society for Industrial and Organizational Psychology, 7*(1), 35–38. doi:10.1111/iops.12101.

Zammito, J. H. (2004). *A Nice derangement of epistemes. Post-positivism in the study of science from Quine to Latour*. Chicago: The University of Chicago Press.